Treasures of Islam

Published by
WELLFLEET PRESS
110 Enterprise Avenue
Secaucus, New Jersey 07094

Published by arrangement with Philip Wilson Publishers

ISBN: 1-55521-514-9

Printed and bound in Singapore

Contents

The Aesthetics of Islam

A.S. MELIKIAN-CHIRVANI

As visitors to the Treasures of Islam exhibition wind their way between illuminated manuscripts, pottery and bronzes, they will set eyes on many works of art that have never been publicly displayed until now.

Yet many are of great beauty, and some may be considered of primary importance in their own field. The 10th-century dishes from Nishapur in Iran with sepia calligraphy on ivory ground (nos 205-209) compare with the finest to be seen in museums. The brass vessel from 16th-century Iran (no. 297), which is designed as a ship, has no parallel in public institutions. More astonishing still to a non-specialist, a whole style of monumental carving from the Umayyad period in the Syrian sphere is revealed by the architectural remains sent to the exhibition by the Kuwait National Museum (nos 353 and 354).

While it is perhaps understandable that archaeological finds mostly made by commercial diggers should yield important objects that remained unknown for long periods, it is more surprising to discover to what extent the greatest works of painters and calligraphers have remained hidden from public view. Until it reached the Kuwait Museum last year, less than a thousand people of our time had seen the 15th-century miniature on silk (no. 30), probably painted in Herat, which ranks among the greatest ever created in the Iranian world. Few Persian books have been scrutinized with as much attention as the 16th-century manuscript, the *Shāhnāmeh* (Book of Kings) (nos 40-61) from which the *Court of Kayumars* (no. 41) is perhaps the greatest painting created in Iran at that time.[1] The significance – and perfection – of the manuscript stands comparison, in its own sphere, with that of the *Creation of Man* in the Sistine Chapel in the sphere of Italian Renaissance art. It was commissioned by a King, Shah Tahmasp of Iran, and executed by some of the greatest painters. The difference is that while millions of visitors have seen the Sistine Chapel, only a few thousand have set eyes on the miniatures from the Book of Kings and less than a hundred may have seen some of those now shown here.

Discoveries are not confined to individual masterpieces. Entire categories of works of art from the world of Islam have come to light in recent decades. The calligraphic pottery of 10th to 11th-century Khurasan and Transoxiana was first dug up in small quantities in Samarkand early this century and really became familiar when thousands of pieces streamed out of Iran, following the excavations by the Metropolitan Museum, New York.[2] The history of these diverse pieces still has to be written, together with the tracing to their sources of the numerous maxims to be read on them.[3] Khurasan metalwork of the 12th and 13th centuries was known only through a handful of pieces until recently, and these were not even identified for what they are. The Fars school of the 14th century, represented in the exhibition by one bowl, was first recognized in 1968. Many questions of art history remain unanswered. The emergence of the earliest lustre-painted pottery is still shrouded in mystery. How did it come into existence? Where? Much of it is ascribed to 'Mesopotamia', essentially because German archaeologists found a few fragments there at the turn of the century. But the overwhelming

1) S.C. Welch, *A King's Book of Kings* (New York, 1972); p. 39-117; M.B. Dickson and S.C. Welch *The Houghton Shahnameh* (Harvard, 1981)

2) The excavations were conducted without much planning and were more like a succession of scattered digs. See Wilkinson *Nishapur Pottery of the Early Islamic Period* (New York, 1973) introduction p. XXVIII-XLII for an account. No stratigraphy was worked out

3) Only one article dealing with the epigraphy has been published: Lisa Volov, 'Plaited Kufic on Samanid Epigraphic Pottery', *Ars Orientalis*, VI (1966), p. 107-33. Scattered inscriptions have been mentioned here and there, often calling for emendations. No attempt has been made so far to trace the inscriptions to their literary sources which can be done in a number of cases

4) Charles Vignier, a French officer turned dealer, whose brother conducted commercial digging in Iran for four years between 1910 and 1914 and who handled thousands of pieces of Iranian pottery, already warned in 1925 against the wholesale attribution of the early so-called Mesopotamian pottery to Iraq. Vignier may not have been a professional art historian but he was highly cultivated and knew about the provenance of his pieces. The excavated pieces from Iran are largely unpublished. A major dish from Istakhr near Persepolis excavated before World War II was only reproduced in 1972 (A.S. Melikian-Chirvani 'Baba Hatem, Un chef d'ouvre inconnu d'époque ghaznévide en Afghanistan' 5th International Congress Iranian Art and Archaeology, (Tehran, 1972) pl. 10, p. 122. For the contrary argument see O. Watson *Persian lustreware*, London 1985, p. 26-28

majority of the pieces now known come from the Iranian art market, a factor that has never yet been seriously taken into account, not to mention the pieces properly excavated on some Iranian sites.[4]

Serious research has barely begun concerning some areas at certain periods. Islamic India in the early stages preceding the advent of the Mughal dynasty in 1526 is but hazily known to us.[5] Many more manuscripts will have to be published before we can form a precise idea of what 15th-century book painting by artists following the Iranian model to varying degrees really looked like.

When basic facts have yet to be established it is hardly surprising that the purpose of the art should have been barely considered.

Old misconceptions linger. The most persistent one is that figurative art in Islam was either banned or at best tolerated in a more or less 'heretical' context.[6]

This mistaken idea owes a lot to the circumstances under which the art of the various Islamic cultural areas was discovered by the West. For a long time Islamic painting was essentially known through Iranian miniatures – and indeed the production of Iran outnumbers that of the other Islamic countries, much as Chinese painting towers above the art of the Far East. Thus figurative art in Islam came to be equated, wrongly, with Iranian painting. A second reason is that 19th-century Europeans, particularly the French in North Africa, were in touch with peripheral areas where the prejudice against figurative art was deeply rooted. It was therefore easy to assume, as has been asserted more than once, that the art of painting flourished in supposedly 'heterodox' Iran, meaning the Shi'a minority of Islam in contrast to the Sunni majority. But this is an anachronistic view. The vast majority of the Iranian world adhered to Sunnism until the Safavid takeover in the early 16th century. Most of the rulers who patronized the art of the book in Iran were Sunnis. And the Sunni Ottomans, embattled against Shi'a Iran as well as their own Shi'a subjects, fostered the development of the art of the book in their capital by attracting hundreds of Iranian painters and calligraphers.

It is possible to go still further. The Arab world itself cultivated figurative art from the beginning on a spectacular, monumental scale. It thrived for centuries in greater Syria including its southern extensions Palestine – reckoned part of Syria – and in Egypt. Every important structure erected by the Umayyad Caliphs that is known to us appears to have been covered from ceiling to floor with frescoes, low reliefs and mosaics. Indeed figurative art in various media existed continuously for seven hundred years. If Arab painting came to a virtual end in the late 14th century, it is for reasons unrelated to 'orthodoxy' dealt with elsewhere by this writer.[7]

Unfortunately manuscripts that are more than six centuries old survive only in small numbers. There are few Arab manuscripts with miniatures just as there are few early Iranian manuscripts with miniatures that predate the

5) Most of the research deals with manuscript painting, A 15th-century miniature in the manner of the Shiraz school of the 'forties was first published by the writer 'L'école de Shiraz et les origines de la miniature moghole' in Ralph Pinder-Wilson (ed.) *Painting from Islamic Lands* (London, 1969), pp. 124-41. See p. 128 where it is suggested that the painting must have been executed in India within the two decades or so following the emergence of that style in Shiraz. In the same year an article by Irma Fraad and Richard Ettinghausen 'Sultanate Painting in Persian Style, primarily from the first half of the fifteenth century' in *Chhavi* (Benares, 1969) pp. 48-66 reascribed to India a number of provincial 'Persian paintings' echoing views previously expressed by B.W. Robinson and Stuart Cary Welch. A number of reassessments have since been made by B.W. Robinson, See B.W. Robinson, *Persian Paintings in the John Rylands Library* (London, 1980), p. 95-115

6) See Thomas Arnold, *Painting in Islam. A Study of the Place of Pictorial Art in Muslim Culture*, (London, 1928), new edition with a preface by B.W. Robinson (New York, 1965). The scholar refutes many of the unfounded theories about the ban on figurative art in a remarkable essay written at a time when he did not have the advantage of knowing about the Umayyad palaces excavated later in the century. A year earlier, Gaston Migeon, *Manuel d'Art Muselman*, Paris 1927 (second revised edition, 2 volumes) I pp. 101-9, independently refuted the idea producing evidence relevant to Iran *and* the Arab world

7) For an overall view of figurative art in Arab countries see the writer's forthcoming *Sulwān al Muta' fi 'Udwān al-Atba*: A rediscovered masterpiece of Arab literature and painting. On the various Umayyad structures with frescoes and bas reliefs, see particularly the following: Daniel Schlumberger 'Les Fouilles de Qasr el-Heir Gharbi' *Syria* (1939) 3-4, pp. 195-373 (see carvings presumably representing the caliph pl. LXV 3, and XLVI, 1; a carved group continuing the Parthian tradition pl. XLVI, 2 and a man carrying a sheep pl. XLVII, 38); Daniel Schlumberger 'Deux Fresques Omeyyades' *Syria* XXV (1946-48, 1-2) p. 86-102 (concerns the frescoes from the same site); R.W. Hamilton, *Khirbat al Mafjar*, (Oxford, 1959); Martin Almagro et al. *Qusayr 'Amra' (Madrid, 1975)*

mid-14th century. The extinction of Arab book-painting around that time accounts for the present scarcity of examples and the impression that it was never highly developed. Such delusions are in part responsible for the insufficient attention that has been paid to the nature and purpose of figurative art in the Islamic world. The criteria that have been applied when assessing Iranian painting – the best known and therefore most widely commented upon – have too often been those applied to Western painting since the Renaissance.[8]

A long-cherished view in the West has it that calligraphy and abstract designs consisting of formal motifs developed in the East as a compensation for the 'forbidden' living image. Confining the debate to the case of Iran for reasons of space, a glance at Persian literature on painting and calligraphy is enough to disprove the contention. Historians, as well as artists, writing about the art of the book note that calligraphy is the source of all art, which certainly does not mean that painting is deemed inferior. The great historian of the Safavid period, Qazi Ahmad, compiled what we would call a biographical dictionary of calligraphers and painters, in which he quotes these verses: 'Of the key of intellect art has become the banner – And what is the key of art? 'Tis the tip of the calamus – The calamus contrives designs and reveals faces – God has created the pen as of two kinds.'[9] Art in general is thus held to be the essential part of human perception – 'the banner' of the key is the element at the end that does the opening – and, within art, it is the work of the calamus or pointed reed, used in calligraphy as in drawing. The words 'two kinds' refer to the vegetal nature of the reed-calamus and the animal nature of the hair used for brushes, also called calamus. They underline the fact that writing and painting are seen as two branches of the same art.

This is technically true. In a manuscript, the lay-out of the image and the columns of text were determined simultaneously. The format of the image, including its asymmetrical extension, was established in relation to the columns of text, following proportions calculated in modular units derived from the calligraphy – the measuring unit is the diagonal of the square serving as a dot to the letters.[10] The composition of the image similarly follows proportions worked out in modular units.

What is more, the calligrapher and the painter use the calamus in the same way. In the exhibition miniature from the *Book of Kings* commissioned by Shah Tahmasp (no. 48) in which the simurgh brings its catch to the infant Zal, the rocks sway with the same rhythmical effect as the slanting letters. The curves of the flaming tail are drawn in single strokes like the letters, without the calamus ever being lifted from the sheet of paper. The variations in the light pressure on the paper as the calamus runs over it, result in strokes of a typically calligraphic nature.

Not surprisingly, beings and objects are seen by the artist as outlines. What the West calls a 'painting' – emphasizing the act of spreading colour – is referred to in Persian as *nigār* or *naqsh*, an Arabic loanword which never means 'incising, engraving' as its etymology has led some English specialists to believe, but 'design', figurative or abstract. The pre-eminence of outline is demonstrated by the fact that in contrast to Western painting since the Quattrocento it is not submerged by paint but serves as a boundary to flat areas of colour.

The paramount importance attached to outline in the East which has not been the object of any comment in the West, comes out strongly in Persian historical and technical literature. When Prince Muhammad Heydar Dughlat, a cousin of Babur, celebrates Bihzad and Shah Muzaffar as the two greatest painters of his time, he remarks that 'the calamus of the former is firmer and his outline [*tarh*] and composition are better.'[11] In the late 16th century, the historian Iskandar Munshi, wrote of Shah Tahmasp, a pupil of the great Sultan Muhammad of Tabriz that 'he had raised the art of the outline [*tarrāhī*] and the fineness of the calamus to perfection.'[12]

This emphasis on outline is not simply a matter of individual taste, it is the recognition of the fundamental nature of figurative art in Iran which is to convey in visual terms the mental images of which the metaphors in poetry and prose are the written expression.

One of the most striking expressions of the intimate link between figurative and literary archetypes is the image of perfect beauty, the moon-faced Buddha or *But-i Māhrūy*.[13] Originally rooted in the pre-Islamic Buddhist background

8) In his important book produced in the form of an exhibition catalogue, *Persian Miniature Painting* (London, 1967), B. W. Robinson has produced an anthology of judgements titled 'Preliminary Symposium Impressions of Persian Painting' p. 13-17 that has at times the irresistible humour of parody

9) Translated from the Persian original by Qadi Mir Ahmad, *Golestān-e Honar*, ed. Ahmad Soheyli Kh^W^ansari, (Tehran, 1952), p. 9. The English version by V. Minorsky *Calligraphers and Painters. A Treatise by Qadi Ahmad, son of Mir-Munshi* (Washington, 1959) calls for numerous emendations, including the translation of these lines on pp. 49-50

10) C. Adle 'Recherche sur le module et le traçé correcteur à partir d'un exemple' *Le Monde Iranien et l'Islam*, III (1975), pp. 81-106

11) The text is quoted in an article by Sir Thomas Arnold carried as appendix II in Binyon, Wilkinson and Gray, *Persian Miniature Painting*, (London, 1933) p. 190. 'Tarh means drawing,' Arnold writes in a footnote. It is in fact more precise. It is the outline or contour drawn before the details are supplied. *Ustukhwān* struck Arnold as 'rather obscure' and he suggests 'main design'. This is about right though 'structure' might be a better word

12) Iskandar Beg Turkaman known as Iskandar Munshi *Tārīkh-i 'Ālamārā-yi 'Abbāsī*, ed. I. Afshar, Tehran 1350 s./1971, (2 volumes), I, p. 174

13) On the *But-i Māhrūy* in a 13th-century manuscript and its literary sources, Melikian-Chirvani, 'Le Roman de Varqe et Golšāh', *Revue des Arts Asiatiques*, XXII (1970), particularly p. 43.

of eastern Iran, as has been shown elsewhere, it survived by many centuries the total oblivion into which Buddhism sank in Iranian culture around the second half of the 11th century.[14] The face round as the full moon, with eyes slit as almonds [*bādāmī*] and eyebrows arched as a bow [*kamān*] changed only slowly. While it may have been influenced by the sight of certain Turkish and Mongol types that matched the archetypal description so well, it was never perceived as the characteristic of one race as distinct from another. On the contrary, beauty was given the same features regardless of the race indicated, by the conventional colour ascribed to it. The beautiful 'Indian' would be given the outline of the moon-faced Buddha with its slit eyes and the contour filled with purplish black – 'Indians' were understood to be 'black' according to literary convention.

In such a system, colour does not convey visual impressions. It serves as a codeword in painting as in literature. This is not only true of human types but also of landscape painting, where colour faithfully transcribes the literary metaphors. Just as the poet alternately characterizes the sky as having the hue of lapis lazuli or turquoise, so does the painter give it the colour of lapis lazuli or turquoise – ground lapis lazuli and turquoise being actually used to produce the colour. The image of the 'golden' sky when filled with light as the sun reaches the zenith is represented, literally, as a uniform, glittering gold surface. The metaphorical colours of Iranian painting carry to an extreme the precedence of mental archetypes that is a fundamental characteristic of this art.[15]

A great change occurred in the 14th century when painting began to achieve a degree of autonomy in relation to the repertoire of literary images. Certain types, certain details of landscape painting appear that are no longer matching clichés to the written word. However, they continued to follow the general principles of stylization. This innovation changed the appearance of miniature painting. It did not fundamentally alter its nature. It might be said to have introduced autonomous archetypes devised by the painter alongside the archetypes found in literature.

The predominance of the system of mental images – of ideas in the etymological Platonic sense of the word – in the art of Iran over visual art is not confined to painting. It extended to architecture and to objects.[16] It would be hopeless to try and compress into a few lines the complex array of metaphors that governed the selection of shapes, of motifs, and of colour, be it in metalwork, pottery or any other medium over the centuries. But a few glimpses into it are indispensable if one is to have an idea of the fundamental Middle Eastern approach to *objets d'art.*

Of all the themes underlying the symbolism attached to objects, none recurs as frequently as that of the universe and its corollary, world kingship, God being the King of the world and 'the king' – whichever human ruler might be intended – 'the shadow of God on earth'. The world is symbolized in literature by the celestial sphere or rather the hemispheric dome to which the sky, as seen by the human eye, is constantly compared. Because early bowls could be hemispherical, the sky was alternatively referred to in literature as the 'upturned bowl' (*tās-i nigūn*), a metaphor already used in pre-Islamic times – and a 'rotating dome' (*gunbad-i gardān*). These two sets of images are the key to the motifs – and colour – on pottery vessels.

Every metaphor used in Persian literature for the sky can be matched in pottery and metalwork. The stereotype of the 'turquoise dome' or 'azurine dome' (*Gunbad-i fīrūzeh, Gunbad-i lāzvard*) is echoed a thousand times in turquoise or lapis lazuli blue pottery bowls. The lotus dome (*gunbad-i nīlūfarī*), an early image predating Islam,[17] accounts for the many pottery and metal bowls with lotus chalice motifs on the underside.[18] The sky could also be signified by the representation of its attributes such as the twelve signs of the Zodiac and/or the seven planets.

Just as the sky will be compared in the same poem with an upturned bowl, a lotus chalice or a rotating dome, so could the corresponding images be associated on the same object. This leads to a complex interplay of visual symbols, undecipherable without the key provided by the explicit metaphors of literature.

As time went by the full representation of the visual symbol was more and more frequently replaced by a quasi-pictogrammic allusion to it. The lotus chalice gave way to a single lotus blossom within a circle or rosette. Allusions to the dome of heaven could be made in the form of an encircled geometrical pattern of a kind used in vaulting designs.

14) A.S. Melikian-Chirvani 'Le legs littéraire du Bouddhisme iranien' *Le Monde Iranien et l'Islam*, II (1974) pp. 1-79 particularly pp. 35ff. On the literary survival of a Buddhist ritual, the worship of the Adorned Buddha (which also left traces in early Iranian figurative art). A.S. Melikian-Chirvani 'The Buddhist ritual in the literature of early Islamic Iran' in B. Allchin ed., *Proceedings of the Sixth International Conference of the Association of South Asian Archaeologists* (Cambridge, 1984) pp. 272-79

15) Colours, in addition, had a symbolic value which led to a further interplay of ideas suggested by the contemplation of the images

16) A.S. Melikian-Chirvani 'Le Grand Livre des Bronzes Iraniens' *Connaissance des Arts* (December, 1983) p. 102-7

17) A.S. Melikian-Chirvani 'Recherches sur l'Architecture de l'Iran Bouddhique' *Le Monde Iranien et l'Islam* III (1975) p. 39. That the image of the upturned bowl as a symbol of the sky was fully alive by the late 16th century is demonstrated by the gloss provided by Inju Shirazi, *Farhang-i Jahāngīrī*, ed. R. 'Afifi, Meshed 1351–54s./1971-75 (3 volumes), III, *tās-i nigūn, tās rāzhgūn* s.v.

18) It already occurs in the 9th-century poems of Kasa'i Marvazi, quoted in the 13th century by Mohammad 'Awfi, *Lubab ul-Albab*, ed. Edward G. Browne, (London-Leiden 1903), 2 volumes, II, p. 35 lines 18 and 20 which specifies that the 'blue lotus' [*nīlūfar-i kabūd*] has the same colour as the sky and has the *appearance* of the sky

This trend towards greater abstraction went further still. It became customary to convey themes through texts as much as visual symbols. Persian poems occur with increasing frequency on metalwork in the 14th century. A century later, their use had become systematic. The growing role of the written word went together with the new emphasis on mystical themes.

On a show-piece drinking vessel of the type called in Persian *mashrabeh* (no. 277), the theme of the world – and of world kingship – is struck up in one of the most famous odes by Hafiz 'He that has the bowl in hand – Has the kingship of Jamshid for ever – The water through which Khizr found eternal life – Seek it in the tavern, for there is the bowl . . .'.[19] These are complex allusions to Jamshid, the mythical king of Iran who had a world-revealing cup, to Khizr, the mysterious prophetic figure who led Alexander the Great to the Source of Life in his initiatory quest through the world. The mug – called a wine bowl in reference to its function: it is a drinking vessel – looks like an illuminated page designed in an atelier of painters, illuminators and calligraphers, as was no doubt the case.

Indeed, a bowl in the Victoria and Albert Museum, London, made like the *mashrabeh* at Herat, in 1510, formally establishes the part taken by calligraphers and literati in the creation of objects and the selection of their symbols.[20] Visual and literary images combine to make the bowl a symbol of the sky as well as a 'fount' sending back the reflection of the Beloved One, i.e. God. The celestial theme is rendered by several visual metaphors on the outside and inside – trilobate arches standing for 'the arcade of heaven' (*rivāq-i falak*) a metaphor used in poetry down to the 15th century, wavy cloud bands associated in literature with celestial space and, on the outside, 'the garden of heaven' (*bāgh-i mīnū*) or Paradise seen through the lunette of the dome of heaven. Inside, six tiny fishes engraved on the walls swim down towards the centre designed as a rosette, in Persian *turanj-i zar*, 'the gold rosette', a metaphor for the sun. The fishes signify the 'pool' or 'fount', with which bowls are commonly compared. Associated with the gold rosette, they identify the bowl as a fount of sunlight, the red light of mystical illumination created by wine.[21] This is the theme so often expressed on bowls in a poem by Hafiz 'Cupbearer illuminate our bowl from the light of wine' (*Sāqi bi nūr-i bādeh bar afrūz jām-i mā*). On the 1510 bronze it is conveyed in verses by Hilali 'As the Beloved One [=God] considers His rose-coloured Face in the wine bowl – The reflection of His Face turns the bowl into a Fount of Sun . . .'. The calligraphy is signed by Sultan Muhammad (*Nūr*) one of the most famous calligraphers of the Herat school. Hilali, who died a quarter of a century later, must have composed the poem for this very bowl clearly designed in the royal atelier.

Such a work of art is both visual and conceptual. It may be approached on several levels and requires the simultaneous perception of form, visual ornament conveying the theme, calligraphy and literature. In no other culture are the multiple facets of the arts so utterly integrated.

While it appears, for the time being, that this multiple approach was primarily confined to the world of Iran, the celestial symbolism and the theme of the world Kingship were probably shared by the Arab designers. The early Caliphs adopted wholesale the regalia of pre-Islamic Iran. Themes such as the Fount of Sun occur in Arabic literature. They are dealt with visually on many *objets d'art*, even if the aesthetic effect sought after is different, just as German Renaissance painting is utterly different from its Italian source, their common Biblical iconography notwithstanding. If we may now be under the impression that Arab literature was not so intimately linked to Arab visual art it may be in part because research is less advanced. Fewer pieces have been properly published as *objets d'art* from the Islamic world must be – with all their inscriptions duly read and as many as possible traced to their literary source.

Whether in the Arab, the Iranian, the Turkish or the Indian field, the arts of Islam are only just being unveiled in their full complexity. The novelty of many objects is suitably matched by the novelty of the *Weltanschauung* that is at last beginning to be surmised.

19) *Dīvān-e Kh^{w}āje Hāfez-e Shīrāzī*, ed. sayyed Abo'l Qasem Anjavi Shirazi, Shiraz 1346 s./1968, p. 46
20) A.S. Melikian-Chirvani, *Islamic Metalwork from the Iranian World*, (London, 1982), p. 332-3
21) On all these images see the writer's forthcoming essay 'The metaphorical art of Islam'

Private Collectors and Islamic Arts of the Book

STUART CARY WELCH

In 1771, William Beckford, one of history's most discerning and omnivorous art collectors, then a mere boy, was caught by his tutor copying Indian miniatures. The deed was reported to Beckford's guardian, the Earl of Chatham, who ordered that the Indian pictures be destroyed, an act unthinkable to us, if only because Indian miniatures are now accepted as significant, and valuable, works of art.

A taste for such things had been growing in Europe at least since the 17th century. (But did the Crusaders bring home miniatures along with the rock crystals, textiles, and bronzes still admired in Church treasuries?) Rembrandt, a keen collector who drew inspiration as well as motifs from his pictures and objects, dashed off lively sketches of his Mughal portraits, before impecuniousness forced them to the auctioneers. Several of them, including a magnificent miniature dated 1627/28 of four holy men, attributable to Govardhan, were acquired later by Empress Maria Theresa of Austria, for whom they were set along with many other Indian miniatures into the rococo panelling of the so-called *Millionenzimmer* in her palace at Schönbrunn. Unmindful of the picture's quality, decorators overpainted a splendid tree and cropped the miniature to suit their ornamental purposes.

Works of art follow patterns of power and taste. The locations of Islamic calligraphies, manuscripts, and miniatures were at times shuffled on a grand scale. Many fine manuscripts given by the Safavid shahs to the Shrine at Ardabil were carried off to St Petersburg after the Russian campaigns in the Caucasus; and the Uzbek royal library was incorporated into the Public Library of Tashkent after the Russian Revolution. Another major change of ownership took place in Turkey, when the uniquely rich Ottoman library, incorporating several others captured by the Turks, became part of the Topkapi Saray Museum, where it is now expertly preserved and available to art lovers and scholars.

Other royal libraries fared less well. That of the Mughals, assembled since the 16th century by generations of immensely civilized emperors, was pillaged on several occasions. It was first sacked in 1739 by Nadir Shah, who took marvellous material back to Iran, whence much of it eventually went to Europe, Britain, and America. In the late 18th century it suffered again, from the Rohilla Afghans; and much of the remainder was ransacked following the Sepoy Rebellion of 1857.

Although many extraordinary Mughal manuscripts and miniatures remain in India, few are easily accessible. To survey adequately the arts of the Mughal book, one must travel widely not only in India but in Europe and America, visiting countless public and private collections. Studying other Indian schools is even more challenging. Paintings of the Persianate pre-Mughal sultanates and of the lyrically delightful Deccani traditions of Ahmednagar, Bijapur, and Golconda, always scarcer, have been scattered yet farther and wider.

Ordinarily, the great libraries and collections of the Islamic world were less cruelly treated. It is apocryphal that the great colonial powers, such as the British in India, calculatedly appropriated private and public libraries. Museum and library collections in Britain indicate that the acquisitors were usually rather bumbling enthusiasts, and that most of the miniatures and manuscripts they bought were artistically modest, hardly a treasure of 'masterpieces'. Indeed, these 'looters' probably were seen all too accurately by fellow colonialists as harmless aesthetes or deluded madcaps, hoodwinked by the denizens of the bazaars.

One views more admiringly than accusingly the discerning scholarship of a Warren Hastings or Richard Johnson, who found time despite arduous administrative duties to pursue pictures and manuscripts, which, it could be argued, they sought to preserve. Although the Hastings collection was dispersed, Johnson's survives. In penurious old age, eager that it be maintained, he offered the collection for a minimal sum to his former employers, the East India Company, which acquired it reluctantly, after painful bargaining. Johnson's beloved albums and manuscripts are now suitably housed and scrupulously cared for in the India Office Library, London.

Far more menacing to the national heritages of the Islamic world were the late-19th-century European collectors, true connoisseurs whose enthusiasm and aesthetic insights might have been enjoyed by a Shah Tahmasp or Emperor Jahangir. Sharp-eyed and mad for art, they were in the sophisticated tradition of the brothers Goncourt, the French novelists and men of letters who surrounded themselves with orientalia, which they described in elegantly printed books.

With the invention of the steam engine, the world had 'shrunk'. Objects from shores as distant as India and Japan were imported by ambitious merchants for the delectation of amateurs. Collectors also travelled, and became increasingly knowledgeable. Acquisitiveness knew no limits: a few trinkets were not enough; whole environments became the vogue. If one could not recreate an entire Japanese garden, at least one could receive guests in a Turkish corner.

Sections of *boiserie*, marble pools and fountains, costumes, textiles, silver-inlaid bronze lamps, carpets, shields and daggers – all these and more were gathered by a generation of romantics aspiring for stagy atmosphere. The arts of the book were also admired; and by the end of the nineteenth century, when eastern collections were most vulnerable, European and English *cognoscenti* happily paid generous sums for miniatures and manuscripts. Once-humble merchants from Istanbul, Damascus, and Cairo – erstwhile peddlers of the odd coin to tourists and diplomats – became art experts. Donning suits, stiff collars, ties, and spats, they foresook the bazaars of the East for the boutiques of the West. As anyone knows who has tried since to see manuscripts or miniatures in Iran, Egypt, or Afghanistan, they were extremely thorough.

Many dealers were Armenians, with talents for international trade and entrees to the crumbling palaces of eastern nobles, from whom they bought everything from brocades, Isnik dishes, and tiles to calligraphies and miniatures. Most of these engagingly multilingual entrepreneurs came from the town of Kayseri, whose merchants it is claimed not only could outwit all other Armenians but were craftier than the Chinese or the Jews. (According to the New York version of this legend, only the Yankee could outsmart them . . . but one suspects that Frenchmen, Britishers, or Eskimos heard flatteringly adjusted variants.)

By the late 19th century, Professor F.R. Martin was the quintessence of a new breed of collector, the art-loving scholar and 'man of the world'. This knowledgeable Swedish gentleman's enthusiasm for Islamic art was contagious – some might claim to the point of virulence. His life was a continuous buying spree, punctuated by lavishly produced publications on carpets, metalwork, manuscripts and miniatures. Martin's *The Miniature Painting and Painters of Persia, India and Turkey*, published in London in 1912, is still essential for scholars and collectors. A 'pioneer work', its floridly 'art nouveau' prose vivifies hundreds of excellent collotype reproductions of well-chosen miniatures and calligraphies.

Sadly for Mr Martin, whose finances did not always match his enthusiasms, he occasionally had to play the role of dealer-amateur, not a difficult task when interest in Islamic art was spreading. Many of his exciting discoveries were sold to maintain his Florentine villa, where he entertained *à la* Berenson. Distinguished guests from Europe and America, drawn to Florence by medieval and renaissance monuments, were introduced to Islamic art by Mr Martin, who occasionally obliged them by relinquishing a 'duplicate'. Mr Berenson's distinguished Islamic manuscripts and miniatures, still at *I Tatti*, as well as those passed on by him to Mrs Gardner of Boston, probably came from his Swedish neighbour.

The decades preceding and following the first world war were a 'golden age' for collectors in our field. Antiquities regulations did not exist. (If they had, Mr Martin and many other amateurs of the arts would have languished in highly atmospheric jails!) The flow of magnificent goods to the marketplace seemed endless. Exhibitions intensified the ardour of collectors and scholars (Paris 1903, Munich 1910, Paris 1912) and publications proliferated. To sense the ferment, one need only skim the massive catalogues and books by Friedrich Sarre and F.R. Martin, Georges Marteau and Henri Vever, E. Blochet, Ph.W. Schulz, Ernst Kühnel, Sir Thomas Arnold, and Percy Brown.

Although British and German scholars and collectors were excitedly busy, Paris was the centre of collecting. Not a time for extreme specialization, connoisseurs such as Jacques Doucet, Arthur Sambon, or the Comtesse de Béhague acquired Islamic art with eyes educated and broadened by classical, Chinese, and European pictures and objects. Refreshingly, their *objets de haute curiosité* were arranged with artful abandon, medieval bronzes cheek-tojowl with Chinese terracottas, Islamic metalwork, or miniatures. Elsewhere in Europe, there were other admirable collectors such as the scholarly German Friedrich Sarre and the discerning Belgian, Adolf Stoclet, whose Islamic material shared his museum-like house with wondrous antiquities and pictures by Giovanni de Paolo.

These outstandingly personal collections were formed during the years of art nouveau and art deco, both of which were reflected in penchants for particular Islamic styles. The vegetal sinuosity of Riza 'Abbasi was harmoniously attuned to the 'floral' Paris of Mucha and the Metro, whereas a few years later, more architectonic, sparer idioms appealed to Louis J. Cartier, whose brilliant art deco jewellery designs benefited from his unrivalled early Safavid and Mughal miniatures. Although the inventive craftsman René Lalique is not known to have owned Islamic pictures, it is not surprising that one of his leading patrons did, the notable Calouste Gulbenkian.

Collectors occasionally manifested themselves in dynasties, as did the Medici and the Rothschilds. From the late 19th century through the 1920s, Barons Edmond and his son Maurice de Rothschild chose marvellous Iranian and Indian miniatures. Although the 'Gout Rothschild' evokes mansard-roofed mansions of flamboyant grandeur aglow with old master paintings and gilt bronzes, it did not exclude smaller, subtler splendours, works of art to be enjoyed in the mood of chamber music. Safavid and Mughal pictures delighted Barons Edmond and Maurice. The former acquired the extraordinary early Safavid *Shāhnāmeh*, a virtual portable art gallery which until recently contained 258 miniatures by Shah Isma'il's and Shah Tahmasp's court painters (see nos 40–61). His son opened baronial doors to the poetic naturalism of the Mughal school, of which he bought pre-eminent examples, although this tradition was then deemed inferior to the Iranian, astonishing as this might seem to us in 1984. Even the finest Mughal miniatures then cost less than Timurid or Safavid ones, despite efforts by dealers to elevate prices with the phrase 'Indo-Persian'.

While the French bought manuscripts and miniatures from Iran and Turkey, often through an international network of dealers, the English formed collections in India. The Marquess of Bute and Lord Teignmouth, among others, brought home excellent Mughal and Iranian manuscripts. Then, as now, Jaipur was a centre of miniature painting, and the Jeypore Exhibition of 1884, of which a four-volume catalogue was produced, was an influential international event. When the 1911 Durbar was held in Delhi, a local dealer named Imre Schwaiger, who specialized in Mughal and Rajput art, was honoured by a visit from the King-Emperor George and Queen Mary, who autographed one of his offerings (see no. 133). Although Schwaiger also sold textiles, jades, and other objects, he was a major source for Indian pictures; and dealers from Europe, England, and America as well as collectors bought from him.

Stimulated by European example, wealthy Indians such as A.C. Ardashir and Sir Cowasji Jahangir, both of Bombay, also collected. There was precedent in India for this activity. Hindu and Jain temples as well as Muslim shrines maintained ever-increasing treasures of sacred texts and objects, to which were added secular works of art received as offerings. Princes and merchants also collected. Particularly dedicated and perceptive was Emperor Jahangir, who gathered manuscripts, miniatures, and objects with the same energetic zeal and sensitivity he expressed as a patron. Maharajas and nawabs bought, too, often with imaginative flair. According to records maintained in the Sawai Man Singh Museum of Jaipur, a Mughal album was acquired by the Maharaja from Delhi dealers in the early 19th century, which offers intriguing evidence of the art market.

In the early 1900s, C.W. Dyson Perrins, the youthful heir to the Lee and Perrins sauce concern, acquired Indian and Iranian as well as European manuscripts in a brief, passionate fling. These included two superb Mughal manuscripts, a *Khamseh* of Nizami and a *Dīwān* of Anwari, both illustrated for Emperor Akbar by his most esteemed court painters. When he died at a great age in 1958, the former was bequeathed to the British Museum; and the latter was sold with the rest of his extraordinary library at Sotheby's, where John Goelet bought it for the Fogg Art Museum.

Although an American by birth, Sir A. Chester Beatty ranks high among British collectors. To quote an aside from his librarian, J.V.S. Wilkinson, 'Sir Chester *knows* a good miniature', implying that he bought from the heart rather than through a specialist's discipline. Instinctively acquisitive, he was as gratified to find a Safavid manuscript as a promising lead mine. Since Indian and Turkish material was more easily available than Iranian, his library, which he bequeathed to Ireland, contains magnificent Mughal, Deccani, and Ottoman pictures.

Art collecting usually follows economic trends, and the depression years which began in 1929 brought a lull to the field of Islamic art, particularly in Europe. Most of the veteran-collectors withdrew from the chase, perhaps as much due to failing eyesight as to weakened finances.

(Might not this affliction also have contributed to Shah Tahmasp's and Aurangzeb's dramatic change of heart towards miniature painting in middle age?) Before the crash, however, a great exhibition of Persian art had been planned for 1931 at Burlington House. Warmly received, it was commemorated two years later by the publication of *Persian Miniature Painting*, by Lawrence Binyon, J.V.S. Wilkinson, and Basil Gray, a substantial volume devoted to a major section of the exhibition.

Sparked by the 1931 exhibition, a new generation of British collector-scholars emerged, of limited means but quick of eye and mind. B.W. Robinson recalls the thrill of his childhood visit to the Royal Academy show, which inspired him not only to learn about miniatures but to acquire them and paint a few of his own. At the same time, another discerning English lad, Edward Croft Murray, later Keeper of Prints and Drawings in the British Museum, received a guinea for Christmas. With it, he bought a superb early Mughal portrait.

During the years of doldrum, which lasted until the later 1950s, there were extraordinary opportunities for collecting. Several dealers carried on from livelier days; and it was exciting to visit their establishments in Paris, London, or New York and thumb through stacks of pictures, manuscripts, and calligraphies, which could be bought for prices that now seem laughable. A prowl in Paris, stopping off to see Messrs Kevorkian, Soustiel, Hindamian, or Injoudjian was likely to turn up splendid works of art for the cost, today, of a good luncheon. Across from the British Museum, Luzac's, the orientalist booksellers, sold assorted antiquities and miniatures in a small upstairs room. Mounted and kept in stacks, the pictures varied in quality; but with luck one could find excellent Akbar period pictures for seventy-five pounds. Minutes later, at Maggs Brothers in Berkeley Square, rummaging through their piles of pictures, it was possible to buy an Imperial Shah Jahani miniature for a few pounds. Few took the trouble to look.

Comparable, if costlier, thrills rewarded one in New York at Adrienne Minassian's warehouse storage rooms, where a gladdening cache of calligraphies and fine miniatures awaited. The search was accompanied by educational discourses on art and humanity, with particular reference to collectors and collecting. (One recalls Miss Minassian's tale of a passionate Frenchman, who softened dealers' hearts, and reduced prices, by lowering himself to his knees and sobbing.) Excellent miniatures and manuscripts also awaited at the Kelekian gallery; and H. Khan Monif was eager to show his appealing signed pictures by Mu'in Musawwir ($80.00), folios from the South Kensington *Bāburnāmeh* ($250.00), and outstanding 14th-century paintings from the so-called Ajit Ghose *Shāhnāmeh* ($350.00 to $1,000.00). A man of peace, Mr Monif's prices for miniatures were inversely proportioned to the amount of bloodshed represented. Battle scenes were bargains.

In more elegant surroundings, remarkable works of art could be enjoyed with Nasli and Alice Heeramaneck, who had acquired *en bloc* the stock of the late Parisian dealer Demotte, which contained important Mughal material. Their artistic insight spurred on by venturesomeness, Alice and Nasli Heeramaneck were unafraid of styles unrecorded in academia; and they tempted one with exciting, often unfamiliar, miniatures or drawings. Inasmuch as earlier US collectors (such independent spirits as Henry Walters, Alexander Smith Cochran, Charles Lang Freer, and George D. Pratt were now part of history, and Abby Aldrich Rockefeller and Cora Timken Burnett) had turned to other pursuits, miniatures were 'slow movers'. In the language of the marketplace, 'it was a buyer's market'. Upon hearing that a well-preserved *Hamza-nāmeh* page was available, I recall the luxury of deciding to buy it *only* if it contained lively trees. Not many years later, circumstances had changed. One could no longer buy single items from the Heeramanecks, who found it more congenial to part with entire collections. Nevertheless, upon being shown a particularly attractive and humorous Akbari drawing I asked if I might buy it. As I had feared, Nasli refused to sell; then he insisted upon giving it to me.

Although English by birth, Eric Schroeder was markedly American as a collector. Responsive to pictures in a most personal way, he was neither influenced by French aestheticism nor by German or English academic methodology. Before joining the Fogg Art Museum as keeper of Islamic art, he had worked with Arthur Upham Pope, the P.T. Barnum of Islamic art, at the Iranian Institute in New York. When the Institute held a large exhibition of Persian art in 1940, Eric inspected most of the potential loans, both in the hands of established collections and dealers. He remembered what he had seen, and despite extreme paucity of funds, he chose a small number of superb miniatures and drawings for the Fogg, which already possessed a fine group of miniatures, including excellent folios from the Demotte *Shāhnāmeh*. When we met him in 1948, by which time our addiction to Islamic art was already fatal, he had turned his attention from Islamic art to astrology; but his guidance was stimulating, often controversial, and inspiring.

Despite the lack of Islamic art courses at the Fogg, a circle of enthusiasts formed there. One of the early converts was John Dolliver MacDonald, who gained from the Fogg's tradition of wide-ranging connoisseurship, which through comparison encouraged high standards within each specialty. His eye for fineness led him to buy small Chinese objects, paintings by Andrew Wyeth before they were widely admired, and Indian and Persian miniatures, most of which he acquired in New York or through Maggs Brothers of London, who also represented him at auction sales.

The saleroom had long been an active arena for buyers and sellers, one where the flavour of gladiatorial combat could still be sampled, as when a bold American collector enlivened a Paris sale by raging at an American dealer who was bidding against him. More often, controversy preceded the sales, with sly, *sotto voce* insinuations that lot such and such had been repainted or another was a pastiche by the drug-addicted genius to whom many 1930s fakes have been ascribed. But skullduggery was less common than sociability; and most auction sales, whether in Paris, London, or New York, were virtual indoor garden parties, with a décor of 'blossoms' available for a price.

With the passing of the old collectors and dealers, auctions became more exciting. Supreme among them was the cycle of Kevorkian sales, for instance, at which so many mouth-watering (tear-producing?) items changed hands to benefit the Hagop Kevorkian Fund; or the astonishing Sevadjian sales of 1961, when stuning miniatures and drawings, often of the greatest rarity but barely described in the catalogues, sold for pittances. Yet another memorable sale was that of Jean Pozzi, who had left his Iranian material to Geneva's Musée d'art et d'histoire, but whose heirs, in 1970, disposed of the Indian items. Among them were folios from the *Shāh Jahān-nāmeh* and several soul-stirring Deccani miniatures.

Sales catalogues from the auction houses of Paris and London document the re-emergence of interest in Islamic art. Prior to the later 1950s, 'oriental miniatures' were humble addenda to more briskly moving European lots, and they were rarely illustrated in the catalogues. Even eye-catching and *rarissimus* pictures, accurately described (at Sotheby's, at least, with the advice of Messrs Robinson and Skelton) sold for negligible sums. Gradually, the number of illustrations increased; and before long not only were entire sales devoted to Iranian, Turkish and Indian material, but some of the lots were reproduced in colour.

Nevertheless, Islamic arts of the book were not quite fashionable. Chic households sprouted contemporary art or impressionist pictures; aristocratic ones, impressively oblivious to 'taste', were hung with inherited portraits, old masters, and assorted hand-me-downs: miniatures *et al* were for eccentrics, and they were kept in cupboards. Among enthusiasts of miniature painting itself, curious vogues prevailed. In 1955, when a recently acquired picture by Akbar's great painter Basawan was shown to a noted London authority, he asked why anyone would have paid one hundred pounds for it when the same price would have brought an 18th-century miniature from Kangra.

Islamic activity was increasing at the Fogg Art Museum. Small exhibitions of Islamic art were held far more frequently. Students as well as visitors responded enthusiastically, and friends began to share my mania for pictures and objects. All activities, from meals to squash games, were interrupted to discuss them. Especially keen was Prince Sadruddin Aga Khan, whose background was exhilaratingly appropriate. Once, when he and I entered Eric Schroeder's drawing room, he recognized a majestic, black-bearded ancestor gazing down from the wall: Fath 'Ali Shah! Excitedly, Prince Sadruddin joined in the search, and he rarely returned from the bazaars of New York without exciting discoveries.

Another close friend with Islamic interests was John Goelet, who then as now was always keen to travel and to see works of art. Admirably benevolent, John baffled me by his determinedly unpossessive attitude towards pictures and objects but he was most kindly disposed towards museums, as we shall see further on.

As a volunteer at Harvard, I could come and go freely; and I spent much time visiting and photographing collections, in England and Ireland, in Europe, and in the USA. Inasmuch as no courses in my field were accessible (which forced me to be an autodidact), the help of English friends such as B.W. Robinson, W.G. Archer, Robert Skelton, and others was a blessing. Guided by Robinson's notes to many library and museum collections, I systematically, and joyfully, went through them; and ordinarily I was allowed to take colour slides.

Art education requires seeing and touching at least as much as reading; and I was fortunate in finding pictures to study intensively often through magnifying glasses, in bed. These 'study-pieces' were usually souvenirs from energetic walks through Paris and London with eyes peeled for antiquities and picture dealerships. Miraculous discoveries occurred in unpromising places, as when a fine portrait of a dancing girl that had once belonged to Emperor Jahangir was sighted in the Paris flea market on the tabletop of an outdoor stall, seconds before a rainstorm.

In 1957, during one of our extended London visits, *The Times* reported the death of Baron Maurice de Rothschild. Moments later, I cabled John Coolidge, then the director of the Fogg Museum, suggesting that we try to acquire the legendary Rothschild *Shāhnāmeh*, said to have been illustrated for Shah Tahmasp and not seen by 'specialists' since the early part of the century. Several years later, the topic came up again, when John Coolidge told me of an acquaintance bent upon acquiring a major work of art, regardless of period or style. I reminded him of the Rothschild manuscript, and soon discussed it with his friend, Arthur A. Houghton, Jr. To make my remarks convincing, I showed him the spectacularly beautiful Safavid miniatures from the Cartier collection, given to the Fogg in 1958 by John Goelet.

A glorious few hours soon followed, when Arthur Houghton and I met at the firm of Rosenberg and Stiebel, art dealers representing the Rothschilds. We stood in front of a marble-topped Louis Quinze table onto which was placed a very simple wooden box. I opened it, removed the weighty manuscript, and slowly turned its pages. Thinking of Dust Muhammad's account of the sublime *Court of Gayumars* in Shah Tahmasp's *Shāhnāmeh*, I was impatient to find it, although the opening pictures in the volume were thrilling. Suddenly, like a flock of tropical birds soaring from a pond, Sultan Muhammad's masterpiece was revealed (see no. 41). One knew for certain that the Rothschild manuscript was Shah Tahmasp's greatest. The experience could be likened to entering an unknown Sistine Chapel.

Well over two hundred more pictures remained to view; and after a few awed minutes, we turned to Sultan Muhammad's sprightly and heroic comedy *Hushang slays the white div*, perhaps the only picture that could follow the great *Gayumars* without being anticlimactic. But the creative wizardry of decades awaited, and we soldiered on, flipping through the large folios until one's arms hurt, elated by the dazzle, often deeply moved. I was not surprised to learn a week or so later that Arthur Houghton had bought the majestic manuscript. When we next met, I asked if he would consent to my publishing it in collaboration with Professor Martin B. Dickson of Princeton University. He agreed; and the most fascinating, arduous, and time-consuming work of my life began.

Very quietly, the Fogg collections were being strengthened, largely through the help of John Goelet, who had encouraged us to persevere in acquiring the legendary collection of Louis J. Cartier, which had been inherited by his son Claude, an acquaintance from schooldays. To our delight, the Cartier purchase came to pass, due to John Goelet's benefaction. It was soon followed by a remarkable group of calligraphies, another splendid Goelet gift, gathered by the late Helen Temple Cook, a schoolmistress of Wellesley. In retrospect, one can boast that the Fogg in those days was decades ahead of the art market.

Islamic activities spread at the Fogg. Informal seminars were begun, illustrated by colour slides of miniatures, including many dazzling close-ups, taken during our travels. Several undergraduates, such as Milo Beach, became interested; and a graduate student, Anthony Welch, after a spirited conversation over luncheon, changed his field from European medieval art to Islamic. Eventually, when Prince Sadruddin asked me to catalogue his expanding collection (at a time when I was writing day and night for the Houghton project), I suggested that Tony write it, which he has done with distinction, challenged by the diverting problem of keeping pace with princely acquisitions.

Auditors also attended the Fogg seminars, one of whom was at least as devoted to the field as the students. This was Edwin Binney 3rd, always eager to expand his knowledge of miniatures and to learn where to find them. He was introduced to scholars, to the dealers in New York and London, and to the auction houses, whose sales he attended with unequalled regularity, soon becoming the Paganini of bidding. Passionately interested in pictures and art historical niceties, Ed Binney now possesses many splendid pictures and the most complete representation of Indian miniature painting in any collection, private or public. He also owns a remarkable Ottoman collection, which, with the rest of his material, he has catalogued admirably and lent with invariable generosity.

Although one never questioned the beauty and importance of Islamic art, it was satisfying when the international art world concurred, as became apparent from the art market. Rising prices demanded revised insurance valuations. If in the mid-1950s a well-preserved folio from Emperor Akbar's *Hamzanāmeh*, was estimated at two thousand dollars, it had risen to twenty thousand or so a decade later, and to sixty by the mid-1970s. The field was no longer a cosy little backwash of art enjoyed, and controlled, by a dozen or so enthusiasts. Exhibitions and publications burgeoned, and ever-increasing numbers of collectors possessed both knowledge and aesthetic discrimination. If a fine drawing or miniature appeared in some remote shop, its date, provenance, and a valuation based upon recent auction records, were likely to be known.

A yet more revolutionary change occurred when new and enthusiastic collectors from Islamic countries began to reacquire works of art that had gone to Europe or America many years before. Prince Sadruddin, a pioneer among Muslims buying back their cultural heritage, was soon joined by highly intelligent, strongly motivated *confrères* from Iran and the Arab world.

In 1976 a remarkable occasion linked old and new collectors and collections and showed the way of the future. This was the sale at Colnaghi's in London of the remaining miniatures from the Rothschild collections to which had been added most of Edwin Binney 3rd's Fatimid, Abbasid, Mamluk, and Iranian material. For those who had sighed enviously for decades over the soulful elegance of the Rothschild pictures, known from books and articles but seldom seen, the great moment had arrived. And for those eager to buy consequential early Islamic paintings, Edwin Binney's were perhaps the last to be found.

The stage was set for a grand international art scramble, with a cast of players suited to a James Bond film. Indeed, the Colnaghi's sale invites interpretation in filmic terms, with Jacob Rothschild, owner of the venerable dealership, as producer, and as director, Michael Goedhuis, an ingratiating former banker with a yen for the arts. A battery of technical consultants (including B.W. Robinson, Toby Falk, Robert Skelton, and Ralph Pinder-Wilson) waited off-stage; and Colnaghi's stately galleries (a large mouse-trap for collectors!) provided a drawing-room-comedy setting, relieved by occasional sequences set in distinguished hotels and restaurants. Inasmuch as the epic was planned to coincide with the major exhibition of Islamic art at the Hayward Gallery, a large number of 'stars' had come to London and there were enough extras (spears, or chequebooks, in hand) to staff a Hollywood epic.

At times, the plot verged on comedy. One day, while cooling our heels in an exhibition gallery, we sighted a most Edwardian client, packed into a mink-collared coat, his moustachios pricking the air like Rustam's before a dragon combat, eager to buy miniatures. Alas, his ardour for acquisition was soon dampened, we heard, when government inspectors at his Teheran bottling works found a soft-drink bottle containing a dead mouse.

For all concerned, whether buyer or seller, the overriding problem was the plot. One assumed it was a siege – the storming of the Rothschild/Binney castle – but the identity of the attackers was uncertain. Were they mere art fanatics, such as ourselves, or was this a drama sparkling with royalty? According to rumour, negotiations were proceeding to sell the entire collection to the Iranian court, a discouraging scenario to private buyers.

Shortly before the private viewing, one's hopes rose. Clients for specific pictures were invited to discuss prices. Mr Goedhuis aired them with aplomb, like golden rabbits from a magician's diamond-studded top-hat. They seemed forbidding, in 1976, but unarguable. Now, they seem cheap.

In 1970, public gratitude was occasioned by the generous gift by Mr Arthur A. Houghton, Jr of seventy-nine miniatures from Shah Tahmasp's *Shāhnāmeh* to The Metropolitan Museum of Art, an event followed by a series of sales, both public and private, from the same manuscript. The first, at Christie's occurred in November of 1976, when seven miniatures, of varying importance, were acquired by private collectors for sums that set new standards in the field. Collectors of European art, accustomed to such prices for small pictures by French impressionists or old masters, were astounded when even smaller Iranian ones achieved the same level, even though they could admire the brilliance of Sultan Muhammad, Aqa Mirak, or Mir Musawwir, and realize that their paintings are as scarce as those by Vermeer, and considerably rarer than Rembrandt's. For those of us convinced long ago that non-western art qualitatively ranks as high as European, the new prices offer, albeit in worldly terms, corrective poetic justice.

Treasures of Islam is the most impressive showing of the arts of the Islamic book since the London exhibition of 1931. It marks another 'golden age' of collecting, when connoisseurs of the stature of the Comtesse de Béhague, Baron Edmond de Rothschild, Louis Cartier, or Sir Chester Beatty have assembled miniatures, manuscripts, and calligraphies of the utmost importance and beauty. But there is a major and refreshing difference: most of the present collectors are not foreigners attracted to the arts of another culture but Muslims who have re-acquired masterpieces from their own traditions. Happily, in this remarkable exhibition they share them.

ANTHONY WELCH

The Arts of the Book

The Arab Lands

In the 7th and early 8th centuries Islam expanded from its spiritual core in south-western Arabia to rule over regions such as Andalusia, the Maghrib, Egypt, and Mesopotamia that had rich and ancient cultural traditions. Through the Arabic language, script, the Qur'an, and the new Muslim faith, Islam brought religious and cultural unity to this vast geographical expanse. Traditional Arab passion for language was focused through Islam on the Qur'an – God's Revelation through Muhammad to humanity – and Islam's fervent adherence to its scripture is directly connected to traditional Islamic passion for the written word and books. Here was the beginning of the great tradition of the arts of the Islamic book. The art of the precious manuscript was a collaborative art, requiring the talents of paper-makers, binders, illuminators, calligraphers and painters. Products of the highest calibre were the result of specific commissions by wealthy patrons. Thus most of the finest manuscripts were created in libraries that were part of princely establishments: indeed manuscript patronage was regarded as a manifestation of power and ability.

Calligraphy was and still is Islam's most distinctive art, and the flowing, versatile Arabic script was ideally suited to the dozens of major writing styles that developed from it. Many variations of stately, angular styles are incorporated under the loose term Kufic, while cursive styles like *naskh*, *muhaqqaq*, and *thuluth* acquired particular prominence after the 12th century. There were regional styles too, notably the North African *Maghribī* that was the only cursive style to develop directly out of Kufic. Scriptures such as the Qur'an and the *Hadīth* were never illustrated with figural images, but they could be splendidly illuminated with abstract geometric and vegetal designs. Books with secular content, such as works of literature or histories or scientific treatises, could be figurally illustrated, and the tradition of the illustrated Islamic manuscript begins in the early 11th century.

Arab patrons ranged from the amirs of Granada to the caliphs of Baghdad, but with the conquest of that city in 1258 by the non-Muslim Mongols the centre of traditional Arab culture shifted decisively to Egypt where amirs and sultans of the Mamluk dynasty were active and energetic patrons of architecture and the portable arts. By the end of the 13th century those parts of eastern Islam conquered by the Mongols were recovering in prosperity and stability, but their cultural focus had altered: the central influence in language, manners, and the arts came now from Iran.

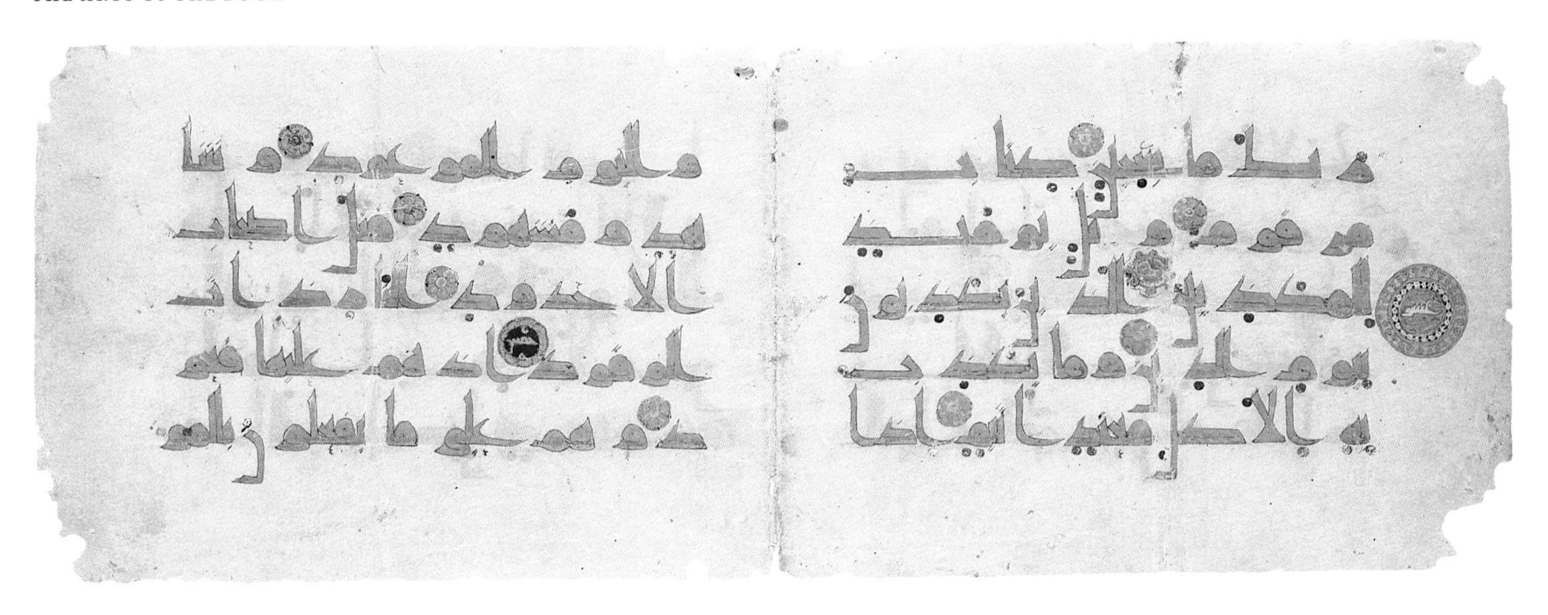

I

Suras LXXXIII *Al-Tatfīf* verses 3–12 and LXXXV *Al-Burūj* verses 2–9

Two pages from a dispersed manuscript of the Holy Qur'an, written in gold Kufic on vellum
14.5 × 40.5 cm
Previously in the collection of the Qadi of Jerusalem
Tunisia, probably Kairouan, 9th century

Paper had come into use in Islamic lands in the middle of the 8th century, but vellum was still employed for the most precious Qur'ans. The value of this manuscript was even more substantial, for its text was written entirely in gold. It must have been destined for a wealthy and pious patron. In keeping with the Kufic of 9th-century Kairouan, the letters are angular and compact, and the five lines on each side are composed as dense horizontals, enlivened by diacritical marks in blue, red, and green.

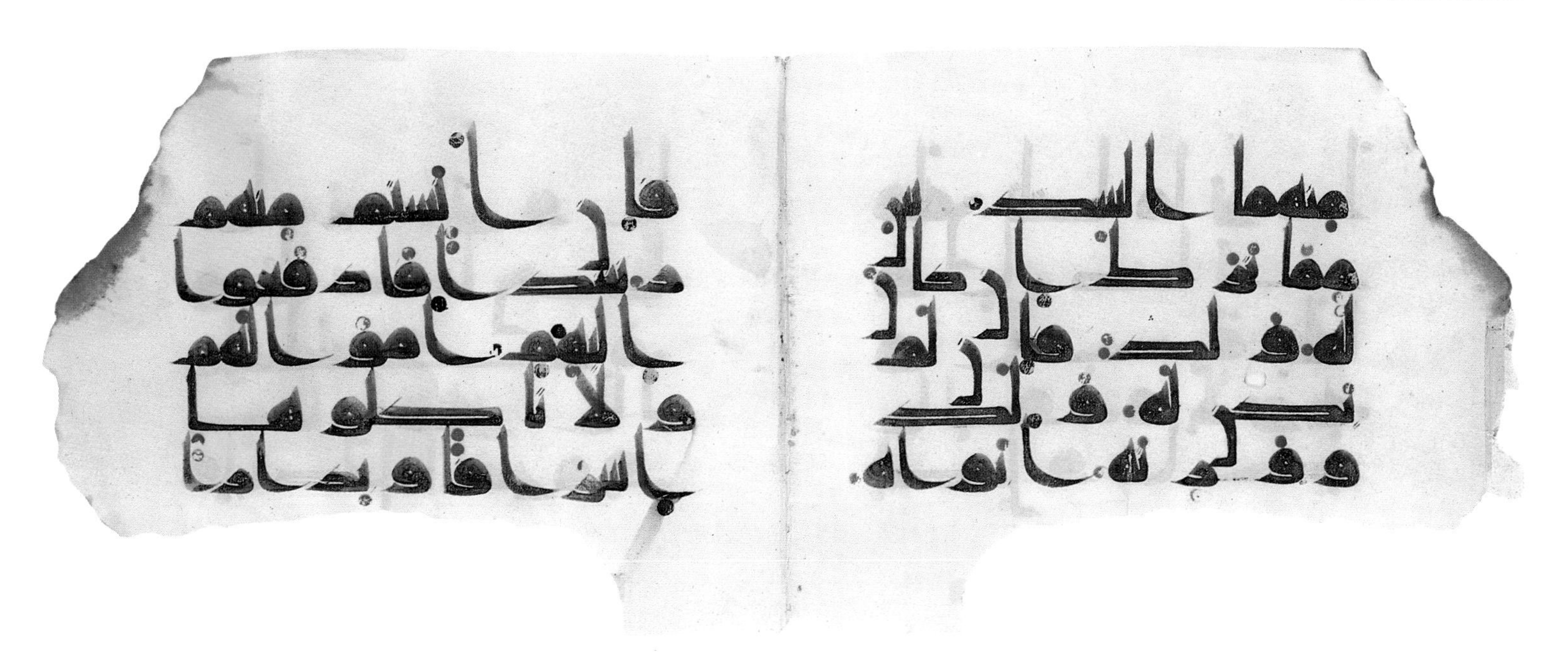

2
Sura IV *Al-Nisā* verses 6 and 11
Two pages from a dispersed manuscript of the Holy Qur'an, written in Kufic on vellum
21 × 50 cm
Tunisia, probably Kairouan, late 9th century

Verse 6 deals with a guardian's responsibilities towards orphans; verse 11 expounds the right distribution of inheritance. In keeping with the flexible canons of Kufic script, individual letters are extended or compacted for aesthetic reasons, and easy legibility is sacrificed to visual rhythms. Short, faint diagonal lines serve as diacritical marks, and the variously coloured dots are decorative and bear no relationship to the text. The bold dimensions of this writing style were influential far beyond the land where it was written. Kairouan was one of the major centres of medieval Islamic culture, and its Qur'ans must have been eagerly sought, for they became treasured possessions of religious institutions and pious individuals from North Africa to Iran.

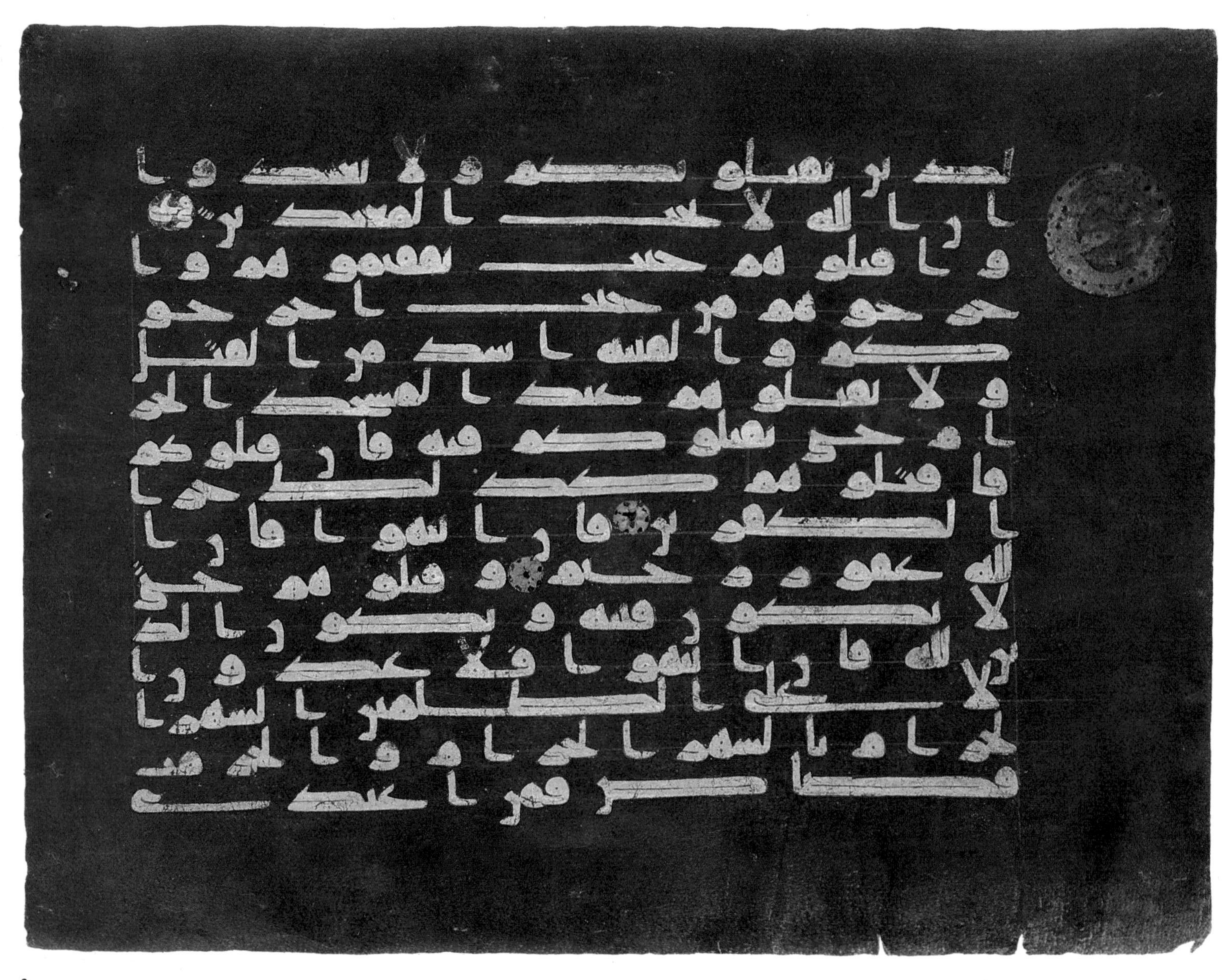

3

Sura II *Al-Baqarah* verses 190–194

Page from a manuscript of the Holy Qur'an, written in gold Kufic on blue vellum

25.7 × 37.5 cm

Tunisia, probably Kairouan, early 10th century

In this remarkable Qur'an the left-hand page generally precedes the right, the reversal of normal pagination. Letters are unpointed and diacritical marks are omitted. Official Byzantine documents were sometimes written on blue or purple vellum in gold or silver ink, and the patron of this Qur'an probably wished to emulate Byzantine practice, at a time when Byzantine artistic prestige was high throughout the Mediterranean area. The text proclaims the right of Muslims to defend themselves against aggressors and the duty of Muslims to forgive those who desist from fighting. Vertical letters have been compacted, and curving letters have been compressed so that the fifteen lines of text emphasize horizontality and create a stately image as regal as the colours chosen.

Most of this manuscript is in the Museum of Islamic Art, National Institute of Archaeology and the Arts, Tunis. A number of pages from it appeared on the art market in the early part of the 20th century and are now in various public and private collections.

4
Sura XVII *Al-Isrā'* verses 76-81

Page from a dispersed manuscript of the Holy Qur'an, written in Kufic in dark brown ink on vellum
28 × 33 cm
Tunisia, probably Kairouan, late 10th century

The unknown scribe responsible for this Qur'an clearly intended that each page be seen as a unity and not as an assemblage of words or lines, for these sixteen lines of Kufic establish a ladder-like linear pattern. Most curving letters have been subdued, so that a few stand out as dramatic highlights; verticals have been restrained so that they slow down but do not halt the almost overpowering horizontality of the script. It is an incisive and measured style – the work of one of Kairouan's great masters. After the 13th century Kufic was rarely used for writing the texts of Qur'ans, but this kind of western Kufic became the basis for the *Maghribī* script – the only kind of cursive style to evolve directly out of Kufic – that was widely used in Qur'ans of Spain and North Africa after the 12th century.

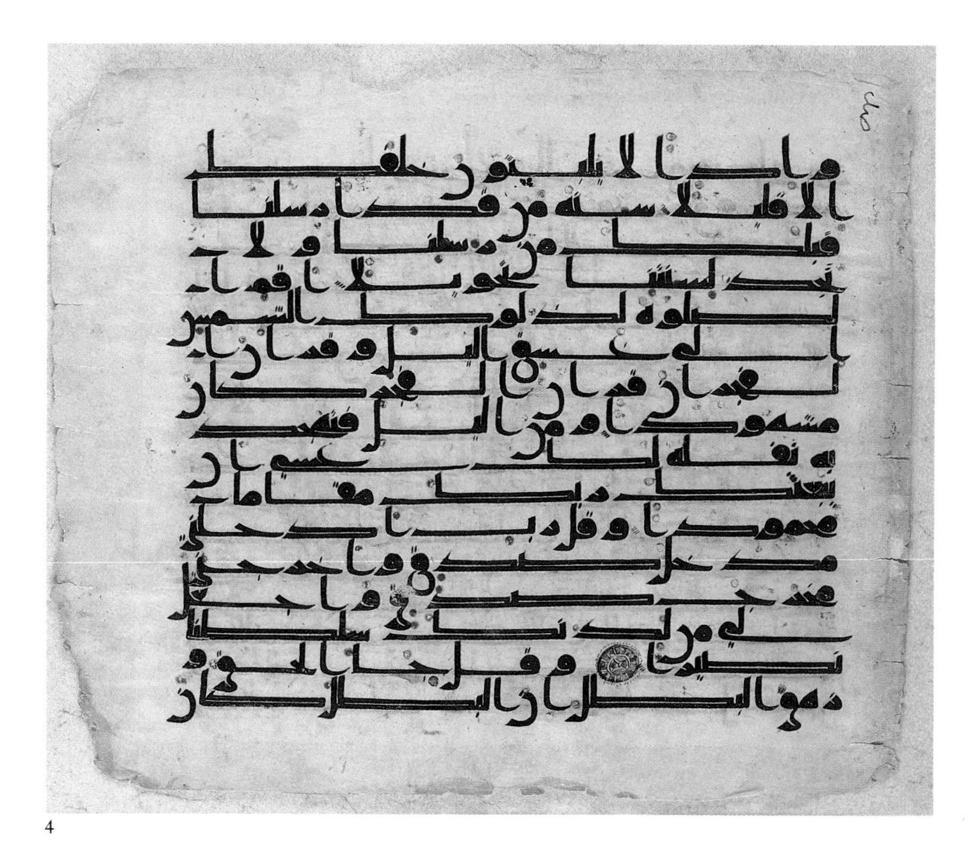
4

5
Holy Qur'an

Manuscript of sixty-five pages written in *Maghribī* script and illuminated
18th-century light brown leather binding
17.9 × 16.5 cm
A. Welch (1972), vol. 2, MS 3, pp. 22–33
North Africa, 13th century

These *Qur'an* pages are written on vellum in a small, fine *Maghribī* script, twenty-five lines to the page. Verse markers consist of triangles, bell-shapes, and circular medallions in gold, blue, green, and brown; the illuminated pages are distinguished by complex geometric designs in gold. *Maghribī* was a style of writing indigenous to Spain and North Africa, and, as Ibn Khaldun noted in the 14th century (*Al-Muqaddima*, book 1, chapter 5, section 30), its aesthetic principles were different from those of script styles found in Egypt and further east: while most calligraphers taught students to write according to established forms for each letter, *Maghribī* was based upon the formation of whole words. Despite its cursive appeal, its regularity, and its striking forms, *Maghribī* was never used outside of North Africa and Spain.

5

6
Sura XVII *Al-Isrā'* verses 71-79

Page from a dispersed Qur'an written in *Maghribī* script with nine lines of text to the page
Gold and some colours on light brown vellum
25.4 × 17.8 cm
A. Welch (1972), vol. 2, Cal. 3, pp. 11-13
North Africa, 13th-14th century

This fluid, rounded script is written in gold with diacritical marks in red and blue. The text speaks of the opposition that existed to the Prophet and of the punishment awaiting those who oppose the Revelation.

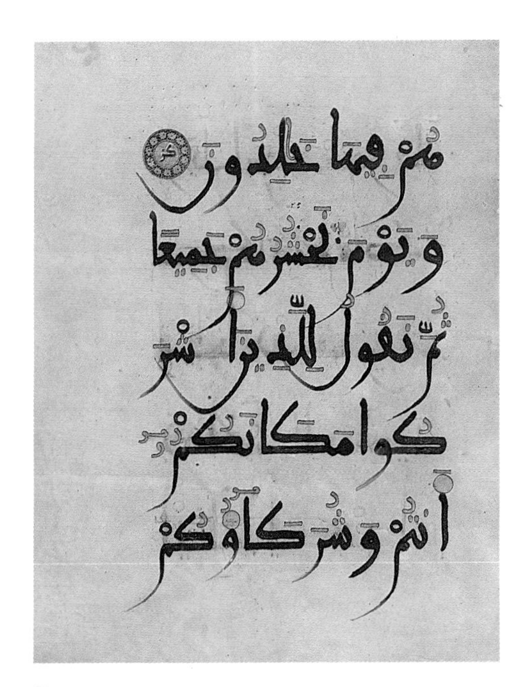

7
Sura X *Yūnus* verses 28-29

Page from a manuscript of the Holy Qur'an
Dark brown ink on pink paper; diacritical marks in blue and gold
32.2 × 25.3 cm
Spain, probably Granada, 13th century

Beginning with the last words of verse 27 and ending on the overside with the first words of verse 29, most of the text here comes from verse 28 which describes the fate awaiting polytheists who associate other gods with Allah.

Qur'an pages from the Muslim state of Granada are rare, and they are generally on tinted paper, ranging in colour from purple to pink. The *Maghribī* script here is still closely related to the Kufic from which *Maghribī* derives.

8
Sura II *Al-Baqara* verses 4-61, 76-89, 93-129, 135-139

Twenty-five folios from a manuscript Qur'an in *muhaqqaq* script
29.7 × 22 cm
Previously in the Kevorkian Collection
Sotheby's, 23 April 1979, lot 142
Egypt, *c.* 1320

These pages from the second sura of the Qur'an are written by an unidentified scribe in five lines of gold *muhaqqaq* on a plain ground. Diacritical marks are in blue, and there are circular verse markers in the margins: some markers are filled with fine floral ornamentation; others are simple, small gold medallions. Though Central Asian Turks of slave origin, the Mamluk sultans and amirs who ruled Egypt from 1250-1517 were some of the most energetic patrons of traditional Islamic arts, particularly calligraphy, and this Qur'an portion must have been created for a Mamluk of high standing.

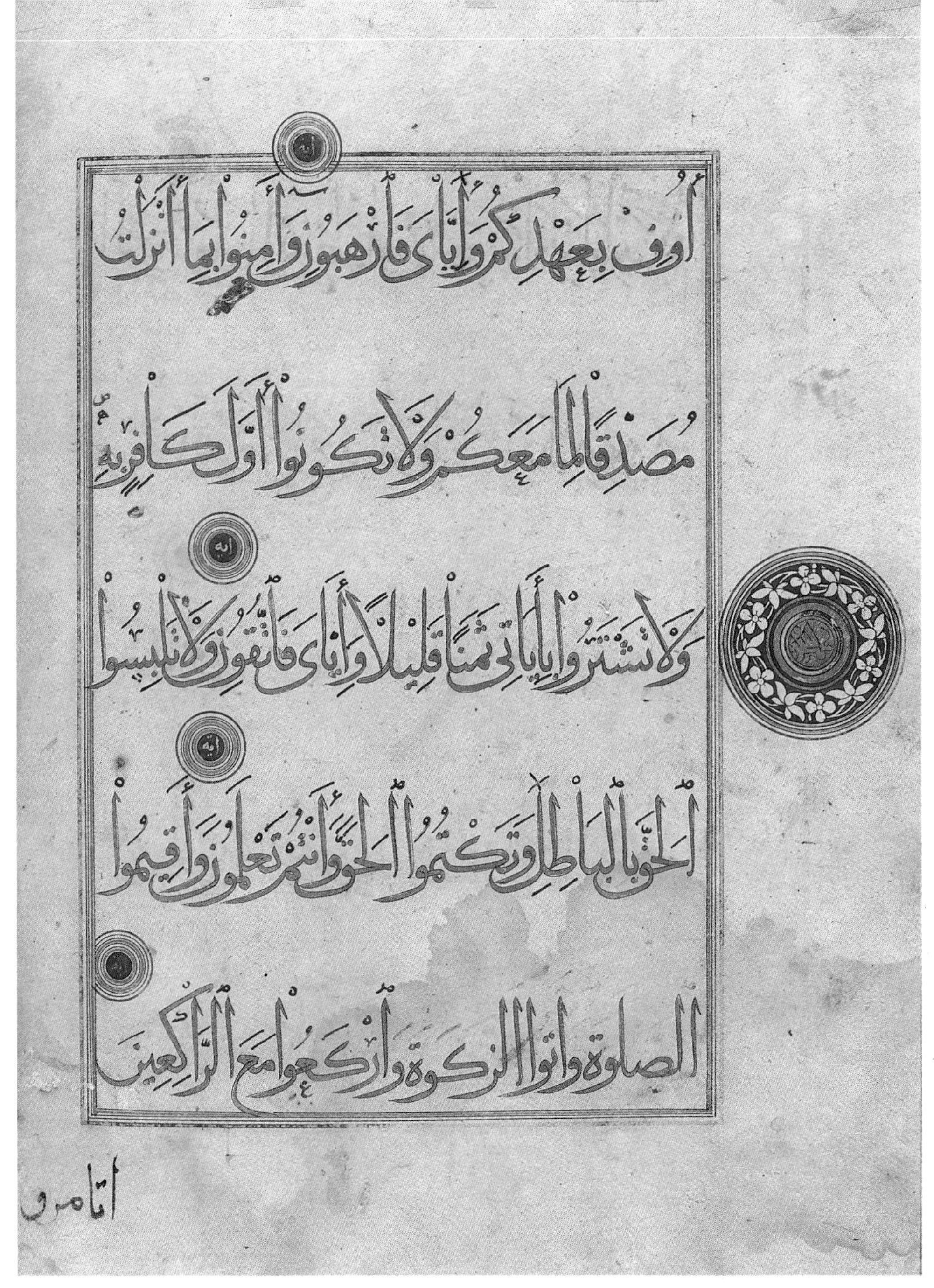

8

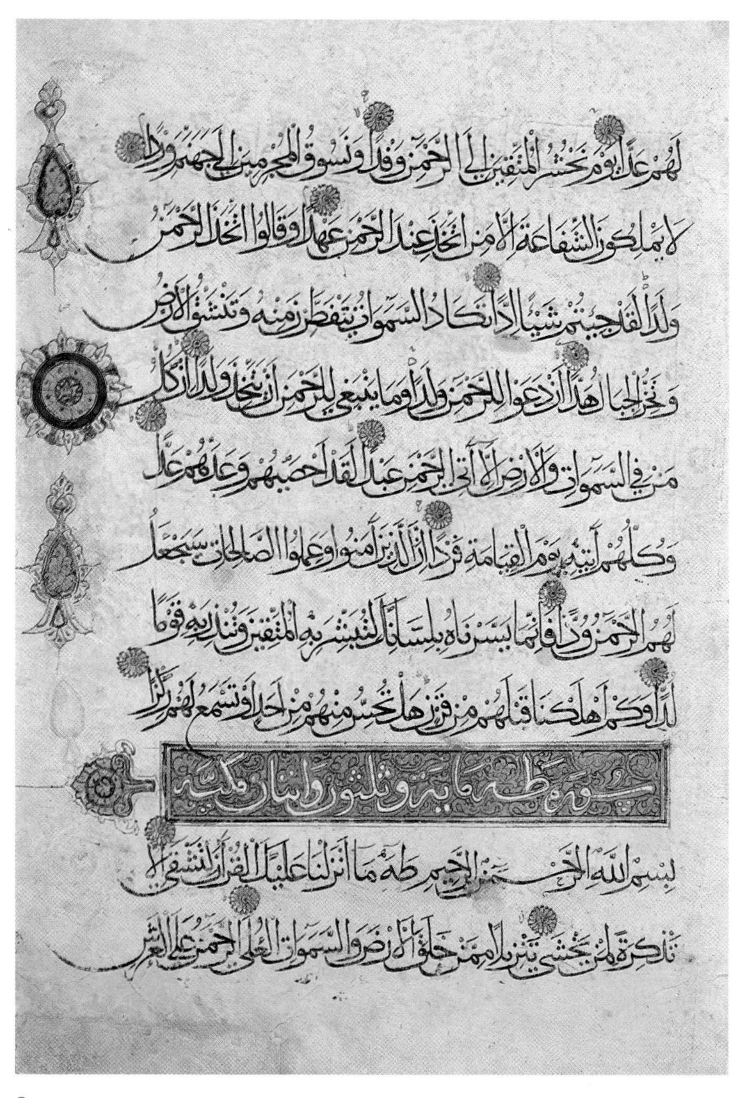

9
Suras XIX *Maryam* verses 85–98 and XX *Tā Hā* verses 1–23
Page from a dispersed manuscript of the Holy Qur'an, written in black *naskh* on paper
42 × 30 cm
Egypt, 14th century

Pages from this Mamluk Qur'an are in several collections, and some of them have the word *waqf* (endowment) written at the top, an indication that the book was given at some time to a religious institution. The text is written in a tall, elegant *naskh*, and the title of Sura *Tā Hā* is written in white on a gold ground. In the margins, pear-shaped medallions mark each fifth verse, while larger circular medallions indicate each tenth verse.

10
A medicinal plant
Page from an Arabic manuscript of the *Khawāss al-Ashjār* (*De Materia Medica*) of Dioscorides
Two lines of text describing the properties of the plant
24.1 × 16.5 cm
A. Welch (1972), A.M. 1, vol. 1, p. 21
Mesopotamia, first half 13th century

The first-century Greek physician, Pedanius Dioscorides, had compiled the ancient world's most famous medicinal herbal. A handbook for locating and identifying useful plants and preparing remedies, it functioned as an essential physician's tool in the medieval Islamic world, and it must have been one of the most copied books. Illustrations in the Arabic manuscript were clearly based on earlier Greek images. This particular page describes a medicinal plant used for the treatment of various skin disorders, such as ulcers, pustules, and itching.

11
Three courtiers

Right half of a double-page frontispiece from a manuscript of the *Sulwān al-Mutā'* of Ibn Zafar
Painting on paper
24.6 × 17 cm
Hotel Drouot, 26 October 1973, lot 19; A. Welch (1978), A.M. 4, vol. III, p. 8
Egypt, probably Cairo, *c.* 1325-50

Ibn Zafar was probably born in Sicily in 497/1104, when it was under the rule of the Norman kings of Sicily, who were noted for their encouragement of Islamic learning. The author travelled widely in the Mediterranean lands and completed thirty-two books on a variety of subjects. His *Sulwān al-Mutā'* (The Prescription for Pleasure) is a collection of animal fables, based on the earlier *Kalīla wa Dimna*, and like its prototype intended to provide moral instruction. The manuscript to which this frontispiece originally belonged is now in the Freer Gallery of Art and was presumably produced for a notable Mamluk amir in Cairo.

12
A mechanical device

Page from a manuscript of the 'Automata' of al-Jazari
Inscription names the Mamluk sultan al-Malik al-Salih (1351-54)
40 × 23.5 cm
Martin (1912), p. 2; Blochet (1929), pl. XXXVIII; Binney (1962), no. 17; Robinson (1976), no. 5
Egypt, 1354

'The Book of Knowledge of Ingenious Mechanical Devices' (more simply, the 'Automata') included descriptions of fifty devices that al-Jazari had designed. This copy, made for a prominent Mamluk amir in Egypt, was copied by the scribe Muhammad ibn Ahmad al-Izmiri, and it was illustrated by some of the finest painters in Mamluk employ. This device, designed to pour liquid from the flask into the basin of the woman at the base, depended upon musicians, an acrobat, and the horseman on the dome, all of whom rotated as the liquid was poured.

Iran, Afghanistan and Central Asia

In the middle of the 7th century Muslim Arabs conquered the rich, distinctive Sasanian empire of Iran. While Sasanian arts continued to exert a powerful impact on subsequent Islamic culture in Iran, the power of the new faith and its new art of calligraphy dramatically affected Iran. For centuries, despite the re-emergence of Persian as a literary language and the appearance of definite regional styles in the arts, Iran remained strongly under the influence of Arab culture emanating from Baghdad. Calligraphy in particular developed richly in Iran, and some of the finest medieval Qur'ans were produced by Iranian scribes.

The Mongol conquest of Iran was complete by the 1258 seizure of Baghdad. Under the dynastic name of Il-Khans, monarchs of Mongol descent ruled Iran, but initially they were not Muslim. Ghazan Khan (1295-1304) had been raised as a Buddhist and accepted Islam only on his accession to the throne. His successor Uljaytu had been baptized and brought up as a Nestorian Christian before, influenced by one of his wives, he became a Muslim. But by the end of the 13th century the Il-Khans had become an indigenous, Muslim dynasty with a strong devotion to patronage of Iranian Islamic culture that is perhaps most noticeable in the arts of the precious book. Under the influence of powerful viziers Il-Khan rulers commissioned the greatest extant 14th-century manuscripts – the 1306 and 1314 manuscripts of the *Jāmi' al-tawārikh* and the *c.* 1335-36 Demotte *Shāhnāmeh*, and they established a model of centralized, style-setting, royal patronage that was to be the pattern for the development of the art of the illustrated manuscript in Iran.

With the death of the ruler Abu Sa'id in 1335 the Il-Khan state broke up and was supplanted by regional powers and patrons like the Injus in Shiraz and the Jalayrids in Tabriz. Timur's invasion and conquest in the late 14th century shifted the royal centre east to Herat. Timur's son and successor Shah Rukh (1404-47) supported an archaicizing style of painting based on the Tabriz style of a century before, while Shah Rukh's son Baysunghur distinguished himself as one of the most gifted royal artists and connoisseurs in Islamic history. He established an image of princely culture and patronage that was to serve as a model for many later rulers, particularly those of Timurid descent. For eastern Islam, strongly under the influence of Iranian culture, Herat remained the leading cultural centre well into the 16th century, and its leading artists – painters like Bihzad and calligraphers like Mir 'Ali – established methods and styles that would be perpetuated as ideals of elegance for many decades.

In 1501 Shah Isma'il I established the Shi'a Safavid dynasty with its political and artistic centre in Tabriz. His son Tahmasp (r. 1524-76), only ten years old when he came to the throne, immediately exerted himself as an energetic and imaginative patron. Gathering around him the finest calligraphers and painters in Iran and taking a keen personal interest in their work, Tahmasp oversaw the creation of an astonishing number of remarkable manuscripts of which the single most impressive was a great *Shāhnāmeh* (the 'Houghton' *Shāhnāmeh*, see nos 40-61), produced over a twenty-year period. Not only one of the masterpieces of world art, it dramatically displayed the talents of brilliant painters like Sultan Muhammad and Aqa Mirak. Despite his earlier dedication to precious books, Shah Tahmasp lost interest in the visual arts after about 1545, renounced his previous passion for painting, and dismissed most of his painters. Some of them found other patrons in Iran; others moved to India, where they were instrumental in forming Mughal painting.

Tahmasp's grandson 'Abbas I (r. 1587-1629) brought the Safavid state to a peak of disciplined strength and established a new capital in Isfahan which was to remain Iran's chief metropolis until the 18th century. A determined patron of architecture, calligraphy, and painting, 'Abbas encouraged styles that were to remain essentially in place for a hundred years. His successors had less directed aesthetic senses and a far less keen sense for patronage, and during their reigns painters and calligraphers did fine work for non-royal patrons and sold finished paintings and drawings (not part of manuscripts) in bazaars. This expansion of the art market brought with it greater diversity of styles and more pronounced individual manners: thus a master like Mu'in Musawwir could demonstrate a marvellous range of styles and media, over an extraordinarily long career. 'Abbas' successors were for the most part inept rulers, and the state suffered a slow decline. In 1722 Iran fell to Afghan conquerors. The arts of painting and calligraphy did not recover until the 19th-century Qajar dynasty when Europeanizing taste and technique was briefly synthesized with traditional Iranian styles to produce the last florescence of manuscript art in Iran.

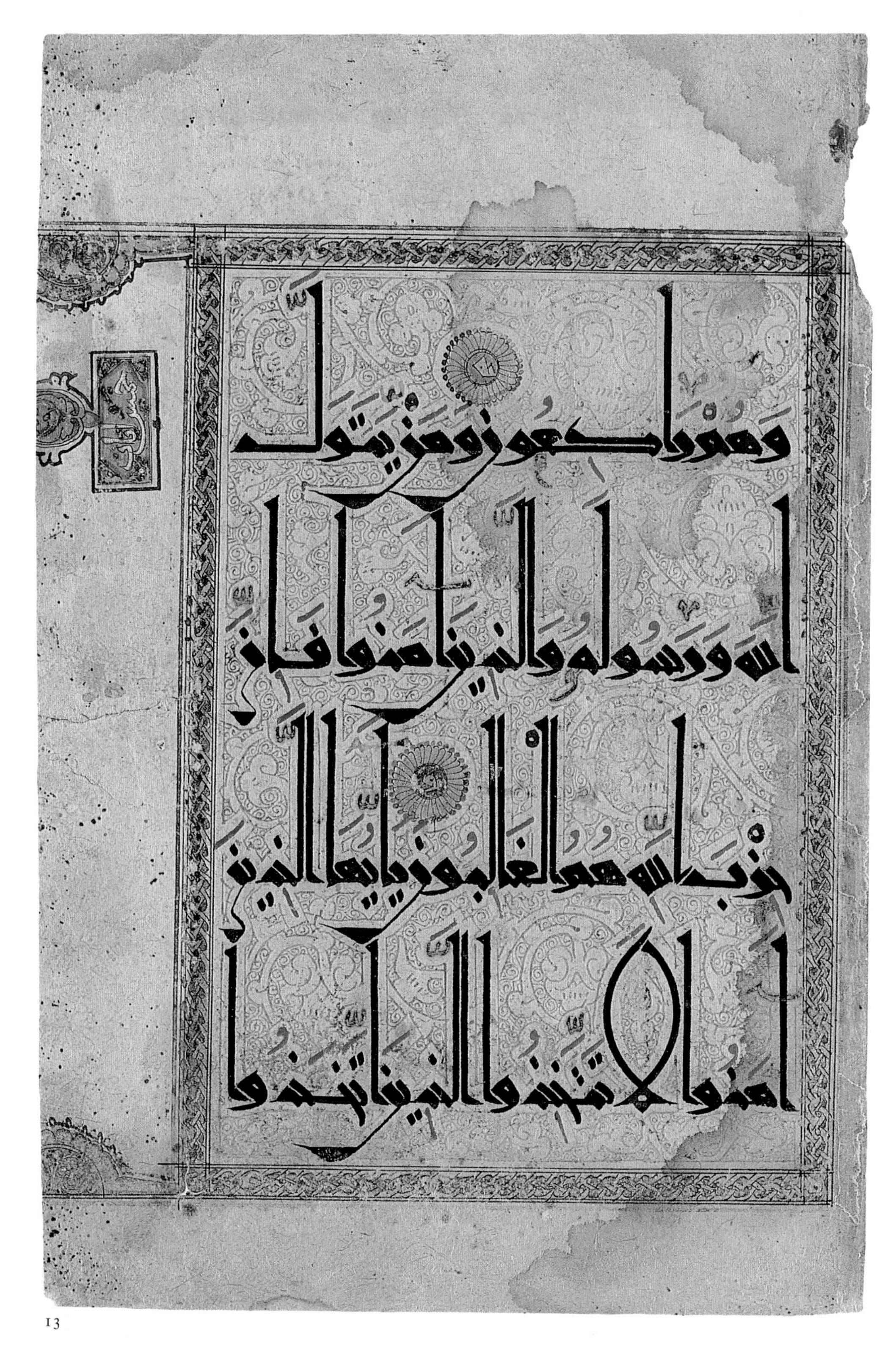

13

13
Sura V *Al-Mā'idah* verses 55-57

Page from a dispersed manuscript of the Holy Qur'an, written in black ink on paper in Kufic
23.5 × 16.5 cm
Iran, perhaps Meshed, late 11th century

North-eastern Iran was one of the creative centres for medieval Islamic literary and visual culture, and this Qur'an – now widely dispersed – was probably produced in the holy city of Meshed under Seljuq patronage. Its background is composed of pale arabesques, almost fading beneath the intense boldness of the script. Here horizontal letters have been compacted so that verticals soar to six or seven times their height; in some instances even letters normally vertical have been compressed for dramatic emphasis. Thus, at the beginning of the second line, the word Allah has the initial *alif* towering above the two succeeding *lams* which have been not only compressed but tilted to the left. In this form God's name resembles the single lozenge mark made by the impression of the reed pen on paper. In shape and size this lozenge is the basic 'building block' of Islamic calligraphy, for it is used to measure the length and breadth of letters. Thus the foundation of the script reflects the faith's true centre.

14
Sura VI *Al-An'ām* verses 1-2

Page from a dispersed manuscript of the Holy Qur'an, written in black Kufic on paper
26.5 × 20 cm
Iraq or Iran, 12th century

Sura headings generally employed a different and more ornamental style of script than the text, and the Kufic in the decorative *'unwān* at the top of this page is appropriately more formal and complex than the black lines below. At the left is a box containing the word Makka, identifying the sura as one that was revealed while the Prophet was in that city. These two initial verses of this sura announce God's power as sole creator. This page comes from the same original manuscript as no. 15.

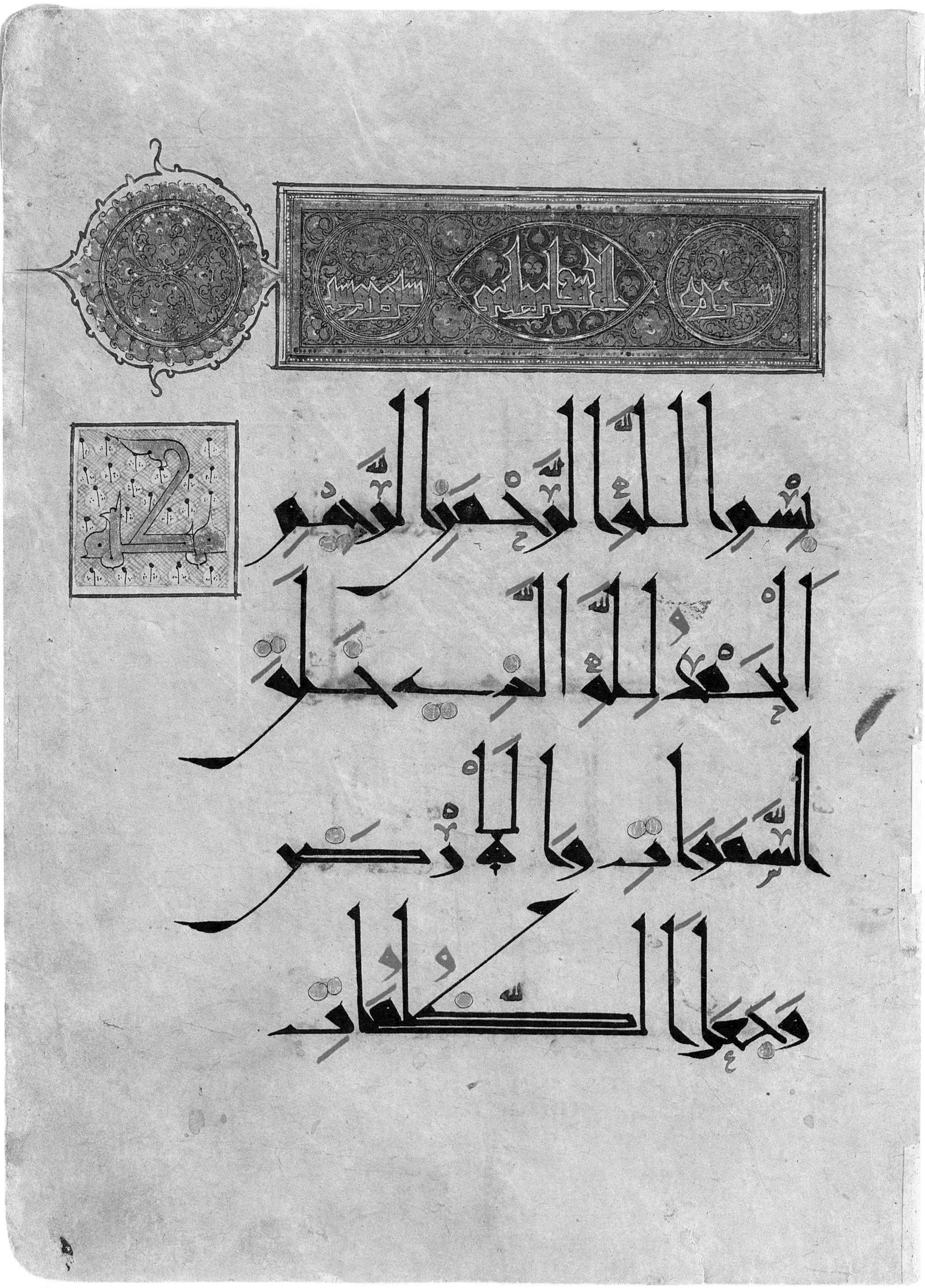

14

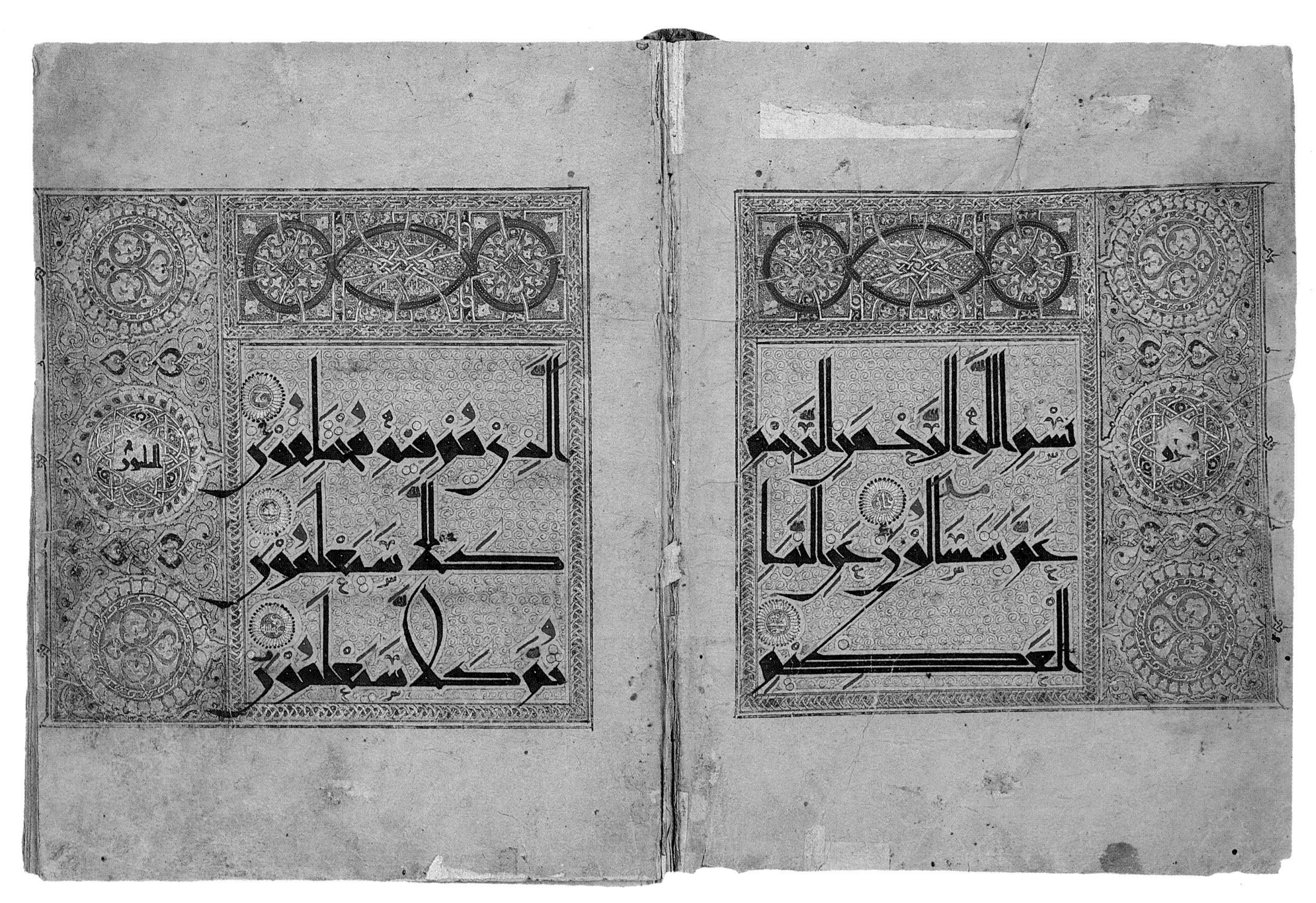

15
Sura LXXVII *Al-Naba'* (opening verses)
Illuminated frontispiece to Section 30 of the Holy Qur'an, written in Kufic from a Qur'an fragment of thirty-six pages
25.4 × 19.5 cm
A. Welch (1972), vol. 2, MS 2, pp. 21-22, 25-27; Lings and Safadi (1976), no. 37; Lings (1977), p. 18, and pl. 12; A. Welch (1979), no. 12; A. Welch and S.C. Welch (1982), no. 12, pp. 48-50
Iran or Iraq, 12th century

These pages are the remnants of what must have been one of the great Qur'ans, and they were preserved by an unknown connoisseur in the late eighteenth or nineteenth century who had them bound in a simple leather binding. (See no. 14 for an additional page from this manuscript.) The text is written in eastern Kufic script, and its stark letters move with a slow, measured rhythm. Red diacritical marks indicate vowels, and small blue cursive letters explicate Kufic forms too difficult to read easily. The script moves against a background of minute arabesques. The calligrapher was obviously an artist of the highest calibre, as was the illuminator who made the two pages mirror-images of each other. Roundel, medallions, and panels are filled with fine gold arabesques, and blue, white, and red are used to outline geometric forms that express Islamic artists' fascination with mathematics as a metaphor of divine order and presence.

16
The *ghawwās*, (water bird)

Page from a manuscript of the *Manāfi' al-Hayawān* of Ibn Bakhtishu'
Chapter headings in Kufic; text in *naskh*
22.3 × 16.5 cm
A. Welch (1978), vol. III, pp. 34-35
Iran, late 13th century

The *Manāfi' al-Hayawān* (The uses of animals) was a bestiary that enjoyed particular popularity in Il-Khanid Iran, and this page (also illustrated on the reverse) comes from a dispersed manuscript that was probably done in the last decade of the 13th century in Maragheh or Tabriz in north-western Iran. According to the Persian text, the *ghawwās* is a bird that lives in streams near Baghdad and dives under water to catch fish. Ibn Bakhtishu' relates a story of a *ghawwās* whose snaring was repeatedly interrupted by a raven that stole the captured fish. Its patience at an end, the *ghawwās* finally attacked and killed the raven. The unknown illustrator seems to have chosen not to illustrate this story but instead to show three of the *ghawwās* birds in their natural habitat.

17
Bahram Gur at the house of Mahiyar the Jeweller

Page from a manuscript of the *Shāhnāmeh*
Text in *naskh*
23.8 × 19.4 cm
Pope (1945), pl. 121; A. Welch (1972), vol. I, Ir. M. 1, pp. 44-45
Iran or Iraq, *c.* 1300

Unknown patrons, probably either in Baghdad or Tabriz, commissioned the earliest extant illustrated copies of Firdawsi's great epic, the *Shāhnāmeh* (Book of Kings). Four of these early manuscripts have survived and, due to their relatively small size, are known now as the 'small' *Shāhnāmehs*. They are key documents for the development of Iranian painting and testify to a wide range of astute patronage and skilled painters during the Golden Age of Il-Khanid culture. This particular episode recounts the visit of the disguised Shah Bahram Gur – one of the epic's great hunters and lovers – to the home of a wealthy jeweller whose daughter sings in praise of his good looks. The story ends with their marriage.

18 *Folio 3r*

18 *Folio 7r*

18

The *Jāmi' al-tawārikh* (World History) of Rashid al-Din

Manuscript of sixty-three folios, written in Arabic in thirty-five lines to the page in a clear *naskh* by an unidentified scribe
43.6 × 29.1 cm
Previously in the library of the Royal Asiatic Society, London
Gray (1978) (with complete bibliography); Sotheby's, 8 July 1980
Iran, Tabriz, dated 714/1314

It would be hard to overestimate the importance of this remarkable manuscript. It is not only a superb work of art but also stands near the beginning of the great tradition of the Iranian precious book. This fragment of sixty-three folios originally belonged to a royal copy of the *Jāmi' al-tawārikh* (World History) of Rashid al-Din, one of the most noteworthy figures in Islamic history. The text contains portions of four sections of the original work: a history of Muhammad (fols 2-8); the history of China (fols 9-18); the history of India (fols 19-41); and the history of the Jews (fols 42-60). Chapter titles, key sentences, and important names are written in red, and the manuscript contains two *shamsas* (illuminated roundels, fols 19r and 42r) and two illuminated *'unwāns* (headings, fols 19v and 42v), as well as thirty-five pages illustrated with one hundred miniature paintings by several different, unidentified artists.

On folio 41v is written the information that the manuscript was created in 714/1314 on the order of the Il-Khanid ruler Uljaytu (r. 1304-16) in his capital city of Tabriz. The author, Rashid al-Din, was at the height of his political power as the vizier of the monarch, and the manuscript was produced in the Rashidiyya, the intellectual and artistic quarter that had been constructed under his patronage in the late 12th and early 13th centuries. The vizier also established an endowment to support scholars and students in the Rashidiyya and to enable the scriptorium there to produce two copies (one in Arabic and one in Persian) of the *World History* each year for distribution to the major centres of the Il-Khanid state. This manuscript is one of the very few fragments that were produced during the author's lifetime and perhaps even under his supervision. The other substantial fragment is dated 1306-7 and is in the Edinburgh University Library (Rice and Gray, 1976).

The 1314 *World History* was perhaps destined for Herat, since on folio 11r is the library seal of Timur's son and successor Shah Rukh (r. 1405-47). No surviving seals attest to the manuscript's subsequent history, though at some point before the 19th century it came into the possession of an Indian prince. On folio 1v is a note that it was owned by the British officer John Staples Harriot in Patna (Dinapur); Harriot was stationed there in 1813. Between 1818 and 1838 Harriot returned three times to England. During one of these trips he sold it to Major-General Thomas Gordon who bequeathed it to the Royal Asiatic Society in 1841. It was on loan to the British Museum and British Library from July 23, 1948, to July 8, 1980, when it was sold at Sotheby's in an auction that occasioned world-wide interest. One of the most widely exhibited and widely published works of Islamic art, this *Jāmi' al-tawārikh* has now returned to Muslim ownership.

The author of the *Jāmi' al-tawārikh*, Rashid al-Din, was born in 1247 in Hamadan in western Iran. He was a physician by training and it was in this capacity that he served under the Il-Khanid ruler Abaqa (r. 1265-82). In 1298 under Ghazan Khan (r. 1295-1304) this capable and ambitious man was appointed deputy to the vizier Sadr al-Din Zanjani and was commissioned to serve as court historian. A few months later Sadr al-Din Zanjani was deposed and executed, and Rashid al-Din and his colleague Sa'd al-Din Savaji were appointed joint viziers. Both men presumably participated in Ghazan Khan's effort to rebuild Iran's economy, social structure, and artistic traditions. The monarch commissioned Rashid al-Din to complete the history of the Mongols begun by the Iranian historian Juwayni, and Ghazan Khan's successor, Uljaytu (r. 1304-16) extended the commission to include the history of the Far East, Europe, and South Asia from Adam to contemporary times.

The production of appropriately fine copies of the *World History* was entrusted to Rashid al-Din's scriptorium in the Rashidiyya (*Rab'-i Rashīdī*), a suburb east of the centre of Tabriz. Under the vizier's patronage the Rashidiyya became a focus for intellectual, artistic, theological, and cultural life under the Il-Khans, and the scriptorium used not only the finest materials but also employed the best calligraphers, painters, and other masters of the book. They came not only from Mesopotamia and Iran but also from Central Asia and the Far East, and their diverse cultural heritages reflected the cosmopolitanism of the Il-Khanid state.

The *Jāmi' al-tawārikh* was an ambitious historical work. For information about the Mongol tribes and conquests, Rashid al-Din relied upon Pulad, the Mongol emissary at the court of the Il-Khans in Tabriz, and in a similar fashion he carefully consulted appropriate authorities for the other historical sections. Thus while the history of the prophetic tradition from Adam to Muhammad was a traditional Islamic intellectual concern, the history of areas outside Islam was not. For his section on China the author, who was familiar with Chinese painting and calligraphy, consulted Chinese scholars resident in Tabriz who translated Chinese texts for him. The history of India and its religions was developed with the assistance of Indian scholars, and the large Christian communities in Tabriz probably supplied him with information about Byzantium and Western European Christendom. In its scope and scholarship the *Jāmi' al-tawārikh* was one of the most impressive accomplishments of medieval Islamic culture.

This manuscript belonged to a copy of the entire book completed in 1314. The only other portion known to have been completed during the author's lifetime and presumably under his supervision in the Rashiddiya is a volume containing 277 folios and seventy miniatures dated 706/1306. Though in a similar text format and style of painting, it is a separate manuscript (also incomplete), originally destined for another location. Together, these two splendid fragments are the most important surviving creations of the atelier in the Rashidiyya and represent some of the finest achievements of Il-Khanid painting. They are crucial documents for an understanding of Il-Khanid culture and the subsequent evolution of Iranian art. For neither manuscript are calligrapher and artists known. An analysis of the Edinburgh miniatures has identified five different painters,[1] and it is apparent that several painters also worked on the creation of the paintings in the 1314 volume.

The Rashidiyya lost its great patron in 1318. The Il-Khanid ruler Abu Sa'id (1317-35) dismissed, imprisoned, and then executed the vizier, Rashid al-Din, and the Rashidiyya was attacked and looted.

18 *Folio 14v*

18 *Folio 19r*

Undoubtedly many of its artists and intellectuals moved to safer quarters or sought new patronage. But in 1328 Rashid al-Din's son Ghiyath al-Din, a man of learning well-known as a connoisseur and collector of manuscripts, became vizier. He restored and expanded the Rashidiyya, and it is likely that the last great manuscript of Il-Khanid art, the fragmentary Demotte *Shāhnāmeh*, was worked on there between November, 1335, and May, 1336, when Ghiyath al-Din was murdered.[2] Father and son had served Iranian culture well. The illustrations of the manuscripts produced under their auspices were characteristic of Il-Khanid culture in Tabriz: they were eclectic blends of different artistic traditions, chiefly those of China and Iran, and in this regard they reflected eastern Islam's continuing fascination with the arts of the Far East.

Folios 2-8 of the 1314 *Jāmi' al-tawārikh* are concerned with the history of the Prophet Muhammad. Due to Islam's well-known avoidance of figural imagery in its sacred arts, manuscripts of the Qur'an and the *Hadīth* were never figurally illustrated, though they were often lavishly illuminated with non-figural decoration. But the *Jāmi' al-tawārikh* was a history rather than a sacred text, and neither patron nor the Tabriz *qādīs* who examined the text for accuracy seem to have objected to its figural illustrations. The iconography of the Prophet, his family and descendants, and the history of Islam is thus largely to be found in histories, biographies, and mystical literature. Folio 3r (page 48) describes the submission of a Jewish tribe – the Banu'l-Nadir – to the Muslims. Il-Khanid eclecticism is evident: one of the figures in the castle stretches his hands beyond the picture's borders, a compositional idiosyncrasy found in earlier Mesopotamian painting. Pre-Islamic Sasanian Iran is probably the source for the sun's form, while the sense of depth and the expanse of empty space is the result of Chinese influence. In folio 7r (page 48) Muslim nobles consult before the 624 battle of Badr in which the Muslims defeated the Makkans. Landscape is again strongly influenced by Chinese convention.

The history of the rulers of China (fols 9-18) was compiled with the assistance of Chinese scholars, manuscripts, and printed books, the latter being the likeliest source for these 'portraits' of the rulers of China that make up the only illustration of the section on China in the *World History*.[3] On each page there are several images; folio 14v shows five figures – in the centre the emperor Hsuan-ti of the Later Liang dynasty (555-62) (illustrated) and in separate panels beside and below him four attendants.

The nine illustrations in the section on the history of India (fols 19-41) present historical scenes, images from Hindu and Buddhist scriptures, pure landscape, and architecture. The Buddhist monk Bakshi Kamahshri at the Il-Khanid court was the chief source of information about Buddhism for Rashid al-Din. On folio 34r (opposite) the Buddha offers fruit to the devil; both wear the headgear of Chinese scholars. Strong in Central Asia, Buddhism was still very much part of the larger Il-Khanid world: Ghazan Khan had been a Buddhist before his conversion to Islam in 1295. Folio 36v (page 52) is one of two pure landscapes in the manuscript and shows the grove of Jetavana which the wealthy man of Sravasti had bestowed on the Buddha. The representation of this sacred landscape is based on Chinese scroll painting, though here rendered in a more decorative manner by the bunching of leaves and silver shading.

The final section (fols 42-60) deals with the history of the Jews, and its first illustration (fol. 45r, page 52) shows Noah reclining near the ark's bow; adjacent to him are his three sons, while three other men guide the ship. Though the boat's form is probably derived from Mesopotamian tradition, the representation of water and landscape is strongly Chinese. As in the other miniatures, this eclectic utilization of different traditions reflects the cosmopolitan nature of Tabriz under the Il-Khans.

1) Rice (1976), pp. 5-9
2) Grabar and Blair (1980), p. 48
3) Rice (1976), pp. 25-30

انا خير منكم لان رياضتي ومجاهدتي اكثر فقطع سرهارتسد شعره ورمى السيف في الماء وترك الدنيا كلها واعطى بعض شعره لذلك السايس وبعثه الى امه
وابيه والباقي من شعره اخذته الملائكة وحملوه الى السماء الثامنة الى مقام الابرار وكانوا يزورونه المشائخ الذين كانوا على صورة اهل ثم انكروا
عليه وقالوا ابن انت وان هذا الشغل نحن نجتهد الليل والنهار ونعبد الله ونرتاض رياضة صعبة ناكل الحشيش بدل الغذاء وانت فقد ربوك في
نعمة وثروة فكيف تطيق مشقة الجوع والغذاء [illegible] ثم يا ابن الملك من واشتغل بامر الدنيا والخيل والصيد فلما سمع سرهارتسد كلامهم ظهر له غيرة
فاختار القناعة وقعد ست سنين على راس صخرة وكان غذاؤه في كل يوم حبة من الماش وابتت قدمه على ذلك فمن كان اقرب الى الخلق ما كان شاهده
هزيلا ونحيفا بل شاهده على حالته الاولى وبلونه وقوته قاعدا على سرير مرصع معلق في الهواء والذي كان منهم ضعيف اليقين وبعيدا من الحق وجدوه ضعيفا
نحيفا وقد مد عظامه وعروقه واعصابه في جلد مرميا فوق حجر وكان في خدمته خمسة نفر من تلك الجماعة يلازمونه ليلا ونهارا فلما تمت المدة و
ست سنين جاء اليه ملك اسمه اندر وهو الذي له الف عين فقال له قد آن الزمان الذي تخرج فيه من هذا المقام وفي تلك الحالة جاء صوت النداء
من السماء وسمي شاكموني وهو الذي يسميه اهل المذاهب والاديان آدم والآن اثر قدمه موجود في حجر على جبل سرنديب عند معدن الياقوت
الاحمر وكان اسنة باق ثم عند المحتشين في مقام يقال له سادبل وكانت الملائكة الذين حضروا من جبل قاف لاجل افطار شاكموني اربع قصاع معي بعضها
فوق بعض وهي عند مجاوري سرنديب باقية الى الآن والسلم ٥

الفصل

السادس في خروج شاكموني من الخلوة والمجاهدة ٥

فلما خرج من الخلوة ووصل خبره الى الخاص والعام والزهاد والعباد علموا بانه قد خرج من الخلوة والانزواء وهو يطلب الماكل والمشارب
وكان له بنت فخطر ببالها ان تعمل له طعاما وتقدمه بين يديه ليكون اول اكله عندها وكان لها سرح من البقر فامرت حتى اتي بمائة بقرة وحلبها وطبخت بالارز
والسكر طعاما وكذا اباقي اصحابه واصدقائه طبخوا مثلما طبخت ابنته فلما فرغوا من الطبخ احضروا الطعام بين يديه فمد يده الى الاطعمة واعطاها لسطل جائع لياكلها

فتخيل لكل واحد منهم ان شاكموني اكل من طعامه ففرحوا غاية الفرح وافتخروا بذلك وكان يقول كل واحد منهم ان شاكموني اكل من طعامي فلما عرف
بعض المشائخ والزهاد وبعض مريديه تلك الافعال منه انكروا عليه وقالوا انه لما اكل الطعام وترك الخلوة تكدر صفاء قلبه وتزول عنه المكاشفات
ومعرفة الاسرار الالهية والعلوم اليقينية ومهما يكون لنا فكيف ربنا وتوصلنا الى مشاهدة عالم النور والقدس والمكاشفات فاختاروا انهاجروا
على صحبته وتركوه فلما راى شاكموني افعالهم وسمع اقوالهم اخذ القصعة التي كان فيها الطبيخ ورماها في البحر وقال ان كنت نبي الخلائق ومقتدهم
[illegible] هذه القصعة الى اعلى الماء فلما رماها صعدت وسارت الى اعلى الماء وفي مقدار ساعة وصلت الى العين التي كانت تخرج منها الماء [illegible]
[illegible] وقعدت على الاقصاع التي كانت للانبياء الستة المتقدمين عليه وكان داخل العين ملك اعمى على صورة ثعبان يسمونه كالك فلما [illegible]
[illegible] امتلا بيته ضياء ونورا من كثرة اشعة انوارها وصحت عين الملك من [illegible] كالك وقال يا للعجب كيف خرج نبي [illegible]
[illegible] يوم واحد وكان مقدار يوم كالك كلب فقال شاكموني وباقي الانبياء ان مقدار كلب هو انا لو وضعنا ارضا مساحتها اربعة فراسخ [illegible]
[illegible] فراسخ عرضا في اربعة فراسخ عمقا قد مليت من السمسم ونطرح في كل سمسمة واحدة فيكون حاصل [illegible] هذه المدة من طوفان الى [illegible]

18 *Folio 34r*

18 *Folio 36v*

18 *Folio 45r*

19

The fable of the lion, the fox, and the ass

Page from a manuscript of the *Kalīla wa Dimna*
28 × 18.5 cm
A. Welch (1972), vol. I, Ir. M. 3/A, pp. 61 and 63
Iran, Shiraz, 1333

The *Kalīla wa Dimna* were enormously popular animal fables based ultimately on the Sanskrit Tales of Bidpai. This page, from a dispersed Persian manuscript of the stories, is written in a legible, though inelegant, *naskh*, and is illustrated by painters unacquainted with the achievements of Il-Khanid painting in northern Iran. Despite the typically somewhat sloppy application of colour, the drawing is direct and simple, appropriate to the tale itself. Wasting from illness, the lion was prescribed the heart and ears of an ass as a cure. His courtier, the fox, cajoled an ass to come close enough so the lion could kill him, but as the lion washed before beginning his meal, the fox devoured the ass's heart and ears.

19

20

Garshasp enthroned

Page from the Demotte *Shāhnāmeh*
Inscribed with heading: 'The reign of Garshasp (was) nine years.'
Miniature 28.5 × 29 cm, page 41 × 29 cm
Musée d'art et d'histoire, Geneva (Pozzi Collection)
Robinson (1974), no. 1; Grabar and Blair (1980), no. 15
Iran, Tabriz, *c.* 1335

Much of the miniature is badly abraded, and a triangular piece is missing from the upper left. The son of Shah Zav, Garshasp ruled for nine largely peaceful years. When he died, the hostile Turanian king Afrasiyab invaded Iran. In an elaborate palace setting sits the grand figure of Garshasp on a huge throne. Not mentioned in the text, a large group of unidentified, very busy courtiers surround the throne.

21
Bahman meeting Zal

Page from the Demotte *Shāhnāmeh*
Inscribed with heading: 'Bahman comes to Zal'
Miniature 21 × 21 cm, page 41 × 29 cm
Musée d'art et d'histoire, Geneva (Pozzi Collection)
Robinson (1974), no. 2; Grabar and Blair (1980), no. 18
Iran, Tabriz, *c.* 1335

The miniature is in good condition, except for slight abrasion of Zal's face. According to the text, Shah Gushtasp dispatched his son Isfandiyar to Zabulistan to bring the champion Rustam back in chains to the Iranian court. In an effort to persuade Rustam to come peacefully with him, Isfandiyar first sent his son, Bahman, to Rustam's citadel. Here he is greeted by Rustam's father Zal who is, like Bahman, anxious to avoid a confrontation.

22
Ardashir and Gulnar in bed

Page from the Demotte *Shāhnāmeh*
Inscribed with heading: 'Gulnar coming to Ardashir's pillow and sleeping by his side'
Miniature 20 × 20 cm, page 41 × 29 cm
Musée d'art et d'histoire, Geneva (Pozzi Collection)
Robinson (1974), no. 3; Grabar and Blair (1980), no. 40
Iran, Tabriz, *c.* 1335

Much of the miniature has been damaged, and the blanket over the loving couple has been partially repainted. The young Ardashir was of noble descent and great prowess. The Parthian king Ardavan brought him to his court, but after seeing that he was more able than his own sons, the king banished him to the stables. Ardavan's favourite slave girl, Gulnar, fell in love with Ardashir and secretly spent the night with him. Despite the fact that the future Sasanian ruler is not yet shah, Ardashir wears a crown in bed, and another crown rests on his clothes in the lower right. (cf. no. 57)

23

Bahram Gur sends Narsi as Viceroy to Khurusan

Page from the Demotte *Shāhnāmeh*
Inscribed with heading: 'Bahram Gur talks to Narsi'
Miniature 21 × 20 cm, page 41 × 29 cm
Previously in the Kevorkian Collection
Sotheby's, 3 April 1978, p. 23, Grabar and Blair (1980), no. 52
Iran, Tabriz, *c.* 1335

Famed as a hunter and lover, the Sasanian shah Bahram Gur was also concerned with justice, and when he sent his brother Narsi to govern the rich province of Khurasan, he instructed him to rule fairly and treat the poor with generosity and justice. Seated on a large throne, the shah extends his right hand toward Narsi, while a young page listens to their conversation. Two women lean over and eavesdrop. The archway at the left and a large rectangle to the left of the pageboy have been repainted. Enthroned kings are a common motif in the Demotte *Shāhnāmeh*, since the presumed patron was interested in images of royal power and legitimacy.

24
Forest conflict

Page from a dispersed album
Ink drawing bordered by six panels of verse
Drawing 8.4 × 18.5 cm
Ackerman (1940), p. 203; A. Welch (1972), vol. I, Ir. M. 7, pp. 93-95; A. Welch and S.C. Welch (1982), no. 14, pp. 53-55
Iran, *c.* 1400-5

The drawing reverberates with chaos and panic: a lion mauls a deer while its mate screams in fear; a lone warrior grips and stabs a dragon; two ducks turn in a swirling sky; disputing monkeys quarrel in the lush vegetation. Although it may have illustrated a now lost tale, this superb drawing was not made for inclusion in a manuscript. Instead, it was a *tour-de-force* presumably intended for inclusion in an album for an imaginative patron like the great sultan Ghiyath al-Din Ahmad Jala'ir, the foremost opponent of Timur in Iran. The verses in *mathnawī* metre that border the drawing are written in a handsome *ta'līq* script, but bear no direct relationship to the drawing itself.

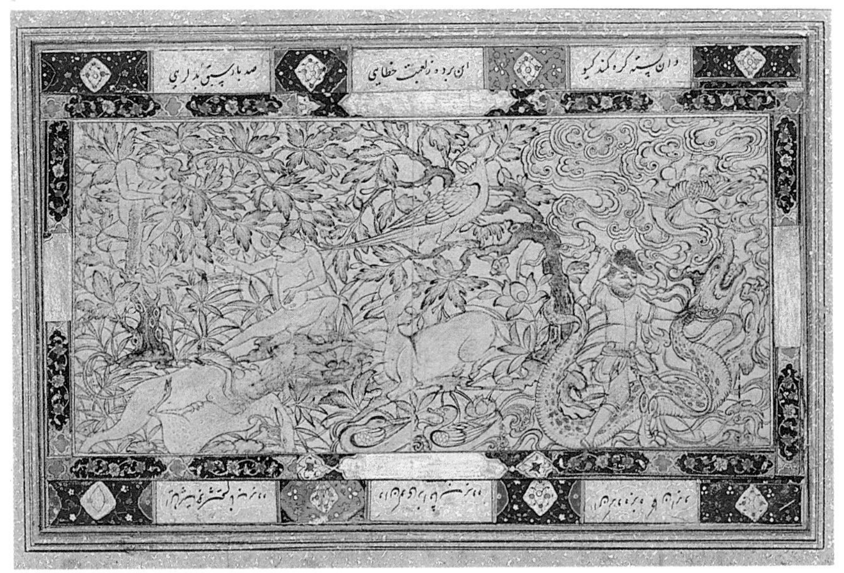

24

25
Monkeys taunting a lion

Page from a dispersed album
Ink drawing
Drawing 24.1 × 15.6 cm
Martin (1912), vol. 2, pl. 64; A. Welch (1972), vol. I, Ir. M. 8, pp. 96-97; A. Welch and S. C. Welch (1982), no. 15, pp. 54-55
Iran, *c.* 1400-10

It is plausible that this drawing may have been done for the same spirited patron as the previous one, and it too may have been based on a story no longer known now. Clearly, both were done in north-western Iran, perhaps Tabriz. The landscape is nearly as animated as the enraged lion, roaring at the mischievous monkeys who insultingly wave leaves in his face.

25

26

Sura XXIX *'Ankabūt* verses 25-27

Page from a large manuscript of the Holy Qur'an, copied by Prince Baysunghur
177 × 101 cm
Iran, Herat, *c.* 1420-33

The son of Shah Rukh who ruled Iran from 1404 to 1444 and the grandson of Timur, Prince Baysunghur spent most of his life in Herat, where he devoted himself more to the arts than to the governmental offices he nominally held. Thoroughly trained as a calligrapher and a connoisseur of painting, he established a model of princely patronage that later Timurid, Safavid, and Mughal rulers emulated. Trained by a follower of Yaqut al-Musta'simi, he must have learned the six cursive scripts practised by Yaqut, and this splendid page demonstrates his mastery of the majestic *jalīl al-muhaqqaq*, the grand cursive script that was the favoured script for large Qur'ans in the 14th and 15th centuries. As the only example of Baysunghur's art, pages from this now-dispersed Qur'an have enormous historical significance.

These seven lines deal with the line of prophethood and the punishment of disbelievers on the Day of Resurrection.

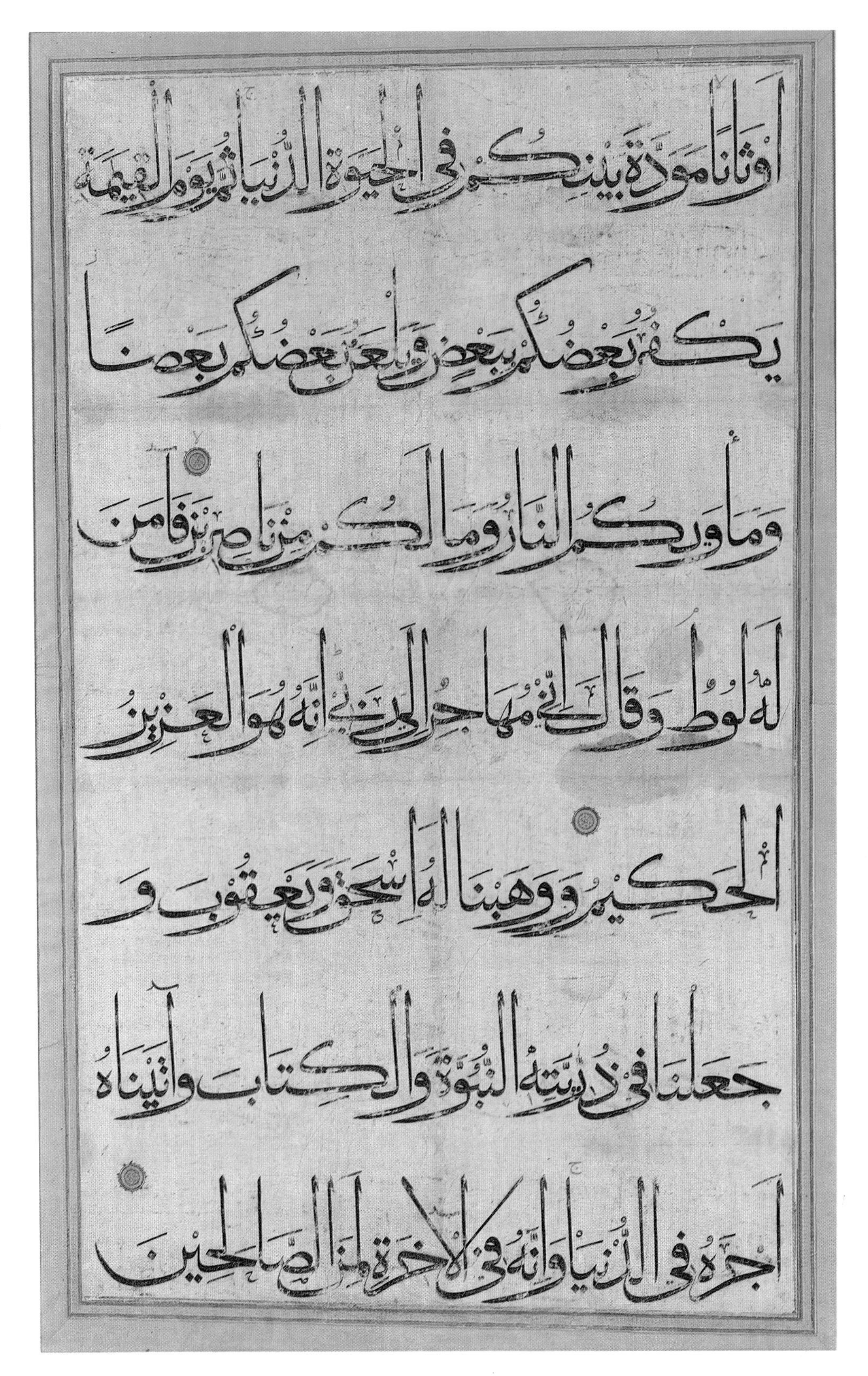

اوثانا مودة بينكم في الحيوة الدنيا ثم يوم القيمة
يكفر بعضكم ببعض ويلعن بعضكم بعضا
وماويكم النار وما لكم من ناصرين فامن
له لوط وقال اني مهاجر الى ربي انه هو العزيز
الحكيم ووهبنا له اسحق ويعقوب و
جعلنا في ذريته النبوة والكتاب واتيناه
اجره في الدنيا وانه في الاخرة لمن الصالحين

27

The last of the Abbasid Caliphs, Musta'sim

Page from a manuscript of the *History* of Hafiz-i Abru
Inscribed with Persian historical text in *naskh*
36 × 25 cm
A. Welch (1978), vol. III, Ir. M. 57, pp. 46-49
Iran, Herat, *c.* 1425

Court historian to Timur's son and successor, Shah Rukh (r. 1404-44), Hafiz-i Abru was commissioned by his patron to revise and bring up to date several distinguished histories, including the *Universal History* of Rashid al-Din. This page from a dispersed manuscript of his History describes the defeat, surrender, and death of the last of the Abbasid caliphs of Baghdad, Musta'sim (r. 1242-58), in the 1258 capture of Baghdad by the Mongol armies under Hulagu. Presumably it is the martyred caliph who is represented standing in an aura of fire. The structure in which he stands bears no relationship to Islamic architecture in Herat, and though the figure of Musta'sim conforms to contemporary Timurid style, the vegetation and rudimentary landscape are based upon types prevalent in Il-Khanid painting of more than a century before.

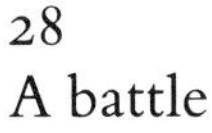

28

A battle

Double-page from a dispersed manuscript of Sharaf al-Din Yazdi's *Zafarnāmeh*
Miniature 27 × 19 cm, page 35.5 × 23.75 cm
The manuscript was previously in the Kevorkian Collection
Sotheby's 7 April 1975, lot 187
Iran, Shiraz, 1436

Sharaf al-Din Yazdi's *Zafarnāmeh* is a panegyric Persian history of the conquests of central Asia, Iran, and northern India by Timur (Tamerlane). Here his army encounters that of Amir Haji Sayf al-Din. The right-hand page is dominated by Timur who sits astride a gigantic, mailed horse and gestures with his whip toward the enemy. One of his soldiers holds a regal umbrella over his head. His followers, crowded in a narrow defile in the lower right, follow two horsemen, who 'leap' across to the left-hand page in pursuit of the fleeing enemy. Above them Timur's hapless opponent looks helplessly across at the victor, and the soldiers crowding behind him are as frightened as he is.

For Timur's descendants this History was obviously a book of signal importance, and this copy of the *Zafarnāmeh* was probably produced for his grandson Ibrahim Sultan, the governor of Shiraz, who was a devoted patron of the arts of the book. During the reign of Timur's son Shah Rukh (1404-44), Iran's major cities were closely linked, and there was frequent exchange of artistic talent and transmission of artist styles. Thus while this miniature is clearly a work of Shiraz painters, it resembles in its simplification of action and its large figures the 'Shah Rukh historical style' that was used for the illustration of historical manuscripts in Herat under the patronage of Shah Rukh.

29
Kay Kavus tries to fly to Heaven

Manuscript of Firdawsi's *Shāhnāmeh* written by the scribe Mahmud ibn Muhammad ibn Mahmud al-Jamali in *nasta'līq*, illustrated with fifty-three miniatures; one double-page and four single-page illuminations
Given in India to John Shore, first Baron Teignmouth, *c.* 1775
33.5 × 24.5 cm
Previously in the Kevorkian Collection
Robinson (1951) no. 14, (1952) pls 10 and 11; A. Welch, (1978), vol. 4, MS 11, pp. 12-22; A. Welch and S.C. Welch (1982), no. 16, pp. 57-60
Iran, Shiraz, 1 Rabi' al-awwal 861 (27 January 1457)

This manuscript's 554 pages are written in a crisp, fine *nasta'līq*, and the scribe, who also wrote a volume of Qasimi-i Anwar in Vienna (Flugel, 583), and perhaps a *Khamseh* of Amir Khusraw in the Bodleian Library, Oxford, (MS Elliot 189), was evidently a master of the first rank. Equally distinguished was the anonymous illuminator whose work here places him among the best Timurid masters of this art. The governor of Shiraz at this time was the Turkman Pir Budaq, and if he was the patron of this *Shāhnāmeh*, he was obviously a man of taste. A single painter, also unnamed, was responsible for fifty of the book's illustrations, and the imaginative rendering of a palace interior here indicates that he was a skilled and innovative artist in the Timurid tradition of mid-15th-century Shiraz.

30

Four figures beneath a tree

Painting in colours and gold on silk
19 × 28 cm; page 32 × 43 cm
Previously in the collection of the Comtesse de Béhague, France
The al-Sabah Collection, *Dār al-Āthār al-Islāmīya*, Kuwait National Museum, LNS 77 MS
Hillenbrand (1977), no. 13, p. 17. For other references see Hillenbrand's bibliography
Iran, Herat or Tabriz, 15th century

This breathtakingly beautiful miniature belongs to a very rare group of paintings on silk executed during the second or last quarter of the 15th century in Iran, in either Herat or Tabriz. By his skilful rendering of the facial expression and the demeanour of each participant in this charming scene, the artist has imbued his creation with the tension and relief proper to such an encounter. The expert handling of the psychological element in the painting, further enhanced by its setting on a cool Spring day, is matched by the masterful depiction of the details of the costumes on the four stately figures.

M.J.

31
Golandam and a suitor

Page from a manuscript of Ibn Husam's *Khāwarānnāmeh*
Inscribed with four columns of text in a good *nasta'līq*
40 × 29.2 cm
A. Welch (1972), vol. I, Ir. M. 13, pp. 107-108, 11; A. Welch and S.C. Welch (1982), no. 17, pp. 60-62
Iran, probably Herat, 1477

Composed in the same metre as Firdawsi's *Shāhnāmeh*, the *Khāwarānnāmeh* is an epic life of 'Ali, the Prophet Muhammad's cousin and son-in-law and the most important saint and hero of Shi'a Islam. It has been plausibly suggested that this widely dispersed copy of the book was produced in a Sufi centre near Herat, and, if this is the case, it indicates that patronage of illustrated manuscripts took place not only at the courts of secular rulers and in commercial ateliers but also under the aegis of clerical patrons. While the illustration of scripture was never sanctioned, works of religious history and poetry could be provided with suitable figural images.

32
Gushtasp works as a smith

Page from a manuscript of Firdawsi's *Shāhnāmeh*
Inscribed with four columns of text in *nasta'līq* written by Murshid ibn 'Izz al-Din
33 × 22.9 cm
Previously in the Demotte Collection
A. Welch (1972), vol. I, Ir. M. 14/C, pp. 108-115
Iran, Shawwal 887 (October, 1482)

This simple, straightforward painting style (closely similar to that of the dispersed *Khāwarānnāmeh*) was pan-Iranian in scope and probably more favoured by lesser aristocratic and even bourgeois patrons than by royalty. It survived for about a hundred years, well into the sixteenth century, and exerted a significant effect upon the development of Safavid painting.

33
Rustam fells Ashkabus

Page from a *Shāhnāmeh* made for Sultan Mirza 'Ali
Text in four columns of competent *nasta'līq* written by Salik ibn Sa'id
34.6 × 24.5 cm
A. Welch (1978), vol. III, Ir. M. 60/A, pp. 52-57; A. Welch and S.C. Welch (1982), no. 18, pp. 62-65
Iran, Gilan, 1494

The Iranian army at the right and the Turanian forces at the left exchange flights of arrows that form a decorative 'ladder' ascending towards rocks vitalized by minute natural and supernatural faces. An arrow from the champion Rustam, the towering figure at the right, topples the Turanian hero Ashkabus from his horse. Important provincial styles of art flourished at independent political centres in late 15th-century Iran. Sultan Mirza 'Ali, the ruler of the southern Caspian state of Gilan from 1478-1504, was one of the most energetic patrons, for he commissioned an enormous *Shāhnāmeh* with approximately 350 illustrations by many different painters. The two volumes of the manuscript are now in Istanbul and retain 311 illustrations; the remainder were apparently separated from the first volume about sixty years ago.

34

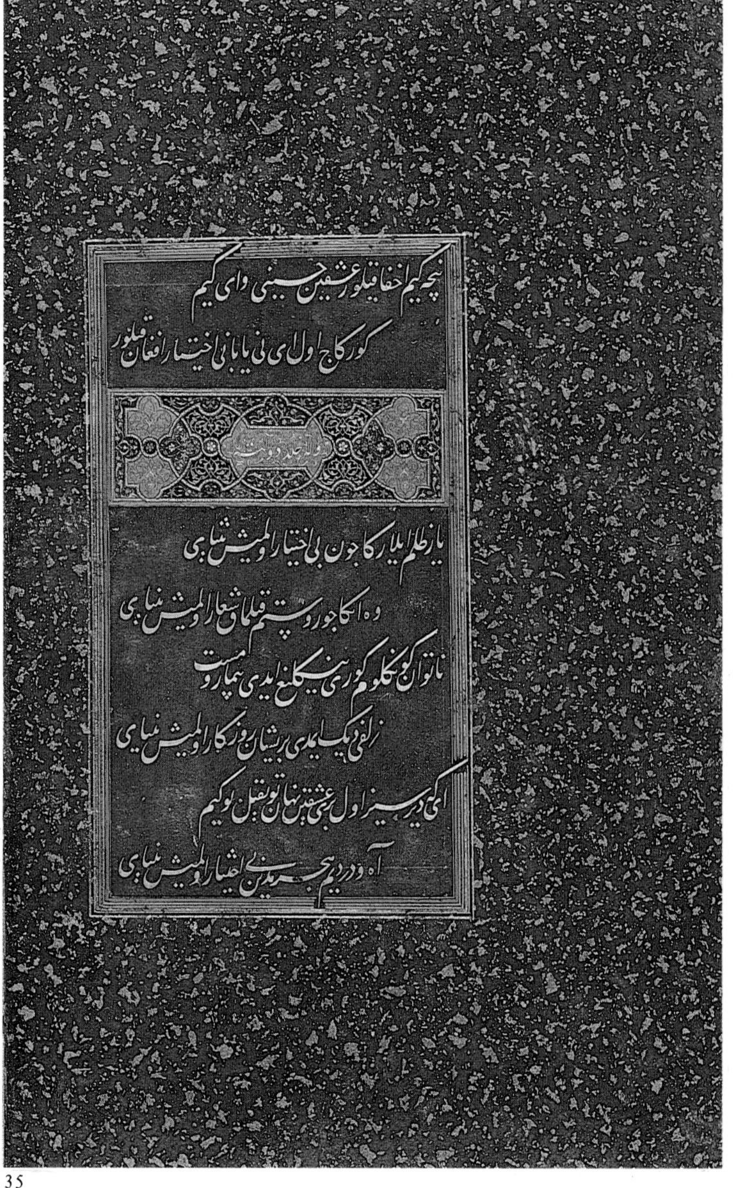

35

34
Page from a poetical manuscript of Jami

14 × 8.5 cm
Iran, Herat, late 15th century

Sultan Husayn Bayqara ruled a stable and prosperous kingdom from his capital in Herat from 1467-1506. One of the greatest of Timurid patrons, he assembled at his court the most talented artists of his time. His vizier and close friend, Mir 'Ali Shir Nawa'i, was a patron and poet of distinction. Noted historians, theologians, and philosophers wrote and taught in Herat. Painters, like Bihzad, and calligraphers, like Sultan 'Ali Mashhadi, flourished under his patronage, and among a number of other poets was Jami, the last great classical master of Persian poetry and the author of the *Haft Awrang*.

This page is inscribed on both sides with Jami's poetry. The light brown margins are flecked with gold. Against a light blue ground are written horizontally four lines in pink and yellow and diagonally twelve lines in white and pink. Coloured *nasta'līq* letters against a blue background was a favoured technique in Timurid Herat at the end of the 15th century (see no. 35), and these lines may also be the work of the celebrated Timurid master of *nasta'līq*, Sultan 'Ali Mashhadi.

35
Page of *découpé* calligraphy

From a dispersed manuscript of the *Dīwān* of Sultan Husayn Bayqara
15.9 × 10.3 cm
A. Welch (1972), vol. 2, MS 5, pp. 12 and 17
Iran, Herat, late 15th or early 16th century

Its margins sprinkled with gold, this dark blue page comes from a now dispersed manuscript of the Chaghatay Turkish *Dīwān* of Sultan Husayn Bayqara, the last great Timurid ruler of Herat (r. 1467-1506). He not only presided over one of the most illustrious courts in Islamic history but also composed Turkish poetry under the pen-name Husayni. The two top lines here conclude one *ghazāl* (ode), and the fine illuminated heading introduces six lines of another *ghazāl*. Notably, these six lines in yellow and white *nasta'līq* were not written with a pen. Instead, these letters were cut from coloured paper in an art form known as *qit'a* (calligraphic *découpage*). It may be that Sultan Husayn's celebrated master of *nasta'līq* Sultan 'Ali Mashhadi was the creator of these lines.

36
Page of *nasta'līq*, calligraphy

From an album made for Shah Jahan
Inscribed with Persian poetry
Signed by Mir 'Ali al-Katib
35 × 28 cm approx.
Iran, Herat, *c.* 1520

A Persian poem is written in four lines of diagonal *nasta'līq* across the central rectangle; it is bordered by ten panels containing poetry in a minute *nasta'līq*. A horizontal panel at the bottom of the page contains lines of both large and small *nasta'līq*. Mir 'Ali al-Katib, whose name appears in the triangular area in the lower left of the central rectangle, came from a prominent family in Herat and studied calligraphy under the great Sultan 'Ali Mashhadi. He soon gained renown as a master of *nasta'līq* and worked for Timurid and Safavid patrons in Herat. When that city was captured by the Uzbeks in 1528-29, he was taken to the Uzbek capital of Bukhara, where he remained until his death around 1544. The Mughals in particular admired his script, and this page was bound in an album presumably compiled for Shah Jahan: its floral borders closely resemble other pages from that monarch's albums.

37
Portrait of Hatifi

Page from an album made for Prince Bahram
Inscribed: 'Portrait of Mawlana 'Abdullah Hatifi; the work of Master Bihzad.'
Miniature 9.9 × 6 cm, page 11.8 × 7.7 cm
Sakisian (1929), pl. 74 and fig. 129; A. Welch and S.C. Welch (1982), no. 20, pp. 67-69
Iran, Herat, 1511-12

Often cited by Islamic sources as the greatest of Iranian painters, Bihzad was born about the middle of the 15th century. By 1485 he was flourishing under the patronage of the Timurid ruler of eastern Iran, Sultan Husayn Bayqara, and his vizier, Mir 'Ali Shir Nawa'i. When Herat was conquered by the Uzbeks in 1507, he entered the service of their sultan Shaybani Khan until he was killed and the city taken by the Safavid shah Isma'il I in 1510. This portrait of the eminent Shi'a poet, Hatifi, may have been one of Bihzad's first commissions for his new patron, for Isma'il paid a visit to Hatifi in 1511, when the poet recited a thousand-line panegyric on the new king. Possibly this portrait commemorates the event.

The portrait was valued by later Safavids. In 1546 the Safavid painter and calligrapher, Dust Muhammad, assembled a splendid album for Shah Tahmasp's brother, Bahram Mirza, and at that time supplied the informative inscriptions above and below the portrait.

38
Khusraw kills the lion

Page originally intended for a manuscript of Nizami's *Khamseh*
Inscribed in the upper left with a Persian love poem and with three smaller couplets in *nasta'liq* describing the scene
20.3 × 17m
Sakisian (1929), fig. 118; A. Welch (1978), vol. III, Ir. M. 62, pp. 60-61
Iran, Tabriz, *c.* 1525

This fine painting must date to the very early years of the reign of Shah Tahmasp and was executed by a master clearly under the influence of Sultan Muhammad. It must have been created for inclusion in a copy of Nizami's *Khamseh*, but the picture was never finished, for though the painting was completed, the text frames were left uninscribed. At some point in its later history the page ended up in India, where a competent calligrapher inscribed the verses from a mediocre love poem that has nothing to do with the miniature. At the same time he apparently supplied the three couplets in the three smaller frames: here the story of Khusraw killing the lion is retold, not in Nizami's classical Persian, but in a Persian markedly Indian in style.

38

39

The Feast of 'Id begins

Signed (on throne) by Sultan Muhammad
Page from a *Dīwān* of Hafiz made for Sam Mirza, whose name and titles appear above the doorway at the right
An inscription in four panels at the top of the building may be rendered in prose

> The 'Id (*al-Fitr*) has come; the roses are in season; our friends are waiting. Saqi, see the new moon in the shah's face and fetch the wine. Fair is this flourishing kingdom and fair its generous prince; Lord, keep him safe from the evil eye.
> TRANSLATED BY C.G.

28.9 × 17.8 cm
Previously in the Cartier collection
S.C. Welch (1972) fig. 12; (1976) pl. 17; (1979) no. 43
Iran, Tabriz or Herat, *c.* 1526–7

As the month of Ramadan draws to a close, a princely court prepares to celebrate the holiday. Attention focuses on the prince (surely a portrait of Shah Tahmasp's younger brother, Sam Mirza, for whom this copy of the *Dīwān* was made) at the top of a circle of courtiers, busily engaged in conversation or eagerly anticipating the feast. Servants bring food; musicians start to play. On the palace roof those who are ostensibly pious gather to pray as Ramadan ends, but it is clear that while some are earnest, others are hypocritical or even besotted.

The greatest of Safavid artists, Sultan Muhammad was close to the royal family and must have viewed scenes like this one, which he recorded with a sense for luxury and the humour of human foibles.

The *Shāhnāmeh* (Book of Kings) of Shah Tahmasp

Shah Tahmasp's *Shāhnāmeh* (Book of Kings), known as the 'Houghton' *Shāhnāmeh* after its last owner, was the grandest and most fully illustrated royal copy of the Iranian national epic. The most splendid of all Safavid manuscripts, it contained no colophon, but the titles of Shah Tahmasp (r. 1524-76), its major patron, appear several times in the volume, and one of the miniatures, *Ardashir and the slave girl* (fol. 516v, no. 57 below) is dated 934/1527-28. The miniatures can be assigned on stylistic grounds to the years between *c.* 1515 and 1535, after which two further pictures were added in about 1540 (see nos 55 and 58 below).

No scribe's name is given, but the manuscript was probably copied by several calligraphers one of whom may have been Shah Mahmud of Nishapur, whose name appears as scribe of another of Shah Tahmasp's magnificent volumes, the British Library's *Khamseh* of Nizami dated from 1539 to 1543 (Or. 2265). Until recently, the *Shāhnāmeh* contained 759 folios, measuring about 470 by 31.8 cm. Text areas measure approximately 26.9 by 17.0 cm, inside the marginal rulings.

Inasmuch as the earlier miniatures in the volume can be no later than 1515 to 1520, the project must have been initiated by Shah Isma'il (r. 1501-24), the first Safavid ruler, who probably presented it to his son Prince Tahmasp in 1522, soon after his return from Herat, where he had served as nominal governor. These miniatures, of which *The death of King Mardas* (no. 42) and *Zahhak receives the daughters of Jamshid* (no. 43) are excellent examples, can be assigned to the great early Safavid court artist, Sultan Muhammad. He served both Shah Isma'il and his son, who inherited the throne in 1524 as Shah Tahmasp. Stylistically, they are attuned to the personality and aesthetic of Shah Isma'il, who was related to the royal family of the *Aq-Koyunlu* (white sheep) Turkmans, whom he defeated in 1501. His artistic tastes were moulded at Tabriz, capital of the Turkmans, where painting flourished in the western Iranian tradition. Earthy, expressive, and broadly dramatic, rather than naturalistic, the style was especially well suited to their delightful orientalizing motifs, the demons, dragons, and flowers which were adapted from ceramics, textiles, and gilt bronzes imported from China prior to 1480.

Shah Isma'il, like many founders of political dynasties, was an exceptionally charismatic, physically powerful visionary. Descended from a family prone to mysticism, he was creatively attuned to Sultan Muhammad, his court painter, who was of like mind and spirit. Sultan Muhammad's pictures for Shah Isma'il are often pictorial equivalents of the religious verses with which the shah harangued his armies before battle. 'I am Moses; I am Zahhak!' he proclaimed in statements that would have caused him to be stoned to death during the more orthodox times that prevailed under his son not many years later. Although Isma'il remains a rather shadowy patron, his encouragement of Sultan Muhammad reveals a taste for comedy, satire, and paradox raised to visionary forcefulness. Sultan Muhammad's paintings, especially those of this early period, bring to mind Zen koans as well as Sufi mysticism.

Shah Isma'il's artists – along with his calligraphers, textile makers, and other artisans – were gathered as part of the spoils of conquest. Upon the defeat of the Turkmans, he took over their libraries, treasury, and workshops. When he added eastern and southern Iran to his broad territories, he assembled further manpower as well as rich booty. Sultan Muhammad, we believe, joined Shah Isma'il during the military campaigns near Herat in 1504. With him came other artists represented in the great *Shāhnāmeh*, including the second of its three senior painters, Mir Musawwir. Both had contributed miniatures to a manuscript of Asafi's *Jamāl and Jalāl* now in the Uppsala University Library. It was copied by the scribe Sultan 'Ali (presumably of Qazvin) 'at Herat' in 1503, and a few of its thirty-four miniatures, painted in a lively, considerably less refined variant of the style favoured at the Timurid Sultan's court, are dated to that year and to 1504. Apparently, it was begun for Prince Muhammad Husayn, a rebellious son of Sultan Husayn Bayqara, the last of the Timurid Sultans of Herat and a greatly discerning patron of the arts. When the son defected to Shah Isma'il, he seems to have brought the unfinished manuscript, along with its leading artists, to Shah Isma'il, for whom it was completed. Although the additional miniatures are akin to the earlier ones, they contain new elements typical of the formative Safavid style. Crucial for establishing Safavid provenance is a detail of costume, the Safavid *tāj*, an upright baton round which the turban was wrapped. Another Safavid characteristic is stylistic: an extra surge of imaginative potency evoked from his new artists by the fervid young shah's exhilarating patronage. Colours became richly, flamingly vivid; people, demons, and trees gained romping, comical expressiveness; and compositions vibrantly reflected Isma'il's buoyant spirits.

In 1514, after having carved out his kingdom, Shah Isma'il settled at Tabriz, the former Turkman capital, to enjoy the pleasures of peace, and to consolidate his power, which was threatened from the west by the Ottomans and from the east by the Uzbeks. He spent much time in the former Turkman library, delighting in the great albums of paintings, drawings, and calligraphies, and sharing them with Sultan Muhammad, whose eastern artistic ways gained expressive exuberance from the experience. In all likelihood, the *Shāhnāmeh* project was initiated at this time.

During the years when Shah Isma'il and Sultan Muhammad thrilled to the wonders of the Turkman collections, absorbing ideas and motifs, a concurrent development was to bring eastern elements into the Safavid artistic synthesis. Two years after his birth in 1514, Prince Tahmasp, was sent eastward as nominal governor to Herat, the former Timurid capital and erstwhile centre of the court of Sultan Husayn Bayqara. Under the tutelage of regents, Prince Tahmasp grew up in an atmosphere quite different from that of his father's court. Apollonian as opposed to Dionysian, Herat was the Athens, as compared to Rome, of its day, a centre of fine manners, of highly refined poetry and painting. Sultan Husayn's great artist Bihzad still practised his art, known for its extraordinary delicacy of finish, psychological nuances, naturalistic proportions of people and animals, and logical disposition of space. At Herat, the precocious little prince learned to admire ways of life and art that he would bring back with him to Tabriz.

When he was summoned home in 1522, and was received by his father, a virtual stranger, the confrontation must have been unnerving, if not awkward. Happily, the royal pair shared at least one profound interest: painting. To Prince Tahmasp, however, accustomed to Bihzad's subtleties, Shah Isma'il's pictures, with their rampaging demons and dragons, surging rhythms, and blazing palette, must have seemed at first startlingly coarse and raucous, better suited to barracks than to a royal court.

Tensions were eased by laughter. The king and the prince both enjoyed a good joke; and Sultan Muhammad's pop-eyed, flailing, often irreverent characterizations of mighty Iranian heroes surely delighted the boy-patron, who several years later himself painted and drew comparably satirical spoofs of personages in the royal household, one of whom revelled in the name Melon-Sultan.

Few Iranian patrons can have been as talented at painting and calligraphy as Prince Tahmasp, or as articulate. His comical portraits (preserved at Istanbul in an album assembled by his brother, Bahram Mirza) are masterful as well as extremely funny. Another fascinating and beautiful document attests to young Tahmasp's artistic acumen, a small manuscript of 'Arifi's mystical *Gūy wa Chawgān* (The ball and mallet), copied in 1524/25 by Shah Tahmasp himself. Now in Leningrad, this engaging, poignant little book, given by the very young shah to his regent/father-figure Qadi-i Jahan, is also a crucial art historical monument. Its miniatures can be assigned to the leading court painters, working at a particularly crucial time. By now, the ageing and somewhat dim-eyed Bihzad had come to Tabriz, along with several of his followers. Although the double page frontispiece of the little volume can be ascribed to him on grounds of composition and characterizations, its uncertain brushwork explains why the revered old master served at Tabriz as artistic mentor rather than painter. Liveliest and finest of the miniatures are those by Sultan Muhammad, whose zestfulness shines through the newly acquired manner of Bihzad. These tiny pictures were art historically momentous. With them, Sultan Muhammad, the humble painter from Herat who had become the leading master of Tabriz, strove to delight not only his eager boy patron but also the living legend, Bihzad, in whose shadow he had once laboured. And he had to accomplish this not in his own style but in theirs.

He succeeded; and his combination of eastern and western traditions, of the fantastic and the naturalistic, of styles favoured by a father and by a son, won the day. Moreover, Sultan Muhammad's miniatures for the pocket-size *Gūy wa Chawgān* of 1524/25 enable us to date his stylistically similar paintings for the much larger *Shāhnāmeh*, in which one can trace the emergence of the new synthesis. If *The death of King Mardas* (no. 42) typifies Sultan Muhammad's zestful, early work for Shah Isma'il, and *The court of Gayumars* (no. 41) marks his personal mode of merging Turkman expressionism with Timurid fineness, *Zahhak slays the cow Birmayeh* (no. 44) exemplifies a more strongly disciplined attempt in about 1525 to bring together the best of both schools. In this picture, Sultan Muhammad's innate humour overflows in the characterizations of the goats and sheep, his profound sympathy for nature moves us in the superb plane tree, and his ability to paint *à la Bihzad* abounds in the minutiae of brushwork, realistic scaling of figures, and special clarity.

Shah Tahmasp's highly ambitious *Shāhnāmeh* project required as much attention as a military campaign, and, we suspect, as much expense. For the boy shah (who brings to mind the connoisseurly Mughal Emperor Jahangir as compared to his father, Akbar, whose dynamically unselfconscious patronage of art recalls Shah Isma'il's) painting provided salvation. During the early years of his reign, Shah Tahmasp was frustrated by regents who denied him all political power. Painting, therefore, offered a happy outlet for youthful energies; and he spent much of his time cultivating artists as well as making his own pictures.

If we are correct in singling out the artists of the *Shāhnāmeh* (only one painting for the original project bears its artist's name) sixteen were employed, of whom Sultan Muhammad and Mir Musawwir were seniormost. Somewhat younger was Aqa Mirak, described by contemporary sources as a boon companion of the shah and a specialist in portraiture. Also at work on the project was a pupil of Bihzad, Dust Muhammad, whose most ambitious composition for the volume, *Haftvad and the worm* (no. 58), was painted, signed, and inserted several years after the rest of the manuscript had been completed. Several young apprentice masters or journeymen also painted for the project. Two were sons of senior masters: Mir Sayyid 'Ali, whose father was Mir Musawwir, and Mirza 'Ali, son of Sultan Muhammad. Another apprentice, Muzaffar 'Ali, was related to Bihzad, while the still younger Shaykh Muhammad, whose *Fariburz against Kalbad* (no. 55) was added to the manuscript at the same time as the *Worm*, was a follower of Dust Muhammad, whom he assisted. Another youthful artist was 'Abd us-Samad, who joined the workshop towards the end of the project, after proving his talents as a painter at Shiraz, his native city.

The artistic talent assembled at Shah Tahmasp's court rivals that of other art historical peaks. Could ancient Athens or Rome, or renaissance Florence boast more artists of genius? Men of the power and depth of Sultan Muhammad, Mir Musawwir, and Aqa Mirak were always rare; and when one adds to them the younger artists, the concentration of masters is remarkable.

But projects on the scale of Shah Tahmasp's required a corps of artists. Planned under Shah Isma'il, the *Shāhnāmeh* was to contain hundreds of illustrations, more than could be supplied by Tahmasp's outstanding masters, especially as they were called upon to paint not in the dashing manner enjoyed by Shah Isma'il but in the new, far more time-consuming mode, with its Bihzadian elaboration. Although Sultan Muhammad and his fellow artists had already painted dozens of lively if old-fashioned illustrations, many, many more were needed to complete the volume. New, quicker ways of painting were necessary, if possible without loss of quality.

Visual evidence suggests that Shah Tahmasp and Sultan Muhammad, probably with the advice of Bihzad, decided to concentrate the efforts of the major artists on a small number of masterpieces, some to be finished by outstanding apprentices. In addition, the leading artists would paint a number of less highly finished miniatures, and they would direct the atelier's apprentices and lesser painters as best they could. Occasionally, the senior artists supplied under-drawings, of varying completeness, to be coloured by assistants. Thus the project moved ahead.

The court of Gayumars (no. 41), which was singled out for the highest praise by Dust Muhammad in his preface to the album gathered by Bahram Mirza, can be seen as Sultan Muhammad's final masterpiece for Shah Isma'il and first for Shah Tahmasp. So fully wrought and detailed as to make Bihzad's greatest pictures seem spare, it remains loyal to the Turkman idiom admired by Shah Isma'il. Its soaring grandeur, profundity, and bubbling wit mark the end of the early phase of Safavid painting under Shah Isma'il, while intricacy and eye-trapping fineness herald the beginning of Shah Tahmasp's inspired patronage. Sultan Muhammad lingered over *Gayumars*, and probably returned to it, for nourishing communion with his late shah, even after he had reshaped his style in the light of Bihzad. For the *Shāhnāmeh*, he painted only one Bihzadian picture without assistance, *Faridun crosses the River Dijla*. Usually, he worked with brilliant young Mir Sayyid 'Ali, whose concern for detail verged on mania. Together, they painted a pair of superb compositions on the theme of evil and its rewards: *Zahhak slays the cow Birmayeh* (no. 44), and *The death of Zahhak* (no. 45).

Mir Musawwir and Aqa Mirak also painted a small number of highly finished miniatures for the project, the former in his elegantly lyrical, immaculately harmonious, but unchanging style, exemplified here by the supremely lyrical and romantic *Ardashir and the slave-girl Gulnar* (no. 57). He also helped in the training of apprentices, and directed the lesser artists. Aqa Mirak, Shah Thamasp's closest friend among the artists, was honoured with the commission to paint the opening picture of the volume, *Firdawsi encounters the three poets of Ghazna* (no. 40), in which the personage at the right, the first figure in the manuscript, is a portrait of the patron. He is shown as a beardless young man, which dates the picture to the early 1530s. Characteristically, its lightness of mood belies serious painterliness and daringly spontaneous compositional invention, resolved and finished to elegant perfection. Aqa Mirak also supervised lesser painters and supplied a considerable number of far less fully detailed miniatures, immaculately hued, thoughtfully and innovatively composed, but broadly painted. At least one of them, *Bizhan forces Farud to flee* (no. 52), with its magically jewel-like rock formations, ranks with this mysterious yet courtly artist's most memorable work.

The lesser masters also served with distinction. Qadimi, a brusque, lively painter from Gilan with tendencies towards Sufism and raw humour, proudly contributed *The court of Faridun* (no. 46) to the project; Qasim son of 'Ali rose to considerable heights, under the watchful eye of Mir Musawwir, when he painted *Siyavush and Afrasiyab in the hunting field* (no. 51). Perhaps the most appealing of the humbler men was 'Abd ul-'Aziz, whose *Zal is sighted by a caravan* (no. 48) is positively incandescent in palette and composed with arresting sinuousness. The less gifted painters of the *Shāhnāmeh* are not represented here, perhaps because their miniatures seemed monotonous and repetitive.

Shah Tahmasp, it appears, was similarly unenthusiastic. Turning the pages of the *Shāhnāmeh*, which is still possible in the monograph devoted to it, reveals a crowding of excellent paintings by major artists towards the beginning, and a gradual decline in quality as one progresses through the dozens of battle and court scenes by the assistants, with just enough exceptional pictures sprinkled here and there to sustain one's interest.

The artists themselves usually worked excitedly, although healthy artistic rivalry occasionally sparked them to new heights. Sultan Muhammad's great *Gayumars*, seems to have inspired both Aqa Mirak and Mir Musawwir to outshine it just as the young contenders (Mirza 'Ali, Mir Sayyid 'Ali, Muzaffar 'Ali, *et al*) and the lesser masters (Qadimi and his *confrères*) also vied with one another. As the manuscript grew, the eager patron expressed his admiration for certain artists by commissioning miniatures for prominent positions, or by assigning them particularly attractive pictorial themes.

Young Mirza 'Ali, for instance, was chosen to paint *Gushtasp slays the dragon on Mount Saqila* (no. 56), a subject that inspired them not only to devise a writhingly credible monster but to place it in a refulgent mountainscape. Another of his commissions, *The parable of the ship of Shi'ism*, given by Mr Houghton to the Metropolitan Museum of Art, was singled out for placement as the third picture of the volume. Less appealing painters, such as Qadimi and Qasim son of 'Ali, increasingly fell from favour as Shah Tahmasp's connoisseurship reached ever new pinnacles. Their work was not included in Shah Tahmasp's other great manuscript, the *Khamseh* of Nizami, bearing dates from 1539 to 1543 but probably started earlier, of which a good part has survived more or less intact in the British Library.

For decades, under two reigns, the *Shāhnāmeh* was the focal point of Safavid art. The showplace for the senior masters, the training ground for the next generation, and the summit which lesser artists tried to scale, it was also the field upon which the Turkman and Timurid traditions met and merged. Most movingly, it embodied the ideas and energies of Shah Isma'il and of his son, whose maturing tribulations and pleasures it intimated. Although most of its miniatures have been scattered, many of the liveliest ones are reassembled here, proclaiming the spirits of its creators, inspiring reverence, lending delight and laughter.

40
Firdawsi encounters the three poets of Ghazna
Folio 7r of Shah Tahmasp's *Shāhnāmeh*
Attributable to Aqa Mirak
47 × 31.8 cm
Iran, Tabriz, *c.* 1532

Particularly lyrical, this picture was commissioned by Shah Tahmasp as the 'fanfare' to his *Shāhnāmeh*. His 'boon companion' among the painters, Aqa Mirak, was honoured by the commission; and into it, as the first figure among the thousands depicted in the manuscript, the courtier-painter placed a sensitively royal portrait of the young shah himself, standing at the extreme right of the composition, somewhat behind the poets. The shah is beardless, and seemingly very young, as he looked in the early 1530s.

Although the first painting in the volume, its style is fully developed, scarcely less progressive than Aqa Mirak's miniatures for Shah Tahmasp's *Khamseh* of Nizami in the British Library (Or. 2265), a manuscript dated 1539 and 1543 but likely to have been initiated earlier.

Conceivably, an earlier miniature, painted for Shah Isma'il, the founder of the Safavid dynasty and the father of Shah Tahmasp, was replaced by this happy picture, a most suitable opening to one of the world's outstanding manuscripts.

41
The court of Gayumars
Folio 20v of Shah Tahmasp's *Shāhnāmeh*
Attributable to Sultan Muhammad
47 × 31.8 cm
Iran, Tabriz, *c.* 1522–25

One of the supreme masterpieces of Iranian art, this miniature is unique in having been discussed specifically in a contemporary document, Master Dust Muhammad's characteristically florid preface to an album he assembled for Prince Bahram Mirza, Shah Tahmasp's brother. On Sultan Muhammad's work, he wrote: 'painting rises to the heights, where skies, for all their thousand-starred eyes, have yet to see the like. . . . Among his creative works are those he painted and sketched in a *Shāhnāmeh* done for his Alexandrous Majesty in whose person is Jamshid's right reserved, the True Creed conserved, and the True Rite preserved.' *The court of Gayumars* is identified as 'a scene with figures clad in leopard skins', and is singled out for highest praise: 'Lions fierce in the field of painting, as awesome tigers drawn to the arts, stung at heart by the smart of his brush, cower in hurt, overpowered by this work.' (Translation quoted from Professor Martin Bernard Dickson, in Dickson and Welch (1981), vol. II no. 7.)

By a visionary artist, Sultan Muhammad's *Gayumars* reveals a world yet untainted by evil, but soon to be visited by the devil. Seemingly, the artist included all good things in his candle-flame composition. People of all kinds – Central Asians, Indians, Mongols, Chinese, and Europeans – are shown among the courtiers; and close inspection reveals an *omnium gatherum* of flora and fauna. After exploring the denizens of *this* world, the actual participants in the painted drama, one should search out myriads more, of the *other* world, hidden in the mystical mountain. Sultan Muhammad spent many years, it seems, lovingly enriching this astonishingly spiritual picture.

41

42
The death of King Mardas

Folio 25v of Shah Tahmasp's *Shāhnāmeh*
Attributable to Sultan Muhammad
47 × 31.8 cm
Iran, Tabriz, *c.* 1522

Good and evil are basic themes of the *Shāhnāmeh*. Sultan Muhammad, a Sufi at heart, explored them deeply and seriously, always with compelling lightness of touch. Here, in one of the half dozen miniatures commissioned for the manuscript not by Shah Tahmasp but by his father, Shah Isma'il, Sultan Muhammad dazzles us with *bravura* brushwork, infectious wit, and some of his most brilliant draughtsmanship. A favourite passage is the veritable dance of flowers, protesting the dread episode, above and to the right of the benevolent greybeard, Satan in disguise.

In this miniature and the other five of the series, Sultan Muhammad, cheerily reverts to his archaic 'roots' in the vigorous, breezy manner known from the late-15th-century *Khāwarānnāmeh* of Ibn Husam, and from the early-16th-century romance of *Jamāl and Jalāl*, by 'Asafi. Nevertheless, the rhythmic dash of the dancing flowers can be traced to the exuberantly enthralling court style of pre-Safavid Tabriz, which made its mark not only on Sultan Muhammad but on artistic traditions as distant as Turkey, India, Tibet, and Europe.

43

Zahhak receives the daughters of Jamshid

Folio 27v of Shah Tahmasp's *Shāhnāmeh*
Attributable to Sultan Muhammad
47 × 31.8 cm
Iran, Tabriz, *c.* 1520–30

A prolific creator of styles, Sultan Muhammad's essential nature remained constant regardless of the one in which he worked. For the *Shāhnāmeh*, in a surge of energy, he painted a suite of six swashbuckling miniatures, one of which we have already seen (no. 42, fol. 25v), which stand apart from the rest of his work. Although one finds in them every earmark of his wizardry, down to the last prancing gesture or comet-like eye, these pictures possess extra sparkling humour and gusto.

Sultan Muhammad's characterization compare in range and depth to those of a Shakespeare. Note here, the anxiousness underlying the well-born demeanour of the princesses, Zahhak's blend of lust, fear, and guilelessness, and the spectator's puzzled concern.

Note, too, the hungry, dragonish snakes emerging from Zahhak's shoulders, and the marvellous frieze of dragons and other orientalizing, Turkman creatures on Zahhak's throne.

44
Zahhak slays the cow Birmayeh

Folio 30v of Shah Tahmasp's *Shāhnāmeh*
Attributable to Sultan Muhammad assisted by Mir Sayyid 'Ali
47 × 31.8 cm
Iran, Tabriz, *c.* 1520–30

Few Iranian pictures can be so closely linked to three major masters. In this instance, the planning, with its logically ordered space, naturalistic canon of proportions, and subtle characterizations stem from the supervision of the renowned master, Bihzad of Herat. The actual drawing and painting are the work of Sultan Muhammad, with the help of his very young, but brilliantly talented apprentice, Mir Sayyid 'Ali, who became one of the major masters of Shah Tahmasp's ateliers. Later, he was one of the founders of the Mughal school of painting.

To please his new boy-patron, Shah Tahmasp, whose taste in painting reflected his childhood at Herat, where Bihzad was the leading artist, Sultan Muhammad merged his earlier idiom with that of Bihzad, in a new Safavid synthesis. Occasionally, one senses a degree of reluctance on the part of Sultan Muhammad, who may at first have been troubled by the demand for Bihzadian finesses. Happily, the young Mir was well suited to sustained, rigorous work of this sort; and most of Sultan Muhammad's later pictures for the *Shāhnāmeh* project reveal his patient hand.

Very close observation of this miniature discloses that most figures, animals, and trees are in effect 'translations' from Sultan Muhammad's earlier mode into the new one; and very often, the artist has merely reduced them in scale and added details of handling to harmonize them with Bihzadian ways.

45
The death of Zahhak

Folio 37v of Shah Tahmasp's *Shāhnāmeh*
Attributable to Sultan Muhammad and Mir Sayyid 'Ali
47 × 31.8 cm
Iran, Tabriz, *c.* 1535

Sultan Muhammad's latest major painting for the *Shāhnāmeh* carries one into a world in which good triumphs over evil – or does it? As interpreted by the painter-saint, Sultan Muhammad – aided by skilful Mir Sayyid 'Ali, who painted many of the faces – heroic Faridun's accusing finger waggles all too schoolmarmishly, while the stealthy executioners scale the heights of Mount Damavand in spooky slow-motion. All seem more cruel than wicked Zahhak, whose snakes have now shrunk into ineffectual wormishness, and whose acquiescence to his grim fate evokes our sympathy. Below, a foppish musician charms a horse and an ass; overhead, more-real-than-life spirits peep out from the rocks, and a great whispy tangle of cloud-dragons sports above it all.

46

46
The court of Faridun

Folio 38v of Shah Tahmasp's *Shāhnāmeh*
Attributable to Qadimi
47 × 31.8 cm
Iran, Tabriz, *c.* 1520–30

With expansive pride, Qadimi of Gilan demonstrated to Shah Tahmasp, to Bihzad, and to his mentor, Sultan Muhammad, that he, too, had mastered the new Safavid blend of styles. The picture is one of his largest, laid out according to the new demands for spacial coherence, and painted with his utmost exquisiteness. But always-confident Qadimi cannot quite hide his amiably zany nature, prone to bombast and garrulousness. His horses are a kick-line of coquettes reborn; trees and flowers thrash in the air like dust-mops; and the swarms of courtiers and attendants evidently have dined on well-sauced rocks that have lodged prettily in their bellies and ankles. These indelicacies notwithstanding, one is happy that Qadimi, the dependable clown of the atelier, painted on and on. One of the *Shāhnāmeh*'s more prolific veterans, he survived into the 1550s, and lent earthy humour to Sultan Ibrahim Mirza's splendidly eccentric, world-weary Jami manuscript.

47
Salm and Tur receive the reply of Faridun and Manuchihr

Folio 53v of Shah Tahmasp's *Shāhnāmeh*
Attributable to 'Abd ul-'Aziz
47 × 31.8 cm
Iran, Tabriz, *c.* 1520–30

Like Qadimi, 'Abd ul-'Aziz was one of the lesser royal artists who had long been affiliated with Sultan Muhammad, but who strove heartfully to adjust to the Bihzadian mode. An original, individualistic colourist, he took pleasure in the superb pigments available to the shah's ateliers.

48

48
Zal is sighted by a caravan

Folio 62v of Shah Tahmasp's *Shāhnāmeh*
Attributable to 'Abd ul-'Aziz
47 × 31.8 cm
Iran, Tabriz, *c.* 1525

Despite Bihzad's restraining advice, 'Abd ul-'Aziz's vast, long-tailed, unabashedly Turkman simurgh undulates freely through the golden sky. A non-conformist by nature, 'Abd ul-'Aziz, perhaps encouraged by Sultan Muhammad, painted this soaring bird in response to Shah Tahmasp's stylistic revolution. Whatever his motive, the picture was so admired – and rightly so – that a sequel was commissioned (fol. 63v) which is now in the Berlin State Museum.

49

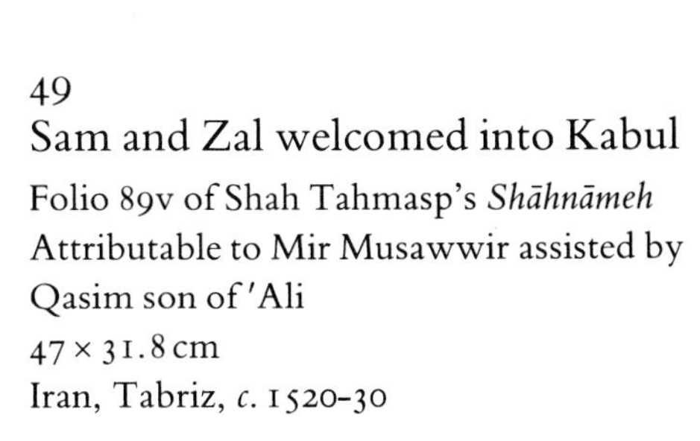

49
Sam and Zal welcomed into Kabul

Folio 89v of Shah Tahmasp's *Shāhnāmeh*
Attributable to Mir Musawwir assisted by Qasim son of 'Ali
47 × 31.8 cm
Iran, Tabriz, *c.* 1520-30

More charmingly than Shah Tahmasp's other artists, Mir Musawwir brought to life the colourful festivity of the royal court. Intriguingly, his curvaceous elephant was derived not from observation but from a Chinese *objet de vertu*, perhaps a gilt-bronze or ceramic. Many years later, Mir Musawwir followed his son to the Mughal court, where he must have seen many living elephants. In India, he painted miniatures in a style almost identical to the one seen here.

50

50

Rustam and the 'seven' champions hunt in Turan

Folio 135v of Shah Tahmasp's *Shāhnāmeh*
Attributable to Mir Sayyid 'Ali
47 × 31.8 cm
Iran, Tabriz, *c.* 1530

Mir Sayyid 'Ali's first 'solo' painting for the *Shāhnāmeh* borrows freely from such pictures as Sultan Muhammad's *Zahhak slays the cow Birmayeh* (no. 44), upon which he had worked as an apprentice. Given access to Sultan Muhammad's sketches and tracings, he also purloined the stalking lion from the lower left-hand corner of *Faridun crosses the River Dijleh*, (fol. 33v). Ungentlemanly and painful as it might be to 'rake over old coals', one is reminded that years later in India, Mir Sayyid 'Ali signed his own *nom de plume* to verses entrusted to him by a dying friend.

More significantly, Mir Sayyid 'Ali was an extraordinary artist, with a particular gift for bold composition, unique concern for exacting still life, and the highest standards of detailed finish – qualities already apparent in this picture, which must have been painted when he was hardly older than seventeen. Like most Safavid artists, he painted seeming portraits into his miniatures. One would greatly like to know the identity of the lightly bearded gentleman conversing with a youth (Mir Sayyid 'Ali himself?) atop a hill at the right horizon. A haunting personage to the young artist, who painted him at various ages, he might portray the Mir's mentor, Sultan Muhammad.

51

Siyavush and Afrasiyab in the hunting field

Folio 182v of Shah Tahmasp's *Shāhnāmeh*
Attributable to Qasim son of 'Ali
47 × 31.8 cm
Iran, Tabriz, *c.* 1525-30

Often, the *Shāhnāmeh* project served as an academy of art. In this case Mir Musawwir and Qasim son of 'Ali, as mentor and painter, resulted in one of the liveliest pictures by a lesser master in the entire volume. Apparently, the collaboration also changed the course of Qasim Son of 'Ali's artistic career; for a signed miniature (now in the Soviet Union) in his pseudo-Mir Musawwir manner reveals that the Mir's instructions were well learned. It also made it possible for us to assign his name to many pictures in the *Shāhnāmeh*. An artist who needed lessons in figure drawing (he tended to cram heads onto neckless shoulders), Qasim greatly profited from Mir Musawwir's expert advice. Nevertheless, this hunting scene also contains strongly Turkman elements derived from another mentor, Sultan Muhammad.

52

53

52
Bizhan forces Farud to flee (*page 84*)

Folio 234r of Shah Tahmasp's *Shāhnāmeh*
Attributable to Aqa Mirak
47 × 31.8 cm
Iran, Tabriz, *c.* 1530

Aqa Mirak's daring composition, dramatic silhouettes, and vibrantly crisp palette are here be-jewelled by one of his most inspired and painterly passages – the glassily transparent outcropping of rocks. As was often the case, rock-painting liberated Aqa Mirak, who delighted in laying watercolour washes and brushing on richly opaque accents of dots, dashes, and blobs. For viewers, these painted gems offer a hide-and-seek of bears, frogs, and very old courtly friends.

Aqa Mirak's style, while markedly his own, was developed under the direction of Shaykh-zadeh, a follower of Bihzad who worked on several royal Safavid manuscripts. Like Bihzad himself, however, he was more influential to Safavid art as a teacher than as an artist. Outstanding as a composer of arabesques, Shaykh-zadeh was also notable for his precisely balanced colour areas, and for his masterfully fine brush handling, all of which he passed on to Aqa Mirak.

53
The combat of Rustam and Shangul (*page 85*)

Folio 279v of Shah Tahmasp's *Shāhnāmeh*
Attributable to Aqa Mirak
47 × 31.8 cm
Iran, Tabriz, *c.* 1525

Pictures such as this one explain why Shah Tahmasp appointed Aqa Mirak to be in charge of selecting pigments for the royal ateliers. Of all the shah's artists, Aqa Mirak was the most fastidious colourist.

Dateable to *c.* 1525, this miniature shows the strong influence of Shaykh-zadeh on Aqa Mirak, whose hand is evident in several miniatures for the Paris Nawa'i (Bibliothèque Nationale, supp. turc 316) and Metropolitan Museum *Khamseh* of Nizami (Cochran collection, MS no. 8). The thick turban batons support this early date, and invite comparison with the leaner, more elegant one worn by Shah Tahmasp in Aqa Mirak's later *Firdawsi encounters three poets of Ghazna* (no. 40).

54
Rustam pursues Akvan the onager-div

Folio 294r of Shah Tahmasp's *Shāhnāmeh*
Attributable to Muzaffar 'Ali
47 × 31.8 cm
Iran, Tabriz, *c.* 1530–35

One senses Muzaffar 'Ali's purity of soul in this romping miniature, with its sweetly innocent foal and aspiringly bounding horses. Perhaps the most cheerful composition in the *Shāhnāmeh*, its silhouetted quartet of horses in the centre is rhythmically echoed throughout the picture, particularly in the bosky trees on the horizon.

55
The first 'joust of the rooks': Fariburz against Kalbad

Folio 341v of Shah Tahmasp's *Shāhnāmeh*
Attributable to Shaykh Muhammad
47 × 31.8 cm
Iran, Tabriz, *c.* 1540

Shaykh Muhammad's only picture for the *Shāhnāmeh* harks back to the chivalrous archaicisms of Timurid painting, and ahead to his disturbing – even alarming – explorations of singular goings on at the court of Sultan Ibrahim Mirza, as depicted in the Freer Gallery of Art's Jami manuscript. Along with Dust Muhammad's *Haftvad and the worm* (no. 58), this miniature was inserted in about 1540, well after the completion of the *Shāhnāmeh* project.

Shaykh Muhammad was trained by Dust Muhammad, for whom he served as colourer or finisher. A fine craftsman, bold designer, and expressive innovator, his artistic personality flowered under the sympathetic patronage of Sultan Ibrahim, for whom he painted a series of extraordinary, somewhat frenzied miniatures, epitomizing the mood of Ibrahim's court at Meshed. When Shah Tahmasp removed Sultan Ibrahim from the governorship of Mashhad and sent him to the remote town of Sabzevar, Shaykh Muhammad and Mirza 'Ali remained loyal to their imaginative patron and accompanied him into exile, where they painted some of their most extreme pictures.

55

54

56
Gushtasp slays the dragon on Mount Saqila

Folio 402r of Shah Tahmasp's *Shāhnāmeh*
Attributable to Mirza 'Ali
47 × 31.8 cm
Iran, Tabriz, *c.* 1530-35

The sun seemingly pulls the trees towards it, and a mountain goat looks away in terror as straight-armed Gushtasp stabs a fellow beast, the dragon. Although other dragon pictures might be more convincing anatomically, the impact of this one is unsurpassed. Much of its dramatic effectiveness stems from the vivid actuality of the sunstruck landscape, a new achievement in Iranian painting. Better known as a painter of court life and intrigue, Mirza 'Ali surprises us by his success in depicting the open air. Not until the late Akbar period in Mughal India would such out-of-door settings again be painted so convincingly.

57
Ardashir and the slave-girl Gulnar
Folio 516v of Shah Tahmasp's *Shāhnāmeh*
Attributable to Mir Musawwir
47 × 31.8 cm
Iran, Tabriz, dated 934/1527-28

Bracketed by their slippers, arranged like quotation marks below the dais, Ardashir and Gulnar make love, beneath an elegantly suggestive coverlet. This is the most lyrical, moon-struck, romantic picture in all Safavid art. It also provides the only date in the *Shāhnāmeh* – 1527-28, inscribed above the portico. Coincidentally, this is also the year of Shah Tahmasp's first recorded love affair.

58
The story of Haftvad and the worm

Folio 521v of Shah Tahmasp's *Shāhnāmeh*
Signed 'Dust Muhammad painted this'
47 × 31.8 cm
Iran, Tabriz, *c.* 1540

Fairly bursting its borders, this picture is the largest in the *Shāhnāmeh* and the only fully signed one in the manuscript. Its borders, lacking gold flecks, are atypical, and the paper is thicker than usual. Perhaps as a gift to the project, upon which he had worked in its heyday, this enterprising miniature was inserted into the manuscript in about 1540, a few years before Master Dust wrote his art-historical preface to the album assembled for Prince Bahram Mirza.

Impressive, odd, and mysterious, this miniature exemplifies the troubled soul of its creator, who was a man of letters, calligrapher, and poet as well as artist. Characteristically, he signed his verses *Kāhī*, which means 'The waner' or 'The straw man'. Among its myriad motifs are several genre subjects strongly reminiscent of Mir Sayyid 'Ali, whose poetical name was 'The Loner'.

An Indian copy of *Haftvad*, made for the Mughal Emperor Jahangir, is in Berlin, part of the so-called Jahangir Album. Presumably, it was made from another version of the picture, or from a tracing, taken to the Mughal court by Dust Muhammad, when he left Iran and went to Kabul, where he arrived in 1549.

59
Burzuy brings Nushirvan the book of Kalila and Dimna

Folio 649r of Shah Tahmasp's *Shāhnāmeh*
Attributable to Aqa Mirak
47 × 31.8 cm
Iran, Tabriz, *c.* 1530

This handsome, sturdily patterned, artfully balanced composition exemplifies Aqa Mirak's concern for architectonic structure. Within it, one finds several of the artist's oft-repeated motifs, such as the young man with lightly pencilled moustache, seated in the doorway, and the interlocking pattern of tiles surrounding Nushirvan. Eminent artists of Shah Tahmasp were called upon to provide designs for carpets and other textiles, for tiles, and all other decorative arts, perhaps even for architecture, a factor which lent harmonious unity to the court and its surroundings.

60

60
Nushirvan records his sage counsel for Hurmuzd

Folio 654r of Shah Tahmasp's *Shāhnāmeh*
Attributable to Muzaffar 'Ali
47 × 31.8 cm
Iran, Tabriz, *c.* 1530

In Shah Tahmasp's ateliers, the artists exchanged ideas about art and inspired one another to new heights. Muzaffar 'Ali's debt to Aqa Mirak is apparent here in the figures, plane tree, streams, rocks, and clusters of flowers. Despite their copy-book relationship to the older painter's motifs, Muzaffar 'Ali's picture is unmistakably original. Several of Aqa Mirak's miniatures for the British Library's *Khamseh* contain passages attributable to the sensitive younger man, who seems to have worked with Aqa Mirak in the same way that Mir Sayyid 'Ali painted under Sultan Muhammad.

61
Barbad the concealed musician

Folio 731r of Shah Tahmasp's *Shāhnāmeh*
Attributable to Mirza 'Ali
47 × 31.8 cm
Iran, Tabriz, *c.* 1535

Bulky, ponderous Barbad strains the sturdy cypress tree in which he is so ingeniously hidden. A stickler for accurate detail, Mirza 'Ali 'camouflaged' the up-and-coming musician by tailoring him in the perfect costume for secrecy, a flaming orange coat! To fully appreciate Safavid pictures, one must be attuned to their uproarious humour. Shah Tahmasp, Mirza 'Ali, and the courtiers fortunate enough to have attended the unveiling of this picture, must have laughed hysterically over the burlesque Barbad, whose likeness may have been taken from a familiar figure at court.

NOTE TO NOS 40–61

Readers wishing to learn more about early Safavid painting and painters should consult the following publications, details of which are given in the Bibliography: S.C. Welch (1972), (1976), (1979), (1981).

The author is thankful to Mr Arthur A. Houghton, Jr for allowing Professor Martin Bernard Dickson and himself to study his *Shāhnāmeh* manuscript. He is also very grateful to Professor Dickson, from who he has learned a great deal about Safavid history, life and art, for many years of happy and productive collaboration.

61

The *Fālnāmeh* (Book of Divination) of Shah Tahmasp

The impact of a patron's personality on art history is dramatically apparent in the development of Safavid painting under Shah Tahmasp. An ardent calligrapher, painter, and patron as a boy and young man, he altered the course of Safavid painting by bringing together in a new Safavid synthesis the styles of Turkman Tabriz and Timurid Herat. Artists of the calibre of Sultan Muhammad, Aqa Mirak, and Mir Musawwir responded to his artistic direction, and they were followed by a new generation of distinguished masters. Two of the world's most remarkable manuscripts, his *Shāhnāmeh* and *Khamseh*, the illustrations of which include fifteen or twenty truly great pictures and many more excellent ones dating from the early 1520s through the 1540s, underscore and commemorate his creative artistic discernment.

By 1549, when Shah Tahmasp was thirty-seven years old, his intense interest in painting had lessened. Several of his notably talented artists (Mir Sayyid 'Ali, 'Abd us-Samad, Mir Musawwir, and Dust Muhammad) became discouraged and moved away, casting their lots with the Mughals; and most of the other artists once busy in his ateliers were compelled to seek patronage elsewhere.

The shah's disinclination towards painting developed gradually, and must be seen in the light of his total personality. Despite his august position in the world, life was not easy. Sent away from his family at the age of two, he spent his early boyhood in the charge of *lalehs* or tutors, and when he inherited his father's throne, he was ruler in name only. Not until 1536 did he gain control of the reins of government.

Shah Tahmasp's sensitivity and vulnerability are revealed in his memoirs. In 1534, threatened by enemies from within and without, he equated the troubles with his own failings and resolved to 'wash away the stains . . . of pulverized emerald (hashish) and liquefied ruby (wine).' 'Thenceforward', he wrote resolutely, 'debauchery and licentiousness were suppressed throughout our land.' The still young ruler, it seems, was becoming increasingly orthodox, partly but not entirely in keeping with the ethos of the times. In 1537, he attended the trial and execution in Teheran of extremist Sufis, holy men who would have been admired during the latitudinarian days of Shah Isma'il; and four years later, a military campaign was sent into Khuzistan to quell similarly extreme political and religious elements.

His attitude towards the arts reflects increasing rigidity. Qadi Ahmad, the calligrapher and man of letters, wrote from his own observations and those of his circle that Shah Tahmasp's turn against painting occurred in about 1544-45, 'when the monarch, having wearied of the field of calligraphy and painting, occupied himself with important affairs of state, with the well-being of the country, and the tranquillity of his subjects.' By 1556, his disaffection for painting was so complete that he issued an edict of 'sincere repentence' formally banning the secular arts throughout the realm.

The Pozzi collection in the Musée d'art et d'histoire, Geneva, contains four strikingly large illustrations to the *Fālnāmeh* (Book of Divination) which shed light on Shah Tahmasp's patronage in *c.* 1550, during the years when his encouragement of painting had greatly lessened but not ended. The text is traditionally ascribed to the Shia Imam

Ja'far al-Sadiq. It was intended for consultation, offering omens and their interpretations. If one's omens were *Dajjāl*, for instance, much grief, countless worry, and pollution of mind lay ahead. It was not deemed propitious to travel, to buy or sell, or to enter into contracts, either economic or matrimonial. Indeed, one should neither move things from one place to another, nor move oneself. Moreover, one to whom this omen applies should not mix with people who are outwardly friendly but inwardly inimical; and he must leave their company lest his affairs enter a state of total confusion. Further, he must not neglect remembrance of God Most High, and must give alms and gratuities to the dervishes and to the deserving, according to his capacity. He must also carry out the prescribed prayers, and on Monday and Friday nights he must offer candles and lamps at the blessed graves so that he may reach his goal if God Most High, He alone the Strong, Willeth.

Although the subject matter is surprisingly folkloristic and magical, samples of the text, such as the lines we paraphrased above from a translation prepared by Dr Annemarie Schimmel, are entirely consistent with the Shah's phases of intense religiosity and with his occasional fickleness. One can believe that he regularly consulted it, presumably from the very copy represented here, for its superb *nasta'līq* calligraphy, impressively composed on the illuminated pages facing the miniatures, is clearly a royal commission.

The huge, majestically designed miniatures are equally royal, as can be seen not only from their compelling artistic quality but from their being attributable on grounds of style to two of the Shah's painters, Aqa Mirak, the courtier-artist cited as a boon companion of the Shah, and 'Abd ul-'Aziz, who had worked with him on the *Shāhnāmeh*. Even when the ateliers were suffering royal neglect, Aqa Mirak was awarded this exciting commission.

To one whose happiness depended upon painting, the project encouraged daring experimentation; for manuscript illustrations so large as to evoke wall paintings had never before been attempted in the Islamic world. Although Aqa Mirak's broadly composed miniatures for the *Shāhnāmeh*, such as *Bizhan forces Farud to flee* (no. 52), stem from a mentality suited to grandeur of scale, the *Fālnāmeh* stimulated him to explore expansive, new vistas. The fifteen complete miniatures and three fragments known to us from it are attributable either to Aqa Mirak himself, sometimes assisted by 'Abd ul-'Aziz, or to the secondary artist working under close supervision. Apparently, the series was well known among artists and patrons. Its giantism and fervid religiosity inspired comparably large, intense pictures both in Ottoman Turkey and in Mughal India, where Emperor Akbar's *Hāmzanāmeh* was illustrated by artists formerly employed by Shah Tahmasp, who must have been spurred on by Shah Tahmasp's innovative achievement.

I am beholden to B. W. Robinson, whose *Catalogue des peintures et des calligraphies islamiques leguées par Jean Pozzi au Musée d'art et d'histoire de Genève*, Geneva, 1973, has been very helpful. I am also particularly grateful to Dr Annemarie Schimmel for the translation of a section of the *Fālnāmeh*, which I have attempted to paraphrase, and for suggestions as to the iconography of several of the miniatures. For an earlier discussion of this important manuscript, see A. Welch and S. C. Welch (1982), no. 25.

62
The dying Dara comforted by Iskandar

Illustration to the *Fālnāmeh*
Attributable to Aqa Mirak
59 × 44.5 cm
Musée d'art et d'histoire, Geneva, 1971-107/34 (Pozzi collection)
Robinson (1974), no. 34
Iran, Tabriz, *c.* 1550

While Dara (Darius) expires, with his head on the lap of Iskandar (Alexander the Great), a scribe takes notes from an astrologer, who consults an astrolabe. Aqa Mirak's mind and hand are omnipresent in this miniature, which recalls his smaller but equally bold designs for the *Shāhnāmeh*. Figures such as the almost imbalanced kneeling mourner behind Iskander are strongly reminiscent not only of his miniatures in simplified style but also of his more finely detailed figures in the British Library's *Khamseh*. Colouring, gestures, ornamental clusters of flowering plants, turban-forms, the treatment of hands, and many other details support the attribution to Aqa Mirak.

63
Scene in a Mosque (?)
Illustration to the *Fālnāmeh*
Attributable to Aqa Mirak
59 × 44.5 cm
Musée d'art et d'histoire, Geneva,
1971-107/35 (Pozzi collection)
Robinson (1974), no. 35
Iran, Tabriz, *c.* 1550

This striking composition, with its two huge feet placed at either side of a noble, emblematically simplified Qur'an on a stand, is one of the more impressive religious pictures in Islamic art. Dr Annemarie Schimmel has suggested to us that the feet are effigies of the Prophet's sandals (*ni 'āl-i sharīf*), especially valued because the Prophet touched them on the apex of the divine throne during his heavenly journey. Throughout the Islamic world, they are often seen in mosques and tombs. Once again, design, colour, figures, arabesques, and such minor but telling details as formulae for eyes and mouths, point to Aqa Mirak's artistry. His life-long fascination with symmetry, for him a serious compositional challenge, further supports our unqualified attribution.

64

A greybeard threatens a camel

Illustration to the *Fālnāmeh*
Attributable to 'Abd ul-'Aziz, directed and aided by Aqa Mirak
59 × 44.5 cm
Musée d'art et d'histoire, Geneva, 1971-107/36 (Pozzi collection)
Robinson (1974), no. 36
Iran, Tabriz, *c.* 1550

Far less classic in composition, this miniature, with its remarkable camel, whose hump is surrounded by heavenly flame, was designed by 'Abd ul-'Aziz. Although the camel and greybeard are well drawn, the figures on the horizon loom too large, depriving the design of coherence, and the space-filling flowers and rocks are uneasily congested. The crawling figure in the foreground, with his cracker-jaw and acquiline nose is a stock-character found in many of 'Abd ul-'Aziz's pictures.

65
Scene at the Ka'ba in Makka (?)
Illustration to the *Fālnāmeh*
Designed and partly painted by Aqa Mirak, assisted by 'Abd ul-'Aziz
59 × 44.5 cm
Musée d'art et d'histoire, Geneva, 1971-107/37 (Pozzi collection)
Robinson (1974), no. 37
Iran, Tabriz, *c.* 1550

Dr Annemarie Schimmel has pointed out that there are many Sufi stories of dervishes clinging to the door of the Ka'ba and praying there. But she questions the identification of the Ka'ba, which is not usually depicted as hexagonal or domed. The fully frontal, bearded figure, standing on the wall with arms upraised is often seen in Aqa Mirak's miniatures.

66
Holy Qur'an

Illuminated manuscript on paper, probably made for Shah Tahmasp
43 × 30 cm
Iran, probably Qazvin, 959/1552

This complete Qur'an of two hundred and two folios is bound in a contemporary dark brown leather binding: a large, gilded rectangle, embossed in gold arabesques, is bordered by cartouches, alternately filled with arabesques and with *Hadīth* expounding the importance of reading the Qur'an. The inside cover is a superb combination of gilded embossed arabesques and gold, *découpé* arabesques over a blue background. It is testimony to masterful workmanship.

On the first folio is an effaced inscription with the name 'Shah Jahan' still legible, perhaps the holograph of the Mughal emperor. The frontispiece (fols 1v-2r) is a striking composition in gold, blues, red, white, pink, and green that indicates the presence of a gifted and highly trained illuminator. The two geometric gold borders have been abundantly pricked so that they catch and reflect light. The text of the frontispiece is written in two scripts: the sura heading is in gold *thuluth*, and the text of Sura I *Al-Fath* is in white *naskh*.

The second sura (fol. 2v) is titled in white *thuluth*, and the text is written in two alternate styles, beginning on page 3r, that will continue throughout the manuscript: lines 1, 9, and 17 are written in blue *muhaqqaq* and the remaining fourteen lines are in gold *naskh*. Both are composed with flawless distinction. Gold panels frame lines 1, 9, and 17, and four vertical panels – usually gold arabesques or cloud forms over a blue (or sometimes pink, green, brown, or red) ground frame the *naskh* lines. The text is fully vocalized and pointed in gold and blue. Verse markers in blue and gold are in the margins to indicate every fifth and tenth verse.

The colophon on page 203r unfortunately does not identify scribe, patron, illuminator, or place of production, though it does give the date: the month of *Sha'bān* 959/July-August 1552. By 1545 Shah Tahmasp had overseen the completion of his last great secular manuscripts – the 1539-43 *Khamseh* of Nizami (British

66 Inside cover of binding

Library) and Shah Tahmasp's *Shāhnāmeh* (see nos 40-61). The text of the former manuscript had been written by Shah Mahmud Nishapuri, the most honoured, versatile and gifted scribe at the royal court, and though the illuminator is not identified, he could have been 'Abdullah Mudhahhib (see nos 76 and 77) or Zayn al-'Abidin (see no. 72), master illuminators who are mentioned with great praise in contemporary texts. After completion of these works the shah is said to have lost interest in the art of painting, but he must have still retained a commitment to the art of calligraphy, Islam's great sacred art. Few great royal Qur'ans from Tahmasp's reign are known and everything about this book – from its lavish illuminations, its gold script, its consummate mastery on every level – indicates that this Qur'an was the shah's great Qur'an, commissioned as an act of piety after the completion of the *Khamseh* and the *Shāhnāmeh* and employing the finest, appropriate talents. It is plausible that Shah Mahmud Nishapuri was the calligrapher honoured by this commission and that 'Abdullah Mudhahhib and/or Zayn al-'Abidin were its illuminators. This book deserves to be included in the small group of unquestioned Safavid masterpieces of the art of the book.

On folio 203v are the seals of the Mughal emperors Awrangzib (1658-1707) and Shah 'Alam (1707-12) who preserved this Qur'an in the royal library.

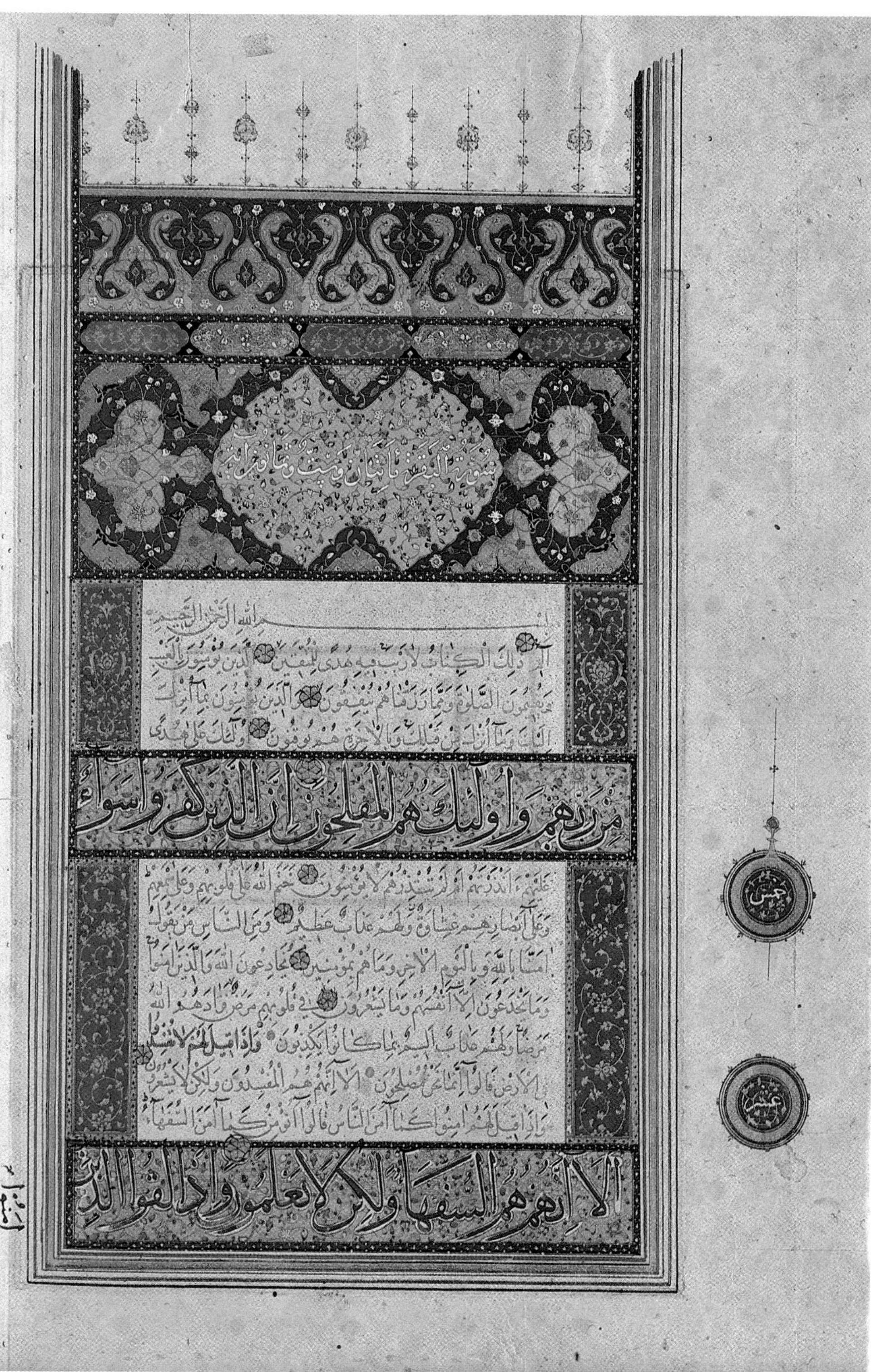

66 *Folio 2v*

66 *Folio 1v*

67
Crystal seal of Shah Tahmasp

3 × 2.5 cm
Iran, Qazvin, dated 963/1555-56

Signed on 29 May, 1555, the Treaty of Amasiya ended years of conflict between Ottoman Turkey and Safavid Iran and initiated a period of relatively peaceful relations that was to endure until the end of Shah Tahmasp's long reign (1526-76). The shah's capital had recently been established at Qazvin, where a modest building programme was underway. Outlying areas such as Georgia had been subdued, and the aristocracy had been brought firmly under the control of the central government. The shah's son Isma'il, a popular military hero, had been installed as governor of Khurasan to protect it from Uzbek incursions, and his trusted nephew Ibrahim had been appointed governor of Meshed. The year in which this seal was made was therefore a period of great personal and dynastic security for Tahmasp.

This thin, light crystal seal is delicately and densely incised. In the four corners are multi-lobed cartouches containing four lines of Shi'a devotional verse, as follows:

Chūn nāma-yi jurm-i mā baham pīchīdand
Burdand ba-mīzān-i 'amal, sanjīdand
Bīsh az hama kas gunāh-i mā būd walī
Mārā ba-mahabbat-i 'Alī bakhshīdand

When they rolled up the book of our transgressions,
They took it away to the balance of deeds and weighed it.
Our sins were greater than any man's, but
They forgave us for the love of 'Ali.
TRANSLATED BY A.H.M.

These verses are also found inscribed in ornamental Kufic on mosaic tile-work dated 1112/1700 inside the west *iwān* of the Friday Mosque in Isfahan (see Seher-Toss, *Design and Colour in Islamic Architecture*, Smithsonian Institute, 1968, pl. 85, and Yusuf Ghulam *Arabic Calligraphy in Iran*, Asia Institute, Shiraz, pp. 40-41). In the middle of the top side is God's name, Allah; in the middle of the right side is the name Muhammad, and in the middle of the left side is the name 'Ali. At the bottom is the date AH 963. In the large central area is the most frequently used Safavid royal titulature, commonly found on manuscript pages: *Banda-yi Shāh-i wilāyat Tahmāsp*, 'Tahmasp, servant of the King of Holiness (i.e. 'Ali).' Though by this time when he was in his early forties, Tahmasp was no longer a major patron of the arts of the book, this seal is one of the masterpieces of Safavid calligraphy and lapidary art.

67 (Actual size)

68

A love poem

Page from an album
Signed by Shah Mahmud Nishapuri
26.6 × 16.7 cm
Ackerman (1940); A. Welch and S.C. Welch (1982), no. 24, pp. 76–78
Iran, Tabriz or Meshed, *c.* 1540–50

Mahmud Nishapuri was one of the most celebrated of Safavid calligraphers, but he also had a reputation as a poet, and this poem, though not of great distinction, may be part of his literary *oeuvre*. The calligraphy, however, is a splendid example of *nasta'līq*, and it is enclosed by delicate floral illuminations in the corners and rich, blue marbled and gold-flecked margins. Born in 1487, Mahmud attained high position under Shah Tahmasp and worked in association with the most celebrated Safavid painters. He was a pious man, and while he worked for the shah in Qazvin, he lived in a *madrasa* (theological seminary), and when after 1545 he moved to Meshed, he also dwelled in a *madrasa*. He had no family, and in his later years he earned his living by teaching calligraphy and selling samples of his art, such as this one. He died in 1564–65.

69
Holy Qur'an

Illumination signed by Nasir ibn Muhammad
25 × 16.5 cm
Iran, perhaps Shiraz, *c.* 1550

Shiraz in southern Iran was a major centre for the art of the book in the 16th century, and it is likely that this fine Qur'an was produced in one of its ateliers. In style its frontispiece and its organization of text can be compared to no. 66, produced almost certainly at the same time. Although this Qur'an carries no information about scribe, patron, place of production, or date, its fine frontispiece bears near the bottom a minute white signature 'illuminated by Nasir ibn Muhammad'; illuminators rarely placed their names on their creations, and this is an unusual and discreet personal testimony by an illuminator of great ability. The text on following pages is written in eleven lines to the page: one line of blue *muhaqqaq*; four lines of black *naskh*; one line of gold *muhaqqaq*; four lines of black *naskh*; and one line of blue *muhaqqaq*.

70
Album page with *nasta'līq* calligraphy

Signed by Malik al-Daylami
14 × 7.5 cm
Previously in the Kevorkian Collection
Sotheby's 2 May 1977, lot 24
Iran, *c.* 1550-60

Four diagonal lines of large *nasta'līq*, recording a poem, are framed by an inner border of ten panels, also filled with poetry in *nasta'līq*. In the lower left corner of the central rectangle is the name of the scribe, 'the humble Malik al-Daylami'. The outer margins are filled with gilt animal and plant decoration.

At first on the staff of Shah Tahmasp's vizier, Qadi-i Jahan, Malik al-Daylami became a favourite of Shah Tahmasp, who allowed him to work for Ibrahim Mirza in Meshed from 1556-59. The king recalled the scribe to Qazvin in that year in order to provide inscriptions on his palaces and gardens, and, though Ibrahim Mirza pleaded with Tahmasp to allow him to return to Meshed, Tahmasp steadfastly refused. Malik al-Daylami died in 1561-62. This fine calligraphy was probably produced either in Qazvin or Meshed.

71
Young man playing a *Yektār*

Attributed to Mirza 'Ali
34.4 × 23.7 cm
A. Welch (1978), vol. III, Ir. M. 71, pp. 100-101; A. Welch and S.C. Welch (1982), no. 27/B, pp. 84-88
Iran, probably Sabzevar, *c.* 1570-74

The son of Sultan Muhammad, Mirza 'Ali had worked with his father illustrating Shah Tahmasp's *Shāhnāmeh* (see nos 46-61) and the 1539-43 *Khamseh* of Nizami in the British Library. After Shah Tahmasp's 1556 Edict of Sincere Repentance in which the king formally renounced his patronage of figural painting, Mirza 'Ali began working for Ibrahim Mirza, the son of Tahmasp's brother Bahram. He was one of the major painters of the 1556-65 *Haft Awrang* of Jami in the Freer Gallery of Art, and when Prince Ibrahim was exiled in Sabzevar in eastern Iran from 1567-74, Mirza 'Ali apparently kept him company by painting portraits of wistful youths like this one, apparently removed through his own music from the tiny oasis in which he sits. The attenuated figure and elongated neck are characteristic of his art, and both manner and motif strongly influenced later Safavid painting.

71

72

72
Illuminated *shamsa*

Perhaps the work of Zayn al-'Abidin
Page from a manuscript of Firdawsi's *Shāhnāmeh* made for Shah Isma'il II
41 × 27 cm
Previously in the Rothschild Collection
Robinson (1976), no. 19i
Iran, Qazvin, 1576-77

Precious manuscripts were often introduced by illuminations such as this one, known as a *shamsa* (or sun), that had several metaphoric and symbolic purposes: to shed light on the book's pages; to symbolize the life-giving vitality of God's light; and to honour the names of author and patron. Thus this *shamsa* is inscribed with words in praise of the poet Firdawsi, and the facing page would almost certainly also have displayed a *shamsa* that would have contained the name and title of Shah Isma'il II (1576-77). Cited in contemporary sources as a notable painter and illuminator, Zayn al-'Abidin had been trained in Shah Tahmasp's atelier and signed the illuminated heading for the great fragmentary *Shāhnāmeh* for Shah 'Abbas, produced probably between 1587 and 95. As a member of the atelier assembled by the short-lived king Isma'il II, Zayn al-'Abidin worked in association with painters like 'Ali Asghar, Sadiqi, and Siyavush. The shah, who suffered from drug- and alcohol-abuse and periodic bouts of paranoia and violent insanity, did not live to bring this 1576-77 *Shāhnāmeh* to completion. Apparently a patron of taste, he nevertheless nearly brought to extinction the tradition of Safavid patronage, for he murdered almost all of the royal princes, including his gifted cousin Ibrahim Mirza (see no. 71).

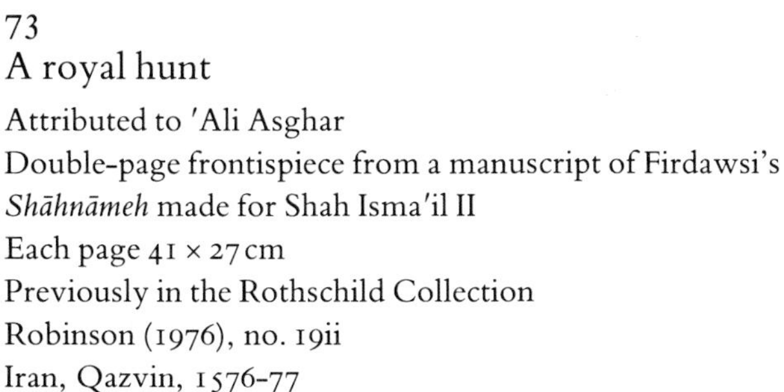

73

A royal hunt

Attributed to 'Ali Asghar
Double-page frontispiece from a manuscript of Firdawsi's *Shāhnāmeh* made for Shah Isma'il II
Each page 41 × 27 cm
Previously in the Rothschild Collection
Robinson (1976), no. 19ii
Iran, Qazvin, 1576–77

Illuminated *shamsas* (such as no. 72) were frequently followed by elaborate double-page compositions. One of the most common frontispiece subjects was the royal hunt, a suitable visual introduction to a manuscript of *The epic of the kings*. It is a reasonable hypothesis that the ruler – shown at the right seated under a canopy and on the left mounted on a white horse – is meant to represent the king who commissioned the manuscript. Royal hunts of this sort were carefully managed affairs, meant to demonstrate the monarch's special powers, and usually only the king was allowed to kill the animals that had been driven into an enclosed space.

It has been plausibly argued by B.W. Robinson that the painter responsible for this impressive frontispiece was 'Ali Asghar who had already served under Shah Tahmasp and his nephew Ibrahim Mirza. He was probably the most senior artist in the employ of Shah Isma'il II, and it would have been normal that he be awarded the task of painting the frontispiece. A very competent, though not strikingly original master, he responded to this honour by basing his composition on a well-known double-page frontispiece to a somewhat earlier Safavid manuscript, a copy of Jami's *Haft Awrang*, painted about 1540. A sensitive connoisseur, though a short-lived and paranoid ruler, Isma'il II most likely understood this visual reference to a respected prototype, and other pages in the 1576–77 *Shāhnāmeh* make respectful obeisance to Shah Tahmasp's *Shāhnāmeh*.

74
Isfandiyar kills the simurgh

Signed by Siyavush
Page from a *Shāhnāmeh* made for Shah Isma'il II
Inscribed with four columns of text in excellent *nasta'līq*
40.5 × 29.7 cm
Marteau and Vever (1912), pl. CIV, fig. 128; Robinson (1976), no. 48; Robinson (1976), no. 19xxi; A. Welch (1976), p. 25 and fig. 2 A. Welch (1978), vol. III, Ir. M. 69/D, pp. 94-97; A. Welch and S.C. Welch (1982), no. 29/B, pp. 90-94
Iran, Qazvin, 1576-77

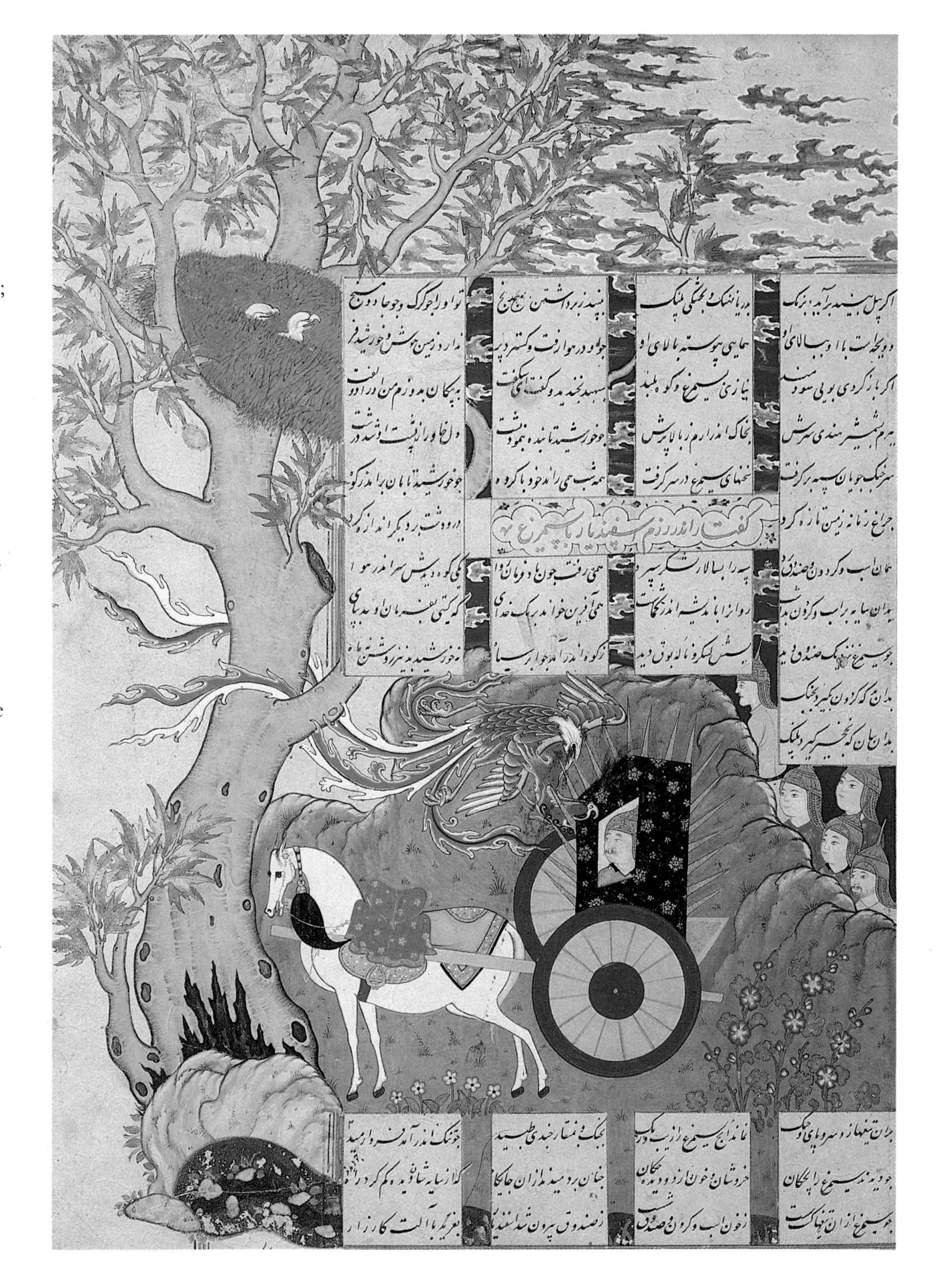

In his struggle with an unfriendly simurgh (a phoenix-like bird of great power) the Iranian hero and king's son Isfandiyar made use of an armoured chariot bristling with spikes. Defending its nest, the unfortunate bird impaled itself and died before the eyes of unmoved spectators. In the lower left is the name of the painter Siyavush, one of the most well-known figures in late-16th-century painting in Iran. He may originally have been a Christian, for he came from Georgia, presumably as a captive. He was one of Shah Tahmasp's pages in the 1530s, and the perceptive king, noting his talent, assigned him to be trained by the great master of painting, Muzaffar 'Ali. Siyavush was an established artist in his own right when Isma'il II succeeded his father in 1576 and commissioned a royal *Shāhnāmeh*, for which Siyavush eventually supplied at least thirteen illustrations. During the reign of Shah 'Abbas I (1587-1629) Siyavush executed a number of fine drawings for the king before he retired to Shiraz, where he died some time between 1606 and 1616.

75
Seated princess

Signed by Sadiqi
Tinted drawing on paper, on an album page
Inscribed with a Persian quatrain, glorifying God:

> No living being has ever found your favour disappointing,
> For he whom you accept enjoys nothing but good fortune.
> And any particle joined to your favour for even one instant
> Glows with a brightness greater than one thousand suns.

Calligraphy signed by Mir Husayn al-Sahvi al-Tabrizi
Page 33.8 × 22.3 cm
Binyon, Wilkinson, Gray, (1933), no. 302;
A. Welch (1973), no. 1, pp. 22 and 63;
A. Welch, (1976), pp. 88-90 and fig. 18
Iran, Qazvin, *c.* 1578

Mouth, sash, handkerchief, and undergarment are coloured a delicate red; the long cloth dropping from her headdress is light blue. Such tinted ink drawing became popular in 16th-century Iran and India, and this fine example is by one of Iran's most fascinating artists. Born into the military aristocracy that supported the Safavid house, Sadiqi served initially as a soldier and travelled widely in Iran and the Near East. In 1565 at the age of thirty-two he left his first career to devote himself to art; for three years he studied calligraphy in Tabriz and then in 1568 began the study of painting with the great Safavid master, Muzaffar 'Ali, in Qazvin. By 1576 when Isma'il II came to the throne Sadiqi was well enough established to become, along with Siyavush, one of the major artists of the king's *Shāhnāmeh*. After the monarch's death in 1577 Sadiqi spent a number of years in the service of provincial nobles. With the accession of Shah 'Abbas in 1587, Sadiqi came into his own, for he was appointed Director of the Royal Library, a post which he held until 1598 when he was dismissed for malfeasance. From then until his death in 1610 Sadiqi devoted himself largely to literature: his *Qānūn al-Suwar* is an invaluable treatise on the techniques of painting, while his *Majma' al-Khawāss* is a biographical memoir giving short, and often nasty, accounts of the hundreds of persons Sadiqi had known in his turbulent career. A bitter and often self-serving individual, he surely left behind him as many enemies as friends.

76
Camp in the mountains

Page from a manuscript of the *Sifāt al-'Āshiqīn* (Dispositions of lovers) of Hilali
Inscribed with two couplets in *nasta'līq*
24 × 16 cm
Previously in the Binney Collection
Grube (1968), no. 79.1; Binney (1966), frontispiece; Robinson (1976), no. 24ii; Kevorkian and Sicre (1983), p. 225
Iran, dated 990/1582

Hilali wrote under the patronage of Sultan Husayn Bayqara in late-15th-century Herat, and his *Sifāt al-'Āshiqīn* was popular in Safavid Iran. The manuscript from which this fine miniature comes was the most impressive copy of Hilali's poem produced in Safavid Iran. Of its three miniatures, only one, the double-page frontispiece, is signed (by 'Abdullah al-Mudhahhib, q.v. nos 66 and 77). Though this mountain encampment is not signed, the master responsible for it also worked on the *Dīwān* of Ibrahim Mirza that was completed in the same year. He had clearly studied similar scenes in the 1556-65 *Haft Awrang* of Jami (Freer Gallery of Art, Washington) and may have been trained by Mirza 'Ali or Muzaffar 'Ali.

77
Prince visiting a hermit

Manuscript of the *Dīwān* of Ibrahim Mirza written in *nasta'līq* script by an unidentified scribe, illustrated with six single-page and one double-page illustrations
Preface probably by Gawhar-sultan, daughter of Ibrahim Mirza; sixty-eight pages of Persian poetry; twenty pages of Chagatay Turkish poetry
Miniature signed on rock in lower left: 'On this stone the painter has written that this humble world lacks constancy. Therefore be happy. Work of 'Abdullah al-Mudhahhib in the year 990.'
Page 24.7 × 17.1 cm
Marteau and Vever (1912); A. Welch and S.C. Welch (1982), no. 30, pp. 94-98
Iran, Qazvin, 990/1582

Born in 1543-44, Ibrahim Mirza was the son of Shah Tahmasp's brother Bahram Mirza, and like his father and uncle the prince was a gifted artist, connoisseur, and patron of the arts, as well as a poet and scholar. Favoured by his uncle, he married the shah's daughter, Gawhar-sultan, in 1555-56, and in the same year was appointed to the prestigious governorship of Iran's holy city, Meshed. There Ibrahim assembled a splendid court, noted for its literary and artistic talents, and his atelier busied itself with the creation of the great 1556-65 *Haft Awrang* of Jami in the Freer Gallery of Art. Between 1565-74 his unpredictable uncle exiled him to minor posts, but in 1574 he returned to Qazvin to serve as grand master of ceremonies. He brought with him a library of more than 3000 volumes. Despite a careful apolitical stance, he was murdered by the shah's paranoid successor, Isma'il II in 1577; his devoted daughter, Gawhar-sultan arranged that he and her mother be buried in Meshed. As a tribute to her father, she also compiled the poems in this *Dīwān* and gave the task of writing and illustrating them to the foremost calligraphers and painters.

Only one of the manuscript's illustrations is signed, but the artist 'Abdullah al-Mudhahhib ('Abdullah the Gilder) is well known. A native of Shiraz, he was famed for his skill in gilding and illumination and worked for twenty years in the service of Prince Ibrahim. His devotion to the prince was so great that after Ibrahim's murder, 'Abdullah moved to Meshed and assumed the post of attendant at his grave. Evidently he did not retire from the practice of his art, since he was prepared to paint and sign one of the miniatures in this manuscript; it is quite possible that he was responsible for the gilding and illumination in the book as well.

78
Holy Qur'an

Illuminated manuscript on paper
21.5 × 13.5 cm
Uzbekistan, Samarkand, dated 994/1585-86

The first folio of this fine Qur'an of 324 folios is illuminated with an uninscribed *shamsa* in dark blue, gold, light blue, green, white, and red, and the same colours are used in the double-page frontispiece that has been slightly retouched. Sura titles are illuminated in narrow cartouches in the same colours. The text is written in thirteen lines of clear, fine *naskh*, and the margins are illuminated with gold vegetal and floral patterns. The colophon, written in a more cursive hand, states that the book was completed in Samarkand in 1585-86 by 'Abd al-Faqir al-Raji al-Rahmatullah al-Bari' (the poor slave, the one who hopes for the mercy of God the Creator).

Rivals in the east to the Safavid shahs of Iran, the Uzbek khans established a large, Sunni state in Central Asia and made their chief cities of Samarkand and Bukhara into major cultural centres. A number of Uzbek rulers were notable patrons of architecture and the arts. Seizing Bukhara in 1557, Sultan 'Abdullah ibn Iskandar took Samarkand in 1578 and from his vast realm led fierce raids into Iran in the last decade of the 16th century. A number of important manuscripts were produced during his reign, though only one – a 1563-64 *Tuhfat al-Ahrār* of Jami (A. Welch (1979) no. 74) – specifically names 'Abdullah ibn Iskandar as the patron. From its date and quality this Qur'an can be plausibly attributed to his patronage: it was created at the height of the sultan's power and prestige.

77

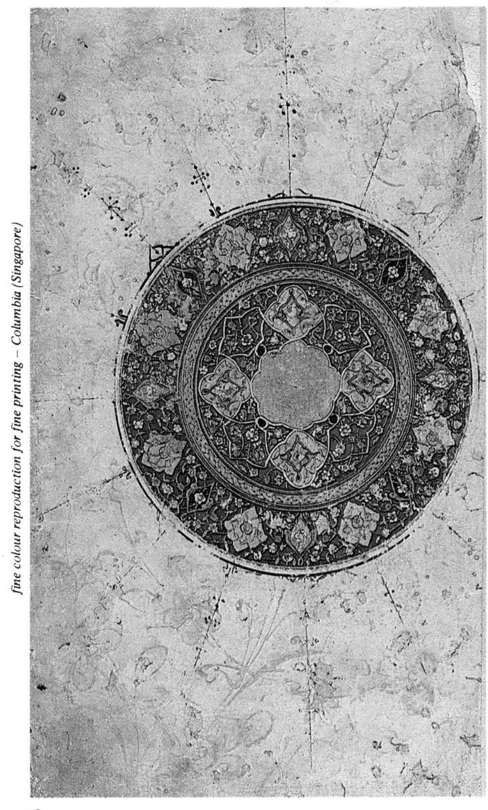

78

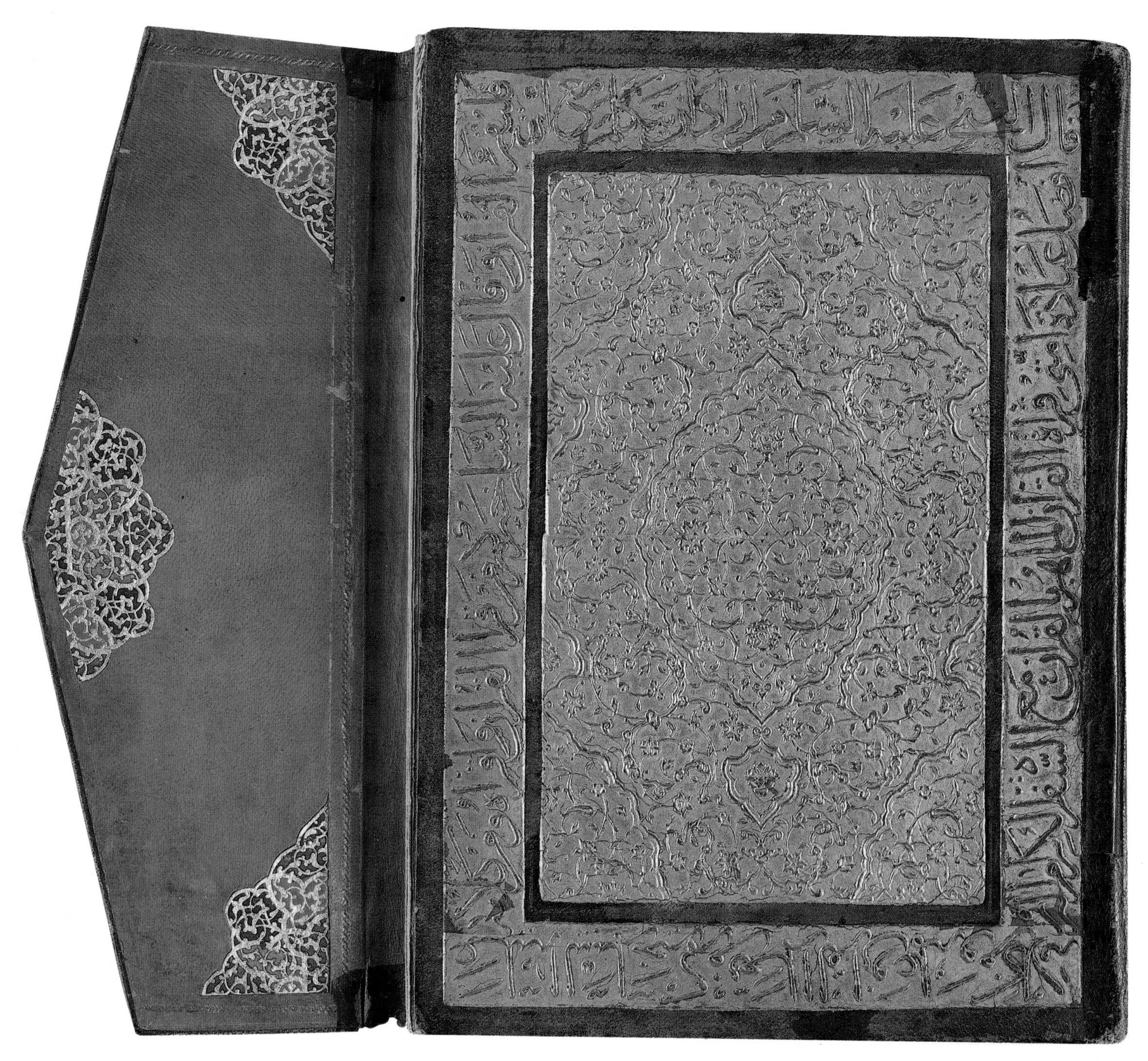

79
Gilt leather binding for a Holy Qur'an

Manuscript of Sura XXI *Al-Anbiyā*, and Sura XXII *Al-Hajj*
24.5 × 17.8 cm
Previously in the Kevorkian Collection
Sotheby's 12 Jan 1969, lot 184; A. Welch (1978), vol. 4, MS 10, pp. 6–11
Iran 14th century; binding 16th century

This manuscript of twenty-nine pages (the seventeenth section of the Qur'an) is written with seven lines of *muhaqqaq* to the page, four lines in black alternating with three lines in gold. In the 16th century an appreciative owner supplied this Qur'an section with a new binding: the exterior is gilded, black leather with raised arabesques in a central rectangle and *Hadīth* (sayings of the Prophet Muhammad) extolling the virtues of reading the scripture inscribed in the outer border. The light brown leather interior has a central medallion and four corner cartouches decorated with gold *découpé* arabesques against backgrounds of black, red, blue, and green.

80

Bazindeh and the sudden storm

Manuscript of the *Anwār-i Suhaylī* of Husayn Wa'iz-al-Kashifi, written by the scribe ibn Na'im Muhammad al-Husayni al-Tabrizi, illustrated with 107 miniatures
Note of front flyleaf stating that in 1618 the manuscript was received at Dar al Sa'ada, Ahmedabad, in Gujerat, where Jahangir's court was at the time
Contemporary green lacquer binding with arabesques in red, black and gold
Commissioned and presumably illustrated by Sadiqi
30 × 21 cm
Previously in the collection of the Marquess of Bute
Robinson (1974); A. Welch (1976), pp. 125-143; London (1976), no. 621; A. Welch and S.C. Welch (1982), no. 32, pp. 100-10
Iran, Qazvin, dated 13 Safar 1002/8 November 1593

The moralizing animal fables of the *Kalīla wa Dimna* were rendered in elaborate Persian prose by Husayn Wa'iz al-Kashifi in the late 15th century at the court of the Timurid sultan, Husayn Bayqara, in Herat. They were popular in 16th-century Iran, and Shah 'Abbas' *kitābdār* (director of the royal library) commissioned this impressive volume for himself in 1593. For an artist to assume the role of patron indicates the high status and respectability of painters and calligraphers in Safavid times. Indeed, the manuscript's lengthy colophon not only supplies the information cited above but also describes Sadiqi as 'the rare man of the time, the second Mani and the Bihzad of the age.' It was high praise, though the self-appreciative Sadiqi surely felt he deserved it.

Folio 22a (Bazindeh and the sudden storm) illustrates the first tale in Book 1. Bazindeh was an adventurous pigeon, anxious to travel and see the world. But when, after a day of travel, he was settling down for the night near a mountain, a sudden storm swept down upon him. It was not long before Bazindeh concluded there was no place like home. This dramatic illustration is one of the most impressive depictions of wind and storm in Iranian art; like many other paintings in the manuscript, its iconography is more radical than those done for royal patrons, and it can be suggested that Sadiqi's very independent temperament responded well to the artistic freedom of self-patronage.

81
Three *ta'līq* calligraphies by Mir 'Imad

On an Indian album page signed by Muhammad Hadi and dated 1171/1757-8
29.5 × 21.5 cm
Iran, *c.* 1605

Safavid and Mughal albums generally alternated paintings with calligraphies in order to present a rich diversity, and on the reverse of this fine Indian album page is a picture of four holy men near a water-wheel. The three calligraphies, written in the flowing, floating *ta'līq* script, are the work of Mir 'Imad, and his signature 'Imad al-Husayni appears in the upper and right-hand panels. One of the most celebrated Iranian scribes and a consummate master of *ta'līq*, Mir 'Imad was highly regarded by his chief patron, Shah 'Abbas I, and worked in the court atelier in Isfahan. A devout Sunni in officially Shi'a Iran, he made enemies, particularly the ambitious and envious 'Ali Riza 'Abbasi, as gifted a calligrapher as he was. Ruthless in his rivalry, 'Ali Riza engineered the assassination of Mir 'Imad.

The scribe's fame survived his death. Connoisseurs in Iran, Central Asia, and India in the 17th and 18th centuries eagerly collected his writings, which often fetched very high prices. These three fine samples of his work were put together for an unknown patron in India, but the gilder identified himself and dated his work in the margin.

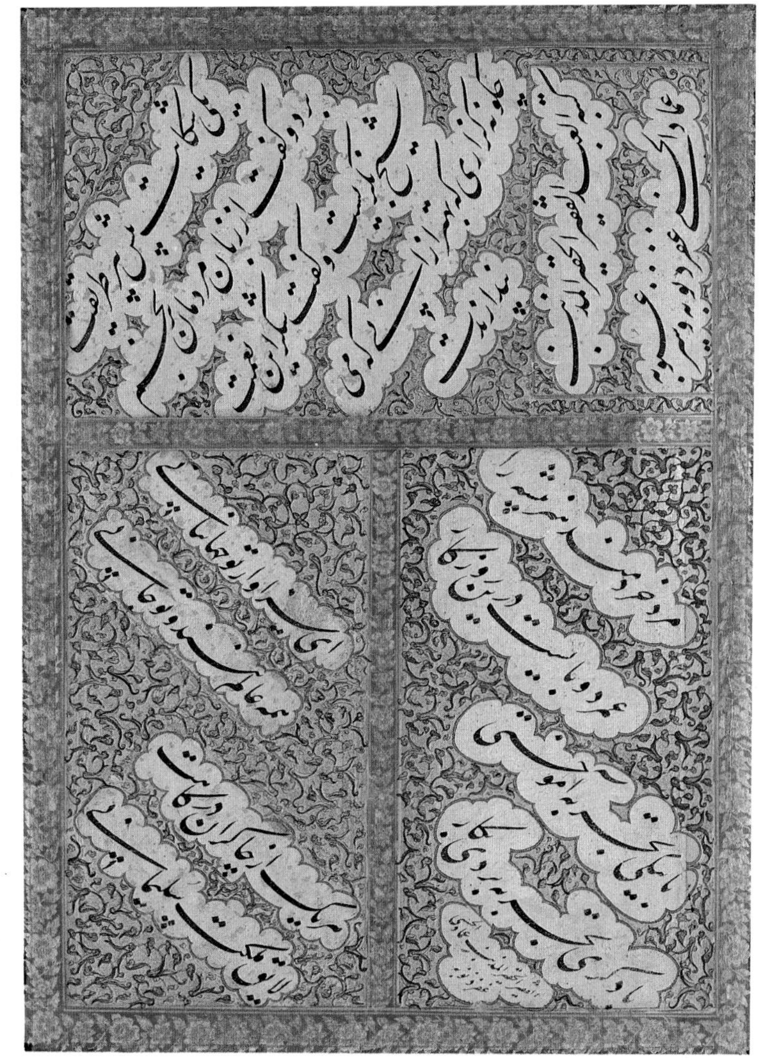

81

82
Jade bowl with Persian calligraphy

Inscribed with a *waqf* dedication to the Ardabil shrine in the name of Shah 'Abbas I
14 cm diameter
Christie's 15 October 1980, lot 173; see also Pope (1956) p. 51; Transactions of the Oriental Ceramics Society, vol. 25, 1949-50
Probably Samarkand, 15th century; engraved in Iran *c.* 1612

Like the Ottoman sultans, the Safavid shahs made an impressive collection of Chinese wares and in 1021/1612 Shah 'Abbas I deposited, according to the annalist of his reign, about 1215 pieces of porcelain and six of jade in the shrine of Shaykh Safi, the eponymous founder of the Safavid dynasty, at Ardabil in Azerbaijan, whence they were removed to Tehran during the reign of Riza Shah.

The Ardabil pieces were engraved by a noted artist with the personal seal of Shah 'Abbas recording their presentation to the shrine, as follows:

> *Bandeh-i Shāh-i Wilāyat 'Abbās waqf bar āstāneh-i Shāh Safī namūd*

> 'Abbas, slave of the King of Holiness (i.e. 'Ali), made (it) *waqf* of the shrine of Shah (sic) Safi

This light green jade oviform bowl with short foot and moulded rim carries an identical inscription (rubbed with red pigment to make it more easily legible) and therefore must have formed part of Shah 'Abbas' collection and been deposited at Ardabil.

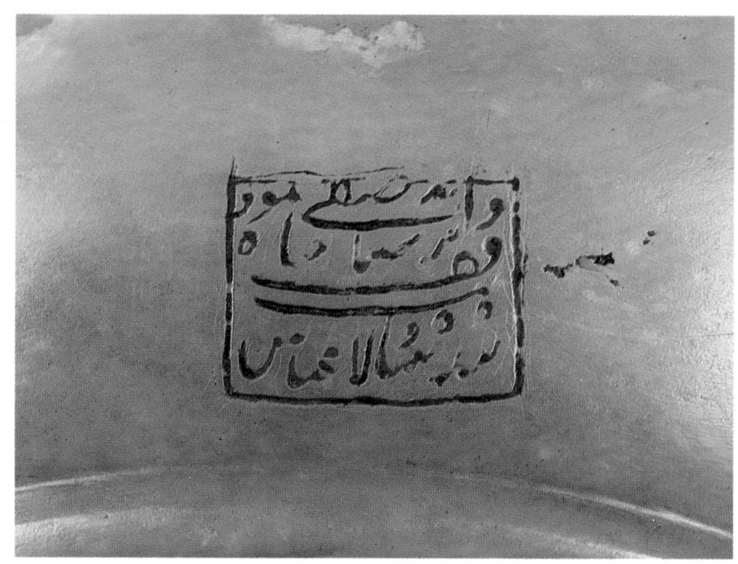

82

83
Youth with burn marks

Album page
Reverse: a page of calligraphy, including an Arabic *Hadīth* and four lines of Persian poetry, written in *nasta'līq* and signed by Mir 'Ali al-Katib
Miniature 18.5 × 11 cm; page 44.5 × 31.5 cm
Previously in the Everitt Macy Collection
Iran, early 17th century

This flaccid dandy is a youthful lover of leisure: his double chin puffs from too much alcohol or too many sweets. Despite the delicacy of his appearance and the landscape in which he sits by himself, he is engaged in a serious exercise. The small cotton roll in his left hand and the roll resting on his right forearm are burning, and he has already inflicted two wounds on his skin. This kind of localized immolation was a recognized practice in Safavid Iran. Originating probably as a dervish practice to demonstrate self-control and submission to God, it acquired more worldly meaning in 17th-century Iran, where a young man would prove his devotion to his beloved by inflicting himself with burns. The youth with the most burns would be considered the most desirable marriage prospect. The young man portrayed here is obviously just beginning his candidacy. The pomegranates in front of him were standard symbols of love. The painting is unsigned but may be the work of Riza 'Abbasi (see nos 84-86). The margins are ornamented with animals in subtle gold – a hare, a kylin (winged lion), a dragon, a simurgh (phoenix) and a forlorn duck.

84
Portrait of Dervish Ghiyath

Miniature signed by Riza 'Abbasi
Inscribed in *nasta'līq*: '. . . Portrait of Dervish Ghiyath . . . It was finished on the fifth day of (the month of) *Rabi' al-ākhir* 1032 (6 February 1623). The work of the most humble Riza 'Abbasi.'
18.3 × 12.5 cm
Iran, Isfahan, 1623

A dervish was a mystical devotee of God in Islamic tradition, and dervishes were favourite subjects of painting in 17th-century Iran. Holding out a fruit and a leafy twig, Ghiyath appears to be making a humble offering to someone, perhaps a potential donor. Dressed in simple garb, the holy man is a stout middle-aged man whose face, filled with worldly wisdom, is brightened by a cunning smile. While he may have commissioned this painting himself, it is more likely that he was portrayed for a connoisseur assembling an album of interesting characters and well-known types. In the last decade of his life (he died in 1635) Riza developed a keenly naturalistic manner, far broader in scope than the idyllic renderings that characterize his early art. Many are humorous, even caricatural, and their vivid recording of Safavid society was the basis for much of the work of Riza's most gifted student, Mu'in (see nos 90 and 91, 94-97).

85
Page boy

Album page
Signed by Riza 'Abbasi
18.9 × 9.2 cm
A. Welch (1978), vol. III, Ir. M. 83, pp. 127-129; A. Welch and S.C. Welch (1982), no. 34, pp. 107-109
Iran, Isfahan, *Rabi' al-awwal* 1034/December 1624-January 1625

Elegant, affluent, and dressed *à la mode*, this aristocratic dandy appears to be self-centred and absent-minded at the same time. Portraits of this sort were enormously popular in 17th-century Iranian art, and Riza 'Abbasi was the great master of the genre. First known simply as Riza or Aqa Riza, he flourished at Shah 'Abbas' court from the time of the monarch's accession in 1587 until about 1605, when the artist, despite high favour, experienced a kind of 'mid-life crisis', largely gave up the practice of art, and spent his time with persons of low repute. After a decade of what stern contemporary chroniclers obviously considered dissolution, he returned to his vocation, and after 1605 until his death in 1615 devoted himself with skill and energy to art. This portrait was done mid-way in this second part of his career, when he also functioned as a gifted teacher who trained most of the distinguished painters of the later Safavid period.

86

Seated youth

Miniature signed by Riza 'Abbasi
19 × 10.5 cm
Previously in the Kevorkian Collection
Sotheby's, 21 April 1980, lot 80
Iran, Isfahan, *c.* 1630

Although earlier masters like Mirza 'Ali had excelled at rendering delicate dandies in wistful contemplation, it was Riza who during his long career established this motif as one of the major subjects of later Safavid painting. The master's signature at the right is clear, even if the date when it was done has been effaced. An inscription in the same hand in the upper left names one Mirza Muhammad Shafi', for whom this picture may have been done.

(Actual size)

87
Young man drinking
Miniature painting
Miniature 16 × 11.5 cm; page 32 × 27 cm
Iran, Isfahan, *c.* 1630

The margins are decorated with falling leaves and unusually flecked with silver. In the miniature, the young man assumes a comfortable pose: he leans against a bolster and a pillow supports his right arm, weakly holding a half empty glass flask. Drained to the last drop, his wine cup is upside-down in his left hand. His clothing is in the latest fashion and not a hair is out of place in his *coiffure*. Images of youth, luxury and drinking were common in Persian poetry and often had mystical overtones. This elegant 'fashion-plate' seems far removed from this spiritual tradition but represents one of the most frequent subjects in 17th-century Iranian art.

88
Bearded dervish
Attributed to Shafi' 'Abbasi
Miniature 16.5 × 8.6 cm, page 20 × 19 cm
Previously in the Rothschild Collection
Robinson (1976), no. 47
Iran, Isfahan *c.* 1640

In the 17th century, the depiction of dervishes or holy men, whether portraits or idealized images, became very popular in both Safavid Iran and Mughal India (see no. 98). The drawing here represents a well-known type of Safavid album page painting. Several versions of the identical idealized figure exist but he is usually shown seated alone or in the company of a youth.[1] Shafi's fluid calligraphic style not only confirms his superb draftsmanship, but provides his standing dervish with a remarkable presence and sensitivity.

Muhammad Shafi' 'Abbasi was not only trained by Riza 'Abbasi but according to an inscribed drawing in the Los Angeles County Museum[2], he was also his son. Shafi's earliest signature appears on a recently published work dated 1028/1618-19[3], but the majority of his paintings fall under the reign of Shah 'Abbas II (1642-66). His interest lay primarily in bird and flower studies which were inspired by both Indian and European examples. He also provided several drawings in the same genre for textile designs. Shafi' numbered among the highest revered artists of his period for he not only provided paintings for the royal collection[4] but like his father, received the honorific title ''Abbasi' from the shah, in his case, 'Abbas II.

M.F.

1) Topkapi album H 2162 fol. 3a; Metropolitan Museum of Art 25.68.5; Sotheby's, 7 April 1975, lots 44; 45
2) *Man with a pitchfork* (1044/1634), Pal (1973), no. 237; Sarre and Mittwoch (1914), p. 13
3) Rogers (1983), no. 58
4) Blochet (1929), pl. CLXVIII, the only known work which bears a specific dedication to 'Abbas II

89
Portrait of a Persian lady of the Court of Isfahan

Signed by Muhammad Qasim-i Tabrizi
28 × 17 cm
Previously in the Tabbagh Collection and the collection of Dr Schaurte
Blochet (1929), pl. CLXVII; Sotheby's, 12-13 December 1929, lot 257 and 16 April 1984, lot 111
Iran, Isfahan *c.* 1640-50

Muhammad Qasim-i Tabrizi contributed to a number of important mid-17th-century manuscripts[1] but his fame rests primarily on album page painting. These usually consist of carefully drawn, intimate images of elegant, somewhat wistful, figures. Although this portrait resembles these single works in subject matter, its rather large format and sumptuous finish, especially of the background, is more akin to the artist's manuscript illustrations. The overall nature of the painting suggests that it was commissioned by a high-ranking patron for an oversized de luxe album. In fact, Muhammad Qasim has executed another equally large and lavish single page now in the Topkapi Saray Library, possibly meant for the same collection.[2]

Although known as a portrait, the elegant young girl resembles more an idealized 17th-century female figure, identical to numerous others in Muhammad Qasim's work. She represents a highly sophisticated *saqi* (cupbearer) seen in an imaginary setting offering worldly pleasures in the form of the waterpipe and the wine cup.

Muhammad Qasim-i Tabrizi, a native of the old Safavid capital Tabriz, numbered among Riza 'Abbasi's foremost followers. Although one of his drawings was executed in Baghdad,[3] his style indicates that he was primarily active in Isfahan. He was not only revered as a painter excelling in the application of colour, but was also known as an accomplished poet.

Muhammad Qasim's date of death is given as 107 (presumably meaning the year 107 [0]/1659) and he lies buried in the Takht-i Fulad cemetery in Isfahan.[4]

M.F.

1) *Shāhnāmeh* 1058/1648 Windsor Castle, Royal Library, A/6 see Stchoukine (1964), pls LII-LXV
2) Topkapi Saray Album H2162 f 20b; 24.7 × 16.7 cm
3) Bibliotèque Nationale O.D. 41 f.33; see Martin (1912) pl. 165c
4) Wali Quli Shamlu *Qisas al-Khāqānī* British Library, Add 7656 f. 175a

90
European youth
Signed by Mu'in Musawwir
Miniature on cream paper, background details and borders decorated in gold
20.5 × 10 cm
Previously in the Rothschild Collection
Robinson (1976) no. 55i
Iran, Isfahan *c.* 1648

Mu'in Musawwir, considered the most gifted and prolific follower of Riza 'Abbasi, was active between 1635 and 1697. His work ranges from the illustration of large-scale manuscripts to individual sketches of daily events, portraits and idealized images. Little is known about his life but his paintings are usually signed and inscribed (see nos 96 and 97), providing an invaluable source for understanding 17th-century painting. Although Mu'in always adapted his style to his subject matter, his work remained unaffected by the introduction of European elements into Persian painting. This portrait and its counterpart (no. 91), however, illustrate that he was not unaware of this great western influx. The young man is dressed meticulously in a European costume while casually resting his weight on one foot. His elegance and sophistication is such that even the white lap dog at his feet cannot help but gaze up at him in total admiration.

Mu'in has drawn three other versions of this figure, whose smooth, generalized features suggest an idealized rather than actual person.[1] But in each case, despite his interest in the outward trappings, the style and treatment of his subject has remained within the mainstream of traditional Persian painting.

This version, which is the finest of the group and obviously meant for an album, was painted curiously among the pages of a *Shāhnāmeh*. The reasons for this are not clear but as the manuscript has been illustrated by Mu'in, we may assume that its date, 1058/1648 also applies to this portrait and its companion (no. 91)

M.F.

1) Topkapi album H2142 f. 15b; Binney (1962), no. 55; Metropolitan Museum of Art, 55.121.23.

91

Girl in European costume

Signed by Mu'in Musawwir
Miniature on cream paper, background details and borders decorated in gold
20.5 × 10 cm
Previously in the Rothschild Collection
Robinson (1976), no. 55ii
Iran, Isfahan *c.* 1648

The graceful swaying figure of the idealized young girl holding a bottle and a cup, complements the companion portrait (no. 90) in its elegance and refinement. An identical drawing of the same girl, but in reverse, has also been attributed to Mu'in.[1]

M.F.

1) Los Angeles County Museum of Art, Pal (1973), no. 251, p. 140

92

The constellation centaur

Manuscript of the *Book of fixed stars* of 'Abdulrahman ibn 'Umar al-Sufi, copied in *nasta'līq* and illustrated with sixty-five ink illustrations
On the first page library seals of 'Alamgir (Awrangzib), 1103/1691-92, and Shah 'Alam, 1123/1711-12
31.4 × 18 cm
A. Welch (1972), vol. 2, MS9, pp. 69-73
Iran, probably Isfahan, mid-17th century

Among the earliest illustrated Islamic books are copies of scientific treatises – natural histories, astronomies, and herbals, among others – and the production of classics of science remained an important task of calligraphers and painters well into the 19th century. 'Abdulrahman ibn 'Umar al-Sufi was a celebrated 10th-century Arab astronomer, and his *Suwar al-Kawākib al-Thābita* (Book of fixed stars) became the single most important Islamic astronomical text. The Arabic text generally is written in seventeen lines to the page, while a Persian translation fills the margins. There are numerous charts. The illustrations are the work of a highly trained Isfahan artist, strongly influenced by the art of Muhammad Yusuf. Not too long after this book was finished, it was taken to India and became part of the Mughal royal library.

92

93

93

Page holding a bowl on a gold tray

Signed by Muhammad 'Ali
Miniature painting on cream paper
11.6 × 4.3 cm
Sotheby's, 7 April 1975, lot 49
Iran, Isfahan *c.* 1650

The small painting of a pageboy holding a blue-and-white bowl on a gold tray bears the signature of the 17th-century artist, Muhammad 'Ali. The son of the painter Malik Husayn Isfahani, he ranked among Riza 'Abbasi's foremost followers and like his contemporaries Mu'in, Muhammad Yusuf and Muhammad Qasim, drew upon Riza's artistic achievements to develop his personal calligraphic style. (Malik Husayn Isfahani is responsible for the double frontispiece 'Solomon and the Queen of Sheba enthroned' of the *Shāhnāmeh* (1058/1648) Royal Library Windsor Castle; Holmes 151 (A/6); Stchoukine (1964), pls LII, LIII.) The crisp, clean lines delineating the figure of his pageboy have been reduced to the most essential, while Muhammad 'Ali has alternated clearly defined areas of green, orange and gold to create a subtle interplay of colours. Equal attention has been lavished on the carefully composed flower bushes and wisp of clouds of the background, producing an effect not unlike that of some Safavid textiles. Although dealing with a common subject-matter, Muhammad 'Ali's rather abstract drawing style has provided yet another interpretation of the idealized Safavid youth.

M.F.

94
The fire-ordeal of Siyavush

Volume One of a *Shāhnāmeh* made for Shah 'Abbas II, written in *nasta'līq* by an unidentified scribe, illustrated with a double-page frontispiece and twenty-nine other miniatures
Twenty-eight miniatures signed by Mu'in Musawwir
Three miniatures dated 1065/1654-55; frontispiece dated 1067/1656-57
19th-century Indian binding
35.3 × 24 cm
Sotheby's, 25 November 1968, lot 179 (Thomas Phillipps Collection); A. Welch, (1973), no. 57, pp. 87 and 99; A. Welch (1978), vol. IV, MS 22, pp. 89-97; A. Welch and S.C. Welch (1982), no. 38, pp. 117-120
Iran, Isfahan, 1654-57

Like many of his predecessors, Shah 'Abbas II (r. 1642-66) commissioned his own royal copy of Firdawsi's epic, and as a gifted connoisseur of painting, he had the good sense to select Riza's foremost student, Mu'in Musawwir, as its chief painter and the director of the project. Born in 1617, Mu'in had been only eighteen when Riza died and was thirty-seven when he began the formidable task of illustrating this *Shāhnāmeh* (the second volume of which is in the Chester Beatty Library, Dublin). An artistic prodigy, he was also enormously productive and vastly diverse in style, and he dominated Isfahan art until his death in 1708. He paints in a fluid but conservative manner, and his miniatures here belong to the established iconography of Iran's epic. That he signs nearly all of the paintings surely indicates not only his own sound sense of self-worth but also his patron's appreciation of his ability.

95 *(Actual size)*

95

Loving couple and a servant

Signed by Mu'in Musawwir
14 × 20 cm
Iran, Isfahan, dated 1081/1670

It is a warm embrace, and while the young woman daintily reaches for the wine cup extended to her by the servant, her lover's left hand pulls his fine gold-embroidered coat around her and discreetly keeps our eyes from their right hands. Solitary youths are more common in later Safavid painting than couples, and there are few extant group portraits as tender as this one. An inscription below their feet identifies the artist as Mu'in Musawwir and dates it to the month of *Jumādā al-ākhira* 1081/October-November 1670. Mu'in was at the height of his artistic power at this time and was illustrating *Shāhnāmehs* and producing individual drawings with a profusion that is one of the wonders of later Safavid art. He was a keen observer of life around him and of human emotion, and this touching love portrait is rendered with a sympathetic hand.

96

Portrait of Mirza Muhammad Taqi

Signed by Mu'in Musawwir
Miniature painting on light brown paper
Inscribed in Persian: In the likeness of his excellency, the exalted and lofty refuge, the source of glory and justice(?), of praiseworthy qualities, known for virtue and piety, pilgrim to noble places and sites, [who] does not need titles and epithets, the Mirza (Mirza Muhammad Taqi, may God keep him from evil and misfortune) upon his return from [the] holy [city of] Meshed. Painted by his highness, the rarity of his time, Aqa Mu'ina . . . (?) May God bless it. 1[0]96
25 × 18 cm
Iran, Isfahan 1[0]96/1685

As the Safavids adopted Shi'ism as their new state religion, pilgrimages to the various Shi'ite shrines became an essential part of religious life. The most frequented site was Meshed, the burial site of Imam Riza, the eighth Imam, in north-eastern Iran. This demonstration of Shi'ite devotion was not limited to the populace alone. Safavid monarchs and their ruling élite not only visited Meshed regularly but continuously strove to commemorate their piety by expanding and embellishing the shrine complex. Thus Mu'in's two paintings of Mirza Muhammad Taqi (see no. 97) serve not only as portraits but also as a confirmation of the sitter's religious devotion.

Although Mu'in has painted numerous portraits, the two here are undoubtedly among his finest. Mirza Muhammad Taqi's elegant appearance suggests that he was a man of high rank. Firmly seated on his horse led by a groom, he is dressed in a

96

simple red robe with frogging and a blue fur-trimmed cap. He is carrying a set of bow and arrows, while balancing a slender staff with his left hand. Details have been kept to a minimum and Mu'in's selection of few yet striking colours against the light brown background has created a warm, highly refined visual effect.

The inscription along the left edge claims that the miniature commemorates Muhammad Taqi's return from his pilgrimage to Meshed in 1096/1685. Although the script resembles Mu'in's, its laudatory tone suggests that it may have been added by a pupil and great admirer rather than by Mu'in himself.

M.F.

97

Portrait of Mirza Muhammad Taqi

Signed by Mu'in Musawwir
Miniature painting on light brown paper
Inscribed in Persian: 'In the likeness of his excellency, the exalted and lofty refuge, of praiseworthy qualities, known for virtue and piety, [who] does not need titles and epithets, the mirza of pilgrims to noble and blessed places and sites. Painted towards the end of Sha'ban the year 1096 at Isfahan, the seat of government. Illustrated by the mastery of the pearl strung pen of Aqa Mu'in, the rarity of his time. May God bless and exalt it.'
Above: 'Mirza Muhammad Taqi Tabrizi. May his glory and fortune endure for ever'
23.5 × 18 cm
Iran, Isfahan *Sha'bān* 1096/July 1685

A second painting commemorating Mirza Muhammad Taqi's pilgrimage to Meshed reconfirms the importance of this occasion. The figure is shown in a different costume but the format and composition of the work suggests that the two were conceived as a double equestrian portrait to be seen side by side. Muhammad Taqi is now shown in a dark purple robe with small clusters of white dots. Instead of a fur-trimmed cap, he is wearing a tightly knotted turban. While still holding a thin staff in his left hand, his right rests elegantly on the opposite side. His more sombre and formal attire contrasts with the bright red robe of the groom, leading his horse.

Continued overleaf

Just as the two representations of the figure complement each other, so do the inscriptions. They are quite similar in content, but here, instead of referring specifically to Muhammad Taqi's return from Meshed, we are told that the miniature (presumably both) was completed at Isfahan towards the end of *Sha'bān* 1096/July 1685.
M.F.

98
Indian holy man walking by an encampment

Signed by 'Ali Quli Jabbadar
Gouache and gold on paper set in floriated borders. Seal and *waqf* inscription; inscribed at the bottom: 'He has reached his goal, and we are still searching.'
Miniature 14 × 11 cm, page 21.6 × 34.4 cm
Hotel Drouot, June 23 1982, lot 12
Iran, Isfahan, dated 1068/1657-58

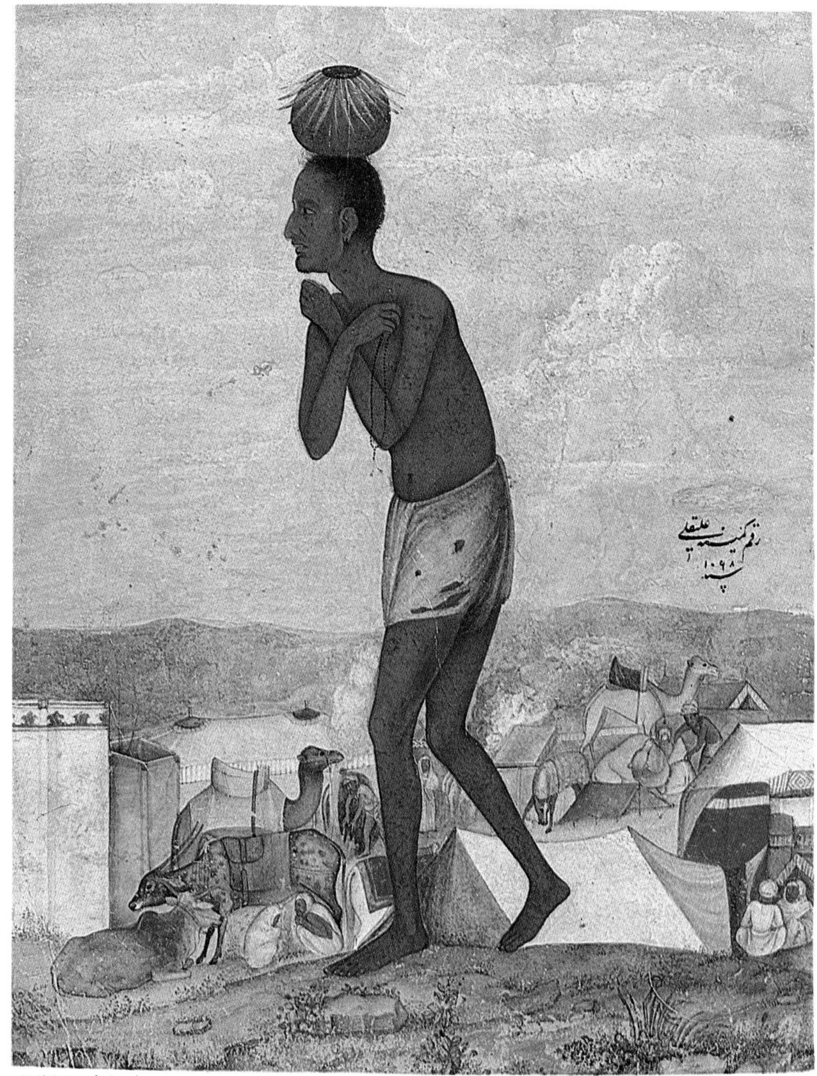

98 *(Actual size)*

In the mid-17th century, a number of European artists, attracted by the Safavid interest in western art, came to Iran in search of patronage. Although 'Ali Quli's origins are still unknown, his title *farangī* meaning European, suggests that he, too, belonged to this group. He migrated to Iran in the reign of 'Abbas II (1642-66) and, having converted to Islam, began working for a number of high-ranking patrons. He is also known by the *nisba* Jabbadar indicating that he was officially associated with the arsenal (*jabbakhāneh*), though his appointment was surely a sinecure.

'Ali Quli's work is primarily Europeanized but he also expressed an interest in Mughal painting which he probably regarded as a bridge between Persian and European painting traditions.[1] One of his earliest dated works, this miniature is in fact modelled after an original Mughal miniature *c.* 1630-40 attributed to Govardhan.[2] 'Ali Quli has faithfully recreated the man's total self-absorption and vacant gaze as he slowly walks past the busy encampment. The same overall muted tones, delicately outlined and modelled, predominate whereby the refined haunting quality of the original has been captured.

'Ali Quli may not have been a first rate western artist, but as his work here suggests, he possessed an almost unrivalled ability to grasp the exotic nature of non-Persian painting and interpret it according to Safavid taste.
M.F.

1) See Ivanov (1926), nos 76, 77, 78
2) This miniature appeared together with 'Ali Quli's version in the same album Hotel Drouot, 23 June 1982, lot 11

99
Young prince receiving instruction

Tinted drawing on paper
Page 15.9 × 11.9 cm
Hotel Drouot, 23 June 1982, lot 4
Iran, Isfahan, *c.* 1675

European prints and Indian painting strongly influenced the art of two of the leading painters of the second half of the 17th century in Iran – Muhammad Zaman and 'Ali Quli Jabbadar, to whose hand this work may tentatively be attributed. His art was clearly valued by the Indian connoisseur who assembled a number of them in the important Indian album from which this miniature comes. The floral border dates from the end of the 17th century.

99 *(Actual size)*

100
Shah 'Abbas II and the Mughal ambassador

Miniature painting on an album page
Attributed to Muhammad Zaman
20.3 × 31.8 cm
A. Welch (1973), no. 63, pp. 84-85, 100;
A. Welch (1978), vol. III, Ir. M. 93, pp. 154-157; A. Welch and S.C. Welch (1982), no. 37, pp. 115-117
Iran, *c.* 1663

The king sits in the middle of the picture, and an inscription in the *īwān* (arched niche) behind him identifies him as Shah 'Abbas II. To his left, his hand upon his *katar* (dagger) is the ambassador from the Mughal emperor Awrangzib (r. 1658-1707). Flanking these two personages are officials, courtiers attendants, entertainers, and servants. Although the composition is based upon the well-established Mughal genre of the imperial court reception, facial types, trees, and architectural perspective strongly suggest that the artist was Muhammad Zaman, a Europeanizing master who, if he did not actually spend time in India, was well acquainted with Indian painting. His contemporary at the Safavid court, Shaykh 'Abbasi, also represented the meeting of 'Abbas II and the Mughal ambassador in a group portrait dated 1663-64.

100

101

Album page with four miniatures

Tinted drawing, inscribed in upper left: *Ya Sāhib al-Zamān 1086/1675*
Page 44.5 × 29 cm, miniature 28 × 18 cm
Sotheby's (New York), 9-10 December 1977, lot 76
Iran, 19th century, miniature 17th century

The precious *muraqqa'* (album) was one of the major art forms of the 16th and 17th centuries. Selected paintings and drawings could be preserved in it, and these works often had not been intended as illustrations of particular texts. This shift from illustration to independent works of visual art was an important element in the development of portraiture and naturalistic painting in later Safavid Iran. In most albums, pages with figural art alternated with calligraphies: the two great arts of the book were thus maintained without the literary content that earlier sustained them. Thus on the reverse of this page is a page of calligraphic exercises in *ta'līq*.

In the upper left a couple embrace. The inscription indicates that the artist was probably Muhammad Zaman, working in the year 1675. The solitary picnic in the upper right can be attributed to his contemporary Shaykh 'Abbasi. In the lower right is a lightly tinted drawing of a kneeling dervish by an unidentified artist working in the style of Mu'in Musawwir. The drawing in the lower left is by an unknown Mughal artist *c.* 1610-20.

102

Judith and Holofernes

Signed *Yā Sāhib al-Zamān*
Miniature painting set in floriated borders with seal and *waqf* inscription
Miniature 20 × 17 cm, page 33.5 × 21 cm
Hotel Drouot, 23 June 1982, lot 16
Iran, Isfahan *c.* 1680

This painting is based on a 17th-century European engraving, after Guido Reni and Alessandro Torchi's *Judith*. It has been generally agreed that the inscription *Yā Sāhib al-Zamān* (O Lord of Time) is that of Muhammad Zaman, the late-17th-century artist. This invocation appears on a number of works which are stylistically similar to his signed ones.

Although Muhammad Zaman has been regarded as one of the most important Safavid painters, he is also the most enigmatic. The son of Haji Yusuf Qumi, he has been traditionally accredited with introducing the Europeanized style into Persian painting. This has led to the assumption that he in fact studied in Italy. But the general westernized elements in his work as well as the specific biblical scenes have been based on Flemish engravings which had become widely available in 17th-century Iran. Thus, the idea of an Italian study trip has now been largely discarded.[1] Muhammad Zaman began his artistic career during the reign of 'Abbas II, attested by a lacquered pen box dated 1070/1059-60,[2] bearing the same invocation as the painting here. Most of his work, however, was carried out under the patronage of Suleyman I (1666-94) who expressed a keen interest in his Europeanized style and subject-matters.

Apart from the miniature here, Muhammad Zaman painted four other known biblical works whose dates range from 1678 to 89. The stylistic and thematical similarity of *Judith and Holofernes* to this group suggests that it was executed during the same period.

M.F.

1) See A.A. Ivanov 'The Life of Muhammad Zaman: A reconsideration' *Iran* XVII (1979), pp. 65-70
2) Niavaran Collection

103
Susannah and the Elders

Signed by Muhammad Baqir
Miniature painting set in a floriated border
Seal and *waqf* inscription
Miniature 16 × 11.5 cm, page 33.7 × 21 cm
Nouveau Drouot, 23 June 1982, lot 8
Iran, Isfahan, 1178/1764-65

The Safavid interest in Europeanized painting outlived the dynasty which fell in 1722 and as the painting here indicates, persisted well into the 18th century. Muhammad Baqir's *Susannah and the Elders* is based on an identical work by 'Ali Quli Jabbadar (see no. 98) modelled after an engraving by the Flemish master Lucas Wasterman, which was in turn inspired by Rubens' *Chaste Susannah*. Both Muhammad Baqir's and 'Ali Quli's versions of this biblical theme appeared side by side in a remarkable album of Persian and Indian paintings and calligraphy.[1] In fact, all our knowledge about Muhammad Baqir stems from this album which contains two of his signed sweetbrier watercolours (lots 19 and 20). Moreover, one of the flower borders (lot 25) also bears his signature and as several of the pages are embellished with similar margins, it appears that Muhammad Baqir played a central role in assembling this album.

The three works bearing his name are all dated to 1178/1764-5, the last date in the album, suggesting that the artist produced his works to coincide with its completion.[2]

M.F.

1) The entire album is reproduced in the sales catalogue of Nouveau Drouot, 23 June 1982. Nos 98 and 102 are also part of this album

2) B.W. Robinson has pointed out that from the beginning of the 18th century a great variety of works bear the name of Muhammad Baqir (*Highlights of Persian Art*, chapter 14, p. 344). However, several paintings in the style of the above Muhammad Baqir also appear in the 'Falak album' no. 1644 of the Golistan Palace Library (see B. Atabay *Catalogue of albums in the Royal Library*, Tehran 1353/1974)

103 *(Detail)*

104
Roses

Miniature painting on an album page
Signed by Muhammad Baqir
19.2 × 13 cm
Hotel Drouot, 23 June 1982, lot 20
Iran, perhaps Shiraz, dated 1178/1764-65

Ruling most of Iran from his capital in Shiraz, Karim Khan Zand (r. *c.* 1751-79) established a reign of relative peace and prosperity and became a significant patron of the arts, particularly architecture. Strongly influenced by late-17th-century Isfahan painting – particularly that of Muhammad Zaman and Hajji Muhammad – Muhammad Baqir seems to have flourished during the reign of Karim Khan for whom he may have worked. His extant *oeuvre* is limited to a number of impressive floral and figural paintings.

104 *(Actual size)*

Turkey

Turkish-speaking Muslim peoples began settling Anatolia after the 1071 battle of Manzikert, but it was with the conquest of Constantinople in 1453 that an empire based in Turkey came to dominate the eastern Mediterranean. The Ottoman Turks were fortunate in a succession of capable rulers from the late 13th to the 17th century who expanded their state, established a capable and effective administration, and upheld Sunni Islam against Christian Europe to the west and Shi'a Iran to the east. Ottoman sultans ruled into the 20th century, and many of them were gifted, energetic patrons of architecture and the portable arts. Some of the greatest calligraphers in Islamic history flourished under Ottoman patronage and enjoyed enormous favour and reputation. Iranian culture was markedly influential, and Persian was the language of poetry and much of the court.

Painters illustrated not only traditional Islamic classics but also Ottoman epics, histories, and geographies. Where Iranian painting tended to focus on the illustration of high literature or the depiction of a fairly narrow set of appropriately high themes, Ottoman patrons and their painters were fascinated by the here-and-now of their world. Portraiture flourished, and the physical forms, social strata, and military campaigns of the enormous empire were depicted with a naturalism and attention to detail that gives the impression of authentic documentation.

بسم الله الرحمن الرحيم
الحمد لله رب العالمين الرحمن الرحيم
مالك يوم الدين اياك نعبد واياك
نستعين اهدنا الصراط المستقيم
صراط الذين انعمت عليهم غير
المغضوب عليهم ولا الضالين

بسم الله الرحمن الرحيم
الم ذلك الكتاب لا ريب فيه
هدى للمتقين الذين يؤمنون
بالغيب ويقيمون الصلوة ومما رزقناهم
ينفقون والذين يؤمنون بما انزل
اليك وما انزل من قبلك وبالاخرة هم

105
Holy Qur'an

Illuminated manuscript of 278 pages written in thirteen lines to the page; text copied in *naskh* by Shaykh Hamdallah
38.8 × 26.3 cm
A. Welch (1972), vol. 2, no. 5; Lings and Safadi no. 129; A. Welch (1979), no. 29; A. Welch and S.C. Welch (1982)
Ottoman Turkey, probably Istanbul, *c.* 1500–10

Although this superb Qur'an's colophon bears neither date nor the name of the patron nor the name of the master illuminator who ornamented its pages, it does identify with exactitude the scribe: 'Shaykh Hamdallah ibn Mustafa, the perfect *hajji* and the head of the scribes.' The most celebrated of Ottoman calligraphers, Shaykh Hamdallah was born in Amasiya in 1439 or 1440 and was the calligraphy tutor of the heir apparent, Bayezid. When the prince became sultan in 1481, Shaykh Hamdallah moved to Istanbul and was appointed chief court calligrapher: he enjoyed high esteem and an impressive salary. He lived until 1519 and was extremely prolific: he is said to have completed forty-six Qur'ans and a thousand Qur'an sections (*ajzā'*). He was also a gifted teacher, and his many students and their artistic descendants perpetuated his style until the end of the Ottoman sultanate. Since this manuscript is unquestionably of royal quality, it is reasonable to assume that it was created for Sultan Bayezid in the final years of his reign.

106
Portrait of Sultan Selim II

Page from a royal Ottoman album
Attributed to Ra'is Haydar
Painting 37.4 × 24.5 cm; page 44.1 × 31.2 cm
A. Welch and S.C. Welch (1982), no. 6, pp. 32–34
Ottoman Turkey, Istanbul, *c.* 1570

A poet and a gifted, energetic patron, Sultan Selim II (r. 1566-74) inherited from his father Sultan Suleyman I (1520-66), an empire of vast wealth and power that was sustained by a well-trained and effective bureaucracy. His interest in government was small, but his attention to architecture and the arts was intense. The sultan was about forty-five years old when this portrait was painted by Ra'is Haydar, more commonly known as Nigari. Dressed in a brilliant scarlet coat, the sultan, who had a pronounced penchant for wine, sits in state with a wine cup in his right hand. His portraitist had a previous career as a successful naval captain, and when he executed this powerful and discerning portrait, he was director of the great imperial shipyards in Istanbul.

107
Firmān of Sultan Murad III

Inscribed in *dīwānī* script
142 × 45 cm
Ottoman Turkey, Istanbul, dated 983/1575

Despite his years of war with Iran and Austria and severe economic and social problems at home, Murad III (r. 1574–95) presided over a period of notable achievement in Ottoman culture, especially in calligraphy, painting, and the arts. This *firmān* (royal epistle) was composed in the second year of his reign. The sultan's name and titles appear in the complex, formal intertwinings of the black-and-gold *tughrā*, the work of a specialist calligrapher and high official known as a *tughrākesh*. Separated by small gold discs, the forty-four lines of text are rendered in the tight energetic, and rather busy *dīwānī* script, particularly favoured by Ottoman officialdom.

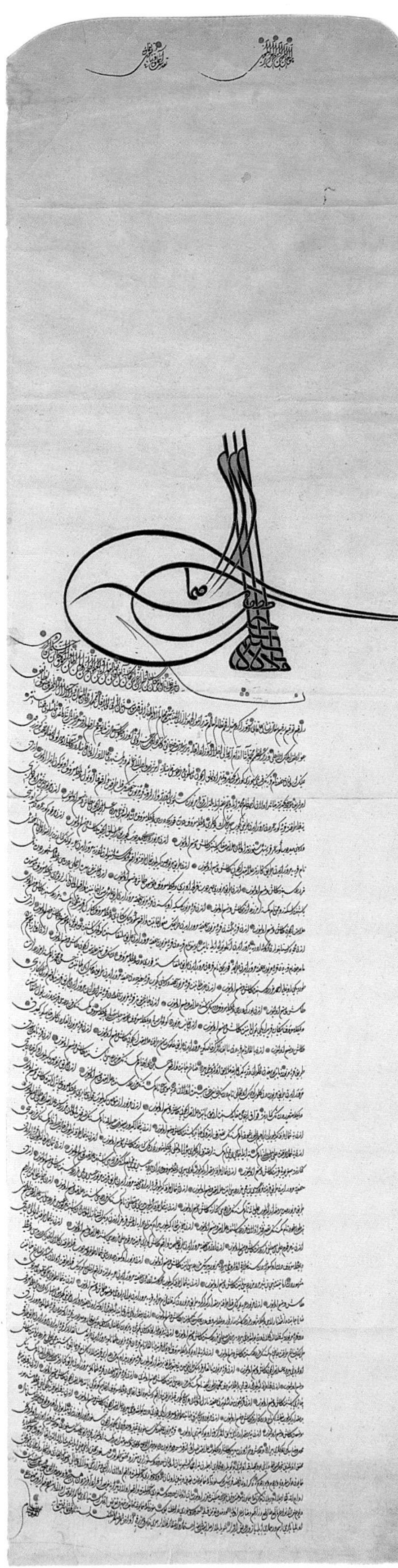

107

108
Portrait of Tatar Hasan Khan

Folio 119r from a Turkish manuscript of the *Durr-i Shāhvār*
Written by Sayyid 'Ali ibn Sayyid Mustafā al-Bursawi
21 × 13.5 cm
Christie's, 21 July 1971, lot 113; Sotheby's, 9 October 1978, lot 103
Ottoman Turkey, probably Istanbul, dated Friday, 15th of Ramadan, 997/29 July 1589

This anthology of poetry entitled *The royal pearl* has 135 pages and contains fifty-one miniatures that are identified as individual portraits of aristocrats, warriors, poets, and other notables. Text and miniatures are bordered by broad arabesques in gold. The contemporary binding is of dark brown leather, the exterior is embossed with gold arabesques and cartouches, and the interior is inset with dark blue medallions decorated with *découpé* arabesques.

109

109 Kayter Khan receives Shah Ramin in his pavilion on his return

109

Manuscript of the *Tuhfet ul-Letā'if* of 'Ali ibn Nakib Hamza made for Sultan Murad III

Turkish manuscript of 300 pages with eight double-page and sixty-one single-page illustrations
Written in a large, clear *naskh*
Each page 34.5 × 21.9 cm
A. Welch and S.C. Welch (1982), no. 9, pp. 38–42
Ottoman Turkey, Istanbul, 1002/1593–94

Compiled during the reign of the Ottoman sultan Murad II (1421–51), the *Tuhfet ul-Letā'if* (A collection of strange and entertaining tales) is a series of stories centring around the romance of Shah Ramin, the son of the King of Ghazni, and Mah Parvin, the daughter of the king's vizier, Shahruz. These Persian stories must have been popular in the Ottoman empire, and this – the only extant copy of the *Tuhfet ul-Letā'if* – was created for one of the most discerning of Ottoman patrons, Sultan Murad III (r. 1574-95). In his palace studio a major, though unidentified, scribe copied the text, while unnamed painters of the highest stature provided its illustrations. One of the finest illustrated Ottoman manuscripts, this *Tuhfet ul-Letā'if* is also a book of major importance for the history of Ottoman literature.

110

Subduing a dragon

Page from volume IV of a manuscript of the Turkish *Kitāb-i Siyār-i Nabī* (Book of the life of the Prophet) by Darir of Erzerum
Written in *naskh* by Mustafa ibn Vali, whose name appears in the colophon
Miniature 28.6 × 18 cm; page 37.2 × 26.5 cm
Previously in the Collection of Major Gayer-Anderson
Nouveau Drouot, 23 March 1984, lot 1
Ottoman Turkey, Istanbul, 1594

Under the Sultan Murad III (1574-95) Ottoman painters and calligraphers made some of their most notable achievements. During the final years of his reign this astute patron commissioned one of his most grandiose projects – a six-volume copy of the *Kitāb-i Siyār-i Nabī* (Book of the life of the Prophet). As an historical study of the life of Muhammad and events in the early history of Islam, the book was not scripture in a formal sense, and illustration of it did not fall under Muslim strictures against the illustration of holy writ. As a result, illustrations of this text (and others like it, such as the *Qisas al-Anbiyā* (*Lives of the Prophet*) that was popular at this time in Iran) are essential documents in elucidating the religious iconography of Islamic art.

The six volumes of this manuscript were completed in 1595, the first year of the reign of Murad III's successor, Mehmet III (1595-1603). When completed, they contained a total of 814 miniatures. Volumes I, II, and VI are still preserved in the Topkapi Saray Museum; Volume III is in the Spencer Collection of the New York Public Library; volume V is apparently lost. Volume IV is largely preserved in the Chester Beatty Library, Dublin, and the colophon provides the information that it was completed in 1594 by the scribe Mustafa ibn Vali. He appears to have been the scribe responsible for copying the text of the great *Tuhfet al-Letā'if* (no. 109), created also for Murad III. Originally this volume was illustrated with 158 or 159 miniatures, of which 137 are still in the Dublin manuscript.

The manuscript's painters did not sign their names, but it is known that the painter Lutfi 'Abdullah was in charge of the project. Stylistic evidence indicates that six painters were employed on the illustrations, and they must have included not only Lutfi but also his major associates, Hasan and Osman. The manuscript's finest paintings, such as this one, testify to the boldness and technical virtuosity of Ottoman painting at the end of the 16th century.

110

111

112

111
Seated Peri

Miniature painting
Inscribed with incorrect attribution to Bihzad
13.8 × 11 cm
Previously in the collection of Vera Amherst Hale Pratt
Christie's, 19 April 1979, lot 44
Ottoman Turkey, late 16th century

There are numerous extant drawings and paintings of angels or peris from Ottoman Turkey, and this small painting is one of the finest. The peri's multi-coloured wings rise behind it, and its moon face contemplates a large rose. The gold outer garment is richly decorated with gold, blue, and white arabesques, and the undergarment is a brilliant red.

112
Portrait of an Ottoman official

Page from an Ottoman album
Inscribed in the reverse with lines from the *Gulistān* of Sa'di (Book II, story 31)
Painting 22.3 × 13 cm
A. Welch (1978), vol. 3, T.M. 3; A. Welch and S.C. Welch (1982), no. 8, pp. 36-38
Ottoman Turkey, *c.* 1650

Neither the official nor the portraitist is identified, but this individual was clearly a person of status and authority. His lavender turban is vast, and his swelling brown robe is lined with white fur. That he stands under a golden arch only underscores his high position. The text on the reverse was bound in this album as an example of calligraphy and has no relationship to the portrait. An almost identical portrait was in the collection of John Lord Northwick (Sotheby's, 21 November 1928, lot 112).

113
Views of Makka and Medina

Manuscript of the *Dalā'il al-Khayrāt* of Muhammad ibn Suleyman al-Jazuli
Contemporary Ottoman binding: outer cover of brown and gold lacquer; inner cover of blue and red with gold arabesques
14.6 × 8.5 cm
A. Welch (1978), MS29, vol. 4, pp. 137-143
Ottoman Turkey, Muharram, 1233/November, 1818

The *Dalā'il al-Khairāt* is an Arabic devotional work particularly popular in Turkey and Morocco. The text in this copy was written by an unidentified calligrapher in a stately *naskh* on gold-flecked paper. The manuscript consists of 219 pages, many with fine margin illumination; there are ten richly illuminated double pages. Folios 117v-118r show detailed views of the holy cities of Makka and Medina painted in gold and several hues of blue and red.

113 folio 117v (*Actual size*)

India

Muslim armies under Turkish-speaking leaders invaded India from Afghanistan in the late 12th century and laid the foundation of Islamic rule that was to endure until the last Mughal emperor was exiled to Burma in 1858 by the British. Turkish remained the mother language for most of India's Muslim rulers; Persian was the language of high culture; and Arabic was the language of the faith. Great numbers of Muslims from Islam to the west migrated to India over the following centuries, some in search of refuge, others in pursuit of the generous patronage for which India's Muslim rulers were famed. Despite this influx and the sheer wealth of the land and the efforts of thousands of Muslim missionaries, the majority of the population remained Hindu, and Jains and Parsees remained influential minorities. After the initial occupation of the area around Delhi in 1192 the relationship between Islam and India's other faiths remained the essential problem for India's Muslim rulers and had a powerful effect upon Islamic culture in India.

Manuscripts from the Sultanate period (1192–1526) are rare, and the history of Sultanate painting and calligraphy is still to be written. Painters from Iran seem to have exerted a strong effect, and already by the 14th century a distinctly Indian Islamic style is evident in calligraphy and architecture. But it is under the Mughal emperors from the 16th through the 19th centuries that the Islamic art of the precious book achieves some of its most notable expression. Descended from Timur, Mughal rulers consciously emulated a Timurid ideal of princely patronage in keeping with their imperial image: the art of the book became an expression not only of royal aestheticism but also of the power of the state and the dynasty. Possessed of wealth, intelligence, and taste, the six great Mughal rulers from 1526-1707 marked the arts under their patronage with their distinctive personalities and created a synthesis of Muslim and non-Muslim styles that was to exert a wide international influence.

It was under the third Mughal ruler Akbar (r. 1556-1605) that Mughal painting and calligraphy came of age. A military genius who brought nearly two-thirds of India under Mughal rule and an administrative genius who organized a governmental system that preserved a centralized state for more than a hundred years, Akbar was also a passionate patron of the arts. He planned cities and built an abundance of sacred and secular structures, and though illiterate, he was devoted to literature and the arts of the book. His taste was dynamic and eclectic, and he supported a vast atelier of painters, calligraphers, and other manuscript artisans which created a profusion of finely illustrated histories, dynastic memoirs, works of literature, and even Persian translations of Hindu religious texts. Safavid painters worked under his aegis, as did gifted Hindu masters, and they studied the European prints that the emperor admired. The classic Mughal style emerges under Akbar's patronage as a unique blend of indigenous Indian, Iranian, and European styles that was strongly directed toward realism and the observation of the natural world ruled by the Mughals.

Akbar's spiritual nature was similarly eclectic and individual, and he espoused a set of beliefs (his *Din Ilahi* or 'divine faith') which many Muslims, including his son Jahangir, regarded as deviant from orthodox Islam. Less inclined to military adventure and more devoted to connoisseurship and elevated taste, Jahangir (r. 1605-27) was one of the most brilliant patrons of calligraphy and painting in Islamic history. Akbar's huge atelier was reduced in size to include only the very finest masters, and while Akbar's artists had been engaged in producing dozens of large manuscripts, Jahangir directed his masters towards smaller books and exquisite single-page drawings, paintings, and calligraphies where their virtuoso talents and his virtuoso connoisseurship would be most apparent. It was, as a result, a great age of portraiture, whether of people, animals, or plants, and a painter who sought out the essence of forms, like Abu'l-Hasan, could flourish under his patronage.

Jahangir's son Shah Jahan (r. 1627-57) was fascinated by the rituals of government and the liturgical requirements of rule. His empire was the wealthiest in the world, and the emperor displayed a nearly fanatical passion for jewels and jewel-like creations, whether the Taj Mahal or the cool, structured, and gem-like paintings issuing from his atelier, to satisfy his well-known taste. His final years were plagued by civil disorder while his four sons struggled for power. His youngest son and successor Awrangzib (1657-1707) had been a sensitive patron of painting and calligraphy in his youth, but soon after his accession to power he devoted himself almost singlemindedly to the expansion of the Islamic state. Briefly he brought nearly all of India under Mughal control, but the effort exhausted the emperor and the state. Revolts broke out, and during the course of the 18th century the fragmenting Mughal empire was slowly absorbed by the British crown. Even during this period of decline painters and calligraphers produced impressive works, either for lesser Mughal patrons or for princes in the Muslim Deccan.

114
Holy Qur'an

Manuscript written by the scribe Mahmud Sha'ban in *Bihārī* script
Thirty-four illuminated double pages
24 × 17 cm
Sotheby's, 10 December 1974, lot 473; Hayward Gallery (1976), no. 635; A. Welch, (1979), no. 75, pp. 14 and 178; A. Welch and S.C. Welch (1982), no. 47, pp. 141-144
India, Gwalior Fort, 1399

According to the informative colophon of this rare Qur'an, the copyist finished his task on 7 *Dhū'l-qa'da* 801 (21 July 1399) in the massive Gwalior Fort south of Agra. It is likely that he began the manuscript in Delhi where two rival members of the Tughluq family quarrelled over the control of the Delhi Sultanate. Their feud was interrupted and ended by Timur's devastating raid on the capital in 1398-99. Mahmud Sha'ban probably took refuge at Gwalior along with other notables from Delhi. The 550 pages of this Qur'an are written in the *Bihārī* script, a regional variant of eastern *naskh*. In a smaller style of script, Mahmud Sha'ban has added an interlinear Persian translation: presumably his patron was not entirely fluent in Arabic.

115
Sura XVII *Al-Isrā'* verses 75-85

Page from a dispersed manuscript of the Holy Qur'an
37 × 28 cm
India, *c.* 1400

Like the great Sultanate Qur'an (no. 114), this single page is written in *Bihārī* script: its letters move in stately grace, three gold and ten black lines to the page. Here too there is in red a minute Persian interlinear translation. These verses specify the times of daily prayer, the power of the Qur'an, and God's omniscience and omnipresence.

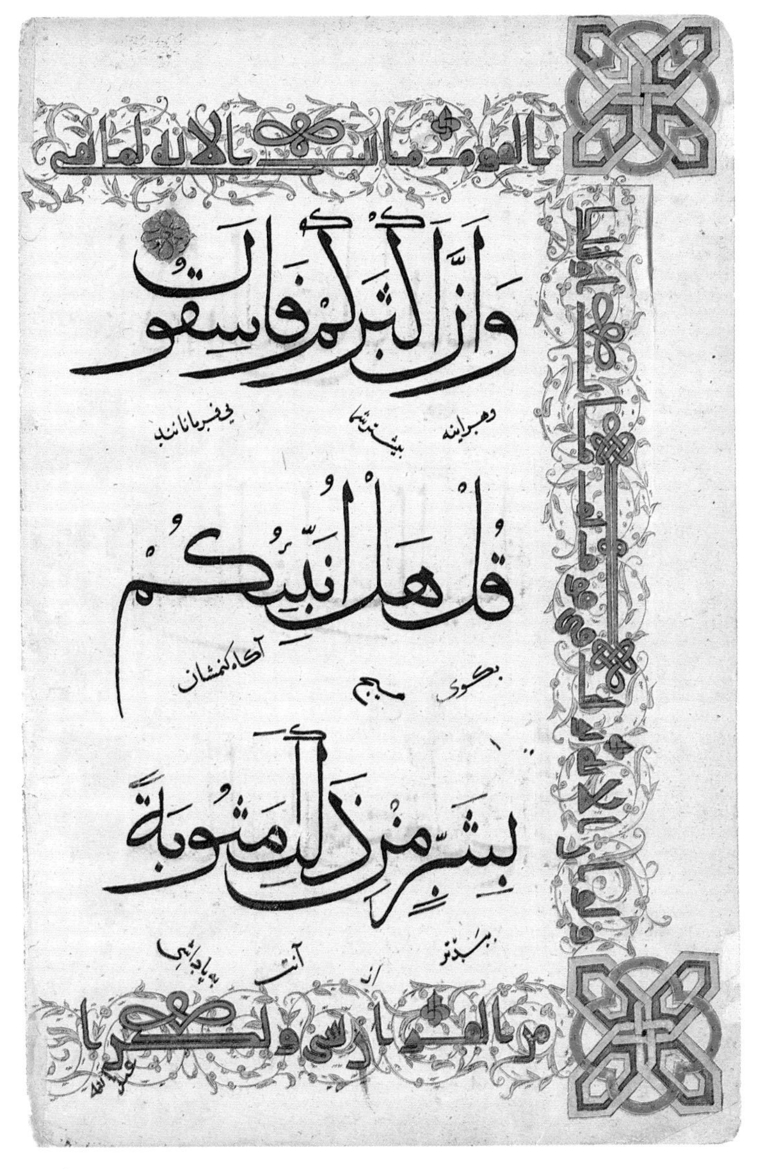

116
Sura V *Al-Mā'idah* verses 59-60

Page from a dispersed manuscript of the Holy Qur'an, written in black *Muhaqqaq* and blue Kufic on paper
28 × 18 cm
India, 15th century

The patron for whom this Qur'an was intended must have been, like many Muslims in northern India, more familiar with Persian than Arabic, for there is a Persian interlinear translation in a minute *naskh*. Corners are marked by an interlocked geometric design in blue, gold, and red, and through a delicate gold arabesque in the margins runs a stately blue Kufic.

117
The night of power

Page from a dispersed manuscript of the *Khamseh* of Amir Khusraw Dihlavi
Miniature 8 × 20.1 cm, page 34.3 × 25.3 cm
A. Welch and S.C. Welch (1982), no. 48, pp. 144-146
India, perhaps Delhi, *c.* 1350-1450

The miniature illustrates the story of a saint who unsuccessfully tried to remain awake until the twenty-seventh day of Ramadan (The night of power). It commemorates the evening when Muhammad was called to his mission and when the Qur'an's initial verses were revealed. Amir Khusraw entered the service of the Delhi sultans in 1290 and became one of the most celebrated Indian poets writing in Persian. The *Khamseh* is the best-known of his many works. While the unknown painter was obviously well acquainted with the traditions of Iranian painting, his art reveals the strong impact of Hindu and Jain art.

118
Portrait of Shah Abu'l-Ma'ali

Signed by Dust Muhammad
Album page with four lines of poetry in *nasta'līq* written by Muhammad Riza on the reverse
17.5 × 14.5 cm
Previously in the Collection of Sir Robert Dent
S.C. Welch, (1979), no. 75; A. Welch and S.C. Welch (1982), no. 49, pp. 146-148
India, Mughal, *c.* 1556-60

Shah Abu'l-Ma'ali was one of the eminent scoundrels at the early Mughal court. Handsome, well-born and brave, he was overbearing to those around him, devious, disloyal, and inclined to murder. None of these attributes seems immediately apparent in this portrait by Dust Muhammad, an accomplished Safavid painter who emigrated to join the Mughals in India (see no. 58). The paper held by Shah Abu'l-Ma'ali identifies both him and the portraitist and informs us that it was made after the death of the emperor Humayun in 1556.

119
Hamza escapes from prison

Page from a manuscript of the *Hamzanāmeh*, made for the emperor Akbar
Miniature 64.5 × 46 cm, page 72 × 57 cm
Falk and Digby (1979), no. 11
India, Mughal, *c.* 1565

The uncle of the Prophet Muhammad, Amir Hamza was one of the heroes of early Islamic history, and the *Hamzanāmeh* is an epic account of his exploits that was extremely popular in Abkar's India. According to Akbar's friend, adviser, and boon companion, Abu'l-Fazl, the copy produced for Akbar early in his reign contained originally some 1400 paintings. It was the most grandiose single manuscript project in the history of Islamic art, and its ambitious scale is very much in keeping with the energy and enthusiasm of its youthful patron. In charge of the illustration of the manuscript were two former Safavid painters – Mir Sayyid 'Ali and 'Abd al Samad (see nos 50 and 121) – who had come to India during the reign of Akbar's father Humayun and whose presence was instrumental in the creation of the classic Mughal painting style. Much of the evolution of this synthesis took place during this massive undertaking.

Unlike most Islamic painting, these illustrations were painted on cloth, not paper, and they were huge in size, large enough to have been seen by many people at court at the same time. In this illustration Hamza has just escaped from imprisonment in a camp in the Caucasus. Comfortably riding a palanquin supported by peris and submissive demons, Hamza is borne away from his captors who are bombarded with huge rocks thrown by the demons. One boulder has smashed part of the pavilion at the right, while other stones crush bodies and break necks. It is a scene mixing vibrant colour, frenetic activity, and a sometimes gruesome realism, a combination of elements characteristic of the manuscript and, presumably, the patron's taste and gusto.

119

120

Hamza fighting demons

Page from a manuscript of the *Hamzanāmeh*, made for the emperor Abkar
64 × 55.5 cm
India, Mughal, *c.* 1565

Although this scene is not specifically identified, it most probably relates to the early part of the *Dastān-i Amīr Hamza* or *Hamzanāmeh* and to one of Hamza's many adventures in either the Caucasus or Abyssinia. Despite his small size in comparison to the huge monsters who attack him, the hero is more than able to take care of himself, and one of the demons already lies wounded. From the early 16th century, Safavid painting had been rich in paintings of demons, and these three creatures are similar, though bulkier and coarser, than demons in Shah Thamasp's *Shāhnāmeh*, the Safavid manuscript project on which both Mir Sayyid 'Ali and 'Abd al-Samad had worked.

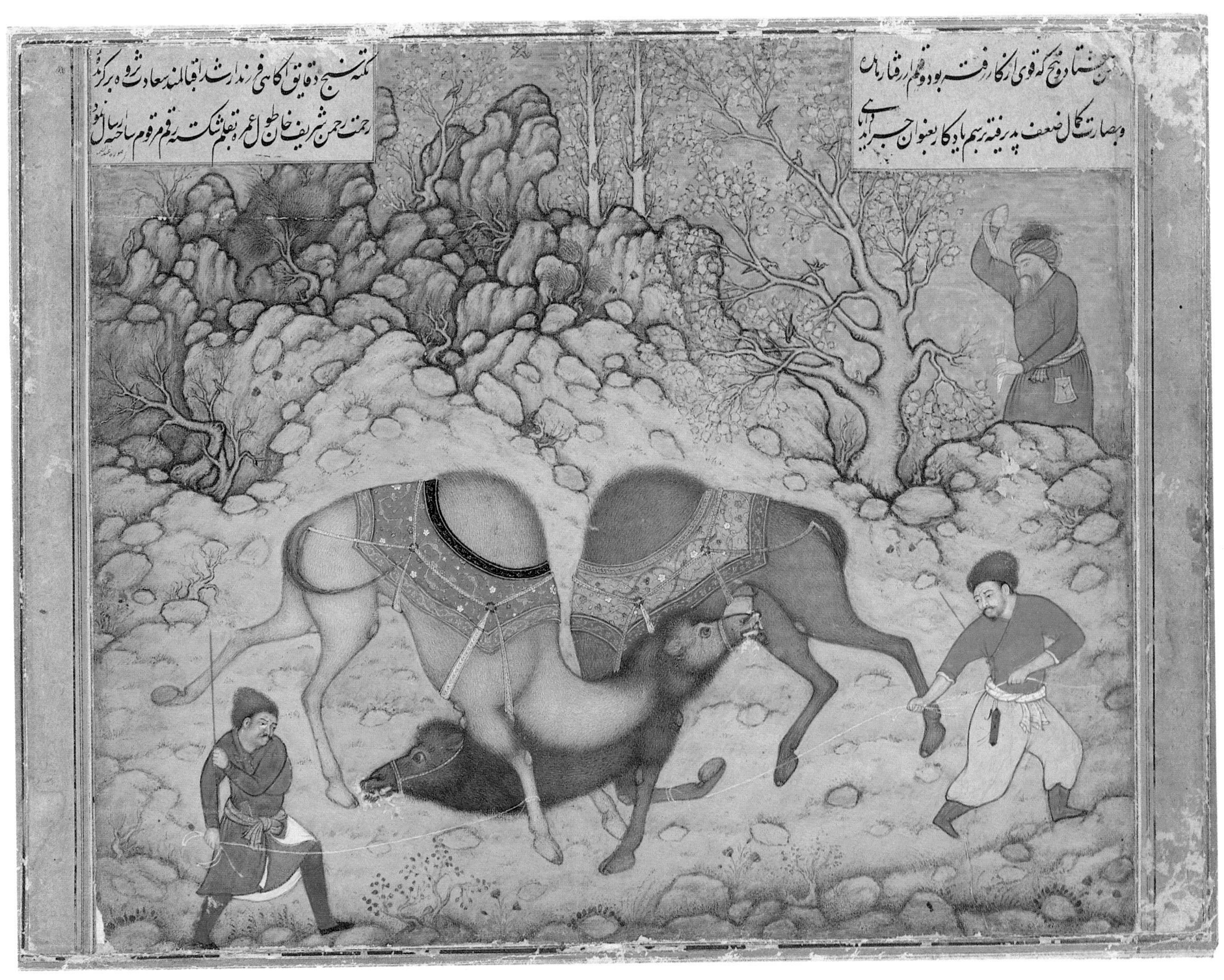

121
Two fighting camels

Signed by 'Abd al-Samad
Miniature painting
Inscribed with four lines of black *nasta'līq*
18.8 × 24 cm
India, Mughal, *c.* 1570

'Abd al-Samad had been a prominent artist in the court atelier of Shah Tahmasp at Tabriz; during his exile at the Safavid court the Mughal emperor Humayun became acquainted with him and his work. On his return to India Humayun induced the painter to enter his service, and 'Abd al-Samad, along with his compatriot Mir Sayyid 'Ali, was instrumental in the great *Hamzanāmeh* project begun by Humayun's son Akbar. Abu'l-Fazl recorded the emperor's appreciation of the artist's talent: 'Khwaja 'Abd al-Samad, styled Shirin-Qalam, or Sweet Pen. He comes from Shiraz. Though he had learnt the art before he was made a grandee of the court, his perfection was mainly due to the wonderful effect of a look of His Majesty, which caused him to turn from that which is form to that which is spirit.' (Abu'l-Fazl, I, p. 114.) Under Akbar's benevolent aegis, the painter did well in India. He first received a sinecure command of four hundred troops, and then in 1578 was given the lucrative job of master of the mint. Still later in his career he was given authority over the city of Multan.

Like their Iranian counterparts, Mughal artists often demonstrated their skill by rendering well-known compositions of earlier masters, especially Bihzad. There are a number of versions of Bihzad's original picture of two fighting camels, but 'Abd al-Samad's ranks among the very finest. It may have inspired the later Mughal artist Nanha to make his own version of the subject in 1608-9. The centre of 'Abd al-Samad's picture is dominated by the stuggle of the two animals whose keepers are unable to restrain them. In the upper right stands a bearded man with a spindle. On the reverse are a number of owners' seals and an inscription that provides the date 23, October 1541: it is probably meant to refer to the date when 'Abd al-Samad entered Humayun's service. If it does, it is inaccurate, since he did not join the Mughals until 1549.

122
Discussion on a verandah

Page from a dispersed Persian manuscript of Ziya al-Din Nakhshabi's *Tūtīnāmeh* (known as the Chester Beatty *Tūtīnāmeh*), written in *nasta'līq*
Miniature 15.5 × 12.5 cm, page 25.5 × 16.5 cm
Falk (1978), no. 4
India, Mughal, *c.* 1580

The *Tūtīnāmeh* (Tales of a parrot) was a collection of moralizing stories that was one of the most popular books at the Mughal court. About 1560 the emperor Akbar ordered a royal copy of the book (preserved now almost in its entirety in the Cleveland Museum of Art) that is one of the most important documents for the study of the evolution of early Mughal painting. About twenty years later a second manuscript, somewhat larger in format, was commissioned by an unknown Mughal patron. The largest part of this is in the Chester Beatty Library, Dublin, but a number of pages are dispersed in public and private collections. Seven lines of text appear above and below the miniature; fifteen lines are on the reverse. The number 228 appears in the upper left. As with no. 123, it is probably indicative of the work of painters, well trained in the Mughal court styles, who are in the employ of sub-royal patrons. The closeness in style with no. 123 supports dating this page to about 1580.

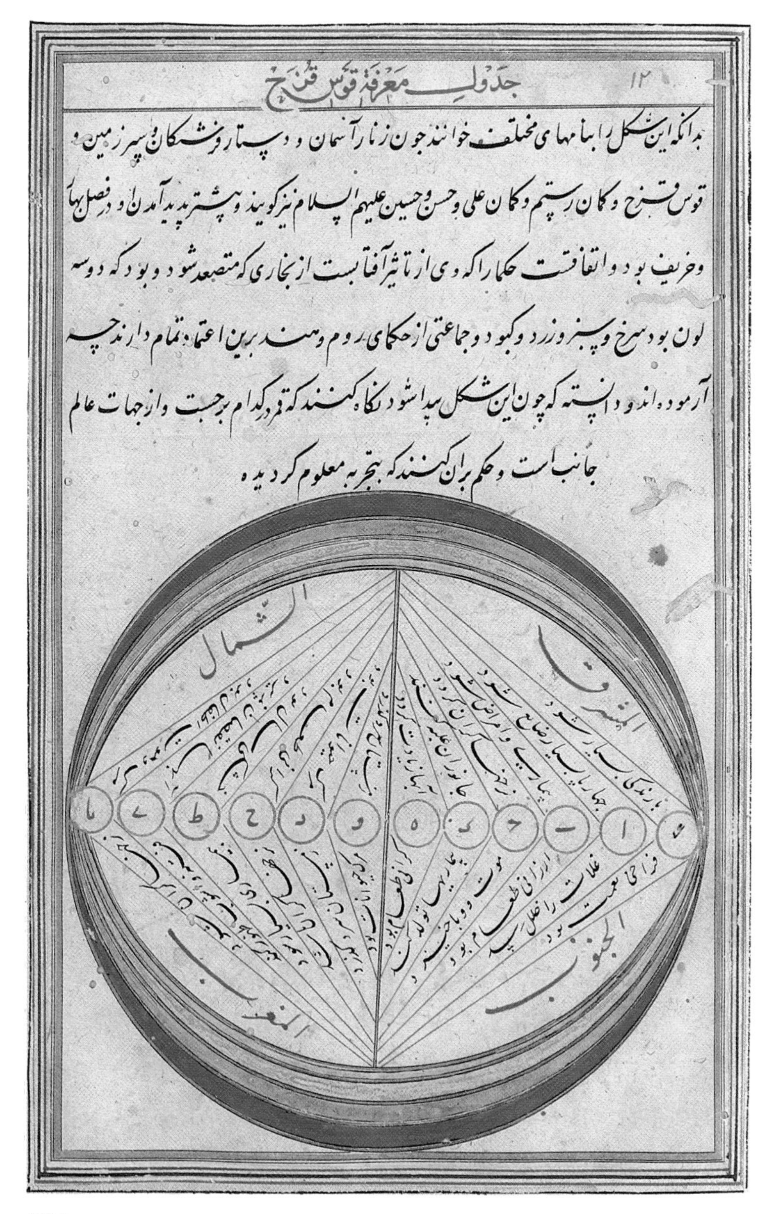

123

The *Kitāb-i Sa'āt* (Book of Hours)

Manuscript of 51 folios written in *nasta'līq* by the scribe Muhammad Yusuf for Mirza 'Aziz Koka at Hajipur with twelve miniatures and four zodiac diagrams
Text 20 × 11.7 cm, page 27.4 × 19.8 cm
Previously in the Kevorkian Collection
Falk (1978), no. 5
India, Mughal, dated 21 *Shawwal* 991/7 November, 1583

This treatise on astrology was made for Mirza 'Aziz Koka, one of the most prominent and influential officials in the service of the Mughal emperor Akbar. Its twelve miniatures by an accomplished but unidentified Mughal painter illustrate the twelve signs of the Zodiac. Despite the concentration of artistic talent at Akbar's court, where contemporary painters and calligraphers were engaged in producing the many illustrated histories and religious classics that characterize Akbar's patronage in the late 16th century, there were skilled painters in the Mughal court style who were available to work for sub-royal patrons, like 'Aziz Koka. Though past Islamic princes had been keenly interested in astronomy and astrology, these disciplines particularly flourished in Mughal India.

The manuscript is bound in a contemporary leather and lacquer binding with gold floral borders and central arabesque medallions.

Illustrated here are *left: Houses of the Zodiac*, folio 12r and *right: A lion regarding the sun* (Constellation Leo), folio 28r.

124

124
Elephant procession

Miniature painting
28.6 × 19.2 cm
Sotheby's, 10 October 1977, lot 27
India, Mughal, *c.* 1585

This page was originally the left-half of a double-page and may have been part of an unidentified historical manuscript, perhaps an *Akbarnāmeh*, a book that amply records the emperor's fascination with elephants. Indeed, these magnificently caparisoned adult and half-grown animals may have been some of his favourites. The larger elephant's mahout (keeper and driver) bows his head toward the right, and two of the soldiers in the lower right bend low. These gestures of obeisance are evidently for the emperor who must have occupied centre-stage in the right half of the double-page.

125
Prince Salim and the dervish

Dispersed page from a royal album
Tinted drawing
Inscribed: 'The son of the emperor Akbar; the work of 'Abd al-Samad Shirin-Qalam'
39 × 25.4 cm
S.C. Welch (1976), no. 10; A. Welch and S.C. Welch (1982), no. 56, pp. 162-167
India, Mughal, *c.* 1586-87

A frequent theme in Islamic literature and art, this encounter of prince and dervish (or worldly and otherworldly power) may actually have taken place, for the inscription along the right side identifies the future emperor Jahangir, seated in the centre of the picture. The use of an established literary conceit to portray his favourite son must have pleased the emperor Akbar for whom it was made. The painter's epithet, Shirin-Qalam, means 'sweet pen', and he was greatly honoured by the emperor who first gave him an honorary command of four hundred troops, then placed him in charge of the royal mint, and finally appointed him governor of Multan. For a painter who had left Iran in search of more understanding patronage, 'Ab al-Samad had done very well indeed.

125

126
Babur directs the laying out of a garden at Istalif

Double page illustration from a dispersed manuscript of the *Bāburnāmeh*
Mounted on 17th-century album leaves
Right half inscribed 'design by Miskin; execution by Sanwala'
Left half inscribed 'Design by Miskin; execution by Nand Gwaliori'
Miniatures *right* 25.2 × 13.6 cm; *left* 25.4 × 13.7 cm
Falk (1978), nos 93 and 94
India, Mughal, *c.* 1589

Composed originally in Chaghatay, an eastern Turkish language, the *Bāburnāmeh* (Memoirs of Babur, the first Mughal emperor) was one of the favourite books of later Mughal rulers and served as a model for their own memoirs. To make its remarkable text more accessible to the Muslim élite in India, it was translated into Persian in the 1580s, and Akbar commissioned at least five impressive copies of it. These two pages come from the earliest of these containing 191 miniatures, of which 108 are still extant. (The largest single group is twenty-one miniatures in the Victoria and Albert Museum, London.)

Like his descendants, Babur was passionately fond of gardens, and long before he invaded India in 1526, he was devoted to landscape architecture. In the summer of 1504 he resided near Kabul at the village of Istalif which he describes in detail: 'Few villages match Istalif, with vineyards and fine orchards on both sides of its great torrent, with waters needing no ice, cold and, mostly, pure . . . I took over (its great garden), after paying its price to the owners . . . A one-mill stream, having trees on both banks, flows constantly through the middle of the garden; formerly its course was zig-zag and irregular; I had it made straight and orderly, so the place became very beautiful.' (Beveridge (1969), p. 216.)

Major painters, including Basawan and Miskin, were responsible for designing the illustrations in this manuscript; as was often Mughal custom, assistants did most of the actual painting. Mughal patrons were keenly interested in supplying historical data, and here, as in many Mughal manuscripts, information about the production of paintings is written in red ink below the miniatures. Miskin was the son of the painter Mahesh. Initially working in collaboration with his father, Miskin had become by the late 1580s one of the major talents in Akbar's large atelier. As in these two miniatures, he invests his landscapes with a sense of vital energy and renders human faces with a high degree of individuality.

127
An Atelier at work

Ascribed to Sajnu
Manuscript of the *Akhlāq-i Nāsirī* of Nasir al-Din Tusi, 254 pages, text written in a fine *nasta'līq*, probably by 'Abdulrahim 'Anbarin-Qalam
Illustrated with seventeen miniatures, many inscribed with the names of members of Akbar's royal atelier: Kanak Singh, Dhanraj, Tulsi Kalan, Phim Gujarati, Sajnu, Khim Karan, and Nand Gwaliori
23.7 × 14.3 cm
Previously in the collection of Sir Thomas Phillipps, Sotheby's, 27 November 1974, lot 684
A. Welch and S.C. Welch (1982), no. 58, pp. 171-175
India, Mughal, *c.* 1590-95

One of the great intellects of 13th-century Iran, Nasir al-Din Tusi wrote the *Akhlāq-i Nāsirī* (Nasirean ethics) *c.* 1235. The Mughal emperor Akbar held its presentation of ethical, social, and political questions in high esteem, and frequently had it read to him. In the last decade of the 16th century he commissioned this fine manuscript of it, and since the painters were younger artists trained by Akbar's major masters, the task of selecting the subjects for illustration may have been assigned to Akbar's friend and adviser Abu'l-Fazl. Without narrative, heroes, or established iconography, the *Nasirean ethics* did not offer ready subject matter, and as a result relatively minor elements of the text are selected for illustration. The text here deals with urban and class organization, including specialists in communication who utilize the disciplines of scholastics, jurisprudence, public speaking, poetry, and calligraphy. Focusing on this last field, Sajnu shows us an active manuscript atelier: two painters, a scribe, and a paper maker are at work, while a second scribe is supervised by his master, presumably the director of this project and perhaps 'Abdulrahim 'Anbarin-Qalam himself. Representations of artists working are not common in Islamic art, and this is one of the most informative.

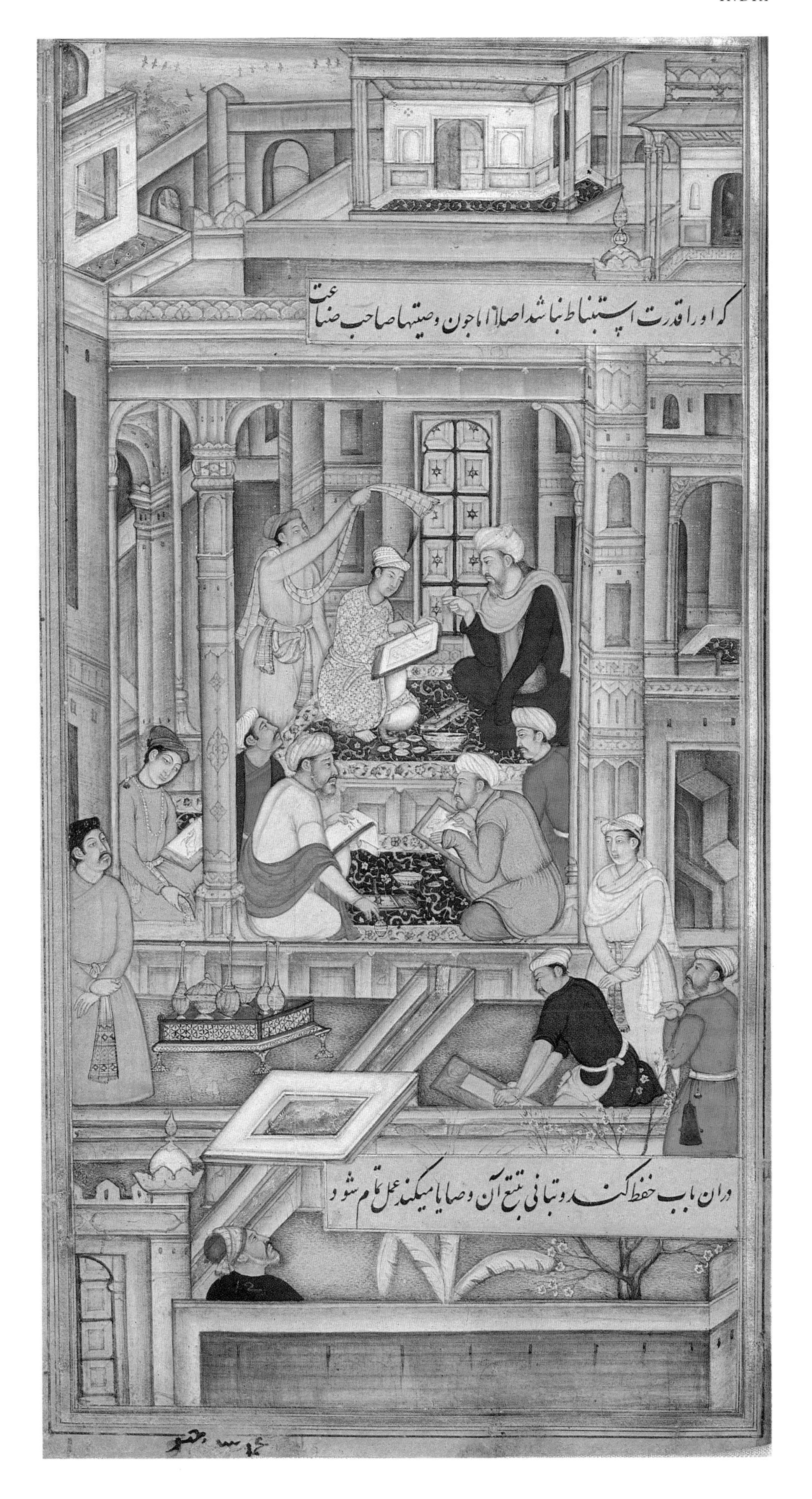

128

Portrait of a Chaghatay woman

Miniature painting
22.6 × 13.1 cm
Previously in the Kevorkian Collection
Falk (1978), no. 8
India, Mughal, *c.* 1595

Although the sky was added in the 17th century when this miniature was probably mounted on this page for inclusion in an album, the portrait reflects the characteristic Mughal interest in the diversity of nature and the human condition. The Mughals were of Chaghatay Turkish origin, and this rotund lady may have been one of the emperor Akbar's relatives or a distinguished visitor from the north. She certainly must have attracted some attention, for she is as well stuffed as the bolster that props her up, and she is about to embark upon the kind of feast that brought her to this stage of plumpness. The unidentified artist has transformed this portrait into a study of curves and volumes from the woman's knees, abdomen, and face to the bolster and the hill behind her.

129

Humayun defeats Kamran at Kabul

Page from a manuscript of the *Akbarnāmeh*
Ascribed to Mahesh with some faces painted by Padarath
Miniature 32.8 × 21.1 cm
S.C. Welch (1959), p. 138, fig. 7; A. Welch and S.C. Welch (1982), no. 52, pp. 153-155
India, Mughal, *c.* 1595-1600

The Mughal emperor Akbar's boon companion and adviser, Abu'l-Fazl, was a prolific writer, and his *Akbarnāmeh* supplies us with vast information about the emperor and his empire. Akbar ordered his atelier of painters and calligraphers to produce at least two lavish copies of the *Akbarnāmeh*, and this page originally belonged to the earlier copy. It accompanied text describing the successful assault on Kabul by Akbar's father Humayun who seized the city back from his rebellious brother Kamran. Humayun occupies the centre of the painting, where in gilded armour he sits on a magnificently decked-out horse.

130
Abaqa Khan and his court

Page from a manuscript of Rashid al-Din's *Jāmi' al-Tawārikh* made for the Mughal emperor Akbar and written in *nasta'līq*
Miniature 34.2 × 21.1 cm, page 35.8 × 24.4 cm
Sotheby's, 13-14 October, 1980, lot no. 239
India, Mughal, *c.* 1596-1600

Akbar's interest in histories that related to the Mughal dynasty was enormous, and some of his most impressive commissions were for splendid copies of historical texts. The *World History* of Rashid al-Din (see no. 18) wss one of the most treasured histories, and on 25 May 1596, the text for Akbar's copy of this work was completed. Most of this manuscript is in Tehran. Other miniatures bear the names of major Mughal masters like Basawan, L'al and Mansur. As descendants not only of Timur but also of Chingiz Khan, the Mughals were keenly interested in Mongol history, and this miniature illustrates part of the history of Abaqa Khan. The inscription at the top reads: 'Portrait of the court of Abaqa Khan, son of Hulagu Khan, son of Tului Khan, son of Chingiz Khan.' Abaqa, the second Il-Khanid (mongol) ruler of Iran (r. 1265-82), strengthened the state he had inherited from his father and was noted for his tolerance of different faiths: he was himself a Buddhist. The Mongol ruler is enthroned in a polygonal pavilion and converses with two Mongol officers. Attendants, courtiers, and officers wear the distinctive Mongol headgear. At the bottom of the page is an inscription stating that the picture's design and portraits were done by Farrukh, while its painting was executed by 'Ali Quli. This kind of division of labour with a senior master responsible for composition and portraits along with an assistant doing the actual laying-on of paint is characteristic of Akbar's atelier, and made it possible for its huge staff to produce rapidly and efficiently large numbers of high-quality paintings.

131
King Solomon's court

A page from a dispersed manuscript (perhaps a *Dīwān* of Hafiz) made for Akbar
Attributed to Mahesh
Inscribed with a couplet of Persian poetry in *nasta'līq*:

> With the compassion of Jacob, and the countenance of Yusuf,
> With the piety of Yahya (John the Baptist) and the sovereignty of Solomon

Miniature 27.4 × 15.5 cm
Grousset (1932), fig. 218; Strzygowski (1933), pl. 80, fig. 216; S.C. Welch (1959), no. 8 and fig. 11; Welch and Beach (1965), no. 6; A. Welch and S.C. Welch (1982), no. 64, pp. 188-190
India, Mughal, *c.* 1600

For Muslims Suleyman (Solomon) was the model of the perfect king. Through divine favour he had been given great gifts, especially the knowledge of all human and animal languages. With unparalleled understanding he not only ruled human and animal kingdoms but also controlled natural forces, like the wind, and supernatural beings, like the jinn. Here, enthroned, the king sits listening to the hoopoe at his left hand who is telling him of the imminent arrival of the Queen of Sheba. Respectfully gathered around and above him are his subjects, and the composition recalls formal *darbār* scenes in Mughal art. The image of the haloed Suleyman – ruling wisely with uncontested authority – appealed to autocratic emperors and sultans, and for the Mughal ruler Akbar, whose empire was far more heterogeneous than any other Islamic state, this image must have been particularly appealing.

131

132
Elephant of many parts

Page from a royal album
13.4 × 20 cm
India, Mughal, *c.* 1600

The King is more than regal, for flames blow behind his crown, and his pale white guide seems also out of this world. But the elephant exceeds them both in otherworldliness, for it is a composite of dozens of creatures – predators, those preyed upon, birds and human beings – who are packed in a complex creation. Such composite animals are not uncommon in Islamic art, but it is here invested with unusual vitality and special puzzles: a snake hangs from the elephant's trunk, though elephants and snakes are inveterate enemies. Only a semi-divine king could control such a world, and the Mughals saw themselves as Solomic rulers invested with divine authority. Thus the birds – symbols of the soul in Islamic literature – form the feet that lift the weight of the world and carry the ruler on it.

132

133
Sa'di preaching

Page from a manuscript of Sa'di's *Gulistān*
Miniature 16 × 11.3 cm; page 25.7 × 13 cm
Falk (1978), no. 9
India, Mughal, *c.* 1600

The *Gulistān* (Rose garden) by the great 13th-century Iranian poet Sa'di is a collection of stories and anecdotes designed to edify and instruct the reader. Akbar, Jahangir, and Shah Jahan commissioned fine copies of Sa'di's works. The volume from which this miniature almost certainly comes has an unusual history. Now in the British Library, its text was copied in Bukhara in 1567 probably for the Uzbek ruler Iskandar Khan. Several of its miniatures were done by Bukhara artists. Around 1600 the manuscript apparently was presented to the Mughal emperor Akbar who ordered his atelier to add a number of miniatures. Six of them are still in the book. Eight more are in the Cincinnati Museum and bear inscriptions to major Mughal masters, like Dharmdas, Farrukh Chela, and Manohar. Two other miniatures are thought to belong to this group – one page inscribed with the name of Basawan (now in the Los Angeles County Museum of Art) and this present page, attributed to Miskin. This miniature was on exhibition in Delhi in 1911 when it was much admired by King George V and Queen Mary who signed their names in pencil at the top of the page.

The story illustrated (*Gulistān* Book II story no. 10) tells how Sa'di, preaching in the congregational mosque at Baalbek, here represented by a pavilion in a garden, could not move his audience. As, however, he began to expound the Quranic verse 16 from Sura L *Qāf* 'It was We (God) who created man; We know what dark whispers come to him from his soul; for We are nearer to him than his jugular vein', he became drunk with his own eloquence and at that moment a passer-by hearing him cried out aloud and the congregation followed the man's example.

133 *(Actual size)*

134
Sa'di and the idol of Sumnath

Signed by Dharmdas
Manuscript of Sa'di's *Kulliyāt* written by the scribe 'Abdulrahim al-Haravi 'Anbarin-Qalam, illustrated with twenty-three miniatures, illuminated with five title pages
Library seal of Shah Jahan on folio 1a
42.5 × 27.5 cm
Pinder-Wilson (1976), no. 72; Beach (1978), pp. 25, 66, 69, 175, 176; Beach (1981), pp. 107, 111, 115-116, 228; A. Welch and S.C. Welch (1982), no. 64, pp. 191-198
India, Mughal, *c.* 1604

Sa'di's works were enormously popular throughout the Islamic world, and Mughal patrons commissioned sumptuous copies of his *Bustān* (Garden) and *Gulistān* (Rose garden). His *Kulliyāt* (Collected works) was, because of its size and complexity, a more grandiose undertaking, and this manuscript is the only extant imperial Mughal *Kulliyāt*. It was a treasured possession of Shah Jahan (1627-58). The book was probably begun in the last year of Akbar's reign and completed in the first year of the reign of his successor Jahangir, whose taste it reflects in important ways.

Dharmdas had served in Akbar's atelier for many years, and it is not surprising that folio 78b should bear his name. It is one of the most celebrated stories in the *Bustan* where it ends Book VIII. During his travels in India Sa'di visited the great Hindu temple at Sumnath. To his praise of Islam the Brahmin priests answered by demonstrating that the temple's idol gestured in response to their supplications. Though at first puzzled, Sa'di reserved judgement until he could inspect the statue at night. On the next day he defended his position by showing that a mechanical device moved the idol's arms.

135

The emperor Akbar crossing a river

A miniature from the 'Chester Beatty' *Akbarnāmeh*
21.5 × 12 cm
Previously in the Pozzi Collection
Palais Galiéra, Paris, 5 December 1970, lot 59; Blochet (1928) pl. XXVII, no. 4
India, Mughal, *c.* 1605

Akbar commissioned at least two copies of the *Akbarnāmeh*, the panegyric biography composed by his close friend and boon companion, Abu'l-Fazl, at the emperor's request. Along with Abu'l-Fazl's *'Ayn-i Akbarī* (which is more concerned with encyclopaedic information about India and Mughal administration than with Akbar's career), it is one of the most important sources of historical information about the Mughal state and the personality of the emperor most responsible for creating it. His first copy of the work (known as the Victoria and Albert Museum *Akbarnāmeh*) was produced in the last years of the 16th century. A somewhat smaller copy was produced a few years later between 1602 and 1610 and is now divided between the Chester Beatty Library, the British Library, and numerous other public and private collections. This fine miniature has been subsequently remounted with gold-illuminated margins. Akbar's river-borne fleet is substantial and includes not only platform-ships for elephants in the lower right but also protective *howdas* (compartments) for the women in his entourage in the upper right. As in many *Akbarnāmeh* paintings, the emperor is located in the centre of the painting, and dominates not only composition but all those around him. Mughals artists were keen observers and careful recorders of visual information, and this painting provides us with valuable information about the types and construction of Indian vessels in the 16th century.

135 *(Actual size)*

136

136
Manuscript of Sa'di's *Bustān*

Written by the scribe 'Abdulrahim al-Haravi 'Anbarin-Qalam, illustrated with twenty-six miniatures
19.1 × 10.1 cm
Previously in the Rothschild Collection
Stchoukine (1937), pp. 68-74; S.C. Welch (1963), nos 23, 24; Beach, (1978), passim; Beach (1981), passim; Das (1978), pp. 76-77; A. Welch and S.C. Welch, (1982), p. 196
India, Mughal, Agra, dated 1014/1605-6

According to the informative colophon on folio 198, this precious, portable copy of Sa'di's *Bustān* was completed in Agra in 1014/1605-6 by 'Abdulrahim al-Haravi 'Anbarin-Qalam.

137
Jahangir's lion hunt

Attributed to Farrukh Chela
Page from a royal album
On the reverse are *nasta'līq* inscriptions identifying Jahangir and Prince Parviz; a second inscription, perhaps in Jahangir's handwriting, ascribes the painting to 'Farrukh-i Khurd-i Chela'
Miniature 26.8 × 20 cm
A. Welch and S.C. Welch (1982), no. 66, pp. 201-202
India, Mughal, *c.* 1610

In the lower left and upper left calm reigns, but elsewhere this is a scene of turmoil and fury. It is dominated, however, by the central figure of the emperor Jahangir, with total concentration leaning from his elephant and spearing the lion that is mauling one of his officers. Jahangir's son Parviz rushes in on his horse to give the lion another mortal blow. Royal hunts had been expressions of kingly strength and authority for over two thousand years, but like 'Abd al-Samad in no. 121, Farrukh Chela has combined a real event with a rich iconographic tradition.

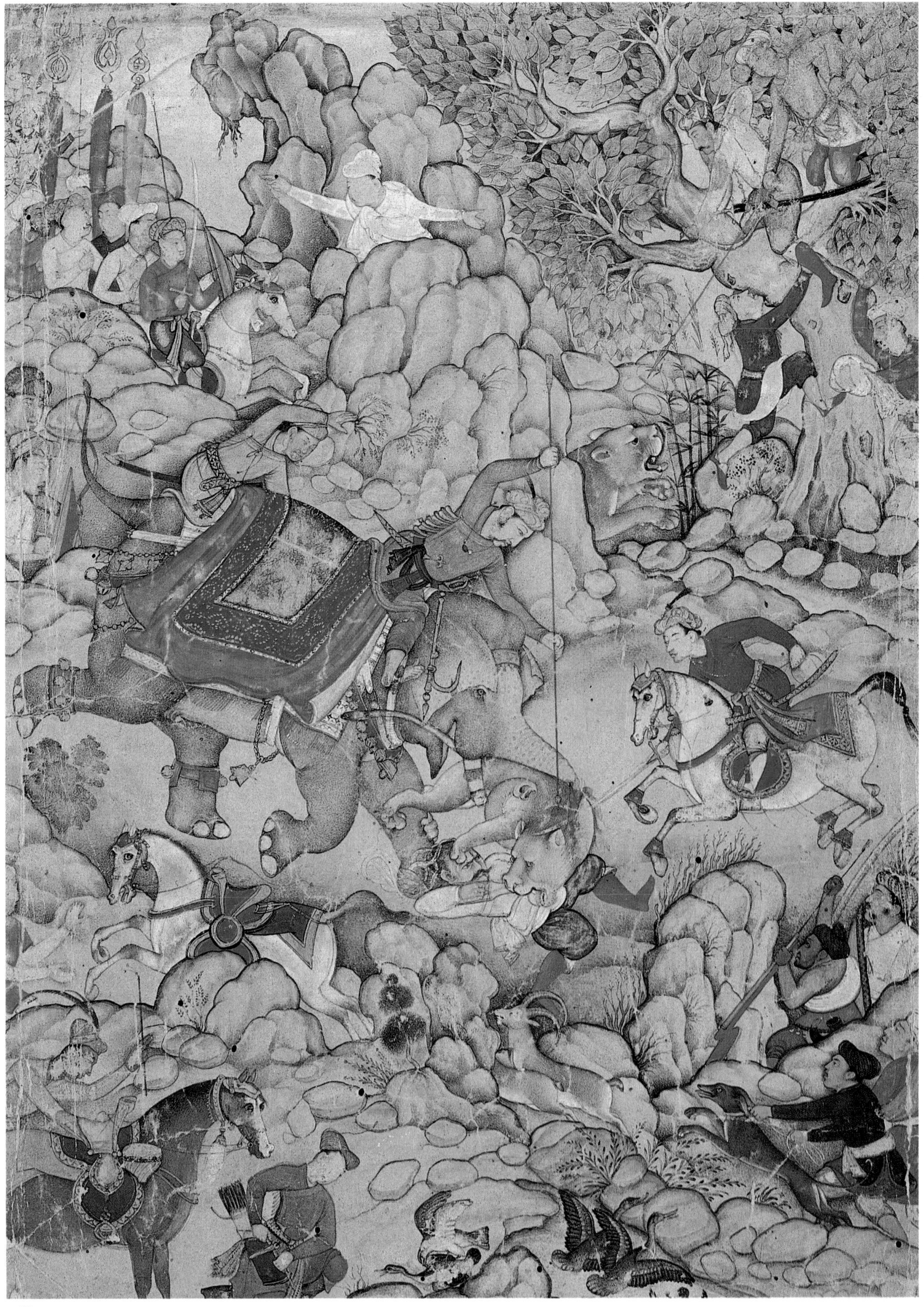

137

138 *(Actual size)*

138
Couple before the muftis

Page from a dispersed manuscript of Sa'di's *Gulistān*
Miniature 8.5 × 13 cm; page 36 × 28.2 cm
Previously in the Rothschild Collection
Robinson (1976), no. 89i
India, Mughal, *c.* 1610-15

Jahangir's fondness for Sa'di's literary works is evident from other items in this exhibition (nos 133, 134, 136) that were created several years earlier. The copy of the *Gulistān* from which this miniature comes was probably intended as a companion volume to the 1605-6 *Bustān*, and some of the same painters illustrated both manuscripts. But, sadly, Jahangir's copy of the *Gulistān* did not survive intact. Probably early in the 19th century it was dismembered, and its miniatures were mounted on album pages. Even in their present state they indicate that this *Gulistān* must have been one of Jahangir's finest manuscripts. In this miniature an old man and a young woman argue a case before three muftis (expounders of Islamic law).

139
Youth by a stream

Miniature painting
14.7 × 8.3 cm
Previously in the Rothschild Collection
Robinson (1976), no. 91
India, Mughal *c.* 1615

The setting is idyllic. A blossoming tree curves around a cypress – one of the standard literary and visual metaphors for the intertwining of lovers – and small birds fill the air with melodies. Seated on a stool beside a stream, the young man reads a small, green book, presumably containing love poems, and his elegant clothing bespeaks his rank and sophistication. In Safavid art the image of the solitary, refined, and presumably lovelorn young man (who can be interpreted as a representation of the earthly beloved or as a metaphor of the divine beloved) occurred with great frequency in the late 16th and 17th centuries. It was a motif so well tried that only an artist of great talent – like the Safavid masters Mirza 'Ali, Muhammadi, or Riza – could lift it above triteness. During Jahangir's reign there was a vogue for solitary images based on Safavid models, and the gifted Mughal master responsible for this painting was obviously well acquainted with the art of Muhammadi.

139

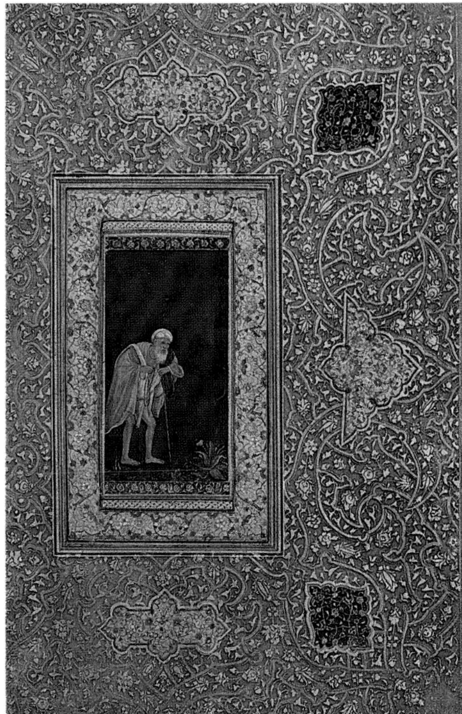

140
An aged pilgrim

Inscribed 'The work of Nadir al-Zaman'
Page from a royal album
11.6 × 6.4 cm
Previously in the Rothschild Collection
Brown (1924), pl. XVII and fig. 1; Robinson (1976), no. 93, pp. 180 and 212; Beach (1978), p. 91 A. Welch and S.C. Welch, (1982), no. 68, pp. 206-208
India, Mughal *c.* 1615-20

The painter Abu'l-Hasan who bore the honorific epithet of Nadir al-Zaman (Rarity of the Age) must have known how this small portrait would please the emperor. Jahangir was fascinated by wondrous and strange sights, and, while his India was crossed by many wandering pilgrims, few could have been possessed of such spiritual dignity as this holy man who seems to have been walking in search of salvation all of his life. Eyes locked on the distant goal we cannot see, he transforms his spare environment into a space filled with promise. Keenly sensitive to outer form as a mirror of inner self, the imperial connoisseur surely found this portrait of a humble subject as revealing as Bishndas' portrait of Shah 'Abbas.

141
Portrait of Shah 'Abbas I

Attributed to Bishndas
Page from a dispersed royal album
Inscribed: *lower right* – Likeness of 'Ali Khan; *lower left* – Bishndas
15.8 × 8 cm
Previously in the Rothschild Collection
Stchoukine (1935), pp. 190-208, no. 2; Robinson (1976), no. 112, pp. 190-192; A. Welch and S.C. Welch (1982), no. 67, pp. 203-206
India, Mughal, *c.* 1618-20

Despite the inscription, this is not a portrait of 'Ali Khan but of Shah 'Abbas I (r. 1587-1629), the most powerful and successful of the Safavid rulers of Iran. The Mughal emperor Jahangir was not wholly at ease with his powerful neighbour and wisely wondered about 'Abbas' intentions. The Indian ruler had long had not only an 'addiction' to realistic portraiture but also a firm belief in its power to reveal the mind and personality of the individual portrayed. When he sent a splendid mission to Isfahan in 1618, he ordered his court painter Bishndas to go along and 'take portraits of the Shah and the chief men of his state'. This is one of several fine portraits of 'Abbas by the painter: 'Abbas' intelligence, determination, and confidence are readily apparent, and one can imagine that Jahangir must have felt some apprehension, even while he admired these portraits.

141

142

142
Mongol warrior

Miniature painting
Miniature 16 × 10.3 cm, page 22 × 16 cm
Previously in the Kevorkian Collection
Falk (1978), no. 19
India, Mughal, *c.* 1620

This soldier kneels on a dark blue carpet ornamented with flowers and arabesques, and except for clouds and a blue and a red flower, the space behind him is empty. Underneath a light blue hat is a face that is ruthlessly confident, and his stout body expresses muscular strength. A bow, a quiver of arrows, a sword, two daggers, and a mace are the evident tools of his trade, and he is clearly a man who is competent in his profession. He is posed, in fact, as if he were at a court reception: the little finger of his left hand is delicately placed on his knee, and his face seems to be turned toward his employer. At the courts of India and Iran, Central Asia's warriors were both feared and admired, and this 'portrait' is based upon a well-established tradition of renderings of solitary, seated Mongol soldiers in 15th- and 16th-century Iranian art. The unidentified painter knew this tradition well, and, in keeping with customary practice in Islamic art, was testing his talent against the achievements of his predecessors.

143
Shah Jahan and Jahangir

Portrait of Jahangir signed by Balchand; portrait of Shah Jahan signed by Abu'l-Hasan (Nadir al-Zaman)
Page from an 18th-century album
Portrait of Shah Jahan inscribed: 'Written in the first year of the fortunate ascension; presented to the sight of the most pure; the work of the humblest of the servants Nadir al-Zaman.'
Page 55.2 × 34.5 cm
Beach (1978), pp. 92, 101; A. Welch and S.C. Welch (1982), no. 71, pp. 215-217
India, Mughal, 1628

Both connoisseurs of painting, father and son had very different taste, to which their court artists responded. Balchand's portrait of Jahangir at the top of this page is small but reveals character shaped by emotion, and in its shading and volume gives a sense of a solid, vital person. Though Abu'l-Hasan was more than capable of rendering the same qualities, he was working in 1628 for a different patron, and his portrait of the new emperor reveals an icier and more detached personality, fonder of jewels than of flowers and more interested in surface than in depth. He favoured iconic poses of this sort in which he is as still and locked in place as a gem in a precious setting, and he stares fixedly at his accession seal on which is written: 'Abu'l-Muzaffar Muhammad Shihab al-Din Shah Jahan Padishah Ghazi, Second Lord of the (auspicious) Astral Conjunction, (in the) year one.'

On the reverse are four lines of *nasta'līq*, signed by Akbar's famous calligrapher, Muhammad Husayn.

144

The honourable qadi caught by surprise with a young man

Page from a manuscript of Sa'di's *Gulistān*
Miniature 9.2 × 12.5 cm; page 32.5 × 20 cm
Hotel Drouot, 23 June 1982, lot 31
India, Mughal, *c.* 1630

Early in his reign, Shah Jahan commissioned a very fine, small copy of the *Gulistān* (Rose garden) of Sa'di that was intended to rival in form and quality the one commissioned by his father Jahangir between 1610 and 1615, and its illustrations share the same oblong format as the earlier manuscript. At some point, this precious manuscript was broken up, and a number of its illustrations were mounted on album pages. This miniature was placed in a blue mount, illuminated with small gold vines and flowers and a lush pink rose and tulip: both flowers are metaphors of love and lovers in Islamic art, and they obviously refer to the miniature below. Less directly, however, the rose indicates the source of the miniature, Sa'di's *Gulistān*.

To the left of the flowers is a Persian notation – 'perpetual endowment' – indicating that the page (and perhaps the entire album from which it came) was once given as a valuable endowment to a religious institution.

The miniature illustrates a well-known tale in the *Gulistān* (Book V, story no. 20): a qadi (Muslim religious judge) who was otherwise famed for his modest and honourable comportment fell head-over-heels in love with a handsome youth, ill-befitting his social status. Since he had not concealed his feelings, he was soon discovered by the king after a night of love and drinking. In this miniature, the couple are exhausted and oblivious to the consternation around them. The king is reacting in shock; the betrayer, who has just pulled away the sheet, is pointing the couple out with ill-concealed malice and the faces of the king's attendants represent a wide range of emotions: pious shock, wide-eyed astonishment, vicarious glee, malicious gloating, curiosity and revulsion. Some faces are brightly lit, others are partially hidden in the night. Despite the threatening atmosphere here, the tale has a happy ending, for in spite of his immediate disgrace the qadi wins the king's pardon by means of adroit and witty argumentation.

Although this superb painting is not signed, it can be attributed to Payag, the brother of the Mughal painter Balchand, and one of the most gifted artists working for Shah Jahan. A master of sombre tones and night scenes, Payag may have examined European chiaroscuro techniques and acquired from them his interest in single light sources (here the candle by the qadi's bed). Payag was also a keen observer of human personality and emotions.

Above the miniature is a superb illuminated panel and below is an additional panel that contains eight lines of a poem in *nasta'līq* script.

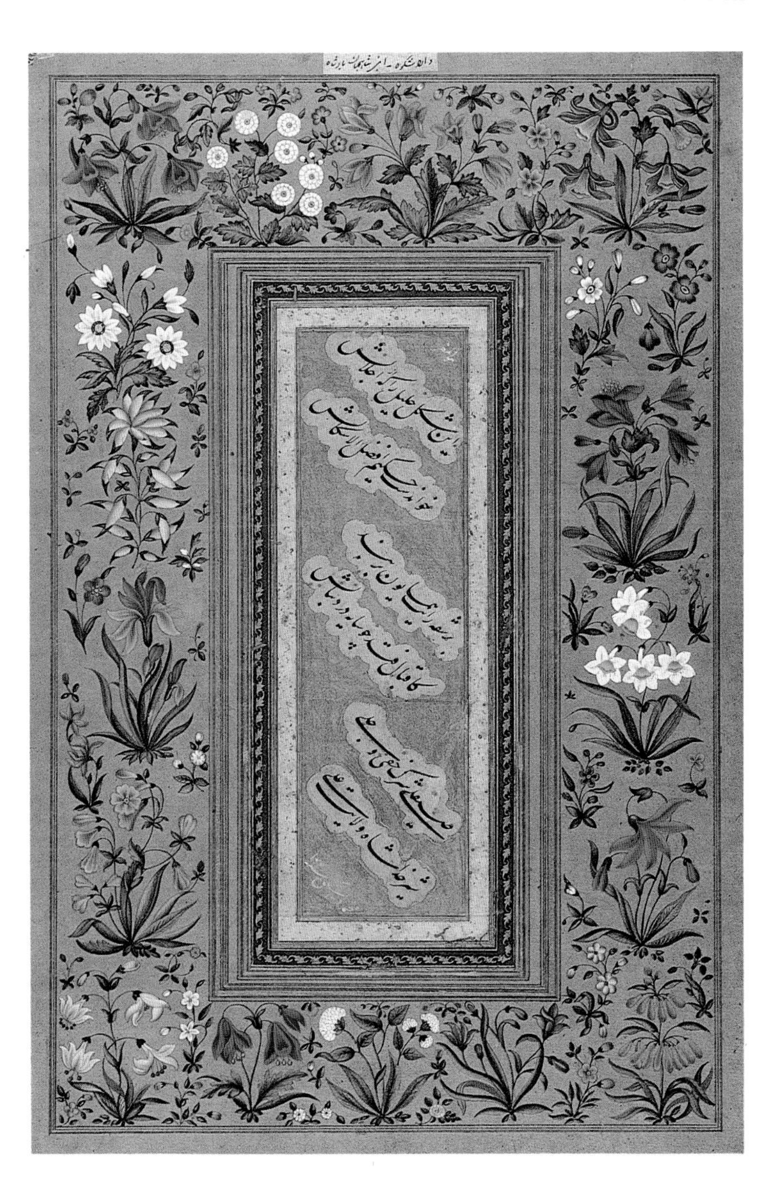

145
Calligraphy by Muhammad Dara Shikoh

Page from an 18th-century Mughal album
21.7 × 6.4 cm
Sotheby's, 17 July 1978, lot 9
India, Mughal, Burhanpur, 1041/1631-32

Six lines of Persian verse are written diagonally in a fine, black *nasta'līq* on a gold ground. The margins are decorated with an abundance of flowers, painted in the early 18th century when the calligraphy was mounted on this album page. The signature – Muhammad Dara Shikoh – and date – 1041 – appear in white in the lower left. The favourite son of Shah Jahan, Dara Shikoh was one of the most brilliant members of the Mughal family. A sufi by training and inclination, he associated with Muslim and Hindu mystics and even translated Hindu scriptures inro Persian. A productive writer, he was also a talented calligrapher. Born in 1615, this gifted prince was sixteen years old when he wrote these lines. The Mughal army was engaged in a lengthy campaign in the Deccan, and the prince resided in the central Indian city of Burhanpur with his father and mother (for whom the Taj Mahal was built). This calligraphy is dated the year of her death.

146

147

146
Love poem

Page from an album made for Shah Jahan
Inscribed with four lines of *nasta'līq* poetry, signed 'Ali al- Katib
Calligraphy: Afghanistan, Herat *c.* 1525
Page 37.8 × 25.6cm
Previously in the Kevorkian Collection
Sotheby's, 21 April 1980, lot 23; A. Welch and S.C. Welch (1982), no. 73, pp. 220-223
India, Mughal, *c.* 1635-40

According to the inscriptions in the upper right and lower left corners, 'Ali al-Katib composed this love poem and wrote it down in this splendid *nasta'līq*. Of all Iranian calligraphers Mir 'Ali al-Katib al-Haravi received the greatest acclaim at the Mughal court in India, and specimens of his script (see no. 36) were sought for inclusion in royal albums. Calligraphies were frequently decorated with illuminated margins when they were bound in albums, and the superb border here is the work of one of the greatest artists in Shah Jahan's employ – the anonymous Master of the borders (see no. 150). Like jewels in fine settings, flowers are bordered with shining gold; animals sit in silence within the precise turnings of an arabesque; birds poise in flight. It is an ideal world, too pristine and too ordered to be real, a paradise removed from care to frame a plaint of love.

147
Akbar offering a sarpech to Jahangir

Page from an album made for Shah Jahan
Miniature 24.2 × 15.7cm, page 38.1 × 26.8cm
Previously in the Rothschild Collection
Robinson (1976), no. 119
India, Mughal, *c.* 1640

As in nos 148-149, the margins here signify royal power and heavenly blessing on the Mughal dynasty. Authority is officially transferred in the miniature, for the emperor Akbar (r. 1556-1605) hands a *sarpech* (jewelled turban pin) to his son and successor Jahangir (r. 1605-27). Mughal imperial patrons were avidly interested in visual statements of royal rituals, genealogies, and transfers of power.

148
Portrait of the emperor Shah Jahan

Possibly by Bichitr
Page from an album made for Shah Jahan
Miniature 24.2 × 15.7cm; page 38.1 × 26.8cm
Previously in the Rothschild Collection
Robinson (1976), no. 120
India, Mughal, *c.* 1640

This page originally belonged in an album compiled for Shah Jahan, and the margins are replete with references to royal authority. A cheetah, wearing a royal collar, stalks three antelope; at the right three courtiers stand in quiet obeisance and hold regal paraphernalia; at the top two angels hover as they bring celestial grants of power – a sword and a necklace. The emperor, here about forty-eight years old, faces to the left. The aura round his head emits a green glow that separates the emperor's space from the blue-green sky behind him. One of the most gifted portraitists in the atelier of Jahangir and Shah Jahan, Bichitr continued painting until about 1645.

149
Akbar in old age

Page from an album made for Shah Jahan
Miniature 21.6 × 12.7 cm
Brown (1924), pl. 26; S.C. Welch (1963), fig. 17; A. Welch and S.C. Welch (1982), no. 74, pp. 223-225
India, Mughal *c.* 1645

Painted approximately forty years after Akbar's death, this posthumous portrait represents the great emperor as his grandson wished him to be seen. His head set in a halo and his body frozen in formality, he stands on a hillock that is a metaphor for the world ('Shah Jahan' means 'king of the world'), while two putti hold a regal canopy over his head and three courtiers with the regalia of power stand in the margin at the left. It is an image of the Mughal state under divine blessing, and its static, established iconography is sharply in contrast to the real Akbar – a man of high intelligence, great physical strength, and enormous energy whose exuberant vitality was the driving force behind the creation of the Mughal empire.

150
Poetry

Page from a dispersed album compiled for Shah Jahan
Fourteen lines in *nasta'līq*
38 × 25 cm
India, Mughal, *c.* 1650

These lines come from an unidentified Persian heroic poem and were copied here by an unknown scribe of great ability. An equally anonymous specialist in decoration supplied the floral ornament in the margins: flowers bounded by gold and represented with great richness and vitality characterize the art of the 'Master of the borders' who was responsible for illuminating many pages from Shah Jahan's albums. (For a discussion of this master see A. Welch and S.C. Welch (1982), no. 72, pp. 217-220.)

151 *(Actual size)*

151
Floral fantasy

Miniature painting
20.5 × 13.1 cm
A. Welch and S.C. Welch (1982), no. 75, pp. 225-227
India, Deccan, *c.* 1650

This is an exuberant garden, less ordered than the formal paradise-landscape the Mughals built around royal tombs and filled with movement: birds, bees, and butterflies animate the space around the blossoms. Patrons in Safavid Iran, Mughal India, and the Netherlands were all attracted to images of flowers, but the master responsible for this painting was at home in India's Deccan. Although he had surely seen work from all of the lands noted above, his vision is a different one, less decorative than the Iranian, less realistic than the Mughal, less moralizing than the Dutch. Most likely, he worked at the court of Golconda, a Shi'a kingdom and major commerical centre in south-eastern India that did not become part of the Mughal empire until 1687. (Toby Falk informs me that a smaller flower painting by this artist is in the Royal Library, Windsor, Album A 13, folio 50 b, signed 'Amin', and dated 1069/1658-9.)

152

152
Timur, Babur, and Humayun

Signed by Hashim
Page from an album made for Shah Jahan
Miniature 26.7 × 18.7 cm;
page 36.9 × 25.2 m
Previously in the Kevorkian Collection
Sotheby's, 3 April 1978, lot 99;
Martin (1912), pl. 14
India, Mughal, 1064/1653

A gold sky with clouds touched by sunlight extends above a green hill. On a dais covered with a splendid carpet are three thrones. According to an inscription on the white marble dado, the central king is 'Amir Timur Gurkan' or Tamerlane, the Central Asian conqueror whose victories in Afghanistan and northern India in the late 14th century were the formal basis for the claim of his descendants, the Mughals, to rule India. To his right sits Babur, the first Mughal emperor, to whom Timur (who died in 1405, while Babur established his kingdom in India in 1526) hands a *sarpech* (jewelled turban pin) in a symbolic transfer of authority (see no. 147). To his left sits Humayun, Babur's son and the second Mughal emperor, holding what appears to be a compass. For these two figures inscriptions are not necessary, for their portraits are convincing likenesses. In its entirety this group portrait is a statement of political legitimacy – with careful references to the origins of the Timurid line and the Mughal dynasty – a type of symbolic statement of which both Jahangir and Shah Jahan were particularly fond.

But the painting's references are more complex. The arabesque carpet is a type almost always reserved for members of the royal house. The flowers inlaid in the dais' marble dado are like the semi-precious stone inlays of the Taj Mahal, the tomb of the emperor Shah Jahan's wife Mumtaz Mahal that was nearing completion when this painting was finished. On his lap Babur has a book, most likely a copy of the *Bāburnāmeh* (his memoirs) that was Shah Jahan's favourite reading and the literary foundation for Mughal family reminiscences. Remarkably, the poppies filling the meadow behind the dais recall descriptions of the flower-studded fields of Afghanistan in the *Bāburnāmeh*. The Mughal throne depended upon its military, and the attendants in the lower corners represent its pillars – a Hindu Rajput at the left and a Muslim Turk at the right. Perhaps also a metaphor of lineage, five couples of different species of bird inhabit the tree behind Timur. Thus nature too is not haphazard. Even the green hill is probably a studied reference to the 'world' that Timur ruled: 'Shah Jahan' means 'king of the world', and this great Mughal used as a regnal title 'Lord of the Auspicious Astral Conjunction' – an ambitious nomenclature that Timur had also liked.

Next to the attendant at the right is the notation 'the work of Hashim (in the) year 1064'. One of the most accomplished of Shah Jahan's artists, Hashim was a gifted portraitist and a master of formal compositions replete with political references.

The page's margins, cruelly trimmed, are illuminated with birds, butterflies, and flowers outlined in gold. This stunning assemblage of plant and animal life is the work of an anonymous artist of the highest calibre, known as the Master of the Borders, whose paintings of animals, flowers, and arabesques illuminate many pages from Shah Jahan's albums and who may well have been the designer of the floral inlays of the Taj Mahal (see no. 150).

153
Woman amid blossoms

Miniature painting
19.1 × 10.6 cm
Colnaghi (1982), no. 30
India, perhaps Golconda, *c.* 1670

Artists in the Deccan, particularly Golconda, were able to combine Safavid decorativeness with Mughal realism and create landscapes that were both ordered and lush and that gave the impression of textile-like patterns ornamented with convincing natural forms. This is a landscape under the spell of flowers so believable that their imagined odours permeate the air. Orange poppies in the lower left and mauve roses in the lower right stabilize the composition; irises flower near the young woman's feet, and tiny white or orange flowers dot the landscape, a luxuriant green carpet of grass and vegetation. The young woman is elegantly and richly dressed, and she holds roses, plucked from the bush, in her right hand. Her left hand rests on the bending branch of a blossoming tree as gently as it may rest upon the arm of the beloved for whom she waits. Her finger tips and nails are covered with henna patterns, indicating that she is married.

153

This painting's appeal goes far beyond the visual. We can smell the different scents in the air and feel the soft, warm breeze that stirs the woman's diaphanous dress. The sun is rising, and birds sing in the morning sky. It is a love painting masked in flowers, and its blend of mystery and realism, of verisimilitude and fantasy, of delicacy and innuendo, admirably evokes the subtle ambience and refined sensuality of Deccani painting.

154
Sea serpent swallows a royal fleet

Page from a manuscript of a Deccani Urdu epic written in *naskh*
Inscribed on the reverse in two columns of text
Page 39 × 23.5 cm
Christie's, 10 October 1979 lot 185;
A. Welch and S.C. Welch (1982), no. 77, pp. 229-231; Zebrowski (1983), pp. 222-4
India, Bijapur, *c.* 1670-86

Although the colophon of this manuscript does not name the epic, author or patron, it has since been identified as the *Gulshān-i 'Ishq* by Nusrati. The colophon tells us that the poet 'grew prosperous . . . during the reign of 'Ali 'Adil Shah' who ruled Bijapur from 1656 to 72. In fact Mian (Master) Nusrati was the court poet and boon companion of Sultan 'Ali and dedicated the *Gulshān -i 'Ishq* to him. The manuscript may have been produced during the latter part of his reign or that of his successor, and it is possible that it was made for a prominent aristocrat. In any case from 1489, when Bijapur emerged as an autonomous Shi'a kingdom, until 1686, when it was annexed to the Mughal empire, this Deccani city was a major centre of Islamic culture and attracted talent from all over the Muslim world.

154

155
Dancing cranes and ducks

Miniature painting
26.9 × 17.5 cm
India, Deccan, *c.* 1700

Four white cranes with reddish heads pirouette around the blue banks of a silvery stream in which white ducks swim and dive. Their elegance and grace testify to the hand of a master painter who took a theme – animals in nature – that Mughals might have found attractive but who invested it with the finesse of a stylish dance and a sense of lyrical romance that is Deccani rather than Mughal in spirit. The unknown artist may have been trained in Hyderabad.

155

156
Night celebration at the wedding of Prince Dara Shikoh

Miniature painting
Miniature 40 × 28 cm, page 42.8 × 30.8 cm
Falk (1978), no. 36
India, Oudh, *c.* 1760

Dara Shikoh (1615–59) was the eldest son of Shah Jahan and a brilliant scholar and connoisseur of the arts, as well as a talented calligrapher (see no. 145). When he was eighteen years old he was married to his first cousin, Nadira Banu. He continued to serve his father loyally but was murdered by his younger brother Awrangzib. His wedding in 1633 was a sumptuous affair, and this painting records both its visual splendour and its noises, as massive drums reverberate from elephants' backs and fireworks burst in the distance. Illuminated night scenes were a favourite challenge to later Mughal painters, and precise portraiture had always been a Mughal concern.

The veiled prince is shown in the picture's centre, while his father – his head in a green aura – rides close behind him. Their many attendants, as well as the bride's welcoming party, are represented with convincing individual likenesses.

The Mughal empire essentially collapsed in the early 18th century, though its legendary power and wealth exerted an enormous influence on successor states until the 20th century. The northern state of Oudh inherited a tiny portion of the empire in the 18th century, but its *nawābs* aspired to all the trappings of the empire. There are numerous examples of copies of Mughal paintings by later Oudh artists, though most are on a less ambitious scale than this grand composition. The original painting, presumably done in 1633, was surely intended for inclusion in the *Shāh Jahān-nāmeh*, now in Windsor Castle. This page is now lost but it was still available around 1760 for the gifted anonymous Oudh painter who has left us this record of a splendid event.

B.W. ROBINSON

Lacquer, Oil-paintings and Later Arts of the Book

It is no more than a generation ago that the arts of the Zand and Qajar periods were the object of derision or plain neglect. On the one hand admirers of classical Persian painting of the Timurid and Safavid periods felt that the artists of the 18th and 19th centuries had somehow let the side down by adopting certain European conventions; and on the other hand, critics with a background of western painting looked in vain among their works for the qualities of realism and spirituality which classical European painting habitually displays. In short, these later Persian paintings, it was felt, fell between two stools, and they were damned accordingly.

A similar condemnation, be it noted, was at the same time extended to most European works of the Victorian era. But from the 1950s onwards a more sympathetic view was gaining ground. Pre-Raphaelite and High Victorian academic pictures began to command respectable – and now very high – prices; Victorian silver, furniture, and ephemera were eagerly collected; and scholarly works in these hitherto neglected fields began to proliferate. This movement set off a similar reaction in the oriental field. With the successive centenaries of Hokusai (1949), Hiroshige (1958) and Kuniyoshi (1961), and their attendant celebrations, the later, erstwhile 'decadent', Japanese prints came into their own; Chinese 19th-century export works – sidelines of the tea-trade – found a ready market; and finally the despised Qajar oil-paintings and painted lacquer began to enjoy an unprecedented popularity, the sometimes undiscriminating enthusiasm of Persian collectors and dealers pushing up prices to an incredible and, it must be admitted, quite unrealistic level.

What has brought about this radical change of attitude? Partly, perhaps, a justifiable impatience with the *ex cathedra* pronouncements by pundits of the artistic establishment. Ordinary people of culture and intelligence felt that they had a right to form their own preferences. They decided that they liked these 19th-century works, and they were not prepared to submit unconditionally to the opinions (for they were no more) of 'experts'. But such an alteration in taste could not have taken place unless the objects themselves had considerable merit, and nobody can have any doubts on that score in face of the objects here described.

First and foremost, the artists of the Zand and Qajar periods carried on the classical Persian miniaturists' tradition of meticulous craftsmanship and a rich colour scheme. They also followed their Safavid predecessors in striving after a portrayal of the ultimate in youthful beauty of both sexes, and of the luxuriance of nature manifested in flowers and birds. The development of a partly Europeanized style gives Qajar representations of such subjects a warmth and, perhaps, a sentimentality not found in the classical periods, and in this they reflect the spirit of their period in both East and West. There is indeed something intriguing in the actual hybrid nature of the style, for which we can find a parallel in the early 14th century. The combination of largely undigested Chinese and even Byzantine elements with remnants of the old Baghdad style and of a native Iranian tradition would, one would have thought, prove disastrous, or at least unsatisfactory. But it produced on the one hand the austere and dignified miniatures of the Rashid al-Din manuscripts, and on the other the monumental and dynamic illustrations of the Demotte *Shāhnāmeh*. So it was with the western elements incorporated in Iranian painting in the period with which we are here concerned. In the face of foreign influences, it seems, the Iranian artists knew instinctively what to adopt (and adapt) and what to reject in order to produce the effect at which they were aiming. In the Zand and Qajar periods, of course, these aims were very different from those of the 14th-century painters. Epic illustration – indeed, book-illustration of all kinds – was virtually 'out'. What was called for was, firstly, large portraits and other mural paintings in oils, and secondly exquisitely decorated small objects of everyday use – pen-boxes, mirror-cases, and caskets.

The origins of the Europeanizing style are to be sought in the reign of Shah 'Abbas the Great, when European pictures were included amongst ambassadorial gifts, and a handful of European artists and craftsmen are found settled in Isfahan. By the 1670s a thoroughgoing European style of painting had become fashionable at court, its foremost exponents being Muhammad Zaman (nos 100-102), 'Ali Quli Jabbadar (nos 98 and 99), and Shaykh 'Abbasi. It may be appropriate to observe here that the old legend of Muhammad Zaman's studies in Italy and his conversion to Christianity has been convincingly demolished by the Russian scholar Ivanov; the European influences under which these painters worked seem to have been Flemish rather than Italian (no. 157).

What with the Afghan occupation and Nadir Shah's campaigns of liberation and, later, conquest, the generation after the Safavid collapse in 1722 can show little in the way of painting. Two good oil portraits of the great soldier, one in the Commonwealth Relations Office and the other in the Victoria and Albert Museum, are in fact the only works worth mentioning. But the court of Karim Khan Zand at Shiraz (1750-79) provided an oasis of peace and culture in the barren desert of the 18th century. It was probably at Shiraz that Sadiq, the leading painter of his time, made his début and formed the style which the Qajars inherited and developed. He worked on a large scale in oils, and also produced miniature paintings and lacquer; he seems to have had a long working life, spanning almost the entire second half of the 18th century.

His style was closely followed by Mirza Baba, who was in the service of the Qajar family at Astarabad before they attained the throne, as testified by a painting of 1794 in the present exhibition (no. 184). Fath 'Ali Shah (r. 1797-1834) made him *naqqāsh-bāshī* or Painter Laureate, which seems to be the first use of this title; it became quite common as the 19th century proceeded. His chief rival was Mihr 'Ali who outlived and, it might be said, surpassed him. 'Abdullah Khan, who survived into the reign of Nasir al-Din Shah (reigned from 1848), makes the third in this trio of leading painters of the early Qajar period; all three produced impressive life-size portraits of their royal master – Mihr 'Ali no less than ten.

European envoys and travellers were numerous in Iran from the reign of Fath 'Ali Shah onwards, diplomatic activity having been stimulated by Anglo-French rivalry in the Napoleonic wars. Traders soon followed, and it is amusing to recall that bottles of Rowland's Macassar Oil, obtainable in London until comparatively recently, bore the legend 'by appointment to the Shah of Persia 1828'. The paintings of the time show European decanters, watches, candle-sconces, and furniture. Later, it appears, European pictures and prints, often of a rather dubious nature, found a ready market in Qajar Iran, and caused a proliferation of dissipated youths in smoking-caps and dressing-gowns, and of simpering young Cyprians in poke-bonnets and crinolines, in the work of many mid-19th century lacquer painters (nos 166 and 170). But their transference to this medium effectively filtered out any vicious qualities the originals may have had, leaving the youthful figures all pretty, naive, and apparently innocent. Innocent and unsophisticated charm is, indeed, the most endearing feature of Qajar painting, which is given piquancy by the highly sophisticated and accomplished techniques used in presenting it.

The style of Mirza Baba and his contemporaries was carried through, with slight modifications, to the end of Fath 'Ali Shah's reign by painters such as Sayyid Mirza, Ahmad, and Muhammad (nos 185 and 186), and indeed continued through that of his grandson and successor Muhammad Shah (1834-48). But a further strong injection of European influence was on the way. Abu'l-Hasan Ghaffari, a pupil of Mihr 'Ali, was sent to study painting in Europe, and returned shortly after the accession of Nasir al-Din Shah in 1848. He had developed a notably realistic style, particularly effective in portraiture (nos 190 and 191), and such was his reputation and ability that his new style was everywhere imitated, not only in full-size paintings and lithographed book-illustrations, but also in lacquer and enamel.

Exquisite painted enamel work had been produced for Fath 'Ali Shah by his court painters 'Ali and Baqir, examples of which were formerly to be seen among the Persian crown jewels. But some of the work done for Nasir al-Din, especially by Muhammad Kazim, son of the celebrated lacquer painter Najaf, is even finer. It is notable that the Comte de Rochechouart, who was in Tehran in the 1860s and had some scathing things to say about Persian painting in general, was captivated by these painted enamels, finding that he far preferred them to the imported Swiss examples by which, in all probability, they were originally inspired.

Nasir al-Din's first European tour of 1873 set off a further train of European influence. On his return he stripped from his palace walls most of the large oil-paintings of Fath 'Ali Shah's time, which were sold off at ridiculous prices; a fine full-length portrait of Fath 'Ali

Shah by 'Abdullah Khan, now in the Victoria and Albert Museum, was bought for £3 10s. They were replaced by European pictures, tapestries, and mirrors acquired on his travels.

Abu'l-Hasan, better known by the title of *Sani' al-Mulk* (Painter of the Kingdom), conferred on him in 1861, had died in 1866. But the realistic style was ably carried on by his long-lived nephew Muhammad Ghaffari *Kamal al-Mulk* (1852-1947), whose genre scenes are particularly effective. He also studied in Europe, and established an art school of his own on his return.

So we see that during the 18th and 19th centuries Iranian painting was washed over by a series of waves of western influence, usually set in motion by political events, and always reinforced by the passion for novelty inherent in the lively Iranian mind. The ablest painters were successful in absorbing these influences into their style without losing their individuality or national character, but it must be admitted that a good deal of inferior work has survived, which for some time gave Qajar painting as a whole a bad name. But the more sympathetic study to which it has been subjected in the past thirty years or so has enabled us to sort the wheat from the chaff, and to recognize and applaud its very considerable achievements, especially the magnificent royal portraits and the unassuming but exquisite work in painted lacquer and enamel.

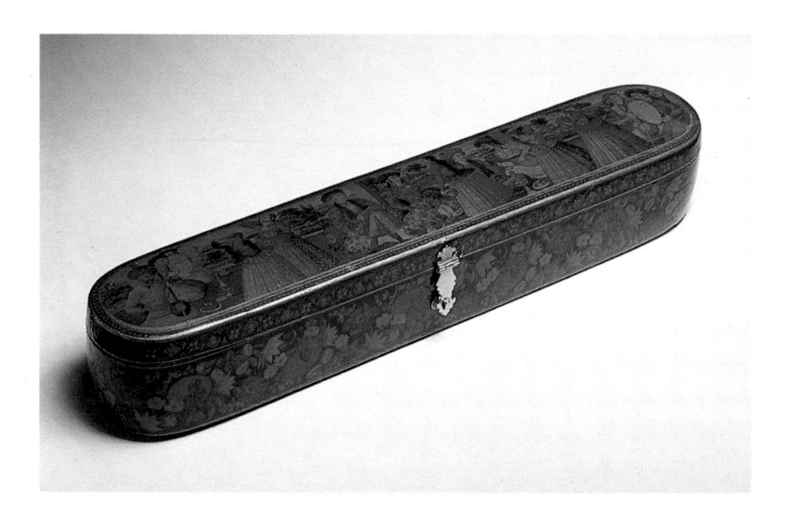

157
Pen-box

Signed *Muhammad 'Alī ibn Muhammad Zamān*
Papier mâché, painted and lacquered
Oblong with rounded ends and hinged lid. On the top, a prince and princess being entertained by dancers and musicians on a terrace with wooded landscape behind; rich floral designs round the sides, and a reclining courtesan on the interior of the lid
Length 29.7 cm
Iran, dated 1130/1718

Safavid lacquer is very rare, and this is an outstanding example. The artist's father Muhammad Zaman was the leading spirit in the thoroughgoing westernization of Persian painting in the late 17th century. The best-known work of Muhammad 'Ali is a painting in the British Museum of the last Safavid monarch, Shah Sultan Husayn, and his court, dated 1133/1721, the year before the Safavid *débacle* (no. 1920-9-17-0299).

158
Mirror-case

Papier-mâché, painted and lacquered
Cover A girl reclining on a terrace playing the *sehtar*, behind her a bare-headed youth with a large flat drum; landscape background. This is derived from an oil painting by Sadiq in the Negarestan Museum, Tehran. On the reverse, hyacinths and roses.
Case A girl with closed eyes reclining against a seated youth on a terrace, two seated cats in front of them
25.75 × 18.25 cm (cover 21 × 13.5 cm)
Iran, Zand style, late 18th century

159
Pen-box

Papier-mâché, painted and lacquered
Oblong with very slightly convex detached lid. Top of lid painted with Fath 'Ali Shah and his army routing the Uzbeks, the king himself spearing the Uzbek leader; behind him rides the young Crown Prince 'Abbas Mirza.
Interior of lid and sides of box painted with hunting scenes
27 × 6.25 × 5 cm
Iran, Early 19th century

The style is characteristic of the reign of Fath 'Ali Shah, and is perhaps best exemplified in manuscripts of the *Shāhinshāh Nāmeh*, the epic celebrating his exploits, by Fath 'Ali Khan (Saba), the Poet Laureate, of which copies exist in the Bodleian Library (Oxford), the India Office Library (London), the National Library (Vienna), the Majlis Library and the Negarestan Museum (Tehran).

160
Apothecary's box

Wood, painted and lacquered, containing two balances and a set of seven weights, the tops fitted with rings set in rosettes of blue enamel, all in shaped compartments. Underneath is a sliding mirror with mosaic frame. The box fitted with a small key of finely pierced steel. The top of the hinged lid painted with a design of massed flowers within a calligraphic border signed *Mīr Muhammad Bāqir b. Abū Tālib al-Husaynī al-Isfahānī.* On the interior, a youth seated with a girl. *Sides* panels of flowers. *Base* a girl dancing between two others playing drums
17 × 10.5 × 4.5 cm
Iran, mid-19th century

161
Pen-box

Signed *Ismā'īl*
Papier-mâché, painted and lacquered
Rectangular with rounded ends, slightly convex top, and sliding compartment. The top and sides finely painted with panels containing groups of figures of European type, divided by oval medallions of European ladies and a youth, the panels and ovals framed in gold rococo scrollwork
24.25 × 4.5 × 3.5 cm
Iran, dated 1277/1861

This is a characteristic work of Muhammad Isma'il in his middle period. He was the younger brother of the celebrated lacquer-painter Najaf, and was nicknamed *Farangī-sāz* (the Europeanizer). See *Iran* V, 1967, pp. 1-6

162
Casket

Signed *Muhammad Ismā'īl naqqāsh-bāshī*
Wood, painted and lacquered
On the top, the siege of Herat by Muhammad Shah in 1837-38: a panoramic view comprising literally hundreds of tiny figures, including Muhammad Shah inspecting severed Afghan heads in the foreground. Round the sides are scenes from the same campaign alternating with others of the defeat of the Turkmans by Mirza Muhammad Khan Qajar about twenty years later. On the interior of the lid, the court of Muhammad Shah, and arabesque designs on the base (both exterior and interior)
Historical Museum, Bern
32.3 × 26.3 × 11.6 cm
Iran, dated 1282/1865

This is perhaps the most spectacular piece of Persian lacquer in existence, and may well have been commissioned by Mirza Muhammad Khan Qajar to celebrate his victories; it was formerly in the collection of Henri Moser of Charlottenfels. See B.W. Robinson, 'Persian Lacquer in the Bern Historical Museum' in *Iran* VIII (1970), pp. 47-50

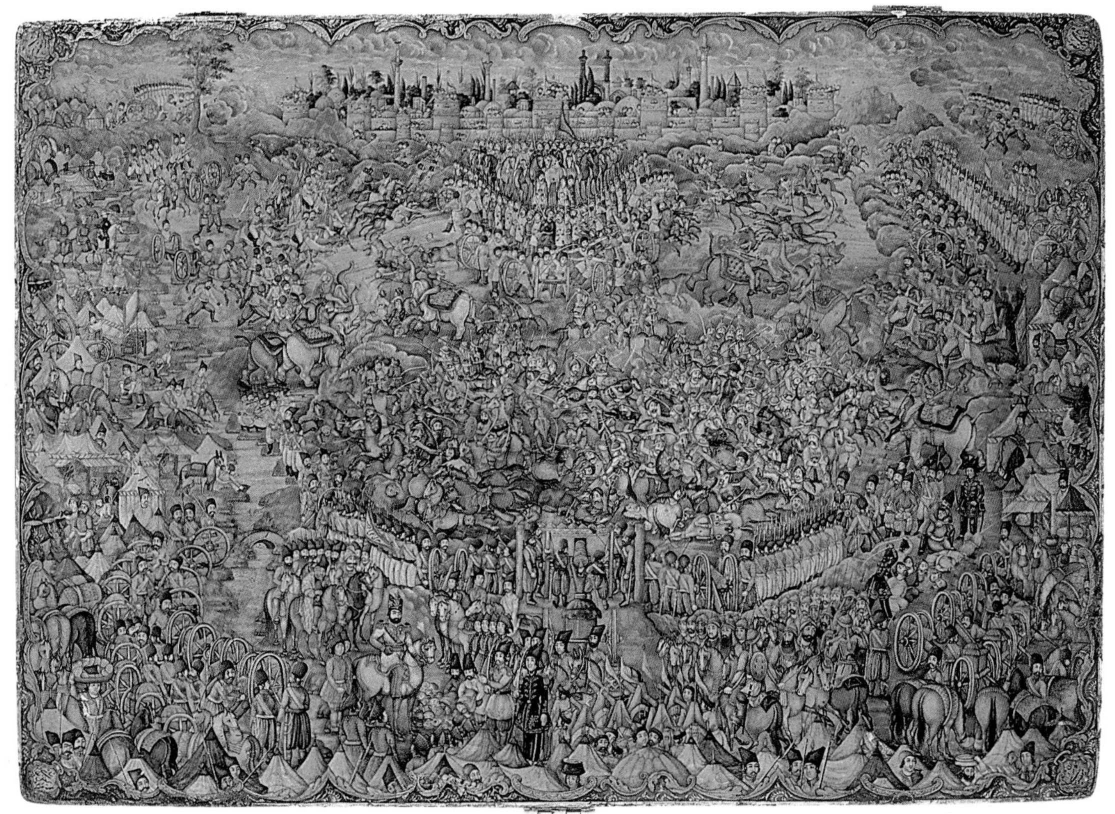

162 *Top of lid*

162 *Interior of lid*

163
Mirror-case
Signed *Muhammad Ismā'īl naqqāsh-bāshī*
Papier-mâché, painted and lacquered
The outer surface of the sliding cover and the case exquisitely painted with an identical design of an oval floral medallion surrounded by interlacing gold scrollwork within a floral border; Historical Museum, Bern
27 × 17.3 cm
Iran, dated 1288/1871

This is the latest recorded work of Isma'il, and one of his finest.

164
Pen-box
Signed *'Ibādallah Mahmūd mudhahhib-bāshī*
Papier-mâché, painted and lacquered
Rectangular with rounded ends, slightly convex top, and sliding compartment. Top and sides black, very finely painted in gold with nightingales among roses, tinged here and there with red; the base, and sides of sliding compartment plain black with narrow gold edging
24 × 4 × 3 cm
Iran, third quarter 19th century

165
Pen-box
Papier-mâché, painted and lacquered
Oblong with rounded ends, slightly convex top, and sliding compartment. The top painted (vertical format) with a blossoming rose-tree, in the branches of which appears a small half-naked figure, and at its base the heads and shoulders of two other figures; birds and flowers on the sides, on black ground
22 × 4 × 3 cm
Iran, third quarter 19th century

The style of the figures still recalls that of the reign of Fath 'Ali Shah, but the painting of the flowers indicates a later period.

166
Pen-box
Signed *Haydar 'Alī ibn Muhammad Ismā'īl naqqāsh-bāshī*
Papier-mâché, painted and lacquered
Oblong with rounded ends, slightly convex top, and sliding compartment. Birds and groups of roses and other flowers on brown ground and, on the top, an oval medallion of a European lady with a fan, with a fine gold rococo frame; on the sides, panels of landscape with figures, similarly framed, between bust-portraits of girls
24 × 4 × 3 cm
Iran, dated 128(0)/1864

Very fine work by the son and pupil of Muhammad Isma'il (see no. 161).

164

165

166

167

168

169

167
Pen-box

Signed *Adarkānī yā Husayn*
Papier-mâché, painted and lacquered
Oblong with rounded ends, slightly convex top, and sliding compartment. The top and sides finely painted with birds, roses, and butterflies on brown ground
25.5 × 5 × 4.25 cm
Iran, dated 1285/1868

An individualistic variation on the favourite *gul-bulbul* design by an otherwise unrecorded artist, whose signature incorporates the pious invocation *yā Husayn*; his actual name may have been Husayn Adarkani.

168
Pen-box

Signed *Mirzā Ahmad ibn 'Abd al-Wahhāb mudhahhib-bāshī*
Papier-mâché, painted and lacquered
Oblong with rounded ends, slightly convex top, and sliding compartment. The top and sides black, very finely painted in gold with sprays of flowers and nightingales
19.75 × 3.75 × 3 cm
Iran, dated 1286/1869

169
Pen-box

Signed *Yā Hazrat 'Abbās*
Papier-mâché, painted and lacquered
Oblong with rounded ends, slightly convex top, and sliding compartment. The top finely painted with nightingales amid roses and other flowers, with central oval medallion framed in feathery gold, in which the Holy Family, with angels, is depicted; the sides similar, with medallions of dervishes
22 × 4 × 3.5 cm
Iran, *c.* 1870

The punning signature in the form of an invocation was common practice in the Zand and Qajar periods; it seems to have originated with Muhammad Zaman (*yā sāhib al-Zamān*) in the late 17th century. The artist of this piece was probably 'Abbas 'Ali of Shiraz.

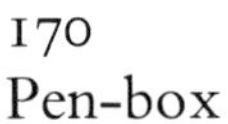

170
Pen-box

Signed *Fathallah Shīrāzī*
Papier-mâché, painted and lacquered
Oblong with rounded ends, slightly convex top, and sliding compartment. Top and sides black with sprays of roses; on the top an oval panel framed with scrolls, beautifully painted with a half-length of a European lady between two smaller ovals of birds on branches; on the sides similar panels
23.25 × 4 × 3 cm
Iran, dated 1293/1876

A fine and typical work of this outstanding artist, who was strongly influenced by contemporary European painted papier-mâché.

171
Pen-box

Signed *Mustafā*
Papier-mâché, painted and lacquered
Oblong with rounded ends, slightly convex top, and sliding compartment. On the top, a rocky desert landscape with Nasir al-Din Shah, dismounted and attended by gun-bearers, shooting a leopard which has just killed an ibex; in the background, a body of cavalry and a coach. The sides painted with landscape panels of European origin, and various animals
23 × 4.5 × 3.5 cm
Iran, dated 1300/1883

This probably represents an actual incident in one of the shah's hunting expeditions. Mustafa was a prominent and versatile artist; in addition to his lacquer painting, he illustrated a lithographed edition of the *Shāhnāmeh* published at Tehran 1307/1890.

172
Presentation pen-box (*qalamdān kiānī*)

Signed *Sānī' Humāyūn*
Papier-mâché, painted and lacquered
Oblong with rounded ends, slightly convex top, and sliding compartment. The top, sides, and base are minutely painted with various kings of Iran, both historical and legendary, either as bust-portraits or represented enthroned and surrounded by massed courtiers. The sides and base of the sliding compartment are painted with scenes from the lives of eminent dervishes and holy men, and its interior with sprays of roses on gold ground
24 × 4.5 × 3.5 cm
Iran, dated 1318/1900

A fine example of the elaborate pen-boxes made for presentation, with every surface covered with painting; d'Allemagne (*Du Khorassan au Pays des Bakhtiaris*, 1911, I. 82–84) describes such a pen-box painted for Nasir al-Din by his Poet Laureate. Sani' Humayun did some fine work under strong European influence; this example is in a more traditional style.

173
Pen-box

Signed *303 Simirumi*
Papier-mâché, painted and lacquered
Oblong with rounded ends, slightly convex top, and sliding compartment. On the top (vertical format) a central panel of a young dervish (probably Nur 'Ali Shah) carrying an axe, between two others, smaller, painted with birds in landscapes; sides with six similar panels, two of them with animals. Black background covered with fine gold floral scrolls
20 × 3.5 × 2.75 cm
Iran, dated 1327/1909

Several painters used the name Simirumi at this time; the significance of the number 303 included by this one in his signature is unexplained. The Simirumi style is strongly influenced by pen-boxes produced and painted in Russia for the Iranian market. In this connection it is interesting to note that lacquered pen-boxes of the normal *qalamdān* form were also made in Japan, presumably also for the Iranian market.

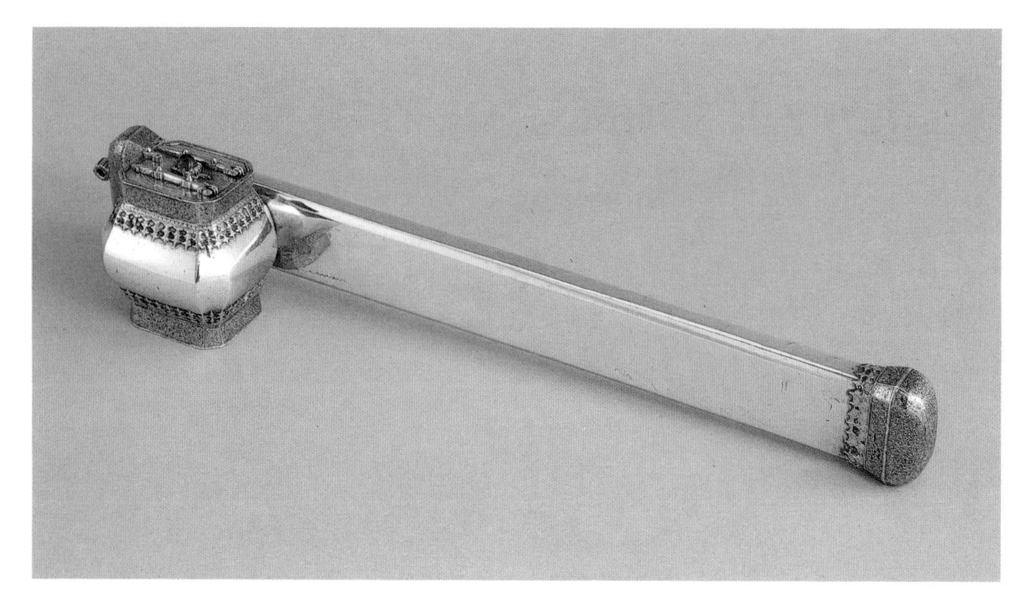

174

Silver parcel-gilt pen-and-ink case

Large pen-and-ink case, silver parcel-gilt, the pen section plain of flattened rounded octagonal cross-section, the ends gilt with fine niello scrollwork and openwork appliqué. The ink-pot of *bombé* octagonal form similarly decorated, with a red stone set in the middle of the lid, which is provided with a double hinge and catch of gilt: interior of lid set with an oval gilt plaque *repoussé* with a calligraphic design. Maker's mark stamped near the hinge end of the pen-section *'amal-i Qaram-safa*.
Tughrā stamp of Sultan Mahmud II on base of ink-pot and on pen-section adjacent
Length 35 cm
Turkey, mid-18th century

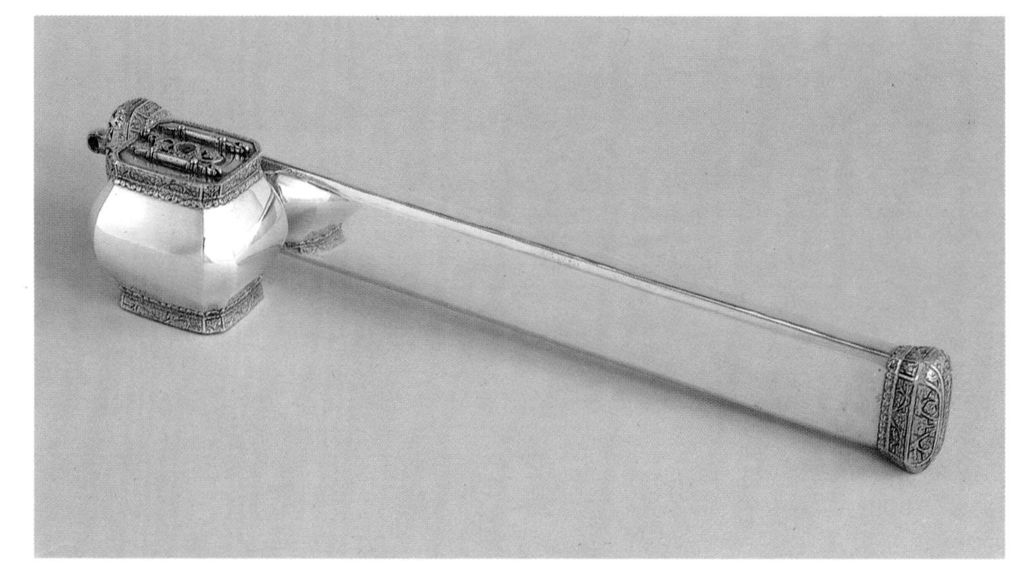

175

Silver parcel-gilt pen-and-ink case

Similar to no. 174 except that the ends of the pen-section and ink-pot are engraved, and the red stone is replaced by an emerald; the interior of the lid is plain
Stamped maker's mark *'amal-i Hasan*
Tughrā stamp of Sultan *'Abd al-Majid* (?)
Length 28 cm
Turkey, mid-19th century

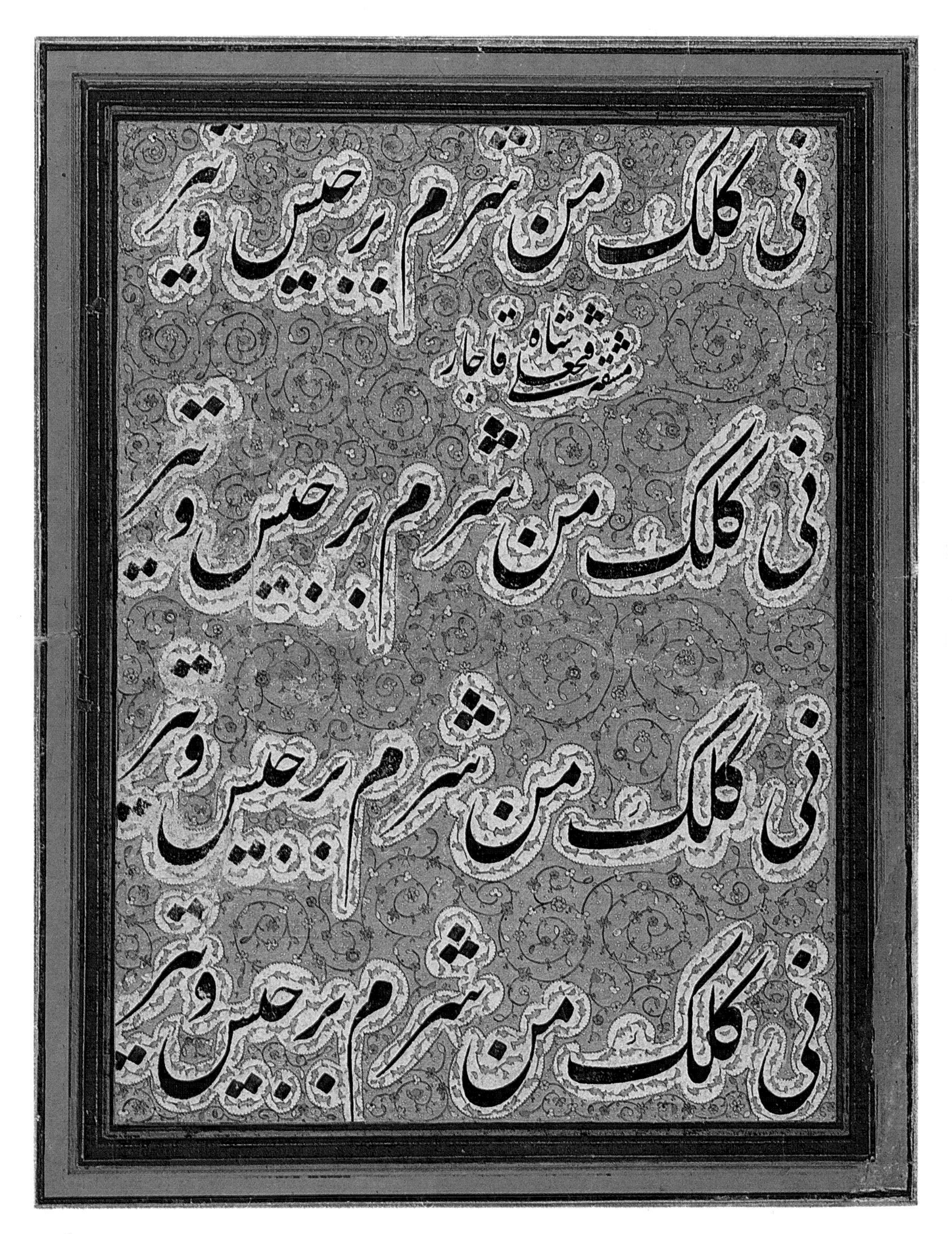

176
Calligraphic exercise
Signed *Fath 'Alī Shāh Qājār*
A line of fine large *nasta'līq* repeated four times; background of gold with floral scrolls
25.4 × 19 cm
A. Welch (1972), vol. III, Cal 12, pp. 196-7
Iran, early 19th century

We know that Fath 'Ali Shah was a great patron of the arts and a respectable poet; this elegant page shows him also to have been an accomplished calligrapher.

177

177
Sheet of decorated calligraphy

Signed *Ismāʿīl al-musawwir al-kātib*

Pious invocations in very large and elegant *nastaʿlīq* against an exquisitely painted background of astonishing variety: *above* a group of monumental domed buildings of semi-European type, and the sun in splendour; *below* masses of roses with groups of shepherds and their flocks, wise men in discussion, ʿAli and the two young Imams Hasan and Husayn, pairs of girls, hunting scenes, birds, and domestic fowls

35 × 53.5 cm

Iran, *c.* 1860

Ismaʿil Jalaʾir was one of the most original and striking painters of the reign of Nasir al-Din Shah, with whom he was a great favourite; sad to say, he went mad in his later years and eventually committed suicide. This and the following item are curiously reminiscent of Ismaʿil's contemporary, the mad English painter Richard Dadd. The sheet is mounted on card, trimmed round the edges and somewhat rubbed. For an album of Ismaʿil's paintings, see Badri Atabai, *Fihrist-i muraqqaʿat-i kitābkhāneh-i Sultānī*, Tehran 1974, p. 386.

178
Sheet of decorated calligraphy

Signed *Ismāʿīl al-musawwir al-kātib Jalāʾir ibn al-marhūm Hāj Zamān Khān*

A quatrain from the *Gulistān* of Saʿdi (preface) in large and elegant *nastaʿlīq* calligraphy against a background very similar to the preceding. Domed buildings again occupy the upper plane, and below, among masses of roses and other plants, are various animals amongst which cats are prominent, with cows, sheep, camels, an elephant, and a giraffe. Human figures also appear, including a group of ladies round a samovar (a large oil-painting of this subject, also by Ismaʿil, is in the Victoria and Albert Museum) – one of them nursing a sheep – a leopard hunt, and a pair of wrestlers

65 × 48 cm

Iran, *c.* 1860

بلغ العلی بکماله
کشف الدجی بجماله
حسنت جمیع خصاله
صلوا علیه وآله

178

179
Sheet of decorated calligraphy

Plain black background with frame of arabesque floral scrolls in gold on red, a short piece of large and elegant *nasta'līq* calligraphy (verse by Hafiz), the letters and dots all minutely painted in grisaille with animals, birds, flowers, and landscape features
31.5 × 46.5 cm
Iran, second half 19th century

This style is known as *gulzār* (filled with flowers), and this example strongly recalls the work of Husayn *Zarīn-qalam* (golden pen) in the late 19th century.

179

180
Sheet of decorated calligraphy

Signed *Muhammad Ja'far Shīrāzī*
On blue ground, a dome-shaped design of faded gold filled with grisaille painting of nightingales and roses; four dark blue arabesque medallions with gold inscriptions (contemporary verses in praise of Imam Riza), the one in the centre with the name of Muzaffar al-Din Shah Qajar
57 × 33.5 cm
Iran, dated 1314/1897

181
Sheet of decorated calligraphy

Circular panel framed by a gold crescent and containing a religious inscription in fine *naskh* calligraphy; at the corners are oval medallions with the names of the first four Caliphs ('Umar, Abu Bakr, 'Uthman, and 'Ali), and a further religious inscription below; the whole against a gold background with coloured floral designs of European inspiration. Wide black margin with European scrollwork designs in gold and silver
59.3 × 44 cm
Turkey, dated 1290/1873

180

181

182
Official letter from the Crown Prince 'Abbas Mirza to Napoleon

Twenty-nine lines of *nasta'līq* script with illuminated heading of fine quality. Inscribed on reverse 'Lettre du Prince Abbas Mirza à S.M. Impériale, écrite a la fin de l'année 1808, et arrivée à Paris le 17 fevrier 1809'
120 × 58 cm
Sotheby's, 24 April 1979, lot 247
Iran, dated 1808

Prince 'Abbas (1789–1833) was the favourite son and heir apparent of the Qajar shah of Iran, Fath 'Ali Shah (r. 1797–1834). A gifted soldier and strategist, he employed various European military advisers and organized his army in Azerbaijan, where he was governor, along European lines. Towards the end of 1808, when he was nineteen, he wrote this letter to the French emperor Napoleon I; according to a note in French on the reverse, it arrived in Paris on February 17, 1809. Although it includes obvious references to Napoleon, his name as 'imperator' and a series of honorifics underlined in gold in the text, 'Abbas Mirza's name is not included, though it may be deduced from the text.

This is a particularly interesting document for the study of Franco-Persian diplomatic relations, for it was written at a crucial moment. Iran had been closed to the West since the fall of Isfahan and diplomatic contacts had really only begun again in the reign of Fath 'Ali Shah, with Great Britain, Russia and France playing the most active roles, each with their own set of interests to further.

Particularly important in this context are the Perso-Russian wars of the early 19th century, which centred on the control of Georgia and Azerbaijan. The Iranian military campaigns were conducted by the Crown Prince 'Abbas Mirza who had his capital at Tabriz.

Initially there had been a period of extensive exchange with France, initiated by Napoleon himself in 1805 and reaching its apogee in 1807 with the signing of the Treaty of Finkenstein and the despatch of the Gardane Mission to Iran. 'Abbas Mirza became very friendly with the young French officers of this mission who came to train the Iranian troops in modern methods of

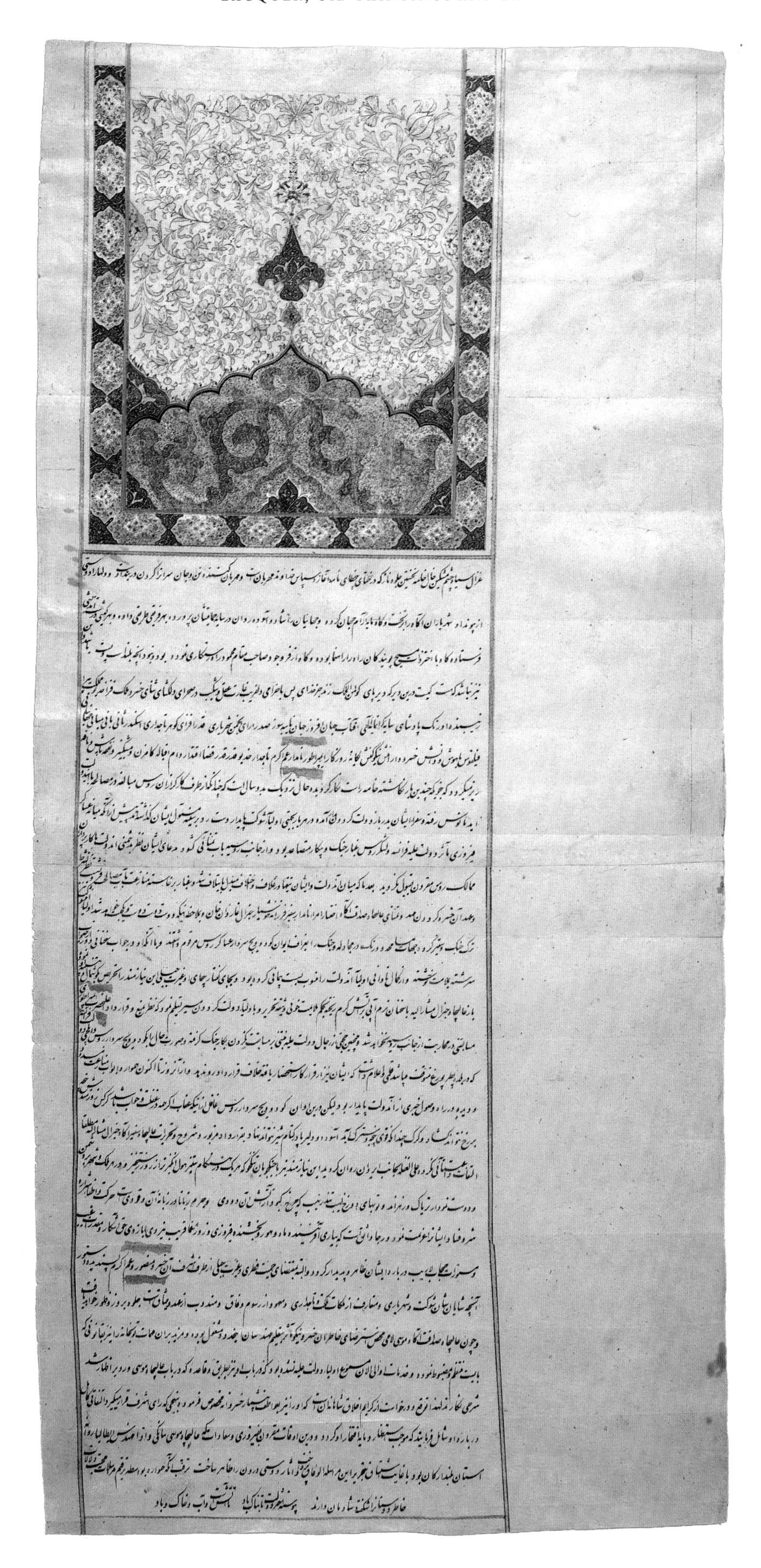

warfare and weapons. However, relations soon cooled due to political events in Europe, and Napoleon did an about face and concluded a new treaty with the Russians in July 1807, thereby betraying his Persian allies. In spite of 'Abbas Mirza's pro-French sympathies, Fath 'Ali Shah subsequently concluded a treaty with the British, even while the Gardane Mission was still in Iran. Their position made untenable by Napoleon's exercise in *realpolitik*, the members of the mission left Tehran on February 17 1809, stayed in Tabriz until March and then continued on to the frontier and their journey homeward.

The letter states, after a preamble of honorifics in Napoleon's favour, that in spite of a lack of news from him for two years (!) the writer is again writing to tell him of the situation with the Russians, particularly that General Goudovich had broken the treaty on numerous occasions, had marched on Erivan and that the writer had only been restrained from military retaliations by General Gardane. What does Napoleon plan to do about the situation? The writer concludes that he is still hopeful of his aid and that his troops are eager for battle. He also requests that Napoleon properly reward a certain 'Monsieur Lamy', teacher to his engineers and cannon makers, a reward that Napoleon had previously given to Monsieur Verdier, who had performed the same duties.

The letter was sent via Mr Bianchi, an Italian engineer travelling to France.

For further reading see: Borgomale (1920), pp. 131-135; Pakravan (1960); Bussé (1965) and (1982).

L.D.

183
Marriage contract

Thirty-seven lines of *nasta'līq* script, with finely illuminated heading and decorated border. The bridegroom was Firuz Mirza *Nusrat al-Dawla*, *Farmān Farmā*, sixteenth son of 'Abbas Mirza, and the bride was his cousin *Shahzādeh* Huma Khanum, daughter of Bahman Mirza *Bahā al-Dawla*, thirty-seventh son of Fath 'Ali Shah. The contract is dated 1270/1853, when the bridegroom was 35 years old
199.5 × 56.75 cm
Diba (1976), no. 18
Iran, Tehran, dated 1853

Late Iranian wedding contracts such as this now serve as a new and valuable source of information on the calligraphy and illumination of the period as known from *firmāns*, royal letters and decrees, and *tughrās*. Further, they serve as a written record of economic and social customs in 18th- and 19th-century Iran, as the earliest extant examples go back almost two hundred years. These contracts usually begin with references to the Qur'an or the Traditions of the Prophet, and then expound on the purpose of marriage, the social status and genealogy of the partners, the all-important 'virginal' attributes of the bride, and the details of the marriage settlement.

L.D.

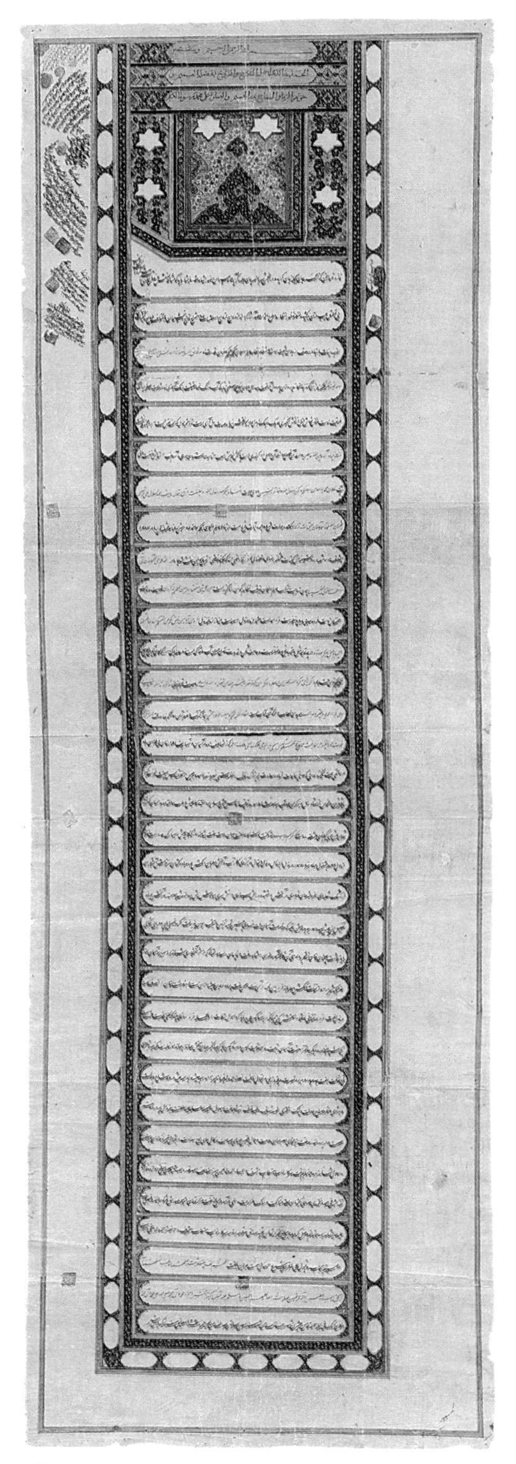

183

184
Oil-painting

Signed *Mirzā Bābā*
Niche form (arched top)
Shirin visiting Farhad as he works on Mount Behistun; she is mounted, and attended by an old nurse, a groom, and a hound; landscape with river, bridge, mountains and trees
145 × 88 cm
Iran, dated 1208/1794

This painting has considerable documentary interest, helping to show that Mirza Baba was in the service of the Qajar family before they obtained the crown. The main evidence is a drawing, formerly in the Pozzi Collection, signed by him and dated 'at Astarabad' 1203/1789.

185
Oil-painting

Attributable to Muhammad
Full-length figure of a court lady standing and partly draped in a black *chādur* with broad bands of gold embroidery, which opens in front to reveal voluminous trousers of striped floral pattern; with her left hand she coyly lifts her veil
145 × 81 cm
Iran, *c.* 1840

This artist, whose style, especially in his girls' faces, is very distinctive, has left us his name on a painting formerly in the Foroughi Collection, Tehran, with the punning invocation-signature *yā Muhammad* and the date 1258/1842.

186
Oil-painting
Attributable to Muhammad (see no. 185)
On tin-plate
Half-length portrait of a court lady holding a bunch of flowers
35.5 × 26 cm
Iran, *c.* 1840

187
Oil-painting
Yusuf (dressed as a young Qajar prince) embraced by his father Ya'qub in the presence of his brethren, grouped on either side
127 × 91 cm
Iran, mid-19th century

188
Portrait of Nasir al-Din Shah

Signed *Muhammad al-Husaynī Qājār*
Seated on a throne of chair-like form, with high decorated back
31.2 × 19 cm
Iran, dated 1265/1849

This portrait is the latest in a group, all very similar, and all signed by Muhammad al-Husayni, who sometimes adds *Sayyid* and *al-Imāmī* to his name. It is the only one dating from after Nasir al-Din's accession in 1848, the others being dated 1260/1845 (Grube, 1962, no. 124) and 1264/1847 (Sotheby's 4. iv. 1978, lot 83), when he was Crown Prince.

189
Portrait of Hajji Mirza Aqasi, chief minister of Muhammad Shah Qajar

Signed *Mirzā Bābā al-Husaynī*
Three-quarter length against a cloudy sky, wearing a white cloak over a coat of Kerman shawl, and holding a walking-stick
24.2 × 17.3 cm
Iran, dated 1262/1846

This portrait also exists in a number of versions. The original, formerly in the Stchoukine Collection, is said to have been by *Sāni' al-Mulk*. Mirza Baba al-Husayni (who must, of course, be carefully distinguished from his namesake at the beginning of the Qajar period – see no. 184) was a court painter to Nasir al-Din Shah. In the Churchill Album in the British Library (Or. 4938) are two works signed by him, one of them a portrait of the Shah, and an unsigned version of the present portrait. Hajji Mirza Aqasi seems to have been the worst type of corrupt vizier, 'ignorant and fanatical, his attitude to all foreigners being one of profound suspicion', as Sir Percy Sykes wrote. According to E.G. Browne he was 'incapable and crotchety', and a satirical poet wrote that he emptied the treasury to buy *qanāts* and guns; the former brought no water, the latter left Iran's enemies intact.

190

191

190

Portrait of Muhammad Yasir Khan *Aqasi-bashi*

Signed *Abū'l-Hasan naqqāsh-bāshī Kāshānī Ghaffārī*
Seated on a rich floral carpet against a wall; he is depicted as a middle-aged man with a full beard, wearing a long fur-trimmed coat of Kerman shawl, his hands joined in his lap, and a long silver-mounted stick on the ground before him
29.8 × 19.8 cm
Iran, dated 1273/1857

A good example of Abu'l-Hasan's genius for realistic portraiture. No particulars of the sitter are so far forthcoming.

191

Portrait

Unsigned, but attributable to *Sāni' al-Mulk*
A seated bearded minister, holding a rosary and with two rolled papers in his girdle; unfinished, apart from the head
30 × 20.5 cm
Formerly in the Rothschild Collection, Robinson (1976), no. 68
Iran, *c.* 1850-65

192

Portrait of Prince Sultan Husayn Mirza *Jalāl al-Dawla*

Signed *Mubārak ibn Muhammad al-Qājār*
Standing by a window holding a toy bow and arrow; he wears a tall lambskin cap, a fur-edged frock coat of Kerman shawl, and dark trousers; books and cushions are on the floor by him, one of the former inscribed with an exhortation to diligent study
27 × 20 cm
Iran, *c.* 1880

This prince was the eldest son of Prince Mus'ud Mirza *Zill al-Sultān*, the celebrated (or notorious) governor of Isfahan, and was born in 1868; he appears to be about twelve years old in this portrait – a true likeness, to judge from surviving photographs, though far from flattering, with its sallow complexion, blank stare, and sulky mouth. The artist was attached to the court of Nasir al-Din Shah, and this candid portrait is very much in the style of Abu'l-Hasan *Sāni' al-Mulk*.

192

193
Persian manuscript of Lutf 'Alī Beg's *Atashkadeh* (The fire-temple), biographies of poets

Text in cursive *nasta'līq*, verging on *shikasteh*, 25 lines to the page, the colophon signed *Mirzā Rahīm son of the late Mirzā Muhammad*, and dated 29 *Jumādā* II 1216/6 November 1801. Illuminated heading of good quality with marginal and interlinear decoration on the first opening, and one or two illuminated section-headings in the body of the volume, which consists of 265 folios. Painted lacquer covers of high quality, the outer surfaces with arabesque medallions and flowers, the doublures red with animals and birds among floral scrolls
29 × 19.5 cm (written surface 22 × 12.5 cm)
Sotheby's, 23 November 1976, lot 419
Iran, dated 1801

There are thirty miniature paintings in early Qajar style, incorporating some late Safavid elements of costume and landscape. Particulars are as follows:

f. 7 b Camp scene: seated prince offered drink by an attendant
f. 41 a Sultan Sanjar with attendants petitioned by the old woman
f. 52 a The three poets 'Unsuri, 'Asjadi and Farrukhi at the court of Sultan Mahmud of Ghazna. (The same three poets are depicted with Firdawsi in no. 40)
f. 67 b A mounted king addressed by an old man in a ruined village
f. 71 a Dervish displaying pearls(?) to an enthroned king
f. 74 a Shirin, mounted, encounters Farhad and his young assistant
f. 112 b Old man debauching a girl, watched by a maid from the doorway
f. 117 a Young huntsman shooting a large bird
f. 126 b Old man listening to a nightingale in a garden by night
f. 132 b Gardener pursuing a bird in a garden; buildings in the background
f. 136 a Peasant addressing a bearded man seated under a tree
f. 138 a Greybeard addressing another on the balcony of a building
f. 155 a Greybeard and four others in a bath-house

193 *Folio 126b*

193 *Folio 206b*

f. 164 b Shirin, mounted and attended, riding past a building
f. 169 a Majnun among the beasts; camp and palm-trees in the background
f. 170 a Majnun encounters Layla's wedding procession
f. 205 b Nadir Shah in battle with the Afghans
f. 206 a Nadir Shah in battle with the Turks
f. 206 b Nadir Shah enthroned, with his son and courtiers in attendance
f. 207 a Defeat of the Mughal army by Nadir Shah at the battle of Karnal
f. 208 a Another victory of Nadir Shah over the Turks
f. 241 a Aziz and three warriors approaching Zulaykha's tent enclosure
f. 242 b Yusuf rescued from the well by merchants
f. 243 a Yusuf being sold in the slave-market
f. 244 a Yusuf, keeping sheep, and Zulaykha in a mountainous landscape
f. 246 a Yusuf enthroned in a walled garden, and surrounded by Zulaykha's maids
f. 247 a Yusuf tempted by Zulaykha in the pavilion of love
f. 247 b Zulaykha and her maids overcome by the beauty of Yusuf
f. 250 a Yusuf, mounted and attended, encounters the aged Zulaykha (slight retouching on her hair and eyebrows)
f. 262 a Discussion between a youth and a bearded man in an interior

Illustrated copies of this work are rare. The fact that no less than five of the miniatures are devoted to Nadir Shah is probably due to the fact that the author was in the service of the Afshar family, and was actually in Meshed when Nadir returned from his Indian campaign. The *Atashkadeh* was compiled between 1760 and 1779.

194 *Doublure*

194 *Folio 17b*

194
Persian manuscript of *Farhād wa Shīrīn* by Wahshi and Wisal

A romantic poem on the theme made famous by Nizami, begun by Wahshi (d. 1583) and completed by Wisal (d. 1847)
Sixty-five folios, text in fine *shikasteh*, four columns (two outer ones written diagonally) to the page in the first part, and two columns in the second part; interlinear gilding throughout. Very fine and minute illumination on ff. 1b, 2a, and 19b, 20a, where Wisal's continuation begins. There are two colophons, both signed by Muhammad Karim, that on fol. 18b dated 8 *Safar* 1272/20 October 1855, and that on f. 65a *Dhū'l-hijja* 1260/December 1844; in the latter he names his patron as Aqa Mirza Muhammad 'Ali, whom it has not so far been possible to identify.
Finely painted lacquer covers: outer surfaces, Khusraw spies Shirin bathing, and Shirin visiting Farhad working on Mount Behistun; doublures, young Qajar prince and his falcon, and young lady in European costume
17 × 10.75 cm
Iran, dated 1844-55

The manuscript contains seven miniatures, of very good quality, by two different painters, in the Qajar style of the time; particulars are as follows:

- f. 17 b Farhad encounters Shirin, mounted and attended, in a landscape
- f. 29 b Farhad at work on his sculpture of Shirin; herdsmen and cattle
- f. 37 b Shirin, mounted and attended, at the rock where Farhad is at work
- f. 48 b Shirin drinking in a landscape with female companions
- f. 58 a Farhad shows Shirin his completed sculpture of her
- f. 62 a The poet Wisal and a pupil seated with books and writing materials before them
- f. 63 a A Qajar nobleman (probably the patron of the manuscript) seated on a terrace smoking; two ministers in attendance

This is an exquisite little manuscript in perfect condition. The second part (by Wisal) was copied during the poet's lifetime, so we may take the portrait on f. 62a as authentic.

195
Qur'an

Arabic manuscript on paper
Two hundred and sixty-eight folios, 15 lines to the page in clear *naskh* script. Rich and minute illumination covers ff. 1b, 2a (all the sura titles on star-shaped gold medallions), 3a, 3b, 4a
Textual adornment and illuminated sura-headings throughout
Covers of painted lacquer with central medallions, pendants, and corner-pieces; the medallions seem to have contained inscriptions which have been erased
28.5 × 17.5 cm (written surface 19 × 10 cm)
Iran, mid-19th century

196 *Cover*

196
Qur'an

Arabic manuscript on paper
Two hundred and sixty-seven folios interleaved throughout with tissue, 17 lines to the page in clear *naskh* script, the colophon signed *al-Haj Mīr 'Abd al-Karīm Muhammad Sādiq al-Husaynī al-Yazdī* and dated 1271/1854. Two double pages of magnificent illumination at the beginning, and textual and marginal decoration and illuminated sura-headings throughout. Covers of fine painted lacquer with floral and arabesque designs
29.2 × 19.1 cm
Iran, dated 1854

OLIVER WATSON

Ceramics

The art of ceramics was one of the major achievements of the Islamic world. From lowly kitchen and storage pots of the pre-Islamic period there developed wares which, in technical inventiveness and artistic creativity, can stand alongside any in the world. This achievement is little known or understood in the West, where connoisseurs of fine ceramics have looked continually to the Far East for the standards by which ceramics are to be judged. This is partly because Middle Eastern wares are much rarer in Europe than Chinese wares, which have been imported in enormous quantities since the 17th century. Furthermore, Islamic pots are often in poor condition, being made of soft earthenware bodies and being largely restored from fragments dug up on archaeological sites. Superficially they suffer by comparison with the brilliant and hard Chinese porcelains which have mostly survived in perfect condition. This unfair comparison hides the real value of Islamic pottery and detracts from its true achievement. The potentials offered by low-fired clay bodies and their appropriate glazes have nowhere else been developed and exploited as in the Middle East. By AD 1200 a range of decorative techniques had been invented which were unsurpassed anywhere in the world until the development of industrial production in 18th-century England. Nor elsewhere in ceramic history has colour and painted design been used to greater effect.

Many readers will be surprised to learn of the contribution made by Islamic potters to European and Chinese ceramics. The technique of painted tin-glazed pottery, which, under various names – Hispano-Moresque, Majolica, Delft and Faience – provided Europe with its luxury pottery for more than three centuries came from the Middle East. This technique was first seen in Mesopotamia in the 9th century (no. 197). Likewise, the technique of underglaze-painting, with blue cobalt pigment, was exported from the Middle East to China in the 14th century, and made possible China's most characteristic ware – blue-and-white porcelain; underglaze painting in blue was seen in Iran more than a century before its first use in China (no. 232). Use of bold colour is often seen as the particular hallmark of the Islamic potter, but perhaps even more important is the use of painted ornament and the design sense with which it was applied. Whether on a vase or a circular dish, whether of extreme simplicity (no. 197), monumental austerity (no. 205), of bewildering complexity (nos. 201 and 211), or of narrative intent (nos 229 and 231), such designs show a sense of proportion and rhythm that characterizes Islamic art as a whole. This does not mean, however, that the potters were unconcerned about the shapes of the vessels or about the quality and textures of glazes, as the monochrome wares amply illustrate (nos 220 and 222). In short, it is only with the hardness and brilliance of the Far Eastern stoneware and porcelain bodies and their glazes that the Islamic potter cannot compete. This deficiency, if deficiency it is, is compensated for by the soft warm texture of the tin glaze (nos 197-203), the brilliant colours of the lead-glazed earthenwares (nos 204-216) and the delicate luminous qualities of the fritwares (nos 220-224), and above all in the sure sense of design in the application of the decoration (nos 197 and 247).

The importance of Chinese influence on the development of Islamic pottery must not be underestimated, however; time and again it provided the initial stimulus from which Islamic potters developed their own skills. In order to simplify the complex history of an art form that developed over many centuries and in countries many hundreds of miles apart, we may divide this section into three periods, each starting from an inspiration given by imported wares. These three periods cover the 9th to the 17th centuries.

EARTHENWARE PERIOD: 9TH TO 12TH CENTURIES

Wares of this period may be divided into western wares, based on the tin-glazed pottery of Mesopotamia and Egypt, and eastern wares, based on the slip techniques of northern and eastern Iran.

It was the importing of white Chinese T'ang porcelains into the wealthy cities of the Abbasid empire that encouraged local potters to develop their wares from simple functional cooking and storage vessels into a luxury product. Since the clays suitable for making porcelain were not available in the Middle East, potters were obliged to develop a counterfeit porcelain in earthenware. This they did by covering a buff or yellow clay body with a glaze made opaque and white by the addition of a small quantity of tin oxide. This duplicated the look of the Chinese prototype but not its hardness nor 'ring'. By way of exchange it gained from the rich and luscious qualities of the tin glaze. The Islamic potter was not content to remain for long a mere copyist, and soon his natural inclination for colour and painted decoration became apparent. First to be adopted were painting in blue and the use of green splashes (nos 197 and 198), then lustre painting, an Islamic invention and characteristic technique *par excellence*. This method, an 'on-glaze' technique, allowed the painter complete freedom of his brush as he painted on the hard surface of the already fired glaze; the pigment was fixed in a second firing. The styles of painting owe nothing to China, though the bowl shapes are based on Chinese porcelain originals (nos 119–202 and 204). Lustre painting, a highly complex technique, seems to have been a monopoly held by a restricted group of potters who moved from country to country seeking more profitable markets as political conditions changed.

After lustre's initial phase in Mesopotamia in the 9th and 10th centuries (nos 199 and 200), the potters moved to Fatimid Egypt where the more naturalistic drawing reflects the Greco-Roman heritage of that country (nos 203 and 204). On the fall of the Fatimids in the late 12th century the potters moved their base once again, setting up kilns in Syria (no. 243) and Iran (nos 224-228), though by now using the frit body (see below) and no longer the tin-glazed earthenware. Lustre eventually even reached Spain.

The wares of the eastern provinces of Iran are the major exception in Islamic ceramics as they appear to have needed no Chinese stimulus and they show no Far-Eastern influence in technique or design. Certain splashed wares resemble those of T'ang China but this is fortuitous, for no authenticated Chinese pieces of this type have yet been found in Islamic lands (no. 216). Vessels were fashioned from a red clay which was then covered with a coating of white slip and a transparent lead glaze. In the 9th and 10th centuries the practice was to decorate with further coloured slips – often black alone, or in combination with red, brown and green (nos 205-215). Another technique which became more common in the 11th and 12th centuries was to cut back through the white slip to the darker red body beneath, giving incised or champlevé designs (nos 217 and 218). Colours which run in the glaze could be splashed on, or the glaze stained a uniform tone, usually green. Similar techniques were used in the Byzantine world, and in Syria in the 12th and 13th centuries (no. 242).

In these eastern wares one notices an almost contradictory aesthetic approach to decoration in wares which if not produced in the same workshops were certainly made in neighbouring ones. At one extreme are pieces relying for their impact on a minimum of decoration, often an inscription or calligraphic device (nos 205 and 206). These refined, intellectual, almost austere, designs, which as Arthur Lane remarked, 'hold the essence of Islam undiluted', are in marked contrast to the colourful, crowded and flamboyant wares shown in nos 211 and 215. Such a contrast is seen in many periods in Islamic pottery; for example between the 9-10th century blue-on-white bowl (no. 197) and the contemporary pieces decorated in lustre (nos 199 and 200), or between the later Iranian monochrome-glazed wares (nos 220-222) and the lustre and minai pieces from the same workshops (nos 224-231).

FRITWARE PERIOD: 12TH TO 13TH CENTURY

At some point in the 12th century a revolution occurred in ceramic technique; inspired yet again by Chinese porcelains. The imports of the 12th century, of Ding and Qingbai types, were no longer of the heavy construction of three centuries before. They were finely thrown, translucent and often decorated with subtle carving or moulding under a thin transparent glaze. These could not be imitated by means of the thick opaque tin glaze over a clay body. Instead the Islamic potters, led by the Iranians, revived an ancient Egyptian technique, in which an artificial body material was made up from ground quartz with a small admixture of white clay and glaze. This somewhat resembles the later European soft-paste porcelain body, and was covered with a thin transparent alkaline glaze. This 'frit' body was white, translucent when thin and capable of an extremely wide range of decorative techniques. As before, the potters at first contented themselves with copying more or less closely the Chinese originals (no. 220). Within half a century, however, we see a burst of creative energy unparalleled anywhere in the world until the rise of industrial pottery in 18th-century England. And indeed not until Wedgwood and the Staffordshire potteries was the range of decorative techniques to be surpassed, even in China. We find monochrome wares (nos 220-222), incised and carved wares (no. 223), wares with moulded and applied decoration, and with underglaze and overglaze painting (nos 229-233). No. 244, from the al-Sabah Collection, is an example of carved decoration under a coloured glaze. Lustre wares, naturally, still accounted for a large part of luxury wares (nos 224-227). We find modelling of small animal figures (no. 233) and of small pieces of furniture. The period sees the first extensive use of tiling in architectural decoration (nos 237 and 238). The most impressive products of this period are without doubt those in overglaze techniques – minai and *lajvardina* enamels and lustre – where the Islamic genius for design and colour is at its most striking. It is the invention of underglaze painting (nos 232 and 233), however, that was the most significant for the future history of ceramics, in China and Europe as much as in the Middle East. For the first time the potters were able to paint freely directly on the frit body under a protective layer of glaze. This technique did not have the disadvantages of the double-fired over-glazed lustre and enamel techniques which involved greater expense in fuel and labour and resulted in a more easily abraded decoration. Even more important, the new alkaline glaze on the frit body did not cause the pigments to run during the firing. In earlier lead-glazed wares the running of colours was inevitable and had to be used as a decorative technique (no. 216) or, where a precise pattern was desired, either thick coloured slips or the more viscous (and expensive) tin glaze were used. Both these techniques were clumsy and restrictive; in underglaze painting the potter's talent with a brush was the only restraint on his freedom of drawing or on the detail required.

14TH TO 17TH CENTURIES

In the last period, underglaze painting on a frit body became the dominant technique, and imported Chinese blue-and-white porcelains the predominant influence. Indeed the vogue for this imported ware was such that the Chinese collections in Istanbul in Turkey and Ardabil in Iran are still the most important of their kind. Shortage of material makes the history of Persian pottery unclear from the 14th to the 16th centuries, but when production started again on a large scale in the 17th century, most of the work was rather uninspired copying after Chinese models. Lustre however enjoyed a brief vogue (no. 250), and the charming 'Kubachi' wares (no. 249) are among the few types that owe little to the Chinese. The Turkish potters on the other hand, unlike the Iranian, were able to break away from dependence on Chinese models, probably because of a shortage of imported pieces for the potters to copy. The Iznik wares (nos 245-248) show vestiges of Chinese influence in the shape of the dishes and in the debased 'rock-and-wave' border, but the colourful floral patterns are amongst the most brilliant of all Islamic designs, and are a fitting culmination to the history of ceramics in the Middle East.

197
Bowl

Tin-glazed earthenware, with Kufic inscription in blue
Diameter 20 cm
Geneva (1981), no. 27
Mesopotamia, 9th–10th century

This bowl shows the first development of 'Islamic' ornament on a bowl which otherwise, in its shape and use of an opaque white glaze, is a close copy of an imported Chinese porcelain. The inscription, placed in startlingly dramatic position, presents problems in its reading. The first two words (*mimmā 'amilahu*) read 'made by . . .'. The last word appears to repeat the second, making no sense. It is possibly a calligraphic conceit, with the name 'Muhammad' disguised in the repetition. These wares give prominence to the name of the artist to a degree unprecedented in any other Islamic pottery, or indeed in artifacts in any other medium. Muhammad, if that be the potter's name, is known through several other surviving works e.g. Düsseldorf (1973), no. 25.

197

198
Dish

Tin-glazed earthenware, with decoration in blue and splashes of green glaze
Diameter 28 cm
Geneva (1981), no. 26
Mesopotamia, 9th–10th century

The motif in blue, divided into hatched and stippled areas is based on similar designs found in contemporary manuscript illumination and on stucco work. The green splashes are intentional but are not, as has been argued in the past, derived from Chinese T'ang splashed wares, no fragments of which have been identified with any certainty on Middle Eastern sites (cf. also no. 216). The shape of the dish, with its three little feet, owes nothing to China, but is a local form.

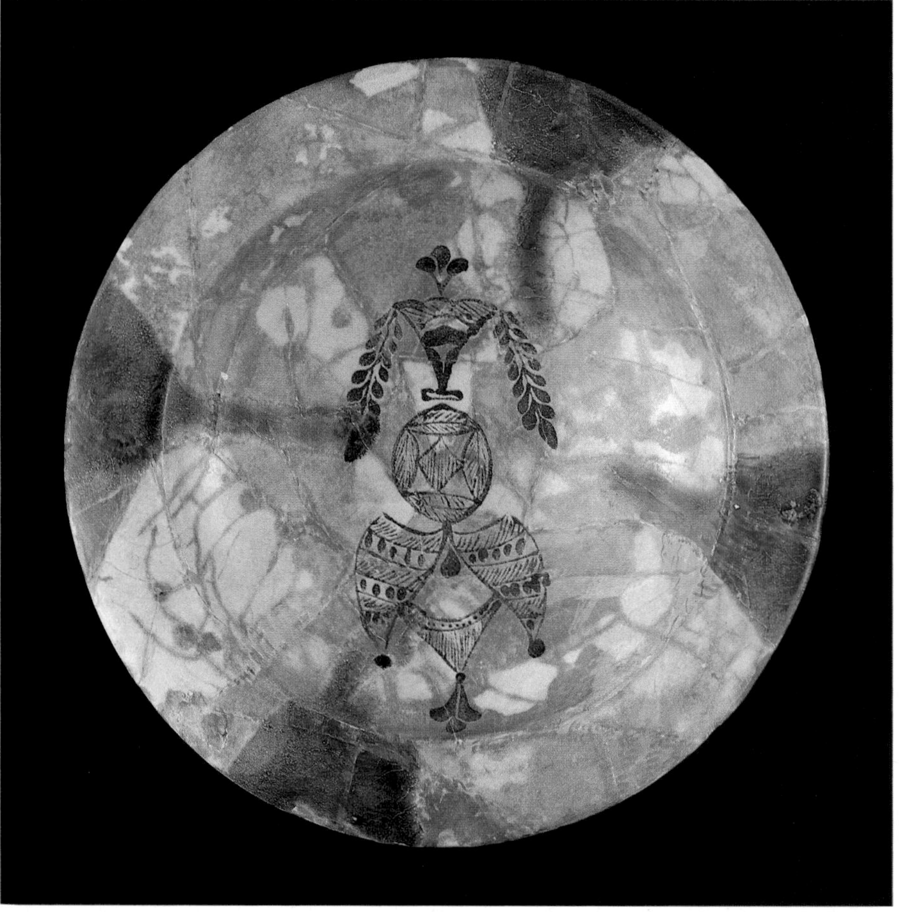

198

199
Bowl

Tin-glazed earthenware with decoration in lustre
Diameter 22 cm
London (1969), no. 21; Sotheby's, 10 October 1978, lot 1; Geneva (1981), no. 28
Mesopotamia, 10th century

This bird with leaf in beak is typical of the stylized designs of the lustre potters in 10th-century Mesopotamia. The source for the design must be sought in textiles, where birds in roundels are a favourite motif, and parallels may be found for the border design of roundels on a stippled ground. The inscription reads *baraka li-sahibihi* (blessing to the owner) and *'izz*(?) (glory). *Baraka* (blessing) is repeated on the base. The shape is an elegant adaptation of an imported Chinese porcelain.

200
Dish with bird

Tin-glazed earthenware with decoration in lustre
Diameter 23.5 cm
A. Welch (1972), vol. II, no. P.2
Mesopotamia, 10th century

This piece is closely related to no. 199 and may well have come from the same workshop. In addition to the bird and band of roundels, the wall of the dish shows alternately inverted 'lotus buds' on a stippled ground. These may have been inspired by similar forms on Iranian metalwork, where they often occur, for example, on the walls of mortars, cf. Melikian-Chirvani (1973), p. 18-19. This dish, like bowl no. 199, has *baraka* (blessing) on the base.

201
Dish with cruciform design

Tin-glazed earthenware with decoration in lustre
Diameter 21 cm
Sotheby's, 10 October 1978, lot 9; Geneva (1981), no. 30
Mesopotamia or Egypt, 10th century

This dish belongs to a group distinct from the main type of Mesopotamian lustres, typified by nos 199, 200 and 202. It is more heavily thrown, less subtle in profile and painted with a type of design not found on the more conventional pieces. It certainly comes from a different workshop, whose location has not been identified. The similarity of the foliate forms in the larger radiating panels to those found on later Fatimid lustre wares (cf. no. 203) suggests that it may be an early Egyptian piece.

202
Small bowl with figure and birds
Tin-glazed earthenware with decoration in lustre
Diameter 15 cm
Geneva (1981), no. 31
Mesopotamia, 10th century

The figure shows the same type of abstraction undergone by the birds in nos 199 and 200. The face, though a little restored, shows features also found on contemporary textiles – the staring wide eyes, the parallel lines for nose and mouth. The symbolism of the designs has never been clearly identified, and it may well be that they were purely decorative.

203
Bowl with hare
Tin-glazed earthenware with decoration in lustre
Diameter 19.5 cm
A. Welch (1972), vol. IV no. P.60
Egypt (Fatimid period), 11th century

While the lustre technique must have come from Mesopotamia to Egypt some time in the 10th century, it is used in a completely new way. The naturalistic drawing of the hare, which contrasts strongly with the Mesopotamian style (cf. nos 199, 200 and 202), is the heritage of Egypt's classical past. The heavily potted, often inelegant, shapes and careless finish in turning and glazing are amply compensated for by the skill in design and exuberance in drawing.

204
Rim sherd of a bowl with man's face

Tin-glazed earthenware with decoration in lustre
8 × 11 cm
Geneva (1981), no. 34
Egypt (Fatimid period), 11th century

Complete Fatimid lustre pots are extremely rare. Most of our knowledge of them derives from the finds of thousands of sherds on the site of Fustat (old Cairo), capital of Egypt up to its destruction in the 12th century at which time the populace moved to new Cairo. However, even a small sherd such as this, shows something of the potters' skill in drawing. The persistence of this style of drawing is remarkable, for it can be traced back many centuries to the pre-Islamic era.

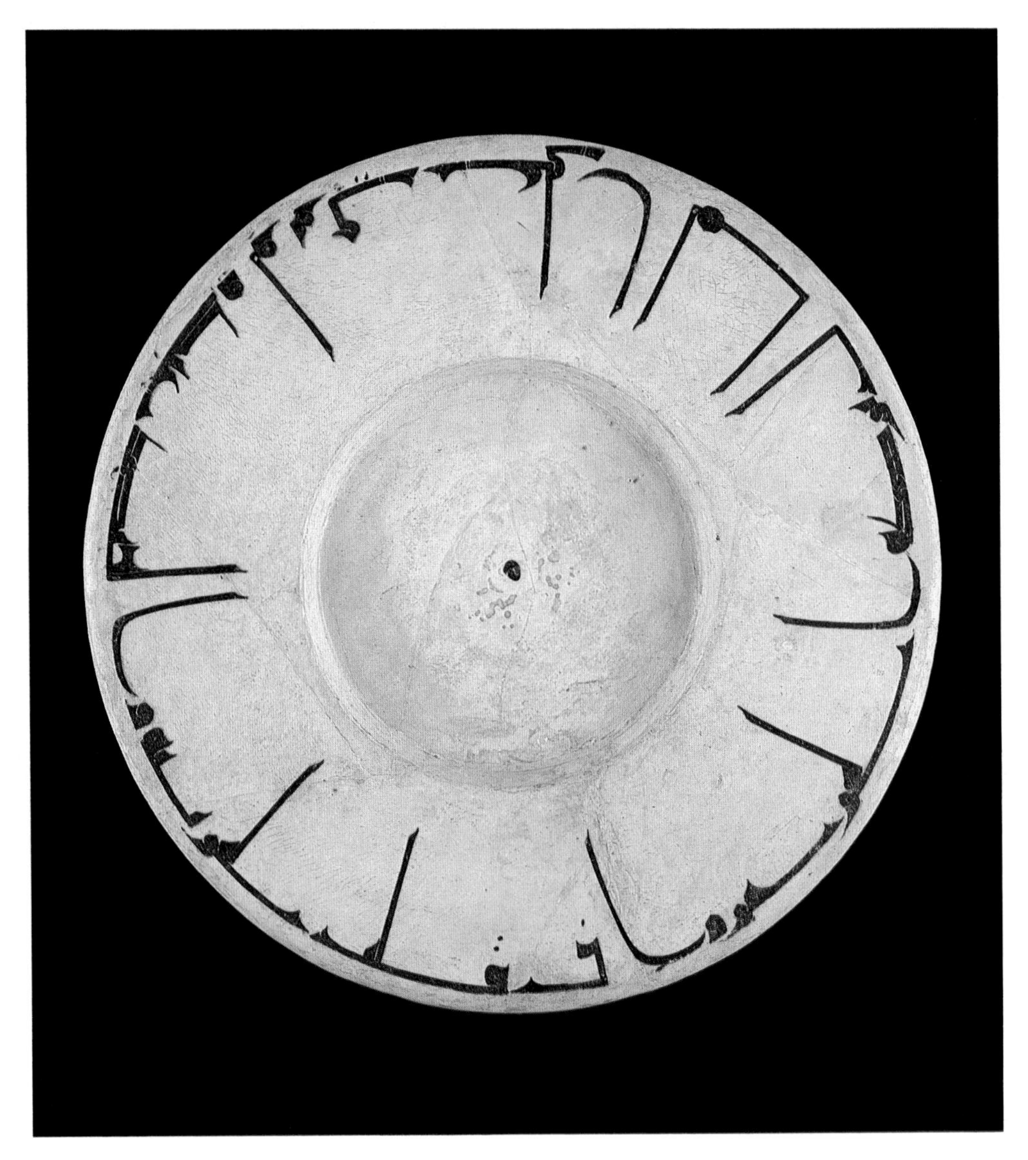

205
Dish with calligraphy

Earthenware with white slip covering and decoration in black slip under a transparent glaze
Diameter 36.5 cm
East Iran or Transoxiana, 10th century

Though simple in technique, the epigraphic wares of the Samanid period in eastern Iran are probably the most refined and striking of all Iranian pottery. At their simplest as well as at their most sophisticated, they rely on the beauty of the script alone. One scholar has commented that 'their beauty is of the highest intellectual order; they hold the essence of Islam undiluted'. The inscriptions, with distortions of letters and absence of pointing are often, as in this case, difficult to read. They usually contain aphorisms and proverbs. Surprisingly, religious inscriptions are almost never encountered, and no signed or dated piece is known.

206
Dish with calligraphy

Earthenware with white slip covering and decoration in black slip under a transparent glaze
Diameter 30 cm
East Iran or Transoxiana, 10th century

Although smaller than no. 205 this calligraphy is perhaps even finer in its sense of rhythm and balance. The inscription, somewhat unusually, is a list of conventional blessings: *al-yumn al-baraka al-salama* (one word illegible) (Good fortune, blessing, well-being . . .). The shape of this plate and that of no. 205 suggests they were intended for display.

207
Bowl with foliated calligraphy

Earthenware with white slip covering and decoration in black and red slip under a transparent glaze
Diameter 27.5 cm
East Iran or Transoxiana, 10th century

The calligraphy here is more ornate than in nos 205 and 206. The adding of foliate sprays and the knotting of certain letters render the inscription even more difficult to interpret. These calligraphic embellishments follow developments in script on monumental inscriptions and coins. The red slip is used for decorative effect, not to stress important parts of the inscription.

208
Bowl with foliated calligraphy

Earthenware with white slip covering and decoration in black slip under a transparent glaze
Diameter 26 cm
Geneva (1984), no. 2
East Iran or Transoxiana, 10th century

So similar is this piece to no. 207 in shape, size and in particular in calligraphic style, that they may reasonably be assigned to the same workshop. Nishapur and Afrasiyab (near Samarkand) appear to have been the main centres of production of the eastern slipwares, but the attribution of the more sophisticated types is not established conclusively. The inscription reads: *al-jūd min akhlāq ahl al-jinna* (Generosity (is) characteristic of the people of paradise), typical of the sentiment of the inscriptions on these wares.

209
Bowl with large calligraphy

Earthenware with white slip covering and decoration in black and red slip under a transparent glaze
Diameter 34.8 cm
East Iran or Transoxiana, 10th century

In striking contrast to the refined and sensitive calligraphy on nos 205–208, this piece relies for its impact on a bold and forceful script, almost too monumental in scale for the piece it decorates. The inscription is the same as that on no. 208.

210
Bowl with bird

Earthenware with white slip covering and decoration in black slip under a transparent glaze
Diameter 32 cm
East Iran or Transoxiana, 10th century

Though made in the same workshop or area as the calligraphic pieces, this bowl is a simpler, and no doubt cheaper, product. Nevertheless, it shows a quite outstanding mastery of design, in the off-centre positioning of the bird, and the sure, calligraphic handling of the drawing.

211
Dish with palmette decoration

Earthenware with white slip covering and decoration in black, red, green and white slips under a transparent glaze
Diameter 36.8 cm
Welch (1972), vol. II, no. P.3; Geneva (1981), no. 7
East Iran or Transoxiana, 10th century

In shape and technique, this dish relates closely to the more restrained wares illustrated by nos 205 to 210. The colourful and lively decoration, however, offers a complete contrast in decorative style, perhaps reflecting a more popular taste. The limitations of painting in the somewhat intractable thick coloured slips is revealed by the rather stiff drawing.

212

Bowl with seated figure

Earthenware with white slip covering and decoration in green slip under a transparent glaze
Diameter 25 cm
Geneva (1984), no. 16
East Iran or Transoxiana, 10th century

This piece is a remarkable example of a rare type of slip ware. In its design, colour and many other details, it shows itself to be an imitation of an imported Mesopotamian lustre bowl (cf. nos 199, 200 and 202). The half-moon border, the birds with leaf in beak, the stippled contour panels in the background, the cross-legged figure holding a goblet, the peacock-eye motif of the man's dress, the drawing of the features of his face, the design on the reverse and the word *baraka* (blessing) on the base – all these are copied faithfully from a Mesopotamian original. Though the potters of eastern Iran and the Samarkand area were second to none in their artistic skill, they did not have the technical expertise to produce real lustre ware, which was much imported from other Islamic centres and which is imitated in this piece in the simpler slip-painting method. The design may simply show a princely figure, or the two 'eye' motifs in his head-dress may indicate that this is a representation of the mythical Iranian tyrant Zahhak, who had snakes growing from his shoulders which had to be fed on human brains. The most famous version of this story was included in Firdawsi's *Shāhnāmeh* composed during the late 10th – early 11th centuries, which may indicate a later date for this bowl.

213
Bowl with bird

Earthenware with black slip covering and decoration in white slip under a transparent glaze
Diameter 22.5 cm
Geneva (1981), no. 2
East Iran or Transoxiana, 10th century

A striking example of a simpler type of eastern slipware, in which the normal slip colours have been reversed. The drawing of the bird is in marked contrast to the more usual calligraphic style typified by no. 210, and may derive ultimately from Mesopotamian lustreware. The peacock-eye motif and the half-moon border support such a derivation, as does the smooth contoured shape of the bowl.

214
Bowl with bird

Earthenware with white slip covering and decoration in black slip under a transparent glaze
Diameter 23 cm
Iran, Nishapur, 10th century

This ware was named 'ware with yellow-staining black' by the excavators at Nishapur where quantities were found, see Wilkinson (1973). The name derives from the fact that to one of the black slips has been intentionally added a chrome compound which, during firing, stains the surrounding glaze a yellow colour. In this piece the yellow-staining black is used for contour panels around the stylized figure of the bird, depicted in the normal black pigment.

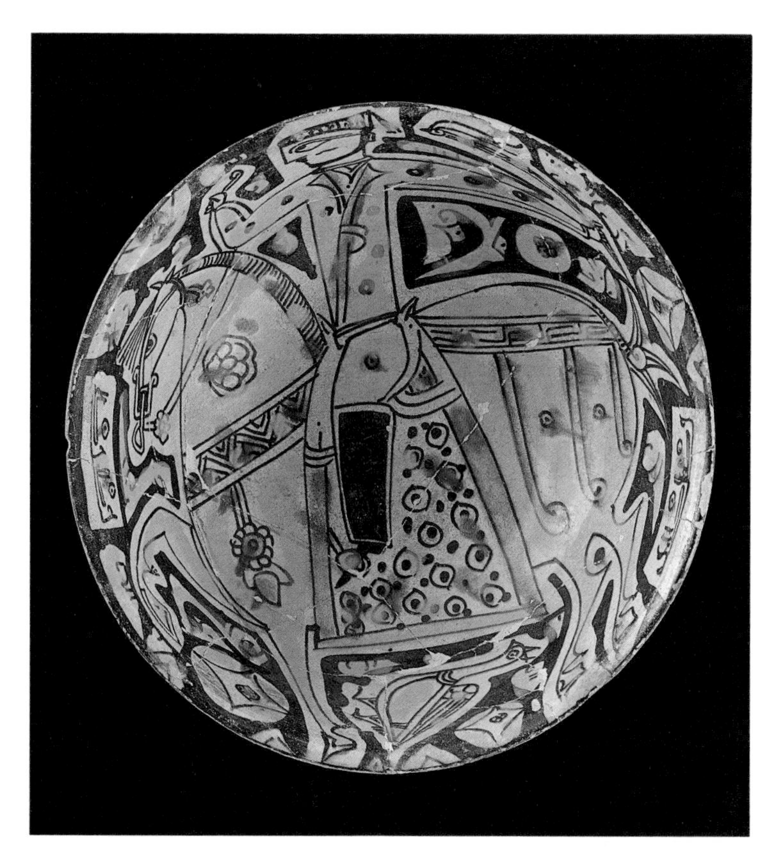

215
Bowl with horserider

Earthenware painted in black, yellow and green slip and pigments under a transparent glaze
Diameter 22.2 cm
Welch (1972), vol. II, no. P.16; Geneva (1981), no. 16
Iran, Nishapur, 10th century

This type of ware was named 'Buff ware' by the excavators at Nishapur, where large quantities were found, see Wilkinson (1973). The pigments are painted directly onto the buff-coloured clay body without any intervening white slip. The bright colour, in which a strong yellow predominates, and the cluttered, strongly stylized decoration mark an extreme contrast with the epigraphic wares (nos 205-209) which were nevertheless made in the same area and at the same period. The buff wares appear unsophisticated, even slightly vulgar, by comparison. The curious stylized drawing is the potters' own invention, and shows an anxious desire to fill the entire space.

216
Bowl

Earthenware with white slip covering and scratched decoration, under transparent glaze with splashes of green and brown
Diameter 30 cm
Geneva (1981), no. 14
Iran, Nishapur, 11th century

Incised wares with colours flowing in the glaze were a staple of potters throughout the Islamic world from the 11th to 13th centuries. They were at one time thought to have been influenced by T'ang splashed wares, but no well-authenticated Chinese fragment has yet been found in the Middle East (cf. also no. 198). The effect is almost inevitable when pigments are used with a lead glaze, which tends to flow greatly during firing. In this piece there has been a moderately successful attempt to confine the colours to parts of the incised pattern. The streaks of colour show that the piece was fired upside-down.

217
Bowl with animals

Earthenware with white slip covering and incised decoration under a transparent glaze, the rim stained green
Diameter 18 cm
Previously in the collection of Charles Vignier
Geneva (1981), no. 23
Iran, 11th – 12th century

This type of slipware, with incised decoration of animals in roundels on the characteristic hatched ground, appears to be confined to the central part of Iran, and has been attributed by some authorities to the city of Rayy. The decoration derives, though not closely, from simple types of incised metalwork.

218
Circular plaque

Earthenware with white slip covering and carved decoration under a transparent green glaze
Diameter 33.7 cm
A. Welch (1972), vol. II, no. P.22
Iran, 'Garrus' ware, 12th century

This plaque was probably originally intended as a border for a window opening. Bowls and dishes occur most commonly in this style, though other plaques and tiles are known. Designs often include rather fantastic figures, but the technique is characterized by the removal of large areas of the slip covering from the background to the design – frequently described as champlevé. They have been attributed, on no sound evidence, to Garrus in North-west Iran.

219
Bowl with bird

Earthenware with white slip covering and decoration in black, green, two shades of brown, and white slip under a transparent glaze
Diameter 19.5cm
Geneva (1981), no. 37; Geneva (1984), no. 23
Iran, 'Sari' ware, 12th century

'Sari' wares are one of the last manifestations of the Eastern slipware tradition. The technique is identical to the 10th-century wares (cf. especially no. 211) but they are identifiable by characteristic designs and motifs. This bowl shows the most typical design of a bird surrounded by flower motifs, with details picked out in white spots. The attribution to Sari in northern Iran is almost certainly wrong, for wasters of this ware are reported slightly further east at Gunbad-i Qabus.

220
Deep bowl

Fritware with carved decoration under an opaque white glaze
Diameter 17.7cm
Geneva (1981), no. 61; Geneva (1984), no. 12
Iran, probably Kashan, late 12th century

This bowl is already Islamic in form, taking its shape from examples in metalwork, but with its white body, white glaze and carved decoration of petal panels shows its initial inspiration in Chinese porcelains. A drop of turquoise glaze inside the bowl fell from another piece in the same kiln during firing.

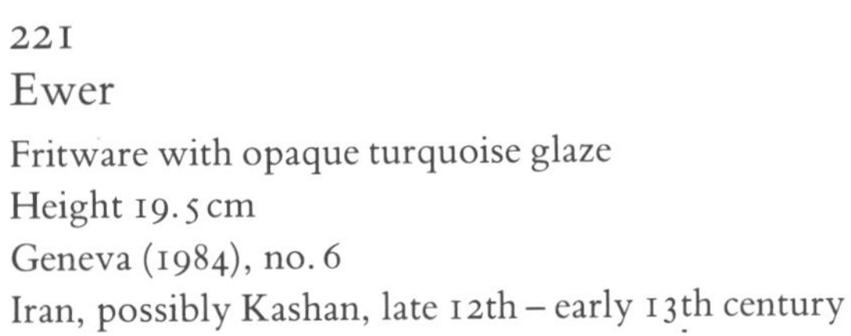

221
Ewer

Fritware with opaque turquoise glaze
Height 19.5 cm
Geneva (1984), no. 6
Iran, possibly Kashan, late 12th – early 13th century

Potters working in fritware mainly produced wares with monochrome glazes. Turquoise was the most popular colour, largely no doubt because of the cheapness of the colouring agent – copper oxide – and also because of the lucky associations which the colour, and the semi-precious stone to which it was compared, was deemed to have. This simple shape, with slight facettings, was probably inspired by forms in glass.

222
Jug

Fritware with opaque turquoise glaze
Height 14.7 cm
Geneva (1984), no. 7
Iran, possibly Kashan, late 12th – early 13th century

So close is the shape of the body of this jug to the ewer, no. 221, that it must have been made in the same workshop. We cannot tell where the workshop was situated, for, by 1200, simple fritwares were being made in a large number of centres throughout Iran. The major centre which produced the best works was Kashan in central Iran. The 'mass produced' nature of this pottery is shown by the fact that a chip on the rim of this piece has not led to its being discarded, but has simply been glazed over.

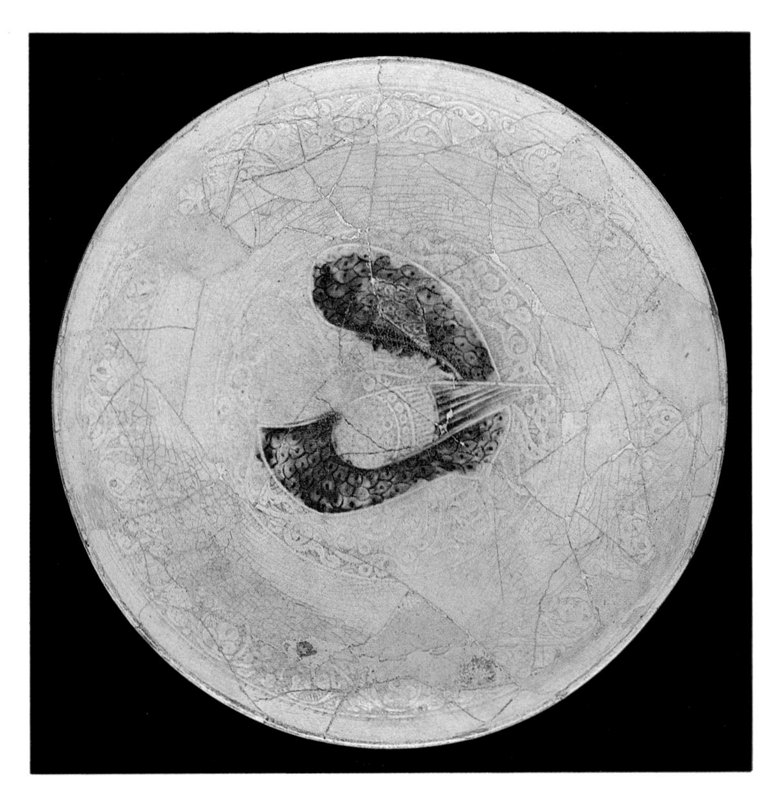

223
Dish with bird

Fritware with carved decoration and blue colouring under a transparent glaze
Diameter 35.5 cm
A. Welch (1972), vol. II, no. P.43; Geneva (1981), no. 55
Iran, probably Kashan, late 12th century

The subtle carved decoration on a white dish such as this was originally inspired by carved Chinese porcelains. The adding of the colour is an Islamic innovation, and the carved decoration shows one of the varied methods used by Iranian potters to fix colour under the glaze in the years immediately preceding the discovery of true underglaze painting (cf. no. 232). The bird is a more sophisticated version of an age-old motif, cf. nos 199, 210, 217 and 219.

224 *(overleaf)*
Bowl with seated figure

Fritware with opaque white glaze and decoration in lustre
Diameter 15 cm
Geneva (1984), no. 26
Iran, Kashan, painted in the 'monumental' style, last quarter of the 12th century

The 'monumental' style of lustre painting in Iran derives from Egyptian Fatimid styles. Characteristic of this style is the naturalistic drawing (cf. no. 204), the design shown in reserve on a lustre ground, and the 'fruit' (?) floating in space. The motif of the cross-legged figure holding a cup (here probably of glass) is one that came into the Middle East from Central Asia in early Islamic times. Its specifically royal connotation in Central Asia had probably been lost by the 12th century, and the image may conjure up nothing more precise than the 'good life'. Though a modest piece in size, this bowl shows that the lustre painters were artists of considerable talent, and that their work matches painting in any other medium of the period.

225 *(overleaf)*
Bowl with two seated figures

Fritware with opaque white glaze and decoration in lustre
Diameter 22 cm
Geneva (1984), no. 29
Iran, painted in the 'Kashan' style, dated *Rabī' al-Ākhir* [6] 10/ August 1213

The 'Kashan' style developed out of the 'monumental' style (cf. no. 224) about the year 1200. It is characterized by the patterning of the whole surface with painted or scratched detail, and a greater use of inscriptions to divide the surface into panels and friezes. The inscriptions are usually love poems bewailing ill-treatment by or separation from the loved one. They may have been composed by the potters for they are in general not of high literary quality. There is some evidence that the images and the inscriptions should be interpreted in a Sufi mystic fashion (cf. no. 238). This piece illustrates the very high technical quality achieved by the Kashan potters, even on unambitious pieces. Dated pieces in the Kashan style are numerous between 598/1202 and 616/1219 when the Mongol invasions caused a major break in production (cf. no. 235).

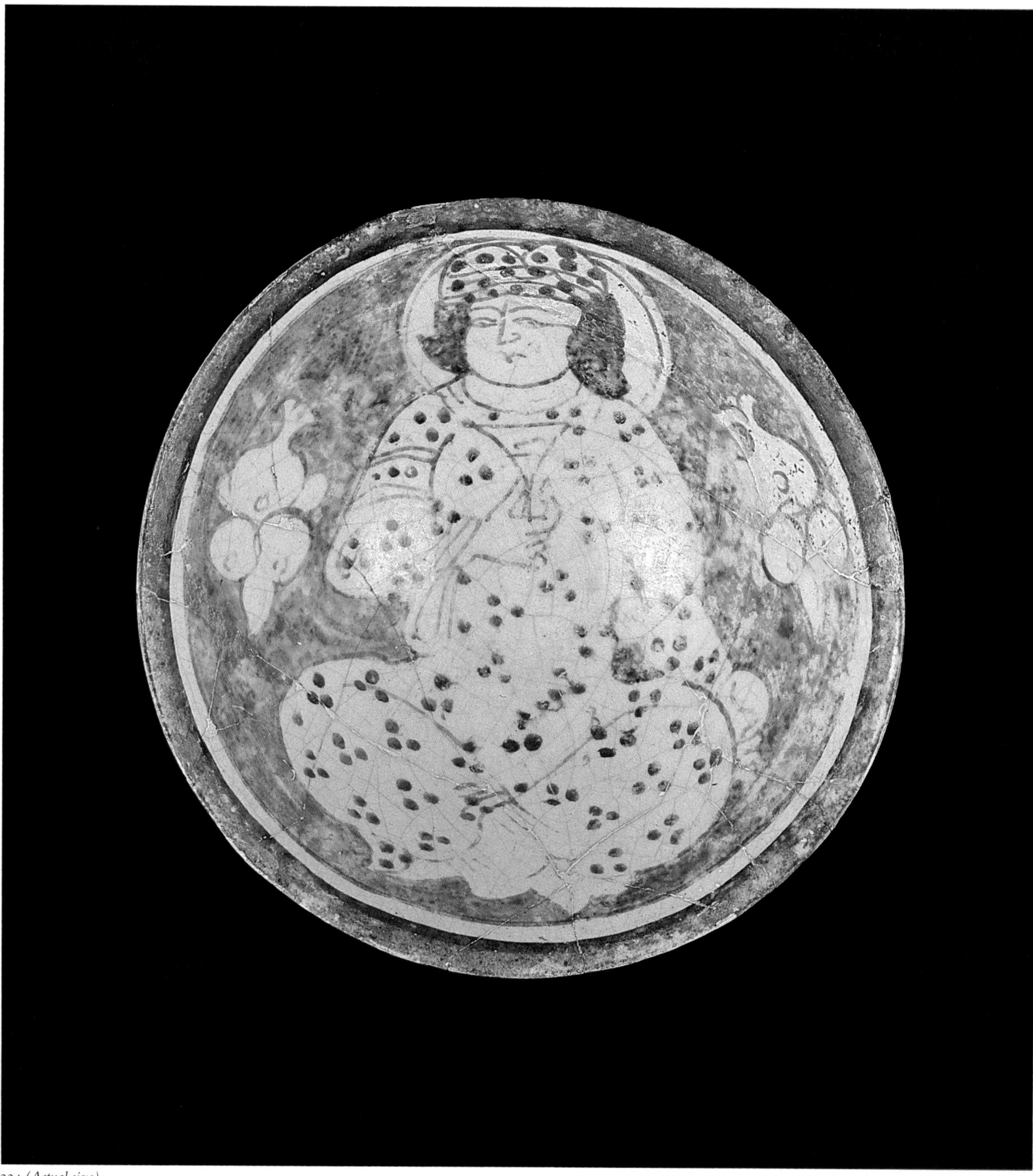

224 *(Actual size)*

225

226
Dish with scalloped rim

Fritware with an opaque white glaze and decoration in lustre
Diameter 27 cm
A. Welch (1972), vol. IV, no. P.69
Iran, painted in the 'Kashan' style, early 13th century

The shape is taken from a metal bowl, but the designs are very characteristic of the Kashan style of lustre painting. The rather repetitive design and sketchy treatment is compensated for by the brilliance of the lustre. The inscriptions here are largely illegible.

227
Deep bowl with lobed sides

Fritware with an opaque white glaze and decoration in lustre
Diameter 16.2 cm
A. Welch (1972), vol. IV, no. P.65
Iran, Kashan, painted in the 'miniature' style, late 12th century

This bowl is based loosely on a metal form and is decorated in a variant of the 'miniature' style, of which here a characteristic hatched lozenge flanked by broad leaves is seen. Pieces in perfect condition such as this are often attributed to Gurgan in North-east Iran (modern Gunbad-i Qabus) where several hundred pieces, all in perfect condition, were discovered during World War II packed into large jars. This was taken by some scholars as evidence that they were made there, but recent research considers them to be the stock of a merchant trading in the area who had imported them from Kashan, a centre that held a monopoly of lustre production in Iran at this period.

226

227

228
Bowl with figures in cartouches

Fritware with painting in blue, purple and green in an opaque white glaze and decoration in lustre, and black and red enamels
Diameter 29.2 cm
A. Welch (1972), vol. II, no. P.41; Geneva (1981), no. 76
Iran, Kashan, late 12th – early 13th century

The lustre technique is often found with in-glaze painting of blue and turquoise, but only very rarely with overglaze minai enamels. This is surprising for we know that both wares were made at Kashan by the same potters, and the few pieces that do exist, like this bowl, show how splendid the combination of colours could be. It may be that the firing schedules and temperatures of the two techniques were difficult to match, making the combination uncertain of success.

229
Bowl with camel riders

Fritware with painting in blue, turquoise and purple in an opaque white glaze and decoration in red and black enamels
Diameter 12 cm
A. Welch (1972), vol. IV, P.64; Geneva (1981), no. 79
Iran, Kashan, minai ware, late 12th – early 13th century

This small bowl is a masterpiece of the minai potters' art. The scene, in brilliant polychromy, shows an episode from Firdawsi's *Shāhnāmeh*. Bahram Gur, the renowned hunter-king, has taken his favourite Greek slave harpist Azadeh out hunting. She asks him, amongst other feats, to pin the rear leg of a gazelle to its head, if he wants to impress her as a marksman. The King is shown about to accomplish the feat having caused with his first arrow the gazelle to scratch itself. The story ends unhappily for Azadeh, as she declares such skill to be demonic, and Bahram, in a fury, crushes her to death under the camel's hoofs. This bowl, and a handful of pieces with other *Shāhnāmeh* scenes are the earliest illustrations to the epic, predating by more than a century the earliest known manuscript illustrations.

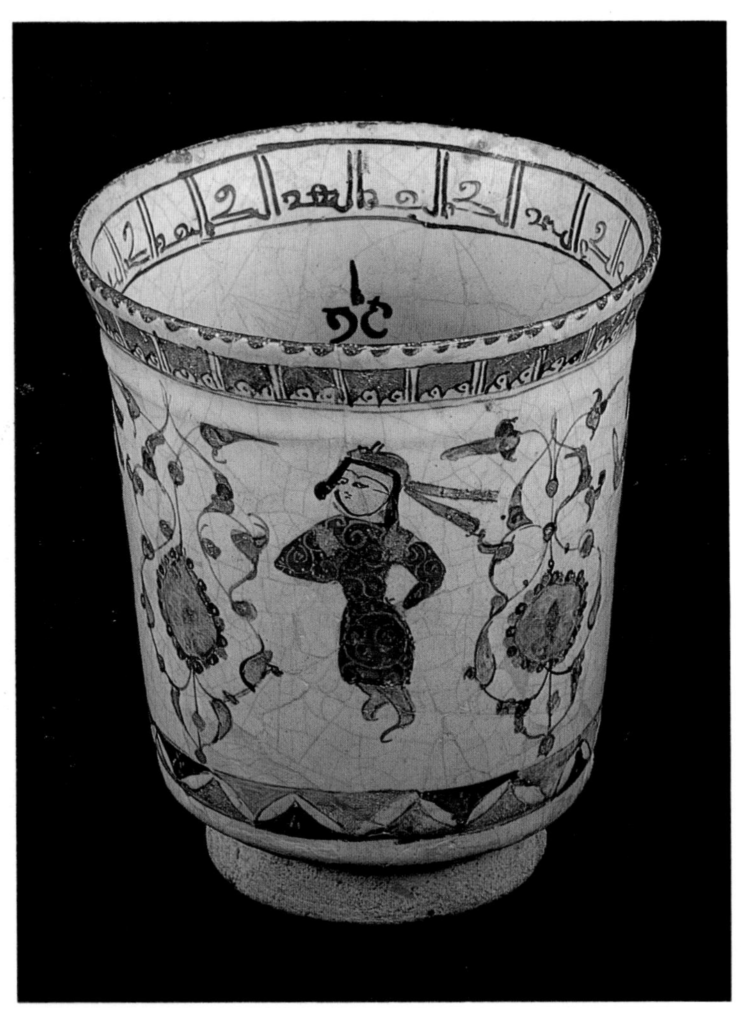

230
Goblet with figures

Fritware with opaque white glaze and inglaze and enamel colours and leaf gilding
Height 12.5 cm
A. Welch (1972), vol. II, no. P.42; Geneva (1981), no. 77
Iran, Kashan, minai ware, late 12th – early 13th century

The goblet is one of a variety of forms decorated in the minai technique. Minai and lustre were always expensive wares, requiring two firings and expensive ingredients, and their decoration, even when simple, is of no mean quality.

231
Bowl with figure on a bull

Fritware, painted with colours in an opaque turquoise glaze and decorated with overglaze enamel and leaf gilding
Diameter 22 cm
Geneva (1984), no. 25
Iran, Kashan, by Abu Zayd, 582-3/1186-7

This bowl, though restored and somewhat repainted, is important for several reasons. Firstly it belongs to a small group of bowls signed by the potter Abu Zayd and dated 582 and 583/1186-7. On this bowl only the beginning of the date survives, but the handwriting is distinctive enough to make the attribution certain. Abu Zayd later in his life is largely responsible for the development of the Kashan style in lustre painting (cf. no. 225) and is a dominant figure in the Kashan potteries. These bowls, though artistically and technically extremely accomplished, must have been done at the start of his career. His latest dated work is 616/1219, some thirty-three years later. The bowl is also interesting for the scene it depicts which appears to be yet another scene from the *Shāhnāmeh* or other epic. The figure on the bull leads a prisoner. In all but detail it follows the iconography of the capture of the tyrant Zahhak by Faridun (see Grube (1976), no. 142), but does not show either Faridun's bull-headed mace, nor Zahhak's shoulder snakes (cf. no. 212). The use of a deep turquoise ground and leaf gilding at this early date is unusual and interesting.

231

232
Dish with radial panels

Fritware with blue-and-black painting under a transparent glaze
Diameter 33.5 cm
Geneva (1981), no. 70
Iran, Kashan, early 13th century

This dish represents the most important technical achievement of the Kashan potters, and one that was to alter ceramic decoration world-wide in years to come. The underglaze-painting technique required a glaze stable enough to prevent the pattern from blurring during firing without resorting to the clumsy slip pigments (cf. nos 205-214) or the opaque tin glaze (cf. nos 197 and 198). The black pigment in this dish is absolutely stable, the only restriction in fluency of style or in fineness of detail being the potters skill with a brush. The blue tends to flow slightly. The use of underglaze blue is very important, for it occurs here in Kashan a full century before its first recorded use in China.

It was from Kashan that the underglaze technique and the cobalt for the pigment were exported to China, where it was so greatly exploited on blue-and-white porcelains. This dish, with its radial panels and half-palmette motifs, is typical of Kashan production in the years immediately preceding the Mongol invasions in the 1220s.

233
Figure of a bull
Fritware with decoration in black under a transparent turquoise glaze
Height 14 cm
A. Welch (1972), vol. IV, no. P.67; Geneva (1981), no. 57
Iran, probably Kashan, early 13th century

Monumental sculpture is virtually non-existent in the Islamic world, yet there was always a tradition of small-scale modelling, the religious prohibition notwithstanding. In the late 12th and early 13th centuries, the Kashan potters developed quite a diverse range of models, in various decorative techniques. The bull figure was perhaps the most popular, along with a seated lion. Human figures exist but are much rarer. All the figures appear to have some function; this piece is an aquamanile, that pours through the animal's snout, and is filled by the spout on the back. The choice of bull and lion may have astrological significance as Taurus and Leo are benevolent zodiacal signs and the domicilia of the benevolent planets Venus and the Sun.

234
Bowl with cruciform device
Fritware with inglaze and enamel colours and leaf gilding
Diameter 17.5 cm
A. Welch (1972), vol. IV, no. P.72; Geneva (1981), no. 82
Iran, probably Kashan, *lajvardina* ware, late 13th century

This bowl and the two following pieces are typical of the wares produced in Iran after the Mongol invasions. For some forty years after the initial onslaught in 1220 virtually nothing was made, but production picked up in the second half of the century. The light-hearted minai wares had gone, to be replaced by the more severely formal *lajvardina* wares. These are so called after the deep blue glaze that characterized most of them (*lajvard* meaning lapis lazuli). This piece is unusual in the blue colour being restricted to the central cross. The small scrolling motif in enamel and the leaf gilding cut in squares are typical of the whole group.

235
Bowl with radial panels

Fritware with blue painting in an opaque white glaze and decoration in lustre
Diameter 22 cm
Previously in the Demotte Collection
A. Welch (1972), vol. II, no. P.38; Geneva (1981), no. 86
Iran, Kashan, late 13th century

This heavy and sombre form of decoration sets the Mongol lustre wares apart from those of the pre-Mongol period (cf. nos 224 and 225). The shape of this bowl is taken from imported Chinese celadons, which arrived in large numbers, thanks to the opening of the trade routes between China and the Middle East, now ruled by related Mongol families. Lustre vessels formed a small part of the output of the lustre potters, who concentrated in this period on tiles (cf. nos 237 and 238). Dates are rare on the vessels, but occur between 660/1261 and 683/1284, indicating a break in production of some forty years from the invasions of 1220 (cf. no. 225).

236
Bowl with floral design

Fritware with grey slip covering and decoration in white slip and black pigment under a transparent glaze
Diameter 17.8 cm
A. Welch (1972), vol. II, no. P.57; Geneva (1981), no. 87
Iran, Kashan, 'Sultanabad' ware, late 13th century

The use of raised slip is a curious reversion to a much earlier technique, but its reason lies more in the desire to model the surface than to fix the pigments, which could by now be achieved (cf. no. 232). The sombre colouring and crowded pattern is typical of the Mongol wares. The four lotus flowers hidden amongst the foliage give evidence of Chinese influence, though in this case probably through the medium of textiles, rather than ceramics. The shape, however, as that of no. 235, is taken from an imported celadon.

237
Tile with inscription
Fritware with painting in blue and turquoise in an opaque white glaze with decoration in lustre
17.5 × 38 cm
A. Welch (1972), vol. IV, no. P.70; Geneva (1981), no. 90
Iran, Kashan, early 14th century

Tiles formed the major output of the lustre potters in the Mongol period. The tiles were destined to decorate the walls and tombs of Shi'ite shrines – a minority sect in Iran at the time, but one to which the potters belonged. Tiles such as this would form part of large panels making up a mihrab, tombstone or sarcophagus covering. The inscriptions are Quranic: the main inscription is Sura LXII, 8, the lower small frieze XLIII, 2. The upper inscription is by chance very appropriate to a potter's tile: 'He created man of clay like the potters, and the Jinn did He create of smokeless fire . . .' (Sura LV, 14). The tile is particularly successful in the quality of its glaze and lustre.

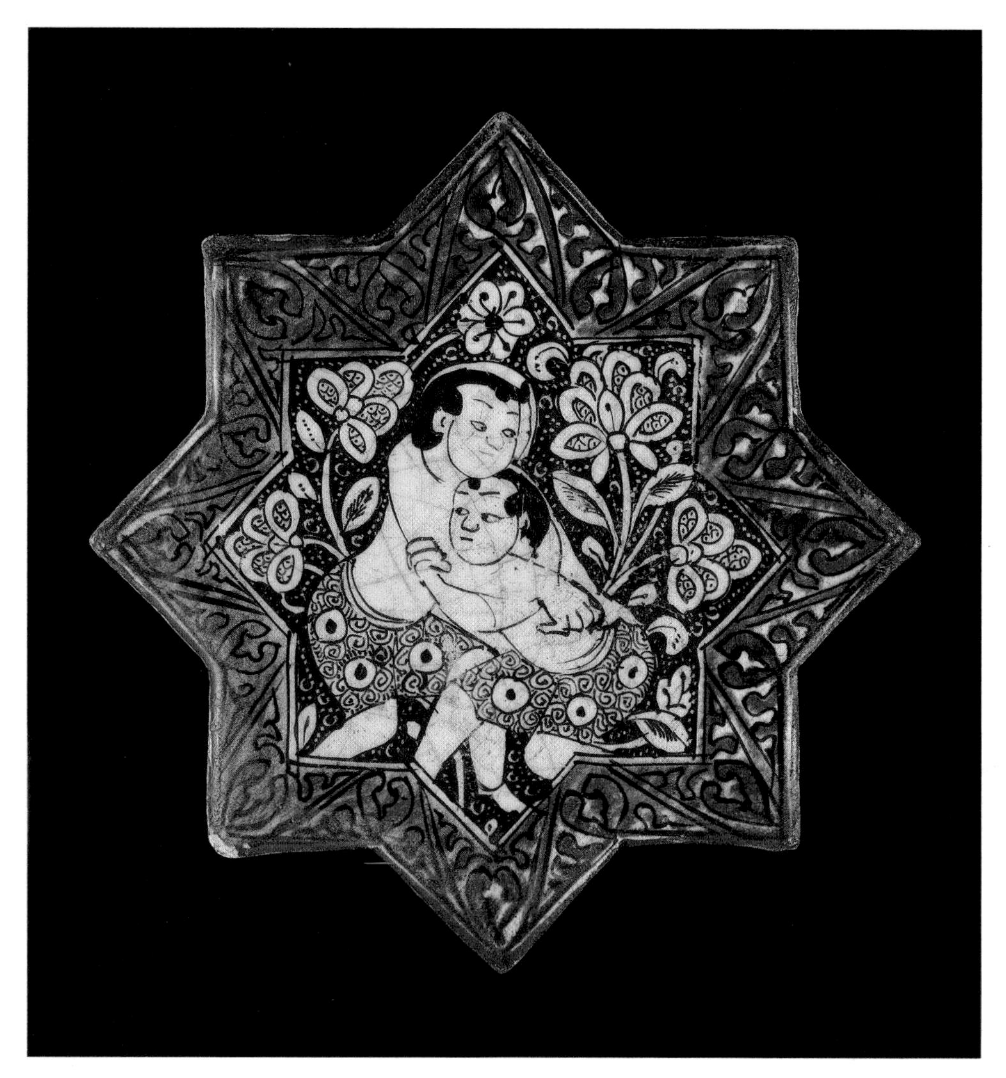

238
Star tile

Fritware with painting in blue in an opaque white glaze and decoration in lustre
Diameter 20.5 cm
Geneva (1984), no. 27
Iran, Kashan, late 13th century

This tile shows what appears to be a purely secular scene – two men wrestling – yet there is evidence that even tiles with such apparently inappropriate images were used in religious buildings. The Shi'ite sect, for whose monuments the tiles were made, were during the Mongol period strongly influenced by the mystic sufi movement, particularly at a popular level. It may thus be that the images on these tiles are either illustrations to popular religious tracts, or illustrate, by analogy, sufi concepts. Traditional Iranian wrestling, practised in *Zūrkhānehs* or gymnasiums, retained till modern times links with semi-secret religious brotherhoods.

239
Two Frieze tiles with inscription

Fritware with painting in blue under a transparent glaze and decoration in lustre
30 × 30 cm
Nouveau Drouot, 9th–10th December 1980, lot 317
Iran, probably Kashan, 860/1455

The main run of lustre tiles from Kashan came to an abrupt halt in 740/1340. The technique of lustre painting was not, however, lost. A series of tombstones dated in the course of the 15th and 16th centuries show how the technique was preserved, albeit in a modest, almost incompetent, form, until the 17th century when it was greatly used again (cf. no. 250). In this period, a series of tiles made for an unidentified building of the Timurid Sultan Abu Sa'id are the most ambitious. These two frieze tiles, designed to run along above a dado, belong to a group out of which are now preserved only two further frieze tiles and two plaques. The two plaques give the Sultan's full titles, the date 860/1455 and the name of the calligrapher – Nusrat al-Din Muhammad. These two frieze tiles give the beginning of the inscription: *('amara bi-binā hadhi) hi 'l-'imāra Sultān al-' (a'zam)*... (The great Sultan ... ordered the construction of this building ...). Two further tiles in the Victoria and Albert Museum give a further title – *al-Muzaffar* – and his name *Abū Sa'īd.*

240
Tile with depiction of the Great Mosque at Makka

Fritware with underglaze painting in blue, black, turquoise, green and raised red
52 × 32 cm
Erdmann (1959), p. 159; Geneva (1981), no. 109
Turkey, Iznik, 17th century

The Quranic inscription at the top reads: 'The first House established for the people was that at Bakka (Makka), a holy place and a guidance to all beings. Therein are clear signs – the Station of Abraham and whosoever enters it is in safety. It is the duty of all men towards God to make a pilgrimage to the House if they are able' (Sura III, 96-97). This verse stresses the prime importance of the pilgrimage – the Hajj – in the Islamic faith. The scene below is a schematic rendering of the Ka'ba, the focal point of all Muslims at prayer, and whose circumambulation marks the most intense moment of the pilgrimage. The Ka'ba itself, the square structure in the centre, is surrounded by various other buildings, enclosed in a courtyard, all of whose doorways are marked. The tile may have been intended to help give instruction on the practices and procedures of the pilgrimage. A number of such tiles are known, all made in the 17th century, as the output of the Iznik kilns was declining.

241
Large jar

Unglazed clay with moulded and applied decoration
Height 88 cm
Nouveau Drouot, 5 May 1981, lot 85
North Mesopotamia, late 12th or early 13th century

The vastly greater part of ceramic production in the Middle East consisted of unglazed wares of various types. Mostly for storage and cooking, they are, in the main, of little interest from an artistic point of view. Rarely do pieces reach the heights of decorative elaboration shown in this large water vase. It was left unglazed for good reason, for the evaporation of water from the porous clay cooled the remaining contents. The vase may also have acted as a filter, the water seeping through the bottom to be collected in a stand underneath. Such vases and stands were once commonplace in mosques and other public places, and may still be found to this day. This vase may be dated to the 12th or 13th century by its form of decoration, in particular by the large 'Persian' faces, characteristic of Iranian and Mesopotamian art just prior to the Mongol invasions.

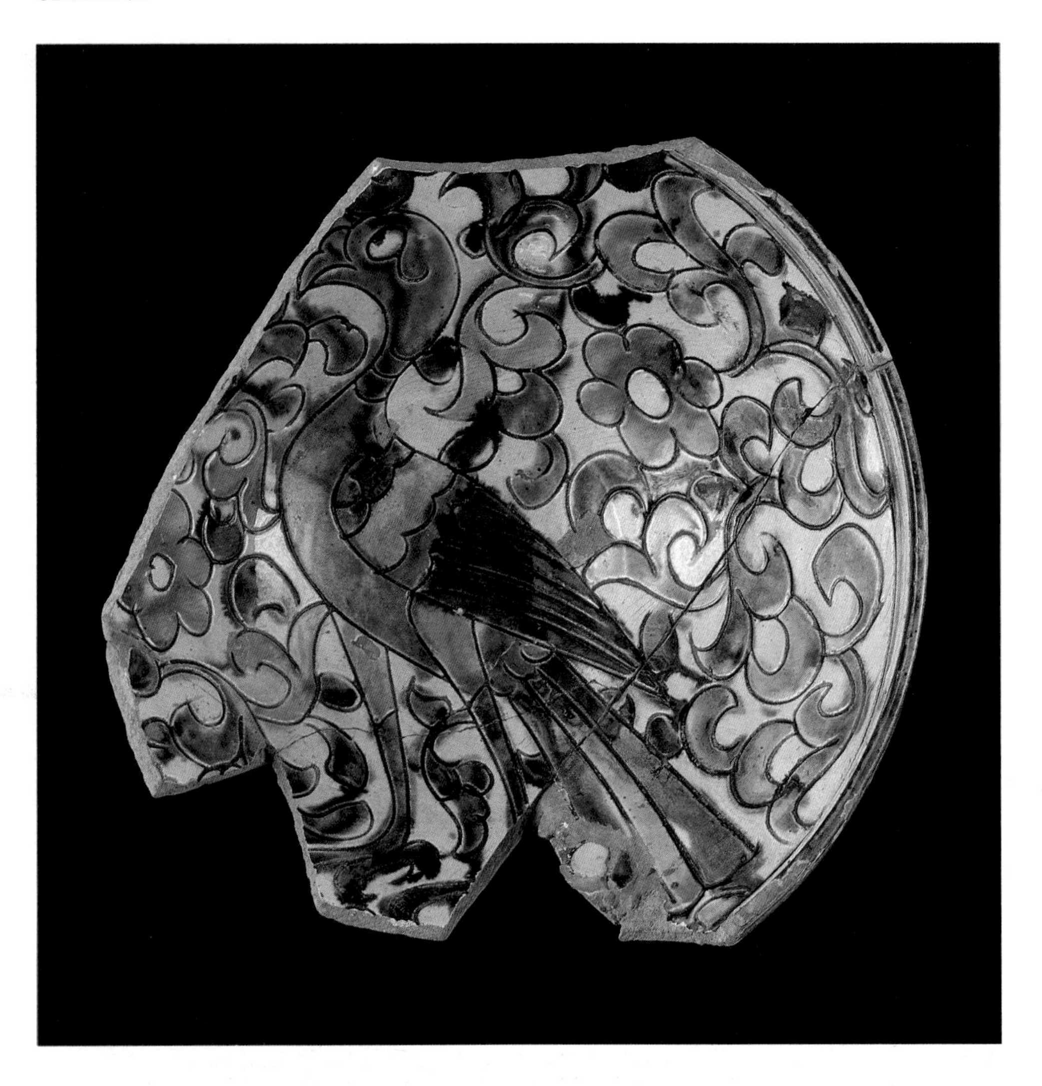

243
Albarello

Fritware with painting in blue under a transparent glaze and decoration in lustre
Height 26 cm
A. Welch (1972), vol. IV, no. P.61; Geneva (1981), no. 69
Syria, Raqqa, early 13th century

The albarello, a form to become very popular with later European potters as a pharmaceutical vessel, was first developed in the Islamic world during the 12th century. The Iranian version had straight sides – the Syrian type with a waisted body was more practical, allowing the hand to grasp it easily in the middle of a row of similar jars. The Syrian lustre potters, like the Iranian, developed their wares after the collapse of the Egyptian kilns at the end of the 12th century, and were no doubt taught by immigrants from Egypt. The Syrian wares were less good technically than the Iranian, having transparent glazes, a less white body, and a duller lustre colour (cf. nos 224 and 225); the painting on the Syrian wares was often of a bolder nature (cf. no. 242). This jar survives in unusually good condition.

242
Fragment of dish

Earthenware with white slip covering, incised decoration and purple, yellow and green colours under a transparent glaze
Diameter 28.5 cm
Geneva (1981), no. 112
Syria, 12th or 13th century

This dish, though fragmentary, retains all of its vitality and strength in drawing and colouring. Related in technique to the slipwares of Iran of the same period (cf. nos 217 and 218), it differs in style of drawing, making the Iranian wares look cramped and timid by comparison.

243

244
Large jar

Composite body (fritware), wheel-thrown, carved and glazed
Inscribed in Arabic: 'Glory and prosperity and . . . and . . . [and] peace and . . . and long life to its owner'
Height 42.5 cm
The al-Sabah Collection, *Dār al-Āthār al-Islāmīya*, Kuwait National Museum, LNS 350 C
Keene (1984), no. 11
Egypt, second half 12th-13th century

While pottery made in various Syrian ceramic centres in the century between 1150 and 1250 has survived in some quantity, objects of contemporary Egyptian production that are complete and of any size are exceedingly rare. Therefore, this large vase is exceptional. It bears close technical comparison, as regards the combination of a transparent glaze on a carved or incised white body, with fragments found in great numbers in Fustat and produced in Egypt, while the shape of the body has parallels in contemporary metalwork, specifically in an inlaid vase in the Louvre bearing the name of Sultan al-Malik al-Nasir II Salah al-Din (1237-60). The layout of its decoration – a series of bands – and the designs, except for the guilloche, are also paralleled in the Paris object.
M.J.

245
Jug with scale pattern

Fritware with underglaze painting in blue, green, black and raised red
Height 23 cm
A. Welch (1972), vol. IV, no. P.82; Geneva (1981), no. 101
Turkey, Iznik, second half 16th century

The Iznik wares of Ottoman Turkey represent in many ways the finest products of the Islamic potters. These wares have a fine white body, unequal to porcelain only in its softness, and a close-fitting brilliant glaze that allows a vibrant range of underglaze colours. From the 16th century onwards they were greatly prized throughout the Near East, as well as in Europe where they are imitated to this day. This jug shows well the sure sense of design of the Iznik painters. The range of colours includes red – the most difficult colour to achieve in ceramics – produced by use of the famous 'Armenian bole', a thick clay slip rich in iron.

245

246

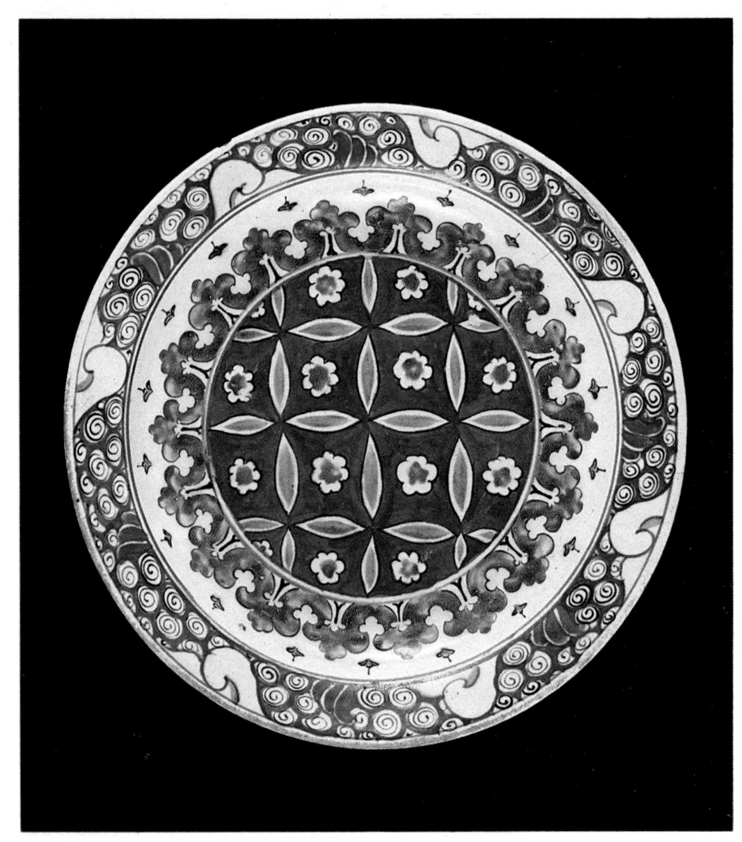

247

246
Dish with rosette

Fritware with underglaze painting in blue and raised red
Diameter 27.5 cm
A. Welch (1972), vol. IV, no. P.83; Geneva (1981), no. 107
Turkey, Iznik, second half 16th century

This dish shows an effective use of a simple concentric rosette device, giving prominence to the high technical quality of the ware.

247
Dish

Fritware with underglaze painting in black, blue, green and raised red
Diameter 28.5 cm
A. Welch (1972), vol. IV, no. P.87; Geneva (1981), no. 106
Turkey, Iznik, second half 16th century

The Iznik potters appear not to have had access to large numbers of Chinese porcelains as they developed their painting styles. Their patterns are largely their own invention or taken from other contemporary Turkish arts. This dish shows vestiges of two Chinese patterns however – in the 'rock-and-wave' rim border, and in the central geometric pattern. The first is an abstracted and garbled version of a border first seen on blue-and-white Chinese porcelains of the 14th century. The central pattern is even more distantly derived from carved ornament in 14th-century celadons, but here adapted and coloured almost beyond recognition.

248
Dish with floral motif

Fritware with underglaze painting in black, blue, green and raised red
Diameter 34.3 cm
A. Welch (1972), vol. IV, no. P.86; Geneva (1981), no. 105
Turkey, Iznik, second half 16th century

The floral style developed in Ottoman decorative arts in the middle of the 16th century. It finds its most natural expression on the Iznik ceramics, whose colours and vivacity of painting match precisely the style's exuberant spirit. We know from archive sources that official design studios in Istanbul provided potters with patterns for tile designs. The potters developed these into suitable ornament for their vessels.

248

249

249
Dish with female figure

Fritware with underglaze painting in black, blue, green with raised red and yellow
Diameter 34.9 cm
A. Welch (1972), vol. II, no. P.59; Geneva (1981), no. 100
North-west Iran, 'Kubachi' ware, early 17th century

The greater part of ceramic production of the Safavid period consisted of copies of Chinese blue-and-white porcelains, to which they evidently had greater access than their Turkish colleagues. A few types of pottery were made, including these polychrome Kubachi ware, that owed nothing in their inspiration to the Chinese. Named after the Caucasian town where many examples were found decorating houses, this pottery was probably made in North-west Iran, possibly at Tabriz. In their colouring they are indebted to some extent to Turkish wares, whose brilliant underglaze painting (cf. no. 247) is here rendered in more muted tones. The drawing, however, is purely Iranian in style, and closely related to contemporary miniature painting.

250
Bowl with floral motif

Fritware with blue slip on the outside under a transparent glaze and with lustre decoration
Diameter 18.5 cm
Iran, late 17th century

In the late 17th century, lustre ware was once again taken up by the Iranian potters and large numbers of vessels were made. The technique had been preserved since Mongol times in the manufacture of a series of tombstones and other tiles (cf. no. 239), but under the Safavids the technique was greatly improved. Brilliant lustres were painted on hard frit bodies of a brilliant whiteness, giving a sparkle and clarity not seen before (cf. nos 224 and 225). The designs, based loosely on manuscript illumination, are rather folksy in their treatment.

JAMES W. ALLAN

Metalwork

Metal objects were among the most important items of equipment among the middle classes in medieval Muslim society. Cooking was almost always carried out in metal basins and pans, though stone was sometimes used; particularly foodstuffs, especially spices and herbs, were pounded in heavy metal mortars (no. 278); cooked food was served in a variety of metal vessels (no. 268), usually placed on a large metal tray. This was generally raised some 30-40 cm off the ground on a metal or wooden stand. Wine and other drinks might be stored in metal bottles (nos 251, 252 and 257), poured from metal jugs (no. 282) and drunk from metal cups (no. 269). After the meal the hands of host and guests would be washed with water from a metal ewer (nos 281, 293 and 294) poured into a metal basin. Incense would be burned for the benefit of the guests in a metal incense-burner (nos 279 and 290). The house itself would have metal fittings on its doors (e.g. no. 275), and would be lit by the wicks of metal lamps on metal stands (nos 258 and 261), by candles in metal candlesticks (nos 285, 286, 288, 289 and 292), or by pitch in metal torchstands (nos 298-300). The literate, especially the administrative classes, would have metal pen-cases (nos 264 and 265) and ink-wells (nos 262 and 263), though pen-cases might also be made of precious woods. The female toilet would be accomplished with pieces of metal equipment, such as mirrors (nos 259 and 260), kohl sticks and tweezers; a lady's gold and silver jewellery might be kept in a metal casket (nos 266, 267 and 272), while the weekly visit to the hammam, or bath-house, would involve the use of a metal pail for dousing one's body with water (no. 301). Horses would be decorated with brasses, while outdoor pursuits such as hawking would entail metal equipment – drums for recalling birds of prey, for example (no. 276). Before battle, as at the time of birth, predictions of good or ill-fortune might be made by using a metal astrolabe (nos 296 and 302), and battle itself would be a mêlée of metal on metal.

Such widespread use of metal had important results for

other crafts in medieval Islam. In virtually every culture craftsmen imitate the most precious materials and skills in less expensive media and techniques, and so it was in the Near East. The pottery jugs of Samarra are of a form derived from metal; they are also decorated with lustre to represent gold. In 12th- and 13th-century ceramics from northern Iran, angular ewer or jug shapes are common, following the large number of such objects made in inlaid metalwork at the time; some of the pottery examples even have imitation rings hanging on the sides of their necks. The bowls of Raqqa and Kashan with their flat base, flaring conical sides, and rigidly cylindrical foot, also follow a metalwork shape.

More important for our understanding of the objects in this section is the dependency of this range of metalwork on more precious metals like silver or gold, or other media. The rectangular box shape (nos 266-7) may well derive from such boxes in precious wood or ivory; certainly this is the source of the round-ended pen-box style exemplified by an object in the Walters Art Gallery, Baltimore, which, though made of soldered metal plates, retains the metal clasps characteristic of ivory work. The whole fashion for inlaid bronze or brass is based on silverwork, in which areas of niello inlay and gilding gave a trichrome palette; in the less sumptuous metal objects the brass is equivalent to the gilding, the silver inlay reproduces the silver but in incomparably cheaper terms, and the niello (compounded of silver and sulphur) is imitated by a black bituminous compound. Specific motifs or designs are taken from costly Quranic illuminated manuscripts: for example, the knot pattern on box no. 267, the base of the handled cup (no. 269) or the tray of incense-burner (no. 279) or the arabesque in a roundel on the base of inkwell no. 263. The illustrations in valuable manuscripts also left their mark. The figure on the cusped roundels on the base of the incense-burner can be paralleled in contemporary book illustrations from Iraq or the Jazira; the planets in their zodiacal domicilia on the Jaziran ewer (no. 281) must be based on illustrated astrological texts, now lost; so too the enthroned figure between dragon-headed staffs who appears on so many Khurasan inlaid metal objects of the 12th-13th centuries (e.g. box no. 266, inkwell no. 262). The numerous equestrian figures, be they hunters or warriors, derive ultimately from wall-paintings – hence the three tiers on inkwell no. 262, which parallels known wall-painting layouts from 8th-century Panjikent, near Samarkand. In that Soghdian city painted depictions of the heroic deeds of Rustam took the place of modern wallpaper. The bands of drinking and gaming figures may come more directly from illustrated manuscripts, though Soghdian wall paintings, alongside the heroic, also included numerous depictions of princes feasting. On the other hand, the slim, elegant lancers on either side of an enthroned seated figure on the Jaziran jug (no. 282) must assuredly draw on the fine draughtsmanship of a book illustrator rather than the monumental wall-painting style. The same should be true of the animated cursive script on this jug, though again no illustrated manuscripts with this type of embellishment have survived.

If the initial inspiration of many designs on inlaid metalwork was from another craft, that is not to say that every decorator of metal objects always copied from another medium. Such figural work could quickly be transformed into designs which much better reflected the nature of the objects they decorated. The human-headed inscription around the rim of the Khurasan dish (no. 268), the animal-headed arabesque in the centre with the band of walking animals around it all have a stylized rhythm which is fully appropriate to the form, the weight, even the restrained golden colour of the object as a whole. So too, the two eastern inlaid caskets (nos 266–7); here the figures and inscriptions are not so much to be read or understood individually as to make up a part of a total design which will give the object stature and add authority to its monumental form. It is presumably this emphasis which explains the complete lack of narrative compositions on inlaid metalwork of this period.

This movement from the naturalistic to the stylized can be seen in metalwork of other periods too. Other Jazira candlesticks of the same form as no. 285 have clearly legible inscriptions around their base and neck. The example in the exhibition, however, has pseudo-inscriptions in Kufic which are designed not to inform or bring good fortune, but to give the required rhythm to the object and thus enhance its monumentality in the eyes of the purchaser. This emphasis on monumentality even occasionally takes on a literal aspect, as when a mortar (no. 278) is designed to look like the body of a building – in this case a tomb tower, though one hesitates to take the comparison too literally!

Although the precious influenced the less precious, it is difficult to be certain of the relative values of different commodities in medieval Islam. Gold, silver and precious stones, were inevitably among the most sought after, as a visit to the treasury in Topkapi or the Bank Melli vaults in Tehran makes clear enough. However, one other particular item stands out in the texts for its enormous prestige: fine quality woven or embroidered textile. Although mosaic work, carved stucco and painted wall decoration must have been in evidence in the apartments of the Caliph's palace in Baghdad, it was the hanging tapestries which most impressed a 10th-century visiting Byzantine embassy. Although gifts of gold and silver bullion might encourage the loyalty of a provincial governor, it was the robe of honour, the outward sign of the Sultan's approval and goodwill, which most effectively enabled an officer-of-state to show off his allegiance, his wealth, and his personal prestige, to his contemporaries. Whereas crafts such as pottery, metalwork, glass and woodwork receive scant attention from medieval geographers, textile-producing centres were almost always recorded in the sources, even if our understanding of the technical terms used is too limited at present to attribute particular fabrics to particular towns or areas.

Among the textiles themselves, on the other hand, relative values are impossible to establish, the more so since the robes of honour mentioned contained a wide variety of woven and embroidered materials, wool, linen, cotton, silk and metal thread, to say nothing of different animal furs. In Ottoman art it is reasonably clear that Iznik ceramic designs owe a great deal to the silk textiles used in the manufacture of royal caftans, still to be seen in the Topkapi Museum in Istanbul. The lack of surviving costumes and the relative scarcity of surviving silks or other materials makes it much more difficult to relate medieval metalwork to its contemporary textile industry. Nevertheless, there are two or three designs on metal objects in this exhibition, which plausibly relate to textiles or costume.

The first of these is the background pattern on the Jaziran incense-burner (no. 279), which is one of a group of geometric designs found on Jaziran and Syrian metalwork of this period. The nearest Islamic parallels are the stucco designs found on the walls of the Umayyad Palace at Khirbat al-Mafjar near Jericho, but there is no reason to relate the two directly. Similar designs are also found on early Chinese silks. Given the continuing desire for these exotic textiles in the medieval world, and the importance of Mosul as a local silk manufacturing centre, such textiles offer a likely source of inspiration for metalwork designs in the 13th century.

A second metalwork design which may originate in textile patterns is the band of interlacing roundels or combination of interlacing roundels and ovals. Examples in this section show interlacing cusped roundels with the signs of the zodiac and the planets (no. 267), and interlacing roundels and ovals in which the roundels contain vegetal, bird or figural designs and the ovals inscriptions (nos 273 and 288). There are no comparable designs in Islamic metalwork from Iran or the Jazira prior to *c.* 1100, and they must therefore come from another source. Their closest surviving parallels are in fact to be found in the designs of Buyid and Seljuq silks, in which interlacing circles, or circles and polygons, are common.

A third parallel relates not so much to textiles as to costume. The Jaziran incense-burner may seem to be wearing not only a Chinese silk, but also a leather belt with two large embossed metal plaques attached to it. It is true that the only surviving Islamic belt hitherto published of this type, is that of Shah Isma'il in the Topkapi Museum, dating from *c.* 1500, but many examples of Jaziran and Syrian metalwork of the pre-Mamluk and Mamluk periods appear to be 'belted' in this way (e.g. the Nuhad Es-Said incense-burner of Sultan Muhammad ibn Qala'un). Moreover, such a direct influence of costume can be seen in other media, such as Kashan lustre ware, in which objects are 'hung' with jewellery pendants, following no doubt contemporary ladies' fashions.

Medieval Islamic inlaid bronzes and brasses, therefore, offer a fascinating view of the arts of their day. Drawing their decorative schemes and motifs from textiles, from precious metal, from wall-painting and manuscript illustrations, they not only reflect the rich variety of contemporary culture, but actually draw the different strands of that culture together visually. Moreover, unusually among surviving objects from medieval Islam, they are very often inscribed with the names of their maker, or their patron, and thus provide important documentary evidence for the taste and wealth of particular individuals or classes in society.

Most commonly found are the names of patrons. This is particularly so in the Mamluk period, from which many hundreds of inlaid brass items survive bearing the names of officers of state, with their titles (e.g. no. 287) and often their blazons. Occasionally objects even bear the name of the ruling Sultan, showing that they would have been used at court. Even where the names of the amirs are not given, Mamluk objects often bear royal titles to indicate the loyalty of the prospective purchaser (nos 286 and 288). Elsewhere in medieval Islam the social structure was less formal and the ruling class less dependent for its acceptance on an outward display of names and titles. This is one reason at least for the comparative lack of such information on medieval Iranian objects. Where they do occur, however, they illustrate a wide range of patrons for inlaid metalwork – 14th-century Inju rulers of Fars, an early-13th-century grand-vizier from Merv, an early-13th-century governor of Peshawar, a merchant from Tabriz, a merchant from Zanjan, an inspector of the court treasury, and a female scholar, for example.

Curiously, in the Mamluk period, makers only occasionally recorded their names on their works of art, whereas considerable numbers of craftsmen are known from the Jazira and Iran. Here we find various indications of the structure of the industry. In the Jazira we find evidence of a pupil-teacher relationship in the works of Ibrahim ibn Mawaliya and his pupil (*tilmīdh*) Isma'il ibn Ward, and possibly of a paid apprenticeship in the use of the title *ajīr* or *ghulām*. More commonly found, though, is evidence of a father-son relationship, and hence of a family industry. This is particularly striking in the Isfahan astrolabe industry, where a certain al-Husayn had two sons and a grandson all known as astrolabists in the first half of the 12th century, while in the second half of the century one Mahmud also had two sons and a grandson in the industry. While the astronomical and mathematical skills required by astrolabists might suggest that they were a special case, there is evidence that family businesses functioned throughout the industry. In the first place the fact that astrolabists bore such appellatives as *al-ibarī* (the needlemaker), *ibn al-naqqāsh* (son of the decorator), *saffār* (bronze/brass worker), *ibn al-saffār* (son of the bronze/brass worker), and *ibn al-nahhās* (son of the coppersmith) shows that they were part of a wider metalworking system. In the second place such relationships are actually attested in inlaid metalwork, witness the two craftsmen Muhammad ibn Sunqur and Mahmud ibn Sunqur in the late 13th and early 14th centuries.

Objects bearing the names of makers and patrons, however, are few compared with the great mass of metal objects which are completely anonymous. Moreover, the percentage of them remaining in private hands continues to decline as they find their way into permanent public collections in different parts of the world. It is largely therefore the anonymous objects that must speak for the industry in an exhibition such as this, and speak they will if we can but free our minds of their traditional artistic and cultural prejudices and open our eyes to the new range of shapes and functions, motifs and designs which lie before us.

251
Bottle
Cast bronze; eight-sided; moulded lotus-leaf on each face; four concentric rings within the foot
Height 17 cm
Egypt, 7th-8th century

Pear-shaped bottles are common in early Islamic Egypt and Iran, but their relationship with one another remains obscure. The Iranian examples probably derive from a style of silver bottle common in the Sasanian period, and this in its turn may be of classical inspiration. If so, both groups may have the same Roman ancestors. Lotus leaf mouldings are common on Egyptian bottles of Islamic date, whereas the Iranian craftsmen went in for almond-shaped bosses (no. 257). The lack of more detailed decoration on such objects makes a close dating impossible.

252
Bottle
Cast bronze; undecorated; three concentric rings around central knop within the foot
Height 17.5 cm
Egypt, 7th-8th century

See note to no 251.

253
Ewer

Cast bronze; six-sided; three legs; traced and punched decoration on the flat rim and beneath the handle
Height 43 cm, diameter 17 cm
Egypt, Tulunid or Fatimid period, 9th-10th century

The dating and determining of provenance of early Islamic bronze ewers is notoriously difficult. However, as a general rule, a spout rising from the body of a ewer points to an Egyptian or Syrian source, and concave-sided bodies also indicate this area. In the case of this ewer, the lightly punched and traced ornament below the handle, and the ring-punch decoration on the mouth, are both types of decoration found on objects associated with the Coptic and early Islamic culture of Egypt, though no detailed study of these has yet been published.

254
Cup

Cast bronze; the handle with a trefoil thumb-piece surmounted by small elephant
Below a Kufic inscription incised below the rim are the words *'amal Muhammad*, 'made by Muhammad'
Height 7 cm, diameter 6.6 cm
Geneva (1984), no. 35
Khurasan, 10th-11th century

Khurasan and Transoxiana inherited cultural traditions from pre-Islamic Soghdia as well as from Sasanian Iran. Among such Soghdian traditions was a widespread use of small ring handles for everyday objects, often bearing a thumb-piece for extra leverage. Soghdia was in fact most unusual in producing large quantities of pottery with such handles, and the continuing tradition can be seen in this small cup with an elephant adorning its thumb-piece, and in cup no. 269, which has a flat thumb-piece, elaborately inlaid like the rest of the object with silver.

255
Bird

Cast bronze; its comb in the form of an antelope's neck and head; a knot pattern is incised on the chest and tail; its eyes were probably inlaid with turquoise
Height 17.5 cm, length 15.5 cm
Khurasan or Transoxiana, 10th-11th century

The Buddhist industry producing images for worship in Kashmir and Afghanistan in early medieval times seems to have had a marked effect on the taste of Islamic patrons of the day. For in eastern Iran in the 10th and 11th centuries, large numbers of animals or birds in the round were made, designed to function as vessels in their own right (e.g. incense burners) or as decorative elements on larger objects. They were occasionally inlaid with copper or silver, as were the Buddhist images, and turquoise – which in Islamic tradition wards off the effects of the evil eye – was also used for the eyes. Nowhere else in the Islamic world does one find such a rich variety of bronze creatures, and the mastery of casting which this implies.

256
Elephant

Cast bronze; decorated with a square within an open work diamond on each side of the back, and a knot pattern on the forehead; three holes underneath
Height 7.6 cm, length 11.35 cm
Khurasan, 10th-12th century

There are indications at the rear of this little creature's back that the object once formed one foot of a much larger item. That such feet were used for animals in the round is attested to by a magnificent horse in the Hermitage Museum (Sarre and Martin 1912, pl. 136, no. 2994), the tail of which ends in a disc and bayonet joint, and an unpublished lion in Berlin-Dahlem, the front legs of which hold a bayonet fixing. No other elephant of this type has ever been published, and its head and trunk are particularly sensitively rendered. Like the cast bronze bird (no. 255), it emphasizes the influence of the Buddhist image-producing workshops in early Islamic times in Kashmir and Afghanistan.

257
Bottle

Cast bronze; decorated with almond-shaped bosses
Height 17 cm
Khurasan or Sistan, 9th-11th century

See note to no. 251

258
Lampstand

Cast bronze; pierced and incised decoration; hexagonal shaft; flat tray missing from top
Height 76.5 cm
Previously in collection of Prince Sadruddin Aga Khan
A. Welch (1972), vol. II, p. 194, no. 11
Iran, 11th century

In a culture where men and women sit on the floor, lamps have to be raised above floor level to be effective: hence the large number of medieval lampstands known from the Islamic world (see also no. 261). The 10th and 11th centuries were the most exciting in eastern Iran in terms of cast bronze forms. Large numbers of different styles of cast bronze lamps were produced, and there is quite a variety of lampstand forms. This period also sees the most extensive use of pierced work, often in the form of palmettes in an ogival lattice; at other times, as here, in interlacing strapwork designs.

260
Mirror

Cast bronze; originally with a handle on one side; in the centre two seated foxes within a band of running animals with a vine-scroll behind
Kufic inscription of good wishes: *baraka wa yumn wa surūr wa sa'āda (wa) salāma wa 'āf(iya) wa 'āfiya wa ta'yīd wa ? wa nasr wa ? wa baqā lisāhibihi*, (Blessing, good fortune, joy, happiness, peace, health, health, (God's) support, ? , victory, ? , and long life to its owner)
Diameter 13.9 cm
Iran, 12th century

The design of this mirror is much less articulate than that of no. 259. A more spacious Kufic with a scrolling stem behind, animals of the hunt merging into their vine-scroll ground, very narrow pearl borders, and a central cusped roundel which should hold a boss but instead is decorated with two rather diminutive foxes, combine to allow the eye to wander over the richly ornamented surface but not to attract or focus its attention. Such a profusion and sometimes confusion of ornament is typical of Khurasan metalwork in the 12th and early 13th centuries, and justifies a dating of the object to this period, even if the style of Kufic looks earlier.

259
Mirror

Cast bronze; handle attached; in the centre a mounted huntsman; around a Kufic inscription of good wishes: *al-'izz al-dā'im wa'l-'umr al-sālim wa'l-surūr (?) al-dā'im wa'l-sa'āda wa'l-(i)dāma lī-sā(hibihi)* (Perpetual glory, safe living, perpetual joy (?), happiness, and perpetuity to its owner)
Diameter 10.1 cm
Iran, 10th-11th century

The huntsman has a hawk on his wrist, and a cheetah on his horse's crupper, and beside the horse marches a hunting dog (or perhaps a hare). The mounted hawker is an image commonly used in the courtly art of medieval Islam, illustrating a pastime popular for centuries in the Arab world. The pearl border and Kufic inscription – the latter with its stress on the vertical – give this mirror back a strength of design which more than balances the ill-proportioned horse with its rather diminutive legs and enlarged head.

260

261
Lampstand

Cast bronze; in three parts – base, stem and tray; inlaid with copper; the base decorated with birds in roundels and a pseudo-Kufic inscription, the shaft with arabesques or pseudo-Kufic, the tray with a central bird and *naskh* and Kufic inscriptions.
The inscription of good wishes in the centre of the tray reads: *al-'izz wa'l-iqbāl wa'l- . . . wa'l-salāma wa'l-dawāla* (Glory, prosperity, . . . , peace and ascendancy)
Height 51.7 cm, diameter 16.5 cm
Geneva (1984), no. 31
Khurasan, 12th or early 13th century

See note to no. 258

262
Inkwell

Cast bronze; overlaid and inlaid with silver; the lid is decorated with six seated figures, the planets in their twelve zodiacal domiciles or the signs of the zodiac alone and a band of gaming figures; inside, it bears an enthroned figure between dragon-headed staffs surrounded by solar rays; the body is decorated with two bands of seated figures and a band of horsemen; on the base is a band of running animals around a central running animal; the inkwell originally had three small feet; two of the suspension brackets on the lid and two of the loops on the body are also missing
On the drip tray is a *naskh* inscription reading: *al-'izz wa'l-iqbāl wa'l-dawāla wa'l-baqā wa'l- ? wa'l-'in(āy)a wa* (Glory, prosperity, ascendancy, long-life, ?, (God's) sympathy, and . . .)
Height 11 cm, diameter 9.4 cm
Khurasan, *c.* 1200

The most unusual feature of this inkwell is the decorative technique used on the flat part of the lid: the bronze alloy is overlaid with a sheet of silver through which the designs have then been cut. An inkwell of similar form found at Ghazni and now in the Museo Nazionale di Arte Orientale in Rome (Scerrato (1966) pl. 16) has a number of smaller sheets of silver attached which have subsequently been incised and inlaid with niello. These two objects suggest that 12th-century inlayers may have been experimenting to find quicker or easier methods of adding richness, colour and decoration to base-metal objects.

262

263
Inkwell base

Cast bronze; inlaid with silver; the body and drip tray decorated with arabesque designs; on the base arabesque and knot patterns around a central interlaced six-pointed star pattern, with solar rays; the lid, three feet and suspension loops are missing
Height 6 cm, diameter 9.5 cm
Khurasan *c.* 1200

The close similarity of the designs of arabesque on this inkwell and on the pen-case (no. 264) suggests that the same inlayers were working on both sheet and cast metal objects. These two objects also show the extraordinary ability of the medieval Islamic designer to cover different shapes of surface with the same sort of abstract ornament. On the inkwell the arabesques give the impression of circular patterns, reflecting the circular form of the object; on the pen-case the arabesque stems multiply and the leaves grow more numerous as the object widens out. On the inkwell one notices too how the arabesques on the drip tray and base have oval leaves whereas those on the sides have diamond-shaped leaves, thus preventing any sense of monotony in the decoration.

264
Pen-case

Brass, inlaid with copper and silver; modern silver mount and inkwell; decorated with arabesques and *naskh* inscriptions
Good wishes inscribed in *naskh* on sides: *al-'izz wa'l-iqbāl wa'l-dawla wa'l-sa'ada wa'l-salāma wa'l-shafā'a wa'l-dawāla*; and *al-'izz wa'l-iqbāl wa'l-dawla wa'l-sa'āda wa'l-salāma wa'l-ni'ma wa'l-bāqiya wa'l-?* (Glory, prosperity, wealth, happiness, peace (Muhammad's) intercession, ascendancy; and Glory, prosperity, wealth, happiness, well-being, favour, long life, and . ? .). On the back in *naskh*; *al-'izz wa'l-i(qbāl)* and *al-'izz wa* and in Kufic: *bi'l-yu(m)n wa'l-*, 'Good fortune and . . .'
Length 23.2 cm, width 4.3 cm
Khurasan *c.* 1200

265
Pen-case

Brass, inlaid with copper and silver; the inkwell and area around modern; decorated with arabesques and *naskh* inscriptions
Good wishes inscribed in *naskh* on sides: *al-'izz wa'l-iqbāl wa'l-dawla wa'l-salāma wa'l-sa'āda wa'l-'i(n)āya wa'l-qanā'a wa'l- ? wa'l-rāha wa'l- ? wa'l-ziyād(a) wa'l-rāha wa'l-tāmma wa'l-ziyād(a) wa'l-baq(ā) (wa'l-) rahma wa'l-shākira wa'l-shukra wa'l-rā'a wa'l-baqā* (Glory, prosperity, wealth, peace, happiness, (God's) sympathy, contentment, ? , ease, ? , abundance, ease, entirety, abundance, long life, mercy, thankfulness, gratitude, protection (?) and long life) On the top in Kufic script: *'amal Shādhī naqqāsh* (Work of Shadhi the decorator).
Length 22.2 cm, width 3.5 cm
Previously in collection of the late Ata Muhammad Naqshbandi, Herat
Melikian-Chirvani, 1974/1, fig. 9
Khurasan, *c.* 1210

Shadhi *naqqāsh*, the decorator of this pen-case, is known from another pen-case of very different form, now in the Freer Gallery of Art (Herzfeld (1936)). This is rectangular with rounded ends, is dated 607/1210, and was made for Majd al-Mulk al-Muzaffar grand-vizier of the Khwarazm-Shah 'Ala al-Din Muhammad and resident in Merv in Khurasan. Its decoration is more elaborate and varied than the pen-case shown here, but is close enough in detail to suggest that the two were made at approximately the same date.

264

265

266
Casket

Cast bronze, inlaid with silver; the body of the box is decorated with enthroned figures between animal-headed staves or mounted archers in roundels, within borders of running animals; on the outer sides of the four feet are mythical creatures; the original domical finial of the lid has been replaced by a plaque with interlacing star pattern; on either side of it are confronted sphinxes; the concave shoulders of the lid bear enthroned figures in roundels and confronted horsemen; hinges and clasp not original

The sides of the lid bear a *naskh* inscription of good wishes which reads: *al-'izz wa'l-iqbāl wa'l-dawla wa'l-sa'āda wa'l-ni'ma wa'l-'āfiya wa'l-'ināya wa'l-dawāla wa'* . . ? . . . *wa'l-rāha wa'l-qanā'a wa'l-dawāma wa'l-shukr(a) wa'l-shākir(a)*

(Glory, prosperity, wealth, happiness, favour, health, (God's) sympathy, ascendancy, ? , ease, contentment, longevity, gratitude and thankfulness)

Length 17.7 cm, width 12.8 cm, height 14.4 cm

Khurasan, Punjab or Hindustan *c.* 1200

Traditionally inlaid bronzes and brasses with decoration like that on this casket and no. 267 have been ascribed to Khurasan, in particular to Herat. This is because the only certain centre for the production of such high-quality work is Herat – witness the testimony of Qazwini, and the inscription on the Bobrinski bucket and the Tiflis ewer. However, study of form and decoration suggests that certain pieces may well come from further east. On casket no. 267 the most striking Indian features are the four-armed planetary figures incised on the base; a jug in the British Museum has an animated inscription in which one letter is in the form of a cobra; an ibex-handled flask in the British Museum is unparalleled in Khurasan forms and was acquired in the Punjab (Barrett (1949) pls 8 and 9); a pair of table-tops recently on the London art market are in the name of a governor of Peshawar; and so on. Hence, it seems likely that in the early 13th century there was at least one school of inlaid metalwork in what are now Pakistan and North-west India.

267
Casket

Cast bronze, inlaid with silver; the body of the box is decorated with riders on camels, elephants and horses, and with enthroned figures between animal-headed staves in roundels; the feet bear pairs of harpies; on the base are seven planetary figures in roundels with a knot pattern between confronted harpies at either end; harpies adorn the domical finial; on either side of it are confronted horsemen with spears; on the edge of the lid, at the front, are figures of the planets, at the two ends are the planets in their domiciles, and on the back are four roundels with a hawk attacking a goose, and a roundel with an enthroned figure between animal-headed staves; at one end of the lid top are four incised florettes, apparently of Mughal date
On the concave shoulder is an inscription reading: *al-'izz wa'l- iqbāl wa'l-dawla/wa'l-sa'āda wa'l-'in(āya)/wa'l- qinā'a wa'l- 'āfiya wa'l-nāsira/wa'l-nusra wa'l-baqā lisāhibihi* (Glory, prosperity, wealth, happiness, (God's) sympathy, contentment, health, victoriousness, God's aid, and long life to its owner)
Length 17 cm, width 12 cm, height 17 cm
Punjab or Hindustan, *c.* 1200

See note to no. 256

268
Dish

High tin bronze, inlaid with silver and originally with a black substance; in the central roundel is an animal-headed arabesque and around it a band of animals
On the rim a band of *naskh* inscription reading: *al-'izz wa'l-iqbāl wa'l-dawla wa'l-salām wa'l-sa'āda wa'l-shafā'a wa'l-'ināya wa'l-qanā'a wa'l-'āfiya wa'l-ta'yīd wa'l-tāmma wa'l-nusra wa'l-nāsira wa'l-shukra wa'l-shākira wa'l-rāha wa'l-tāmma wa'l-nizāma wa'l-dawāma wa'l-riyāsa wa'l-siyāda wa'l-qudra wa'l-qādira wa . . . wa . . . wa'l-baqā lisāhibihi* (Glory, prosperity, wealth, peace, happiness, (Muhammad's) intercession, (God's) sympathy, contentment, health, (God's) support, entirety, God's aid, victoriousness, gratitude, thankfulness, ease, entirety, order, longevity, authority, sovereignty, power, powerfulness, ?, ?, and long-life to its owner)
Diameter 32 cm, height 4 cm
Khurasan, *c.* 1200

High tin bronze, or white bronze, is an alloy containing about 80 per cent copper and 20 per cent tin. It has generally been used in the West for casting bells because of its fine ringing tone, hence its English name 'bell-metal'. It was well known in Iran in pre-Islamic times but became very popular under Islam, perhaps because it is of a similar colour to silver but does not have silver's associations with luxurious living. The main areas of production of this alloy seem to have been Khurasan, Transoxiana and northern Jazira. All three have large deposits of copper, but the tin had to be imported from South-East Asia.

269
Cup

High tin bronze, inlaid with silver and black substance; on the base an interlaced six-pointed star; around the sides enthroned figures in roundels with horsemen between, beneath a frieze of animals; on the thumb-piece an enthroned figure; inside three interlaced sphinxes with fish-pond ornament around
Diameter 9.3 cm, height 3.5 cm
Sotheby's, (Monaco) *Collection de la Villa Ispahan, Monte-Carlo* 28 June 1983, lot 1637, pp. 2 and 51
Khurasan *c.* 1200

For the origin of this type of handle see cup no. 254. Such cups may well have been used for wine, for despite the strict Islamic prohibition on wine-drinking, this activity has a ritual significance for medieval Islamic rulers and for this reason was probably current among the upper classes of society. Different forms of cup were fashionable at different periods and in different areas of the Islamic world: in early Islamic times a wine cup tended to be wide and shallow and was held by its narrow foot; later a beaker form became popular, and it is this latter form which usually appears on inlaid metalwork of the 12th–14th centuries.

270
Covered stem bowl

High tin bronze; cast; base plate soldered in; inlaid with copper and silver
Around knop Kufic inscription of good wishes: *bi'l-yumn wa'l-baraka wa'l-dawla wa'l-sa'āda wa'l-baqā li-sā (hibihi)*, (with good fortune, blessing, wealth, happiness, and long life to its owner); on cover arabesque designs; on body arabesque and lotus design with inscriptions above and below; above more good wishes in *naskh*: *al-'izz wa'l-iqbāl wa'l-dawla wa'l-salāma wa'l-sa'āda wa'l-'āfiya wa'l-'ināya wa'l-qanā'a wa'l-shafā'a wa'l-tāmma wa'l-ta'yīd wa'l-ra'ba wa'l-rahma wa'l-shākira wa'l-shukra wa'l-ni'ma wa'l-nusra wa'l-nāsira wa'l-d b ba wa'l-baqā li-sāhibihi* (glory, prosperity, wealth, peace, happiness, health, (God's) sympathy, contentment, (Muhammad's) intercession, entirety, (God's) support, ease, mercy, thankfulness, gratitude, favour, God's aid, victoriousness and . . . and long life to its owner); below in Kufic similar inscription but miswritten; around foot *naskh* repetition of *al-nā*. Inside foot incised: *bi-rasm* (for) *Ibrāhīm al-Jabalī*
Height 19.5 cm, diameter 17.5 cm
Spink (1977), no. 141
Melikian-Chirvani (1977), pls X-XII
Khurasan, early 13th century

While stem bowls of this shape are relatively common, comparatively few examples have retained their lids. Whether such objects had a practical function is uncertain: they may have been for ceremonial drinking, but they could also have been purely ornamental. Originally published by the present cataloguer as having Timurid decoration on the body, it has more recently been shown by Dr Asadullah Souren Melikian-Chirvani that all the decoration is of one and the same period. It thus provides a good example of the way in which naturalism (on the body) is to be found alongside stylization (on the lid) in vegetal designs at this period.

271

271
Ewer

Beaten brass, inlaid with silver; handle later replacement; various bands of decoration include a *naskh* inscription of good wishes around the neck: *al-'izz wa'l-nasr wa'l-iqbāl wa'l-ni'ma wa'l-jūd*, (Glory, victory, prosperity, favour and generosity); around the shoulder a similar inscription in cartouches interrupted by seated musicians in roundels *al-majd wa'l-afdāl wa'l-karāma wa'l-dā'ima* (Splendour, merit, beneficence and perpetuity); a band of seated musicians in roundels around lower body; bands of ornamental Kufic around mouth, lower neck and foot
Height 33 cm
Western Iran, 14th century

The form of this ewer is quite different from that of ewers in eastern Iran in the preceding century, but very close to those of Mosul and the Jazira (no. 281). It illustrates the common culture shared by western Iran, Iraq and the Jazira under the Il-Khanid rulers, with their capital at Tabriz, and also illustrates the metalworking dominance of the Jazira within that area. The same is true of 14th-century western Iranian bowl shape (no. 273), which is slightly different from those of contemporary Syria or Egypt, but like them is derived from Jaziran bowl forms of the 13th century.

272
Casket

Brass, inlaid with silver; the sides and top decorated with lobed niches containing pairs of birds or arabesques, the bevelled sides of the lid bear the words *al-'izz al-dā'im* (Perpetual glory) in *naskh*
Height 13 cm, width of base 13.5 cm
Western Iran, 14th century

Ducks are common elements in the designs of 14th-century Mamluk metalwork. Their precise significance is elusive though in Rumi's *Mathnawi* the wild duck is a symbol of the soul which wishes to return from the world (land) to the divine (sea), see Okasha (1981) p. 121. Notice the continuing use of the pearl border. This is found in Sasanian times, in Umayyad and Abbasid art, and is common in metalwork from early Islamic times up to the 14th century, as for example in mirrors nos 259 and 260 and around the base of the domical finial of inkwell no. 262.

273
Bowl

Cast brass, inlaid with silver; decorated with a band of oval cartouches containing a *naskh* inscription of a ruler's titles with roundels containing paired standing figures or horsemen between The inscription reads: *al-mawlā al-sultān / al-a'zam mālik riqāb / al-umam al*(sic)*-sultān a / l-salātīn al-'arab[la]*, (The lord, the most mighty sultan, dominant over the nations, sultan of sultans of the Arabs (and non-Arabs))
Height 11 cm, diameter 22.5 cm
Western Iran, *c.* 1350–75

275
Door-knocker

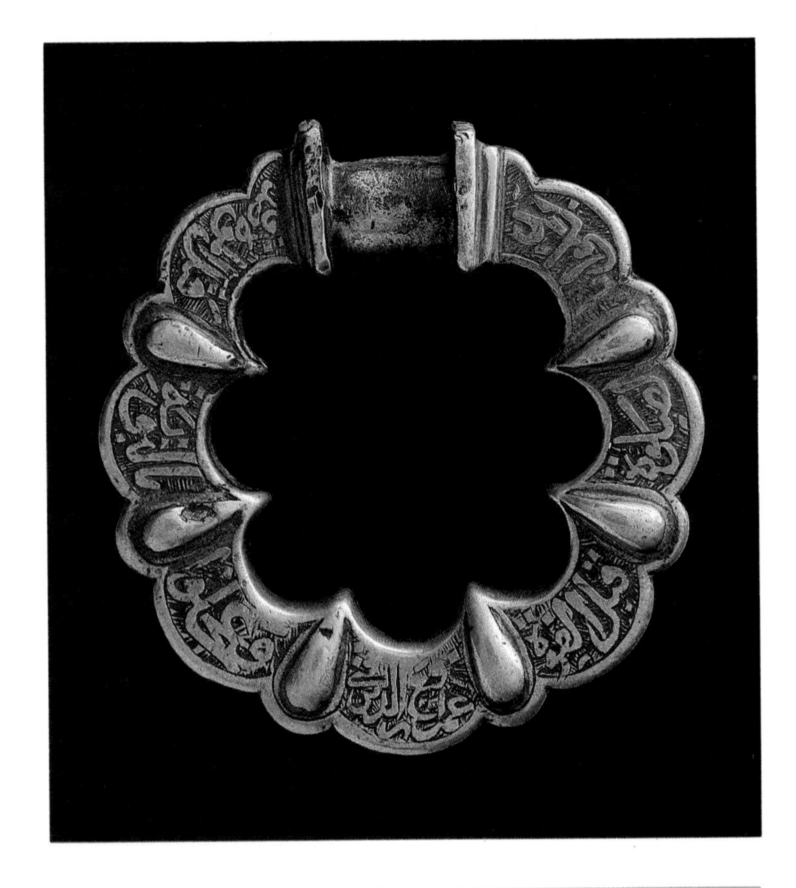

Cast brass; seven-lobed form with six almond bosses
Two-part *naskh* inscription: *'ajalū bi'l-salwa qabl al-fawt/wa 'ajalū bi'l-tawba qabl al-mawt sadaqa* (Hasten to prayer before passing away; hasten to repentance before death. (God) spoke truth)
The maker's signature *'amal Rafi al-Dīn . . . qi* (work of Rafi' al-Din . . .) is placed in a separate cartouche
Diameter 13 cm
Iraq, Iran or eastern Anatolia, 14th-15th century

A study of Islamic door-knockers and handles still has to be written; hence the problem of provenance for this particular example. The inscription suggests that it may have adorned a mausoleum, and is a timely reminder of man's mortality and of judgement to come.

276
Hawking drum

Brass, inlaid with silver and gold; the body is decorated with arabesques, the rim with a band of real and mythical animals against a stippled ground
Height 12 cm, diameter 14.5 cm
Geneva (1984), no. 46
North-west Iran or eastern Anatolia, or possibly India, 15th century

The provenance of this hawking drum is very problematic. Another object with the same style of decoration, which recently appeared on the London art market, is a form of candlestick base which is tray shaped with a conical centre. This form is found in Ottoman Turkey (Petsopoulos (1982), no. 46) but also occurs in India. The arabesques reflect the international Timurid style of the 15th century, and, with the exception of the candlestick base mentioned, the animals and the style of inlay are unparalleled in known pieces. The use of round discs of gold recalls depictions of the stars in constellation drawings, but none of the animals seems to relate to known star groups.

277
Lidded jug

Cast brass, inlaid with silver and gold; handle missing; bands of arabesque ornaments all over; around the centre of the body, in cartouches, four lines from the *ghazal* by Hafiz (see below)
Height 18.5 cm, diameter 15.5 cm
Sotheby's, 12-13 October 1982, lot 59, pp. 74-75
Khurasan, probably Herat, second half 15th century

The spring of Khidir was the mythical source of immortality which, according to the Alexander legend, Alexander the Great sought but never reached. Khidir himself is the prophet who found and drank of the water of life, and who can thereby initiate men into the divine mysteries. The poem on this jug thus emphasizes the mystical outlook of patrons and/or metalworkers in the second half of the 15th century, an emphasis which was destined to leave its mark on Persian metal objects henceforward (see nos 298 and 299). The original handle to this jug would have been of cast brass in the form of a dragon.

Inscription
The inscription starts from the point where the handle has been removed

Ankas ki ba-dast jām dārad
Sultānī-yi Jam mudām dārad.
Ābī ki Khidir hayāt az ū yāft
Dar mishraba jū, ki jām dārad.
Sar-rishta-yi jān ba-jām bigdhār
Kīn rishta azū nizām dārad.
Dar chāh-i zanakh chu Hāfiz, ay jān,
Husn-i tu du sad ghulām dārad.

He who holds the cup in his hand
Forever holds the realm of Jamshid.
The water Khidir found life from
Seek in the jug, for the cup holds it.
Leave the thread of your life to the cup,
For this necklace is strung by it.
In the pit of your dimple, my love, like Hafiz
Two hundred slaves your beauty holds.

The verses, in *hazaj* metre, are the three first and the last line of a *ghazal* of Hafiz (*Dīwān*, ed. M. Qazwini and Q. Ghani, Tehran (1320) p. 80). The first three lines appear on a bronze bowl in the Victoria and Albert Museum and, with a fourth line from the same poem, on a small silver drinking bowl in the Freer Gallery, Washington. (A.S. Melikian-Chirvani, *Victoria and Albert Museum Catalogue, Islamic Metalwork from the Iranian World, 8th-18th Centuries*, London (1982) no. 159; idem, 'Four pieces of Islamic metalwork: some notes on a previously unknown school', *Art and Archaeology Research Papers*, X, 1976, pp. 25-27.)

Occasional letters are pointed, usually correctly, and there are quite a number of vocalization marks, quite often wrong, e.g. *madām* for *mudām* in the second hemistich.

Line 2 *Ābī* appears to be written *āb* at the beginning of the line. In the second hemistich *mishraba*, 'drinking vessel', replaces the *maykada*, 'tavern' of the texts of Hafiz, obviously an attempt to make the verses more appropriate to the object they are inscribed on.

Line 3 *Jān*, which occurs in the printed texts, is defectively written it would seem. On the jug the word looks like *jam*, but that does not appear to make sense. *Mīm* of *nizām* and *rā'* of *dārad* have been run together, or possibly one of them has been omitted.

Line 4 For *zanakh*, 'dimple on the chin' the standard modern editions have its synonym *dhaqan* but the other reading appears to be that of the oldest manuscripts. (See, for example, the editions of early 15th-century manuscripts by Iraj Afshar, Tehran (1348) and Jalali Na'ini and Nadhir-Ahmad, Tehran (1350).)

A.H.M.

277

278
Mortar

Cast lead bronze, in architectural form, with a lobed niche on columns on each of the eight sides; a ring is attached to the base of each column; projecting lion-head handle with large ring on one side
Height 15.5 cm, diameter 23.5 cm
Anatolia, 13th-14th century

This mortar is very reminiscent of the octagonal tomb towers erected in 13th- and 14th-century Anatolia, from Kayseri eastwards. There appear to be no surviving examples with this type of cusped arch on each side, but a similar form is found above the doorways of extant tomb-towers, such as, for example, the Cifte Gunbad (645/1247) in Kayseri and the mausoleum of Khudavend (712/1312) in Nigde (Gabriel (1931), vol. I, pls. XXII and XLVI). It is unusual to find Islamic metalworkers copying architectural forms, though one other example of this phenomenon has been discussed, the Herat late-12th and early-13th-century brass ewers, which appear to follow the forms of contemporary tomb-towers in Khurasan (Aga-Oglu (1943)).

279
Incense-burner base

Cast bronze, with three legs; inlaid with silver; around the body, against a swastika pattern ground, two lobed roundels, each containing a pair of seated figures, either drinking or making music, joined to smaller roundels with arabesques by a band of Kufic inscription; the latter makes no sense; the legs are decorated with arabesques, and the tray with a six-pointed interlaced star within sun-rays and a band of interlace; the handle and lid are missing
Incised *naskh* inscription above one of the seated figures: *bi rasm al-Tāj ibn al- ?* (For al-Taj son of ?)
Height 11 cm, diameter 10 cm
Jazira, *c.* 1240

The decoration on this incense-burner base is so similar to that on an incense-burner in the British Museum dated 641/1243-4 (Barrett (1949), pl. 15c; Aga-Oglu (1945), fig. 6), that it must be of approximately the same date and a product of the same workshop. The main artistic interest of this piece lies in the two groups of figures (the British Museum piece is aniconic), which closely resemble work in early-13th-century Muslim and Christian manuscripts. One of the roundels shows a harpist and a tambourine player, but the other is more unusual, and shows an enthroned ruler being offered a towel by a kneeling servant; the servant is depicted as bearded and has the typically Semitic facial features such as the long nose used to depict the local population by book illustrators at this period, contrasting them with the Turkish mongoloid ruling class.

279

280
Dish

Beaten brass with raised centre; originally inlaid with silver; in the centre a mounted archer shooting a lion; around is a large band of *naskh* inscription interspersed with seated drinkers or musicians in roundels, between two bands of animals, the latter interrupted by roundels containing a (European?) coat-of-arms; three ornamental bands on rim faces
The *naskh* inscription reads: *al-'izz wa'l-iqbāl amān wa'l-baqā laka [al] wa'l-majd wa'l-'adan wa'l-majd khālidan (a)l-ghilāl . . . al-sa'd al-sa'īd min al-dilā'ī* . . . (Glory and prosperity, security and long life to you and splendour and paradise and splendour eternal good crops, . . ., great good luck from misfortunes . . .)
Height 6.5 cm, diameter 43.5 cm
Syria, *c.* 1250

This type of dish with a raised centre is known from Mamluk examples (e.g. Fehervari (1976), pl. L, no. 154), but the form of script, its contents, and the figures in roundels all point to a date late in the preceding period of Ayyubid rule. The band of animals near the edge of the dish curiously includes an elephant. The coat-of-arms in the smallest roundels is not Islamic, and must presumably signify a later European owner of the dish. The purpose of this form of dish is unknown; in Ottoman times a similar form is used as a candlestick base, but in that case the centre is covered by the shaft of the candlestick. A similar use in Ayyubid or Mamluk times is ruled out by the fact that the centre is decorated.

281

281
Ewer

Beaten brass, inlaid with silver; the body decorated with a *naskh* inscription around the shoulder: *al-'izz al-dā'im wa'l-iqbāl al-zā'id wa'l-'umr a/l-sālim wa'l-'ayn al-thāghim wa'l-jann(a) al-qādim (wa)'l-sa'd lisāhibihi* (perpetual glory, increasing prosperity, safe living, clear vision, future paradise and felicity to its owner); below this the planets in their domiciles in roundels, with a frieze of animals above and below; on the neck a *naskh* inscription: *al-'izz al-dā'im wa'l-iqbāl al-zā'id wa'l-'umr (wa)'l-jann(at) al-qādima* (Perpetual glory, increasing prosperity, living and future paradise); below it an ornamental Kufic inscription; handle and mouth-rim modern; spout remounted; neck shortened
Height 29 cm
Previously in the Prince Sadruddin Aga Khan Collection
A. Welch (1972), vol. II, no. 17, p. 204
Jazira, 13th century

The ewer's form is typical of work associated with the Mosul school in the 13th century, and is the source of 14th-century western Iranian ewers (no. 271). The astrological figures around are designed to bring good fortune to both maker and owner, and are as follows, working round leftwards: Sun in Leo, Mercury in Virgo, Venus in Libra, Mars in Scorpio, the pseudo-planetary nodes of the Moon's orbit in Sagittarius (Hartner, (1938)), Saturn in Capricorn, Saturn in Aquarius, Jupiter in Pisces, Mars in Aries, Venus in Taurus, Mercury in Gemini and the Moon in Cancer. These figures would repay detailed study, despite the partial removal of the silver inlay: it is noticeable for example that Saturn is beardless, and that Venus is on one occasion luteless.

282
Jug

Cast bronze; handle separately cast; inlaid with silver; on the front of the body an enthroned ruler between dragon-headed staves in a cartouche; on either side a horseman with a spear. Around the neck an animated inscription of good wishes: *al-'izz wa'l-iqbāl wa'l-dawāma wa'l-sa'āda wa'l-salā(ma)* (Glory, prosperity, longevity, happiness and peace)
Height 16.8 cm, diameter 15 cm
Spink (1977), no. 154
Jazira province, 13th century

Animated inscriptions are found in inlaid metalwork of 13th-century date in both Iran, and the Jazira and Syria (see Rice (1955) pp. 21-33 for examples). The form of dress worn by the figures in this inscription is closer to that of other Jaziran and Syrian examples, and the jug's shape is also to be associated with the metalworking traditions of these areas (e.g. Allan (1982), no. 10; Melikian-Chirvani (1982), no. 8 must be of like origin). At present there seem to be no close parallels for the very slim, almost spindly, drawing of the figures.

283
Jar

Cast bronze inlaid with silver; on each of the nine sides a mace-bearer beneath an ornamental pseudo-Kufic inscription; around lower body off-set panels with rosettes
Height 13 cm, diameter 13.5 cm
Jazira, Syria or Rum, second half of the 13th century

The only published examples of this type of object (Melikian-Chirvani (1982), nos 87, 87a and b) are called 'money-vessels', but the reason for this is as yet unclear. The form was evidently current in the 13th–14th centuries in the Jazira and western Iran, but its origin is uncertain. The main attraction of this particular example is the bold rhythm of the decoration, the stress on the standing mace-bearers, being reinforced by the rectangles of pseudo-Kufic above them.

284
Stem cup

Cast high tin bronze, inlaid with silver; repairs to the stem; the original decoration consists of four roundels beneath a *naskh* inscription of good wishes with another such inscription and a short dedicatory inscription between them; on the foot is an arabesque
The upper band inscription reads:

> *al-'izz al-dā'im wa'l-iqbāl wa'l-dawla wa'l-sa'āda wa'l-salāma wa'l-karāma wa'l-ni'ma wa'l-'āfiya wa'l-nusra wa'l-kifāya wa'l-qanā'a wa'l-dawāma wa'l-'ināya wa'l-rahba wa'l-rahma wa'l-nahy wa'l-bakht wa'l-quwwāt wa'l-baqā lisāhibihi,*
>
> eternal glory, prosperity, wealth, happiness, peace, beneficence, favour, health, God's aid, sufficiency, contentment, longevity, (God's) sympathy, welcome, mercy, command, luck, strength and long life to its owner

The second such inscription, after the word *al-'āfiya* ends *wa'l-kufla lisāhibihi* 'and sustenance to its owner'
The dedicatory inscription reads:

> *sāhibuhu al-amīr Badr al-Dīn Sanjar ibn 'Abdullāh Amāsīrī al-Malikī*
>
> its owner is the Amir Badr al-Din Sanjar ibn 'Abdullah Amasiri, the royal (Mamluk)

The four roundels contain a bull, a mounted hawker, a lion and sun, and a mounted archer shooting at an animal. At a later date the inside and outside have been decorated with astrological figures in roundels, magical letters and Quranic inscriptions
The major inscription (on the outside) reads:

> *hādhihi'l-tāsa al-mubāraka fīhā jumi'at manāfi' wa hiya mujriyya li'l-sumūm wa'l-lusū' wa'l-khamūm wa'l-talqa wa'l-qars (wa) 'l-'illa wa'l-kalb al-kalib wa li'l-maghs wa'l-qawlanj wa li'l-shaqīqa wa'l-darāra wa'l-kabid wa'l-tuhāl wa li'l-qūh wa li ramy al-dam wa li abtāl al-sihr wa li-jamī' al-'ilal wa'l-āfāt wa fīhā yusqā al-sū' . . . ? . . . wa ishrab bi-idhn allāh al-karīm rusidat wa nuqishat bi-rasm nā'ib al-'abd al-faqīr ilā allāh ta'ālā Kāfūr al-Ikhshīdī wa'l-shams fī 'l-asad fī sana hā kāf tā li'l-hijra al-nabawiyya*
>
> This blessed cup has benefits collected within it, and dissolves poisons and stings, putrefaction and labour pains (?) and severe cold and illness, and bite of rabid dogs, indigestion and colic, megrims, and blindness, complaints of the liver and spleen, suppuration, loss of blood, all destruction caused by magic, all illnesses and disasters, and one should be given to drink from it . . . Drink with the permission of God, the generous. (The stars) were observed and (the cup) was inscribed for the deputy, the poor slave of God Almighty, Kafur the Ikhshidid, when the Sun was in Leo in the year 428 of the *hijra* of the Prophet. (428 is in *abjad: hā* 8, *kāf* 20, *tā* 400.)

The roundels on the inside of the cup contain a serpent, a horse, a lion (?), a harpie, a seated figure and a scorpion
Height 11 cm, diameter 14.5 cm
Anatolia or northern Jazira, second half of the 13th century

284

The nisba on this stem bowl, *Amasiri*, points to an Anatolian or possibly northern Jaziran origin for the object, since it must be derived from the town of Amasiya in northern Turkey. Interestingly, the stem bowl is very close in form to a piece bearing the name Khalif ibn al-Julaki, in the Pinacoteca in Naples. This was ascribed by D.S. Rice to Iran, but the *nisba* concerned refers to someone who dies a martyr's death on the frontiers of Islam (Rice (1955) p. 14, pl. XII). This would be much more appropriate to an Anatolian situation and the constant Muslim incursions into Byzantine-held territory, than to Iran.

The ascription to Kafur the Ikhshidid in the magical inscription is purely fictitious, as is the date 428/1036-7. It was no doubt included to add 'authenticity' to an object with supposed magical properties (For other magic bowls see Ittig (1982).) Kafur was incidentally the patron of the great Arab poet al-Mutannabi. The meaning of the curious symbol embedded in the magical inscription is uncertain, though it could, perhaps, be geomantic (Savage-Smith (1980), fig. 2, figure II).

285
Candlestick

Cast high tin bronze, inlaid with silver; around the foot ornamental Kufic inscription and rosettes; on the body four large roundels containing horsemen and four small ones containing seated drinkers in pairs, against an arabesque and rosette ground; on the shoulder pairs of seated figures between rosettes; on the neck an ornamental Kufic inscription; on the candleholder pairs of seated figures between sun-discs
Height 21.6 cm, diameter 19.4 cm
Previously in the collection of Prince Sadruddin Aga Khan
Welch (1972), vol. II, no. 14, p. 203
Northern Jazira (Siirt?), or Rum, second half 13th or early 14th century

Siirt is a likely source of candlesticks such as these, for it is known to have produced fine high tin bronze inlaid cups in a similar style at this period. However, the large quantities of surviving examples indicate a thriving industry and an extensive market, and it is possible that other towns, like Konya further west in the Sultanate of Rum, also manufactured such objects. Thus, there are significant differences in style and costume on different examples of the group which would well be indicative of different cultural centres: some horsemen have the typical Seljuq surcoat with a horizontal hem-line (e.g. Allan (1982), no. 8); some have a robe which hangs diagonally from the knee to a point behind the ankle (Allan (1982), no. 7); on this piece the front of each rider's coat hangs vertically, but the back curves from above and below into a point behind the (theoretical) position of the rider's calf.

286
Candlestick

Cast brass; traces of black, silver and gold inlay; around the body three sections of *naskh* inscription of honorifics divided by rosettes in roundels: *al-maqarr al-'ālī al-mawlawi al-mālikī / al-'ālimī al-'āmilī al-humāmī / al-nidhāmī al-mālikī al-(a)mīr(ī) al-ghāzī* (The lofty authority, the lordly, the possessing, the learned, the diligent, the valiant, the well-ordering, the possessing, the amir, the conqueror); around the neck another: *al-maqarr al-karīm al-'ālī al-mawlawī al-mālikī al-mujā(hidī)* (The honourable authority, the lofty, the lordly, the possessing, the holy warrior); Kufic inscription on shoulder undeciphered
Height 21 cm, diameter 22 cm
Geneva (1984), no. 4
Cairo, first half 14th century

This candlestick follows a form typical of Cairo in the first century of Mamluk rule. The key piece is a candlestick in the Museum of Islamic Art in Cairo which states that it was made in Cairo by Muhammad ibn Hasan al-Mawsili in 668/1269 (Atil (1981), no. 10). Another candlestick of approximately the same date is in the Nuhad Es-Said Collection (Allan (1982), no. 13). They are all of cast brass, and a tell-tale feature is an inverted domical openwork bracket inside the base at the bottom of the neck. The emphasis on inscriptions bearing titles is typical of Mamluk 14th-century metalwork.

287
Vessel

Cast brass; inlaid with silver and black compound; on flat rim vegetal work; on sides *naskh* inscription of honorifics: *al-janāb al-karīm al-'ālī al-mawlawī al-mahr (?) al-makhdūmī al-'(ā)limī 'Alam al-Dīn dāma'izzuhu* (His Excellency, the honourable, the lofty, the lordly, the ?, the masterful, the learned, 'Alam al-Din, may his glory endure). On the base is incised the name 'Ali ibn Muhammad Luqman, presumably a later owner
Height 6.8 cm, diameter 11.7 cm
Egypt or Syria, early 14th century

The purpose of this object is uncertain: it may have been a container for something edible, for incense, or for jewels, or it could possibly have been a spitoon, of which no Mamluk examples are otherwise known. The decoration and form of inscription point to an early-14th-century date, but the inscription unfortunately omits the name and *nisba* of the owner. The *laqab* 'Alam al-Din is usually associated with the name Sanjar. It is therefore possible that the owner was the famous amir Sanjar, well known for his joint mausoleum with the amir Salar in Cairo, and holder of important offices of state and governorships in the first half of the 14th century (Mayer (1933), pp. 197-9). However, given the various other amirs called 'Alam al-Din Sanjar at this period, this is pure conjecture.

288
Candlestick

Beaten brass, inlaid with silver and originally gold; on the body two panels of *naskh* inscription of honorifics divided by roundels: *al-maqarr al-'ālī al-mawlawī al-amīrī al-kabīrī al-ghāzī al-mujāhidī al-dhukhrī al-malikī al-nāsirī* (The lofty authority, the lordly, the great amir, the conqueror, the holy warrior, the treasury of excellence, (officer of) al-Malik al-Nasir); on the drip tray a similar *naskh* inscription: *al-maqarr al-'ālī al-mawlawī al-amīrī al-kabīrī al-mujā hidī al-murābitī al-muthāghirī al-mu'ayyadī al-malikī al-nāsirī* (The lofty authority, the lordly, the great amir, the holy warrior, the guardian of the frontiers, the fortified by God, (officer of) al-Malik al-Nasir); there are the remains of a similar inscription round the candleholder; the neck is decorated with three bands, the central one containing birds in roundels
Height 24 cm, diameter 22 cm
Syria, *c.* 1320–40

Sheet metal candlesticks under the Mamluks are of a quite different shape to cast pieces (nos 285 and 286), and may well be Damascus products, for Damascus had a flourishing candlestick industry in the 1290s (Allan (1982) p. 104). The precise dating of such pieces is also difficult especially when the title used here *al-malikī al-nāsirī* could refer either to a Mamluk of Sultan Muhammad ibn Qala'un (1294-1340) or Sultan Hasan (1347-61). The trellis pattern around the neck, with its quatrefoil insets, appears to be earlier than those on objects associated with the later sultan (e.g. Atil (1981), p. 97), but can hardly be earlier than the middle of Muhammad ibn Qala'un's reign.

289
Candlestick

Beaten brass; decorated with bands of *naskh* inscription divided by roundels with vegetal designs, set between narrow vegetal borders; the inscription on the body reads: *mimā 'umila bi-rasm al-adur al-sharīfa dhāt al-sitr al-rafī' wa'l-hijāb al-manī' Khawand al-kubrā jihat al-maqām al-malik a l-ashraf Abu Nasr Qaītbāy 'azza nasruhu* (One of the things made for the noble princess, the finely veiled, the strongly screened, the great princess, wife of his royal majesty, al-Malik al-Ashraf Abu Nasr Qaytbay, may his victory be glorious); an identical inscription decorates the shoulder; that on the candleholder omits all after 'his royal majesty'; on the neck are the words *al-sultān al-malik Abū Nasr Qaītbāy*; at the base of the neck an incised inscription making the object *waqf*
Height 45 cm, diameter 36 cm
Previously in the collection of M. Rambart Rat, Versailles
Wiet (1970). Its pair is in the Musée historique de Berne and was published by Mayer
Cairo, 1467–98

The lady concerned, Fatima al-Khassbakiya, was in fact married to two sultans, Qaytbay and Tumanbay I. She died in 1503. Despite political, social and economic upheaval in the period around 1400, there is some measure of continuity in the Mamluk minor arts between the 14th and 15th centuries. This candlestick is not only of the same form as no. 288, but also retains a similar layout of decoration with inscriptions separated by roundels in interlacing bands. Decoratively, there have been significant developments in the forms of arabesque used, but the most striking change is the lack of inlay: relatively few 15th-century brasses were inlaid with gold or silver, and only in Qaytbay's reign was there any attempt to revive the luxurious 14th-century polychrome style.

289

290
Incense-burner

Sheet brass, pierced and inlaid with silver, gold and a black compound. Decorated with two bands of pseudo-Kufic interrupted by arabesques in roundels, between scroll borders; interlace pattern on top and bottom
Diameter 12.5 cm
Syria, late 15th century

Spherical incense-burners such as these were introduced into Europe where they were placed on altars in cold cathedrals and used to warm the priest's hands, hence their other common name, 'handwarmers'. Where this particular variety of spherical incence-burner was produced has been much debated: often called Venetian Saracenic, and thus ascribed to a Muslim workshop in Venice, they are more probably Syrian (Melikian-Chirvani (1974/2), 2). There is certainly nothing decoratively to indicate a European ambiance for their production. They probably date from Qaytbay's reign (1468-96) when the political and economic fortunes of the Mamluk empire briefly revived, prior to its destruction at the hands of the Ottoman Sultan Selim early in the next century.

291
Dish

Beaten brass, inlaid with silver; five-lobed centre in *repoussé*; on the inside and rim, bands of cartouches with interlace work or pseudo-Kufic; in the centre a shield with undulating line across
Diameter 40.2 cm
Venice, in the Syrian style, *c.* 1500

Comparing this dish to the incense-burner (no. 290), it appears that the artist has not fully understood the way Islamic arabesques are designed. In particular three of the cartouches in the middle band of decoration contain a mixture of diagonal straight lines and horizontal curving stems which are unparalleled in Near Eastern Islamic art at this period, and indeed would make no artistic sense to an Islamic artist. Nevertheless the decorative influence of Islamic traditions on the designer of this dish would be difficult to underestimate, and shows the close cultural connections between Syria and Venice at this period.

292
Candlestick

Cast bronze; three dragon-headed branches with incised patterning on a twisted stem; otherwise undecorated
Height 45 cm, diameter 33 cm
Turkey, 16th century

The 15th century brought an extraordinary measure of cultural unity in the visual arts of the Near East, stretching from Ottoman Turkey to Central Asia, as arabesque designs of the period show. Forms too show this same phenomenon, and candlesticks with dragon-headed candle-holders are found not only in Turkey, but also in Syria and Iran (e.g. Pope (1938-9), vol. VI, pl. 1377). The absolutely plain body of this candlestick and its slender form make an Ottoman attribution certain.

293

293
Ewer

Cast bronze; the handle and double-mouthed spout adorned with birds; decorative moulded bands around upper body and lower neck; lid missing; on the octagonal neck inscribed *bi rasm al-sharīfa' Atīqa bint al-Mansūr*, (For the noble lady, 'Atiqa bint al-Mansur)
Height 38 cm
Exhibited *Paintings and Sculpture of India*, Michael Goedhuis Ltd., London (1982)
India, Delhi Sultanate (?), 14th century

This ewer is a close relative of the piece in the Nuhad Es-Said Collection (Allan (1982), no. 27) and, with its foot still intact, shows the correct proportions of such objects. However, unlike the latter, it is not inlaid and has relatively unambitious decoration. The provenance of these pieces is unproven, but the name 'Atiqa (meaning literally 'freed female slave') is not found in the Arab Near East at this period, and therefore points to a more eastern origin. There is also a clear link in form between this ewer and the next (no. 294), which can also be put forward as an Indian object.

294
Ewer

Bronze, cast in six pieces: foot, body, neck, spout, handle and lid; lid, neck and foot decorated with incised lotus petal designs with dots around; lion heads at top of handle and spout; bird finial on lid
Height 39.5 cm, diameter 19 cm
India, Mughal period, 16th-17th century

This ewer relates in form to the previous one (no. 293), and also to an 18th-century Mughal blue glass ewer in the British Museum (Victorian and Albert Museum, 1982, no. 393). Since the latter is a rather corrupt and inarticulate rendering of such a ewer shape, one may conclude that the present piece is of an earlier date, but of similar provenance. The present ewer's domical lid suggests the form of lid which may have adorned the previous ewer (no. 293) and the example in the Nuhad Es-Said Collection (Allan (1982), no. 27).

295
Jug

Cast brass; originally with two handles; the octagonal neck decorated with palmettes between two *naskh* inscriptions of good wishes; the upper reads: *al-'izza al-dā'ima wa'l-iqbāl al-'izza al-dā'ima wa'l-dā'ima . . . wa'l-dā'ima* (Perpetual glory and prosperity, perpetual glory and perpetual . . . perpetual); the lower one reads: *al-baraka al-kāmila al-ni'ma al-shāmila wa'l-'izza al-dā'ima* (Perfect blessing, complete favour and perpetual glory). Alternate spiral flutes on the body decorated with arabesques, above a further similar inscription reading: *al-baraka al-kāmila wa'l-ni'ma al-shāmila wa'l-izz* (perfect blessing, complete favour and glory); on each side of hexagonal foot arabesques; underneath foot an interlaced six-pointed star and the name *Yahyā ibn Yūsuf al-s(ā)igh (?)* (Yahya ibn Yusuf the goldsmith (?))
Height 14.5 cm, diameter 10 cm
Nasrid Spain, 14th century

Spanish Islamic metalwork is comparatively rare, but the attribution of this jug to the Nasrid period is certain, both from the form of the half-palmettes and the typical style of Nasrid cursive script. In form, however, the object relates to early Islamic silver, for example two probably Khurasan silver jugs in the Hermitage (Smirnov (1909), nos 127-8, pls 71, 72, 78). This suggests that the Spanish piece is part of a precious metal tradition inherited from the Caliphate in the first couple of centuries of Islam, which spread to the provinces and left its mark on the forms used in those areas in the ensuing periods. The same tendency is found elsewhere in the metalworking industry (in cast bronze ewers), and in architecture.

296
Planispheric astrolabe

Engraved brass, with silver knobs (some missing) on the perforated bases of the star-pointers and on certain cross-bars of the tracery of the *rete* (star-map)
Rete for 30 stars, all but two named, 5 plates
Inscribed, within the horary quadrant: 'Praise be to God. This astrolabe is a pious bequest to the mosque of Qasaba Hadrash'; this information, in a different *maghribi* script, using a different word for 'mosque', is repeated within the shadow-square and, using a third word for 'mosque', on one side of each plate
Diameter 17.2 cm
Phillips sale no. 23, 843, 21 April, 1982, lot 96
Maghrib, probably Morocco, *c.* 1650

The style of this astrolabe, including the characteristic western Kufic script, is typical of the work of Maghrib astrolabe-makers, continuing the traditions of Islamic instrument-makers in Spain before the reconquest.

The plates, engraved on both sides with the usual circles of altitude (*Muqantarāt*), lines for unequal hours, times of Muslim prayer (shown dotted), and dawn and dusk lines (also shown dotted), are for the latitudes of, and inscribed for: Makka, Medina; Taroudant, Marrakesh; Cairo, Tangier; Salé, Algiers; Fez, Meknès. On the back of the astrolabe: a zodiac/calendar scale (0° Aries = 10 March); a sexagesimal sine/cosine quadrant; a sundial-quadrant for unequal hours; a shadow-square. There is some engraved decoration on the back of the suspension bracket, and a petal motif occurs on a fixed silver washer in the centre of the *rete* and on a suspension pivot.
F.R.M.

296

297

Kashkūl (Dervish's begging bowl)

Cast brass; decorated with arabesques in medallions and with an inscription in honour of the Twelve Imams (as Melikian-Chirvani (1982), no. 124, p. 289, with the addition of the word *imām* before each name after that of Muhammad, and with the epithet *al-mujtabā* instead of *al-ridā* for Hasan; the list ends with Muhammad *al-mahdī*); this prayer is set between four lines of a prayer to 'Ali (Melikian-Chirvani (1982), no. 125, p. 292): 'Call to 'Ali who causes wonders to appear. You will find him your help in distress. Every case, every grief will be dispelled through your trusteeship. Oh 'Ali, Oh 'Ali, Oh 'Ali'; in the centre of the inside is a much rubbed inscription in a cartouche

Length 36.5 cm, width 18.5 cm, height 17 cm

Western Iran, *c.* 1550

This form of object goes back to Timurid times and probably earlier (Melikian-Chirvani (1982), no. 112). The Safavid style of this piece is clear not only from the arabesques in roundels and the form of script but also from the dragon heads at either end, which may be paralleled in many religious steel standards of the period. In form this *Kashkūl* is extraordinarily elegant, and this is enhanced by its unusually restrained decorative programme.

298
Torchstand and torch

Cast brass; twelve-sided body with two handles; the handle of the torch is missing; decorated with inscriptions in *nasta'līq* in cartouches (see below), and with a variety of arabesque patterns and palmette borders
Height 72 cm, diameter 30 cm
Pope (1938-9), vol. VI, pl. 1381, from the collection of T.L. Jacks
Western Iran, *c.* 1562

It is rare to find a Safavid torch stand with its torch still intact, and although the torch handle here is missing, the torch itself gives a striking finish to the cylindrical form of the body, and makes it an object of much greater elegance. The close dating of this piece is based on a torchstand in the Iraq Museum, Baghdad, which has very similar decoration and is dated 969/1562.

Inscriptions

TOP REGISTER

Zamānī nīst kaz 'ishq-i tu jān-i man namī sūzad.
Kudāmīn sīna-rā kān ghamza-yi pur-fann namī sūzad?
Chirāgh-i man namī sūzad shab az damhā-yi sard-i man;
Chirāgh-i khāna-yi ham-sāya ham rawshan namī sūzad.

There is no time in which my soul from love of you is not burning.
What breast is there which that artful glance does not burn?
My own lamp does not burn at night because of my cold sighs.
Even in my neighbour's house the lamp does not burn brightly.

These lines are from a *ghazal* of Amir Khusraw. Two more verses from the same poem occur in the next register. The beginning of the inscription is marked by a quatrefoil above the rosette separating the first and last hemistichs.

SECOND REGISTER

Hama shab zār mīsūzam ba-tārīkī [u tanhā'ī]
Ki bā man hīch dil-sūzī/darīn maskan namī sūzad./
Ghamm-i Khusraw hamī dānī u/nādān mīkunī khud-rā;/
Marā in sūkht, war nay/ta'na-yi dushman namī sūzad./

Zi ghayrat sūkhtam, jānā, chu/dar ghayram zadī ātish;/
Tu ātish mīzanī dar ghayr u/ghayr az man namī sūzad./

All night I burn with weeping, in darkness and in loneliness,
For in this house no friendly one burns with me.
You know of Khusraw's pain but make yourself not know –
That burned me; otherwise the taunts of foes don't burn me.

I burned with envy, my beloved, when you set light to another.
You set light to another, and none but me is burning.

The lines in the top register and the first two in the second are from a *ghazal* of Amir Khusraw. The last line, though in the same metre (*hazaj*) and with the same rhyme and in fact by the same poet, is from a different *ghazal*. The first and last lines also appear on no. 299. The first line is found again on the top of the present piece. According to the old Cawnpore edition of Khusraw's shorter poems the first comes from the *Dīwān* entitled *Tuhfat al-Sighar*, which contains the works of his youth and the second from *Wasat al-Hayat* covering his maturity. (*Kulliyāt-i 'Anāsir-i Dawāwīn-i Khusraw*, Cawnpore (1874), pp. 217-8.) The first poem, but not the second, is given in M. Darwish's Tehran edition of 1343 (p. 144), the second, but not the first, in Iqbal Salah al-Din's Lahore one of 1973 (II, pp. 1073-4). These texts are referred to in the notes that follow.

Top register Line 1 The editions give *dast*, 'hand', for *'ishq*, 'love'. The variant also occurs on the top of this piece and on no. 299. *Hā'* of *ghamza* is omitted here and on the top. Compare the treatment of the same letter as an extension of *zā'* on no. 299.

Second register Line 2 *Mī sūzam* and *tārīkī* are partly concealed by the attachment for the handle but there is not sufficient room for *wa tanhā'ī*, which has been restored from the editions. In the second hemistich where the editions give *maskan* the inscription on the lamp seems corrupt. Alternative readings (*gulshan*, *gulkhan*) are just possible but do not seem very suitable and the word as written could easily derive from a misunderstood *maskan*. *Line 3 Dushman* is partly concealed by the attachment.

THIRD REGISTER

Chirāgh-i ahl-i dil-rā/rawshan az rū-yi tu mī bīnam./
Hama sāhib-dilān-rā/rū-yi dil sū-yi tu mī bīnam./
Tu'ī maqsūd-i 'ālam,/kam mabādā az sarat mū'ī/
Ki 'ālam-rā tufayl-i/yak sar-i mū-yi tu mī bīnam./

Chirāghī-rā ki/Īzad bar furūzad/
Har ānkū fuf zanad rīshash bisūzad./

The lamp of men of wisdom I see lit by your face.
All the wise I see wholeheartedly coming to you.
You are the world's goal; may no hair of your head be lost,
For I see the world dependent on the tip of a single hair of yours.

The lamp that God lights up –
Who blows it burns his beard.

The first two lines are from a *ghazal* and are found on several similar Safavid lamps (in Meshed, Baghdad, and London). According to A.S. Melikian-Chirvani, who refers to a manuscript in the Bibliothèque Nationale, the author is Ahli Turshizi. (*Victoria and Albert Museum Catalogue, Islamic Metalwork from the Iranian World, 8th-18th Centuries*, London (1982), p. 327. Cf. Idem, *Le Bronze Iranien*, Paris 1973, p. 125; A.A. Ivanov, 'O pervonachal'nom naznachenii tak nazivaemikh iranskikh "podsvechnikov" XVI-XVII vv.', *Issledovaniya po istorii kulturi narodov vostoka, Sbornik N.A. Orbeli*, Leningrad (1960), p. 345.)

Line 1 Az rū-yi: either *rā'* or *zā'* is omitted by haplography. *Sū-yi tu*: run together as one word in the script.

Line 2 On the lamp in the Victoria and Albert Museum Melikian-Chirvani reads *tu ay sultān* at the beginning. *Tu'ī*, Ivanov's reading, is clear on the present piece. The other published examples also have *maqsūd* rather than *sultān*. For *mū'ī* Ivanov and Melikian-Chirvani read *muy*, which does not scan. For *sar-i mūy* in the second hemistich the Iranian scholar reads *mū-yi sar*, slightly altering the sense and destroying both rhyme and metre. On the present piece there is a superfluous *alif* over *'ālam*.

The third verse is a variant of a saw of some popularity and considerable antiquity. The verse appears again on the top of the piece. The text of the current modern version is given by A. Dihkhudā in his *Hikam wa Amthāl* (Tehran (1310), II, p. 610):

... Har ānkash puf kunad rīshash bisūzad.

The meaning is the same as that of the text proposed here. The currency of the saying in the early 15th century is attested by the appearance of an allusive variant in the *Zafar-nāma* of Nizam al-Din Shāmī (I, Prague (1937), p. 259). Here the second hemistich reads:

Har ānkas puf kunad dānī chi sūzad.

Whoever blows at it – you know what burns.

The first hemistich appears to have *ān rū*, 'that face' for *īzad*, 'God'. There even seems to be the appropriate vowel mark over the *rā'*. It scans and would make good sense but is also an easy corruption of *īzad*. On the top though *īzad* is miswritten it is certainly not intended as *ān rū*.

In the second hemistich the reading proposed assumes that *nūn* has dropped out of *ān kū Zanad* seems to be written in full in the first panel and partly repeated in the second. Thus it is impossible to mark the division in the text at this point. Here and on the top *fuf* appears to follow *Zanad* but the metre requires the opposite.

The inscription on the torch itself consists of the first line of verse on the top register of the body, the third line of verse on the third register, and the following in *mudāri'* metre:

An lāla-rukh ki sūkht dil-i man ba-dāgh-i ū
Rūyash buwad hamīsha ilāhī chirāgh-i ū.

The first verse is the opening verse of the *ghazal* of Amir Khusraw which appears on the top register of the body of the piece and also on no. 299. The second one is also found on the bottom register of no. 298. The third may be translated as follows:

That fair-faced one whose brand has burnt my heart –
His face, O God, serves ever as his lamp.

A.H.M.

299
Torchstand

Cast brass; decorated with diagonal fluting and arabesque bands; on the rim in a cartouche an owner's name – Mashhadi Muhammad 'Ali; Around the top of the neck are verses from two different *ghazals* of Amir Khusraw (see below).
A later crudely scratched inscription on the plain flutes mentions the giving of the object as *waqf*
Height 60.5 cm, diameter 29 cm
Western Iran, late 16th century

The spiral is normally found in Safavid times adorning domical objects (e.g. dish lids – Melikian-Chirvani (1982), no. 145) or objects of related shape (e.g. a hawking drum – Melikian-Chirvani (1982), no. 136). Here, however, it is used to decorate a cylindrical torchstand, a form to which it is equally suited.

Inscriptions

OWNERSHIP INSCRIPTION

Sāhibuhu Mashhadī Muhammad 'Alī.

Its owner is Mashhadi Muhammad 'Ali.

The *nisba* Mashhadi precedes the name, presumably indicating that it is here a title of respect enjoyed by one who has made the pilgrimage to Meshed rather than anything else.

VERSES *(hazaj metre)*

Zamānī nīst kaz 'ishq-i tu jān-i man namīsūzad.
Kudāmīn sīna-rā kān ghamza-yi pur-fann namīsūzad?
Zi ghayrat sūkhtam, jānā, chu dar ghayram zadī ātish.
Tu ātish mīzanī dar ghayr u ghayr az man namīsūzad.

There is no time in which my soul from love of you is not burning.
What breast is there which that artful glance does not burn?
I burned with envy, my beloved. You set light to another.
You set light to another, and none but me is burning.

The verses are from two different *ghazals* of Amir Khusraw which also occur together with other lines from the same poems on no. 298. *Line 1* As on no. 298 *'ishq*, 'love', replaces the *dast*, 'hand' of the printed texts. *Line 2* In the first hemistich *tu* replaces the *chu* of no. 298, an inferior but not impossible reading. *Mīm* of *ghayram* is omitted. In the second hemistich *u*, 'and', is omitted. It is not required by the metre but appears on no. 298 and in the printed text.

Nearly all dotted letters are correctly pointed.

A.H.M.

300
Torchstand

Cast brass; twelve-sided; decorated with bands of arabesques, and lozenge-shape pattern in relief
Around the neck an inscription (see below)
Height 39.5 cm, diameter 21 cm
Western Iran, late 16th century

The lozenge pattern on this twelve-sided torchstand probably derives from an ogival design, with lozenges alternately plain and filled with arabesques (e.g. Melikian-Chirvani (1982), no. 138). The cast flutes in alternate directions give a more interesting visual character to such an object than incised decoration alone, a fact which is equally true of the cast diagonal flutes on no. 299. Thus the Safavid craftsmen avoided the monotony which could so easily have overwhelmed these cylindrical objects.

Inscription (*ramal* metre)

> *'Ishq tābad dar dil-i tārīk tā rawshan shawad.*
> *Sham' gar ātish nabīnad az kujā rawshan shawad?*
> *Gar furūzad sad hazārān sham' bī rukhsār-i tu*
> *Dil az ān sham-i hazāran kay marā rawshan shawad?*

> Love shines in the dark heart so it becomes bright.
> If the candle does not see fire how will it light?
> If hundreds of thousands of candles burn, without your face,
> From that candle of thousands when will my heart be bright?

Some pointing, almost all correct.
A.H.M.

301
Pail

Cast brass; decorated with arabesques, palmette arcading, and a band of inscription in *nasta'līq* (see below)
On the rim, partly invisible owing to the handle, is the name of the owner Ahmad or Muhammad, and the date 1009/1600
Height without handle 16 cm, diameter of mouth 17.5 cm
Western Iran, 1600

Like the *kashkūl* (no. 297) this bath-pail illustrates the elegant forms current in Safavid metalwork, although the form itself certainly goes back to the Timurid period. The decoration is much more profuse here than on the *kashkūl*, but is carefully designed to compliment the shape of the vessel. It displays the rather more rigid arabesque style which occurs on metal objects from the end of the 16th century onwards.

Inscriptions

OWNER'S INSCRIPTION (not fully visible in the illustration because of the handle)

Sāhibu[hu] . . . [A]hmad (or [M]uhammad)

Its owner . . . [A]hmad (or: [M]uhammad)

It is uncertain whether or not there is anything else between *sāhibuhu* and the visible name.

VERSES

Chun ba-hammām dar āyad mah-i man bar khīzam,
Dīda pur āb kunam, bar kaff-i pāyash rīzam.
Bahr-i hammām-i tu, ay shākh-i gul-i naw-rasta
Tās-i zarrīn shuda khurshīd, mah-i naw dasta.
Chun ba-hammām dar āyad mah-i man paywasta
Tās ābīst marā dīda u abrū dasta.

When my beloved Moon enters the bath I rise;
My eye fills with water; I pour it on the soles of his feet.
For your bath, Oh new-blown spray of rose,
The sun is a golden bowl, the new moon its handle.
When my beloved moon enters the bath, constantly
My eyes are bowls of water, my eyebrows handles.

The same verses appear in a different order (1, 3, 2) on a handled pail in the Musée des Arts Décoratifs in Paris published by A.S. Melikian-Chirvani (*Le Bronze Iranien*, Paris (1973), pp. 106-7, where reference is made to two further pieces with part of the same inscription which appear to remain unpublished). Though all three verses are in the same metre Melikian-Chirvani is probably right in saying that they come from two poems but the unidentified metre to which he assigns them is not known to Persian prosody. In fact they are in a common variety of *ramal* (*muthamman makhbūn mahdhūf*).

Line 1 The speaker identifies himself with the pail from which the beloved pours water over himself in the bath. *Dīda*, 'eye', is also applied to the mouth of a vessel. Just as the pail is filled with water the speaker's eyes fill with tears of wonder and passion. In the second verse the rounded pail is compared with the orb of the sun, its narrow curved handle to the new moon. In the third the speaker's eyes resemble the pail in being round with wonder and full of water (tears); his eyebrows rise in a curve of astonishment comparable to the curve of the pail's handle.

Line 2 For *shākh-i gul* the pail in Paris mentioned above has *tāza gulī* (incorrectly, as Melikian-Chirvani notes, for *tāza gul*, 'fresh rose' which does appear on another pail in the same collection. (See Melikian-Chirvani, op. cit., p. 108.) *Shākh-i gul* is found on a handleless, spouted pouring vessel in the Louvre which has the three verses in the same order as the 'Dauphin' pail (Ibid., p. 114). In the second hemistich Melikian-Chirvani reads *īnast* for *ābīst*. There appear to be three dots under the word on the 'Dauphin' piece which would support the more poetic reading *ābīst*. (The photographs available do not show clearly whether there are any dots or a *madda* above the words or not.)

Line 3 Melikian-Chirvani adds *u*, 'and' after *khurshīd* which is possible and may occur on other pieces known to him but is not required by the meaning or metre.

Nearly all the dotted letters in the inscription are given the correct pointing, with *sins* receiving three subscript dots.

A.H.M.

302
Planispheric astrolabe

Engraved brass
Rete incomplete, but pointers for 16 named stars remain. Four plates
On the front of the suspension bracket there is a quotation from the Qur'an, Sura XXXVI, verses 38-40

> And the sun – it runs to a fixed resting-place;
> that is the ordaining of the All-mighty, the All-knowing.
> And the moon – We have determined it by stations,
> till it returns like an aged palm-bough.
> It behoves not the sun to overtake the moon, neither
> does the night outstrip the day,
> each swimming in a sky.
> [Arberry's translation]

Signed, on the back, within and below the shadow-square: 'Made by the poor man Muhammad Muqim al-Yazdi, year 1052, and the designer of its lettering and the engraver of all that is the poor servant Muhammad Mahdi al-Yazdi'
Diameter 18.7cm
Hotel Drouot, 28 April 1977, lot672; Brieux-Maddison, MHMD MQIM YZDI 2
Iran, 1052/1642-3

This is a typically highly decorated Safavid astrolabe, with a characteristic foliate pattern in the tracery of the *rete*. Some of the engraved script is in relief; some delineated in double-outline; mostly *naskh*, with some *nasta'līq* in the signature. The precise workmanship is the result of a collaboration between Muhammad Muqim al-Yazdi, known as the maker of four other astrolabes, and Muhammad Mahdi b. Muhammad Amin al-Yazdi, who signed as the maker of some twenty astrolabes and as the decorator of several others, including two others by Muhammad Muqim al-Yazdi.

On the back, as well as a sine quadrant and a shadow-square and scales of cotangents, are graphs enabling the azimuth of the Qibla (the direction of Makka) to be determined throughout the year by observation of the sun (after noon) from various places, including Isfahan, Yazd, Tus, and Herat.

F.R.M.

302

DAVID ALEXANDER AND HOWARD RICKETTS

Arms and Armour

Islamic miniature paintings gleam with portrayals of warriors and princes clad in gilded armour and engraved war masks, riding richly caparisoned horses with decorated saddles, bearing silk-covered or painted shields, quivers and bow cases, wielding gilded maces, sabres and daggers with gold and silver mounts often studded with gems. Miniature painters also lavishly depicted the paraphernalia of war, such as the intricately wrought belts of the higher-ranking warriors, their fluted war drums, dragon-mouthed trumpets and their sculpted and gilt standards. It is not surprising that court painters so often focused on the beauty of military objects and the accoutrements of war; they were, after all, often employed by masters who were both warriors and lovers of beauty.

Among the great patrons of the arts were the Abbasid Caliphs, perhaps the most notable being al-Mansur (754-75) who extended Abbasid rule as far as India. He was responsible for the building of the city of Baghdad (Madinat al-Salam), at whose centre was a fabulous green dome said to have been topped by a horseman whose lance automatically pointed in the direction from which danger could be expected.[1] In Spain, Islam produced a glorious period of artistic and intellectual activity. One of the great warrior patrons of Spanish Islam was 'Abdulrahman I (755-88) who conquered Cordova, and later turned back the army of Charlemagne, inflicting upon the retreating Franks the disastrous defeat at Roncevalles. As a patron he was responsible for the rebuilding of the Great Mosque of Cordova which became the most important centre of Western Islam.

Practically nothing in the way of arms and armour has survived from this period, although the few pieces which have – several swords and perhaps a helmet from the late Nasrid period illustrate the heights achieved by Western Islamic metalworkers, enamellers and goldsmiths.

The artistic achievements of the 15th century were indebted to the conquests of Timur (1336-1404) who systematically rounded up artists and craftsmen and transported them to his capital at Samarkand. His descendants were famous as patrons of the arts. From among them one could single out Ulugh Beg (1417-49) who scored some notable victories against the Uzbeks, although in his case he was far more important as a patron of science, painting, and jade carving. It is very likely that the jade sword hilt (no. 308) was carved in his workshops in Samarkand.

The inheritors of the Timurid and Turkman artistic traditions were the Safavids, and the chiselled and damascened sword blade (no. 310) was probably made and decorated by a master in the workshops of one of the early Safavid rulers. The best-known ruler of this dynasty was Shah Abbas (1587-1629) who consolidated Safavid power and was responsible for the great building programme at Isfahan. Lovers of Islamic watered steel sabre blades remember him as the patron of the legendary swordsmith Asadullah of Isfahan.

The Ottoman Turks produced a number of great warrior patrons; the most important of whom were Mehmet II (r. 1451-81), the conqueror of Istanbul, Trebizond and much of south eastern Europe, and Suleyman the Magnificent (r. 1520-66) who led his armies on thirteen great campaigns, conquered Hungary and besieged Vienna. The former wrote poetry and was the patron of scores of Near Eastern and European artists including Gentile Bellini; the latter was also a poet and a patron of all the arts who supported numerous artists including Sinan, perhaps the greatest architect Islam has produced.

Beautiful weapons were especially appealing to these warrior patrons, as is shown by surviving examples in many public collections, such as those in the Topkapi Saray Museum and by examples from private collections such as those shown here. Luxurious weapons were often ceremonial and not necessarily used in warfare. It is known, for instance, that most Islamic rulers had special corps of body guards. Such units were generally handsomely equipped; a particularly striking example must have been the palace guards of the Ghaznavids and Saffarids numbering two thousand men, half of whom were armed with gold weapons and half with silver weapons.[2] It is likely that the mace head (no. 304) was carried by such a royal bodyguard.

An even larger display of weapons could be seen at the review (*'ard*) of the troops by the sovereign. This colourful ceremony was probably Sasanian in origin and became a feature of military life in most Islamic societies. Its main purpose was to register the troops, review their martial skills and inspect their weapons.[3] A number of such reviews are described in Islamic chronicles and mention is invariably made of beautiful weapons and armour. In one of these reviews that took place in 1476 before the Aq-Koyunlu Sultan Khalil, we read that the prince sat on 'a golden throne studded with shining jewels', that he was presented by his father with a gem-studded saddle and then reviewed an army that was so resplendent in its armours of iron plates that the court poet compared its brilliance to that of the sun. The parade was so long that it lasted all day and in the evening the prince ordered it to continue by torch and candlelight so that 'their glow and the glitter of arms and armour should make the earth brighter than the heavens.'[4]

Most of the equipment paraded in these reviews was purely military, but even this was often of extraordinary quality. Among the equipment of the army of the great Mamluk sultan, Baybars I (1260-77) we read of 'coats of mail, of silk velvet plated with gold and silver.'[5]

1) P. Hitti, *History of the Arabs* (New York, 1970), p. 293
2) C.E. Bosworth 'The armies of the Saffarids' in *Bulletin of the School of Oriental and African Studies* (1968), vol. XXI, part 3
3) C.E. Bosworth Isti'rad, 'Ard in *Encyclopedia of Islam*, vol. II, pp. 265-9
4) V. Minorsky 'A Civil and Military Review in Fars in 881/1476' in *The Turks, Iran and the Caucasus in the Middle Ages* Variorum Reprints, (London, 1978), p. 155-156, 160
5) S.F. Sadeque (tr.), *Baybars I of Egypt* (Pakistan, 1956), p. 29

Apparently all ranks spent a great deal of their spare time beautifying and embellishing their arms and weapons for such occasions for 'the amirs, soldiers and their Mamluks ... were completely absorbed in preparing the war trappings of horses, making coats of mail, polishing coats of mail, inlaying helmets and making frontals for the horses.'[6]

Beautifully decorated armour or weapons with fittings of precious metal and gems were not only used on parade or carried by royal body guards, but were since the earliest days of Islam given as insignia of rank or as princely gifts. Nizam al-Mulk, who was assassinated by the Isma'ilis in 1092, mentions that the Turkish slave warriors at the Samanid court received such gifts at the end of each year of training. These gifts were clearly intended as marks of rank. In their first year of training the young warriors were forbidden to even mount a horse, but on reaching the second year were given a horse and a plain harness, in the third year they received a long sword, and in the fifth a better saddle, clothing and a mace; in the sixth they received parade dress, etc.[7] A well-known case of the giving of weapons as princely gifts was recorded because of its unfortunate aftermath; the Caliph al-Mutawakkil gave away an 'Indian sword of beautiful workmanship' and then on 11 December 861 he was killed with this very weapon by the trusted guard to whom he had given it.[8]

Protocol, especially during the Abbasid period (750-1258), determined who could receive a particular kind of gift – a merchant for instance would not be given weapons but could receive a robe of honour – and determined who could carry weapons. Only persons of sufficiently high rank could wear a sword, but within this group certain swords could only be worn by certain ranks or individuals. A common soldier could not wear a sword with silver or golden mounts or a silver or gold belt, and only the Caliph could wear the sword of the Prophet. A famous example is related by al-Tabari (838-923) who tells of a manufacturer of umbrellas who dared to put on a sword and sword belt, was severely rebuked by the Caliph and warned never to repeat such a transgression.[9] In a similar instance of self-aggrandizement the offender was ordered to be cuffed a hundred times, put in fetters and made to wear a weaver's shirt as punishment.[10]

Gifts of weapons or garnitures for man and horse were most commonly given to loyal retainers and victorious soldiers; sometimes even in anticipation of victory such as when the Ottoman Sultan Mehmet IV (1648-87) sent to Kara Mustafa Pasha a golden sword and a diamond studded dagger.[11] Unfortunately the Grand Vizier failed to conquer Vienna and the enraged Sultan ordered him strangled with a silken bow cord. It was from this last great Ottoman campaign in the West that nos 317 and 318 were taken as booty.

Garnitures of arms and armour were also traditionally given to foreign princes and rulers. The gifts of Baybars I to King Bereke in 1262 are perhaps the best known and consisted, amongst other things of: 'Qaljuri swords with silver hilts, gilded iron maces ... Frankish helmets with silver collars, painted shields ... bridles inlaid with metal and tops being threaded through with silver ornamented rope, silver jackets inlaid with gold, well-ornamented cruppers, felt covers, saddles from Khwarazm ... cross bows from Damascus with strings of silk ... exquisitely fashioned arrows in leather bound boxes ....'[12] Another spectacular garniture was sent in about 1438 by the Mamluk Sultan Barsbay (1422-38) to John VIII Palaeologus, Emperor of Byzantium. The garniture consisted of a robe of honour, a bow, bow case and quiver, a sabre and belt and possibly a saddle. The Emperor was so impressed that he commissioned Pisanello to make a commemorative medallion. In working on this, Pisanello made a series of drawings of the objects, which are the most detailed and clear representations of Mamluk arms and armour in existence.[13]

Just as arms and armour of high quality could only be worn by the military élite, so the best pieces were often produced in royal workshops and preserved in royal treasuries. It is known that in the early Islamic period rulers often kept collections of arms and armour. The most important instance of this is the preservation by the Umayyads and Abbasids of the weapons of the Prophet. Especially notable amongst these relics was the sword of the Prophet which was used in the inauguration of a new Caliph and was often carried by the Caliph as a symbol of his spiritual and political descent from the Prophet.

A large collection must also have been kept by the Tahirids, for when they were overthrown in 872 their conqueror Ya'qub took as booty from their treasury a large quantity of gold and silver shields, swords and maces.[14] The mace head (no. 304) most probably represents the type

6) Sadeque, ibid., p. 32
7) V. Barthold, *Turkestan down to the Mongol Invasion* 2nd edition (London, 1955), p. 227
8) R. Payne, *The Holy Sword* (New York, 1959), p. 184
9) E. Marin (tr.), *The Reign of al-Mu'tasim* (833-42) by Abu Jafar al-Tabari (New Haven, 1951), p. 19
10) Ibn Miskawaihi, 'The Experience of Nations, in H.F. Amedroz and D.S. Margoliouth (trs. eds.) *The Eclipse of the 'Abbasid Caliphate* (Oxford, 1921), vol. 1, p. 187, 194
11) R.F. Kreutel, *Kara Mustafa vor Wien* (Munich, 1967), p. 57
12) Sadeque, op, cit., p. 189-190
13) M. Vickers 'Some Preparatory Drawings for Pissanello's Medallion of John VIII Palaeologus' in *Art Bulletin* (Sept. 1978), 60, no. 3
14) C.E. Bosworth, *Armies of the Saffarids* p. 546

used by the Tahirids and later by the Saffarids and Ghaznavids.

The Mughal emperors of India must also have had a large, splendid and constantly renewed collection. It is recorded of the emperor Akbar (1556-1605) that all his weapons were ranked and named. These included thirty swords for his special use, a different one of which was sent daily to him. When the number of these had decreased – as the result of gift-giving – to twelve, eighteen new ones were brought from a secondary supply. The different swords, daggers, bows, spears, etc. used by the emperor were apparently ranked and worn according to the day, week or month of the year.[15] It is not known by what special characteristics these weapons were differentiated or ranked, but a small number of imperial Mughal weapons survive, and some of these include in their inscriptions, some hitherto unexplained numbers. Perhaps these will eventually provide the clue to the Mughal classification of imperial weapons.[16]

The contents of the Mamluk treasuries were taken to Istanbul after the Ottoman conquest in 1517. Presumably this was the source of many of the weapons which are now preserved in the Treasury of the Prophet in the Topkapi Saray Museum and of the decorated armours, standards and sabres of such sultans as Qaytbay, Qansuh al-Ghuri and Tumanbay. The Ottomans also took to Istanbul the crusader trophies from the arsenal at Alexandria. These had been engraved with dedicatory inscriptions by their Mamluk captors and as a group provide a comprehensive documentary account of the typology of the European sword in the late 14th and 15th centuries. Most of these swords remain in the Askeri (Military) Museum in Istanbul, but others have entered various public and private collections. An early example, dating to the fourteenth century, is included (no. 307). The collection of arms and armour in the Topkapi Saray is unparalleled today, and probably was the most magnificent and comprehensive collection ever to have been formed in the Islamic world. The description given by the French jeweller Tavernier in the mid-17th century is worth quoting for the light it throws on the collection when it was still in the hands of the Sultans. Tavernier wrote of the extent of the collection and described long bows, cross bows, arrows, muskets, flintlocks, sabres, and swords 'which are all so many masterpieces, that have been presented from time to time to the Turkish Emperor.'[17] He noted that some were in poor condition and neglected because 'there come in daily presents of arms excellently wrought that the novelty whereof makes him forget the old.' In addition there were bridles, breast plates, cruppers, and stirrups set with diamonds, rubies and emeralds, etc., and rich battle axes, swords and sabres set with precious stones. Apparently these latter were given away as gifts for he writes 'that when the Grand Seignor deigns to honour a Pasha he sends him one of those swords or sabres . . . but on the death of the Pasha, they are brought back to the treasury.'[18] Many of the bejewelled and damascened swords and sabres now exhibited in the Topkapi Saray may have made this journey out of and back into the collection. Others, especially those given to foreigners remained outside, and it is possible that the dagger blade (no. 314) was one of these. This blade is of special interest because of its relationship to a *kārd* whose fittings were made by a goldsmith working in the imperial workshops in Istanbul. This craftsman also made a rosewater sprinkler, a jewelled mirror and in 1588/9 a Koran cover for Sultan Murad III (1574-95), illustrating that the same artists worked not just on weapons but also on a variety of objects of courtly and religious use.[19]

The collecting of Islamic arms and armour in the West has recently been fully discussed by Howard Ricketts in his introduction to the catalogue of the Copenhagen exhibition of 1982.[20] Islamic arms and armour entered many royal collections in the West, generally as royal or princely gifts. Of special note here are the collections at Windsor and Sandringham in England and in Europe the collections of Dresden, Stockholm, Paris and Vienna. In other cases objects were purchased by princely patrons such as the Medici or taken as booty such as were many of the weapons now in Poland and Karlsruhe. In addition to these, a number of individuals, such as Frederick Stibbert and George C. Stone assembled large collections of Islamic arms and armour. Most of this private collecting took place during the 19th and early 20th centuries and there has been little activity since. Even so magnificent a collection as that now on exhibition in the Kuwait National Museum contains few arms. For this reason the objects gathered together for this exhibition mark a new and most necessary step in the preservation not only of an important group of beautiful objects but also in the preservation and continuation of an important part of the heritage of Islam.

15) Abu'l Fadl'Allāmi, *Ain I Akbari* tr. H. Blochmann, (Calcutta, 1873), vol. 1, p. 109
16) This problem is being studied by A.S. Melikian-Chirvani, who plans to publish a sabre from the treasury of Awrangzib (1658-1707), which is now in the Metropolitan Museum, New York, acc. no. 36.25.1591
17) J.B. Tavernier, *The six voyages of John Baptista Tavernier* (London, 1677-8), p. 45
18) J.B. Tavernier, *Six voyages*, p. 46
19) The Koran is illustrated in F. Çagman, *The Anatolian Civilizations* (Istanbul, 1983), vol. III. E118, E119, and E199. The fittings of a sabre in the Topkapi storeroom are by the same hand
20) H. Ricketts 'Some Early Collectors and Scholars of Oriental Arms and Armour', in *Islamiski vaben l dansk privateje* (Copenhagen, 1982)

303
War mask

The metal face is forged with delineated eyebrows, cheeks, nose, and moustache. The surface is engraved with interlocking floral forms and, across the brow, with Arabic inscriptions within cartouches and with part of the maker's signature; the forehead is reinforced with a strip of metal and with a lobed 'half moon' of iron set with two rings for the helmet hinge
Length 20 cm, width 16.5 cm
West Iran, 15th century

This mask is one of only three surviving examples. It was originally *en suite* with a helmet to which it was attached by a hinge at the brow, and clamps at either temple (cf. a similar mask of the 16th century with attached helmet, Sarre and Martin (1910), Pl. 230, no. 343). The holes on the sides of the face were probably for the attachment of circular devices to protect the ears and neck (a miniature painting in the Metropolitan Museum, acc. no. 69.74.8 shows a Mongol mask and helmet with protectors of this kind).

War masks were used in the Roman Empire and in the ancient Near East. They are documented in Seljuq and Mongol miniature painting and also in Iranian painting of the 15th century. An Iranian painting of the second half of the 15th century (Topkapi Saray Museum, H. 2123, 53 v) shows a number of warriors wearing masks of this type, and it is possible that this example is from the same period and from the same region.

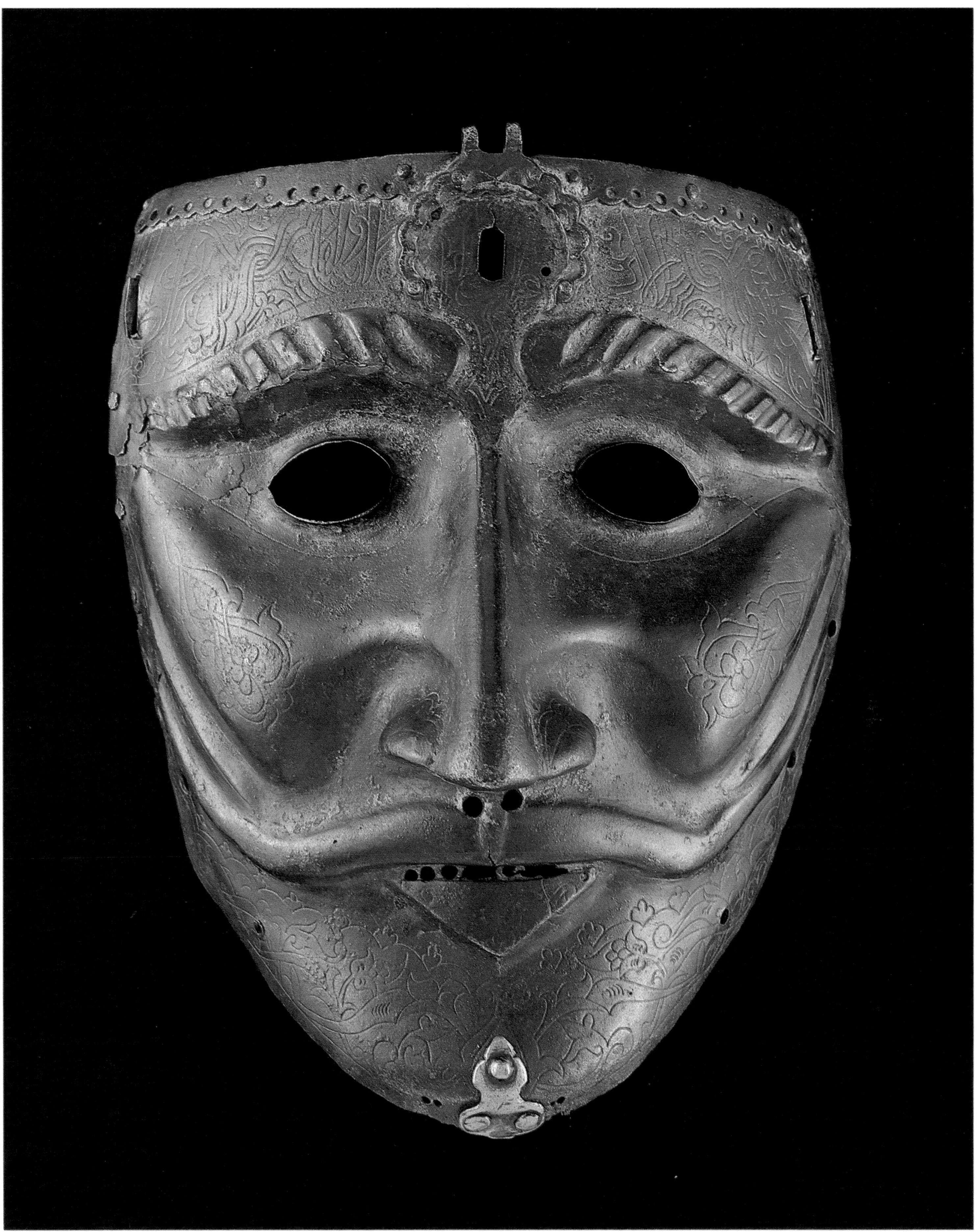

303 *(Actual size)*

304
Mace head

Cast bronze, octagonal in section and deeply fluted with eight heavy ribs, engraved with arabesques and medallions and on the neck with an Arabic inscription, all originally inlaid with silver
Inscribed in Arabic: 'Might, favourable destiny, felicity and good fortune to its owner'
Height 20.5 cm
Khurasan, 12th to 13th century

The mace is primarily a knightly weapon and in Iranian tradition is the weapon of heroes, such as Bahram Gur. A mace inlaid with gold or silver could only have belonged to a warrior of rank, perhaps even to a royal body guard. An elongated mace head of this type was excavated at Nishapur and has been dated to the 11th or 12th century (see Allan (1982), pp. 52 and 94, fig. 142), presumably the Samanid, Saffarid and Ghaznavid palace guards had gilded and silvered maces of this type (see p. 297).

305
Quillon block

Silver gilt and niello made in two identical halves, soldered together; decorated with a star and cross design within gilt borders, and with short stylized foliate quillon tips.
Width approx. 6.5 cm
Seljuq, 12th to 13th century

This quillon block was made for a matrix of the type exhibited (no. 306). The only other surviving example is a quillon block with lion-headed tips in the City Art Museum, St Louis (illustrated in Pope, 1938–9, pl. 1428,b).

306
Matrix for a sword hilt

Bronze, patinated green, consisting of two elements, the pommel and the quillon block; the former with a stylized lion within a roundel, the quillon with lions within foliage flanking a tree
Length 13.25 cm
Seljuq, 12th to 13th century

These matrices would have been used as a master mould from which gold or silver gilt sword fittings were produced. Fittings cast from such matrices can be identified by the seams on their sides. As far as one knows this is the only surviving set to include a pommel.

Matrices of a quillon block and two scabbard mounts are in the Metropolitan Museum of Art, New York (acc. nos 1980.210,1,2,3. See D.G. Alexander, *Notable Acquisitions*, M.M.A., 1979-80, p. 27), a quillon block cast from a similar matrix is also in a private collection (no. 305) and a lower scabbard mount, similarly cast, is in the Kuwait National Museum (LNS 143m). Taken together this group of objects provides a valuable record of the style of the Seljuq sword.

307
Crusader sword

With heavy disc pommel of bronze and spatulate iron quillons; the broad blade straight and double edged with a single groove marked with the letter P in reverse and with a mark consisting of concentric rings

Engraved on either side with an Arabic inscription. *Obverse* 'Made *waqf* by His Excellency, Holder of the Sword, al-Ukuz (officer) of al-Malik al-Ashraf in the year 769(?)/1367.' *Reverse* 'In the *qā'a* (hall) built by him and bearing his name in the well-guarded frontier city (?Alexandria). Whoever shall take it and not return it, that will be imputed to him as a crime.'

Length 109 cm

Previously in the collection of Sir Richard Hyde Parker, Long Melford

Italy, *c.* 1360

Al-Ukuz was a Mamluk of Sultan Sha'ban (al-Malik al-Ashraf), r. 1363-77). Presumably this sword was captured after the Christian withdrawal in 1365 from Alexandria which they had looted and held for a few days as part of a crusade organized by King Peter de Lusignan of Cyprus. To safeguard their booty many of the King's men sailed away with their loot, leaving him with insufficient forces to hold the city.

A number of swords of this type have been preserved, including one in the Kienbusch Collection, Philadelphia, no. 324, another in a private collection in Seattle, and at least seven in the Askeri Museum, Istanbul, including nos 2440, 5924, 5928, 5931, 24147, 14788 and 21661.

The keeping and ritual display of captured weapons, especially swords is well documented. Before Islam captured swords are known to have been ritually displayed in the Ka'ba; there are records from the Ayyubid period of swords and shields captured from the Crusaders in 1157/8 being hung on the walls of Aleppo 'creating a spectacle which people admired for seven days.' The crusader swords kept by the Mamluks and later by the Ottomans demonstrate the continuity of this triumphal tradition.

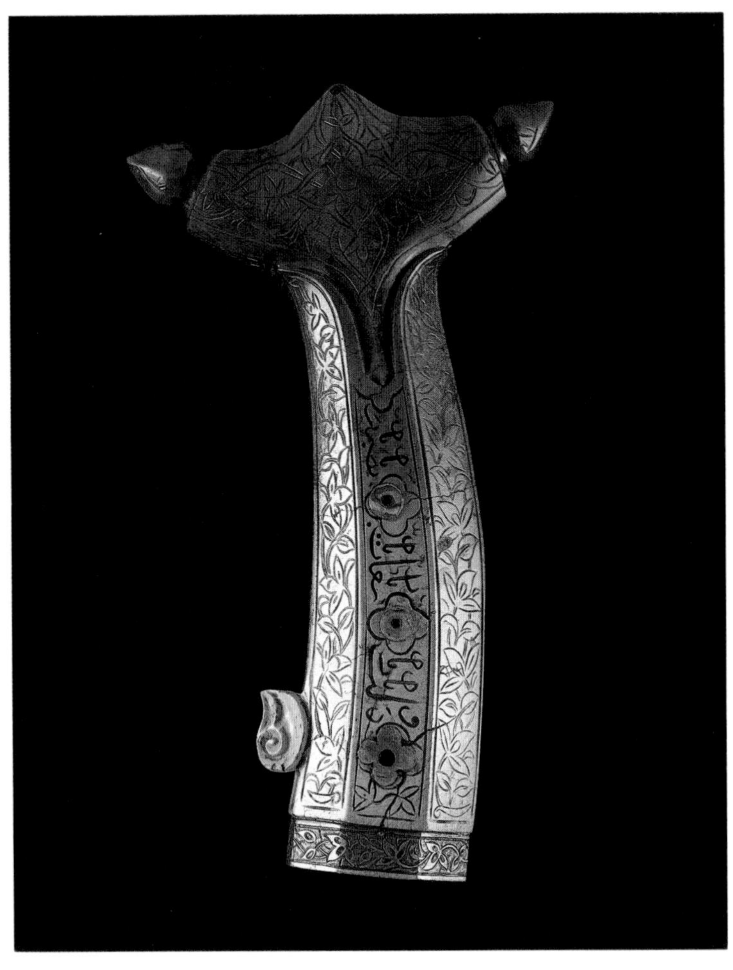

308
Sword hilt

The jade grip, octagonal in section, slightly inclined to one side and tapering slightly towards the quillon block. The thin pommel of silver is chased around the sides with a floral scroll, the quillons carved with bud forms
Inscribed with good wishes in Persianized Arabic
Length 14 cm
Iran, Timurid, probably workshops of Ulugh Beg (1417-49)

This hilt is directly related to the two jade hilted sabres preserved in the Topkapi Saray Museum (nos 1/219 and 1/220, ill. in Pope, 1938–9, vol. XII, pl. 1428, figs C and E), and to a quillon block in the Metropolitan Museum (acc. no. 02.18.765).

The quillons must originally have been carved with dragon heads and then recarved after breaking. By comparison with a jug now in the Gulbenkian Collection, Lisbon (*Arts Council* 1976, no. 114) the entire group can probably be ascribed to the workshops of Ulugh Beg in Samarkand.

309
Helmet

Forged from a single piece of steel, with separate finial set with a cubo-octahedronal plug, each facet with a drilled hole; the bulbous central section with vertical flutings, with two cusped sections for the eyes, the rim reinforced and with vervelles for attachment of the aventail. The surface is engraved and overlaid with silver and with Arabic inscriptions in the upper and lower registers
Inscribed in Arabic with good wishes and the titles of Amir Sultan Bahadur
Height 30 cm, diameter 24 cm
Western Iran or Anatolia, *c.* 1450–1500

Helmets of this type were worn in Iran and Anatolia from the 14th to the 16th centuries. This example is probably of the White Sheep Turkman period and can be dated to between 1450 and 1500 (see D.G. Alexander, 'Turban Helmets' in *Metropolitan Museum Journal*, no. 18).

310
Sword blade

The long tapering blade deeply chiselled in relief with palmettes and half palmettes enclosing a central ribbed panel, damascened in gold below the tang with a palmette and half palmette arabesque
Length 99 cm
Iran, late Timurid or Safavid, *c.* 1500 (probably Tabriz)

No other blade of this type is known, but by comparison with Syrian and Safavid sabres and daggers (especially with the dagger of Selim I in the Treasury of the Topkapi Saray Museum, no. 2/254) it can be dated to *c.* 1500 and like the dagger was probably made in Tabriz.

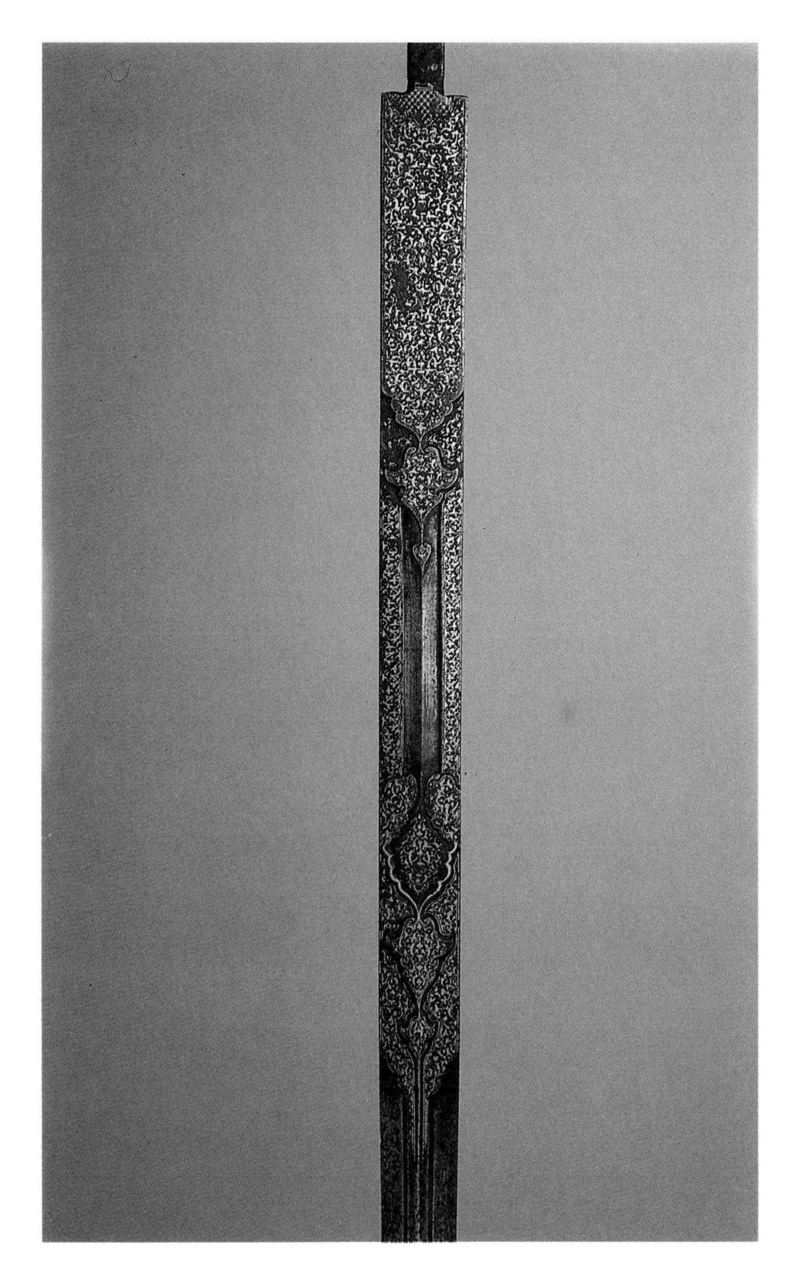

311
Chanfron

The face deeply fluted along the nose and around the ears, forming a flattened triangular brow which is engraved with arabesques and with a cartouche containing an Arabic inscription; the entire face alternately with plain areas and lobed, palmette tipped, cartouches containing arabesques. The cheek plates attached by mail, with traces of gilding and engraved *en suite*
Inscribed with Sura LXI, 13 of the Qur'an: 'Help from God and a speedy victory, so give the good news, to the believers', followed by Shi'a invocations *ya Muhammad, ya 'Ali*
Length 54.5 cm
Probably Ottoman, *c.* 1500–50

Chanfrons of this type were used by the Ottomans, Mamluks and Iranians. A number have survived (in the Askeri Museum, Istanbul) with Ottoman and Mamluk titulature and these enable one to date the group to the early 16th century. The alternation of plain areas and flamboyant lobed cartouches probably indicates that this example was produced in an Ottoman workshop.

313
Sabre

The grip which is lobed at the top consists of two pieces of horn riveted to either side of the tang and framed by a shim of silver. The shim is incised with an inscription in Arabic and Turkish. The quillon block is of silver gilt decorated with a floral design and has short quillons with roundish, ribbed tips. The blade of watered steel is curved and single edged with a double-edged section towards its point. It is engraved on the right side with a roundel below which is a shape comprised of two rounded holes connected to a rectangle and a 'comma' shape. The edges are engraved with a tress design terminating on the back edge with a split leaf form. The scabbard is of wood covered with leather with mounts of silver gilt *en suite* with the hilt
Inscription: verses 1 and 3 of Qur'an XLVIII followed by a garbled version of the end of VII, 89. Then comes the date (1)125/1713 and the name Yakan Ahmad, followed by a couplet in Ottoman Turkish, apparently praying to Allah to make his (Ahmad's) sword into *Dhu'l-faqar* (the sword of 'Ali b. Abu Talib, the Prophet's son-in-law) and himself into the Lion (i.e. 'Ali) when fighting the infidels
Length of blade 81 cm
Fittings Ottoman, dated (1)125/1713; blade Syrian, 1st half 16th century

The hilt and scabbard fittings are very similar to those on a sabre given between 1676 and 1687 by the Ottoman sultan Mehmet IV to

312
Sabre

The blade of steel, curved and single edged with a groove running a third of its length, inlaid in gold on the right side with an Arabic inscription and on the left with an orb mark. The quillon block of steel, decorated with a cloud band arabesque and a floral design against a gold ground, the grip and the pommel restored
Inscription in Arabic from Sura LXV, 3 of the Qur'an: 'And whosoever relies on God, He is sufficient for him; verily God will attain His purpose; God has set for everything a due proportion'
Length 94 cm
Sotheby's, December 1977, lot 51
Quillon block Ottoman, 16th century; blade Eastern Europe, 17th century

The decoration on the hilt is similar to that on the forte of an Ottoman dagger in Edinburgh (see *Arts Council*, 1976, no. 232). The design also occurs on a helmet made for Sultan Bayezid II (1481–1512) (Musée de l'Armée, Paris, no. H445, *Arts Council*, 1976, no. 229), and it is possible that the quillon block was made in the imperial workshops in Istanbul

Michael II Apafi, Prince of Siebenbürgen (Waffensammlung, Kunsthistorisches Museum, Vienna, no. C. 127, Gross and Thomas, 1936, p. 100). This sabre, owned, according to the inscription on the shim, by a warrior named Ahmad, was used in the wars between the Ottomans and the Europeans during the early 18th century. Although the fittings are of high quality, its blade is much more important. It represents a type, the only other examples of which are now preserved in the Topkapi Saray Museum in Istanbul and the Livrustkammaren in Stockholm. The blades in this group are characterized by the same 'decoration' of two rounded holes, comma shape and rectangle. Some examples are signed and one was made for a high Mamluk official. The entire group can be attributed to a Syrian workshop of the late 15th to early 16th centuries. (These weapons will be published by L. Kalus, T. Tezçan and the writer in the forthcoming catalogue of the arms and armour in the Topkapi.) The blade was perhaps a family heirloom, or a piece captured by the Ottomans when they defeated the Mamluks in 1517. It must have been highly regarded and was then re-hilted by its Ottoman owner for use in the wars of the early 18th century.

314
Dagger

The blade of steel is damascened on one side in different coloured golds with dragons, phoenix and kylins(?) against a floral background, on the other side with cartouches containing two lines of Persian verse. The associated hilt of pale green jade carved with a goat's head, the eyes set with rubies
Inscribed in Persian: 'You wield the sword I do not die, What a shame!
Your soul-bestowing sword contains so to speak the water of life' (translated by A.M. Schimmel)
Length 31.5 cm
The hilt Mughal, 17th century; the blade Safavid or Ottoman, *c.* 1580-90

The blade is probably the product of a royal workshop and is probably by the same hand as a *kārd* in the Württembergische Landesmuseum, Stuttgart, no. E.1237. The scabbard of the *kārd* is from the workshop of Murad III (1574-95) which would date its blade to the late 16th century. The reference to the 'water of life' is a pun on the word for watered steel and on the mythical river of Paradise (cf. no. 277). This river, *al-Kawthar*, is the subject of Sura CVIII of the Qur'an. This sura speaks of *Kawthar* as a reward for sacrifice and references to it frequently occur on sword and dagger blades.

The Persian poem seems therefore to allude to the ideals of courage, *Jihad*, and in the event of death, the promise of the incorruptible water of Paradise, see D.G. Alexander, 'Watered steel and the Waters of Paradise' in *M.M.A. Journal* no. 18.

315
Dagger with ivory hilt

The ivory hilt carved with arabesques, out of walrus ivory, the sides with single flowers. Silver ferrule. The blade curved and tapering with a fielded fuller with gilt arabesques and stylized cypress trees against a blackened ground
Length 36 cm
Formerly in the collections of the Earls of Warwick, Warwick Castle, England
Hilt: Ottoman Turkey, 16th century;
Blade: first half 17th century

Turkish ivory hilts of this type seem to date from the middle of the 16th century onwards for about fifty or sixty years. A fine example without a blade is in the Victoria and Albert Museum, whilst Pope, *A Survey of Persian Art*, pl. 1424 (d) shows a yataghan that is related to this series. The shape of the blade and the existence of cypress trees in the decoration suggests a 17th-century dating for the blade.

316
Mail shirt

A long shirt composed of interlocking rings of steel, the cuffs and hem of brass, each ring stamped with an Arabic inscription
Inscribed in Arabic: 'Allah, Muhammad, 'Ali, Fatima, Hasan, Husayn.'
Length 94 cm
Previously in the collection of Richard Whittaker
Iran, 17th century

In contrast to the usual method of cutting the rings from drawn wire, these were punched out on a die, then cut and riveted. The die was presumably cut by a coin-maker. The shirt is actually designed to provide spiritual as well as physical protection as each ring is stamped with the names of God, Muhammad and the *ahl al-Kisā*, people of the cloak, i.e. Muhammad's children and grandchildren, whom, it is said, he gathered one day under his cloak. There are at least seven other surviving shirts of this type which are described by D.G. Alexander in 'Talismanic Shirts of Mail'.

Other talismanic shirts made of textile survive. One, exhibited at Spink ('Islamic Art from India', 1980, no. 78), was inscribed with the Qur'an, the ninety-nine names of

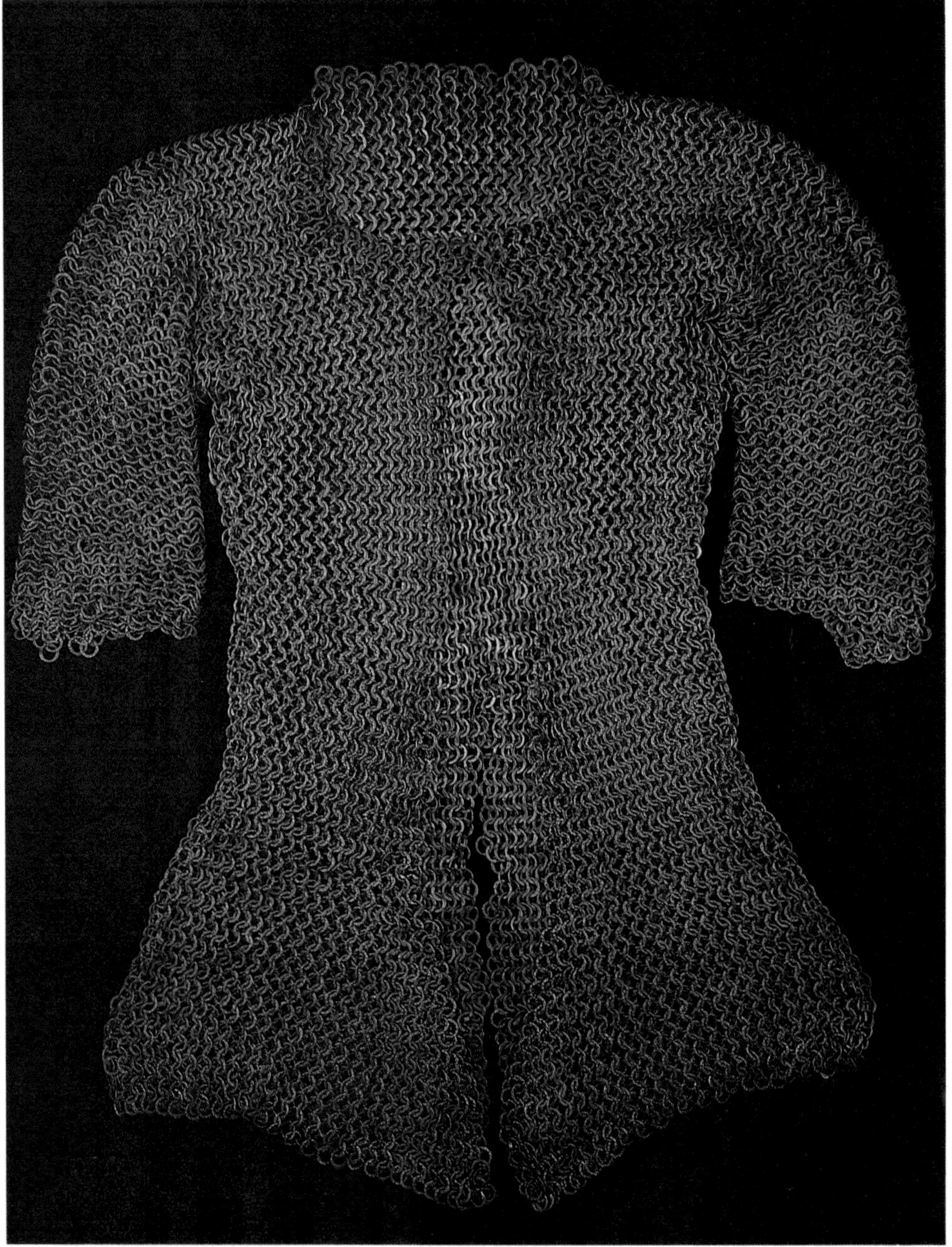

316

316 *(Detail)*

God etc., and two are in the Topkapi Saray Museum, 13/1404 and 13/1408 (Cagman, 1983, E25 and E27).

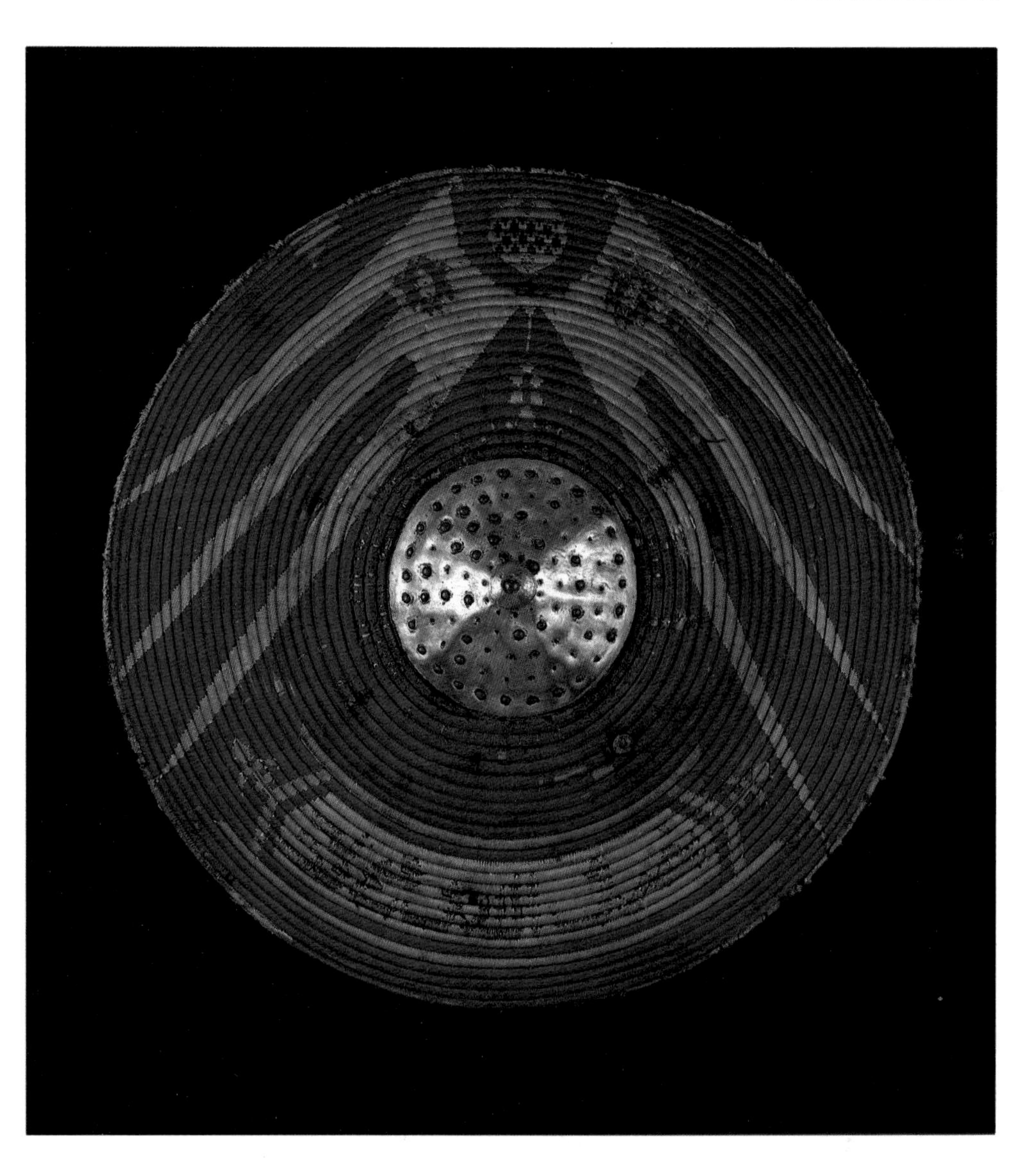

317
Cane shield

Composed of a spiral of cane bound with red and white silk, woven with adossed tailed flags and a cartouche containing an Arabic inscription
.ameter 61 cm
Ottoman Turkey, *c.* 1685

This trophy of the Turkish wars of about 1685 remained from then until the early 1970s in the collection of the Counts von Giech in the armoury at Schloss Thurnau. Similar shields are in Vienna, Dresden and Karlsruhe, (see, for example, E. Petrasch, 1977, pl. 17).

Two Ottoman cane shields of *c.* 1560-70 from the Topkapi Palace Museum were shown at the 1983 exhibition there (Cagman, 1983, E104 and E105). One was made of wicker wrapped in silk thread set round a conical boss of iron; the other carried a text from the Qur'an, Sura XLVIII, *al-Fath*, 1-3.

The flag decoration on this shield is unique and may possibly be an indication of the rank of the bearer.

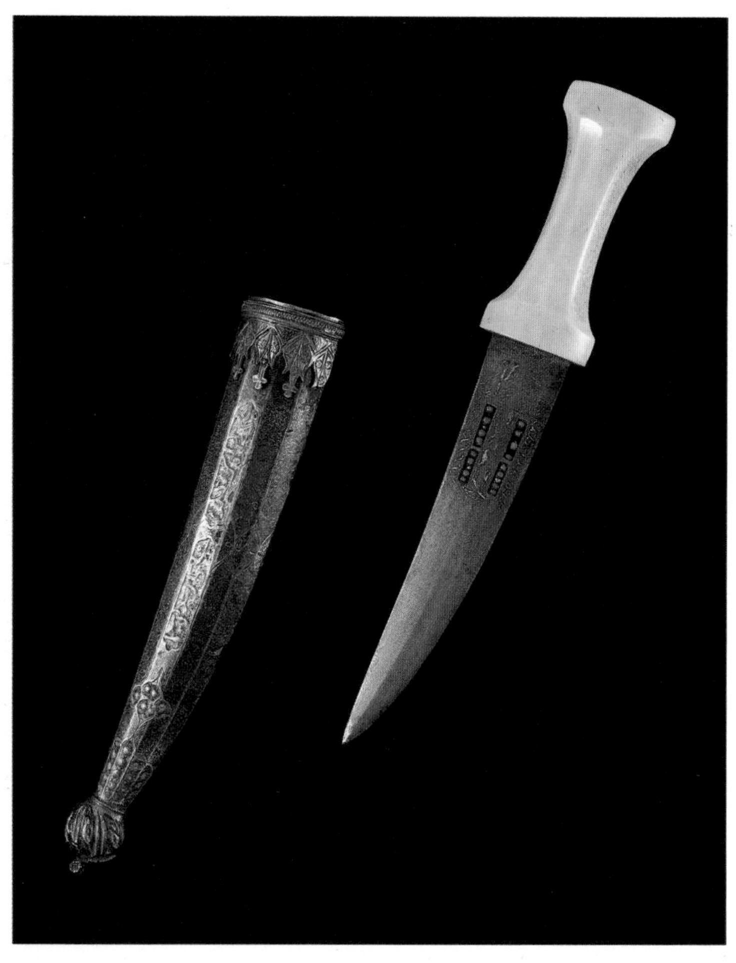

318
Dagger

With waisted hilt of walrus ivory, inscribed on one side and on the other stamped with the *tughrā* of the Ottoman Sultan, Mehmet IV (1648-87); the blade of watered steel with a central pipe containing coral beads; the scabbard of wood covered with silver gilt and decorated in niello with floral forms.
Length 34 cm
Ottoman Turkey, 1648-87

A number of daggers of this type were captured from the Turks at the Siege of Vienna in 1683; see, for example, Schöbel, 1978, no. 154.

319
Field flask

Of hardened leather, pyramidal in form, covered with fabric elaborately decorated in silver wire with floral forms and palmettes
Height 26.5 cm
Ottoman Turkey, *c.* 1683

Water flasks were symbols of rank in both Ottoman and Safavid society and were even considered appropriate as royal gifts, as is seen by the gift in 1581 of a flask by Sultan Murad III to Kaiser Rudolf II (see B. Thomas 'Aus der Waffensammlung in der Neuen Burg zu Wien' in *Gesammelte Schriften*, Graz 1977, p. 192, fig. 8).

Two flask types were in use during the 16th and 17th centuries. One, which has its prototype in early 'pilgrim flasks', had an ovular body and a long tapering neck, the other is of the pyramidal form seen here. Examples of the latter, taken as booty after the siege of Vienna in 1683, survive in the Historisches Museum, Dresden and in Karlsruhe (see, Schöbel, 1974, pl. 23; and Petrasch, 1977, pl. 30).

320
Quiver and bow case

Leather, tooled *en suite* with S scrolls and with silvered mounts
Quiver 71 cm, bow case 51 cm
Ottoman Turkey, *c.* 1683

It is rare to find quiver and bow cases surviving as a set. Similar examples are in the Topkapi Saray Museum, and in several German, Polish and Austrian collections. Most of the latter are booty from the siege of Vienna in 1683 which must be approximately the date of this example (cf. Schöbel, 1974, pls 14-17; and Petrasch, 1977, pls 25-27).

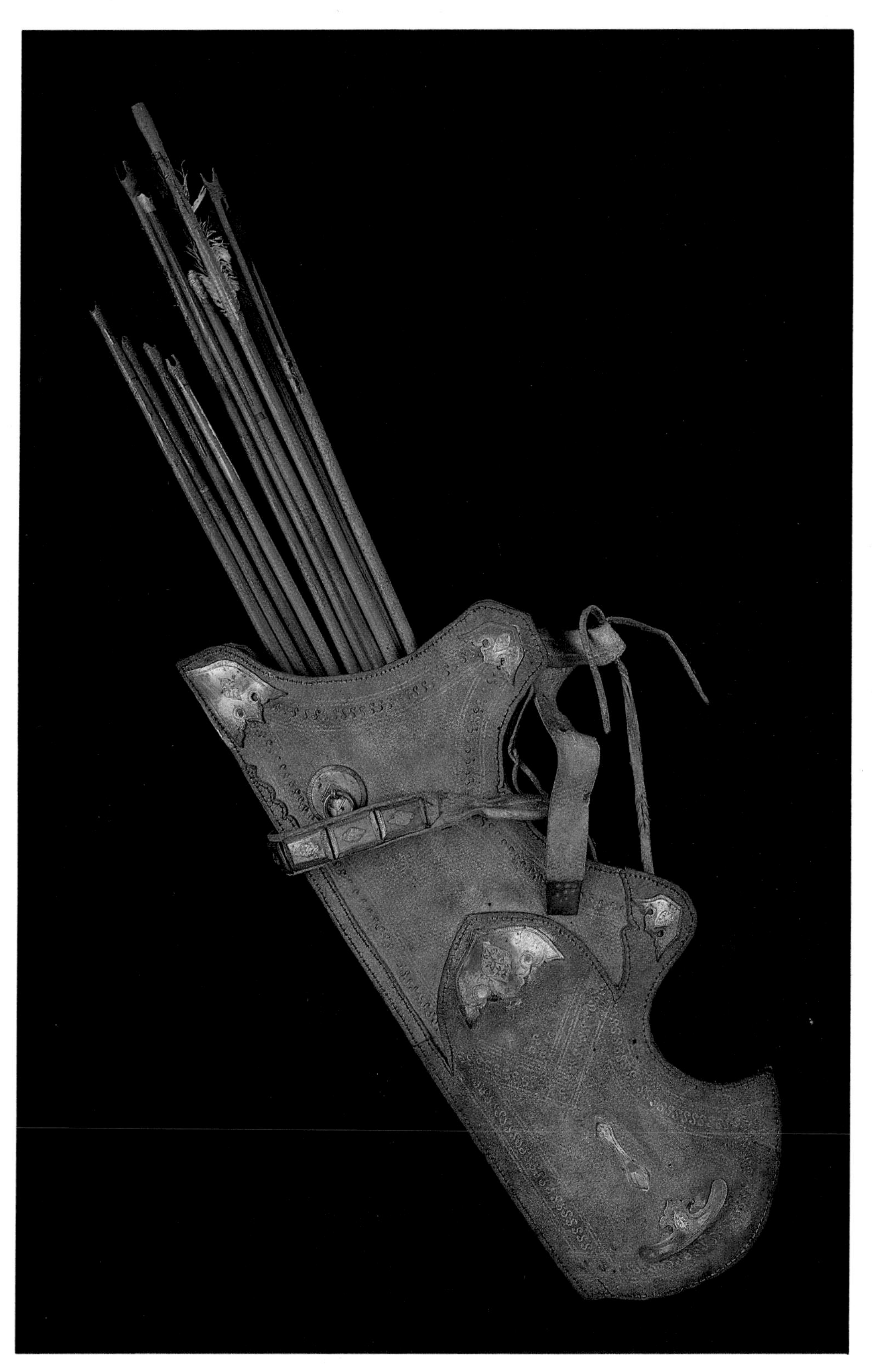

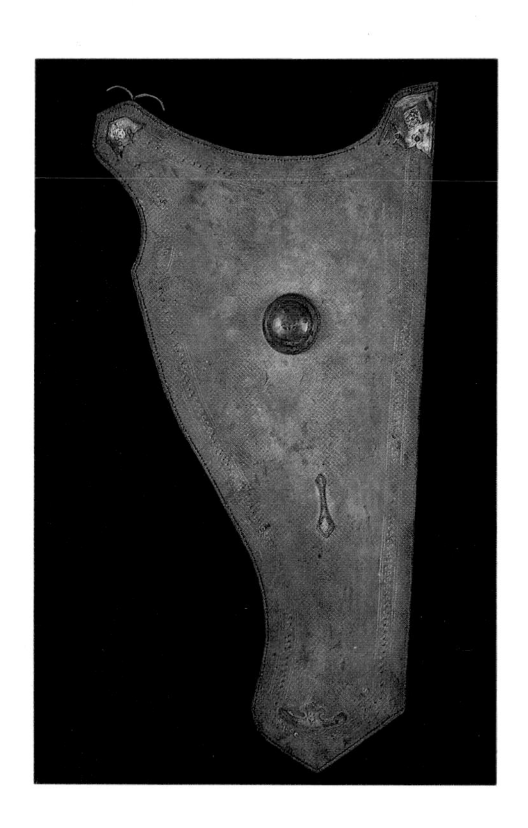

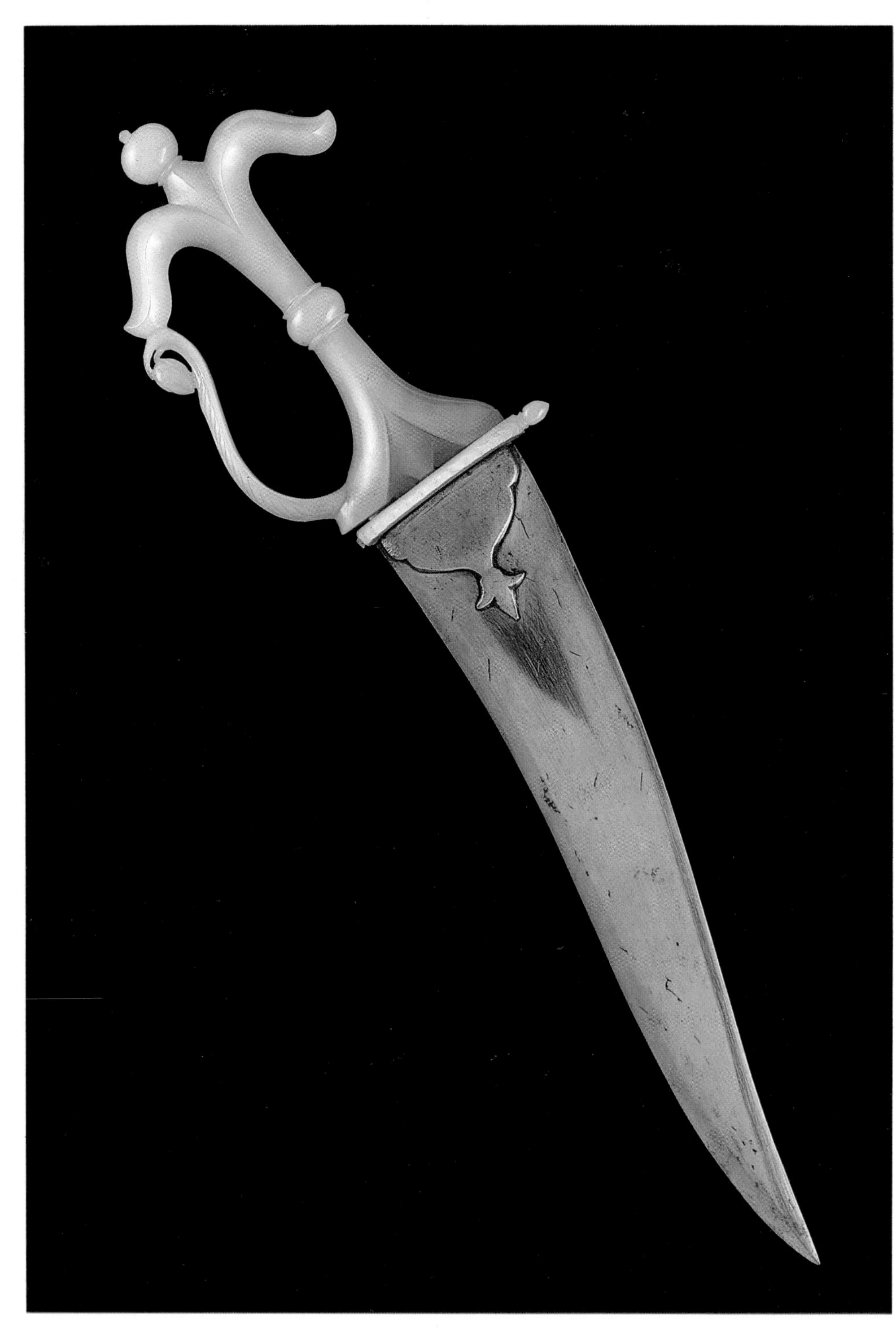

321
Jade dagger

Of pale green jade, of foliate X form with chevron-cut knuckle bow. Scallop-edged guard. Curved blade reinforced at the *forte*
Length 35.5 cm
India, Mughal, first half 17th century

322
Dagger hilt (*Kārd*)

Carved of very pale green jade in the form of a ram's head. The hair well delineated, the eyes set with red stones
Length 11 cm
India, Mughal, 17th century

The *kārd* was mostly worn in conjunction with a dagger and sword in the Islamic world and was more of an all-purpose knife than a functional weapon. It first makes its appearance in miniatures of the late 15th century as a long-bladed knife, almost entirely enclosed by its sheath so that only the pommel is showing, suspended from the belt by a cord.

Seventeenth-century Mughal miniatures show it to be an important accessory to court dress. It is reduced in length but now the pommel is, in grander examples, often carved with animal or occasionally human heads. A miniature from the Minto Album, showing Jahangir as a young man, but painted *c.* 1625, shows such a *kārd* being worn. (Victoria and Albert Museum, I.M. 28-1925.)

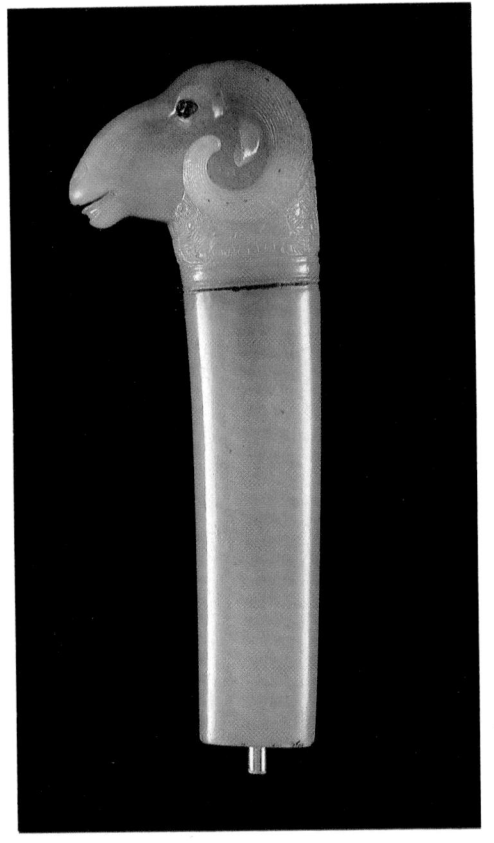

322

323
Gauntlet sword *(Pata)*

The iron hilt richly decorated with gilt flowerheads with russet centres. Imported European blade. Original lining
Length 134.5 cm
India, Mughal or Deccani, 17th century

The gauntlet sword, used on horseback, can be clearly seen in miniatures dating from the 17th and early 18th centuries.

It was a cumbersome weapon that required great strength of the lower arm. It's advantage was that of blade length, but by the middle of the 18th century this 'fixed wrist' weapon had given place to more manoeuverable swords (tulwars and shamshirs).

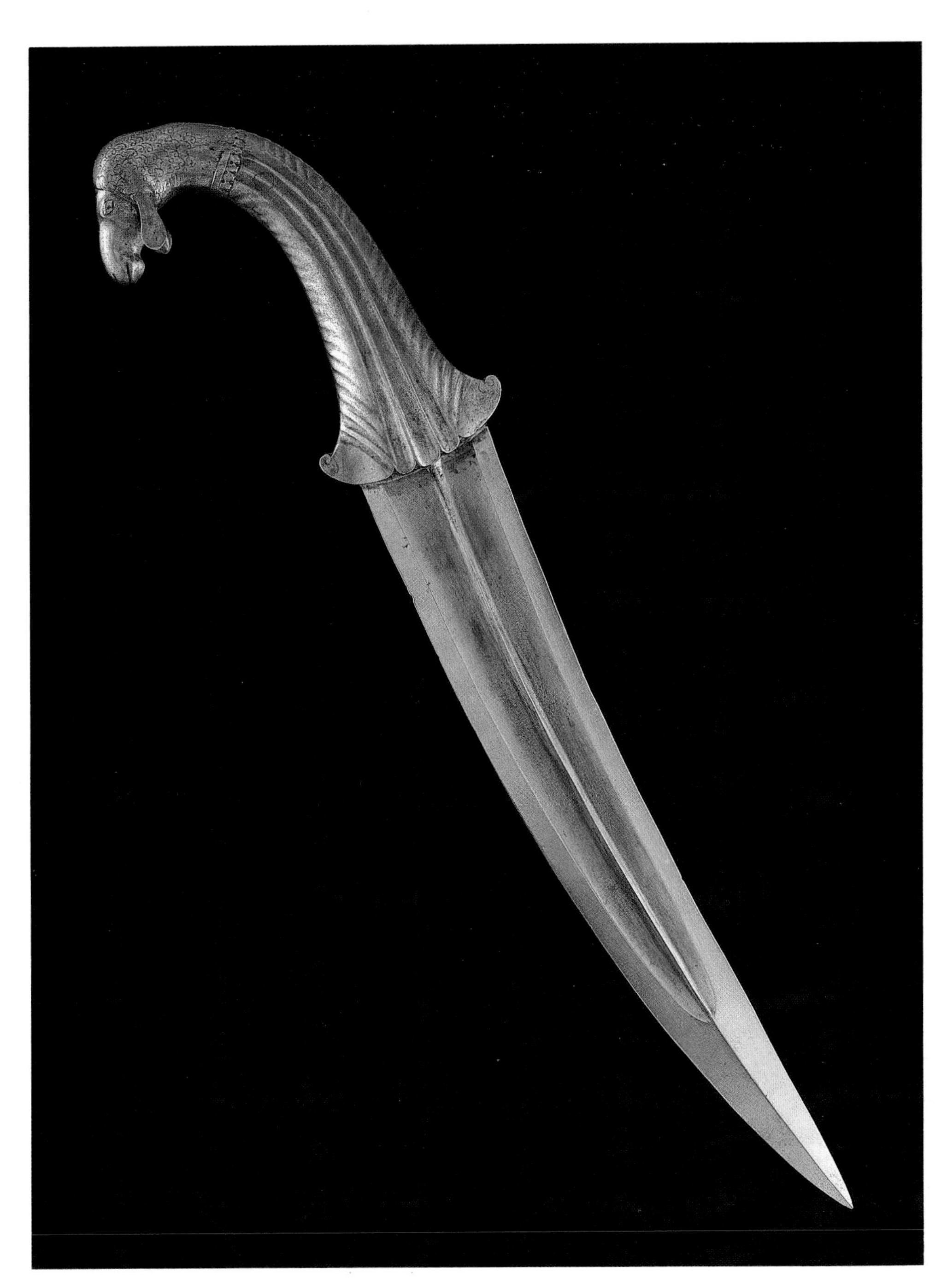

324
All-steel dagger

The pommel in the form of a sheep's head with pendulous ears and engraved curls. The grip with triple flutes within deep chevrons. Watered steel blade
Length 36 cm
India, Mughal, second half 17th century

325
Horse's head dagger

Carved of walrus ivory, the delicate mane heightened in black stain. The bridle and eyes set with rubies. Foliate-carved quillon-block. Damascened blade with gold decoration at the *forte*
Length 36.5 cm
India, Mughal, second half 17th century

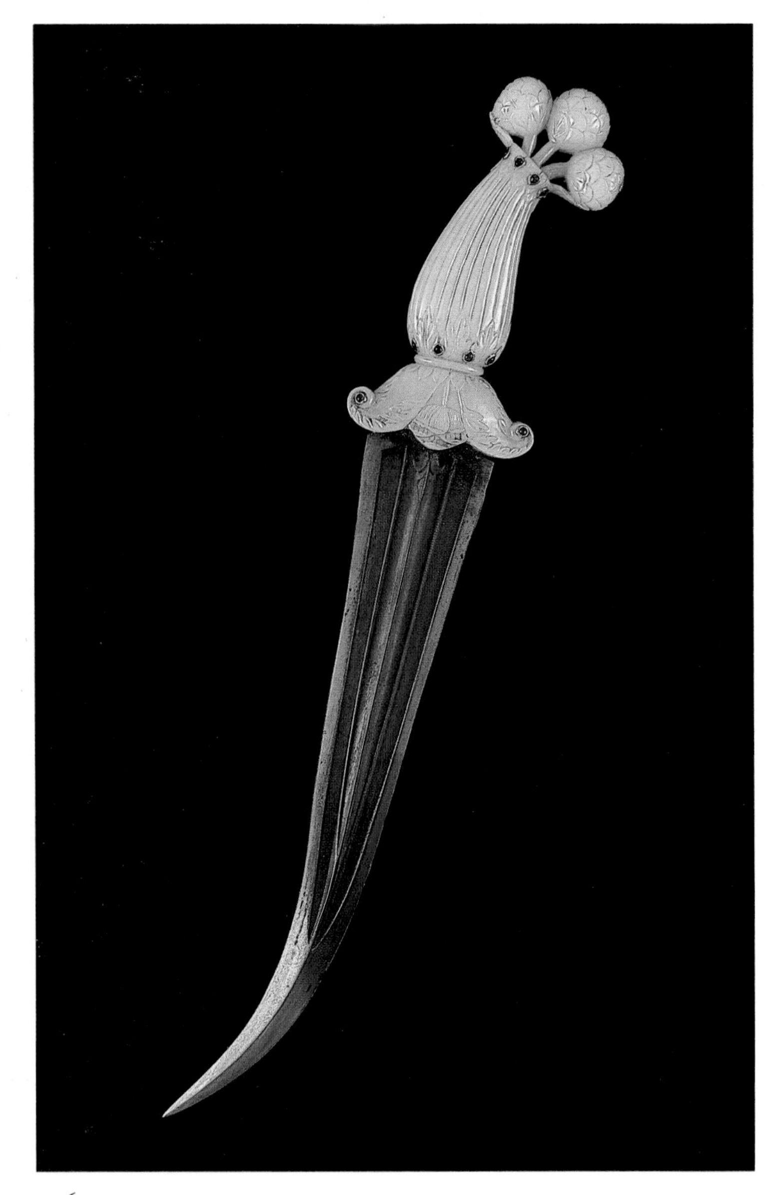

326
Jade dagger (*Khanjar*)

The stone of pale green colour inset with rubies. The pommel formed of three lotus pods. The vase-shaped grip reeded and terminating in scrolled foliate quillons. Watered steel blade
Length 42 cm
India, Mughal, *c.* 1680

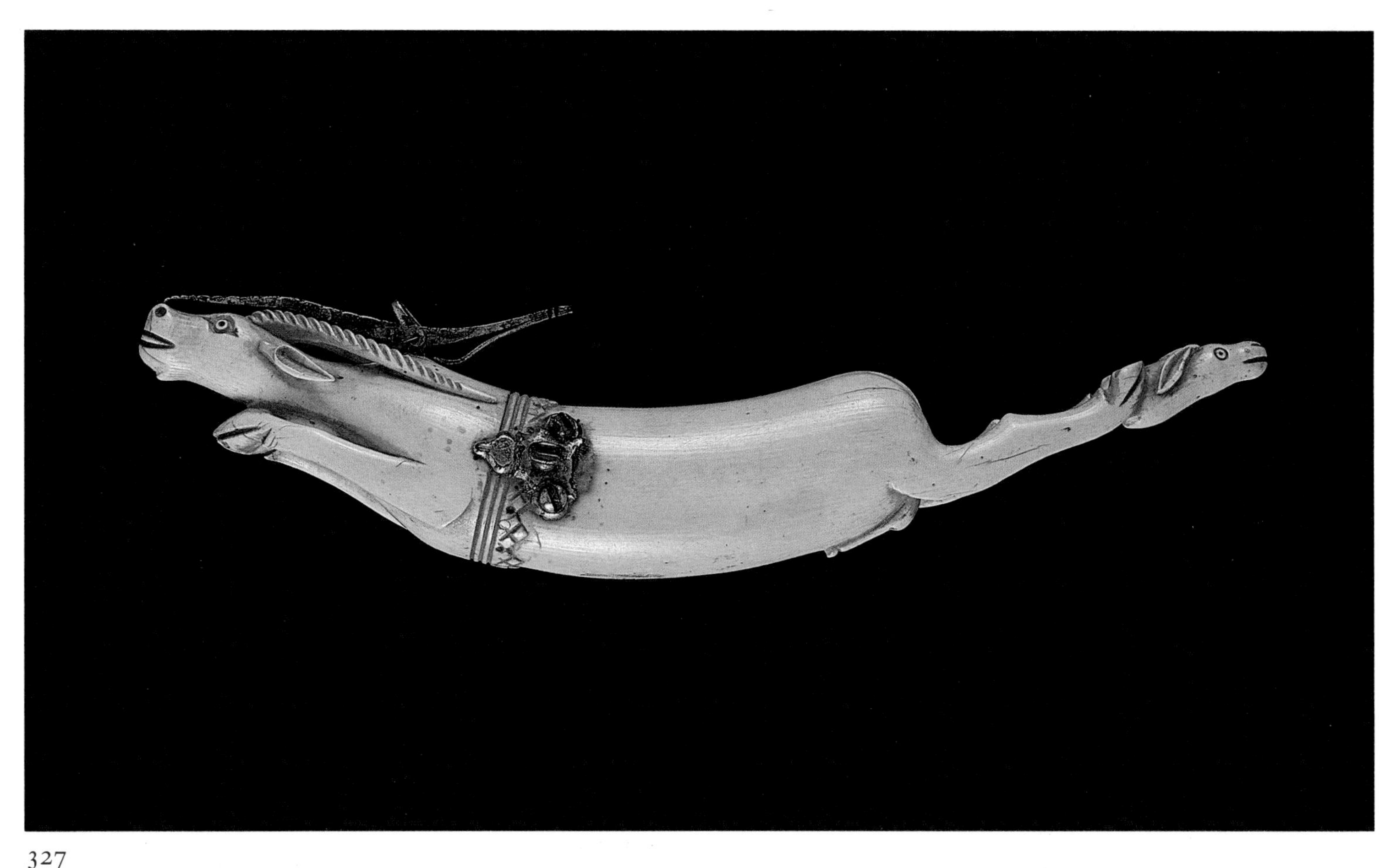

327
Powder flask

Carved in ivory, in the form of a single jumping deer, the animal at full stretch. Gilt-iron mounts
Length 23.5 cm
India, Mughal, 17-18th century

Few Mughal flasks survive carved in the form of a single animal. A slightly more common type is the flask in which the overall outline, in the form of a deer being attacked by lions or tigers, is enhanced by further scenes of animals in relief on the sides. It is this latter type of flask that can be dated to the late 17th century or early 18th century. Three examples entered the Danish Royal Collections from 1690 to 1737. (See *Etnografiske genstande i Det kongelige dansk Kunstkammer 1650-1800*, p. 111, pls EDb62-64.)

328
Jewelled jade dagger (*Khanjar*)
The hilt with scabbard mounts *en suite*, set with sapphires in gold collets. The larger flowers also enriched with further ruby-set ornament
Length 39.5 cm
India, Mughal, 18th century

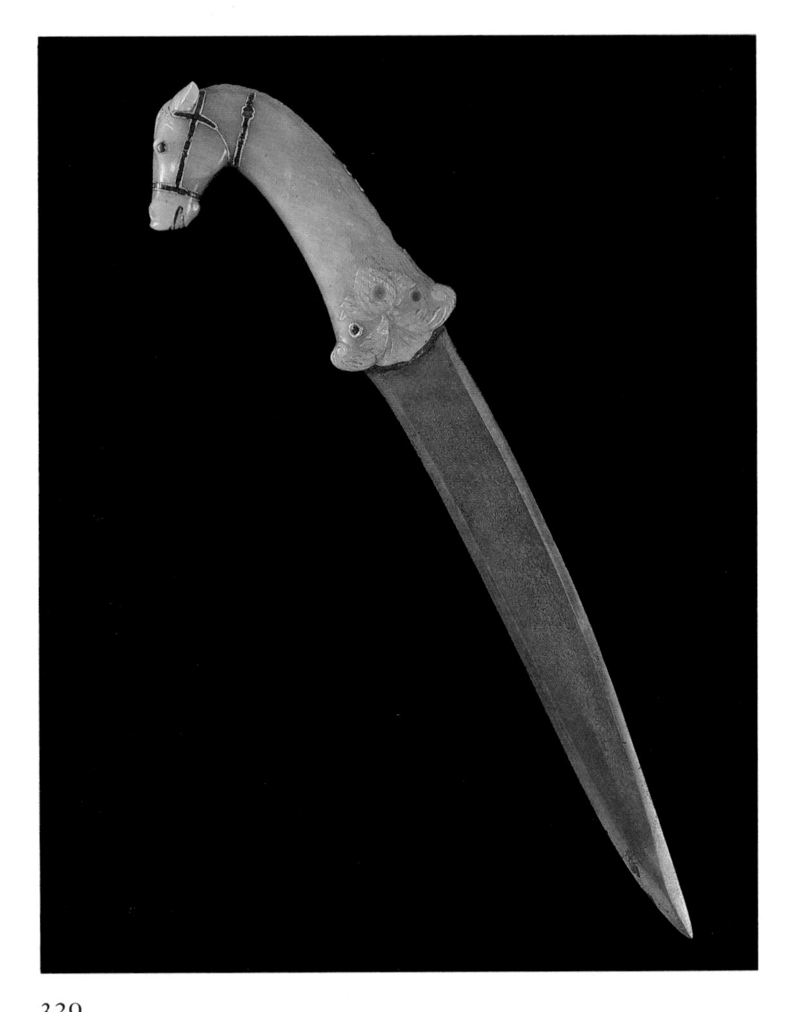

329
Dagger (*Khanjar*)
The hilt of pale grey-greenish jade well carved with the head of a horse, the bridle in gold paved with rubies. Ruby-set eyes and halter. The quillon block centred by a lotus and bordered with scrolled leaves. Watered steel blade with slight curve
Length 34.5 cm
India, Mughal, late 17th century

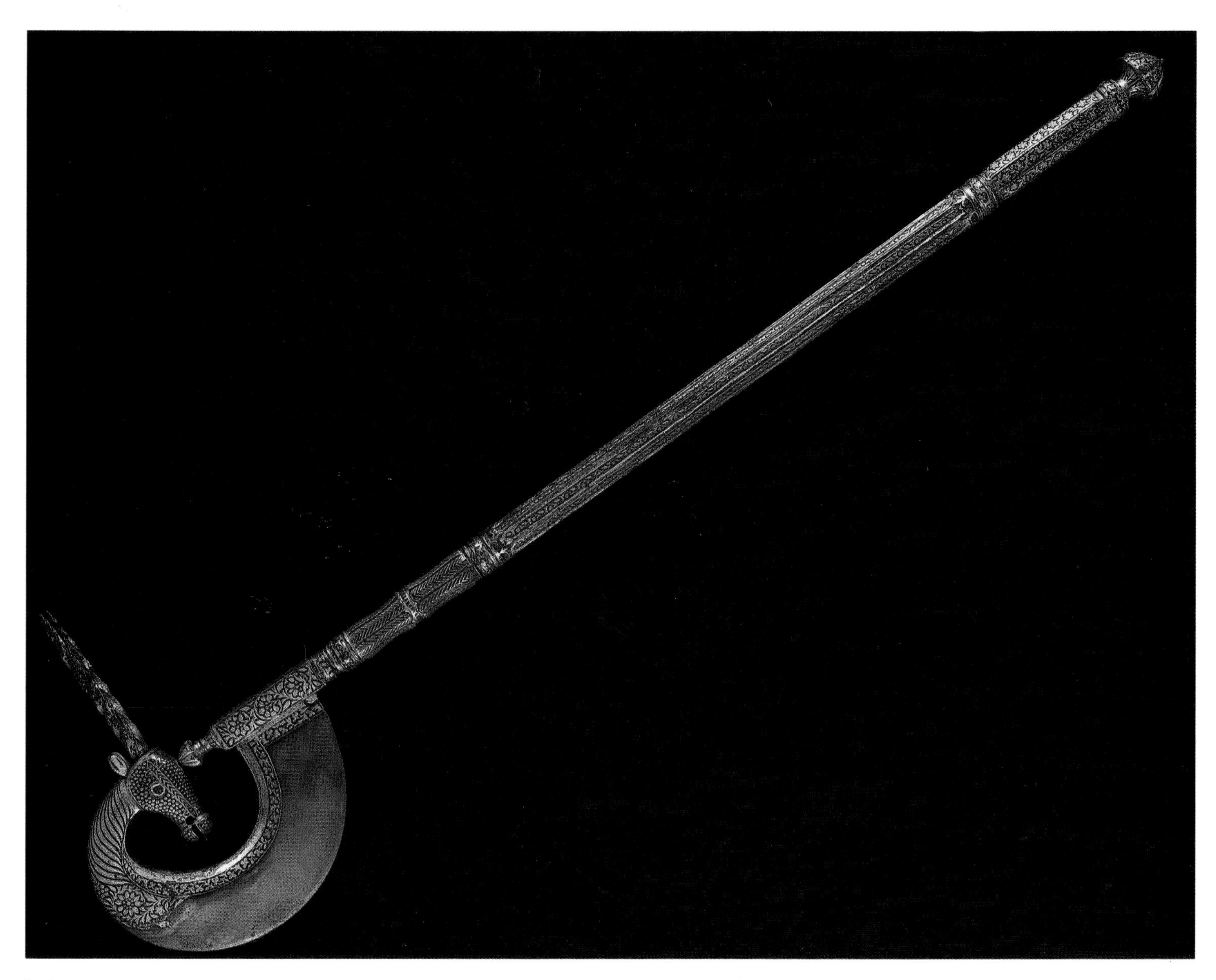

330
Axe

The crescent-shaped damascus steel blade terminating in the head of a gazelle, with ruby set eyes. The head of the animal together with the fluted shaft decorated in *kūftgarī* work with chevrons and floral ornament
Length 64.5 cm
India, Mughal, second half 18th century

Illustrated by Frederick Wilkinson in *Edged Weapons* p. 241. Wilkinson gives it a slightly earlier dating to the 17th century. However, the floral decoration seems to derive more from 18th-century ornament.

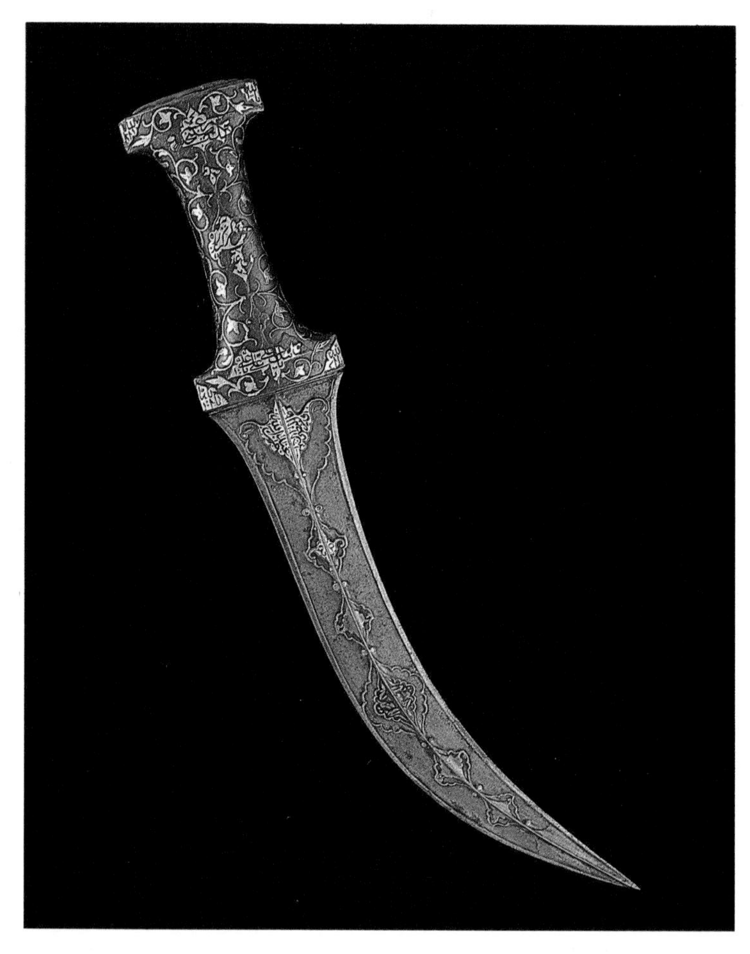

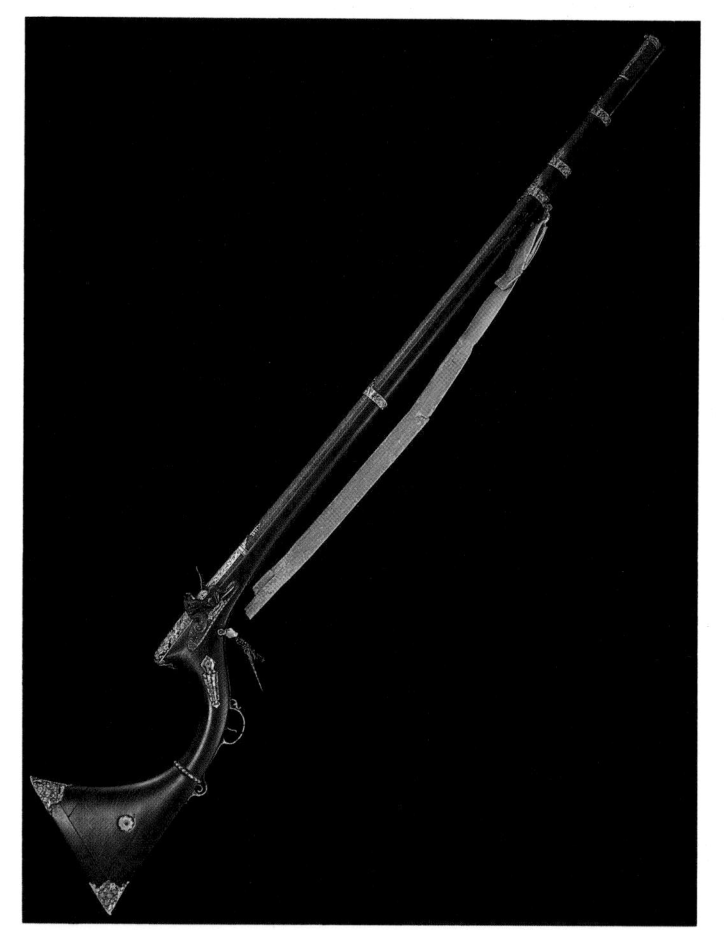

332

331
Dagger

The watered iron hilt well chiselled with a trailing vine pattern, interspersed with cartouches of script reversed out in gold. The pommel in relief with a lion attacking a deer. The watered steel blade with further inscriptions
The inscriptions include a Shi'a devotional poem and give the date as 1770
Length 35.5 cm
Iran, 18th century

332
Two gold and enamel mounted flintlock guns (Jezails)

Both flintlock guns with characteristic hooked butts. The stocks of rosewood with gold furniture richly enamelled *en plein*, in a predominantly rose red palette with flower heads divided by leaves in *basse taille* enamel. The fine damascus-twist barrels with raised gold decoration at both breeches and muzzles. Both bear the name Murad Ali Khan, and one is dated 1192/1778. One imported English lock signed H. Nock, the other signed Perrin
Overall lengths 149 and 151 cm
Scind, one of the barrels dated 1778 but mounted *c.* 1825

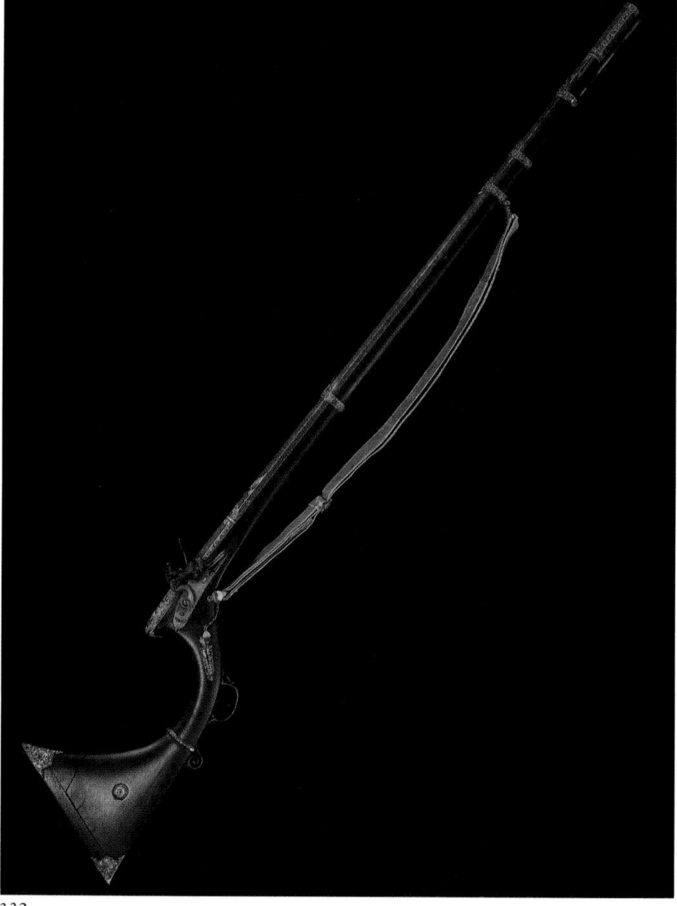

332

333
Helmet

Fine deep bowl decorated with trailing vines, the lower border with panels of inscriptions including couplets from Firdawsi's account of Rustam and Isfandiyar, interspersed with vignettes of birds: Complete with nasal drop, plume holders and camail
Height 26 cm
Iran, Qajar, first half 19th century

DONALD KING

Carpets and Textiles

The Islamic world has long been renowned for the excellence of its carpets and textiles. It has always enjoyed ample supplies of the essential raw materials: silk, wool, linen, cotton, fine dyestuffs and silver and gold thread. At the same time a natural affection among the Islamic peoples for fine colours and patterns in fabrics used for dress and furnishings has ensured very high standards of craftsmanship and design, not only in textiles created for princely courts and prosperous cities, but also in those made in humble villages and nomad tents. For many centuries Islamic carpets and textiles have also been sought after by connoisseurs in Europe. The small group of examples shown here come from the collections of some modern connoisseurs. These objects cannot illustrate all the immense range of fabrics produced, throughout the history of Islam, in many lands from the Atlantic in the west to the Pacific in the east, but they have been chosen with care as fine and characteristic representatives of the various textile materials, the various techniques and various styles of design employed in several different areas of the Islamic world from the 16th to the 19th centuries. A brief study of them will give at least some idea of the wealth of colour and of fine design to be found in Islamic textile art.

CARPETS

In the technique of carpet-knotting, warp threads are stretched on the loom and weft threads are interlaced with them at right angles as in weaving a plain cloth, but after every few weft threads additional lengths of thread, generally wool, are knotted or looped round the warp threads, so as to form a pile which stands more or less erect on the plain woven foundation. The two principal types of knot employed are the symmetrical or 'Turkish' knot (nos 336, 337 and 341) and the asymmetrical or 'Persian' knot (nos 334, 335 and 340), but the superficial appearance of the fabric is the same in either case. Carpet-knotting is well adapted to pattern-making, for each knot produces a coloured spot in the pile, like a cube in a mosaic; by using threads of different colours, the thousands or even millions of knots in a carpet can form designs of every degree of refinement and complexity. An alternative technique used for rather less durable carpets is that of tapestry (nos 338 and 339), in which weft threads of various colours are interlaced with the warp threads only where each particular colour is required by the design, and the pattern is built up bit by bit like a mosaic or map of differently coloured patches. Both techniques allow the weaver, if he or she possesses the requisite skills of hand and eye, to realize every kind of design, from the most geometrical to the most naturalistic. Narrow carpets (nos 337-339) can be woven by a single weaver; wider ones required several weavers working side by side.

Islamic carpet-weavers and designers are the heirs of age-old traditions of carpet production in Asia; both carpet-knotting and the tapestry technique were practised there for many hundreds, and probably thousands, of years before the advent of Islam. One pre-Islamic tradition which still flourishes is the idea of the carpet as a stylized landscape, either a garden full of flowers (nos 335 and 340), or else a hunting park with real and mythical birds and beasts (nos 338 and 341); such designs refer not only to the pleasures of life, but also to the hope of Paradise after death. Another influential concept is that of the carpet as stylized architecture, seen especially in the motif of an arch (or arches), often found in the prayer rugs upon which the devout Muslim, turning towards Makka, recites his prayers; this arch evokes the niche or mihrab in the Makka-facing wall of the mosque, while the stylized lamp suspended from the centre of the arch represents divine illumination (no. 337). Another type of carpet design which perhaps echoes the domes and architectural ornament of the mosque, but which also has close relationships with bookbinding and the other arts of the book, is that with a large medallion in the centre and part-medallions at the sides or corners (nos 335, 336 and 339). The designs of carpets were originated by professional designers, probably painters or miniaturists; but in tribal or village rugs, or in large-scale commercial production such as that of the Ushak area in Anatolia (nos 336 and 337), a successful design, once established, might be repeated and adapted by the weavers for generations, even for centuries, without further recourse to a designer.

The small group of carpets shown in the present exhibition includes excellent examples from several different areas. Cairo, whose workshops were very productive from the 15th to the 17th centuries, exporting large numbers of carpets to Europe, is represented by two fine specimens, rather similar in shape and colouring, but remarkably different in style. One (no. 334), from the early part of the 16th century, illustrates the beautifully complex geometrical style which was current under the Mamluk Sultans. The other (no. 335), made some time after the Mamluks had been overthrown and Egypt occupied by the Ottoman Sultans of Turkey, is in a free-flowing floral style inspired by the tile decorations of the buildings of Istanbul. The very extensive carpet production of the Ushak area in western Anatolia is likewise illustrated here by two contrasted examples, one a splendid large floor-carpet of the medallion type, the other a prayer rug, both with the dominant red and blue tonality of Ushak carpets (nos 336 and 337). Both these rugs are of types which were exported extensively to Europe and can be seen depicted in many European paintings of the 16th and 17th centuries.

Two other rugs shown here, this time of Iranian origin, are both delicate, luxurious pieces woven with soft-toned silks and gold thread in the tapestry technique, but again with contrasting designs, one a lattice pattern containing animals, the other a medallion design with flowers (nos 338 and 339). Such rugs are known to have been woven at Kashan in the late 16th and early 17th centuries. Lastly, two pile carpets illustrate two further aspects of 17th-century

Iranian design. One, a fine example of the so-called vase carpets woven at Kerman, shows a rich and stately floral lattice pattern in harmonious colours (no. 340). The other, woven in the Caucasus, the frontier area between Iran and Turkey, has a lattice pattern with animals and flowers, all vigorously and almost barbarically stylized, with strongly contrasted colours, marvellously decorative in effect.

WOVEN SILKS

Unlike carpets, which are woven on very simple looms, patterned silk textiles have generally been woven on a complex mechanism known as the drawloom, which came into use from about the 3rd century onwards. On this apparatus the skilled professional weaver interlaces coloured weft threads with the coloured warp threads across the width of the loom, while an assistant operates a system of control cords which ensure that each individual thread appears on the front of the textile only when its colour is required to contribute to the pattern, while elsewhere it is rejected to the back. The drawloom is essentially a device for the precise and automatic repetition of a basic unit of pattern across the width and along the length of the textile, so that it naturally produces repeating patterns, generally smaller in scale than the patterns of carpet, which are freely composed and need not be repetitive.

The drawloom can be used to weave repeating patterns with any of the textile fibres, but its finest products are those woven with dyed silks and with gold and silver thread. Such fabrics were widely used in the Islamic world both for dress and for domestic furnishings – hangings, covers and the like. The patterns were invariably devised by professional designers and the textiles in this exhibition illustrate some of the international influences which affected them. For example, the close relationship between the textile designs of Ottoman Turkey and those of Italy is demonstrated by a handsome Turkish hanging of the late 16th century, with a lattice pattern in gold thread on a background of crimson velvet (no. 342). This combines crowns and plant motifs borrowed from Italian models with a power and vigour of drawing and colour which are characteristically Ottoman. Another velvet of about the same period, this time from Iran, has a lattice pattern in polychrome silk pile on a background of cloth-of-gold (no. 343). It includes some motifs, such as tulips, borrowed from Turkish designs and others, such as lotus flowers, derived from China. An Iranian silk cover of the early 17th century (no. 344) is designed like a carpet, with floral borders surrounding a floral lattice pattern in the central field, all in soft colours on a background of cloth-of-silver. Two other textiles, one in coloured silks on a cloth-of-gold background (no. 345), the other in gold, silver and colours on brown satin (no. 346), both have a single repeated motif of flowers growing from a little mound, reminiscent of Iranian miniatures and possibly suggested by European botanical illustrations. The delightful piece with the bird on the rose-stem (no. 345) could conceivably have been woven, not in Iran, but in the Mughal Empire in India, where such naturalistic effects were greatly admired.

EMBROIDERIES

Embroidery, an extremely ancient technique, differs from carpet-making and pattern-weaving in that the pattern is not worked into the textile during the weaving process, but is added to a pre-existing woven textile by means of needle and thread. Although embroidery is often made in professional workshops, the simplicity of the technique and apparatus means that it can easily be made by non-professionals also, and a great variety of domestic embroidery has been produced for furnishing purposes throughout the Islamic world in many different local styles. Most of this embroidery is worked in dyed silk threads on plain linen or cotton cloth, generally undyed. The design which the embroiderer follows is generally drawn directly on the plain ground material, often by a professional designer. There are no technical limitations on the designs, so that absolutely any kind of pattern can be produced, but in practice embroidery designs are often inspired by the repeating patterns of drawloom textiles or the field-and-border designs of carpets.

The embroideries shown here include two cotton covers or hangings from Mughal India, delicately embroidered with silk in fine chain stitch (nos 347 and 348). One has a repeating pattern in the form of a floral lattice, while the other displays a splendid flowering plant beneath an arch. Two others, from Ottoman Turkey, have repeating patterns of flowers in a bolder style and stronger colours on linen backgrounds (nos 349 and 350). Finally there are two from peripheral areas which possessed characteristic styles of embroidery (nos 351 and 352). One, a colourful example from the Caucasus, shows a stylization similar to that of carpets from the same area. The other, with a pattern of great circular flowers, is a fine example of the type of embroidery produced in the Bukhara-Samarkand region of Central Asia.

COLLECTING ISLAMIC CARPETS AND TEXTILES

The carpets and textiles shown here illustrate some characteristic aspects of the styles found in different areas of the Islamic world – the thoughtful geometry of Mamluk Egypt (no. 334), the confident power of Ottoman Turkey (nos 336, 337, 342, 349 and 350), the bold stylization of the Caucasus (nos 341 and 351), the sumptuous elegance of Safavid Iran (nos 338-340), the refined naturalism of Mughal India (nos 347 and 348) – and yet these are only a small sample of the immense variety to be found in this field. Anyone wishing to collect Islamic carpets or textiles will be wise to begin by devoting some study to this complex subject, through books and in museum collections.

Why are Islamic carpets and textiles worth collecting? The answer is, first and foremost, for the sake of their superb decorative qualities. A few well-chosen pieces, judiciously disposed, can make a marvellous contribution to the appearance of a house or flat, and they blend admirably with art-objects of other kinds. Some reasonable precautions must, of course, be taken. It would be foolish to place valuable and frail old carpets on the floors of much-frequented reception rooms; it is infinitely preferable to hang them like tapestries and to use less precious carpets on the floors. Woven silk textiles and embroideries need to be protected with perspex or glass from dust or accidental damage. Obviously no textiles should be exposed to dirty or damp conditions, nor should they ever be exposed to strong daylight, which will first fade the dyes and eventually rot the fabric itself. If it is necessary to store frail textiles, they should be rolled rather than folded.

What should one look for in buying carpets and textiles? This is a question to be decided mainly by the taste of the individual collector. But since the merits of these fabrics reside principally in their colour and design, it is to these aspects that he should give particular attention. The colour schemes of textiles can be splendidly simple, as in the crimson and gold of the Turkish velvet (no. 342), or subtly complex, as the polychromy of Iranian carpets (nos 338-340); what is essential is that the colours chime harmoniously together and are pleasing to the spectator. Similarly, designs can be quite elementary or astonishingly complex and still be of equal merit; what matters is that the design should be suitable to the fabric, pleasantly proportioned and agreeable to contemplate. Then there is the question of condition. Old carpets and textiles are often somewhat faded and worn, and they may be patched and repaired. The vital question here is whether or not the damage or repairs have seriously impaired the harmony of the colours or the clarity of the design. As an example of the kind of decision which has to be made, we may consider the Iranian velvet, no. 343. Its cloth-of-gold background is severely worn, as can easily be seen by comparing it with that of the Iranian silk, no. 345, which is in almost perfect condition; this wear is not at all surprising, since the velvet formed part of a tent which is believed to have been captured at the siege of Vienna in 1683 and which, judging from its style, was by no means new at that time. Though the glitter of the gold has been lost, except near the edge of the piece, the balance and harmony of the colours is otherwise unimpaired, while the handsome design is almost perfectly preserved; this historically important velvet is therefore a most desirable acquisition. If a collector is delighted with the colour and design of a textile, and is satisfied that its condition does not detract from its real quality, then he can scarcely go wrong in acquiring it.

334
Cairene Mamluk carpet

Woollen pile in red, blue, green and yellow
204 × 170 cm
Previously in the collection of Graf Moy, Schloss Stepperg
Erdmann (1961), p. 85 and fig. 11; Schürmann (1966), p. 27
Egypt, Cairo, first half 16th century

This is an excellent example of the kaleidoscopic geometry of Mamluk carpets, in which a limited repertory of ornament is continually reshuffled to produce new compositions. In this case the design seems to expand like concentric ripples on a pool, starting from a central star of interlace, then a circle of arabesques, then an octagon with lancet leaves, then two eight-lobed medallions with umbrella-shaped leaves. Around this are disposed smaller circles, stars and other forms and the whole composition is framed by multiple borders.

Many rugs of this more or less square format were exported from Cairo to Europe, where they were often used as table-carpets. The main border pattern in this example is similar to that of a table-carpet seen in a group portrait with the Venetian Doge, Leonardo Loredano, painted by Giovanni Bellini in 1507.

335
Cairene Ottoman carpet

Woollen pile in red, blue, green, yellow and cream
250 × 222 cm
Previously in the collection of Baron Edmond de Rothschild
Egypt, Cairo, late 16th or early 17th century

The design comprises a central medallion and four quarter-medallions in the corners, with flowers and arabesques; the red field is covered with arrangements of flowers and feathery leaves. The main border, also red, has a pattern of flowers, leaves and cartouches containing arabesques.

A comparison of this fine rug with the preceding example shows very well how, after the middle of the 16th century, the old geometrical Mamluk designs were succeeded in Cairo by a completely new repertory of curvilinear floral ornament. This new style seems to have been inspired by the tile-decoration of contemporary buildings in Istanbul.

336
Ushak medallion carpet

Woollen pile in shades of red, blue, ivory, yellow and brown; symmetrical knot; warp of ivory wool, weft of red wool
544 × 261 cm
Thyssen-Bornemisza Collection, Lugano
Beattie (1972), no. XIV; King (1983), no. 41
Anatolia, Ushak area, 16th or early 17th century

Though somewhat restored, particularly in the bright blue areas, this is a splendid example of the Ushak medallion pattern. The design is given ample space to develop the full effect of its rich complexity, with a great red medallion at the centre and parts of two more at the ends, with four light blue half-medallions at the sides, and a deep blue field overrun with lotus trails inspired by Chinese prototypes.

Carpets of this design appear in paintings of most western European countries from about 1570 to the second half of the 17th century, and even occasionally in the 18th. Dr Julian Raby has recently argued that the style of the design suggests that it must have originated in the second half of the 15th century, but no examples of so early a date have survived. The present carpet resembles others in the Museum für Kunst und Gewerbe, Hamburg, and in the former Stroganoff collection; all three appear to be relatively early examples, probably dating from the 16th century.

337
Ushak prayer rug

Woollen pile in red, blue, yellow, green, cream and brown; symmetrical knot; warp of cream wool, weft of red wool
234 × 139 cm
Previously in the Sherif Sabry Collection
Mustafa (1958), fig. 39; Arts Council (1976), no. 49; Spuhler (1978), no. 24
Anatolia, Ushak area, 17th century

Ushak prayer rugs resemble the larger Ushak carpets in colouring and ornament. Unlike many other prayer rugs, which have an arch at one end only, these have an arch at both ends and a central medallion, in the manner of large medallion carpets. Rugs of this type are depicted in western European paintings from 1519 to 1625. The cloud-band border seen in this example is characteristic of rugs made in the Ushak area in the 16th and 17th centuries.

338
The Figdor silk tapestry rug

Tapestry, on a yellow silk warp, with weft threads of red, orange, yellow, green and blue silk, and gold and silver thread
192 × 125 cm
Thyssen-Bornemisza Collection, Lugano
Previously in the collection of Dr Albert Figdor, Vienna
Pope (1938-9), p. 2404, pl. 1268 A; Beattie (1972), no. III; Cammann (1975), p. 253 ff; Beattie (1976), no. 8; King (1983), no. 71
Iran, possibly Kashan, late 16th century

This famous rug is an outstanding example of a rare class of Iranian carpets, woven in the tapestry technique with gold and silver thread and brightly coloured silks. The design consists of rows of cartouches in various shapes and colours; these, and the sections of ivory ground between them, are occupied by lion masks, dragons, a phoenix and other mythical or natural animals and birds, singly or in combat. The sky-blue border shows arabesques and cartouches containing birds. Professor Cammann has interpreted the whole design as a symbolic view of Paradise beyond the sky.

Only two other silk tapestry rugs with comparable designs are known. One is in the Wher Collection; the other, in Japan, is reputed to have been the favourite campaigning coat of the great Japanese general, Hideyoshi (1536-98).

339
Silk tapestry rug

Tapestry of gold and silver thread, and silk in shades of brown, blue, green, pink, ivory and black
200 × 118 cm
Thyssen-Bornemisza Collection, Lugano
Christie's, 14 April 1976, lot 23
Iran, possibly Kashan, early 17th century

The brown field and sky-blue border have patterns of flowers, palmettes and feathery leaves; there is a scalloped central medallion, with cartouches and finials above and below, and quarter-medallions in the corners, all with similar ornament.

This rug belongs to the same rare class of silk and gold tapestry rugs as the preceding example, but differs in design. Designs of this type, with a central medallion and quarter-medallions in the corners, which had long been in use for book-bindings, were much favoured by Persian carpet-designers in the 16th and early 17th centuries. The present piece is related to other examples which are known, from documentary evidence, to have been woven in Kashan in 1601-2.

340
The Jeziorak vase carpet

Woollen pile in red, pink, orange, yellow, brown, ivory, green and blue; asymmetrical knot; the warp is cotton, the weft wool and silk
269 × 174 cm
Thyssen-Bornemisza Collection, Lugano
Formerly in the church at Jeziorak, Poland; later in the collection of Dr Albert Figdor, Vienna
Beattie (1972), no. I, with earlier bibliography; King (1983), no. 79
Iran, possibly Kerman, second half 17th century

The design comprises three superimposed curvilinear lattices formed by three systems of stems – in sky blue, yellow and white – which carry fantastic blossoms and flower vases; thinner coiling stems bear smaller flowers; the border has arabesques and floral stems.

The numerous group of vase carpets take their name from the vases which figure fairly inconspicuously in their designs, but their principal feature is the astonishing profusion and variety of their floral ornament. There is some evidence to suggest that they were made in the Kerman area. This type of design probably originated in the reign of Shah 'Abbas I, 1587-1629; the present example is rather later, but admirably decorative and beautifully executed.

341
The Cassirer dragon carpet

Woollen pile in shades of red, orange, yellow, brown, ivory and blue; symmetrical knot; woollen warp and weft
431 × 226 cm
Thyssen-Bornemisza Collection, Lugano
Previously in the collection of Mr Alfred Cassirer, Berlin
Beattie (1972), no. XI, with earlier bibliography
Caucasus, second half 17th century

Ragged bands or leaves, with flowers and birds on them, form a complex lattice. At the junctions and in the compartments of the lattice are large palmettes and strangely stylized animals; the latter include dragons (two at the top and two towards the bottom of the carpet) and a lion pursuing a kylin (two groups near the middle of the carpet). The border pattern includes palmettes and an angular ideogram which may conceivably be a stylized phoenix.

The animal figures are of Chinese origin. The design as a whole may have been inspired by Iranian carpets from the Kerman area (compare the overlapping lattice arrangement with that of the vase carpet, no. 340), but is stylized in a manner characteristic of the Caucasus. Such carpets were produced there in considerable numbers in the late 17th and 18th centuries. This is a very fine early example.

342
Velvet with pattern in gold thread

The pattern is in gold thread bound in twill, on a background of crimson silk velvet
165 × 124 cm (two lengths joined side by side)
Previously in the Baron Edmond de Rothschild Collection
King (1980), no. 1. See also Falke (1913), fig. 604; Errera (1927), no. 222
Turkey, possibly Bursa, late 16th century

The large-scale pattern of a curvilinear lattice, formed by double stems linked by crowns, and enclosing enormous thistle-heads of two different kinds, is very similar to Italian textile patterns, and this velvet has sometimes been attributed to Venice or Genoa. It is in fact a typical example of the give and take between Italian and Ottoman textile designers. In this case the materials and technique are clearly Turkish; the Ottoman designer has reduced the three-dimensional effects of his Italian prototypes to flat silhouettes and has transformed one of the thistle-heads into a typically Turkish tulip and carnation. The power and vigour of the design is splendidly set off by the colour scheme of crimson and gold. A related pattern is seen in a silk bed cover in the Topkapi Saray Museum which is believed to date from the reign of Mehmet III (1595-1603).

343

Cloth of gold with pattern in velvet

Silk velvet in shades of blue, red, green, buff and cream, on a background of flat gold strips bound in twill
91 × 42 cm
Previously in the collections of Prince Sanguszko, Adolph Loewi and Dr Jakob Hirsch Loewi (1944), no. 248. See also Reath (1937), no. 82; Pope (1938-9), pl. 1006; Weibel (1952), no. 135; Spuhler (1978), no. 100
Iran, Safavid, late 16th or early 17th century

The pattern is a curvilinear lattice, formed by beaded bands carrying lotus blossoms and rosettes, and enclosing large blooms carried on curvilinear stems; meandering tendrils bear smaller flowers and leaves. The lotus blossoms are derived from China and much of the rest of the design is inspired by Ottoman textiles; but the execution and colouring are clearly Persian, of the time of Shah 'Abbas I (1587-1629).

This is one of a number of shaped panels of velvet, formerly ornaments of a tent, which belonged to the Sanguszko family in Poland and is said to have been captured from the Turkish army at the siege of Vienna in 1683. Other similar panels are in the Keir Collection, the Metropolitan Museum, New York, and the Textile Museum, Washington, D.C.

344

Cloth of silver, brocaded with silk

Silk in shades of pink, green, blue, brown and yellow on a background of silver thread bound in twill
76 × 78 cm
Lefevre sale catalogue, July 4 1980, no. 58
Iran, Safavid, first half 17th century

This square silk cover is designed like a carpet, with central field and borders. The central field shows a curvilinear lattice, formed by double beaded bands, and enclosing three different cross-shaped arrangements of flowers and leaves. The main borders, with their corner compartments and guard stripes, have similar flower and leaf ornament, all strongly stylized.

A number of these bordered silk covers from Iran are known, in various styles, but mostly of 17th-century date. The present piece seems a fairly early example.

344

345
Cloth of gold, brocaded with silk

Silk in shades of red, pink, green and blue, with details in silver thread, on a background of gold thread, all bound in twill
73 × 36 cm
Errera (1927), no. 420E
Iran, Safavid, or India, Mughal, mid-17th century

The motif, a bird perched on a flowering rose bush and catching a fly in its beak, is turned to left and right in alternate rows. It looks like a miniature adapted for silk weaving and is executed with minute delicacy – note the tiny hairs on the rose stems, and the golden stamens of the flowers.

Related motifs of birds in rose bushes are found in many Iranian silks of the 17th century and are sometimes attributed to Isfahan (Pope 1938-9, pp. 2135-36). But the colouring and lively naturalism of this example suggests the possibility of a Mughal origin. Such naturalistic floral motifs, inspired by European botanical illustrations, were adopted by the artists of the Mughal court from the 1620s onwards.

346
Brocaded satin

Silk in shades of red, pink, orange, yellow, green and blue, with details in gold and silver thread, all bound in twill, on a background of dark brown satin
43 × 31 cm
Iran, Safavid, late 17th or early 18th century

The motif, a composite spray of foliage and flowers rising from a little mound, reverses its direction in alternate rows. There is a trace of European influence in the dark brown satin ground and the slightly fantastic stylization of the floral spray, but the details and the delicate execution are characteristically Iranian. A number of more or less related silks are known (e.g. Pope, 1938-9, pl. 1048B).

347
Embroidered cover or hanging

Undyed cotton cloth, embroidered with blue-green, red and yellow silk in chain stitch
114 × 83.5 cm
Spink (1980), no. 79
India, Mughal, 17th or early 18th century

A curvilinear lattice, formed by slender stems with serrated leaves, encloses a delicate flowering plant; the border shows a floral trail. The background is quilted with a straight lattice pattern.

This is a type of floral design which was widely employed in Mughal art over a long period, but this finely executed example must be comparatively early.

348
Embroidered hanging

Dark red cotton cloth, embroidered with white, yellow, green and blue-green silk in chain stitch
178 × 70 cm
Previously in the collection of Mr Vishnu M. Lall
Victoria and Albert Museum (1982), no. 214; Spink (1983), no. 11.
See also Irwin (1973), no. 9
India, Mughal, 18th century

A large flowering plant in a vase beneath an arch. The borders show wavy trails of flowers and leaves. The background is quilted with a straight lattice pattern.

The handsome design is admirably executed. Further hangings from the same set are in the Calico Museum, Ahmedabad, the al-Sabah Collection at the Kuwait National Museum, and the Metropolitan Museum, New York. Such sets of hangings are generally identified as tent hangings, but might also be hung in doorways, windows or palace colonnades.

349

Embroidered cover

Undyed linen cloth, embroidered with silk in shades of red, blue, yellow, cream and black, in oriental couching
117 × 117 cm
King (1980), no. 30
Turkey, Ottoman, late 17th or 18th century

The pattern consists of rows of jewelled arches framing conventional flowering plants. The border shows a repeated leaf and flower. This vigorous design, boldly executed, is not easily datable, but a late 17th or 18th century date seems likely.

Square covers of this kind, called *bohça*, were used as wrappers for costume or textiles.

350

Embroidered hanging or cover

Undyed linen cloth embroidered with silk in shades of red, blue, green, yellow and black, in darning stitch
231 × 150 cm (four lengths of cloth joined side by side)
King (1980), no. 34
Turkey, Ottoman, 18th century

The pattern consists of rows of pointed oval compartments containing sprays of carnation and hyacinths. The narrow border has a wavy stem with hyacinth flowers, and groups of three discs and three crescents.

The design was inspired by Ottoman woven silks of the 16th and 17th centuries, but the light and airy treatment suggests an 18th-century date for this piece. Other examples of similar large size and related design are known (e.g. Petsopoulos 1982, no. 146).

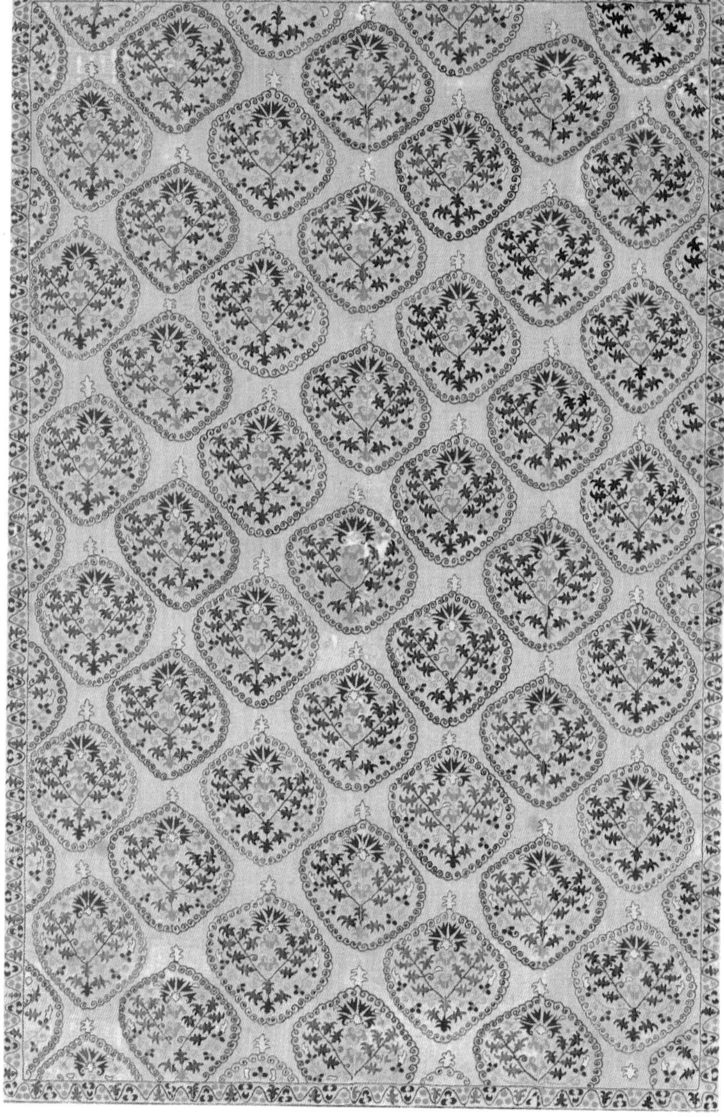

351
Needlework cover

Needlework of silk in shades of black, yellow, red, pink, blue, green, brown and purple silk, in tent stitch on cotton cloth
124 × 71 cm
Lefevre sale catalogue, July 4 1980, no. 78
Caucasus, late 17th or 18th century

From a central medallion, containing stylized plant ornament, various palmettes radiate, and are complemented at both ends by coiling snake-like forms. The border shows small medallions, leaves and birds.

This is an excellent example of a class of Caucasian needlework with designs related to those of the dragon carpets (cf. no. 341) and floral carpets produced in the same area.

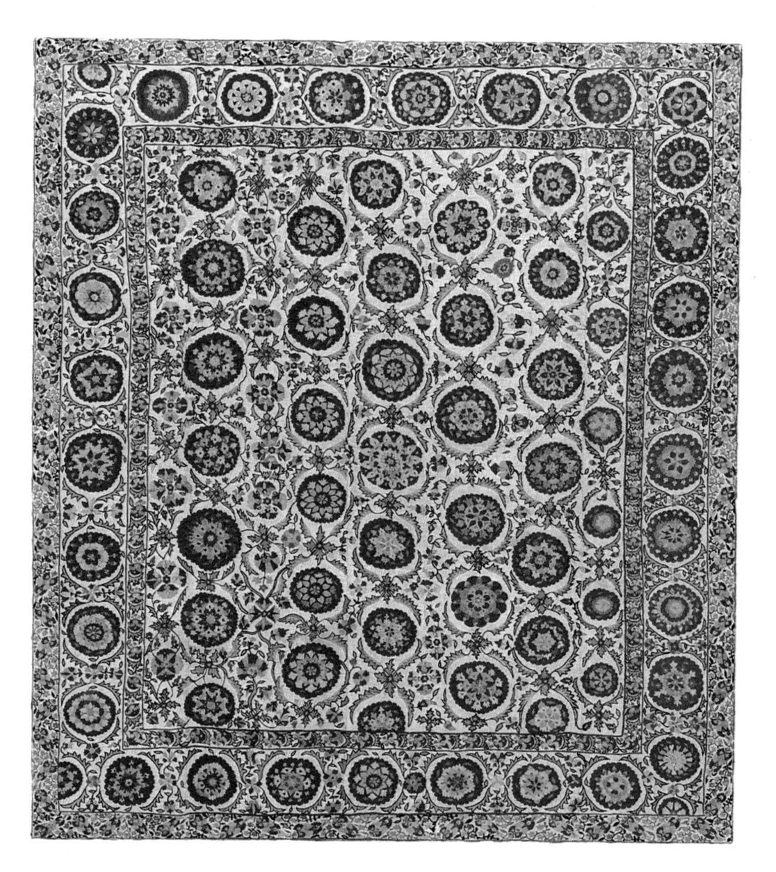

352
Embroidered cover or hanging

Undyed cotton cloth embroidered with silk in shades of red, pink, green, blue, yellow, orange and brown, in Bokhara couching
205 × 187 cm (four and a half pieces of cloth joined side by side)
Lefevre sale catalogue, 4 July 1980, lot 101
Samarkand area, first half 19th century

The pattern consists of rows of large circular flowers, of varying design, surrounded with leaves and smaller flowers; similar motifs fill the borders and guard stripes.

This is a handsome example of a large class of domestic embroideries, said to have been made for bridal dowries, in the Bukhara–Samarkand–Tashkent area. On stylistic evidence it has been suggested that this piece may have been worked in the neighbourhood of Ura-Tyube, east of Samarkand and south of Tashkent.

MARILYN JENKINS

Architectural Ornament and Decorative Arts

This section is devoted to objects selected from a collection which holds a unique position in the field being the most public of all private collections of Islamic art in the world, forming single-handedly the *Dār al-Āthār al-Islāmīya* (The Museum of Islamic Art) in the Kuwait National Museum.[1]

The objects presented here, from the al-Sabah Collection, were not chosen because they share a common theme, medium, period or provenance, but solely on account of their extraordinary quality, rarity and beauty. Consequently, in this sense they are a true miscellany. However, no matter how diverse these objects may seem at first glance, the very nature of Islamic art militates against placing these or any group of Islamic objects into the category of miscellaneous since the cohesiveness of Islamic art is remarkable, given its development over a period of thirteen hundred years and its spread from Spain to the borders of China.

A great deal has been written on the unity inherent in Islamic art despite the great diversity implied in its temporal and geographic expanse. Taking this theme, one could discuss these objects (as I have in other publications) from the point of view of the four elements basic to Islamic decoration: geometric patterns, highly stylized vegetal forms, figural iconography and calligraphy, or how these objects exemplify the cyclical repetition of the processes of adoption, adaptation and creation which insure a continuity over such a long time and wide space.[2]

However, here I would like to take another unifying factor, namely, 'the ready transfer of a technique or pattern – whether appropriate or not – from one medium to another'[3] and apply it to ten of the objects chosen at random from the al-Sabah Collection, ten objects which can be arranged into five pairs, each of which is an example of what I shall call, for the lack of a better term, 'private art' on the one hand and 'public art' on the other. The five examples of 'private art' are items of jewellery – the least public of all possessions, satisfying only in private and reserving their charms for intimacy.[4] The 'public' half of each pair consists of five pieces of architectural decoration, the most publicly accessible category of Islamic art.

The blind niche (no. 353) and the pair of bracelets (no. 355) from the same general geographical area, share a similar series of stylistic conventions and motifs even though they are separated in time by three hundred years. The major border design (which reads as contiguous circles) delimited by a guard band filled with a repetitive design, the tripartite principal decoration with a strong vertical axis and the highly stylized vegetal motifs serve to unite these Umayyad and Fatimid objects despite the differences in medium, scale and period.[5]

Separated by the full width of the Mediterranean Sea, the marble capital (no. 354) and the gold ring (no. 356) share the same lace-like quality in their decoration as if both were executed in the same technique. The common tendency of the Islamic artist to veil a surface in a pattern thus causing the surface to take on a character other than its own can clearly be seen here.[6]

Parallels for the vigorous, beautifully rounded gazelles separated from each other by a five-lobed palmette on the wooden panel (no. 357) are found on the gold bracelet (no. 360), with its equally rounded quadrupeds separated by a filagree-decorated roundel; both groups of animals are set within a band. Although they are executed in totally different techniques, one carved in wood and the other created by hammering a thin strip of gold from the back in the *repoussé* technique, the overall effect is quite similar. The bisecting motif of each band is either completely separate as in the case of the bracelet or, as on the frieze, it has an applied element that is attached by means of a dowel.

The *cloisonné* area of the pair of earrings (no. 359) was made by constructing a cup of gold sheet in which compartments were created by wires or strips of sheet set on edge. The opaque white Quranic inscription is thus seemingly set into the yellow and red highlighted cobalt ground, and closely related to the faience mosaic panel (no. 362) on which letters (also forming a Quranic inscription) are individually set into a plaster background. The great similarity in the basic concept and ultimate realization of these two totally distinct techniques, which are applicable only on objects of greatly differing scale and medium, is striking.

The central, vertically oriented panels on the pair of Timurid doors (no. 366) and the circular area on the obverse of the Mamluk necklace element (no. 363) both contain decoration consisting of two superimposed design networks composed of geometricized vegetal designs.[7] Such a convention was also very popular on carpets and textiles as well as on bookbindings and manuscript illuminations.

Having seen how the application of this single unifying factor to this group of randomly chosen, highly diverse objects moves them out of the realm of miscellany and unites them into a larger whole, let us now turn to each object individually and, within this fundamental unity, see the variety of which Islamic art was capable as well.

1) Catalogue entry 361 was added by the organizers of the exhibition after this chapter was written and has not been seen and examined by the author
2) *Islamic Art in the Kuwait National Museum, the al-Sabah Collection*, ed. Marilyn Jenkins (London, 1983), pp. 11-16
3) Ettinghausen, R., 'The Man-Made Setting', *The World of Islam* (London, 1976), p. 58
4) Goitein, S.D., *A Mediterranean Society*, vol. IV. That jewels intrigue one's close friends, not the crowd in the street is beautifully illustrated by the album page (no. 30) depicting the rendezvous between a chaperoned damsel, adorned with a jewelled gold head-ornament and earrings, and a man with his male servant, both of whom wear earrings
5) Similar stylistic conventions visible on the cylindrical neck and at the waist of the ceramic jar (no. 244) serve to further illustrate this point
6) This veiling can be seen as well on the profusely carved hunting horn (no. 358)
7) This motif occurs as well in the roundel at the centre of the principal band on the glass vessel (no. 364) and on the lid of the wooden Qur'an box (no. 365)

353
Blind niche

Carved limestone
Height 92 cm
Dār al-Āthār al-Islāmīya, Kuwait National Museum, LNS65S
Greater Syria, 1st half 8th century

This blind niche is closely related to those still *in situ* on the upper walls of the gatehouse on the citadel of Amman and those at the summit of the entrance tower of the Lesser Enclosure of Qasr al-Hayr al-Sharqi and should be similarly dated to the first half of the 8th century. On the analogy of the decorative programme of these two buildings, this niche was one of many arranged contiguously so as to form an arcade. The use of arcaded bands as architectural decoration was adopted from the Sasanian repertoire as was the saw-tooth decoration on the arch and the highly stylized vegetal designs.

354
Capital

Signed *Work of Falih*
Carved marble
Inscribed (see below)
Height 38 cm
Dār al-Āthār al-Islāmīya, Kuwait National Museum, LNS2S
Jenkins (1983), p. 44
Spain, dated 362/972-73

This exquisite capital whose filagree-like decoration suggests a Byzantine model rather than a classical one was probably made for Madinat al-Zahra', north-west of Cordova, which was founded by the Spanish Umayyad ruler 'Abd al-Rahman III in 936 and further adorned by his son al-Hakam II (961-76). This city, according to Ibn Khallikan, covered approximately four million square cubits (or two thousand square miles!) and was graced with forty-three hundred columns. Maqqari, quoting Ibn Hayyan, tells us that approximately one-quarter of these columns were imported from Ifriqiya, France or Byzantium and the rest were from Spain itself. Which of these was crowned with the superb work of Falih?

Inscription

Bismillah baraka min Allah/wa 'āfiyya shāmila wa 'izz dā'im/wa surūr muttasil li'l-Imām 'Abdullah/al-Hakam al-Mustansir billah amīr/ al-mu'minīn atāl Allah baqā'hu mimmā a/mara bi-'amalihi wa tamma bi-'awn Allah/('alā yad)ay Talīd al-fatī al-kabīr fī/sanat ithnayn wa sittīn wa thalāth mi'a/'amal Falīh al-asīr 'abdihi

In the name of God. Blessing from God and general well-being and everlasting glory and uninterrupted joy to the Imam 'Abd Allah al-Hakam al-Mustansir Billah, Commander of the Faithful, may God prolong his reign. From among that which he ordered to be made and which was completed with the help of God under the supervision of Talid, the chief servant, in the year two and sixty and three hundred. Work of Falih, the Captive his servant

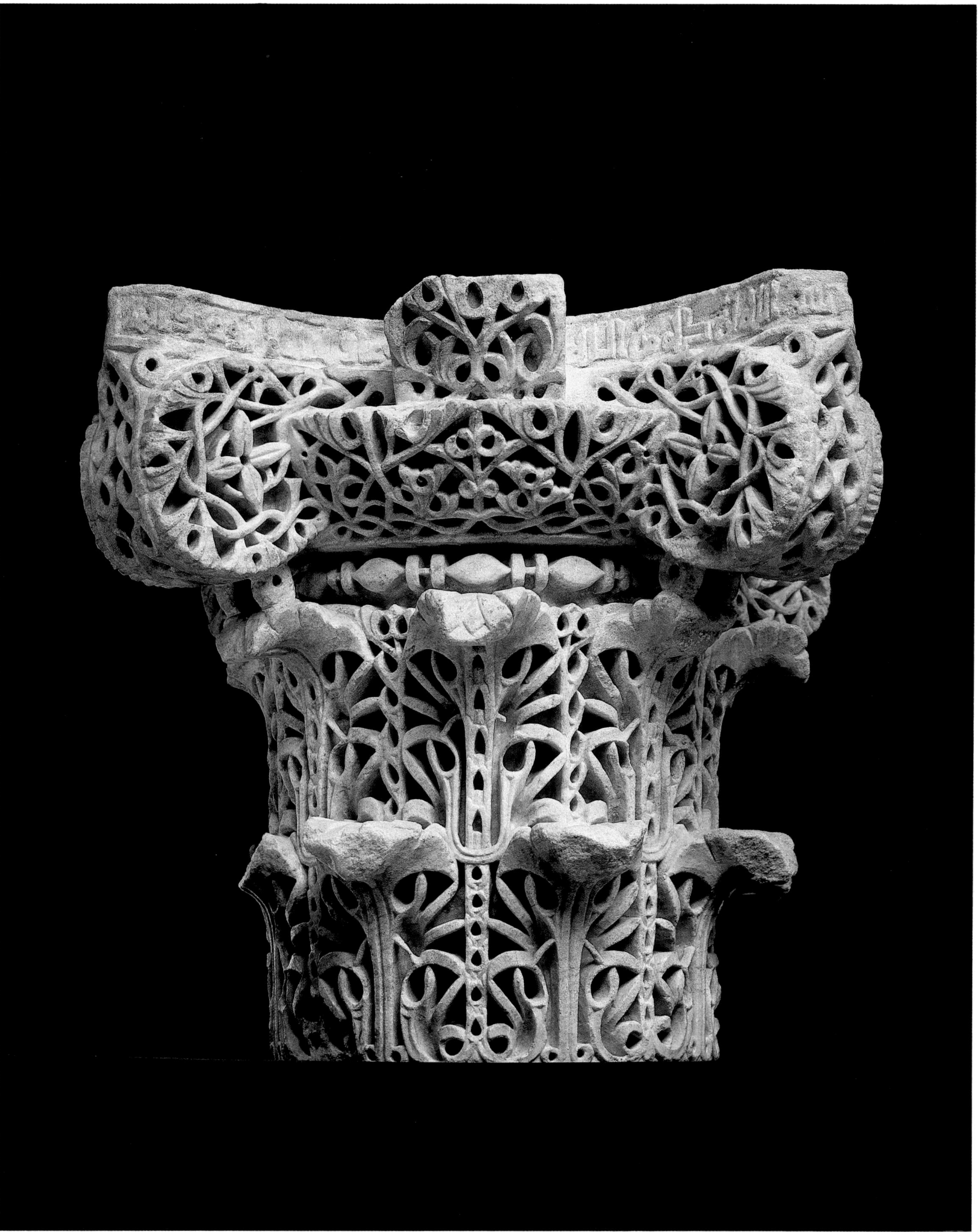

354

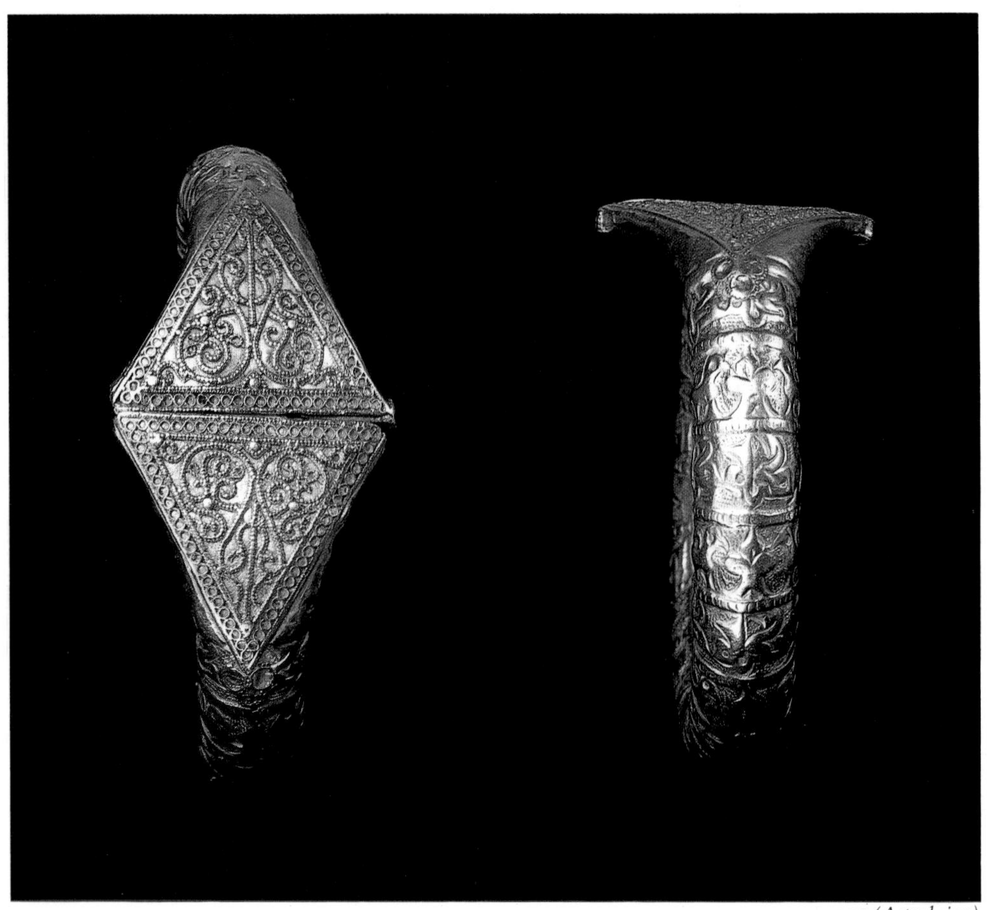

355 *(Actual size)*

356 *(Actual size)*

355
Pair of bracelets

Gold, fabricated from sheet, decorated with punches, granulation, flat and twisted round wire and *repoussé*
Inscribed: *baraka kāmila* (perfect blessing)
Diameter 8 cm
Dār al-Āthār al-Islāmīya, Kuwait National Museum, LNS 7 Ja and b
Jenkins (1983), p. 65
Greater Syria, 11th century

Occurring half way through a two-thousand-year story which is a testament to the conservatism and traditionalism within the art of jewellery making is this pair of bracelets. Their subdivided shanks derive from Roman rings and bracelets formed of ball-shape sections, the basic profile of which has been adapted by the Islamic artist so that only a hint of the precursor remains; while the flat, triangular form of each side of the clasp, as well as the remains of three balls at the apex of each, looks ahead to bracelets made in various parts of the Islamic world in the 19th and 20th centuries.

356
Ring

Gold, fabricated from sheet and wire, decorated with wire and granulation
Inner diameter 1.8 cm
Dār al-Āthār al-Islāmīya, Kuwait National Museum, LNS 35 J
Jenkins (1983), p. 64
Greater Syria, 11th century

This ring is executed solely in filagree with granulation except for the strips of gold placed at critical points to strengthen the delicate network from the back and the tapered band of gold at the inside of the shank which is another practical addition. The two designs of the arabesque and the S-curve (seen forming simple borders as well as the major motif on the sides of the shank) are very characteristic of Fatimid jewellery and are also to be found on the clasps of the pair of bracelets (no. 355) which were executed at the same time and in the same area.

357
Panel

Carved wood (originally painted)
Length 152.5 cm
Dār al-Āthār al-Islāmīya, Kuwait National Museum, LNS 55W
Hali (1984), vol. 6, no. 2, pp. 170-171
Egypt, *c.* 1058

This masterfully carved panel is the most complete of three known parts of a frieze which once adorned the Lesser, or Western Fatimid Palace originally built by the Caliph al-'Aziz (975-96) and completely renovated by the Caliph al-Mustansir in 1058. Their preservation is most probably due to the speed with which the Mamluk sultan Qala'un wanted his great complex built on the site of the Fatimid palace, an order which caused his amir, Sangar al-Shuja'i, to take advantage of the already existing woodwork and other material on the site. This 'recycled' panel is perhaps the single most beautiful piece of Fatīmid woodwork extant.

359 *(Actual size)*

358
Hunting horn

Carved ivory
Length 42.7 cm
Previously in the collection of Mr John Hunt, Dublin, Ireland
Dār al-Āthār al-Islāmīya, Kuwait National Museum, LNS 121
Kühnel (1971), no. 61, pl. LVII; Jenkins (1983), p. 63. For other references see Kühnel's bibliography.
Italy, late 11th-early 12th century

This richly carved hunting horn from Italy, containing a veritable medieval bestiary of real and fantastic animals within the interlocking roundels covering its surface, bears witness to the interaction between countries surrounding the Mediterranean basin at this period. Fatimid influence is obvious when one closely compares the gazelle in the upper row of roundels with those on the Egyptian wood panel (no. 357). Also the arabesque decoration on the tails of the birds and the wings of several fantastic animals is very similar to that on the clasps of the pair of gold bracelets (no. 355) made in Greater Syria.

359
Pair of earrings

Gold, fabricated from sheet, wire and grains, set with cloisonné enamels
Each of the four cloisonné enamels is inscribed with the first two verses of Sura CXII of the Qur'an
Height with earwires 4.8 cm and 4.65 cm
Dār al-Āthār al-Islāmīya, Kuwait National Museum, LNS 30 Ja and b
Davillier (1879), fig. 8, p. 28; Jenkins (1983), p. 91
Spain, 12th century

This beautiful and very rare pair of earrings, while exhibiting an overall shape, calligraphic style and border designs indicative of a Spanish provenance, is also illustrative of Fatimid Egyptian or Syrian influence on contemporary Spanish jewellery. The box-like construction so popular with Fatimid goldsmiths is seen here, as is the convention of attaching loops around the edge of the box which were originally intended to hold strings of pearls or semi-precious stones. The Fatimid proclivity for goldwork with an openwork surface is found here also, as is the combination of the latter with cloisonné enamel. Pieces such as this lead to the simpler, 14th- and 15th-century Nasrid Spanish jewellery.

360 *(Actual size)*

360
Bracelet

Gold, fabricated from sheet and wire, decorated with punches, shot, wire and *repoussé*
Greatest diameter 6 cm
Dār al-Āthār al-Islāmīya, Kuwait National Museum, LNS 31 J
Jenkins (1983), p. 64
Turkey, 1st half 13th century

The construction of this bracelet from gold sheet, the horizontal edges of which are rolled to form a border, and the nature of its inner border of paired twisted wires serving as a mask for the rolled edges, as well as the placement and type of closure, suggest a 12th-century Iranian origin. But the band of running quadrupeds on the shank, and the execution in *repoussé*, set it apart from other Iranian examples of the period. Perhaps a centre in a different, but closely related, country should be sought, namely Seljuq Turkey.

361
Roundel

Stucco, carved with the phrase *al-mulk lillah* (Sovereignty is God's), interspersed with leaf motifs
Diameter 30 cm
North India, Sultanate, *c.* 1480
T.F.

362
Frieze

Composite body, glazed and cut; plaster inscribed with part of the Qur'an, Sura II, verse 286
Length 175 cm
Dār al-Āthār al-Islāmīya, Kuwait National Museum, LNS 234 C
Turkey, 650/1251-52

Originally forming part of the breathtakingly beautiful decorative programme of the Karatay Madrasa in Konya, this frieze is illustrative of an important stage in the history of a technique known as faience mosaic which began with the very sparse and tentative use of small monochrome glazed tiles set into the walls of buildings and culminated in the total blanketing of extensive areas. The intermediate stage represented here, which enjoyed great popularity and reached great heights in the decoration of Seljuq Turkish architecture, consists of individually cut pieces of glazed pottery laboriously fitted together and set into plaster.

363
Necklace element (with two pairs of holes for stringing)

Gold, fabricated from wire and strips of sheet
Diameter 4.2 cm
Dār al-Āthār al-Islāmīya, Kuwait National Museum, LNS 21 J
Jenkins (1983), p. 91
Syria or Egypt, 1st half 14th century

Due to the recent discovery in Simferopol in the Crimea of an important hoard of jewellery and coins, it is now possible to write a chapter (missing so far from the history of the goldsmith's art) concerning the jewellery produced during Mamluk rule. The presence in the Crimea of objects created in the Mamluk period is very easily explained since the trade routes of the Golden Horde, who supplied Cairo with the young boys who would one day become Mamluks, passed through the Crimean peninsula. A major category of jewellery from this period, represented by this necklace element, looks backward to earlier Fatimid jewellery, while at the same time incorporating a number of new features which have echoes in the later Berber jewellery of North Africa and in Russian goldsmiths' work starting from the end of the 15th century.

363 *(Actual size)*

364
Bottle or vase

Glass, free blown and tooled, with plastically applied handles, enamelled
Height 31 cm
Dār al-Āthār al-Islāmīya, Kuwait National Museum, LNS 6 G
Bamborough (1976), p. 98; Jenkins (1983), p. 88
Syria or Egypt, first half 14th century

The technique used to decorate this bottle or vase originated in the early medieval period but it was in the subsequent period, under the Mamluks, that the enamelling of glass reached its zenith. It was the output of this latter period which was to serve as the inspiration for later European glass executed in a similar technique.

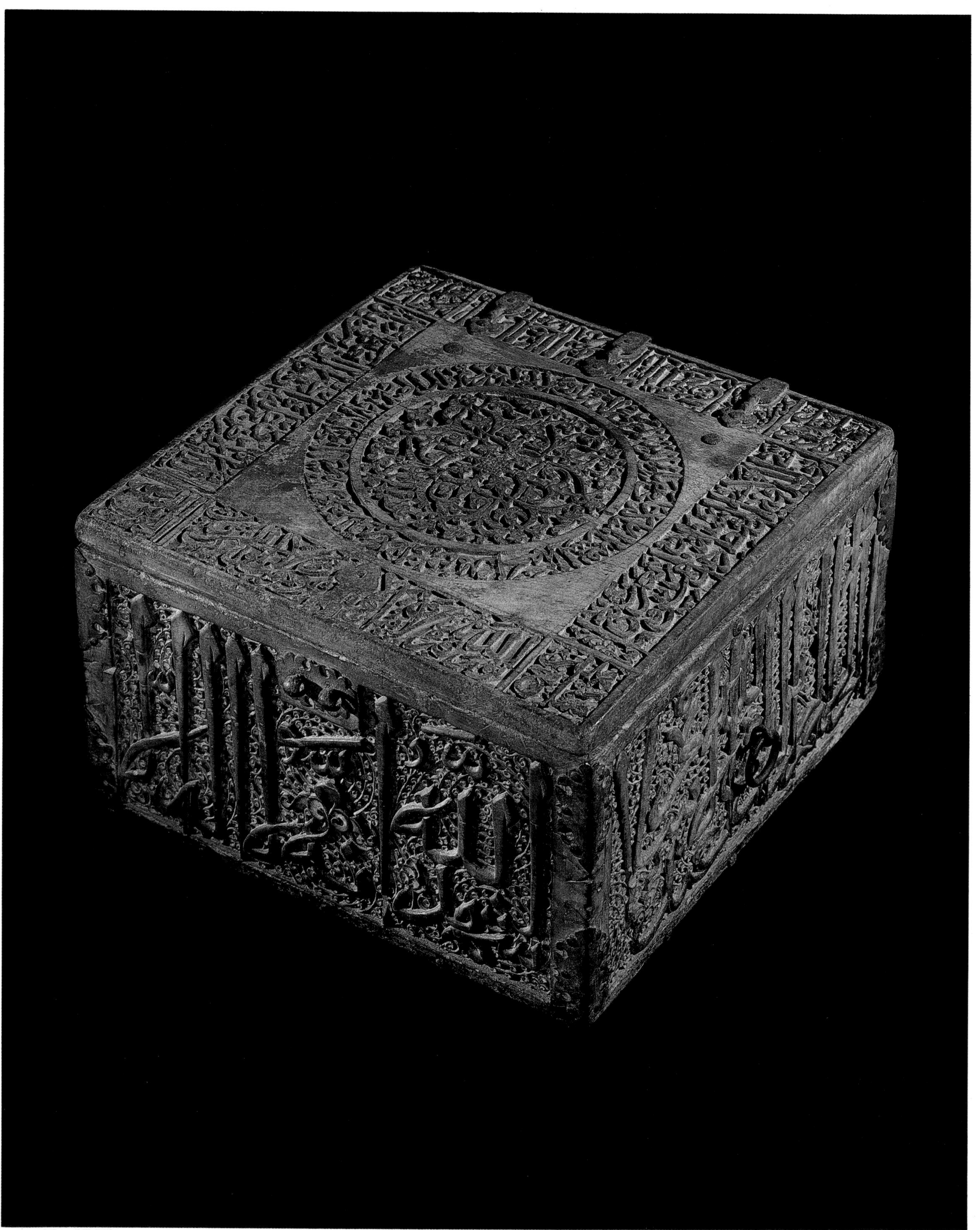

365

365
Box for a multi-volume manuscript of the Qur'an

Presented to the tomb of the late Fakhr al-Din and signed by al-Hasan ibn Qutlubak ibn Fakhr al-Din
Wood, dadoed, mitred, dovetailed and painted; bronze hinges
Inscribed (see below)
Width 43 cm
Previously in the collection of the Comtesse de Béhague, France
Dār al-Āthār al-Islāmīya, Kuwait National Museum, LNS 35 W
Mayer (1958), p. 40, pl. VII; Jenkins (1983), p. 110
Iran, *Rajab* 745/November, 1344

This exquisitely carved box is unique to the best of our knowledge. Consequently, we are fortunate that one of its inscriptions helps us to determine its function. The four interior rectangular compartments which appear to revolve around a small, square, central compartment each held one or more bound sections of the Qur'an. The beautifully executed vegetal design circumscribed in a roundel on the lid of the object is highly geometricized, a sylistic convention which was very popular in Qur'an illuminations of this period and it is tempting to speculate that such decoration on the box may have echoed that in the manuscript it was made to contain.

Inscriptions
Around sides of box: Sura III, verses 18-19; around circular medallion on top of lid: *The revered leader, king of charity and of the notables, 'Izz al-Din Malik, son of Nasir Allah Muhammad, [may God] prolong his exaltedness, entered this august, blessed complete copy of the Qur'an into endowment for the benefit of the tomb of the deceased (received into God's mercy) Fakhr al-Din . . .*; in rectangular compartments around perimeter of lid: *The mentioned one died in the middle of Rajab of the year five and forty and seven-hundred, may God light his tomb. It is not to be sold nor to be given nor to be inherited until God inherits the earth and those who are upon it, and He is the best of the inheritors. Surely, the offence of exchanging it after hearing this is on those who exchange it. Indeed, God is All-Hearing, All-Knowing. The end*; in square compartments at corners of lid: *This is among the works of the poor slave [of God] al-Hasan, son of Qutlubak, son of the deceased Fakhr al-Din . . .*

366
Pair of doors

Inscribed and signed *Ghurra sha'abān al-mu'azzam sana arba' [wa] 'ashrīn wa thamānī mi'a. 'Amal ustādh Qutb al-Dīn ibn 'Alī Nīshāpūrī.* At the beginning of *Sha'bān al-Mu'azzam* four and twenty and eight hundred. Work of Ustad Qutb al-Din ibn 'Ali Nishapuri
Carved wood
Height 171 cm
Dār al-Āthār al-Islāmīya, Kuwait National Museum, LNS 64 W
Bivar and Yarshater (1978), pls 43-45
Iran, 824/1421

This pair of doors is from Roshanabad in the richly wooded Iranian province of Mazandaran which nurtured a number of important woodcarvers, including the master Qutb al-Din who decorated each of the upper, square sections of these doors with an inscription; the lower, rectangular sections with a cartouche filled with a geometricized vegetal design on a background incised with a fish-scale pattern (a design repeated on the central part of the door post); and the central panel of each leaf with a beautifully integrated series of superimposed design networks bearing close comparison with those on contemporary bookbindings and in manuscript illuminations.

366

MICHAEL L. BATES AND

ROBERT E. DARLEY-DORAN

The Art of Islamic Coinage

The artistic quality of a coin often provides a reliable clue to the cultural level of the civilization which struck it. This is especially true of coins found in the lands around the Mediterranean and in the Middle East where coinage was first developed. Because coins represent the authority of the state, their artistic quality naturally influences the way people view their rulers' power and prestige. This in turn depends on the management of the mint and the skill of the workers who make the coins and the dies by which they are struck. Although the skill of die engraving may be seen as one of the minor arts, it calls forth the same talents as that of a sculptor or calligrapher working in miniature. Indeed it would be natural for a capable artist to cut gems, engrave seals or sink dies as part of his daily work. Such skills take years to perfect and can flourish best under rich and stable patronage.

Such conditions were generally lacking in Arabia when the Prophet Muhammad emigrated from Makka to Medina in 622, the first year of the Hijra, for the Arabs of the Hijaz lived on the fringes of the then civilized world and shared few of its benefits. The coins they used came from the Byzantines or Persians, for there was as yet no local political authority which felt the need to strike its own. The first cultural task facing the Muslims after the death of the Prophet in 632 was to transform his oral revelations of God's Word into an acceptable written form. For this a script had to be developed that was sophisticated enough to reproduce with minute accuracy each shade of meaning in the words of the Holy Qur'an. In the first decades, however, the political success of Islam fast outstripped its more tangible cultural achievements, and the Muslims had to rely on local artists and craftsmen who were conditioned by Byzantine and Sasanian art forms. Later, as the Qur'an became part of everyday life, the quality of oral recitation and the calligraphy of the written words of the Qur'an grew to be regarded as the supreme art forms. Thus it was that a new Muslim culture and art based on Arabic calligraphy developed, and in its train came the first coins.

Examples of coins from empires conquered by the Muslims can be seen in the Arab-Sasanian pieces (nos 386-388) where the portrait of the Sasanian emperor and the Zoroastrian fire altar are shown on coins bearing the names of Muslim authorities. Only the briefest of allusions to Islam differentiate these issues from their predecessors. True Islamic coinage originated in the reign of the Umayyad caliph 'Abd al-Malik (685-705), who was also the first caliph to order that the administrative records of his empire be maintained in the Arabic language rather than in Greek or Persian.

At first the policy was simply to adapt the imperial coinage traditions inherited by the Arabs to the needs of the new religion. In fact the very earliest of the new coins of Damascus were fairly close imitations of imperial types, such as the very rare issue (coin no. 368), with three standing figures, that copies a Byzantine issue of some sixty years earlier. On this gold coin the legends are replaced by Islamic inscriptions in Arabic and the three figures are Arabs, not Byzantines. The silver and copper, however, such as the 'Arab-Byzantine' coppers (nos 372-376), even retain the inscriptions and symbols of their prototypes in part. At about the same time the Arabs issued coins in newly conquered North Africa with imperial portraits and inscriptions in Latin, but as on the gold of Damascus the inscriptions were Islamic in content (nos 380 and 381).

The next stage in this rapid evolution was the replacement of imperial symbols with Islamic ones, the most famous being the standing caliph found on gold and copper coins of the years 74-77/694-697 (nos 377-379). Other such experimental Islamic images included the prayer niche of a mosque or the caliph praying. These experiments were not successful, however, for they were no more than adaptations of the western coinage tradition in which images are the primary message bearers on coins (as is still the case today). A fundamental principle of Islam is opposition to the use of religious images, and the caliph was not supposed to be just another emperor with the right to place his portrait on coins.

To meet the needs of the new religion a new coinage was invented. Since worship in Islam centres upon God's Word itself, the new coins carried only religious inscriptions taken from the Qur'an, beginning with gold dinars struck in 77/696-7 (no. 369). With this issue we can begin to speak of the art of Islamic coins. The design is ideally suited to the spirit of the early Muslims – simple, even austere, with no ornamentation apart from the inscriptions themselves which are purely religious except for the date. What is more remarkable about this new issue is the absence of any evolution in its conception. It simply appears in the year 77/696-7, replacing the quite different image-bearing coins that had preceded it. Moreover, its design, with horizontal lines of inscription surrounded by circular legends on both sides, was so satisfactory that this was retained on Islamic coins of the caliphate until the 13th century, along with most of the original inscriptions. There is no evidence in this earliest dinar of 77/696-7 of what can truly be called artistic intention, although the design and epigraphy have the attraction of any object perfectly suited to its use. In the years that followed die engravers developed their crafts into a high art.

To western minds, accustomed to regarding representation as the essence of art, it may seem contradictory to describe coins without images as works of art, but a look with open eyes and mind at these little objects is well worth the effort. The art of Islamic coinage is that of calligraphy and abstract design. Although the mainstream of Islamic coins continue to follow the precedent of the 7th century, there were many variations within the standardized format, as well as new designs that adhered to the principle of avoiding images. In addition, the precedent laid down by 'Abd al-Malik never became a law or religious doctrine – as far as is known, Muslim religious thinkers have practically nothing to say about appropriate coin design – and there are many exceptional Muslim coins with images, both as a result of non-Muslim influence and arising from the use of indigenous motifs.

For nearly a century after the striking of the first Islamic dinar the general format of Islamic coinage remained much the same, as one can see from a survey of the Umayyad and Abbasid coins (nos 389-420). A second look, however, will show that they are not all alike, despite their family resemblance. For example, it is interesting to compare the Umayyad gold coinage of Damascus (nos 389, 392, 393 and 398) with that of North Africa and Spain (nos 394-396), or the earliest dinars (such as nos 368 and 389) with the last of the Umayyad series (no. 398) and the first Abbasid dinar (no. 370). In the latter comparison an obvious feature is the horizontal elongation of the letters, especially in the top line of the reverse. This elongation continued to increase until the beginning of the 9th century, to the point where coins can almost be dated by the length of certain letters. The script on all these coins is an early style of Arabic called Kufic, named after the city of Kufa in Iraq whose calligraphers are said to have brought Kufic to its highest development. This remained in use on all Islamic coins until the 12th century.

The reign of al-Ma'mun (813-33) marked a turning point in the evolution of Abbasid coin design with the creation of what was to become the classical Abbasid Sunni coinage. The development of inscriptions had already begun with the addition of the names of individual rulers and governors on gold and silver coins (as on nos 401-405 and 407). During al-Ma'mun's civil war with his brother, al-Amin Muhammad, (809-13), the coinage of different provinces changed considerably. As far as their appearance goes, these reforms consisted in giving the right to be named on gold and silver coins to the caliph alone, with his designated heir (if there was one), in introducing the names of mints on gold as well as silver coins, in a uniform design for both gold dinars and silver dirhams, and in a second marginal inscription, first used at the time of al-Ma'mun's victory, 'God's is the command, past and future, and on that day the believers will rejoice in the victory granted by God.' All but one of these features continued to characterize the coinage of the Abbasid caliphs and the dynasties that acknowledged them as overlords until the Mongol conquest of Baghdad in 1258.

The exception to this is an important one: al-Ma'mun's prohibition against the naming of subordinate officials on the gold and silver coinage. In fact this prohibition had the contradictory effect of developing into one of the most important features of Islamic coins. Before al-Ma'mun's time many local governors had put their names on coins, but after his reign the only persons to be named were those powerful enough to demand – or simply seize – the right to do so. As a result, the right of *sikka*, a ruler's privilege to place his name on coins issued under his authority, became for medieval Muslims one of the two most important emblems of his independent sovereignty, the other being his right to be prayed for as ruler in the *khutba*, the exhortation which precedes the public act of Friday prayer.

While this new-style coinage became current throughout the Abbasid domains, North Africa and Spain, no longer under Abbasid control, continued to issue traditional coinage. The dirhams of Umayyad Spain still bore the inscriptions seen on those of the Umayyad caliphate (no. 399) and the Aghlabid dinars continued with their original Abbasid design (no. 410). This relatively conservative tradition evolved independently in the 10th and 11th centuries, uninfluenced by political developments in eastern Islam. For example, no. 413 dated 317/929 is one of the earliest Spanish Umayyad gold issues to be struck after 'Abd al-Rahman III (912-61) claimed the caliphate in 928, but it still shows the elongated letters characteristic of Abbasid dinars from the second half of the 8th century. This western Islamic classical style, generally rather austere in its manifestations, was transformed into genuine elegance in the impressive gold coins of the Murabits (*Murābitūn* or Almoravids) from 1056 to 1147 (nos 417-419). So prestigious was this series that it was imitated by the Spanish kings in Toledo after the disappearance of the Murabits themselves (no. 420). The Arabic script on Murabit coins is like no other, unsurpassed for its clarity, proportion and precision.

To the east, from Egypt to central Asia, the new Abbasid style of the 9th century characterized the coinage of all the subsequent dynasties that recognized their authority. The only differences, for example, between a dinar of the Ikhshidid governors of Egypt (no. 427) and a dinar of the Seljuqs of Iran struck over a century later and 2000 kilometres to the east (no. 433) are subtle variations in the arrangement and style of inscriptions which are identical in content except for the rulers' names, the dates and the mints. As time went on the tendency was towards increasingly ornate epigraphy and an increased use of abstract ornament, culminating in the large handsome dinars of 13th-century Iraq (nos 437, 438 and 472). Although images were never used on coins for circulation, abstract symbols are often found, such as the sword (*sayf*) on certain dinars of Mahmud of Ghazna, a reference to his title *Sayf al-dawla*, 'Sword of the Government' (no. 431), or the stylized bow and arrow which was the family emblem of the Seljuqs (no. 433). During this period the Abbasids and the secular rulers often had coins struck for royal donations to court favourites bearing images of various kinds. Not only were these abstract floral designs (no. 551), but also graphic representations of animals and humans. Such pieces, which could also be purely inscriptional, were made with special care and represent the highest peak of the die-engraver's art in the classical era of Islamic coinage.

While the Sunnis adhered to the classical model of 'Abd al-Malik, innovations were introduced by the Shi'i Fatimids as evidence of their rejection of consensus Abbasid Sunni Islam. At first Fatimid dinars were very conservative, perpetuating the Aghlabid tradition, but under al-Mansur (946-53) the traditional coinage was replaced by issues with fine, elegant epigraphy and a more open design. This can be described as the first typically Fatimid coinage which emphasizes the circular elements over the horizontal. Al-Mu'izz (953-75) carried this emphasis to its furthest degree. At the beginning of his reign Fatimid coins carried overtly Ismaili inscriptions for the first time, and it was probably to draw attention to these slogans that a distinctive design was adopted with nearly all the inscriptions arranged in three concentric circles (no. 441). This did not last long, perhaps because the inscriptions were offensive to the largely Sunni population, but its replacement, with no horizontal inscriptions at all was even more extreme in design (as no. 445 of the later caliph al-Mustansir). This is only one of many formats used on the Fatimid coinage which was always characterized by its circular emphasis and by small but precisely engraved inscriptions.

The monetary stability of the Fatimid dinar led to its imitation by other rulers, including not only the Ayyubids, the Fatimids' Egyptian successors, but also the Crusaders, the Seljuqs of Rum (no. 453) and others. The later Ayyubids and early Mamluks revived horizontal inscriptions as the primary design feature, while by the mid-14th century the once important marginal inscriptions had gradually shrunk into what ultimately developed into a purely ornamental border around the outer margins of the dies.

Another new design, again the innovation of religious dissidents, was the square in circle coinage of the Muwahhids (*Muwahhidūn* or Almohads), a fundamentalist movement that emerged from the desert of southern Morocco to conquer all North Africa and Muslim Spain. 'Abd al-Mu'min, the first Muwahhid leader (1130-63) had the central inscriptions of his dinars placed in a square surrounded by a circle, with subsidiary inscriptions in the four segments between the square and the circle. Not only in design, but in their script (a graceful cursive *naskh*), in their varied religious inscriptions (mostly new to Islamic coins), in their lack of a date and often that of a mint name, and in their high and carefully regulated weight, these coins were entirely different from anything that had gone before. Innovation went even further in the silver coins, which were square in shape as well as in design. Although the Muwahhids and their religious movement disappeared within a few short generations, their coinage was perpetuated by all the dynasties of the Muslim West until the Ottoman conquest in the 16th century, and even into the 17th century in unconquered Morocco. The square in circle design was also adopted in Syria, Anatolia, Yemen, Afghanistan, and even on many issues of the Sultans of Delhi, but nowhere did it become standard as it did in the Maghrib.

In one instance the adoption of the Muwahhid square in circle design was the first step in an evolutionary process that transformed the coinage of the eastern Islamic world. This was its use by Salah al-Din (Saladin, 1174-93) for his new dirhams in Damascus in 1175 (like no. 468 struck in 578/1182-3). Although this design became standard at Damascus and a few neighbouring mints for nearly a century, it did not become universal there as it did in the west. Instead it gave the inspiration for an enormous variety of 'cartouches' – ornamental frames surrounding the inscriptions. For example, the late Abbasid dinars of Baghdad have for the first time a quatrefoil, or four-lobed enclosure, for the central legends of the obverse, with a slightly different fourfold enclosure on the reverse (no. 472). These are, however, both merely additions to the classical design which retained horizontal inscriptions within a circular legend. Under the Ilkhans (Mongols of Iran, 1256-1353), the cartouches became the predominant element in the design with many varied forms. The Ilkhan ruler Abu Sa'id issued seven successive coin types in his eighteen-year reign, each with a different obverse and reverse cartouche to distinguish successive reductions in their weight standards. Because of their vast dominions, stretching from western Anatolia to the Oxus River, Ilkhan coinage influenced those of many dynasties between the 14th and 16th centuries. The designs of the early coins of both the Ottoman sultans and the shahs of Iran can be traced back to Ilkhan prototypes.

In the 12th century an interesting, if short-lived, coinage

was issued in Anatolia and northern Mesopotamia by a number of dynasties, mostly Turkish. These are larger copper coins with images of the most varied kind, drawn from ancient Greek, Roman, Parthian and Sasanian coins, from astrology, from Christian iconography, from the repertoire of Near Eastern royal portraiture, or, it seems in some cases, simply from the die engraver's own vivid imagination. Since the first of these were issued by the sons of the warriors who conquered Anatolia from the Byzantines, it is not surprising that they appear to have originated as an offshoot of the large copper coins of Byzantium, for the earliest examples have Greek inscriptions and Byzantine images. In the next decades the coins become more Islamicized, but in some places the custom of using borrowed images continued until the middle of the 13th century. The reason for this peculiar practice is not clear, and was probably not the result of any reasoned mint policy. The best explanation may be simply that images became fashionable for a while, and then died out as the large coppers themselves were replaced by a revival of the use of silver dirhams. Many of the images, of course, can be explained individually as symbols of royal authority, while others may have had some personal explanation.

Egypt itself was little affected by numismatic developments to the east and west. The classical Islamic coin legends persisted there into the 14th century, longer than anywhere else. In the early 15th century, however, a development took place in Egypt that affected Islamic gold coinage for the next 500 years. This was the introduction of the coin known as the *ashrafī*. The reasons for its adoption have more to do with economics than with art. Briefly, at the turn of the 14th century Egypt's gold dinars were nearly driven out of circulation by the Venetian ducat, a coin weighing about 3.5 grammes of fine gold. The *ashrafī*, on the same weight standard, was the last of several attempts to compete with the ducat, and it was so successful that its weight was adopted by the Ottoman sultans and by the shahs of Iran. The latter continued to use the name *ashrafī*, which comes from the title of al-Malik al-Ashraf ('The Most Noble King') Barsbay (1422-37), the Egyptian ruler who introduced it. The Egyptian version is a small, neat gold coin characterized by ornamental 'cables' dividing the horizontal inscriptions (as no. 490, which is not in fact Mamluk, and the Mamluk *ashrafī*, no. 489, a very rare variant design). Like many Islamic coins of this era and later, from Egypt through Iran and into India, both of the dies used were larger than the diameter of the coin itself, so that only a portion of the inscriptions can be seen on any one coin. (The parts of the stamp that do not appear on a particular coin are described as 'off flan', the flan being the metal disc of the coin.) Although other dynasties also adopted the *ashrafī* weight standard, the Egyptian design was used only by the Mamluks' north-eastern neighbours, the Aq Qoyunlu (no. 490).

The Ottomans adopted the *ashrafī* standard directly from western Europe, because the Genoese colony established in Pera, on the opposite side of the Golden Horn from Istanbul, regularly struck imitations of the Venetian ducat which the Ottomans used in their foreign trade. When Mehmed II Fatih, the conqueror of Istanbul, decided to issue his own gold coinage it was known by its traditional Islamic name of dinar as well as *filurī*, an adaptation of the ducat's original name, florin (i.e. the gold coin of Florence). Later the Ottoman ducat was given many different colloquial names depending on important features of the ruler's titulature e.g. *Sulṭānī, Shāhī* or specific style, *sherefī*, 'noble', *ashrafī*, 'the most noble', and *funduqī* or *bunduqī*, itself a corruption of the Arabic name for Venetian commercial establishments in the Near East. The Ottomans did not adopt the Egyptian design for their gold *sulṭānīs*, which have no prototype. The field is filled with horizontal inscriptions, with the words arranged for aesthetic effect rather than straightforward legibility, while the script is a majestic *thuluth*, a calligraphic style more often used for monumental architectural inscriptions than for coins.

Although the Ottoman coinage maintained the 3.5 gramme weight standard for nearly 400 years, its design varied over the centuries. From the end of the 17th century onwards a usual feature was the *tughrā*, an ornamental version of the sultan's name. Aesthetically the highpoint of the Ottoman coinage came in the 'tulip period' of the early 18th century, during the reign of Ahmed III (1703-30), when it attained a standard of elegance and refinement as high as any of the marvellous artistic productions of the era in other genres (no. 496).

The ducat weight also penetrated into Iran, where it was one of several standards used for gold (nos 497 and 499-501). The early coinage of the Safavids, the first great dynasty of shahs (1501-1732), was in the Ilkhan tradition, but in the late 16th century a new script, *nasta'līq*, began to be used. The name of this graceful script means 'hanging', referring to the fall of each letter group as it is written from right to left, and it is characterized on coins by the elongation of certain letters across the face to form dividers between the lines. This inscriptional style was also adopted in Mughal India at about the same time, and its development in the two regions was probably shaped by mutual cultural and economic influences. In both Iran and India the *nasta'līq* style reached its highest development in the 18th century (nos 497, 499 and 512-516).

From the time of India's conquest by the Ghurid sultans at the beginning of the 13th century, Muslim Indian coinage followed its own path, with little influence from other Muslim countries. The coins of the sultans of Delhi (1206-1555) often use the square in circle design which had been adopted by the Ghurids (no. 471) from the Muwahhids, far to the west. They were, however, struck on heavy-weight standards, with the gold muhur and silver rupee both at about 11 grammes, quite different from traditional Muslim coinage weights. Another variation was the frequent use of square coins (nos 503 and 509) and other unusual shapes (no. 561). The most beautiful Indian Muslim coinage is that of the early Mughal rulers, a series of truly imperial splendour. Jahangir, in particular, took special personal interest in the appearance of his coins. He explains in his autobiography that since the coins of his time were dated by the month as well as the year, he conceived the idea of replacing the former by depictions of the Signs of the Zodiac. This resulted in one of the most spectacular and beautiful coin series ever struck (nos 537-548). Issued in both gold and silver, these pieces immediately won popular favour and were often imitated by later generations. It is exceedingly difficult to acquire a complete set of the twelve signs from the original issue.

As we have seen, coinage is generally intended as a store of value and as a medium of trade. However, it also has other more symbolic uses, such as rewards for services, tokens of good luck, marks of prestige, or commemorations of important events. Examples of these special coins are displayed in nos 549-567. Jahangir's die engravers were given the freest rein in the design of his presentation coins that were donated to their recipients as tokens of his esteem and generosity. His portrait medallions are miniature masterpieces of Islamic art (nos 562-566), the most striking examples of an artistic genre appreciated by many other dynasties and rulers.

In the 18th and 19th centuries both the Ottomans and the Qajars also struck a series of medals which, because of their weight could be given a value within the conventional coinage of the time. These special coins were usually intended to be transformed into jewellery by their highly placed recipients, most often for women, but in the case of medals for men as well. Like those of Jahangir, their special design and carefully cut dies distinguish them as artistic productions of the highest order which delight the eye and stand, above all, as witnesses to the faith of Islam.

TERMS AND ABBREVIATIONS

AV	Gold
AR	Silver
AE	Copper
Electrum	Gold alloyed with silver
M	A mark (meaning 40 *nummi*) copied from Byzantine onto early Islamic coinage
Flan	The blank piece of metal to which the dies are applied. 'Off-flan' means that the die has overlapped the flan, thus omitting part of the inscription
r.y.	Regnal year

All coins are illustrated actual size except nos 552, 553, 557, 560 and 567

Coins of special historical interest

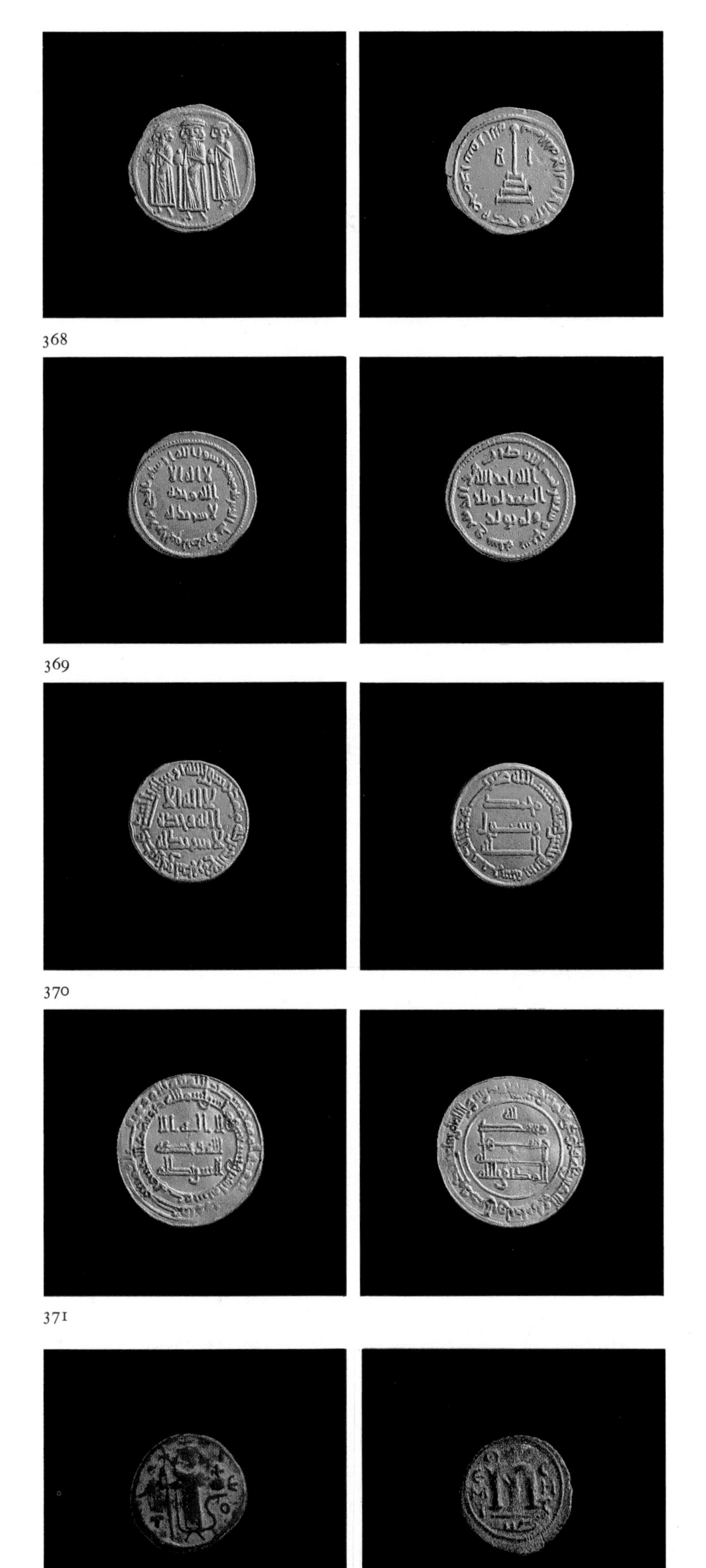

368

369

370

371

372

368
Umayyad dinar, anonymous (time of 'Abd al-Malik b. Marwan)

Without mint name or date, probably struck in Damascus between the years 72 and 74 of the *Hijra* (AD 691-4)
Obverse: 3 standing robed figures, reverse: column surmounted by globe on four-stepped pedestal. Marginal legend in Arabic, 'In the name of God, there is no god but God, He is unique, Muhammad is the messenger of God'
AV 4.35 gm, diameter 20 mm
This dinar marks the first appearance of the profession of faith, the *Kalima*, on an Islamic gold coin.

369
Umayyad dinar, anonymous (reign of 'Abd al-Malik)

Without mint name, struck in the year 77 AH (AD 696-7)
AV 4.24 gm, diameter 20 mm
77 AH was the year in which 'Abd al-Malik introduced his Islamic reform coinage with inscriptions bearing only texts drawn from the Holy Qur'an and a statement of the year in which it was struck.

370
Abbasid dinar, anonymous (reign of al-Saffah)

Without mint name 132 AH (AD 749-50)
AV 4.23 gm, diameter 19 mm
With the defeat of the Umayyads in 132 AH, the first Abbasid caliph, al-Saffah, altered the coinage slightly by giving greater emphasis to the second statement of the *Kalima*, 'Muhammad is the messenger of God'.

371
Abbasid dinar of al-Muktafi billah

Struck in Makka 292 AH (AD 904-5)
AV 4.21 gm, diameter 23.5 mm
Despite its central importance to the Muslim faith, the Holy City of Makka was seldom chosen to be the site of an operating mint. This classic second period dinar is one of those very rare pieces which bear its name.

The pre-reform Umayyad coinage

THE ARAB-BYZANTINE COINAGE OF SYRIA

372
Umayyad fals, anonymous

Struck in Damascus without date
Obverse: standing figure of emperor, reverse: M
AE 4.22 gm, diameter 18 mm

373
Umayyad fals, anonymous
Struck in Hims without date
Obverse: bust of emperor with mint name to right, reverse: mint name in Greek, M
AE 3.29 gm, diameter 21 mm

374
Umayyad fals, anonymous
Struck in Baysan without date
Obverse: two enthroned rulers, reverse: M
AE 12.46 gm, diameter 28 mm

375
Umayyad fals, anonymous
Struck in Ba'albak without date
Obverse: 2 standing imperial figures, reverse: M
AE 4.15 gm, diameter 18 mm

376
Umayyad fals, anonymous
Without mint or date
Obverse: 3 standing imperial figures (similar to coin no. 368), reverse: M
AE 3.33 gm, diameter 20 mm

377
Umayyad fals, anonymous (time of 'Abd al-Malik)
Struck in Iliya Filastin (Jerusalem) without date
Obverse: standing figure of caliph, marginal legend 'Muhammad is the messenger of God', reverse: M
AE 3.08 gm, diameter 21 mm

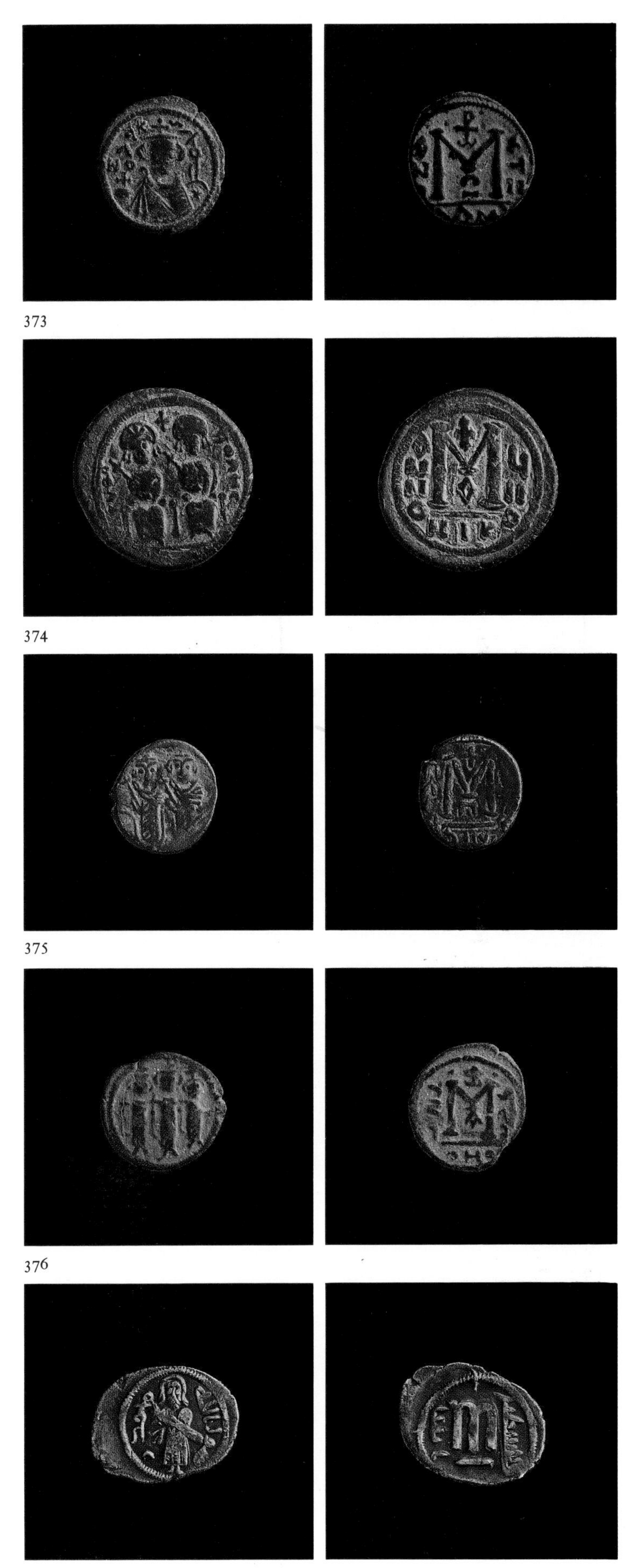
373
374
375
376
377

378
Umayyad fals, anonymous (time of 'Abd al-Malik)

Struck in al-Ruha (Urfa) without date
Obverse: standing figure of caliph, marginal legend *Bismillah Muhammad*, reverse: column on steps, in margin *Kalima* (1st statement)
AE 2.81 gm, diameter 20 mm

379
Umayyad fals of 'Abd al-Malik

Struck in Ba'albak without date (*c.* 73–77 AH/AD 692–7)
Obverse: standing figure of caliph with star to right, marginal legend caliph's name and title, 'Commander of the Faithful', reverse: column on steps bisecting circle, mint name to right, in margin *Kalima* (1st and 2nd statements)
AE 3.29 gm, diameter 19 mm

THE ARAB LATIN COINAGE OF THE PROVINCE OF IFRIQIYA (NORTH AFRICA)

380
Umayyad tremessis (third dinar), anonymous (time of al-Walid I)

Without mint name or date, probably struck at Carthage, *c.* 85 AH (AD 704)
Obverse: 2 imperial busts, marginal legend in Latin, reverse: pole with crossbar on steps, marginal legend in Latin
AV 1.39 gm, diameter 11.5 mm

381
Umayyad fals, anonymous (time of al-Walid I)

Without mint name or date, probably struck at Carthage, *c.* 85 AH (AD 704)
Obverse: 2 imperial busts, marginal legend in Latin, reverse: pole with crossbar on steps, marginal legend in Latin
AE 2.86 gm, diameter 16.5 mm

382
Umayyad solidus (dinar), anonymous (time of al-Walid I)

Struck in Africa Indiction IIII (87 AH/AD 705–6)
Obverse and reverse legends in Latin
AV 4.31 gm, diameter 13 mm

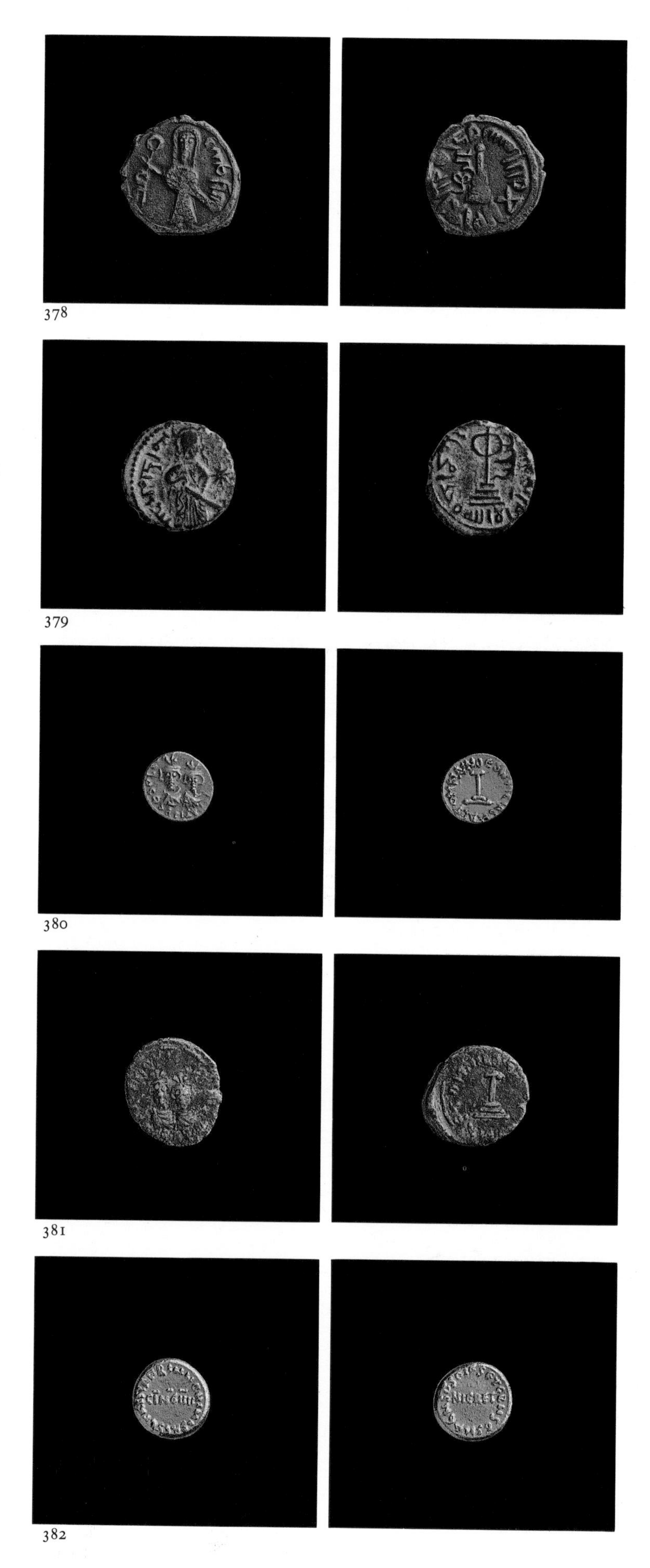

378

379

380

381

382

383
Umayyad semessis (half dinar), anonymous (time of al-Walid I)

Struck in Africa without date
Obverse: legend in Latin, reverse: column surmounted by globe on steps, marginal legend in Latin
AV 2.09 gm, diameter 11 mm

384
Umayyad solidus (dinar), Anonymous (reign of Suleyman)

Struck in Africa 98 AH (AD 716-7)
Obverse: *Kalima* (1st statement), in margin mint and date in Latin, reverse: *Kalima* (2nd statement), marginal legend in Latin
AV 4.24 gm, diameter 13 mm

THE ARAB LATIN COINAGE OF THE PROVINCE OF AL-ANDALUS (SPAIN)

385
Umayyad solidus (dinar), anonymous (reign of Suleyman)

Struck in Spain 98 AH (AD 716-7)
Obverse: in centre eight-rayed star, in margin mint and date in Latin, reverse: *Kalima* (2nd statement), in margin mint and date in Arabic
AV 4.12 gm, diameter 14 mm

THE ARAB SASANIAN COINAGE OF IRAQ AND IRAN

386
Umayyad drachm of Mu'awiya b. Abi Sufyan

Darabjird 41 AH (AD 661-2)
Obverse: bust of Sasanian king to right, in margin *Bismillah, reverse:* fire altar with 2 attendants, mint and date in Pahlavi
AR 3.65 gm, diameter 30 mm

387
Umayyad drachm of al-Hajjaj b. Yusuf

Bishapur 77 AH (AD 696-7)
Obverse: bust of Sasanian king to right, in margin *Kalima* (1st and 2nd statements), reverse: fire altar with 2 attendants, mint and date in Pahlavi
AR 4.02 gm, diameter 32 mm

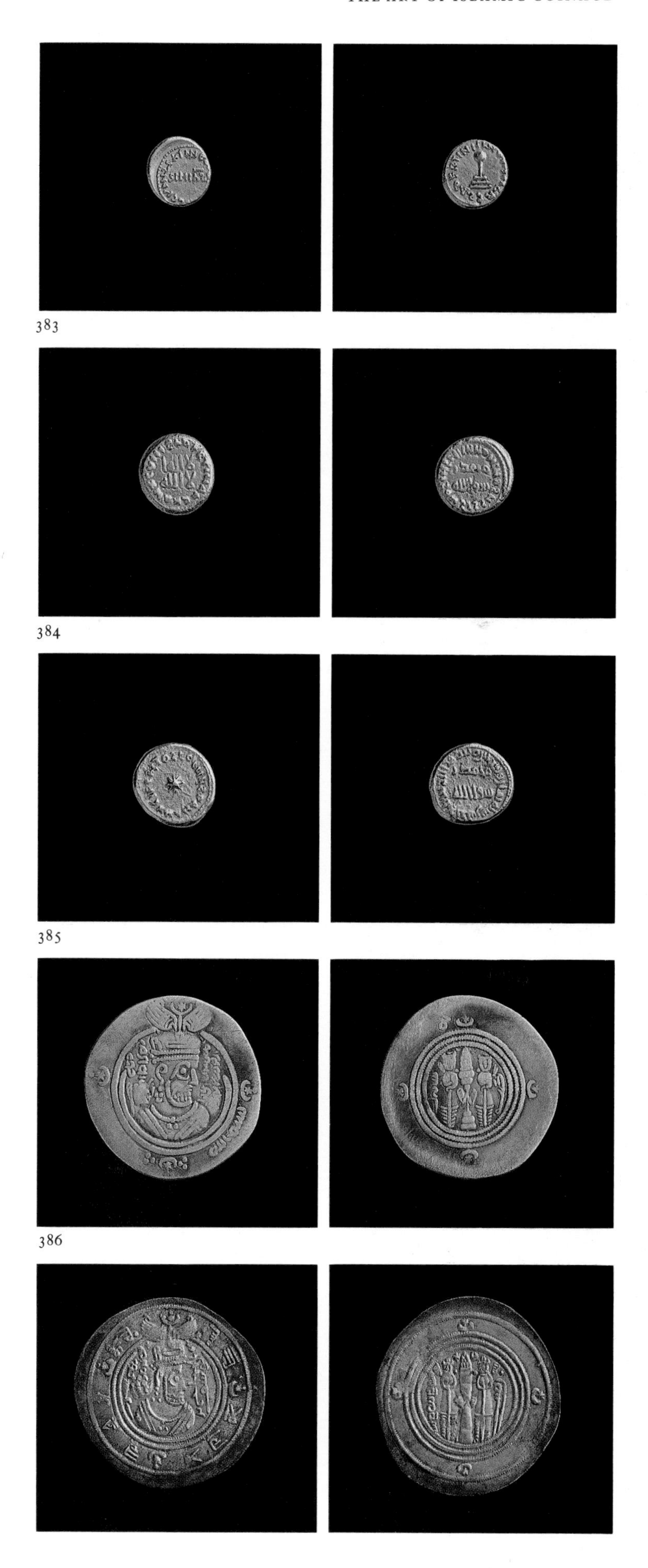

383

384

385

386

388
Umayyad fals of Hisham

Jayy 116 AH (AD734-5)
Obverse: bust of Sasanian king to right, reverse: *Kalima* (2nd statement), in margin mint and date in Arabic
AE2.63 gm, diameter 22 mm

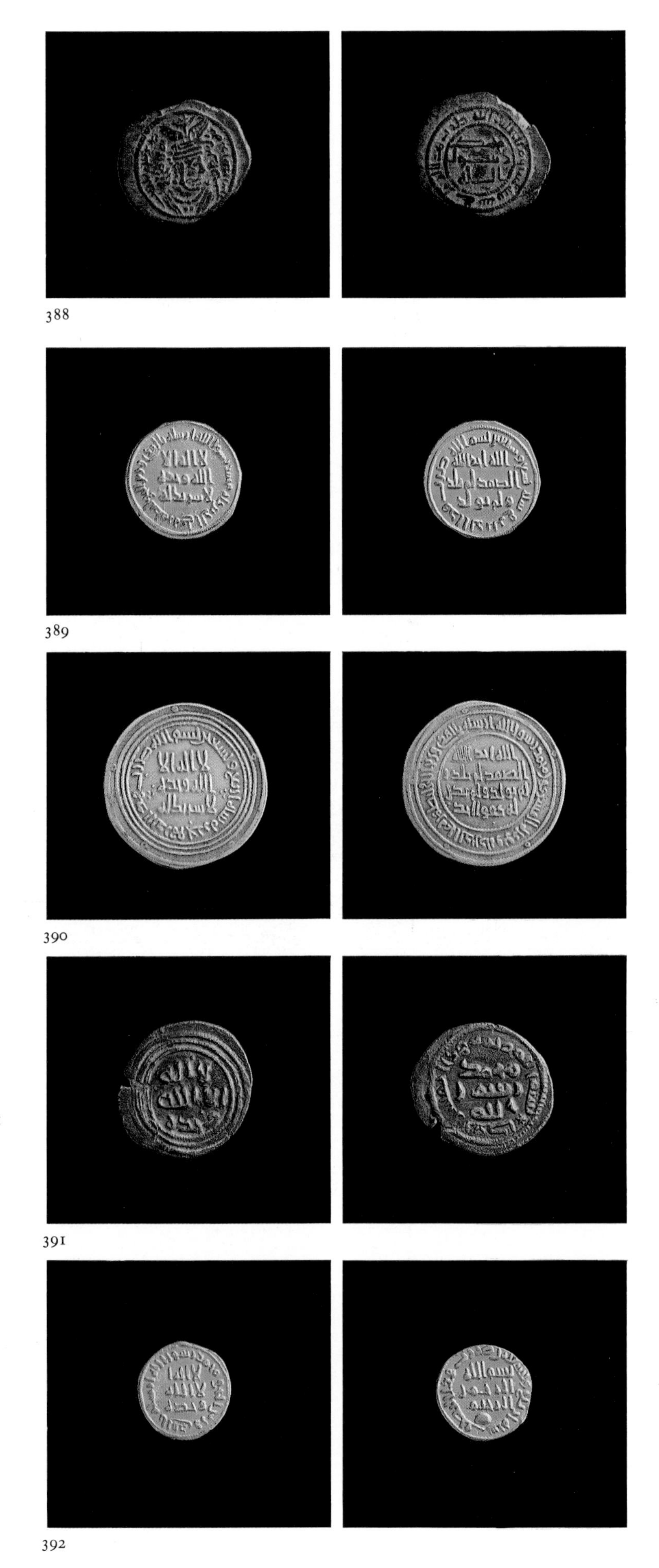

388

389

390

391

392

The Post-Reform Umayyad coinage, the succeeding Abbasid coinage of the first period and its successors in the Maghrib and Spain

389
Umayyad dinar, anonymous (reign of 'Abd al-Malik b. Marwan)

Without mint name 79 AH (AD698-9)
AV4.27gm, diameter 19.5 mm
This is an example of the standard Umayyad dinar, probably struck at the capital, Damascus.

390
Umayyad dirham, anonymous (reign of al-Walid I)

Janza 94 AH (AD712-3)
AR2.87gm, diameter 27.5 mm
This is a standard Umayyad dirham from the exceedingly rare mint of Janza (probably the modern Ganja in Soviet Azarbayjan).

391
Umayyad fals, anonymous

Struck in 'Akka without date
AE3.12gm, diameter 24 mm
Unlike the dinar and dirham, the Umayyad post-reform fals was not struck to a standard weight or design and was generally undated. This example came from the mint of Acre in Palestine.

392
Umayyad half dinar (nisf), anonymous (reign of al-Walid I)

Without mint name 94 AH (AD712-3)
AV2.13 gm, diameter 16 mm
The Umayyad half dinar, a rare denomination modelled on the Byzantine semessis, was struck between 90 and 101 AH (AD708-20). Its reverse carries an extended mint legend and it is always distinguished by a prominent pellet below the third line of the reverse field. Like the dinar it was probably struck in Damascus.

393
Umayyad third dinar (thuluth), anonymous (reign of Yazid II)

Without mint name 103 AH (AD 721-2)
AV 1.43 gm, diameter 13 mm
The Umayyad third dinar, a scarce denomination modelled on the Byzantine tremessis, was struck between 90 and 103 AH. Its obverse legend was shorter than that of the half and it did not bear a pellet in the reverse field.

394
Umayyad dinar, anonymous (reign of 'Umar II or Yazid II)

Struck in Ifriqiya 101 AH (AD 719-20)
AV 4.29 gm, diameter 17 mm
When the distant provincial mints of Ifriqiya and al-Andalus abandoned the former Arab Latin coinage they modelled the legends on those of the Umayyad half dinar adding the name of the mint before the date in the reverse marginal legend. This coin's small size is similar to that of the half dinar, and its thick flan to the Arab-Latin solidus.

395
Umayyad dinar, anonymous (reign of Yazid II)

Ifriqiya 103 AH (AD 721-2)
AV 4.30 gm, diameter 19 mm
This is a handsome example of the Ifriqiya dinar struck on a normal size flan.

396
Umayyad dinar, anonymous (reign of Hisham)

al-Andalus 114 AH (AD 732-3)
AV 4.34 gm, diameter 21.5 mm
During the caliph Hisham's rule the mints of Ifriqiya and al-Andalus abandoned the legends of the half dinar and adopted those of the dinar. Coins of this type are exceedingly rare.

397
Umayyad fals

Struck by the Governor al-Walid in the reign of Marwan II at al-Mawsil (Mosul) without date
Obverse: *Kalima* (2nd statement) in square, in margin name of governor and mint
AE 2.69 gm, diameter 21 mm
See remarks on coin no. 391 above.

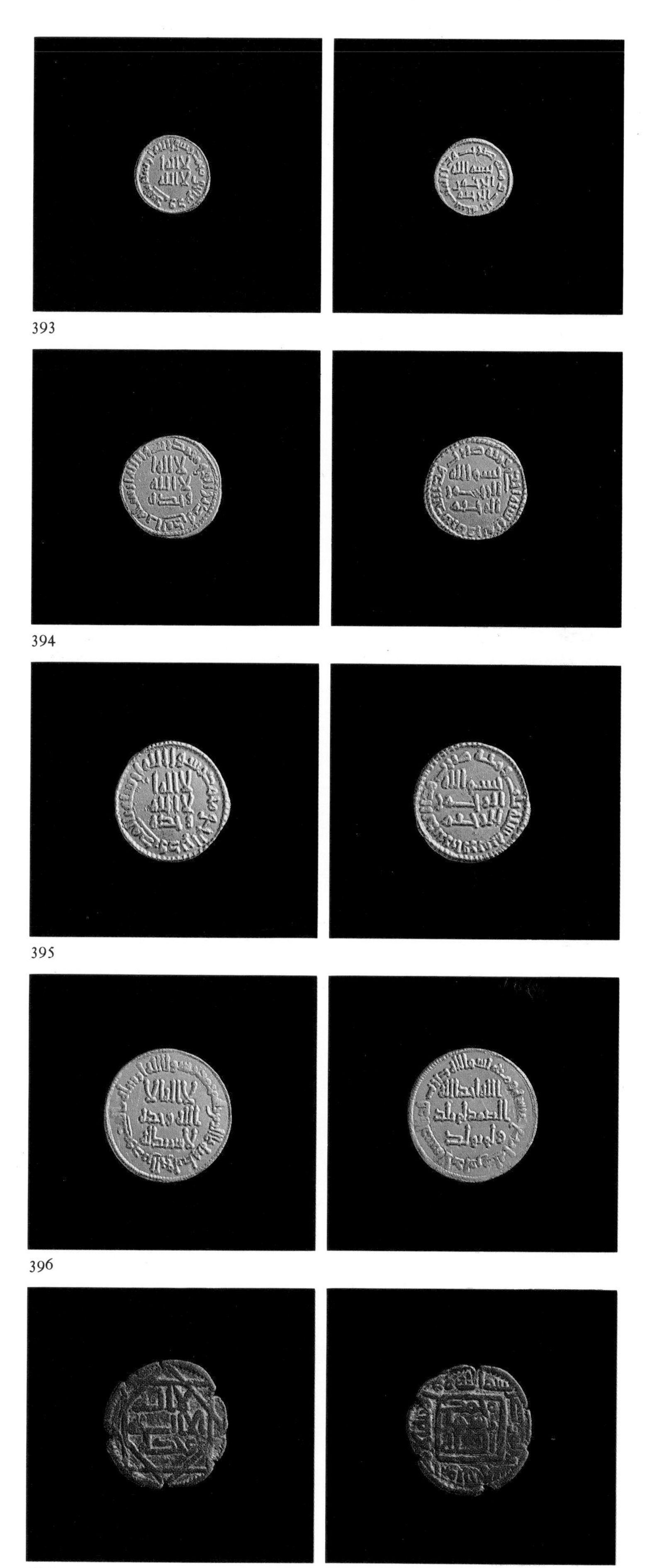
393

394

395

396

397

398
Umayyad dinar, anonymous (reign of Marwan II)
Without mint name 132 AH (AD 749-50)
AV 4.25 gm, diameter 19.5 mm
This is the last date in which the Umayyad dinar was struck.

398

399
Spanish umayyad dirham, anonymous (reign of 'Abd al-Rahman I)
Al-Andalus 165 AH (AD 781-2)
AR 2.73 gm, diameter 29 mm
The Umayyad rulers of Spain continued to strike dirhams identical to those of their Syrian forebears until 'Abd al-Rahman III's monetary reforms in 316 AH (AD 928-9).

399

400
Abbasid dinar, anonymous (reign of al-Mansur)
Without mint name 144 AH (AD 761-2)
AV 4.26 gm, diameter 19 mm
This is a typical example of the Abbasid dinars struck in the reigns of al-Saffah, al-Mansur and al-Mahdi.

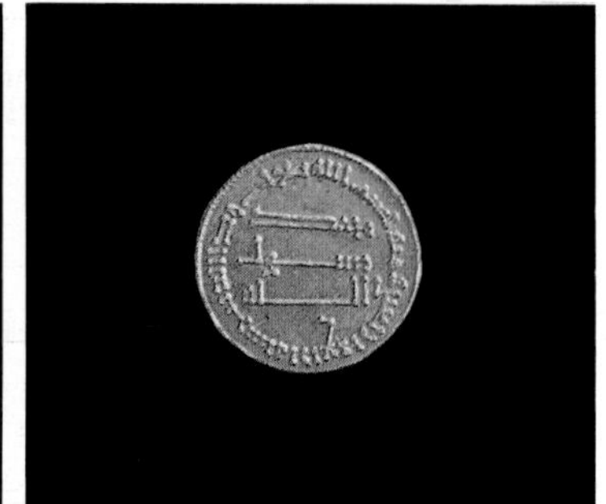
400

401
Abbasid dirham (reign of al-Mansur)
Struck by order of the heir apparent al-Mahdi Muhammad in Arran 153 AH (AD 770)
AR 2.94 gm, diameter 26 mm
This is an early example where the name of the issuing authority appears on an Abbasid dirham. Arran was the Abbasid province with Barda'a in Shirwan, south of the Caucasus, as its capital.

401

402
Abbasid fals
Struck by al-Mansur 'Among those things ordered by the Servant of God, 'Abdallah, Commander of the Faithful' in Madinat al-Salam (Baghdad) 157 AH (AD 773-4)
AE 6.23 gm, diameter 26 mm
The design of this handsome coin is similar to that of the contemporary Abbasid dirham.

402

403
Abbasid dinar of Harun al-Rashid

Without mint name 170 AH (AD 786–7)
Legend in reverse field: 'Among those things ordered by the Servant of God, Harun, Commander of the Faithful'.
AV 4.15 gm, diameter 18 mm
This is the earliest Abbasid dinar to specify the issuing authority.

403

404
Abbasid dinar (reign of Harun al-Rashid)

Without mint name 171 AH (AD 787–8) with name *Mūsā* in reverse field
AV 4.23 gm, diameter 18.5 mm
Starting in this reign the governors of Egypt were authorized to place their names on the coinage.

404

405
Abbasid dinar (reign of Harun al-Rashid)

Without mint name 183 AH (AD 799–800)
Reverse: inner marginal legend: 'Among those things ordered by the Prince, al-Amin Muhammad, son of the Commander of the Faithful'
AV 4.25 gm, diameter 19 mm
This style of dinar was peculiar to al-Rashid's heir, al-Amin.

405

406
Abbasid dirham, anonymous (reign of al-Amin)

Madinat al-Salam 193 AH (AD 808–9)
Reverse field: *Rabī Allah* (God is my Lord)
AR 2.91 gm, diameter 21 mm
Al-Amin assigned the management of his mint to al-'Abbas b. al-Fadl b. al-Rabi who ordered the above inscription to be placed on his coins.

406

407
Abbasid dinar (reign of al-Amin)

Without mint name 196 AH (AD 811–2)
Reverse field: *Rabī Allah/al-'Abbās*
AV 4.29 gm, diameter 18.5 mm
See note on coin no. 406 above.

407

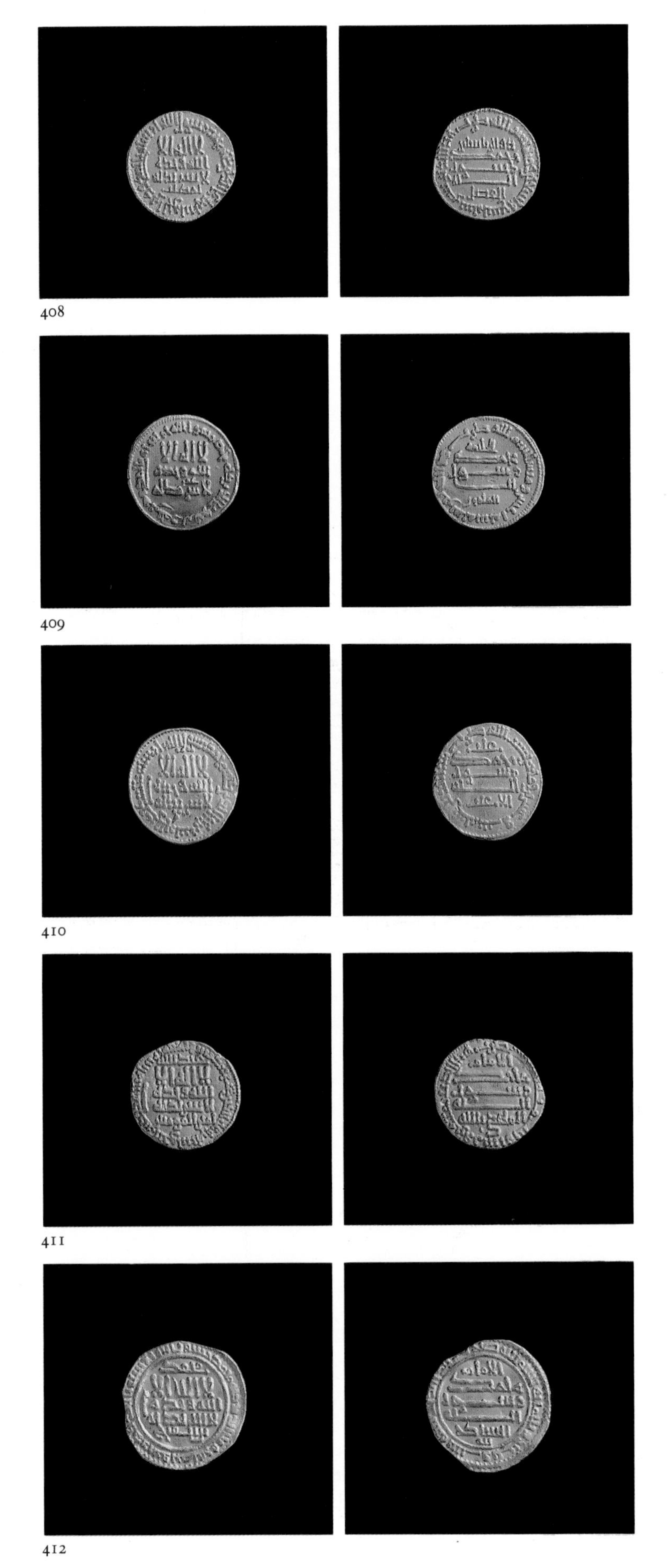
408
409
410
411
412

408

Abbasid dinar (reign of al-Ma'mun)

Misr (Egypt) 199 AH (AD 814-5)
Obverse field: *al-Muttalib*, reverse field: *Dhū'l-Riyāsatayn* 'Master of the two authorities'
AV 4.24 gm, diameter 18 mm
Mint names first appeared on Abbasid dinars in 198 AH (AD 813-4), and 199 AH (AD 814-5) was the first occurrence on the Egyptian coinage. Al-Ma'mun delegated the management of his mint to al-Fadl b. Sahl Dhu'l-Riyasatayn. Al-Muttalib was then the local governor of Egypt.

409

Abbasid dinar of al-Ma'mun

Without mint name 216 AH (AD 831-2)
Between 2nd and 3rd lines on obverse field, in tiny letters the name *'Umar*, Reverse field: *Li'l-Khalīfa/al-Ma'mūn*
AV 4.14 gm, diameter 18.5 mm
This coin's somewhat crude and irregular style and the hitherto unrecorded presence of a name in this position in the obverse legend suggests that it was struck by a local rebel who none the less continued to acknowledge the caliph's overlordship.

410

Aghlabid dinar of al-Aghlab

Without mint name 223 AH (AD 837-8)
In reverse field: *Ghalab/al-Aghlab*
AV 4.22 gm, diameter 19 mm
The Aghlabid Governors of Ifriqiya, whose capital was at Qayrawan in Tunisia, continued to strike traditional Abbasid dinars until the dynasty ended in 296 AH (AD 908-9). They are distinguished by the word *Ghalab* 'Victory' and the name of the governor on the reverse.

411

Fatimid dinar of al-Mahdi

Al-Qayrawan 300 AH (AD 912-3)
Obverse field: *'Abdallah/Amīr al-Mu'minīn*, reverse field: *al-Imām/al-Mahdī billah*
AV 4.05 gm, diameter 18 mm
In 297 AH (AD 909-10) the head of the Ismaili branch of Islam proclaimed himself Commander of the Faithful in opposition to the Sunni Abbasid caliph al-Muqtadir in Baghdad. Al-Mahdi's coinage, however, continued to use the traditional Abbasid legends.

412

Midrarid dinar of Muhammad b. al-Fath

Without mint name 336 AH (AD 947-8)
Obverse field: *Muhammad/ibn al-Fath*, reverse field: *al-Imām/al-Shākir/lillah*
AV 4.01 gm, diameter 20.5 mm
After al-Mahdi had set the precedent of styling himself Commander of the Faithful the title was later assumed by the Berber ruler of Sijilmasa in eastern Morocco whose family had originally given refuge to al-Mahdi before his conquest of Tunisia.

413
Spanish umayyad dinar of 'Abd al-Rahman III

Al-Andalus 317 AH (AD 929–30)
Reverse field: *Lamīr* (sic)/*al-Mu'minīn 'Abd al-Rahmān*
AV 4.24 gm, diameter 19 mm
The Spanish Umayyad ruler met the challenge posed by the Fatimid al-Mahdi by himself assuming the title Commander of the Faithful in 316 AH.

414
Spanish umayyad dinar of 'Abd al-Rahman III

Without mint name 321 AH (AD 933)
Obverse field: *Muhammad*, reverse field: *al-Imām/al-Nāsir li-dīn/Allah 'Abd al-Rahmān/Amīr al-Mu'minīn*
AV 4.13 gm, diameter 20 mm
This coin shows the great ruler's full titulature.

415
Spanish umayyad dirham of Hisham II

Al-Andalus 389 AH (AD 998–9)
Obverse field: *Muhammad*, reverse field: *al-Imām Hishām/Amīr al-Mu'minīn/al-Mu'ayyad billah/'Amīr*
AR 3.20 gm, diameter 25.5 mm
'Amir was the powerful vizier who overshadowed the nominal ruler Hisham II.

416
Abbadid dinar of 'Abbad al-Mu'tadid billah

Madinat Ishbiliya (Seville) 464 AH (AD 1071–2)
Obverse field: *al-Hājib/'Adud al-dawla*, reverse field: *al-Mu'tadid 'ala-Allah/al-Imām 'Abdallah/Amīr al-Mu'minīn/al-Mu'ayyad bi-nasr Allah*
AV 3.80 gm, diameter 26 mm
After the Spanish Umayyad realm collapsed into anarchy a series of small states known as the *Mulūk al-Tawā'if* (party kings) preserved Muslim rule in Spain. The most important of these were the Abbadid rulers of Seville whose coinage, although struck on broader flans, continued to follow Spanish Umayyad and Abbasid prototypes.

417
Murabit dinar of Yusuf b. Tashfin

Shatiba (Jativa) 488 AH (AD 1095)
Obverse: *al-Amīr Yūsuf/b. Tashfīn*, reverse: *al-Imām/'Abd/Allah/Amīr al-Mu'minīn*
AV 4.15 gm, diameter 25.5 mm
This dinar, struck shortly after the Murabit conquest of Spain from the Muluk al-Tawa'if, acknowledged the Abbasid caliph without specifying his name.

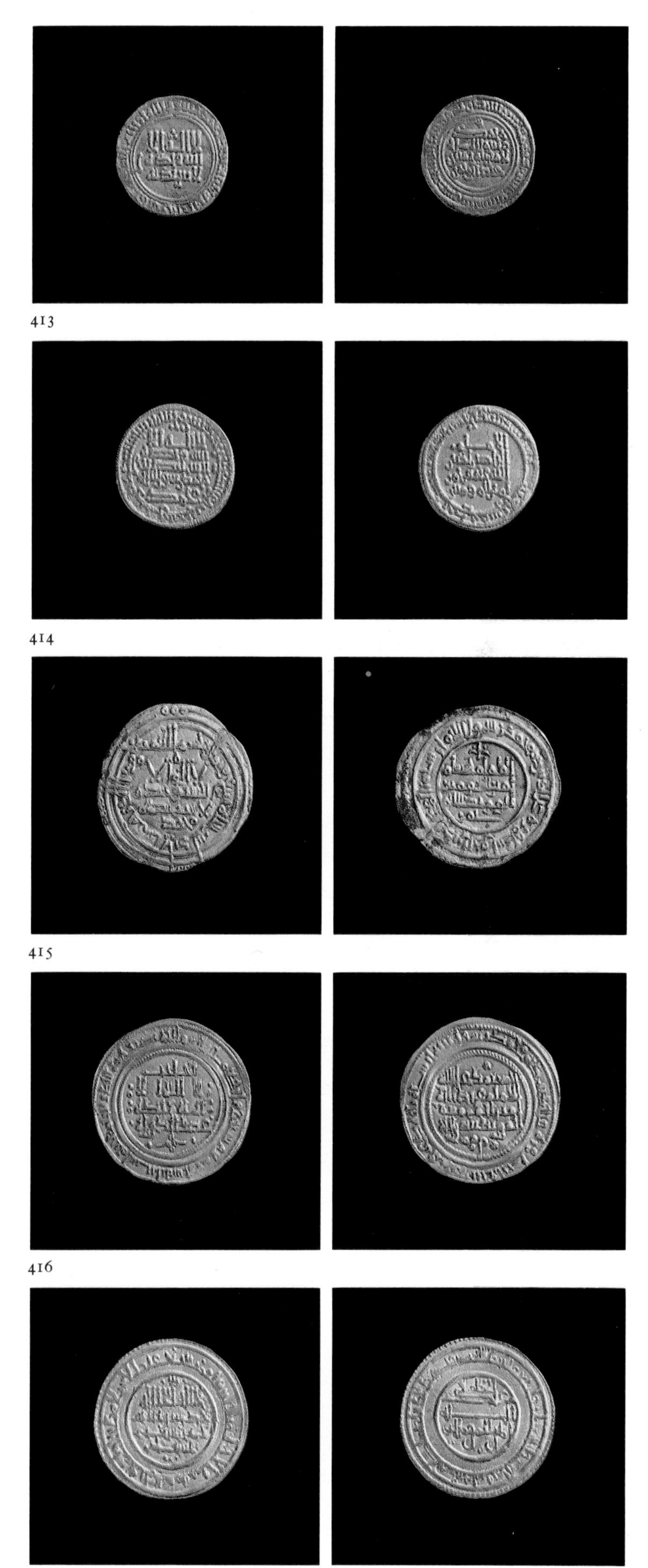
413
414
415
416
417

418
Murabit dinar of 'Ali b. Yusuf

Fas (Fez) 535 AH (AD 1140–41)
Obverse: *Amīr al-Muslimīn 'Alī walī 'ahdihi/Tāshfīn*, reverse: *al Imām/al-'Abbāsī 'Abdallah/Amīr al-Mu'minīn*
AV 4.14 gm, diameter 27 mm
The calligraphy on this and the next coin is particularly artistic.

419
Murabit dinar of Tashfin b. 'Ali

Ishbiliya 539 AH (AD 1144–5)
Obverse: *Amīr al-Muslimīn Tāshfīn b. 'Alī walī 'ahd al-Amīr/Ibrāhīm*, reverse: *al-Imām/'Abd/Allah/Amīr al-Mu'minīn/al-'Abbāsī*
AV 4.11 gm, diameter 26 mm
This is one of the last and most attractive Murabit dinars.

420
Kings of Castille dinar (maravedi) of Alfonso VIII

Tulitula (Toledo) Safar AD 1255
AV 3.84 gm, diameter 26.5 mm
Christian imitations of the Murabit dinar were struck for more than a quarter of a century by the Kings of Castille.

The Abbasid coinage of the second period and its successors in Iraq and Iran

421
Abbasid dirham of al-Ma'mun

Isbahan (Isfahan) 202 AH (AD 817–8)
Obverse field: *al-Mashriq*, reverse: 'al-Ma'mun Vice-Regent of God, among those things ordered by the Prince al-Rida heir of the Muslims, *'Alī b. Mūsā b. 'Alī b. Abu Tālib/Dhū'l-Riyāsatayn*
AR 2.93 gm, diameter 25 mm
This coin commemorates a famous event in Islamic history when the caliph al-Ma'mun, hoping to heal the rift between the orthodox Sunni and the Shi'i followers of the house of 'Ali, chose the eighth Shi'i imam, 'Ali al-Rida, as his heir.

422
Abbasid dinar, anonymous (reign of al-Ma'mun)

Without mint name 206 AH (AD 821–2)
AV 4.25 gm, diameter 19.5 mm
This is the earliest recorded date for the Abbasid dinar of the second period.

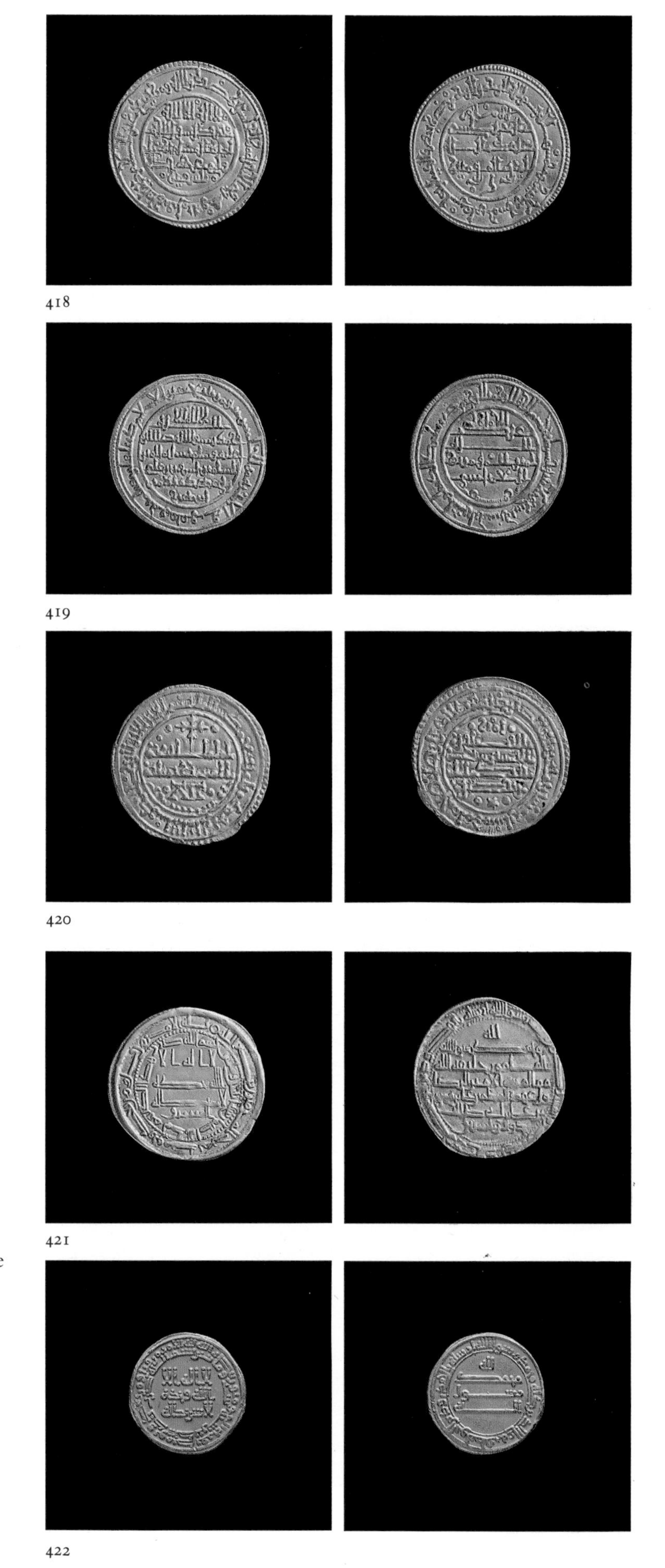
418
419
420
421
422

423
Abbasid dinar, anonymous (reign of al-Ma'mun)

Madinat al-Salam 212 AH (AD 827-8)
AV 4.20 gm, diameter 20 mm
From this year onward both the mint name and date appeared on dinars, and after al-Mu'tasim's accession in 218 AH (AD 833-4) the caliph's name was placed in the reverse field.

424
Abbasid dinar of al-Mu'tamid

Wasit 276 AH (AD 889-90)
Obverse field: *al-Nāsir li-dīn Allah/al-Muwaffaq billah*, reverse field: *al-Mu'tamid 'alā-Allah/Ahmad b. al-Muwaffaq billah*. On both obverse and reverse: *al-quwwa lillah jamī'an*, 'Power belongs to God alone'
AV 3.96 gm, diameter 24 mm
Wasit, the famous Umayyad town on the former banks of the Tigris between Kufa and Basra, had recently been reconquered from rebels by Ahmad, the future caliph al-Mu'tadid, hence the special religious legend on this coin.

425
Rassid dinar of imam al-Hadi

Sa'ada 296 AH (AD 908-9)
Reverse field: *al-Hādī ilā/al-Haqq Amīr/al-Mu'minīn/b. Rasūl Allah*
AV 2.82 gm, diameter 21 mm
Although the Rassid Imams of Sa'ada in the Yemen belonged to the Shi'i branch of Islam and placed unconventional legends on their coins, they followed the style of the contemporary Abbasid dinar.

426
Tulunid dinar of Ahmad b. Tulun

Al-Rafiqa 267 AH (AD 880-81)
Obverse: *al-Mufawwad ilā Allah*, reverse: *al-Mu'tamid 'alā-Allah/Ahmad b. Tūlūn*
AV 3.84 gm, diameter 22 mm
Al-Rafiqa was a town on the Euphrates much favoured by Harun al-Rashid. At this time it lay on the frontier between the lands ruled by the Tulunid governors of Egypt and the Abbasid caliphate.

427
Ikhshidid dinar of abu'l-Qasim Unujur

Misr 336 AH (AD 947-8)
Obverse: *abū'l-Qāsim b./al-Ikhshid*, reverse: *al-Mutī' lillah*
AV 3.53 gm, diameter 23.5 mm
The Ikhshidids were independent governors of Egypt and Palestine from 333 to 359 AH (AD 944-70).

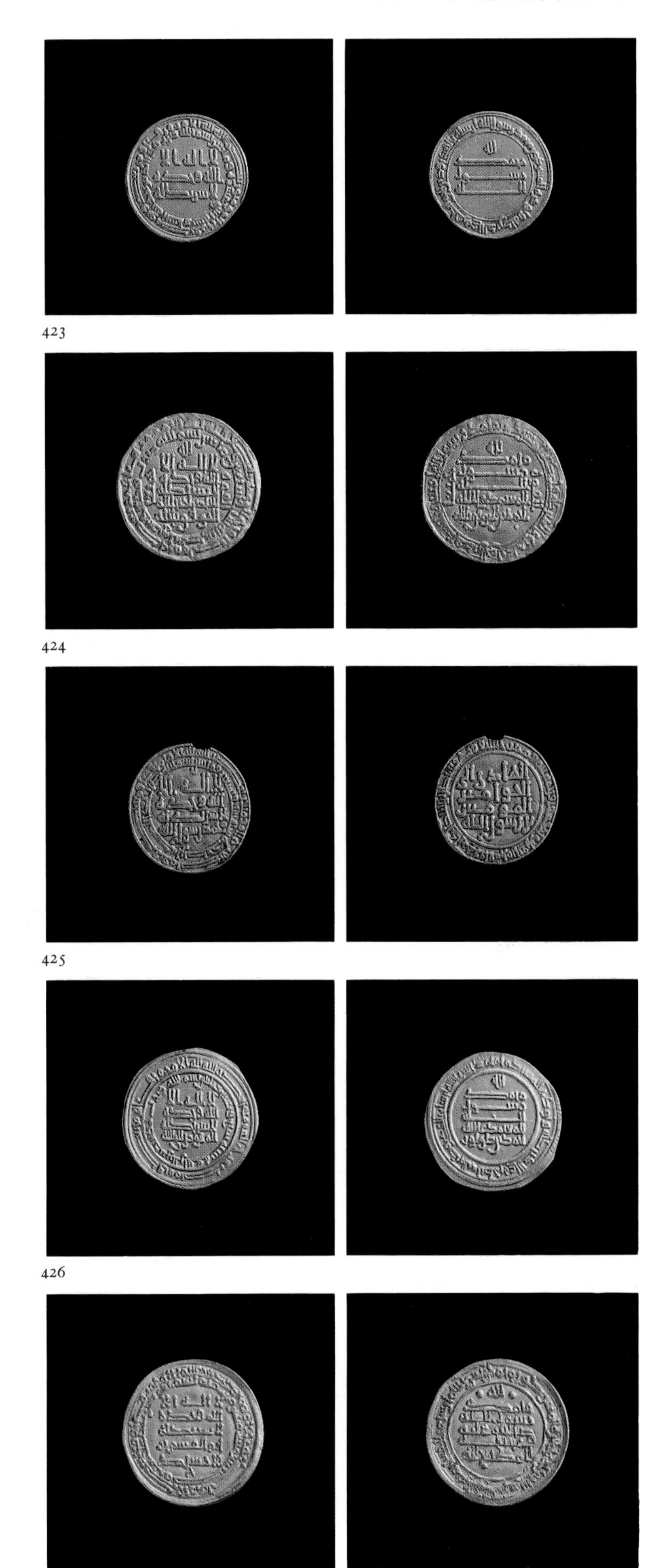

423

424

425

426

427

428
Hamdanid dinar of Nasir al-dawla

Al-Mawsil 348 AH (AD 959-60)
Obverse: *Sayf al-dawla/abū'l-Hasan/ibriz*, reverse: *al-Muti' lillah/ Nasir al-dawla/abū -Muhammad/ibriz*
AV 4.43 gm, diameter 21.5 mm
The Hamdanids ruled the Jazira (northern Iraq) in the middle of the 4th century AH. At this time power was held jointly by two brothers, Sayf al-dawla and Nasir al-dawla. The word *ibrīz* (pure gold) was intended to assure the user of the purity of the metal.

429
Samanid dinar of Nasr II

Al-Shash (Tashkent) 308 AH (AD 920-21)
Reverse: *al-Muqtadir billah/Nāsr b. Ahmad*
AV 4.51 gm, diameter 21.5 mm
The Samanids were governors of Khurasan from about 250 to 389 AH (AD 864-998). They were strongly Sunni in sympathy and their coins, like this one, were often of very high artistic quality.

430
Buwayhid dinar of Rukn al-dawla

Al-Muhammadiya (Rayy, near Teheran) 335 AH (AD 946-7)
Obverse: *al-Mutī' lillah*, reverse: *'Imād al-dawla abū'l-Hasan/Rukn al-dawla abū-'Alī*
AV 4.36 gm, diameter 23 mm
This is the year in which the Buwayhids seized control of Rayy. The unusual floral ornaments on both sides of this coin suggest that it may have been struck to mark the victory.

431
Samanid dinar of Mansur II

Naysabur (Nishapur) 387 AH (AD 997-8)
Obverse: *al-Walī Sayf/al-dawla Mahmūd, reverse: al-Tā'i' lillah/al-Malik al-Mansūr/Mansūr b. Nūh*
AV 5.57 gm, diameter 24 mm
Between 384 and 389 AH (AD 994-99) whenever the Ghaznawid governor Mahmud was in control of Nishapur he struck a special coinage bearing an upright sword (*sayf*), a reference to his name. The Samanids maintained their loyalty to the caliph al-Ta'i' long after his deposition by their rivals, the Buwayhids.

432
Ghaznawid dinar of Mahmud

Naysabur 403 AH (AD 1012-3)
Obverse: *abū'l-Qāsim/wa Amīn al-milla*, reverse: *al-Qādir billah/walī 'ahd al-Ghalib billah/Yamīn al-dawla*
AV 4.37 gm, diameter 23 mm
Mahmud was frequently known by his titles 'the right arm of the state and the security of the people'.

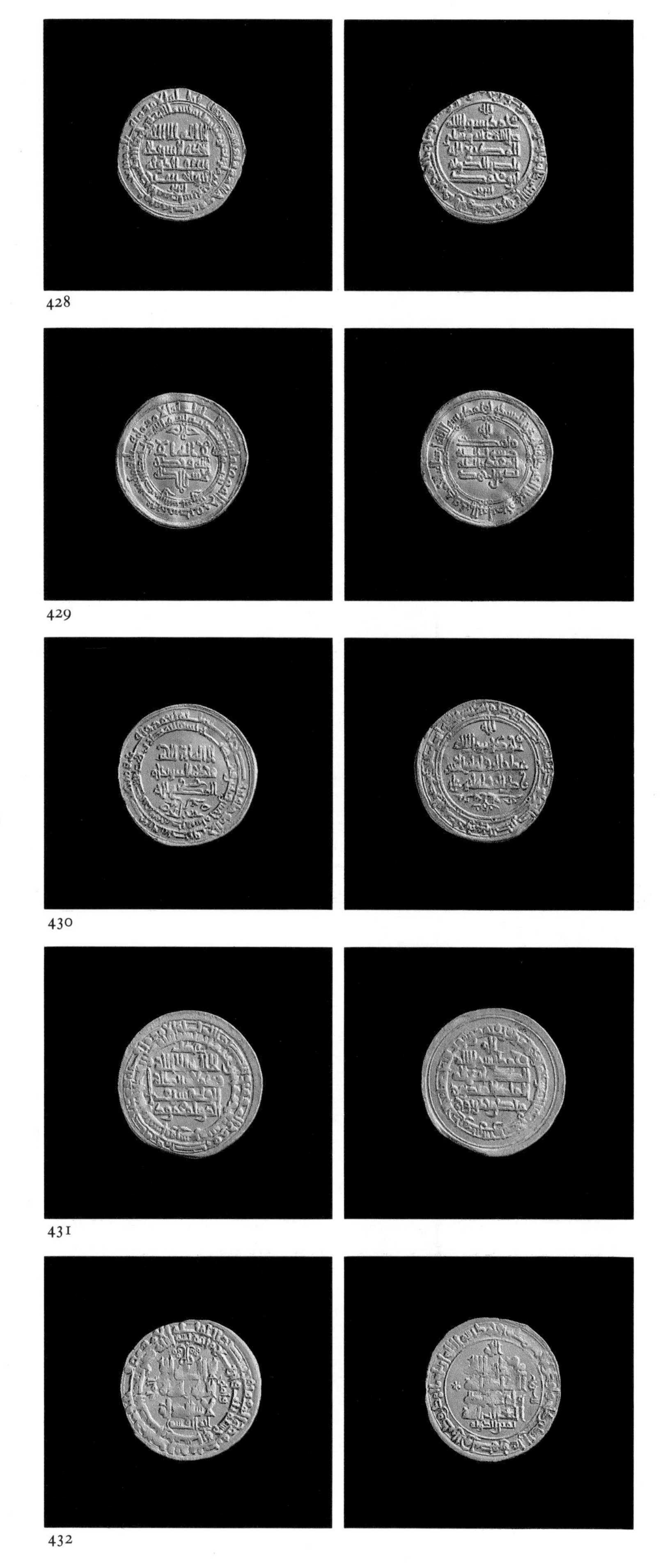

428

429

430

431

432

433
Great Seljuq dinar of Tughrul Beg

Al-Rayy 449 AH (AD 1057–8)
Obverse: *al-Qā'im bi-Amr Allah*, reverse: *al-Sultān al-Mu'azzam/ Shāhanshāh/Tughrul Beg Rukn al-dawla abū-Tālib*
AV 5.02 gm, diameter 21 mm
This coin bears the Seljuq *tamghā* (tribal mark) on both obverse and reverse.

434
Buwayhid dinar of 'Adud al-dawla

Kard Fana Khusraw 362 AH (AD 972–3)
Obverse: *Rukn al-dawla/abū'Alī*, reverse: *al-Mutī' lillah/al-Amīr al-'Adil/'Adud al-dawla abū-Shujā*
AV 3.70 gm, diameter 18.5 mm
This coin and those following lack the outer marginal legend on the obverse, otherwise they follow the design of the conventional Abbasid coinage. This mint was located in a commercial suburb of Shiraz famous for its fine textiles.

435
Hasanwayhid dinar of Badr b. Hasanwayh

Sabur Khwast 396 AH (AD 1005–6)
Obverse: *al-Qādir billah/Badr b. Hasanwayh*, reverse: *Majd al-dawla/ Kahf al-umma abū-Tālib/ibrīz*
AV 4.20 gm, diameter 22 mm
The Hasanwayhids were rulers of a small Kurdish state in western Iran. Badr prided himself on his coinage and struck it in the name of his overlord the Buwayhid ruler of Rayy, whose titles mean 'The glory of the state and the shelter of the people'.

436
Mukramid dinar of Abu'l-Hasan

'Uman 429 AH (AD 1037–8)
Obverse: *al-Qā'im bi-Amr Allah/al-Malik Shāhanshāh/abū-Kalijar b. Sultān al-dawla*, reverse: *al-Amīr al-Sayyid/al-ajall abū'l-Hasan/b. Nāsir al-dawla*
AV 4.33 gm, diameter 24 mm
The Mukramids were governors of Oman under the Buwayhids with their capital at Sohar. Their coinage is exceedingly rare.

437
Abbasid dinar of al-Musta'sim

Madinat al-Salam 656 AH (AD 1258)
AV 10.05 gm, diameter 27 mm
This extremely rare dinar was struck in the month of Muharram in the days immediately before the conquest of Baghdad by the Mongol forces commanded by Hulagu.

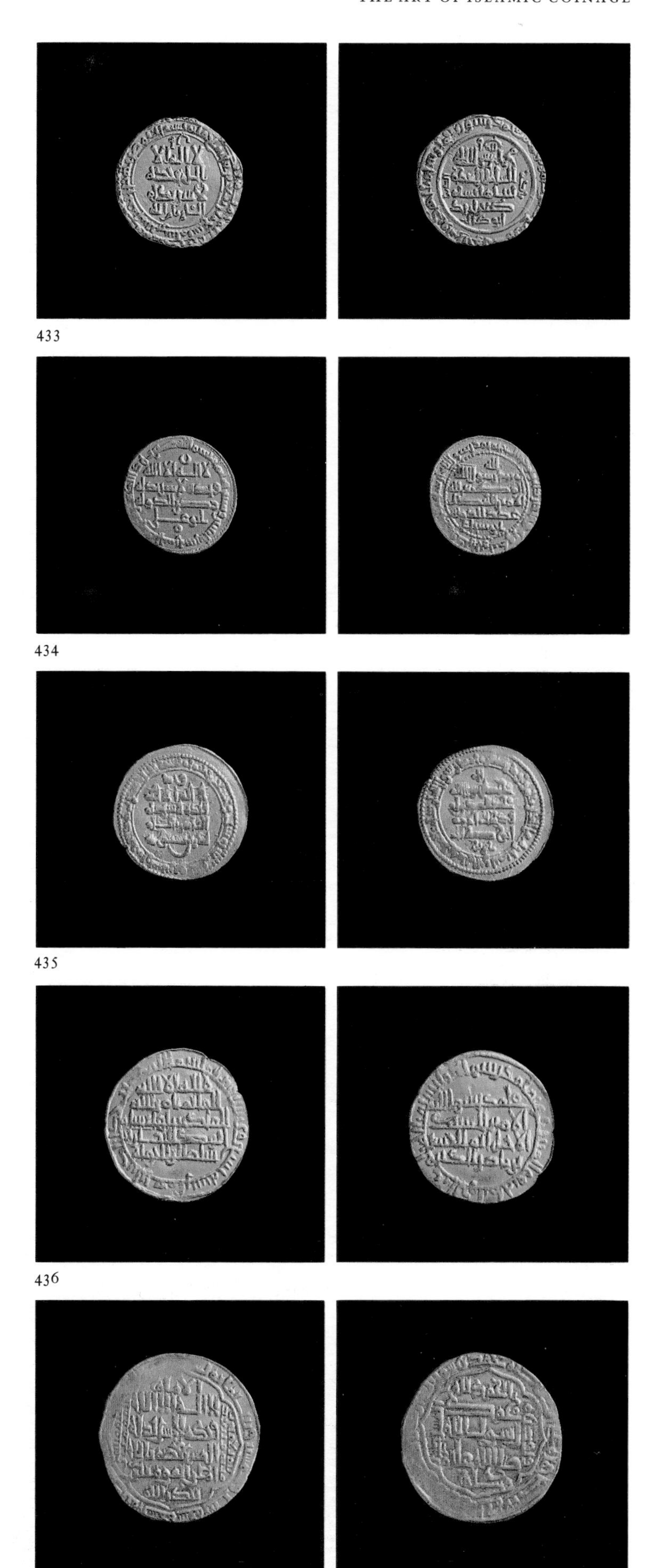
433
434
435
436
437

438
Ilkhan dinar of Hulagu

Baghdad 661 AH (AD 1262-3)
Reverse: *Qa'an/al-A'zam Munka/Qa'an Hūlāgū/Khān Mālik al-Riqab/al-umma Khallada/Mulkahu*
AV 4.18 gm, diameter 28 mm
Hulagu struck this coin in the name of the great Khan Munka and gave himself the title 'King of the Necks of the People'. It was only after the Mongol conquest that the original and colloquial name Baghdad replaced the formal name Madinat al-Salam.

The coinage of the Fatimids and their stylistic imitators the Ayyubids and the Mamluks

439
Fatimid dinar of al-Qa'im

Al-Mahdiya (Tunisia) 324 AH (AD 935-6)
Obverse: *Muhammad abū-Qāsim/al-Mahdī billah*, reverse: *al-Imām/al-Qā'im billah/Amīr al-Mu'minīn*
AV 4.18 gm, diameter 19 mm
On his accession al-Qa'im abandoned the traditional Abbasid coinage used by his father and adopted new legends and a refined calligraphic style for his own coinage.

440
Kharijite dinar of Abu-Yazid

Al-Qayrawan 333 AH (AD 944-5)
AV 4.18 gm, diameter 19.5 mm
This is one of the exceedingly rare coins of the famous Kharijite rebel, Abu-Yazid, who seized Qayrawan in 333 AH (AD 944-5). He held the city until the last months of 334 when he was expelled by the forces of al-Qa'im's son Isma'il al-Mansur. Abu-Yazid's dinars have the same calligraphic style as those of al-Qa'im.

441
Fatimid dinar of al-Mu'izz

Al-Mansuriya 342 AH (AD 953-4)
AV 4.14 gm, diameter 22.5 mm
Al-Mansuriya was a palace suburb of Qayrawan named in honour of al-Mu'izz's father al-Mansur. Al-Mu'izz discarded his predecessors' religiously neutral legends and on his first coinage showed particular reverence to the Prophet's daughter Fatima and his son-in-law and nephew 'Ali. These legends caused such offence among the Sunni population of Qayrawan that their extreme wording was modified shortly afterwards.

442
Fatimid dinar of al-'Aziz

Misr 366 AH (AD 976-7)
AV 4.16 gm, diameter 22.5 mm
All of al-'Aziz's coins were struck with two concentric legends on both obverse and reverse.

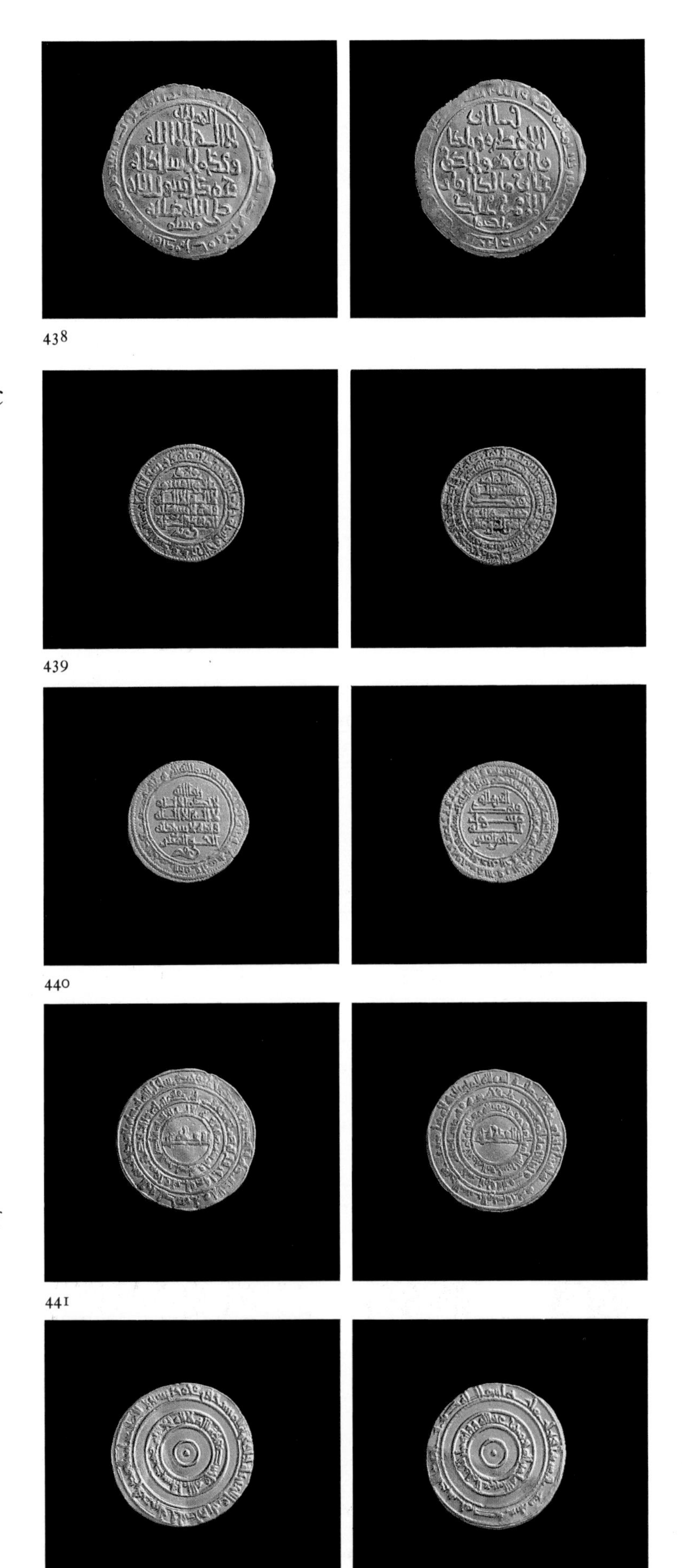

438

439

440

441

442

443
Fatimid dinar of al-Hakim

Misr 387 AH (AD 997–8)
Obverse: *Kalima*, 1st and 2nd statements with the addition of *'Alī walī Allah* which distinguishes all later Shi'i coins. Reverse field: *al-Mansūr/abū-'Alī al-Imām/al-Hākim bi-Amr Allah/Amīr al-Mu'minīn*
AV 3.64 gm, diameter 23 mm
This is the first style of coinage issued by al-Hakim. It is known from two recorded specimens, one from the year 386 AH and this coin from 387 AH.

444
Fatimid dinar of al-Hakim

Misr 387 AH (AD 997–8)
AV 4.19 gm, diameter 23.5 mm
This is an example of the standard coinage issued between 387 and 401 AH.

445
Fatimid dinar of al-Mustansir

Zabid 447 AH (AD 1055–6)
AV 4.19 gm, diameter 22 mm
Zabid was ruled by the Sulayhid princes of the Yemen who declared their allegiance to the Fatimid caliphate.

446
Fatimid dinar of al-Mustansir

Madinat al-Salam 451 AH (AD 1059–60)
Reverse field: *Ma'add/'Abdallah wa waliya/al-Imām abū-Tamīn/al-Mustansir billah/Amīr al-Mu'minīn*
AV 3.01 gm, diameter 22 mm
This coin was struck by the famous Buwayhid general and Fatimid partisan al-Basasiri who seized Baghdad from the Great Seljuq Tughrul Beg in 450 AH and displaced the Abbasid caliph al-Qa'im. He struck coins in the name of the Fatimid caliph until his expulsion from Baghdad in 451 AH.

447
Fatimid dinar of al-Hafiz

Misr 529 AH (AD 1134–5)
Obverse field: *al-Imām/'Abd al-Majīd abū/al-Maymūn al-Hāfiz/li-dīn Allah Amīr/al-Mu'minīn*, reverse: *al-Hasan abū-'Alī/walī 'ahd Amīr/al-Muslimīn*
AV 4.19 gm, diameter 21 mm
This is the second recorded example of the dinar where al-Hafiz named his son as heir to the caliphate.

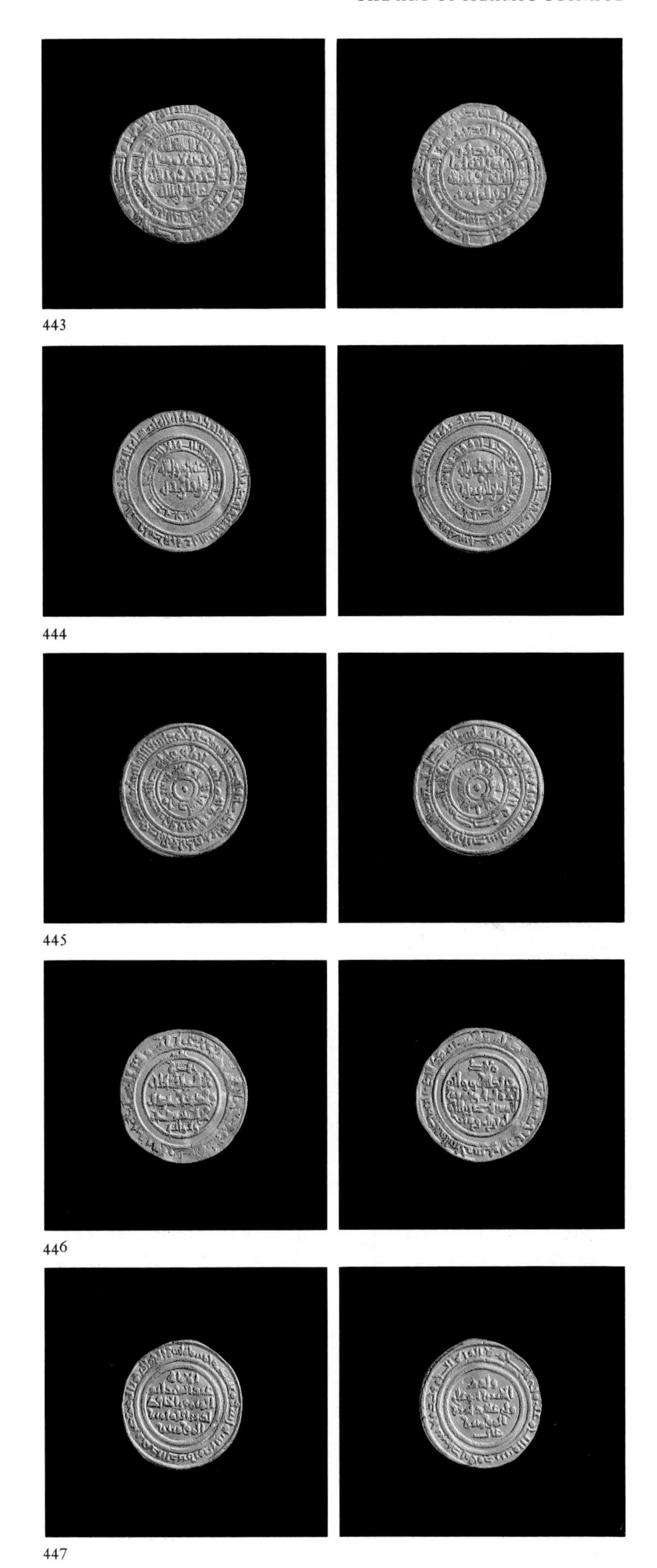
443
444
445
446
447

448
Burid dinar, in name of the great Seljuq ruler Sanjar

Dimashq 531 AH (AD 1136-7)
Obverse in centre: *al-Imam*, reverse in centre: *al-Muqtafi*, inner marginal legend: *Mu'izz al-dunyā wa'l-din Sanjar wa Mas'ūd*
AV 3.39 gm, diameter 21 mm
This very rare dinar, struck during a period of confusion by the Burids of Damascus, acknowledged the overlordship of both the Great Seljuq rulers of Khurasan and Iraq and the Abbasid caliph while copying the design of the contemporary Fatimid dinars of al-Hafiz.

449
Fatimid dinar of al-Fa'iz

Misr 555 AH (AD 1160)
Reverse in centre: *al-Imām 'Īsā*, inner marginal legend: *abū'l-Qāsim al-Fa'iz b. Nasr Allah Amīr al-Mu'minīn*
AV 4.32 gm, diameter 21.5 mm
The arrangement of legends on this coin resembles that of the Burid dinar, no. 448 above.

450
Ayyubid dinar of al-Nasir Yusuf I (Saladin)

al-Qahira 568 AH (AD 1172-3)
Obverse in centre: *Mahmūd ibn Zangī*, reverse in centre: *al-Imām/al-Hasan*, inner marginal legend: *al-Mustadī bi-Amr Allah Amīr al-Mu'minīn*
AV 3.68 gm, diameter 22 mm
Al-Qahira is the Arabic name for the city of Cairo founded by the Fatimid caliph al-Mu'izz. After the death of the last Fatimid ruler, al-'Adid, in 567 AH Saladin returned Egypt's religious allegiance to the Abbasid caliphate. He displayed loyalty to his master, Nur al-din Mahmud, the Zangid ruler of Aleppo, by issuing his early coinage in the latter's name alone.

451
Ayyubid dinar of al-Kamil Muhammad

al-Qahira 618 AH (AD 1221-2)
Obverse: *al-Malik al-Kamil/abū'l-Ma'ālī/Muhammad b. Abī Bakr b. Ayyūb*, reverse: *al-Imām Ahmad/abū'l-'Abbās/al-Nāsir li-dīn Allah/ Amīr al-Mu'minīn*
AV 6.39 gm, diameter 22 mm
While al-Kamil used Kufic inscriptions for coins of the caliphs al-Nasir and al-Zahir, Kufic script was abandoned on the Egyptian coinage after the succession of the caliph al-Mustansir in 623 AH (AD 1226).

452
Ayyubid dinar of al-Kamil Muhammad

al-Qahira 631 AH (AD 1233-4)
Reverse: *al-Imām/al-Mansūr abū/Ja'far al-Mustansir/billah Amir al-Mu'minīn*
AV 4.60 gm, diameter 22 mm
In 623 AH (AD 1226) the Egyptian mint adopted a flowing *naskh* script for its coinage.

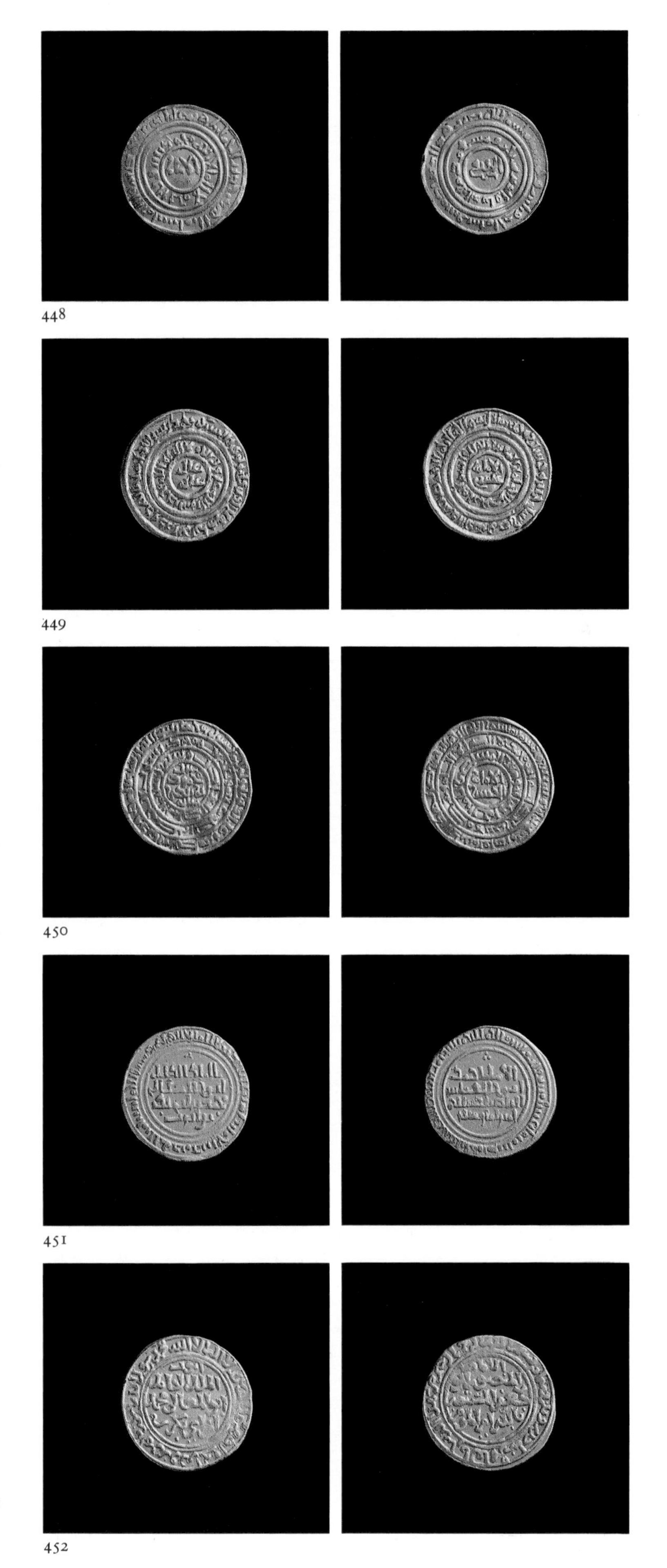
448 449 450 451 452

453
Rum Seljuq dinar of Kaykhusraw II

Qunya (Konya) 635 AH (AD 1237-8)
Obverse in centre: *al-Sultān/al-A'zam*, around: *Ghiyāth al-dunyā wa'l-dīn abū'l-Fath Kaykhusraw b. Kayqubād bi-Qūnya*. Reverse: 'al-Imām/al-Mustansir, around: *billah Amīr al-Mu'minīn fī sanat 635*
AV 4.33 gm, diameter 20 mm
Because Rum Seljuq Anatolia was a silver trading area at this time, its gold coinage is very rare and was probably struck for presentation.

454
Bahri Mamluk dinar of al-Mansur 'Ali

Iskandariya (Alexandria) 655 AH (AD 1257-8)
Obverse: *Aybak/al-Malik al-Mansūr/nūr al-dīn 'Alī bin/al-Malik al-Mu'izz*, Reverse: *al-Imām/al-Musta'sim/billah abū-Ahmad/Amīr al-Mu'minīn*
AV 7.78 gm, diameter 21 mm
Coins of early Mamluks followed style of previous Ayyubid coins.

455
Bahri Mamluk dinar of al-Ashraf Khalil

Thagr al-Iskandariya al-Mahrūsa 690 min al-Hijra (AD 1291-2)
Obverse in field: *Qala'un/al-Sultān al-Malik al-Ashraf/Salāh al-dunyā wa'l-dīn Nāsir al-milla al-Muhammadiya/Muhī al-dawla al-'Abbāsiya/Khalīl bin*
AV 5.69 gm, diameter 28 mm
The mint name means 'The frontier fortress of Alexandria the well-guarded'. This splendid coin is one of the special series struck by Khalil after he reconquered Acre from the Crusaders on which he styles himself 'Help of the Muslim Community and Reviver of the Abbasid State'. A shadow Abbasid caliphate had been established in Egypt by Baybars in 659 AH (AD 1260-61).

456
Bahri Mamluk dinar of al-Nasir Muhammad

Al-Qahira 741 AH (AD 1340-41)
Obverse: *al-Sultān al-Malik al-Nāsir/Nāsir al-dunyā wa'l- dīn Muhammad b./al-Malik al-Mansūr*
AV 6.60 gm, diameter 26 mm
By this time the central area of the Mamluk dinar had expanded to include both the mint name and date leaving only a vestigial marginal legend which in most cases is largely off the flan.

The square in circle coinage of the Muwahhids and their imitations in the Maghrib, Arabia, Anatolia and India

457
Muwahhid half dinar of 'Abd al-Mu'min

Madinat Ishbiliya (Seville)
Without date *c.* 541-558 AH (AD 1146-63)
AV 2.29 gm, diameter 20 mm

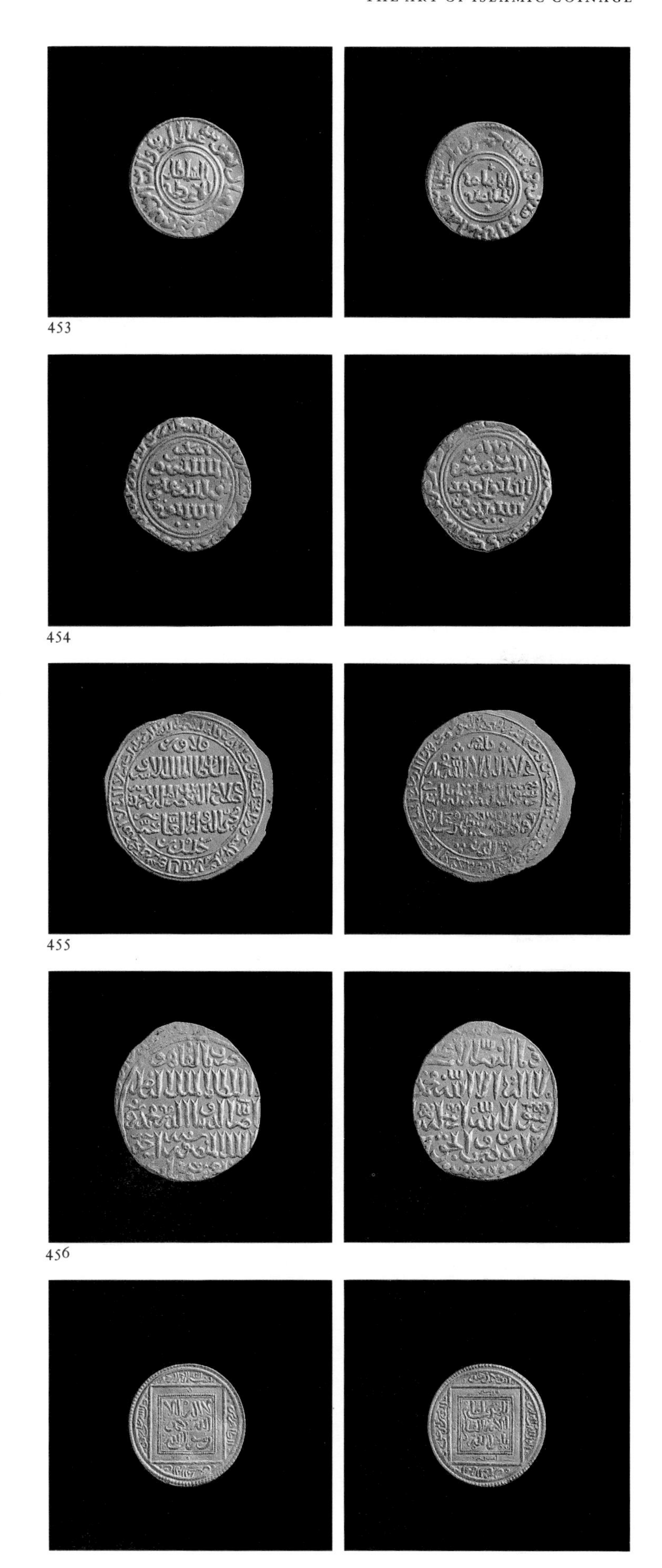
453
454
455
456

457 *continued*

This coin was struck at the weight of a half *mithqal*. Its design is entirely new for the Muslim world with the central legend placed in a square with four marginal segments around. The dies were beautifully engraved in elegant *naskh* script.

458

Muwahhid quarter dinar of 'Abd al-Mu'min

Without mint name or date

AV 1.15 gm, diameter 15.5 mm

The Muwahhids (or Unitarians) had doctrinal affinities with the followers of 'Abd al-Wahhab, the Arabian reformer of the 18th century.

459

Muwahhid half dinar of Abu-Ya'qub Yusuf I

Hadrat Marrakush (Marrakesh)

Without date, *c.* 558-563 AH (AD 1162-68)

AV 2.30 gm, diameter 21 mm

460

Muwahhid dinar (dobla) of Abu-Yusuf Ya'qub

Without mint name or date, *c.* 580-595 AH (AD 1184-1199)

AV 4.64 gm, diameter 28 mm

This coin was struck at the weight of the *mithqal*, the standard weight for a dinar. Because they were twice the size of the preceding coins the Spaniards named them *doblas* (doubles).

461

Hafsid half dinar of Abu-'Abdallah Muhammad II

Tunus without date, *c.* 694-709 AH (AD 1294-1310)

AV 2.36 gm, diameter 23 mm

This is a previously unrecorded denomination for the otherwise rare coinage of Muhammad II. The Hafsid rulers of Algeria and Tunisia continued to use the designs of the traditional Muwahhid coinage.

462

Hafsid dinar of Abu-Faris 'Abd al-'Aziz II

Qusantina (Constantine in Algeria)

Without date, *c.* 796-837 AH (AD 1393-1434)

AV 4.71 gm, diameter 19 mm

The later Hafsids usually struck their dinars on the same size flan as that formerly used for the half dinar.

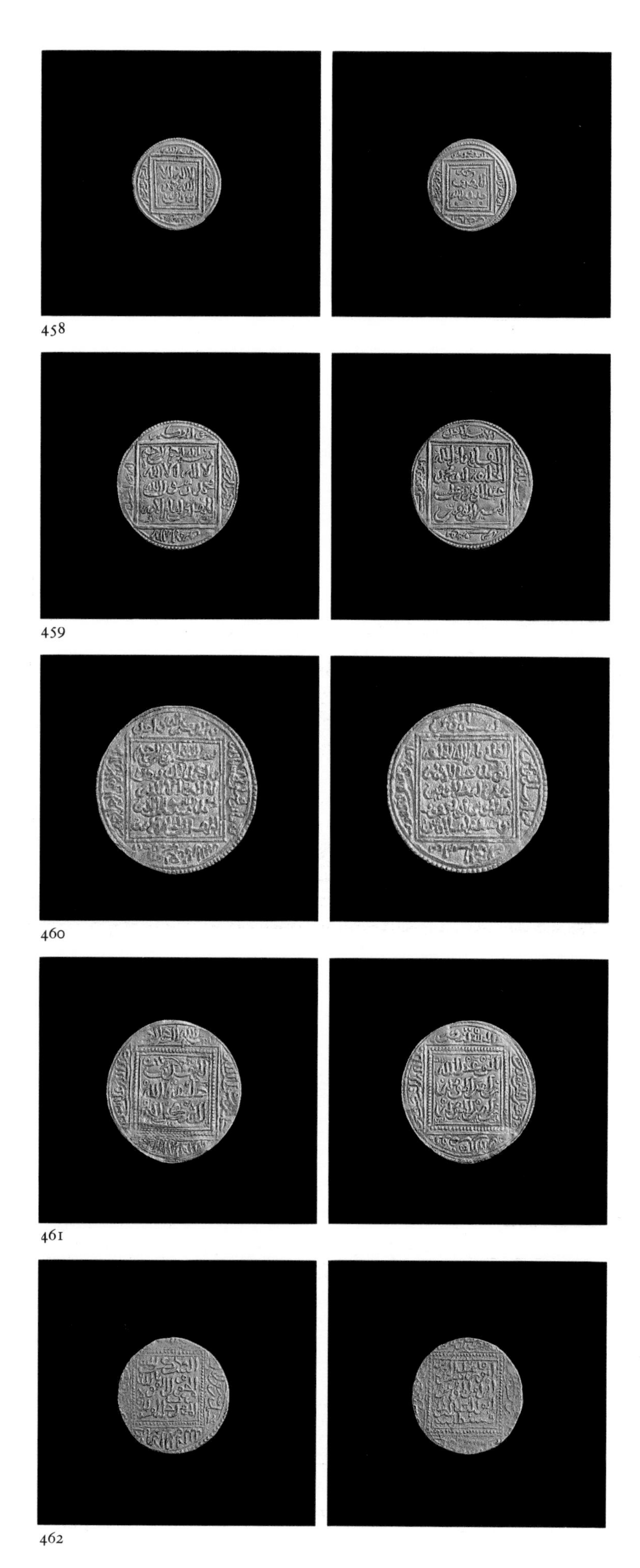

458

459

460

461

462

463
Marinid dinar, anonymous (time of Abu-Yahya Abu-Bakr)

Without mint name or date, *c.* 642–656 AH (AD 1244–1258)
AV 4.69 gm, diameter 31 mm
The Marinids succeeded the Muwahhids as rulers of Morocco, and adopted their style of coinage.

464
Nasrid dinar of Muhammad VIII

Madinat Gharnata without date, *c.* 820–831 AH (AD 1417–1428)
AV 4.62 gm, diameter 33 mm
The Nasrid rulers of Granada probably struck their magnificent dinars in the Alhambra Palace. This one bears their famous motto *La ghālib illā Allah*, 'No victory without God', in the four segments of the obverse field.

465
Ottoman dinar of Murad III

Without mint name but struck in Tilimsan in western Algeria 995 AH (AD 1586–7)
Electrum 4.20 gm, diameter 34 mm
The coinage of Tilimsan (Tlemcen) struck in the name of its Ottoman overlords continued to follow the square in circle design preferred in the Maghrib.

466
Hasani dinar of Ahmad II al-Mansur

Hadrat Sijilmasa 1004 AH (AD 1595–6)
Obverse: *Bismillah al-Rahman al-Rahīm/'Abd Allah al-Imām abū'l-'Abbās Ahmad/al-Mansūr billah/Amīr al-Mu'minīn*, reverse: *b. al-Imām Abī 'Abd/Allah Muhammad al-Shaykh/al-Mahdī b. al-Imām/al-Qā'im bi-Amr Allah/al-Sharīf al-Hasanī*
AV 4.58 gm, diameter 28.5 mm
The last flowering of the Muwahhid style coinage occurred in 17th-century Morocco in the reign of Ahmad al-Mansur II, known as 'the Golden', a title he clearly merited from this superbly artistic coin.

467
Rasulid dinar of al-Mu'ayyad Da'ud

'Adan 718 AH (AD 1318–19)
Reverse field in central square: *al-Sultān al-Malik/al-Mu'ayyad Hizābr/al-din Dā'ūd*
AV 4.66 gm, diameter 31 mm
It is interesting to note that the Rasulids, a Sunni dynasty in the Yemen, briefly adopted the square in circle design and the weight of the *mithqal* for their dinars while the coinage of the Mamluks of Egypt was never influenced by that of the Maghrib despite its much greater proximity.

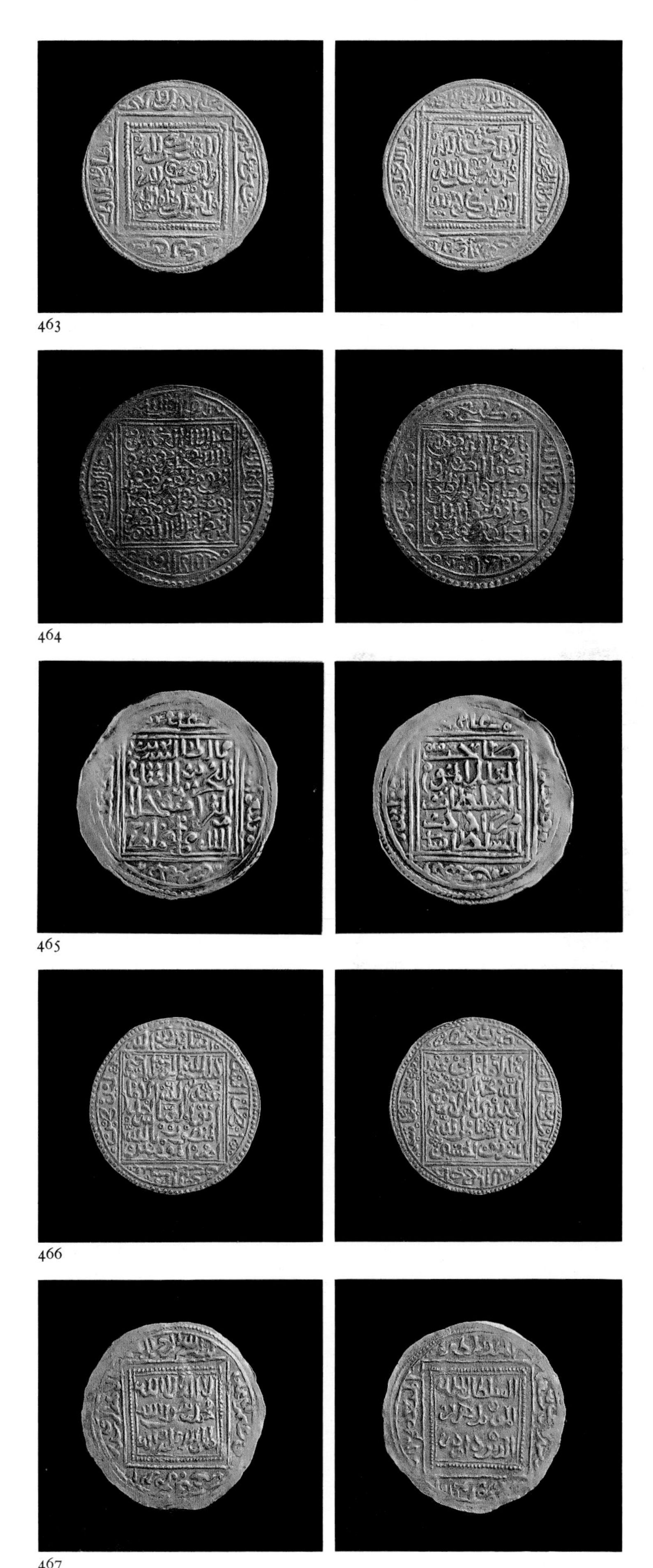

463

464

465

466

467

468
Ayyubid dirham of al-Nasir Yusuf I (Saladin)

Dimashq (Damascus) 578 AH (AD 1182-3)
Obverse in square: *al-Imām al-Nā/sir li-dīn Allah/Amīr al-Mu'minīn*, reverse in square: *al-Malik al-Nā/sir Salāh al-d/unyā wa'l-dīn*, above *Yūsuf b. Ayyūb*
AR 3.01 gm, diameter 21 mm
Saladin, the first Ayyubid ruler, used the square in circle design for his silver coinage most often in the Damascus mint, but occasionally also in Cairo.

469
Rum Seljuq dinar of Kaykawus I

Siwas 614 AH (AD 1217-18)
AV 4.46 gm, diameter 26 mm
This type of Rum Seljuq gold is exceedingly rare and its beautiful dies reflect the high artistry of the Seljuq die cutters.

470
Rum Seljuq dinar of Kaykhusraw II

Siwas 642 AH (AD 1244-5)
Obverse: *al-Sultān al-A'zam Zill Allah fi'l-'Ālam Ghiyāth al-dunyā wa'l-dīn Kaykhusraw b. Kayqubād Qāsim Amīr al-Mu'minīn*
AV 4.53 gm, diameter 27 mm
On this handsome adaptation of Muwahhid gold Kaykhusraw entitled himself 'The Shadow of God on Earth'. Up to the year 641 Kaykhusraw struck his famous lion and sun coinage which, for a devout Muslim, was secular in character (see no. 532 below). After the disastrous defeat of the Rum Seljuqs at the Battle of Kösedağ, he may have introduced this more conventional religious issue in contrition over losing the battle to the pagan Mongols.

471
Ghurid dinar of Taj al-din Yildiz

Balad Ghazna 605 AH (AD 1208-9)
Obverse in square: *al-Nāsir li-dīn Allah/Amīr al-Mu'minīn*, reverse in square: *al-Sultān al-A'zam Mu'izz al-dunyā wa/al-dīn abū'l-Muzaffar/ Muhammad b. Sām*
AV 14.61 gm, diameter 35 mm
The Ghurid rulers of Afghanistan and north-western India adopted several different designs for their coinage. Taj al-din Yildiz, a former slave of Mu'izz al-din, appears to have preferred the square in circle type for many coins he struck in the name of his former master.

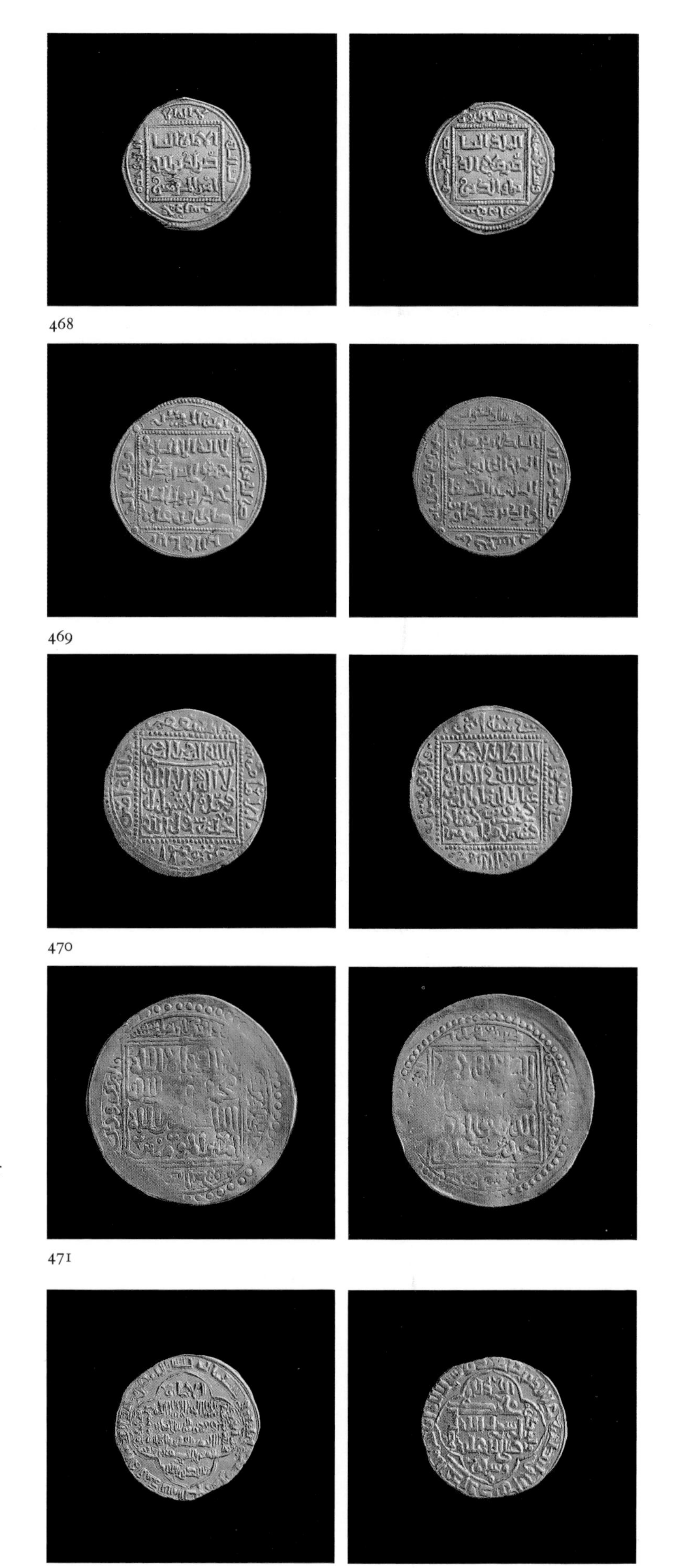
468
469
470
471
472

Ilkhan coinage

472
Abbasid dinar of al-Mustansir

Madinat al-Salam 637 AH (AD 1239-40)
Both obverse and reverse legends in quatrefoil

AV 4.63 gm, diameter 24 mm
In the second period of his caliphate al-Mustansir adopted a new artistic design for his coins, placing the principal legends within an ornamental enclosure. This innovation may have influenced the later coinages of Iraq and Iran.

473
Ilkhan dinar of Arghun

Shiraz 684 AH (AD 1285–6)
Reverse, in Uygur script: 'Coinage struck by order of the Great Khan's Viceroy'
AV 4.72 gm, diameter 27.5 mm
It was usual for the coinage of the Mongols to include a portion of the legend in Uygur script.

474
Ilkhan double dinar of Ghazan Mahmud

Shiraz 700 AH (AD 1300–1)
AV 8.54 gm, diameter 29 mm
Ghazan Mahmud introduced a major coinage reform in 696 AH (AD 1296–7) and silver was widely struck throughout his dominions. Ilkhanid gold is much rarer than silver, and production seems to have been concentrated in a few cities in Iraq and Iran. The coinage of Shiraz seen here is of a particularly high artistic standard.

475
Ilkhan quarter dinar of Ghazan Mahmud

Tabriz without date
Obverse within pentafoil: 'Sovereignty belongs to God, struck in Tabriz', reverse: *Ghāzān/Mahmūd*
AV 1.05 gm, diameter 11.5 mm
The small size and design of this unique coin suggest that it may have been struck for special distribution at a ceremony held in Ghazan's capital city Tabriz, renowned for its active court life.

476
Ilkhan half dinar of Uljaytu

Baghdad 708 AH (AD 1308–9)
First type of reign. Reverse legend in square: *Sultān al-A'zam/ Ghiyāth al-dunyā wa'l-dīn/Khudabanda Muhammad/Khallada Allah-mulkahu*
AV 2.13 gm, diameter 17 mm
Uljaytu struck three coinage types. The first, between 704 and 708 AH, used Sunni legends. After his conversion to the Shi'i branch of Islam in 709 AH the names of the Four 'Rightly Guided' Caliphs were replaced by those of the 12 Shi'i Imams. In 713 AH the third type was introduced and remained in use until Uljaytu's death in 715 AH.

477
Ilkhan double dinar of Uljaytu

Madinat Baghdad 709 AH (AD 1309–10)
Reverse in quatrefoil: *Duriba fi/ayyām al-dawla al-Mawlānā/al-Sultān*

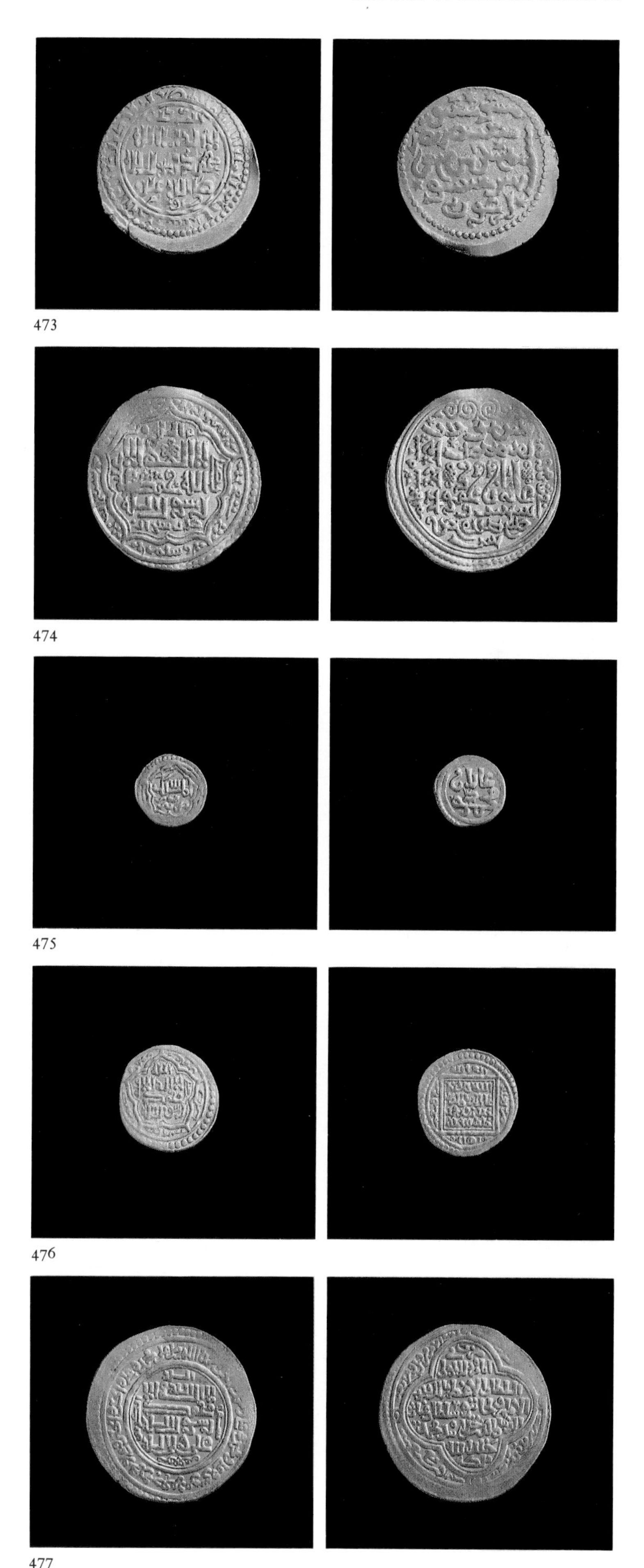
473
474
475
476
477

477 continued
al-A'zam Mālik al-riqāb/al-umma Uljaytū Sultān Ghiyāth al-dunyā wa'l-dīn Khudābanda Muhammad/Khallada Allah mulkahu
AV 8.49 gm, diameter 28.5 mm
This is an example of Uljaytu's second coinage after he adopted the Shi'i faith.

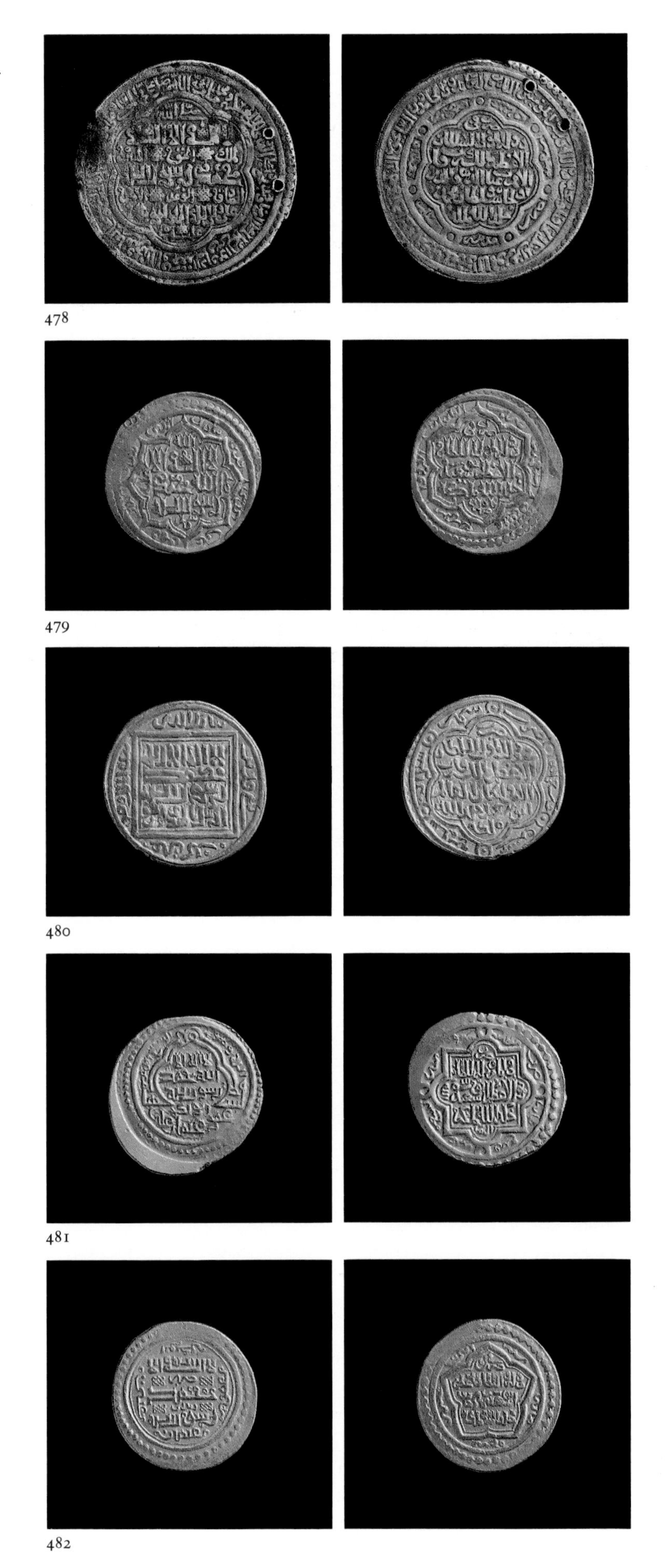

478
479
480
481
482

478
Ilkhan silver dinar (6 dirhams) of Uljaytu

Madinat al-Salam Baghdad 713 AH (AD 1313-4)
Reverse legends (similar to no. 477 above) placed in septafoil
AR 11.41 gm, diameter 37 mm
The Ilkhanid monetary system was based on a dinar valued at 6 dirhams, both of whose weights were regularly debased. This is a particularly handsome example of Uljaytu's third coinage.

479
Ilkhan double dinar of Abu Sa'id

Al-Bazar al-Urdu (the Army Market) 717 AH (AD 1317-18)
Obverse legend in octofoil, reverse in hexafoil
AV 7.97 gm, diameter 27 mm
Abu Sa'id struck seven principal coinage types between 717 and 735 AH, each of which bears its own style of cartouche. These served the practical purpose of distinguishing each successive coinage debasement from the preceding issue.

480
Ilkhan double dinar of Abu Sa'id

Shahr Shiraz 717 AH (AD 1317-18)
Obverse square within circle, reverse with hexafoil
AV 9.18 gm, diameter 28 mm
This style of coinage was only used by the mint of Shiraz.

481
Ilkhan double dinar of Abu Sa'id

Sultaniya 719 AH (AD 1319-20)
AV 8.08 gm, diameter 25 mm
This style is known as the *mihrab* type because of the *mihrab*-shaped ornamental calligraphy on the obverse.

482
Ilkhan double dinar of Abu Sa'id

Zaydan 722 AH (AD 1322-3)
Reverse legend in pentafoil
AV 9.57 gm, diameter 24.5 mm
Zaydan was located in Iran between Kazerun and Bushehr.

483
Ilkhan double dinar of Abu Sa'id

Sultaniya 727 AH (AD 1326–7)
Obverse: square in circle, reverse: circle in circle
AV 6.63 gm, diameter 23 mm
Sultaniya was the capital that Uljaytu established after his conversion to Shi'ism.

484
Ilkhan double dinar of Abu Sa'id

Jajarm 727 AH (AD 1326–7)
Obverse in octofoil, reverse in looped octofoil
AV 6.32 gm, diameter 23.5 mm
Jajarm was an important Ilkhan mint located south of the Caspian Sea.

485
Ilkhan double dinar of Abu Sa'id

Ardharum (Erzurum) 33 Khani (AD 1333–4)
Obverse: the *Kalima* in square Kufic, reverse: Abu Sa'id's name across centre of flan in Uygur script
AV 7.87 gm, diameter 21.5 mm
This was the last coinage type of Abu Sa'id's reign. On it he introduced a remarkable innovation by giving the date in the Khanid era. This was established by Ghazan Mahmud, but apparently was only used on coins during the last two years of Abu Sa'id's reign, i.e. 33 and 34 Khani, 734 and 735 AH (AD 1333–5).

486
Ilkhan dinar of Sati Beg Khan

Baghdad 740 AH (AD 1339–40)
AV 7.62 gm, diameter 23 mm
Abu Sa'id died without any direct male heir; he was succeeded by his distant kinsmen, Arpa, Musa and then Muhammad. On the latter's death in 739 AH. Abu Sa'id's daughter Sati Beg was placed on the throne, but after she married another distant relation, Suleyman, he took the first opportunity to depose her. Although Sati Beg's silver coinage is frequently seen, this is the only gold coin known from her brief reign.

487
Ilkhan dinar of (A)nushirwan

Maragheh 747 AH (AD 1346–7)
Obverse: *Kalima* in lozenge, reverse in looped quatrefoil
AV 5.40 gm, diameter 19 mm
Maragheh is a town located south of Tabriz and slightly east of Lake Urmiya. Anushirwan was the last Ilkhan ruler whose authority was widely recognized on the coinage.

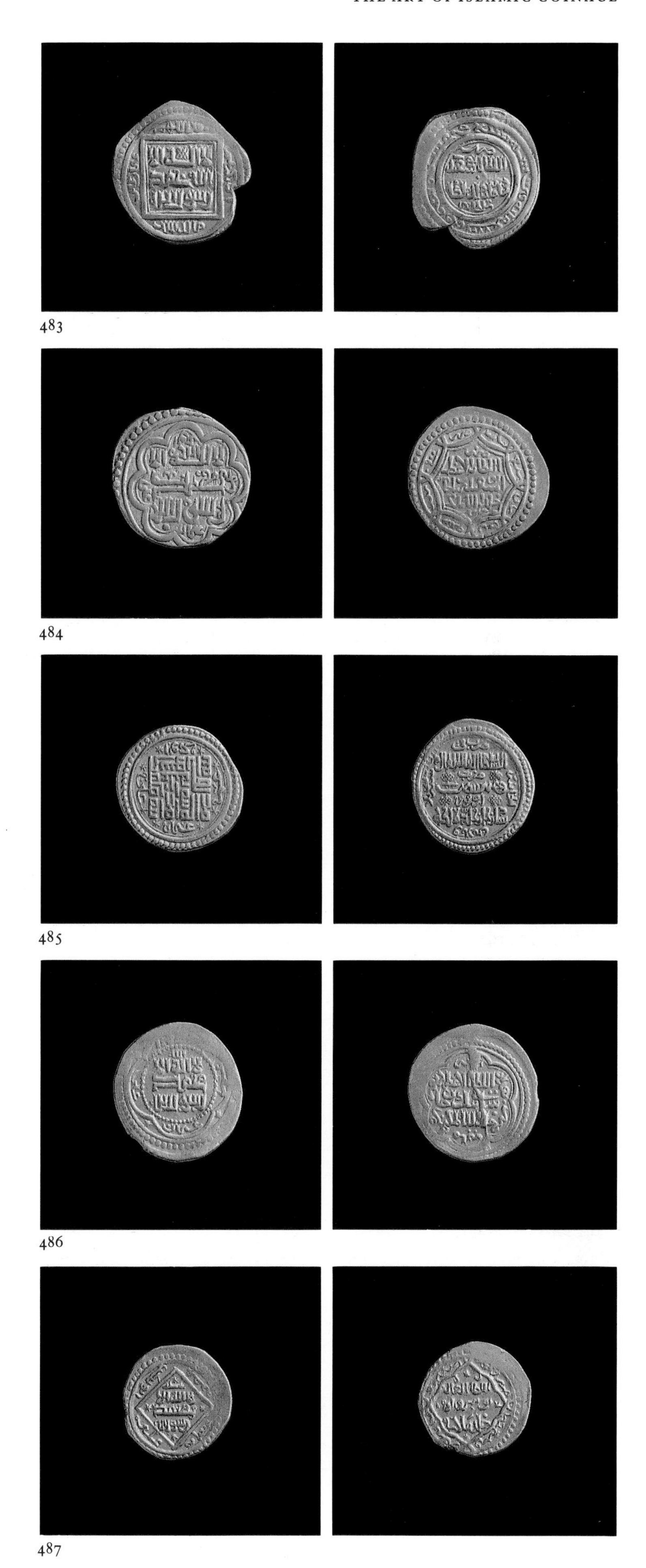

483

484

485

486

487

488
Dinar jalayride anonyme; époque d'Hasan Buzurg

Frappé à Baghdad, en 752 (1351–1352).
Au revers: carré, dans un carré, le carré intérieur contenant ce qui semble être un *tughrā*.
Or, 4,34gr.; d. 19mm.
Le souverain jalayride Hasan Buzurg était un ancien commandant de l'armée ilkhanide; pendant la période de vide politique qui suivit la mort d'Abu Sa'id, il soutint les souverains successifs; lorsqu'ils eurent tous disparu, il finit par prendre le pouvoir, mais, par respect pour l'idéal d'un Etat ilkhanide universel, il ne fit pas apposer son nom sur ses monnaies.

L'influence du ducat vénitien sur la monnaie orientale

489
Ashrafi mamelouk burdjite d'al-Mansur Osman

Frappé en 857 (1453), sans doute au Caire (nom de l'atelier hors flan).
Or, 3,41 gr.; d. 16 mm.
Après une période assez confuse en ce qui concerne le système monétaire, le souverain mamelouk burdjite Faradj frappa pour la première fois une monnaie ayant pour étalon le ducat vénitien, en 810 (1407–1408). Sous le règne d'al-Ashraf Barsbay, cette monnaie fut définitivement adoptée et appelée *ashrafī* (très noble). Les pièces datant du court règne (quelques mois) d'al-Mansur Osman sont rarissimes.

490
Ashrafi al-Qoyunlu de Qasim ibn Jahangir

Frappé à Mardin, date hors flan.
Or, 3,36 gr.; d. 14 mm.
Les rares pièces d'or des souverains al-Qoyunlu de Turquie orientale et d'Iran occidental adoptèrent le poids et la décoration de l'ashrafi mamelouk. Cette pièce est un rarissime exemplaire de la monnaie frappée à Mardin.

491
Filuri ou sultani ottoman de Mohammed II

Frappé à Qustantaniyya (Constantinople), en 883 (1478–1479).
Or, 3,49 gr.; d. 20 mm.
Avant leur conquête de Constantinople, les Ottomans ne frappèrent pas de monnaie d'or; mais en 882 (1477–1478) Mohammed II, qui s'était emparé de la ville, estima qu'il convenait à la dignité ottomane d'avair sa propre monnaie d'or.

492
Sultani ottoman de Selim I (Selim le farouche)

Frappé à Misr (Egypte), en 924 (1518–1519).
Or, 3,32gr.; d. 18,5mm.
Selim conquit l'Egypte en 1517; sa première monnaie adopta le même alliage faible en or des derniers mamelouks burdjites.

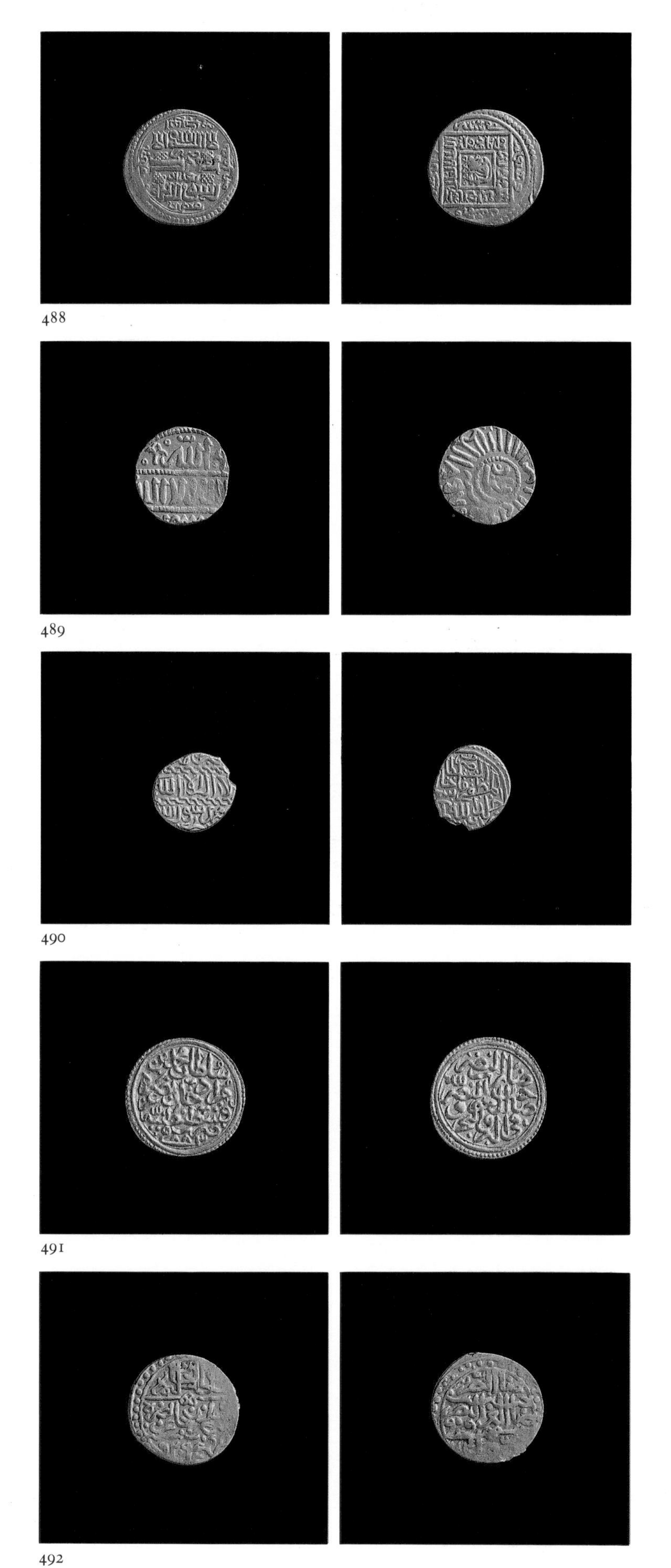

488

489

490

491

492

493
Ottoman sultani of Salim I

Amid (Diyarbakir) date off flan
Reverse field: *duriba/Sultan al-'Adil/abu'l-Muzaffar Salim Shah b. Bayezid/Khan Khallada Allah Mulkahu Amid*
AV 3.59 gm, diameter 19.5 mm
This extraordinary and previously unpublished coin bears the *Kalima* within an oval cartouche on the obverse, a feature only seen on one other of Salim's 'conquest' coins. Its legends and designs suggest that it was struck by the staff of a Safavid mint which may have been operating in Diyarbakir at the time the Ottomans besieged and conquered the city.

494
Ottoman sultani of Suleyman I (Suleyman the Magnificent)

Jaza'ir (Algiers) 926 AH (AD 1519-20)
AV 3.47 gm, diameter 19.5 mm
Algiers was conquered for the Ottomans by the famous corsair Barbarossa.

495
Ottoman sultani of Ahmad I

Toqat 1012 AH (AD 1603-4)
AV 3.43 gm, diameter 21 mm
This obscure central Anatolian town was briefly used as a mint during the Ottoman-Safavid wars of the late 16th and early 17th centuries.

496
Ottoman funduq (zinjirli altun) of Ahmad III

Islambul 1115 AH (AD 1703-4)
sign *ya*
AV 3.49 gm, diameter 18.5 mm
This 'reform' coinage was intended to compete at par with the Venetian ducat. While Qustantaniyya was the formal Arabic name for the city, Islambul, literally 'full of Islam', was an adaptation of its popular name, Stamboul.

497
Safavid ashrafi of Sultan Husayn

Isfahan 1134 AH (AD 1721-2)
Obverse: the Shi'i *Kalima* with the names of the 12 Imams in the margin
AV 3.41 gm, diameter 21.5 mm
The Safavids frequently struck gold coinage on the Venetian standard for trade purposes.

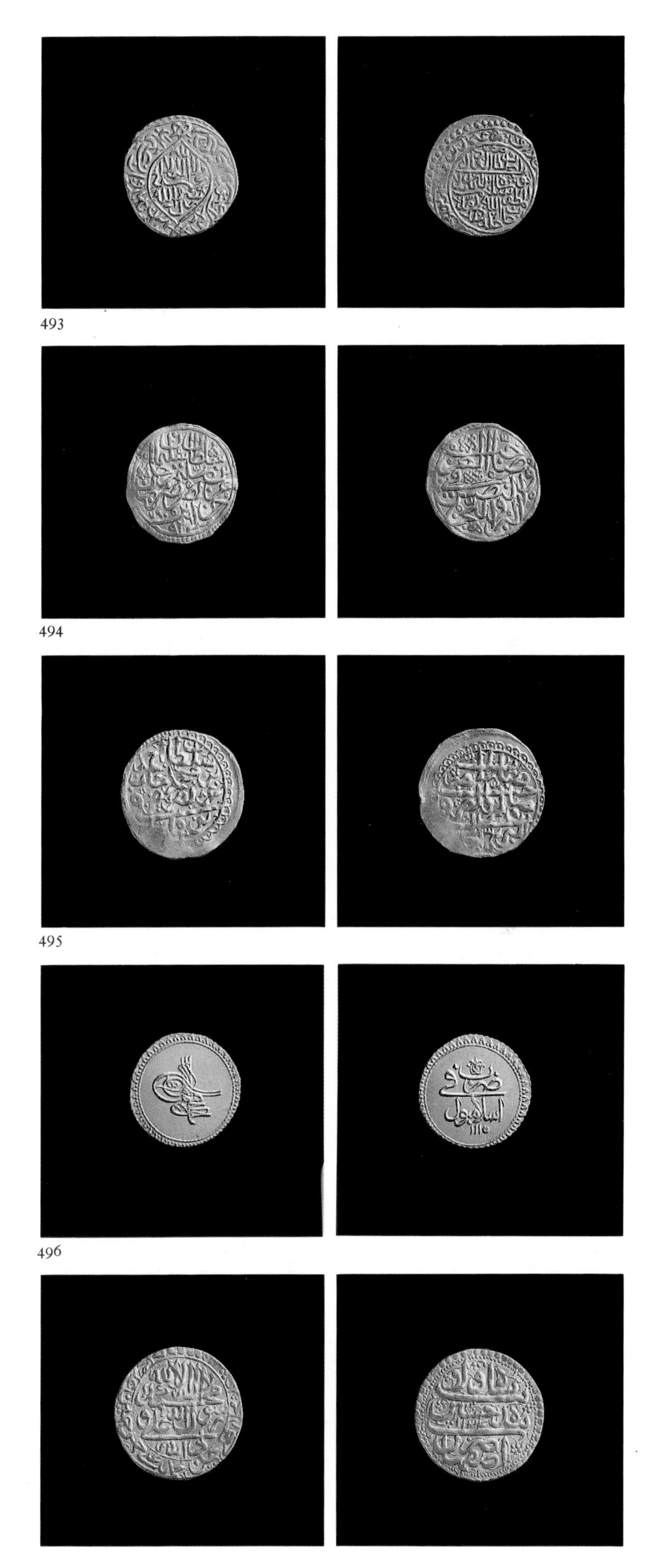
493
494
495
496

498
Filali ashrafi, anonymous (reign of Muhammad I)
Fas 1189 AH (AD 1775-6)
Obverse in octogram: *Ahad (al) Ahad*, 'The Unique of the Unique', i.e. God
AV 3.05 gm, diameter 24.5 mm
Moroccan gold from this period is exceedingly rare, and although normally struck on the ducat standard it is frequently found to be underweight.

499
Qajar toman of Nasir al-din Shah
Astarabad 1277 AH (AD 1860-61)
AV 3.45 gm, diameter 19.5 mm
Astarabad is located south of the Caspian Sea. The toman, originally a unit of account based on the coinage reform of Ghazan Mahmud and valued at 10,000 dinars, had by this time become worth the weight of the ducat.

500
Kashgar tilla of Ya'qub Beg
Struck in the name of the Ottoman ruler 'Abd al-'Aziz, Dar al-Saltanat Kashgar 1292 AH (AD 1875-6)
AV 3.60 gm, diameter 20 mm
Ya'qub Beg revolted against the Manchu emperors of China and sought the assistance of the Ottoman sultan in the latter's role as caliph of Islam. 'Abd al-'Aziz dispatched cannon, standards and presents to his new vassal who repaid the compliment by striking coins in his overlord's name.

501
Barakzay ashrafi of Shir 'Ali
Dar al-Saltanat Kabul 1295 AH (AD 1878)
AV 3.42 gm, diameter 18.5 mm
The rulers of Afghanistan often struck ashrafis when their trade was with Iran, and muhurs when it was with India.

Tankas and muhurs, the heavy gold coinage of India

502
Delhi sultanate tanka of Jalal al-din Firuz Shah
Hadrat Delhi 689 AH (AD 1290-91)
Obverse: *al-Imām al-Musta'sim billah*
AV 10.94 gm, diameter 27 mm
The Delhi sultans often struck their coinage in the name of the Abbasid caliph in Cairo.

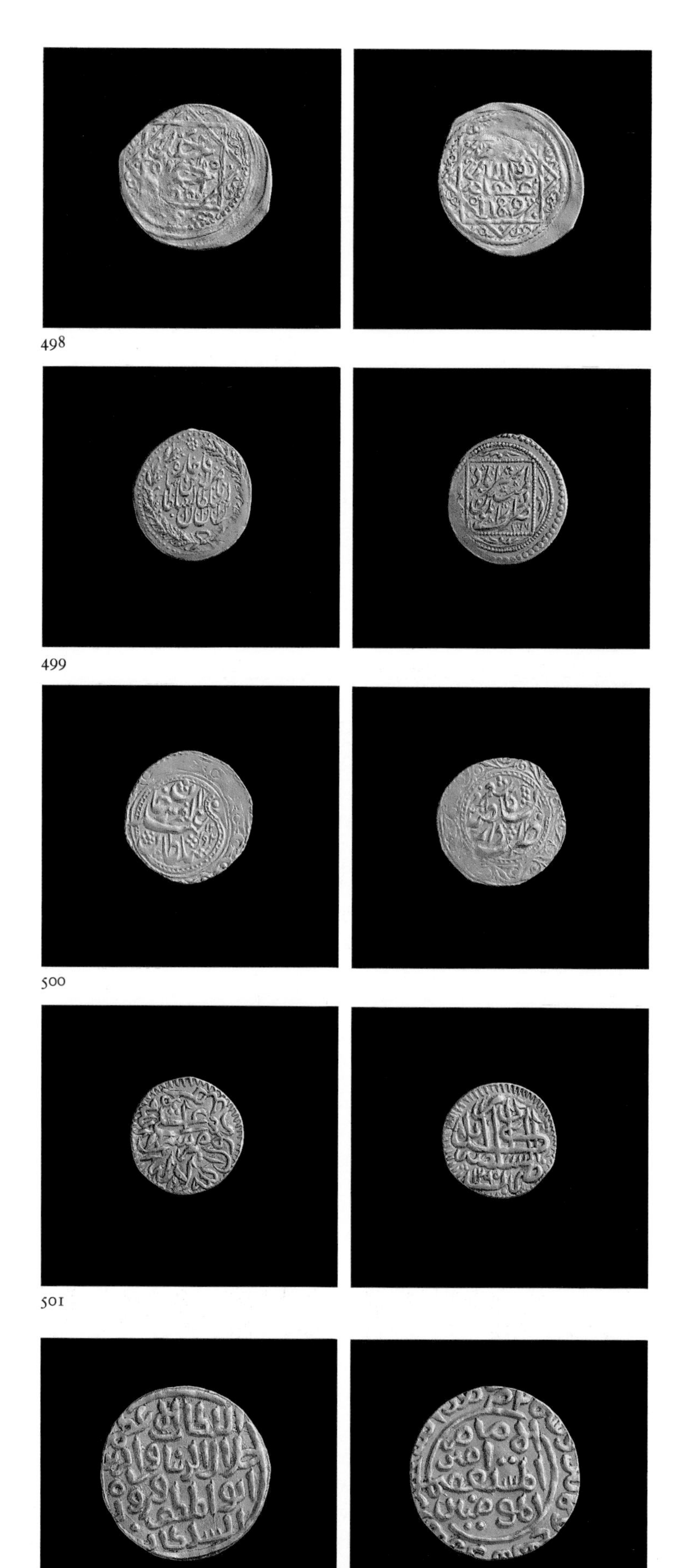
498
499
500
501
502

503
Delhi sultanate square tanka of Qutb al-din Mubarak Shah
Dar al-Khilafat Delhi 718 AH (AD 1318–19)
AV 10.85 gm, diameter 23 × 23 mm
The Indian rulers occasionally struck square coins in both gold and silver.

504
Delhi sultanate 'dinar' of Ghiyath al-din Muhammad II
Hadrat Delhi 727 AH (AD 1326–7)
AV 12.79 gm, diameter 19 mm
An Indian ruler would sometimes strike his coins on a slightly heavier standard to impress people with his generosity.

505
Delhi sultanate tanka of Ghiyath al-din Muhammad II
Without mint name 733 AH (AD 1332–3)
Obverse in pentafoil: similar to the third coinage of the Ilkhan Abu Sa'id
AV 10.71 gm, diameter 22 mm

506
Delhi sultanate tanka of Firuz Shah III
Without mint name or date
AV 11.05 gm, diameter 21 mm

507
Sultanate of Madura tanka of Ghiyath al-din Muhammad Damaghan
Dawlatabad 741 AH (AD 1340–41)
AV 11.94 gm, diameter 28 mm
Madura lies in the extreme south of the Indian sub-continent. The Muslim dynasty which ruled the state lasted for about 50 years.

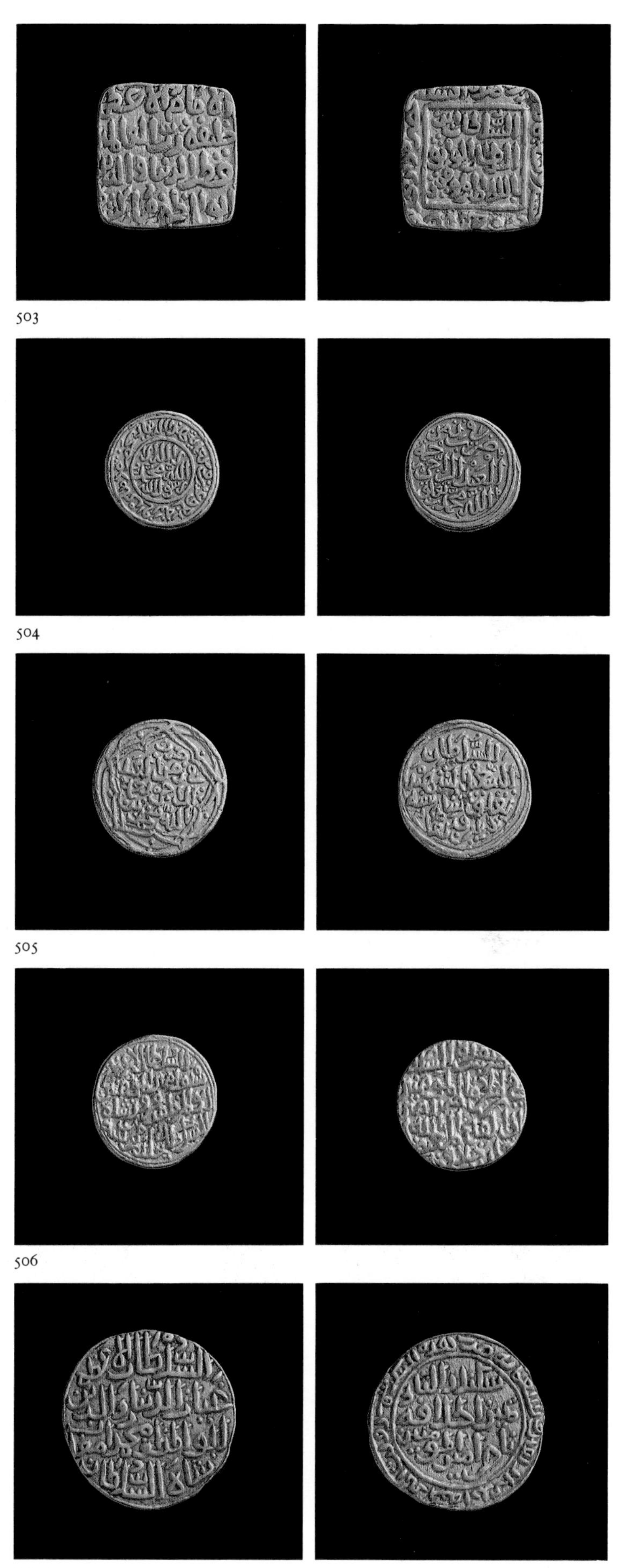
503
504
505
506
507

508
Sultanate of Jaunpur tanka of Mahmud Shah b. Ibrahim

Without mint name 84– AH (AD 1436-46)
AV 11.45 gm, diameter 24 mm
The ruler's name is inscribed in the form of an elaborate *tughrā* on the reverse.

508

509
Sultanate of Malwa square tanka of Ghiyath Shah

Without mint name 883 AH (AD 1478-9)
AV 10.96 gm, diameter 22 × 21.5 mm
This handsome square tanka bears the sign of the swastika on the obverse, an Indian symbol of prosperity and long life.

509

510
Sultanate of Gujerat tanka of Mahmud b. Latif

Without mint name 945 AH (AD 1538-9)
Obverse in central square: *Sultan Mahmūd Shāh bin Latīf Shāh*
AV 11.98 gm, diameter 20 mm

510

511
Mughal muhur of Jalal al-din Akbar

Lahawur (Lahore) 973 AH (AD 1565-6)
AV 10.95 gm, diameter 26.5 mm
This is the first coinage type of Akbar's reign.

511

512
Mughal muhur of Shihab al-din Shah Jahan

Surat r.y. 2 (1038 AH/AD 1629-30) month of Adhar (the 9th month of the Iranian calendar)
AV 10.96 gm, diameter 23 mm

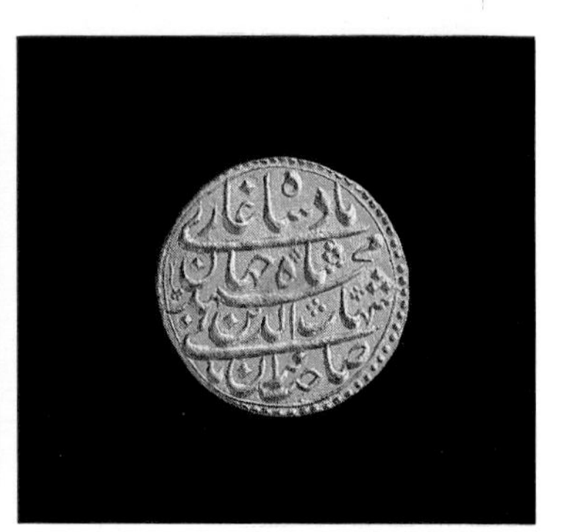

512

513
Mughal Nazarana muhur of Shihab al-din Shah Jahan
Dar al-Khilafat Agra 1038 AH (AD 1628-9) r. y. 2, month of Khurdad (the 3rd month of the Iranian calendar)
AV 10.86 gm, diameter 29 mm
This is an example of a Nazarana or presentation muhur.

514
Mughal muhur of Muhammad Shah
Dar al-Saltanat Lahawur 1155 AH (AD 1742-3) r. y. 25
AV 10.97 gm, diameter 20 mm

515
Afsharid muhur of Nadir Shah
Dar al-Saltanat Isfahan 1156 AH (AD 1743-4) r. y. 6
AV 10.99 gm, diameter 22 mm
After Nadir Shah conquered Dehli from Muhammad Shah in 1152 AH (AD 1739) and looted the Mughal treasury he adopted the Indian muhur standard for the Iranian coinage.

516
Safavid (maternal line) double muhur of Suleyman II
Mashhad Maqdis 1163 AH (AD 1749-50)
AV 22.05 gm, diameter 27 mm
This is an unusually large and rare denomination for the Iranian coinage.

The figured coinage of the late 6th and early 7th centuries of the Hijra

517
Artuqid of Hisnkayfa copper dirham of Fakhr al-din Qara Arslan
Without mint name 559 AH (AD 1163-4)
Obverse: bare-headed half figure towards left, reverse: facing figure

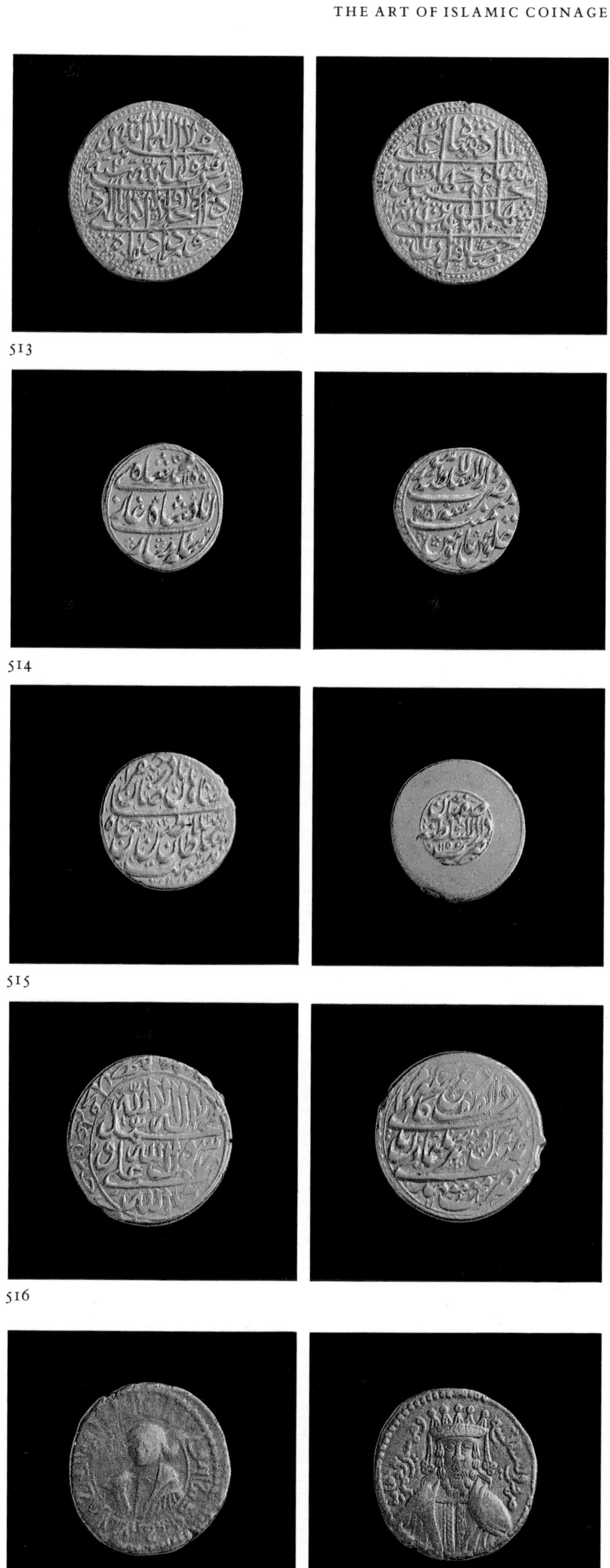

513

514

515

516

517

517 *continued*
of crowned king
AE 11.44 gm, diameter 27.5 mm
The reverse carries one of the most vivid portraits found on any Islamic coin.

518
Artuqid of Hisnkayfa copper dirham of Fakhr al-din Qara Arslan

Without mint name 560 AH (AD 1164–5)
Obverse: head facing towards left, reverse: *Malik al-umara/Qara Arslan bin/Dā'ūd b. Sukman/b. Artuq*
AE 13.62 gm, diameter 29 mm

519
Artuqid of Hisnkayfa copper dirham of Fakhr al-din Qara Arslan

Without mint name 562 AH (AD 1166–7)
Obverse: full-face half figure
AE 11.78 gm, diameter 28.5 mm

520
Artuqid of Hisnkayfa copper dirham of Fakhr al-din Qara Arslan

Without mint name or date
Obverse: winged victory to right (copied from a coin of Constantine the Great struck at Siscia in Pannonia)
AE 11.66 gm, diameter 31 mm

521
Artuqid of Hisnkayfa copper dirham of Nur al-din Muhammad

Without mint name 571 AH (AD 1175–6)
Obverse: nimbate angel with right wing raised and left hand holding scroll which falls over right arm
AE 10.91 gm, diameter 29.5 mm

522
Artuqid of Hisnkayfa copper dirham of Qutb al-din Sukman II

Al-Hisn 581 AH (AD 1185–6)
Obverse: bearded and crowned head of Sasanian king facing left
AE 13.66 gm, diameter 30 mm

518
519
520
521
522

523
Artuqid of Khartapirt copper dirham of 'Imad al-din Abu Bakr

Without mint name 582 AH (AD 1186-7)
Obverse: standing figure riding on writhing serpent
AE 12.86 gm, diameter 29 mm
This design is one of the most striking ones found on the figured coinage.

524
Begtekinid Atabeg of Irbil copper dirham of Muzaffar al-din Kukburi

Irbil 587 AH (AD 1191-2)
Obverse: curly-headed classical bust to left
AE 10.77 gm, diameter 29.5 mm

525
Artuqid of Mardin copper dirham of Qutb al-din Ilghazi

Without mint name, date unclear, probably 578 AH (AD 1182-3)
Obverse: two busts facing forward, one larger than the other
AE 14.81 gm, diameter 34.5 mm

526
Zangid Atabeg of al-Jazira copper double dirham of al-Muzaffar Sanjar Shah

Al-Jazira 600 AH (AD 1203-4)
Obverse: tribal *tamgha* (mark) of the ruler
AE 31.71 gm, diameter 36 mm

527
Ayyubid of Mayyafariqin copper dirham of al-Ashraf Musa

Without mint name 612 AH (AD 1215-16)
Obverse: a Muslim sovereign seated facing, probably al-Ashraf Musa
AE 11.83 gm, diameter 31 mm
The Ayyubids preferred quasi-realistic figures of their rulers on their copper coinage to the classical or mythological subjects used by the Artuqids.

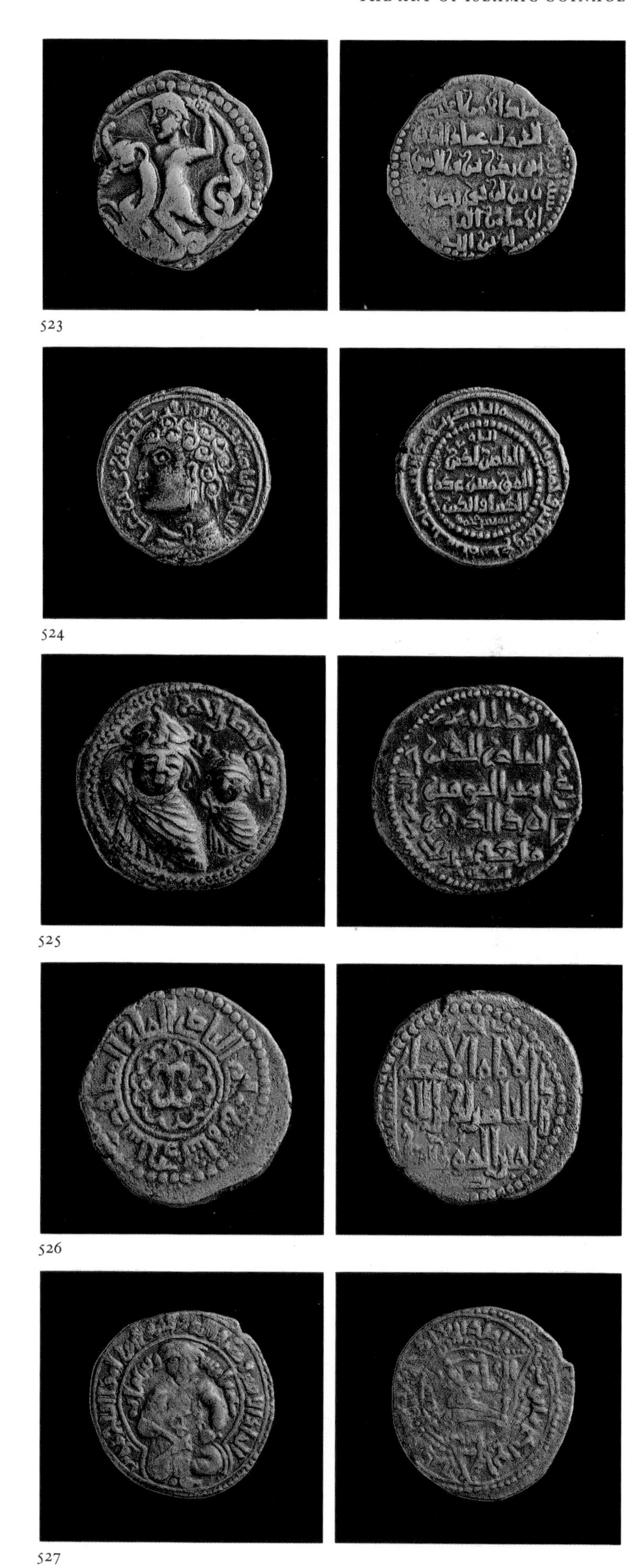

523

524

525

526

527

528
Artuqid of Hisnkayfa copper dirham of Nasir al-din Mahmud

Amid 614 AH (AD 1217–18) (date written in numerals)
Obverse: two-headed imperial eagle poised on perch of interwoven lines with each wing formed by a man's bearded head
AE 12.00 gm, diameter 30 mm
This heraldic design is similar to a carving placed above one of the main gates of the city of Diyarbakir.

528

529

529
Zangid of Mosul copper dirham of Nasir al-din Mahmud

Al-Mawsil 627 AH (AD 1229–30)
Obverse: crowned figure seated cross-legged upholding the crescent of the new moon
AE 8.69 gm, diameter 25 mm

530
Rum Seljuq copper dirham of Suleyman Shah

Without mint name 595 AH (AD 1198–9)
Obverse: nimbate horseman with lance in right hand galloping to right
AE 8.11 gm, diameter 32 mm
In contrast to the dynasties of south-eastern Anatolia, the Rum Seljuqs preferred a galloping horseman on their figured coinage.

530

531
Rum Seljuq dirham of Rukn al-din Suleyman Shah

Madinat Qaysariya 596 AH (AD 1199–1200)
Obverse: figure of horseman (without nimbus) galloping towards right
AR 2.87 gm, diameter 23 mm
This type is exceedingly rare in silver.

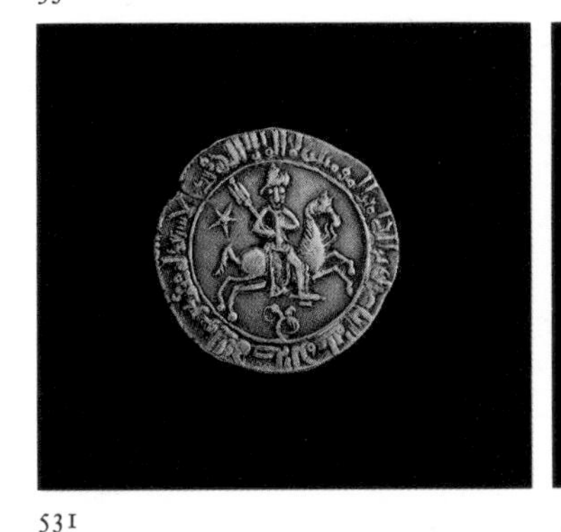

531

532
Rum Seljuq dirham of Ghiyath al-din Kaykhusraw II

Qunya 640 AH (AD 1242–3)
Obverse: figure of lion passant to right above the face of the sun in radiance (the good luck sign of the sun in Leo)
AR 2.96 gm, diameter 22 mm
This coinage design is said to commemorate the great love the ruler bore for his wife, but it is more likely that it symbolized the astral influence that favoured the ruler's power.

532

533
Great Mongol dirham, anonymous (time of the regency of Queen Turakina)

Nakhjawan 6(42) AH (AD 1244–5)
Obverse: mounted archer galloping to right turning backwards in saddle to discharge arrow. Between the legs of the horse a small animal running to left
AR 2.90 gm, diameter 19.5 mm
This design was used on the Mongol coinage only during the regency of Queen Turakina.

534
Bahri Mamluk dinar of al-Sa'id Baraka Qan

Mint off flan (probably Cairo) 67–AH (*c.* 670–78/AD 1271–80)
Obverse: *Amīr al-Mu'minīn/al-Malik al-Sa'id Nāsir/al-dunyā wa'l-dīn Baraka Qan b. al-Malik al-Zahīr Qāsim*, below figure of lion passant.
AV 6.17 gm, diameter 22 mm
Al-Zahir Baybars and his son Baraka Qan were the only Mamluk rulers to use a heraldic device on their gold coinage. Although the figure appears to be a male lion, *Bars* means leopard or panther.

535
Ghurid tanka of Mu'izz al-din Muhammad

Without mint name, month of Ramadan 601 AH (AD 1204–5)
Obverse: horseman with upraised mace galloping to left. Reverse: *al-Sultān al-Mu'azzam Mu'izz/al-dunyā wa'l-dīn/abū'l-Muzaffar Muhammad/b. Sām*
AV 11.15 gm, diameter 23 mm
This is one of two known tankas of this type struck by the famous conqueror of India. The Ghurids frequently adopted previous coin designs for their own uses, and it is possible that this one was inspired by the Rum Seljuq dirham, no. 531 above.

536
Delhi Sultanate silver tanka of Shams al-din Iltutmush

Without mint name or date
Obverse: horseman with upraised mace galloping to left
AR 10.53 gm, diameter 27 mm
Iltutmush copied the device of the galloping horseman from the coins of his illustrious predecessor Muhammad Ghuri.

The zodiacal coinage of Jahangir

537
Mughal muhur of Nur al-din Jahangir

Agra 1028 AH (AD 1618–19) r.y. 14
Aries. Obverse: ram passant to left
AV 10.95 gm, diameter 21 mm

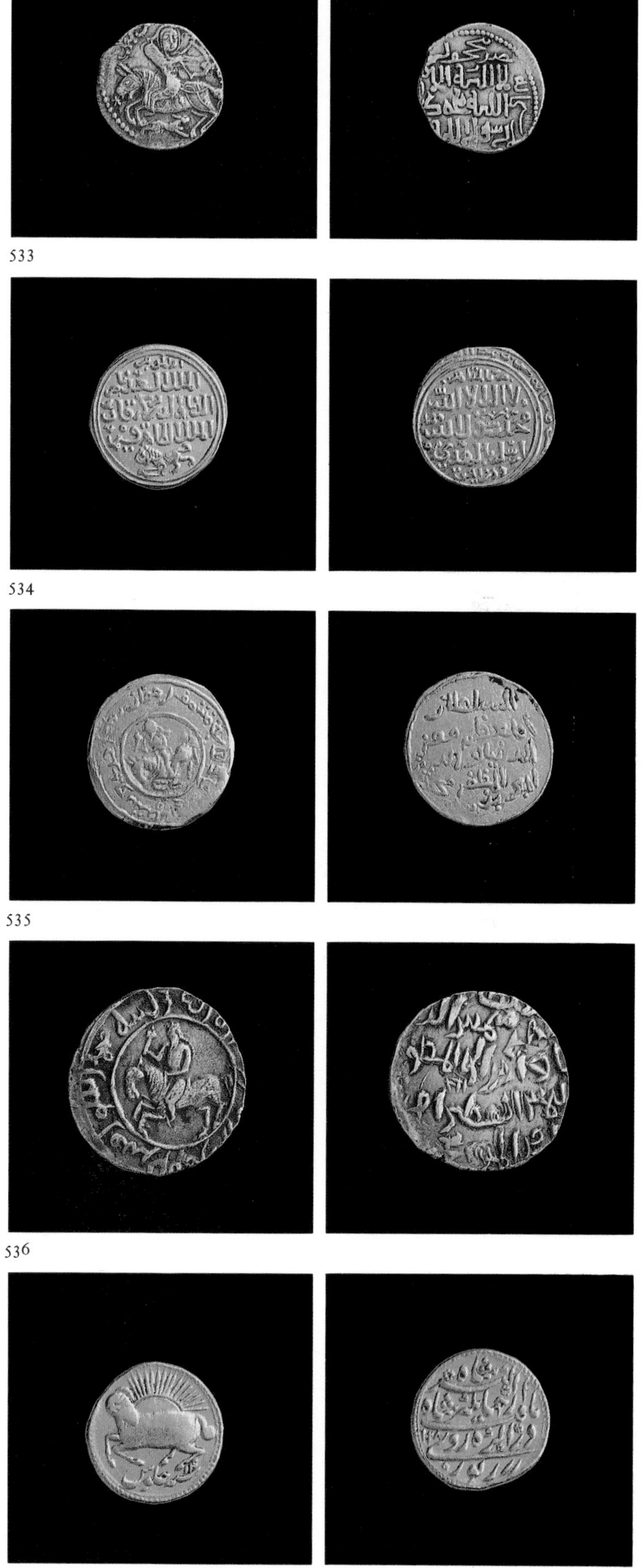

533

534

535

536

537

538
Mughal muhur of Nur al-din Jahangir
Agra 1030 AH (AD 1620–21) r.y. 16
Taurus. Obverse: Brahmin bull to right
AV 10.98 gm, diameter 20 mm

539
Mughal muhur of Nur al-din Jahangir
Agra 1032 AH (AD 1622–3) r.y. 18
Gemini. Obverse: two chubby naked figures embracing
AV 10.88 gm, diameter 20 mm

540
Mughal rupee of Nur al-din Jahangir
Ahmadabad 1027 AH (AD 1617–18) r.y. 13
Cancer. Obverse: crab with claws upraised
AR 11.22 gm, diameter 22 mm

541
Mughal muhur of Nur al-din Jahangir
Agra 1028 AH (AD 1618–19) r.y. 14
Leo. Obverse: lion passant to right
AV 10.94 gm, diameter 20.5 mm

542
Mughal muhur of Nur al-din Jahangir
Agra 1033 AH (AD 1623–4) r.y. 19
Virgo. Obverse: female figure winged and robed
AV 10.98 gm, diameter 19.5 mm

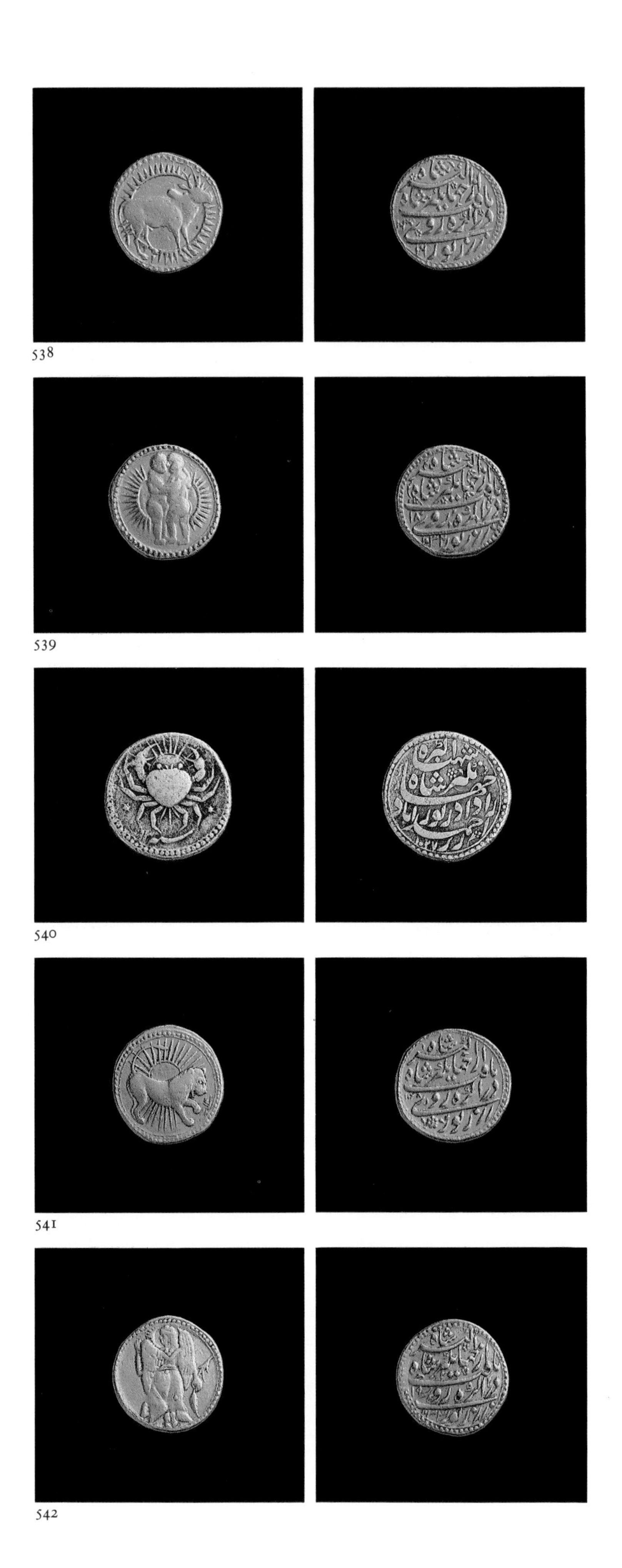
538
539
540
541
542

543
Mughal muhur of Nur al-din Jahangir
Agra 1030 AH (AD 1620-21) r.y. 16
Libra. Obverse: scales, four objects between the balances
AV 10.86gm, diameter 21 mm

544
Mughal muhur of Nur al-din Jahangir
Agra 1030 AH (AD 1620-21) without regnal year
Scorpio. Obverse: scorpion with tail upraised to left
AV 10.81 gm, diameter 20mm

545
Mughal rupee of Nur al-din Jahangir
Agra 1031 AH (AD 1621-2) r.y. 16
Sagittarius. Obverse: centaur galloping leftwards discharging an arrow behind him
AR 11.12gm, diameter 22mm
It is possible that this coin is a later hammered reproduction.

546
Mughal muhur of Nur al-din Jahangir
Agra 1032 AH (AD 1622-3) r.y. 17
Capricorn. Obverse: figure of mythical beast with head of goat and tail of mermaid
AV 10.84gm, diameter 21 mm
This coin is a later imitation of the original.

547
Mughal muhur of Nur al-din Jahangir
Agra 1031 AH (AD 1621-2) r.y. 16
Aquarius. Obverse: figure wearing loincloth and carrying water jar
AV 10.97gm, diameter 21.5mm

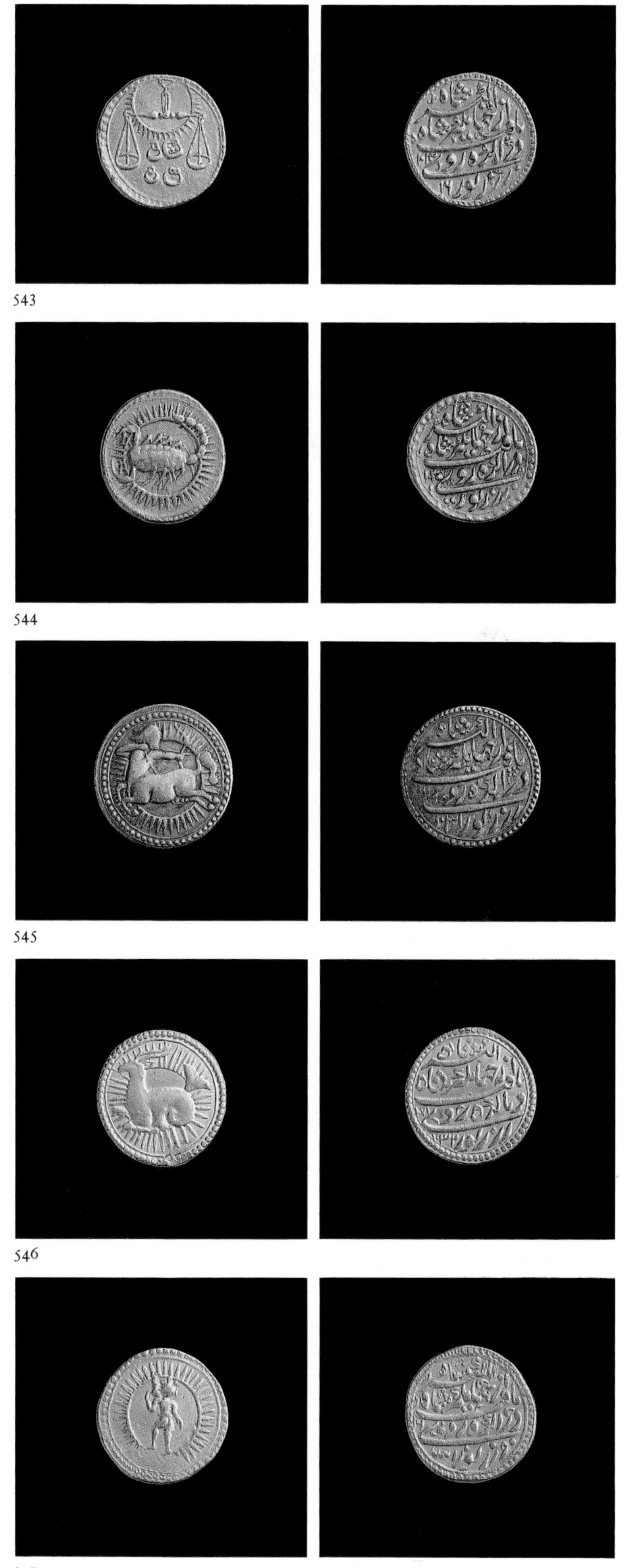

543

544

545

546

547

548
Mughal muhur of Nur al-din Jahangir

Agra 1028 AH (AD 1618–19) r.y. 13
Pisces. Obverse: two fish swimming head to tail
AV 10.89 gm, diameter 20 mm

Coins struck for special occasions

549
Abbasid fractional dinar of al-Mu'tadid billah

Without mint name 280 AH (AD 893–4)
Obverse: name of caliph, in margin the *Kalima*. Reverse: date formula
AV 1.18 gm, diameter 11 mm
This coin and the one following are examples of a special series of Abbasid coins struck at the end of the 3rd and beginning of the 4th centuries AH by the Abbasid caliphs, their heirs apparent or semi-independent governors. Their style gives particular emphasis to the name of the issuer and omits the mint name but retains the year of striking.

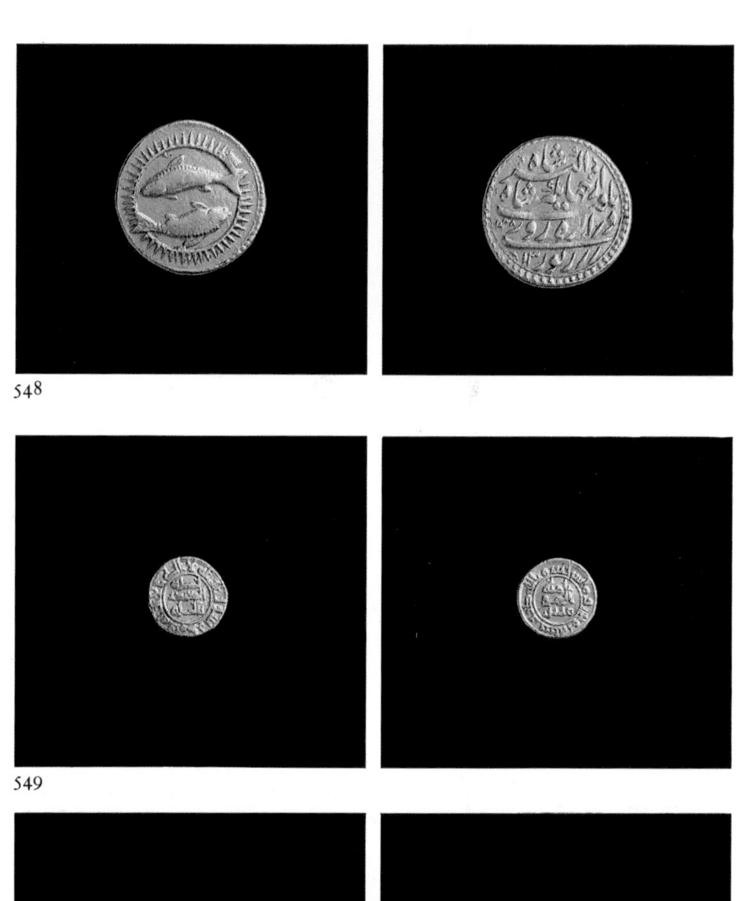

548

549

550
Abbasid fractional dinar, with weight of half dinar, of al-Mu'tadid billah

Without mint name 280 AH (AD 893–4)
Legends similar to no. 549 above
AV 2.12 gm, diameter 14 mm

550

551
Abbasid presentation dinar of al-Muqtadir

Without mint name or date
Obverse and reverse marginal legend: *Ja'far al-Imām/al-Muqtadir/billah*
AV 4.17 gm, diameter 22 mm
The unconventional use of an ornamental design in place of the usual religious legends, and the inclusion of the caliph's *ism* (first name), Ja'far, along with his official title *al-Muqtadir billah* suggest that it was intended as a personal gift from the ruler.

551

552
Buwayhid silver dinar of Abu-Talib Rustam

Al-Muhammadiya 387 AH (AD 997–8)
On both obverse and reverse in outer margin: 4 crescents and 4 good luck words
AR 11.13 gm, diameter 42.5 mm
When a new ruler acceded to the throne it was customary for him to distribute largesse to his troops, although it is not often that one can tell with certainty which coins were struck for the purpose. In this case, however, it is recorded that Abu-Talib did not have access to the treasury because he was besieged in a citadel by mutinous troops demanding payment of salary arrears.

552

553
Ghurid ten dinar of Mu'izz al-din Muhammad b. Sam

Without mint name 598 AH (AD 1201-2)
Struck in the name of his brother and overlord Ghiyath al-din Muhammad b. Sam
AV 44.94 gm, diameter 48 mm
This magnificent coin was struck 10 years after Mu'izz al-din won the Battle of Panipat which delivered the gates of India into the hands of the Ghurids.

554
Ilkhan triple dinar of Ghazan Mahmud

Baghdad 701 AH (AD 1301-2)
AV 12.92 gm, diameter 32 mm
This is believed to be the largest Ilkhan gold coin. It resembles Ghazan's reform coinage, but both obverse and reverse margins have additional legends not normally found on his coins.

555
Ottoman one and a half funduq or double zir-i mahbub of 'Abd al-Hamid I

Islambul 1187 AH (AD 1773-4) r.y. 1
AV 5.26 gm, diameter 30 mm
These coins were specially struck as ornaments for head-dresses and necklaces. It has long been a tradition in Islamic countries for families to convert their portable wealth into jewellery for their womenfolk, and the Ottoman mint made a good business out of striking special heavy, broad flan coins known as *ziynet altun* for this purpose. This custom has persisted until the present day.

556
Ottoman Egypt five guineas or five hundred piastres of 'Abd al-'Aziz

Misr 1277 AH (AD 1860-61) r.y. 11
Obverse: *tughrā, Khān 'Abd al-'Azīz b. Mahmūd al-muzaffar dā'ima*
AV 42.90 gm, diameter 38 mm
The Khedive of Egypt, Isma'il Pasha, struck a small number of these splendid five guinea coins for distribution on such occasions as the opening of the Suez Canal and the weddings of his many children. It is recorded that brides used to be showered with basketfuls of small gold coins during marriage celebrations. This very large coin was probably given to important male guests.

557
Ottoman Ziynet two and a half lira of 'Abd al-Hamid II

Qustantiniyya 1293 AH (AD 1876-7) r.y. 33
AV 17.62 gm, diameter 44 mm
After the introduction of machine-made coins in the 19th century the mint eventually met popular demand for ornamental coins by

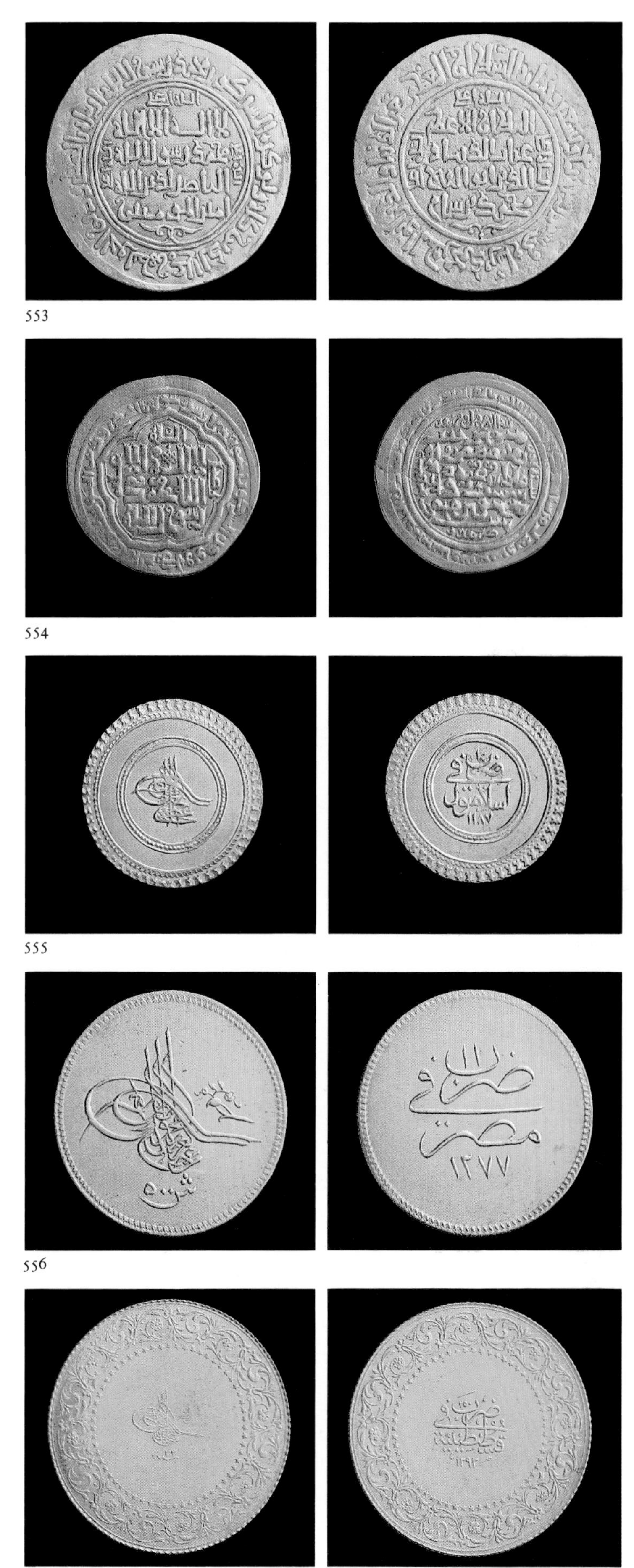
553
554
555
556
557

557 *continued*
designing a special series valued at 500, 250, 100, 50, 25 and 12½ qurush (piastres). Since they were intended to be worn as jewellery, only a very small number have survived in their original unmounted condition. This is one such example.

558
Qajar five ashrafi of Fath'ali Shah

Borujird 1230 AH (AD 1814-15)
AV 23.97 gm, diameter 38.5 mm
Like the Ottomans, the Safavids and Qajars liked to strike coins for ceremonial occasions. This unique example from Borujird may well have been struck for a visit to that city made by the shah. Other coins of the same general type are known from Tabriz and Isfahan.

559
Qajar good conduct medal of Nasir al-din Shah

(Teheran mint) 1300 AH (AD 1882-3)
AV 14.32 gm, diameter 36 mm
This medal contains a particularly handsome representation of the famous lion and sun emblem of imperial Iran. Because it was intended as a medal it is remarkable to find this piece in its original unmounted state.

560
Qajar twenty-five toman of Nasir al-din Shah

(Teheran) 1301 AH (AD 1883-4)
Obverse: portrait bust of Shah facing
AV 71.81 gm, diameter 50 mm
This coin is known in both gold and silver. The silver is valued at one toman and the gold at 25. They were obviously never intended for circulation, but struck as *pièces d'occasion* for presentation to or purchase by members of the court.

561
Mughal mihrab muhur of Jalal al-din Akbar

Balad-i Agra 981 AH (AD 1573-4)
AV 10.91 gm, length 32 mm, width 20 mm
The early Mughal rulers were particularly fond of striking coins of original shape and design for presentation to members of their court. This is one such piece which bears both the Muslim profession of faith and the names of the first four caliphs.

562
Mughal portrait muhur of Nur al-din Jahangir

No mint name 1014 AH (AD 1605-6) r.y. 1
Obverse: portrait of Akbar, to left the legend *Allah akbar*, reverse: the sun in radiance
AV 10.86 gm, diameter 22 mm
This is one of two known examples of this piece which Jahangir struck in homage to his father's memory immediately after his accession. In Akbar's Ilahi faith the sun was the symbol of the unity of God, and the motto of the faith *Allah akbar* was placed beside the portrait of the ruler.

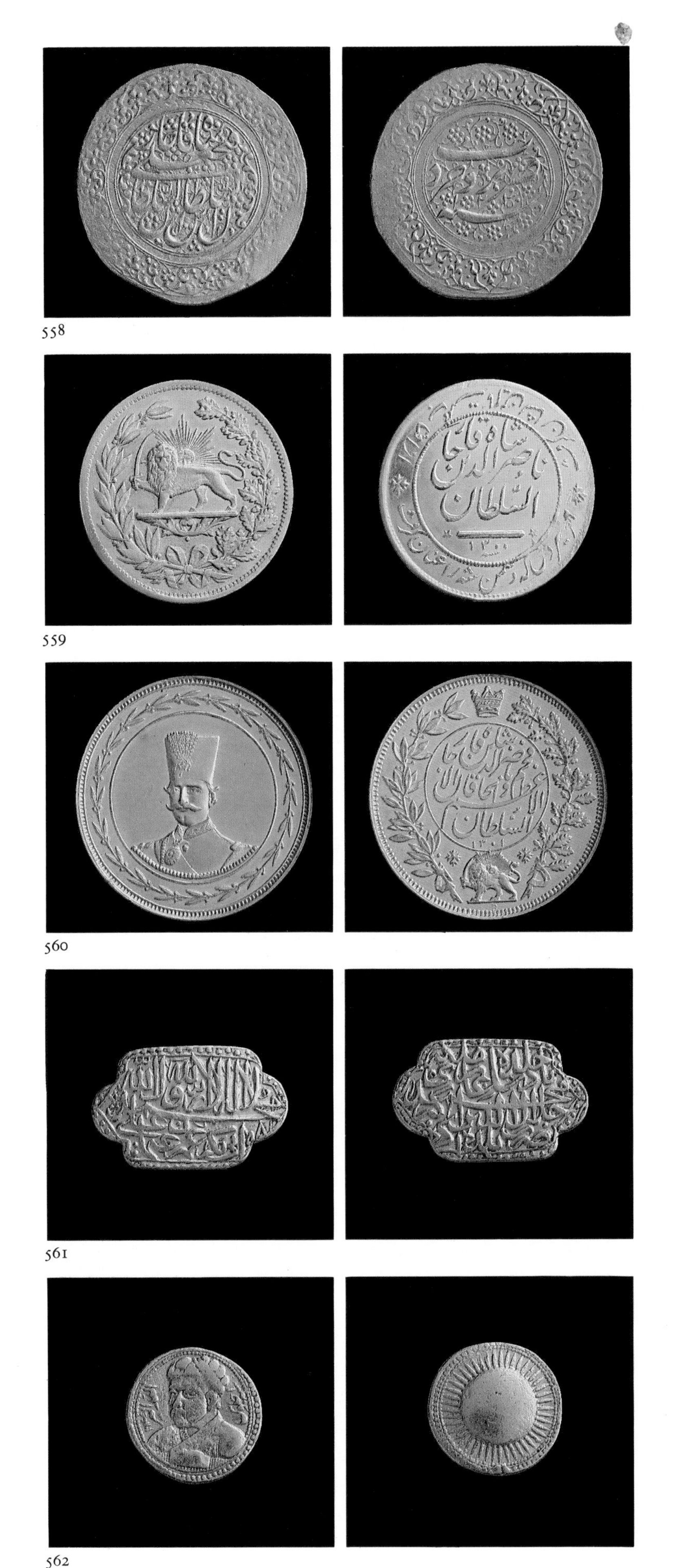
558
559
560
561
562

PORTRAIT COINAGE OF JAHANGIR'S 6TH REGNAL YEAR

563
Mughal portrait muhur of Nur al-din Jahangir
Without mint name 1020 AH (AD 1611–12) r.y. 6
Obverse: nimbate portrait of ruler to left, reverse: lion and sun to left
AV 10.93 gm, diameter 23 mm
On this coin Jahangir rests his hand on a book, possibly the Qur'an or a book of verse.

564
Mughal portrait muhur of Nur al-din Jahangir
Without mint name 1020 AH (AD 1611–12) r.y. 6
Obverse: nimbate portrait of Jahangir with hand on book, reverse: lion and sun to right
AV 10.99 gm, diameter 20 mm
In his memoirs Jahangir records how he presented these coins to members of his court both as signs of imperial favour and as good luck charms. It is possible that this rather austere type may have been intended for members of the religious community.

565
Mughal portrait muhur of Nur al-din Jahangir
Without mint name 1020 AH (AD 1611–12) r.y. 6
Obverse: nimbate head of Jahangir to left holding a ball (or perhaps pomegranate), reverse: lion and sun to right
This coin retains its original gold mount, thus AV 12.14 gm, diameter 20 mm
This type of coin may have been given to civil administrators, the pomegranate being a symbol of fertility, and hence prosperity for the Mughal dominions.

566
Mughal portrait muhur of Nur al-din Jahangir
Without mint name 1020 AH (AD 1161–12) r.y. 6
Obverse: nimbate portrait of Jahangir to right with right hand holding a drinking cup at eye level and left hand resting on book.
Reverse: lion and sun to right
AV 10.95 gm, diameter 21 mm
This masterpiece of the die sinker's art is certainly the finest portrait coin in this series. Special care was taken to give the utmost degree of realism to both the facial features of Jahangir and his clothing. Even the cup has its own floral ornamentation. Jahangir was known as a pleasure-lover and this festive piece may well have been intended for presentation to his boon companions.

567
Mughal portrait medal of Shah 'Alam II
Without mint name 1173 AH (AD 1759–60)
AR 25.95 gm, diameter 48 mm
On this medal Shah 'Alam has the expression of a Sufi mystic.

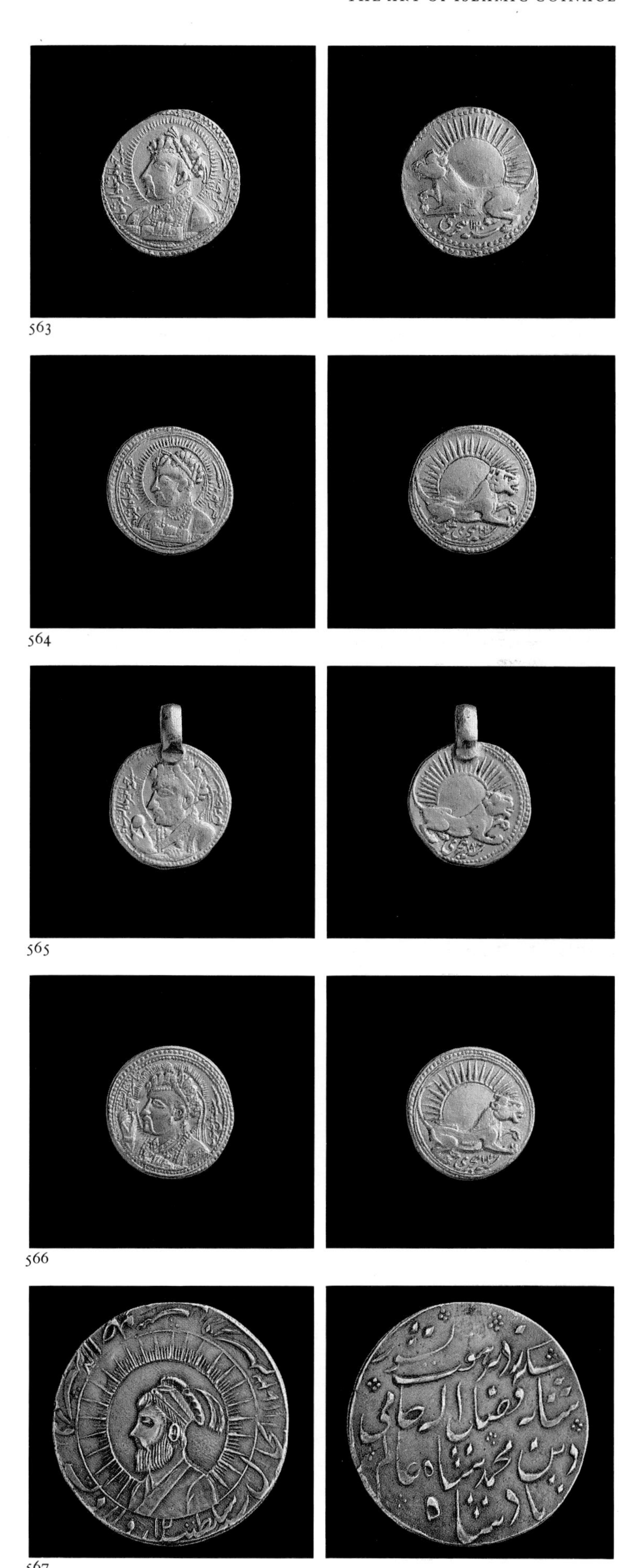
563

564

565

566

567

Bibliography

Abu'l-Fazl, *The A'in-i Akbari*, trans. H. Blochmann, 2nd ed., Calcutta 1927
Ackermann, P., *Guide to the exhibition of Persian art*, New York 1940
Aga-Oglu, M., 'The use of architectural forms in Seljuk metalwork', *Art Quarterly*, vol. VI, 1943, pp. 92–8
Aga-Oglu, M., 'About a type of Islamic incense-burner', *Art Bulletin*, vol. 27, 1945, pp. 28–45
Allan, J.W., *Islamic metalwork: the Nuhad Es-Said Collection*, London 1982
Allan, J.W., *Nishapur: metalwork of the early Islamic period*, Metropolitan Museum, New York 1982
Allan, J.W., 'Manuscript illumination: a source for metalwork motifs in late Seljuq times', *Proceedings of the Edinburgh Symposium on Seljuq Art*, 1985
Arnold, T., *Painting in Islam. A study of the place of pictorial art in Muslim culture*, London 1928
Arts Council of Great Britain, *The arts of Islam*, London 1976
Atil, E., *Renaissance of Islam. Art of the Mamluks*, Washington 1981

Bamborough, P., *Treasures of Islam*, London 1976
Barrett, D., *Islamic metalwork in the British Museum*, London 1949
Beach, M.C., 'The Gulshan Album and its European Sources', *Bulletin of Boston Museum of Fine Arts*, vol. LXIII, no. 332, 1965, pp. 63–91
Beach, M.C., *The Grand Mogul 1600-1660*, exhibition catalogue, Sterling and Francine Clark Art Institute, Williamstown, Mass., 1978
Beach, M.C., *The Imperial Image*, Washington 1981
Beattie, May H., *The Thyssen-Bornemisza collection of oriental rugs*, Castagnola 1972
Beattie, May H., *Carpets of central Persia*, 1976
Beveridge, A.S., *The Baburnamah in English*, London 1969
Binney, E., *Persian and Indian miniatures from the collection of Edwin Binney, 3rd*, Portland, Maine, 1962
Binney, E., *Islamic art from the collection of Edwin Binney, 3rd*, Washington, D.C., 1966
Binyon. L., J.V.S. Wilkinson and B. Gray, *Persian miniature painting*, London 1933
Bivar, A.D.H., and E. Yarshater, ed., *Corpus Inscriptionum Iranicarum, pt IV, Persian inscriptions down to the early Safavid period*, vol VI, *Mazandaran Province*, London 1978
Blochet, E., 'Miniatures orientales de la collection Pozzi', in *Société française de reproductions de Manuscrits à peintures, Bulletin*, XII, 1928
Blochet, E. *Musulman painting 12th-17th century*, London 1929, reprinted New York 1975
Borgomale, Rabino di, 'Une lettre familière du Fath Ali Shah', *Revue du monde Musulman*, vols XL–XLI, 1920
Brieux, A., and Maddison, F. *Répertoire des facteurs d'astrolabes et de leurs œuvres*, première partie, 'Islam, plus Byzance, Arménie, Géorgie et Inde hindoue', Paris (forthcoming)
Brown, P., *Indian painting under the Mughals*, Oxford 1924
Bryan, D., 'A Reconstruction of the Miniature Cycle in the Demotte Shahnama', *Ars Islamica*, VI, 1939
Bussé, H., 'Diplomatic: Persia', *Encyclopaedia of Islam*, 1965, 308–313
Bussé, H. 'Abbas Mirza', *Encyclopaedia Iranica*, vol. I, fasc. 1, London 1982

Cagman, F., and N. Tapan, *The Anatolian civilizations III, Seljuk/Ottoman*, Istanbul 1983
Cammann, Schuyler, 'The systematic study of oriental rugs: techniques and patterns', *Journal of the American Oriental Society*, vol. 95, 1975, p. 248 ff.
Christie, Manson and Woods, London auction sales catalogues
Colnaghi Gallery, *Paintings and sculpture of India*, London 1982

Das, A.K., *Mughal painting during Jahangir's time*, Calcutta 1978
Davillier, Baron Ch., *Recherches sur l'orfèvrerie en Espagne au moyen âge et à la Renaissance*, Paris 1879
Dickson, M.B., and S.C. Welch, *The Houghton Shāhnāmeh*, Cambridge, Mass., 1981
Drouot, Hotel– and Nouveau–Paris auction sales catalogues
Düsseldorf: *Islamische Keramik*, catalogue of an exhibition held at the Hetjens-Museum, 1973

Erdmann, Kurt, 'Kaaba Fliese', *Ars Orientalis*, III, 1959
Erdmann, Kurt, 'Neuere Untersuchungen zur Frage der Kairener Teppiche', *Ars Orientalis*, IV, 1961, p. 65 ff.
Errera, Isabelle, *Catalogue des etoffes anciennes et modernes*, Musées Royaux du Cinquantenaire, Brussels, 1927

Falk, S.J., *Qajar paintings*, London 1972
Falk, T., et al., *Indian painting*, London 1978
Falk, T., and S. Digby, *Paintings from Mughal India*, London 1979
Falke, Otto von, *Kunstgeschichte der Seidenweberei*, Berlin 1913
Fehervari, G., *Islamic metalwork of the eighth to the fifteenth century in the Keir collection*, London 1976

Gabriel, A., *Monuments Turcs d'Anatolie*, 2 vols, Paris 1931
Geneva: *Céramiques Islamiques dans les collections Genevoises*, catalogue of an exhibition at the Musée d'art et d'histoire 1981
Geneva: *Islam et art figuratif*, catalogue of an exhibition held at the Musée d'art et d'histoire, 1984
Goedhuis, M., *Recent acquisitions*, London 1983

Grabar, O., and S. Blair, *Epic images and contemporary history*, Chicago 1980
Gray, B., *The 'World History' of Rashid al-Din: A study of the Royal Asiatic Society Manuscript*, London 1978
Gray, B. ed., *The arts of the book in Central Asia, 14th-16th centuries*, Paris/London 1979
Gross, A., and B. Thomas, *Katalog der Waffensammlung in der Neuen Burg*, Vienna 1936
Grousset, R., *The Civilizations of the East: India*, London 1932
Grube, E., *The classical style in Persian Painting*, New York 1968
Grube, E.J., *Islamic pottery in the Keir Collection*, London 1976

Hartner, W., 'The pseudo-planetary nodes of the Moon's orbit in Hindu and Islamic iconography', *Ars Islamica*, vol. v, 1938, pp. 113-54
Herzfeld, E., 'A bronze pen-case', *Ars Islamica*, III, 1936, pp. 35-43
Hillenbrand, R., *Imperial images in Persian painting*, Edinburgh 1977

Irwin, J.C., and M. Hall, *Indian embroideries*, Ahmedabad 1973
Ittig, A., 'A talismanic bowl', *Annales Islamologiques*, vol. XVIII, 1982, pp. 79-94
Ivanov, A.A., T.B. Grek and O.F. Akimushkin, *Album indiskikh i persidskikh miniatur XVI-XVII v.* ['Album of Indian and Persian miniatures, 16th-18th centuries'], Moscow 1962
Ivanov, A.A., T.B. Grek and O.F. Akimushkin, 'The Life of Muhammad Zaman: A reconstruction', *Iran*, XVII, 1979, pp. 65-70

Jenkins, M., ed., *Islamic art in the Kuwait National Museum, the al-Sabah Collection*, London 1983

Keene, M., *Selected recent acquisitions 1404 AH-1984 AD Dār al-Āthār al-Islāmīya, Kuwait National Museum*, Kuwait, 1984
Kevorkian, A.M., and J.-P. Sicre, *Les jardins du désir*, Paris 1983
King, Donald, *Imperial Ottoman textiles*, London 1980
King, Donald, *The eastern carpet in the western world from the 15th to the 17th Century*, Arts Council of Great Britain, London 1983
Kühnel, E., 'Der Maler Mu'in', *Pantheon*, 29, 1942, pp. 108-14
Kühnel, E., *Die Islamischen Elfenbeinskulpturen VIII-XIII Jahrhundert*, Berlin 1971

Lings, M., *The Qur'anic art of calligraphy and illumination*, London 1977
Lings, M., and Y.H. Safadi, *The Qur'an*, London 1976
Loewi, Gabrielle, *2000 years of silk weaving*, New York 1944
London: *Islamic pottery 800-1400 AD*, catalogue of exhibition at the Victoria and Albert Museum, 1969
London: *The Arts of Islam*, catalogue of exhibition, Arts council of Great Britain, Hayward Gallery, 1976

Marteau, G., and H. Vever, *Miniatures persanes exposés au Musée des Arts Décoratifs*, 2 vols, Paris 1912
Martin, F.R., *The miniature paintings and painters of Persia, India, and Turkey*, London 1912
Mayer, L.A., *Saracenic heraldry*, Oxford 1933
Mayer, L.A., Zwei syro-ägyptische Leuchter im Bernischen Historischen Museum, *Jahrbuch der Bernischen Historischen Museums*, vol. XVI, 1936, pp. 24-7
Mayer, L.A., *Islamic woodcarvers and their works*, Geneva 1958
Melikian-Chirvani, A.S., *Le bronze iranien*, Paris 1973
Melikian-Chirvani, A.S., 'Les bronzes du Khorassan I,' *Studia Iranica*, vol. 3, 1974, pp. 29-50 (1974/1)
Melikian-Chirvani, A.S., 'Venise, entre l'Orient et l'Occident' *Bulletin d'Etudes Orientales*, 1974, pp. 109-6 (1974/2)
Melikian-Chirvani, A.S., 'Les bronzes du Khorassan V', *Studia Iranica*, vol. 6, 1977, pp. 185-210
Melikian-Chirvani, A.S., 'Objets peints d'Iran', *Connaissance des arts*, 302, 1977, pp. 107-11
Melikian-Chirvani, A.S., *Islamic metalwork from the Iranian world, 8th-18th centuries*, exhibition catalogue, Victoria and Albert Museum, London 1982
Mustafa, M., *Unity in Islamic Art*, Cairo 1958

Okasha, S., *The Muslim painter and the divine*, London 1981
Oriental Ceramic Society, Transactions of the

Pakravan, E., *Abbas Mirza*, Tehran 1960
Pal, P., ed., *Islamic Art*, the Nasli M. Heeramaneck Collection, Los Angeles County Museum of Art, 1973
Petrasch, E., *Die Türkenbeute*, Karlsruhe 1977
Petsopoulos, Y., ed., *Tulips, arabesques and turbans*, London 1982
Phillips, London auction sales catalogues
Pinder-Wilson, R., ed., *Paintings from Islamic lands*, London 1969
Pinder-Wilson, R., *Paintings from the Muslim Courts of India*, London 1976
Pope, A.U., ed., *A survey of Persian art*, 6 vols, Oxford 1938-9, reprinted Tokyo 1964
Pope, A.U., *Masterpieces of Persian art*, New York 1945
Pope, J.A., *Chinese porcelains from the Ardabil Shrine*, Smithsonian Institute, Washington 1956

Reath, Nancy Andrews, and Eleanor B. Sachs, *Persian textiles*, New Haven 1937
Rice, D.S., *The Wade Cup in the Cleveland Museum of Art*, Paris 1955
Rice, D.T., *The illustrations to the 'World History' of Rashid al-Din*, Edinburgh 1976
Robinson, B.W., *A loan exhibition of Persian miniature paintings from British collections*, Victoria and Albert Museum, London 1951
Robinson, B.W., *Persian paintings*, London 1952, reprinted 1965
Robinson, B.W., *Persian miniature painting*, Victoria and Albert Museum, London, 1967
Robinson, B.W., *Miniatures persanes, Donation Pozzi*, Geneva 1974
Robinson, B.W., 'Two Persian manuscripts in the library of the Marquess of Bute', *Oriental Art*, spring 1974
Robinson, B.W., 'Isma'il II's copy of the *Shāhnāmeh*', *Iran, Journal of the British Institute of Persian Studies*, vol. XIV, 1976, no. 48
Robinson, B.W., *Persian paintings in the John Rylands Library*, London 1980
Robinson, B.W., et al., *Persian and Mughal Art*, London 1976
Rogers, M., *Islamic Art and Design 1500-1700*, exhibition catalogue, British Museum, London, 1983

Sakisian, A., *La Miniature persane*, Paris 1929
Sarre, F., and F.R. Martin, *Die Ausstellung von Meisterwerke Muhammedanischer Kunst in München*, Munich 1912
Sarre, F., and E. Mittwoch, *Die Zeichnungen von Riza 'Abbasi', Munich 1914*
Savage-Smith, E. and M.B., *Islamic geomancy and a 13th-century divinatory device*, Malibu 1980
Scerrato, U., *Metalli Islamici*, Milan 1966
Schöbel, J., *Türkenschatz*, Leipzig 1974
Schöbel, J., *Splendor of Dresden*, New York 1978
Schürmann, Ulrich, *Oriental carpets*, London 1966
Smirnov, Y.I., *Argenterie orientale*, St Petersburg 1909
Sotheby's, auction sales catalogues, London and New York
Spink and Son, *Persian and Islamic art*, London 1977
Spink and Son, *Islamic art from India*, London 1980
Spink and Son, *Islamic textile design*, London 1983
Spuhler, Friedrich, *Islamic carpets and textiles in the Keir Collection*, London 1978
Stchoukine, I., 'Portraits moghols IV: La collection du Baron Maurice de Rothschild', *Revue des Arts Asiatiques*, 9, 1935, pp. 190-208
Stchoukine, I., 'Un Bustan de Sa'di illustré par les artistes Moghols', *Revue des Arts Asiatiques*, II, 1937, pp. 68-74
Stchoukine, I., *Les peintures des manuscrits de Shah 'Abbas Ier*, Paris 1964
Strzygowski, J., *Asiatische Miniaturmalerei*, Vienna 1933

Thomas, B., 'Aus der Waffensammlung in der Neuen Burg zu Wien', *Gesammelte Schriften*, Graz 1977

Victoria and Albert Museum, *The Indian heritage*, London 1982

Weibel, Adele Coulin, *Two thousand years of textiles*, New York 1952
Welch, A., *Collection of Islamic art, Prince Sadruddin Aga Khan*, 4 vols, Geneva 1972-8
Welch, A., *Shah Abbas and the arts of Isfahan*, New York 1973
Welch, A., *Artists for the Shah*, New Haven/London 1976
Welch, A., *Calligraphy in the arts of the Muslim world*, Folkestone 1979
Welch, A. and S.C., *Arts of the Islamic book. The collection of Prince Sadruddin Aga Khan*, New York, 1982
Welch, S.C., 'Early Mughal miniature paintings from two private collections', *Ars Orientalis*, 3, 1959
Welch, S.C., *The art of Mughal India*, New York 1963
Welch, S.C., 'Mughal and Deccani miniature paintings from a private collection', *Ars Orientalis*, vol. 5, 1963
Welch, S.C., *A King's Book of Kings: The Shāhnāmeh of Shah Tahmasp*, Metropolitan Museum of Art, New York 1972
Welch, S.C., *Persian painting: five royal Safavid manuscripts of the 16th century*, New York 1976
Welch, S.C., *Indian drawings and painted sketches*, New York 1976
Welch, S.C., and M.C. Beach, *Gods, thrones, and peacocks*, New York 1965
Welch, S.C., et al., *Wonders of the age*, Fogg Art Museum, Cambridge, Mass., 1979
Wiet, G., 'Un chandelier en cuivre au nom de la Sultane Fatima epouse du Sultan Qaitbay', *Syria*, vol. XLVII, 1970, pp. 345-55
Wilkinson, C.K., *Nishapur: pottery of the early Islamic period*, New York 1973

Zebrowski, M., *Deccani painting*, London 1983
Zoka, Y., 'Muhammad Zaman', *Nigahi va Nigarkari-yi Iran dar Sadaha-yi Davazdahum va Sizdahum* (in Persian), Tehran 1353 S./1975, pp. 37-80

Index

Numerals in roman type refer to catalogue numbers; numerals in bold type refer to pages in the introductory essays and in the introductions to individual sections of the catalogue. Coinage, and specific issues of coins, are indexed under periods or dynasties (Abbasid, Delhi Sultanate, Ilkhanid rulers, and so on).